European Economic and Monetary Union: The Institutional Framework

International Banking and Finance Law

VOLUME 6

Series Editor

J.J. NORTON

*Centre for Commercial Law Studies,
Queen Mary and Westfield College,
University of London*

The titles published in this series are listed at the end of this volume.

Centre of European Law
King's College, London

London Institute of International
Banking, Finance & Development Law
Centre for Commercial Law Studies
Queen Mary & Westfield College
University of London

European Economic and Monetary Union: The Institutional Framework

Edited by

Mads Andenas
Laurence Gormley
Christos Hadjiemmanuil
Ian Harden

In cooperation with

Faculty of Law, University of Groningen
Faculty of Law, University of Sheffield
European Investment Bank
Financial Law Panel, London
Institute of Advanced Legal Studies, London

KLUWER LAW
INTERNATIONAL
LONDON – THE HAGUE – BOSTON

Published by
Kluwer Law International Ltd
Sterling House
66 Wilton Road
London SW1V 1DE
United Kingdom

Kluwer Law International incorporates the
publishing programmes of
Graham & Trotman Ltd,
Kluwer Law & Taxation Publishers
and Martinus Nijhoff Publishers.

Sold and distributed in
the USA and Canada by
Kluwer Law International
675 Massachusetts Avenue
Cambridge MA 02139
USA

In all other countries, sold and distributed by
Kluwer Law International
P.O. Box 322
3300 AH Dordrecht
The Netherlands

ISBN 90-411-0687-1

© Kluwer Law International 1997
First published in 1997

British Library Cataloguing in Publication Data
A catalogue record for this book is available from the British Library

Library of Congress Cataloging-in-Publication Data is available

Typeset in 10/12 Garamond by BookEns Ltd, Royston, Herts
Printed and bound in Great Britain by MPG Books Ltd, Bodmin, Cornwall

Centre of European Law, King's College
and the
London Institute of International Banking, Finance & Development Law

European Economic and Financial Law Series

The Centre: The Centre of European Law, King's College, University of London, advances research into European Community Law and the laws of European countries. In the years following its foundation by the Lord Chancellor in 1974, it has been internationally recognised as the leading institution of its kind.

The Institute: The London Institute is a privately incorporated, education-based institution. Among its other related educational functions, the London Institute assists the International Financial & Tax Law Unit at the Centre for Commercial Law Studies, Queen Mary & Westfield College, University of London, in directing research seminars, professional conferences, executive training sessions, law reform and consulting projects, and major journals and book series (including the present series).

SERIES EDITOR'S PREFACE

The evolvement of the economic integration of western Europe leading up to the European Union is one of the most important features of history after World War II. It now seems as Economic and Monetary Union is all set to take place as provided for in the Maastricht Treaty through the European Community an Economic and Monetary Union. This is an event of undoubted global importance.

I know that both the Centre of European Law and the London Institute and their joint series are most enthusiastic about publishing this seminal and vanguard book on the public law and institutional dimensions of EMU. It is a joint project which found its home base at the Centre of European Law at King's College, University of London and received financial support from the Centre of Commercial Law Studies, Queen Mary and Westfield College, University of London.

The Centre of European Law has been able not only to harness it own resources but also to involve other University of London institutions with their own EMU projects (such as the CCLS, the LSE Financial Markets Group and the Institute of Advanced Legal Studies). Equally impressive is the way in which the Centre coordinated major contributions from other leading European academic institutions and by individuals in government, Community institutions and from elsewhere.

This book is a collection of a large number of highly substantive chapters which present critical insights into the institutional aspects of the transition to EMU, of its monetary and macroeconomic policy dimensions, and of the European Central Bank. Mads Andenas and his co-editors, Laurence Gormley, Christos Hadjiemmanuil and Ian Harden, are to be commended for this seminal interdisciplinary work of highest quality.

Generous support was received from the European Investment Bank. Special appreciation is also extended to the Legal Department of the European Monetary Institute, Directorate General XV of the European Commission, the Financial Law Panel, London, the Institute of Advanced Legal Studies, London and the SMU Institute of International Finance, Dallas, Texas. Special thanks are also expressed to Douglas W. Arner (CCLS/EBRD) and Matthew S. Morgan (CCLS) for their editorial assistance and to Selma Hoedt at Kluwer for the publication of this volume and this series.

European Economic and Monetary Union: The Institutional Framework

The authors come from different jurisdictions and professional disciplines. A uniform system of citations has been imposed, and generally standard British English spelling is followed. Some inconsistencies are unavoidable. Several of the authors have an institutional affiliation requiring that it is made clear that the views they express are not necessarily those of their employer. A note is made of that here and not, as is sometimes done, with the author's name at the beginning of each chapter. Each author retains the right to use his or her respective chapter for other academic or professional purposes. Finally, some of the chapters are also printed elsewhere. Sir Samuel Brittan's chapter is also his evidence to the House of Lords' Select Committee on the European Communities and is printed with the Committee's report; Professor Daintith's chapter is previously published in Public Law; and Professor Goodhart's chapter is also published in the Scottish Journal of Political Economy.

1 July 1997

Joseph J. Norton

FOREWORD

As a professor teaching European Community Law, but coming from a federation which has (and has had since 1863) a common currency, I find the discussion which takes place in this volume and in the related conferences extraordinarily interesting. In one sense, both the volume and the conferences are truly interdisciplinary. Economists discussing European Economic and Monetary Union normally focus on what might be called the 'macroeconomic' aspects of EMU, particularly the problems with the excessive deficit procedure. On the other hand, lawyers, whether on the public or the private side, are generally interested in the relationship between the use of the currency or, as the case will be between 1999 and 2002, the currencies and the institutional aspects of entrance into the monetary union. If one reads the best-known treatises on the law of money, as exemplified by Mann, the discussion centres on the needs of the lawyer advising the private party who must draw up contracts. (And, however unforeseen by Professor Mann, derivatives are only contracts.) Today's private lawyer must make the best provision that they can foresee for the new world of the monetary union. Since the arrangements that the private lawyers make profoundly affect the working of the institutions, the public lawyers are equally involved in trying to work out any novel legal questions concerning the impact of the Maastricht Treaty provisions and their implementation on the private market.

The great interest of this volume is that the intellectual interests of both economists and lawyers have been, in my view, fully served. The chapters constituting the first section, 'Community Institutions: Preparation and the Transition to EMU', concentrate on what the private lawyers might think to be the 'nitty-gritty' of their practice. Will the Union actually provide in Community law (which will take precedence over Member States' laws) that no doctrine of *imprévision* will apply to preexisting contracts? Will the Union provide a method of translation which will be sufficiently certain to avoid market disruption? As is pointed out by all of the authors in the first section in regard to what might be called private-law issues, a situation where both the common currency and the national currencies will coexist in circulation from 1999 to 2002 is also unprecedented. Where there are no precedents in law, there are great difficulties for the private practitioners in the prediction so necessary for both advice to clients and, above all, drafting for clients. Hence, chapters from actual institutional participants, such as those of Helmut Wittelsberger and Dr. Paolo Clarotti, will be of extremely great utility to practising lawyers.

For the economists, as well as for the public lawyers involved in the drafting of the provisions for implementation of the Maastricht Treaty, the second and third sections introduce the novel problems of this monetary union: the separation of monetary and fiscal policy in Stage Three of EMU, and the role of the European Central Bank in banking supervision. Charles Goodhart's chapter opening the volume raised these novel problems, and the second section of the volume, 'Monetary and Macroeconomic Policy in the EMU', is largely devoted to a full discussion of the difficulties that appear to be inherent in the excessive deficit procedure as presently provided for as well as the analysis of a number of interesting procedures that might alleviate the difficulties. While possibly of less interest to the legal audience than the chapters of the first section, the chapters in the second section provide the indispensable institutional background for any thinking concerning the possible shape of the ultimate institutional mechanisms for the relationship between the European Central Bank's control of monetary policy and the design and implementation of fiscal policy, which remains in the hands of the participating Member States. Since the separation is unprecedented, a review, such as is provided by Professor Goodhart's chapter as well as by most of the chapters in the second section, of the possible future mechanisms is indispensable to the private lawyer contemplating drafting financial products for use in this unprecedented and really most peculiar monetary union.

The final section, 'The European Central Bank', focuses on an area of importance for practitioners, public lawyers and economists: the eventual role of the ECB in EMU, and especially in banking supervision. The various authors present in one single place more significant and scholarly analysis of this topic than appears to have taken place in any other single place. As such, the importance of the writings in this section cannot be ignored. Moreover, readers from many different backgrounds should find them both interesting and thought-provoking.

It is the focus on *both* of these areas of what might be called 'unprecedence', that is, the separation between control of monetary policy and control of fiscal policy on the one hand, and the entrance into a monetary union with a substantial period of the circulation of both national currencies and the common currency on the other, that makes this volume and the event it looks to so interesting. Mads Andenas and his co-editors and the contributors are to be congratulated for a volume of high intellectual level and great practical utility.

Professor Cynthia C. Lichtenstein

CONTENTS

PART I   THE COMMUNITY INSTITUTIONS AND THE TRANSITION TO EMU

Chapter One

The Transition to EMU

C. A. E. Goodhart

Chapter Two

Legal Aspects of the Changeover to a Single Currency

Helmut Wittelsberger

Chapter Five

The Change to a Single Currency: Legal Problems and Solutions

Colin Bamford

Chapter Six

**The Improvement of the European Payment Systems:
Crucial Tool for the Achievement of the Single Currency**

Paolo Clarotti

Part II MONETARY AND MACROECONOMIC POLICY IN EMU

Chapter Seven

EMU in Perspective

Sir Samuel Brittan

Chapter Eight

Monetary-Policy Strategies for the European Central Bank and their Implementation

Claes Berg

Chapter Nine

The European Constitutional Framework for Member States' Public Finances

Ian Harden, Jürgen von Hagen and Robert Brookes

Chapter Ten

The Separation of Monetary and Fiscal Policy in Stage Three of EMU

C. T. Taylor

Chapter Eleven

The Excessive Deficit Procedure: A Legal Description

Alexander Italianer

Chapter Twelve

Towards a Credible Excessive Deficit Procedure

Daniel Gros

Chapter Thirteen

Sound Public Finances and Fiscal Targets

Stephen Matthews

Chapter Fourteen

National Debt Boards: An Institutional Route to Fiscal Discipline

Ian Harden and Jürgen von Hagen

Part III   THE EUROPEAN CENTRAL BANK

Chapter Fifteen

European Monetary Union and Central Bank Independence

Rosa María Lastra

Chapter Sixteen

Independence and Accountability of the European Central Bank

Jakob de Haan and Laurence Gormley

APPENDICES

SOME ABBREVIATIONS AND ACRONYMS

BIS	Bank for International Settlements
DM	Deutsche Mark
ECB	European Central Bank
Ecofin	The Council, meeting in the composition of economic and finance ministers (in accordance with the Declaration on Part Three, Titles III and VI, of the Treaty establishing the European Community, attached to the Maastricht Treaty)
EC Treaty	Treaty establishing the European Community
EDP	Excessive-deficit procedure
EDP Protocol	Protocol on the excessive deficit procedure
EEC Treaty	Treaty establishing the European Economic Community (Treaty of Rome), as amended by the Single European Act
EIB	European Investment Bank
EMI	European Monetary Institute
EMS	European Monetary System
EMU	Economic and Monetary Union
ERM	Exchange Rate Mechanism
ESCB	European System of Central Banks
EUR-12	The Community of twelve Member States, prior to the accession of Austria, Finland and Sweden
G-10	Group of Ten
GDP	Gross Domestic Product
GNP	Gross National Product
IGC	Intergovernmental conference
IMF	International Monetary Fund
Maastricht Treaty	Treaty on European Union

SEA	Single European Act
TARGET	Trans-European Automated Real-Time Gross Settlement Express Transfer payment system
RTGS	Real-time gross-settlement payment system
Statute of the EMI	Protocol on the Statute of the EMI
Statute of the ESCB	Protocol on the Statute of the European System of Central Banks and of the European Central Bank

List of Contributors

Editors (and Contributors)

Dr Mads Andenas. Director, Centre of European Law, King's College, London; Honorary Director of Studies, Institute of Advanced Legal Studies.

Professor Laurence Gormley. Professor of European Law and Jean Monnet Professor, Rijksuniversiteit Groningen; Visiting Professor of EC Law, University College London and Universität Bremen; Professor at the College of Europe.

Dr Christos Hadjiemmanuil. Lecturer in Law, London School of Economics and Political Science; formerly fellow in European Monetary Law, Centre for Commercial Law Studies, Queen Mary & Westfield College, University of London.

Professor Ian Harden. Department of Law and Political Economics Research Centre, University of Sheffield.

Contributors

Colin Bamford. Chief Executive, Financial Law Panel, London.

Claes Berg. Chief Economist, Sveriges Rijksbank.

Sir Samuel Brittan. Financial Times, London.

Robert Brookes. Political Economics Research Centre, University of Sheffield.

Dr Paolo Clarotti. Head of Unit, Banks and Financial Establishments, DG XV, European Commission, Brussels.

Professor Terence Daintith. Professor of Law and Dean of Schools of Advanced Study, University of London.

D. R. R. Dunnett. Head of Legal Division, European Investment Bank, Luxembourg.

Professor C. A. E. Goodhart. Norman Sosnow Professor of Banking and Finance, London School of Economics and Political Science; Deputy Director and Co-Founder, LSE Financial Markets Group.

Daniel Gros. Centre for European Policy Studies, Brussels.

Professor Jakob de Haan. Jean Monnet Professor of European Economic Integration, Rijksuniversiteit Groningen.

Professor Jürgen von Hagen. University of Mannheim, Indiana University and Center for Economic Policy Research.

Alexander Italianer. Cabinet of the President, European Commission, Brussels.

Professor C. S. Kerse. Professor of Law, King's College, London.

Dr Rosa María Lastra. Fellow in International Financial Law, Centre for Commercial Law Studies, Queen Mary & Westfield College, University of London.

Professor Cynthia Lichtenstein. Professor, Boston College Law School.

Stephen Matthews. HM Treasury, London.

Dr Dirk Schoenmaker. Regulatory Policy Division, Financial Stability Wing, Bank of England.

Christopher Taylor. National Institute for Economic and Social Research, London.

Helmut Wittelsberger. Head of Unit, Monetary Union (Legal and Institutional Matters), DG II, European Commission, Brussels.

TABLE OF LEGISLATION

TABLE OF CASES

PART ONE

THE COMMUNITY INSTITUTIONS AND
THE TRANSITION TO EMU

Chapter One

THE TRANSITION TO EMU

C. A. E. Goodhart*

Chapter Outline

1. The Political Nature of the Process

2. Fiscal Problems

3. The Exchange-Rate Question
   3.1 ERM membership as a convergence criterion?
   3.2 How to fix exchange rates among the Ins?
   3.3 Relationships between the Ins and Outs?

4. Thinking the Unthinkable

European Economic and Monetary Union: The Institutional Framework (M. Andenas, L. Gormley, C. Hadjiemmanuil, I. Harden, eds.: 90-411-0687-1: © Kluwer Law International: pub. Kluwer Law International, 1997: printed in Great Britain)

1.   THE POLITICAL NATURE OF THE PROCESS

My subject in this chapter is the transition to Economic and Monetary Union. There were a few moments during December 1995 when I worried whether my chapter might have to be aborted. But the strikes in France and Belgium subsided, and the Madrid summit successfully reaffirmed political commitment to EMU. So for the purpose of this chapter, I shall *assume* that Stage Three of the EMU process will start, as planned, on 1 January 1999. The key to this, of course, lies in the hands of the two main European countries, Germany and France. It depends on whether Germany *will* go on, that is, whether it has the political desire to continue with the exercise, and whether France *can*, that is, whether it can meet the convergence criteria sufficiently to satisfy the requirements exacted by Germany.

I am, therefore, going to assume the long-run steady-state existence of EMU, and to be consistent that this is found to be economically, socially and politically acceptable. Discussions on the possible benefits and costs of EMU for all the prospective participants have gone on for a long time; I want now both to pass on and to narrow my field to discussing some of the problems of the transition to EMU.

Moreover, I shall not, and cannot, deal with *all* the detailed issues involved in the transition process. In particular, I shall have nothing to say about that aspect of most immediate concern to the financial community, which is the specific costs to the banks themselves of the alternative modes of transition. Such costs will be large; Jeremy Peat of Royal Bank of Scotland[1] has reported the British Bankers' Association's first estimate for UK banks of over £900 million per year for three years, if a big-bang transition mode were adopted; a longer process, involving a dual-currency system, would be yet more costly for the banks. However, banking specialists have now focused on this issue. Given their expertise, an outside academic like myself has nothing useful that he could additionally offer on this particular matter.

It is somewhat surprising to me that EMU questions are usually treated as belonging primarily in the realm and discipline of economics; whereas in practice the main issues have, *au fond*, always been political. This was exemplified at the last Madrid summit when, in response to some detailed criticisms of the EMU process by Prime Minister Major, Chancellor Kohl was reported to have replied that EMU would bring 'peace and freedom'. I shall comment on that briefly later.

* I am grateful to many colleagues for comments and suggestions, including W. Allen, J. Arrowsmith, P. de Grauwe, P. Hartmann, P. Minford, P. Mizen, J. Peat, C. Taylor, N. Thygesen and G. Wood. But none of them bear any responsibility for either the views or the remaining shortcomings of this chapter.
1. J. Peat, 'European Union: A New Beginning', speech given in Edinburgh (Nov. 1995).

The essentially political nature of the exercise has also determined much of the transition process. It would have been a simple matter to design a much lower-cost transition. All that would have been necessary would have been to allow those countries meeting the entry criteria to adopt the Deutsche Mark as their own currency, and for the Bundesbank to welcome directors from those countries onto their *Direktorium*, or Board, with the proportional representation matching some index of population and GDP.[2]

There would then have been no transitional costs at all for the largest country in Europe, the country standing to receive the least *economic* benefits from EMU. There would then have been no problems about credibility, or nomenclature. Rather than having to go through the complex task of creating new, and untried, institutions, this would have allowed an evolutionary approach to EMU, and one that built upon monetary foundations, that is, those of the DM and the Bundesbank, universally proclaimed to be the most successful in Europe.

Building monetary union in Europe on the basis of an expanding DM area would have been economically the least-cost method of proceeding. Yet it was unthinkable. There is, of course, the argument that this would have given German banks and financial institutions too much of an advantage. But that problem could, I believe, have been amicably resolved, for example by having an independent assessment of transition costs for countries joining the DM area at the outset, that is, at the equivalent of Stage Three, and then having such total transition costs allocated between *all* the countries involved, including Germany. To put it another way, given its benefits from keeping the DM, Germany could have subsidised the losers and still ended better off.

Instead, the real reason why such an economically sensible design was unthinkable is political. It would have carried the connotation that Europe was becoming a German-led area, at least economically, and in particular that France was a subsidiary nation, at least relative to Germany. That was unacceptable to France. And, since the whole idea was to reinforce the *rapprochement* between France and Germany, Chancellor Kohl's 'peace and freedom', it was not attractive to Germany's political leaders either. The importance of such a *rapprochement* has been considerably increased by Germany's reunification.

What I have sought to establish at the outset is that EMU is primarily a political exercise. This is especially so since the economic arguments are quite finely balanced. EMU will stand, or fall, primarily on its political

---

2. For a similar statement, see W. Buiter, *Macroeconomic Policy During a Transition to Monetary Union*, Centre for Economic Policy Research Discussion Paper No. 1222 (Aug. 1995); see, also, K. Dowd and D. Greenaway, 'Currency Competition, Network Externalities and Switching Costs: Towards an Alternative View of Optimum Currency Areas' (1993) 102 *Economic Journal* 1180.

success. The process is one involving a greater sharing of sovereignty, initially at the monetary level, but undoubtedly also, in due course, at the political and fiscal levels, between federal, national, regional and local governments. In so far as this is recognised, the transition process should have been designed to minimise the *political* objections to that process.

There have been two main strands of such objections to EMU. The first has been felt most acutely among the national political elites in various countries, especially the UK. That concern has centered on the loss by national governments, and by their respective parliaments, of their power of control over the main monetary levers of demand management, interest rates and exchange rates.

What largely drove the actual form of the transition to EMU was that that loss had *already* been accepted by those countries, other than Germany, which had embraced the Exchange Rate Mechanism, especially perhaps the smaller countries. In order to maintain the ERM peg, countries had to follow German interest rates. As has been proven in practice, the problem is that such a pegged system is fragile in the face of self-sustaining speculative attacks.

There could have been, however, an alternative way of moving by stages from national political control of monetary policy to a European single monetary system run by an independent European Central Bank. That would have involved having, as the first stage in the transition process, a shift of the power of control over monetary instruments from national governments to an independent national central bank mandated to achieve a (preferably quantified) inflation target.

Despite the breakdown of the narrow ERM, which has thrown into doubt the interpretation of the exchange-rate convergence criterion, as set out in Article 109j of the EC Treaty, most prospective participants in EMU are still trying, more or less, to follow the ERM transition path. It is, I fear, rather too late to advocate an alternative path towards EMU, based on central bank independence. But in many ways it would have been a preferable route; it would have achieved the vital initial step of removing political power from national ministers without forcing exchange rates into that fragile regime – what Sir Alan Walters termed a half-baked system – of pegged but adjustable rates. It is no more difficult, and perhaps easier, to jump directly to completely, irrevocably fixed exchange rates from a floating than from a pegged system (assuming the same degree of prior economic convergence in both cases), though, as I shall discuss further, the exact modalities of either step are quite complex.

For ministers of finance, Chancellors of Exchequer, etc, losing the power to control interest rates and exchange rates, whether to an exchange-rate commitment or to an independent central bank, is the main cost that must be sustained. This switch of power, however, has less resonance among the general public. They do understand that interest rates have to be varied to control and prevent inflation, but the identity of the person who takes the final decision is usually of less importance.[3] What does concern them are two issues. First, whether painful measures, either monetary or fiscal, will have to be taken, adversely affecting them, in order to achieve and maintain EMU, which would *not* otherwise have been taken in the national interest.

And, second, there is the public's deep-felt, but largely symbolic, concern for the national currency. The strength of the German public's concern for their currency is legendary, partly because it represents for them a visible reaffirmation of sound finance and low inflation. This issue has been epitomised for me in a quotation from the Archbishop of Canterbury, Dr George Carey, who on 15 February 1993, in an interview with the *Financial Times*, was reported as stating that 'he gives a general blessing to European integration, [but] draws the line at the idea of monetary union leading to the head of his Church disappearing from English pound notes'. He is quoted, verbatim:

I want the Queen's head on the banknotes. The point about national identity is a very important one. For me being British is deeply important. I don't want to become French or German.

The elites tend to denigrate the European peoples' attachment to the characteristics of their respective national currencies as immature and irrational. And yet their own rush to try to move from irrevocably fixed currencies, Stage 3A, to a single Euro currency, Stage 3B, on the shortest possible time-scale indicates that they attach just as much importance to the *symbolism* of currencies. By doing so, the authorities are ensuring that deeply felt opposition to the abandonment of national currencies, and concern about the considerable costs of that transition, would surface at exactly the same time that the public in several countries will have to face deflationary pressures, notably as a result of fiscal cuts, in order to seek to meet the Maastricht convergence criteria.

Public opposition to Maastricht has swollen, and has become in many countries a significant factor. Such opposition could have been sensibly

---

3. The locus of power, *eg*, to change the prevailing interest rates in an area, can be justified to the general public *either* by custom and usage, *or* by good results, *or* by fairness and the public's democratic involvement. When the public has no such involvement (*ie*, a democratic deficit exists), custom and usage and a good track record become more important. The Bundesbank has these latter; the ESCB will not have them at the outset. This is why I advocated in earlier papers that the ESCB should have been designed along the lines of the Reserve Bank of New Zealand Act, under which the political authorities retain ultimate control of the objective to be followed by the central bank, and the central bank is made accountable for that. Since that has not been done, there may be more 'political' criticism of the transfer of power from national ministers to the ECB in Frankfurt.

diminished, if only Stage 3B, the move to the Euro, had been deferred indefinitely, until there was much more public support for that, conditional on Stage 3A having been successfully accepted. Why is there such a rush to Stage 3B? Most of the prospective benefits, in terms of lower transaction costs and interest rates, should have been achieved in Stage 3A. The fear, I believe, is that Stage 3A might not be credible, and hence successful; and also that the device of a single currency would cement the system by making withdrawal impossible and unthinkable.

Both those suppositions are, I believe, invalid. So long as the irrevocable fixing of parities has general public and political support, it can be made impregnable. As Peter Kenen has reminded us,[4] there are, in an important sense, 12 separate currencies, rather than a single currency, in the USA. Each Federal Reserve District issues its own greenbacks, and each dollar bill has a letter printed on it identifying the district where it was first issued. Virtually no one looks at that letter or queries the maintenance of the single US currency because of it. Of course, life becomes more complicated when the parities of the separate fixed currencies are not one for one, but are some horrible fraction, to many decimal places; nevertheless, the basic technicalities of running a European system of irrevocably and absolutely fixed currencies would be essentially no different from, and just as immune from speculative attack, as the present American system. The crucial component is that each member national central bank should be prepared to accept *without limit*, and at par with respect to the fixed central parities, the currency issued by any other member central bank. Each national central bank would continue to issue its own currency on demand from the general public as now, but with that demand conditioned by the single interest rate, as determined by the ECB. Should people wish to switch from holding French francs into DM, or vice versa, they could do so without limit; the currencies would be interchangeable, like the various US dollars. This could involve issuing a large volume of notes and deposits denominated in favoured national currencies at the outset (and equally retiring a large volume of notes and deposits denominated in 'suspect' currencies). It is absolutely essential that this implication be willingly and publicly accepted by all the national central banks. It would then soon become realised that that system *cannot* be broken by speculation, only by the politically determined desire of some member country to withdraw; note also that any hint of such withdrawal would force up interest rates on both loans and deposits booked in a country suspected of withdrawing, as depositors would flee to other currencies and banks would seek desperately to square their books.

4. P. B. Kenen, *Economic and Monetary Union in Europe: Moving beyond Maastricht* (1995), ch.3.

By the same token, however, if general public and political support for EMU should fail in some country, then the existence of a common European currency provides relatively little extra disincentive to separation. As W. Robson has pointed out in his discussion of the putative Quebec secession,[5] wherever there has been a major *political* split, currency separation has frequently followed rapidly thereafter, even when that was not intended or desired, as in the Czech–Slovak case, though the link between the Irish and British currencies is a counterexample. Indeed, the question in the Quebec case has been whether an independent Quebec government actually could continue to use the Canadian dollar. The separatists had provisionally committed themselves to doing so under clause 6 of the draft bill on the sovereignty of Quebec in order to appeal to the Quebec voters, partly because the prospect of a separate Quebecois currency had seemed too risky and susceptible to devaluation. But D. Laidler and W. Robson[6] query whether such an option would be sustainable.

The idea that the adoption of the Euro would prevent, or even seriously raise the economic cost of, a Member State deciding to withdraw is just a myth, though it is a myth that seems quite pervasive amongst European authorities. One barrier that does sometimes affect the process of amicable currency separation is how to divide up the, heretofore indistinguishable, national debt. But in the case of EMU there would be no such problem. Each Member State's debt issues in Euros will remain clearly identifiable, and there is no federal debt of any significance now or in prospect.

Thus, if public attachment to national currencies is somewhat irrational, then so too, or even more so, has been the rush of our monetary authorities to junk them. It is said that the adoption of a single currency may be a signal of the authorities' determination to commit themselves to EMU, but it may also be read as a signal of their determination to ignore the preferences of their own public. This has meant that the EMU concept has ranged against it both that strand of public opinion attached to their national currency as well as those now believing that they face painful deflationary measures for the purpose of meeting the convergence criteria.

2. FISCAL PROBLEMS

Apart from the real and the psychological costs of changing from national currencies to the Euro, the main transitional costs of moving to EMU will be

---

5. W. Robson, *Change for a Buck? The Canadian Dollar after Quebec Secession*, C. D. Howe Institute, Commentary No. 68 (March 1995).
6. Ibid; and D. Laidler and W. Robson, *Two Nations, One Money? Canada's Monetary System Following a Quebec Secession* (1991).

felt in the adjustment process to achieve a common low inflation rate, either initially, when having to bring down an excessive starting level, or subsequently in the face of adverse shocks. While it is true that regions within a common currency area have to be able to adjust towards a common inflation rate – otherwise the pressures would become unbearable –, any fool in authority can *temporarily* achieve low inflation by imposing sufficient deflation. But extreme and *continued* deflation is not politically sustainable. Thus, it would, with the benefit of hindsight, have been desirable to supplement the inflation criterion with an unemployment criterion, for example, stipulating that no country could join without simultaneously having had inflation below 3 per cent and unemployment below, say, 7.5 per cent over the previous two years. Several colleagues have pointed out to me that the definitions of unemployment differ among the Member States, and have also been influenced by, possibly country-specific, supply-side differences. Those problems, however, could have been met by designing the criterion in terms of requiring candidate members of the single-currency area to remain below the five-year preceding average of unemployment. But, in any case, that also is water under the bridge.

What is of more immediate importance, is how far public concern about EMU will be stoked up by the need to adhere to the fiscal criteria, whose very rationale is, to say the least, contentious. It is unfortunate that the final path to EMU is coinciding with a phase of low growth and high unemployment in Europe. This not only makes the timing (though not necessarily the extent) of fiscal cuts that may be needed to be consistent with Maastricht cyclically inappropriate, but also means that the EMU process itself may be partially blamed in the public's eyes for the continuation of that very same low growth and high unemployment.

It may well be the case that, with a worsening demographic trend, most European countries should be aiming now for a fiscal surplus on average over the cycle. But whether or not the Maastricht fiscal criteria should happen to be consistent with sound fiscal economics (with the latter based, for example, on a long-term estimate of public expenditure needs, to be financed over that same period by constant expected tax rates), they were not originally designed or justified on such a basis. Instead they were put in place, as far as one can tell, mainly to prevent a Member State choosing to behave fiscally imprudently, for example, by taking advantage of the comparatively low interest rates offered on government borrowing in Euros in order to build up such a large debt that the ECB might suddenly be faced with a choice between an inflationary bail-out and the, barely thinkable, decision to let a Member State actually go bankrupt.

On this issue, the central bank governors, whose prior work, firstly on the Delors Committee and subsequently in their own planning committee, largely laid the foundations for the Maastricht Treaty, have been somewhat inconsistent. Wearing their hats as the Basle Committee on Banking

Supervision, they proclaimed that OECD government debt should bear a zero credit-risk weighting, while at the same time, wearing their Delors hat, they constructed an EMU system in which the default risk on Member State government bonds could become significant.[7] But if such default, or credit, risk on member-government bonds had been, or still could be, properly factored into the various capital adequacy directives, then banks and other financial institutions could only hold large amounts of any government's bonds if they held increasing capital reserves against them. As Graham Bishop has rightly argued,[8] the financial system could be thereby given at least partial protection against such a default, making less pressing the need for the authorities to limit fiscal choice for monetary reasons.

Moreover, Eichengreen and von Hagen[9] have argued that the danger of imprudent fiscal behaviour and of conditions requiring a bail-out, and so the need for prior fiscal restraints, arise

. . . typically where sub-central governments finance only a small share of their expenditures from own taxes. The association of fiscal restraints with the distribution of the tax base makes intuitive sense. When a sub-national government retains significant autonomy over taxation, it can be asked to use tax policy to deal with the fiscal problems it creates for itself. When the tax base is controlled by the [higher-level] government, however, [lower-level] jurisdictions with fiscal problems have only the options of defaulting or soliciting a bailout; raising own taxes is not an option.

This is one reason why one sees a disproportionate incidence of fiscal restrictions in countries where state and local governments retain control of only a relatively small share of the tax base.

In Europe, the EU has only limited taxation and expenditure authority. The vast majority of taxation remains under the control of Member States. This is certain to remain so for the foreseeable future. All this suggests that the rationale for the Excessive Deficits Procedure is weak.

One of the adverse side-effects of the deficit criterion is that this may reduce the flexibility with which fiscal policy may be used by individual Member States in order to offset adverse shocks, just at the moment when monetary policy can no longer be used for this purpose. In this respect,

---

7. As the 1995–96 US budgetary battles should remind us, default risk is present even in the strongest countries. Even before EMU, central bank governors have, however, been reluctant, no doubt for political reasons, to put themselves in a position of having to allocate any risk-weighting to government debt.

8. G. Bishop, *The EC's Public Debt Disease: Discipline with Credit Spreads and Cure with Price Stability*, Salomon Brothers Economic and Market Analysis (May 1991).

9. B. Eichengreen and J. von Hagen, *Fiscal Policy and Monetary Union: Federalism, Fiscal Restrictions and the No-Bail-Out Rule*, Centre for Economic Policy Research Discussion Paper No. 1247 (Sept. 1995).

Minister Waigel's proposed stability pact, whereby Member States aim at a lower deficit in normal times, in order to allow some room for the automatic stabilisers to work during cyclical downturns, makes absolute sense. I have seen, however, no justification for choosing a margin of 2 per cent. It could well be that one should aim for a fiscal *surplus* on average, in order to allow sufficient room for some fiscal stabilisation, both automatic and discretionary, during severe downturns. But perhaps Waigel did not want to frighten the troops.

He did, however, cause a tremor or two with his suggested sanction, whereby any government surpassing the 3 per cent limit for more than one year should be required to pay over to the federal budget a fine representing some significant fraction of the assessed excess. That proposal seems to me to run into all kinds of difficulties. It immediately adds to the fiscal deficit it is meant to prevent. It will encourage accounting stratagems to reduce the estimated fine. Worst of all, the specific extra Waigel tax would inevitably have the effect of raising anti-European venom among the public. And would national parliaments willingly vote for such a tax? And what would happen if they refused? What is needed, instead, is some sanction that would hit the political elite in an offending country *without* impinging on the general public. Perhaps preventing the governor of that country's central bank from participating in the governing council of the ECB, or that country from holding the presidency of the EU, so long as its deficit remained over 3 per cent would be more suitable. I had also thought of requiring the minister of finance of that country to act as host of the Eurovision Song Contest as an appropriate penalty, but perhaps that is too flippant.

If the risk of potential default from a fiscally imprudent Member State is perceived as serious (especially if incremental capital reserves are properly required to be held by financial institutions against such now riskier debt), then the market should price such risk into the interest rates to be paid by each separate governmental borrower. Italian government debt is not going to sell on the same yield as German, whether or not they are both denominated in Euros. Moving to a single currency will mean that fellow Europeans will swap a security with an exchange-rate risk but no default risk for one with no exchange-rate risk but now with a default risk.

We have been told at some length about the advantages in terms of lower real interest rates of getting rid of the exchange-rate risk, but what about the offset in higher default risk? I have seen an exercise run by an American investment firm regressing the credit rating of individual US states on a number of characteristics of those same states, such as income and debt per capita, debt service as a per cent of revenue, unemployment and operating surplus, and then using those same coefficients to estimate the credit rating of prospective EU national governments. All the US states examined, bar one (Louisiana), had credit ratings of A or above. On the firm's estimates, only eight of the fourteen (excluding Luxembourg) Member States would have A rankings, with the lowest being Belgium (C), Italy (B3) and Greece (Ba2). The UK would be Aa2.

There does seem to be a trade-off. The tighter the fiscal criteria that are imposed and maintained, the better the credit rating and the lower the interest-rate risk premium on that country's debt, but at the same time those same criteria will require potentially severe adjustment costs on several countries during the transition period and will continue to constrain national flexibility.

One problem, of course, is that nobody knows exactly what the parameters of this trade-off might be – neither what credit ratings would be established under EMU, nor what will be required to satisfy either the Maastricht fiscal criteria or Minister Waigel's prospective stability pact. Under Article 104c of the EC Treaty, the European Council, on a recommendation from the Commission, can decide whether an excessive deficit exists, with the required ratios of a deficit below 3 per cent and a debt ratio below 60 per cent being interpreted in the light of the qualifying clauses in paragraph 2, clauses (a) and (b), which are mainly about moving in the right direction.

We already know from the Irish case that there is some willingness to interpret these clauses leniently. The Commission is likely to want to bend over backwards to enable Belgium to qualify; but, if the Belgian debt ratio is to be forgiven, how on comparability grounds can others be rejected? Given the keenness of the Commission to extend the coverage of EMU to the greatest extent sustainable, and the willingness of most Heads of State and Government to be similarly generous, the likely arbiter of the composition of EMU at the outset of Stage Three in January 1999 may well be Germany unilaterally, rather than the Treaty modality as laid out in Article 109j. The German authorities may insist that, unless their own interpretation of the criteria is accepted, Germany will not join, perhaps because the Constitutional Court might in this case prevent the country from doing so. So Germany may, in effect, decide who its EMU partners are to be.

3. THE EXCHANGE-RATE QUESTION

3.1 ERM membership as a convergence criterion?

Such uncertainties about the interpretation of the convergence criteria extend beyond the fiscal criteria to the exchange-rate criterion as well. This is set out in Article 109j of the EC Treaty, which states that each Member State shall fulfil 'the observance of the normal fluctuation margins provided for by the exchange-rate mechanism of the European Monetary System, for at least two years, without devaluing against the currency of any other Member State'.

Following the retreat to wider 15 per cent bands in August 1993, quite what is now meant by the term 'normal fluctuation' margins remains obscure. Both the EMI and the Commission have flinched from any attempt at specific quantification. But what is surely crystal-clear is that a Member State must have been a member of the ERM for the years 1996 and 1997 to meet the wording which I have just repeated. Since the UK is not now a member of the ERM, and not intending to become so in the foreseeable future, we *cannot* qualify for EMU at the outset. I have been surprised by comments in the press that the UK may be one of the few countries meeting all the criteria at the outset, even if we should choose to avail ourselves of the opt-out.

I was even more surprised to read a report in the *Financial Times* that Prime Minister Major took the same view, that is, that prior ERM membership was no longer a prerequisite for entry, and even that the Commission had refrained from confirming what seems to me to be patently obvious.[10] The EMI has raised such reluctance almost to an art form, stating that, '[u]nder current circumstances, it is not advisable to give a precise operational content to the Treaty provisions regarding exchange rates which could be mechanically applied also to forthcoming periods'.[11] If so, the exchange-rate criterion must be viewed as abandoned and extinct, which only goes to underline how much the whole exercise is subject to ongoing political interpretation and manipulation.

I have met several academic colleagues from the Continent who take the view that the exchange-rate criterion should be used, if still possible, to *exclude* the UK from initial membership, even should we otherwise both wish and be in a position to join. Their point is that membership of EMU is not widely popular either among the public or among Conservative politicians in the UK. The worst scenario for the continued viability of EMU would be to have one British government take us into EMU, only for another government to be elected subsequently, in the midst, for instance, of a severe slump, on the basis of a mandate to take us out again. It is arguable that federalists, both in the UK and abroad, as well as sceptics, should campaign for a pre-entry referendum, precisely to defend against the disastrous possibility of the UK 'upsetting the apple-cart' by revoking the supposedly irrevocable. As I discussed earlier, the idea that currency union, even when Stage 3B is attained, would be impervious to widespread public

10. L. Barber, 'Brussels Ducks Decision on EMU Requirement', *Financial Times*, 20 Dec. 1995, p.2.
11. European Monetary Institute, 'Progress Towards Convergence' (Nov. 1995), p.x; but later on in this same document, p.33, Box 4.1, the EMI confirms that 'the requirement to be a member of the ERM remains an element of the Treaty'.

and political dissatisfaction in any major country, is just wrong, despite the empty rhetoric to the contrary. Perhaps the ERM-membership issue could be used by our Continental colleagues as a way of *requiring* that the UK holds a referendum before it is *allowed* to opt in, though it might be difficult for politicians on the Continent to appear to propose some prior measure here that could be construed as interfering in our internal political processes!

3.2 How to fix exchange rates among the Ins?

In the context of this discussion of exchange rates, one should also address the question regarding the relationships between those Member States participating in Stage Three and those not participating – the 'Ins' and the 'Outs' of the single-currency area. Let us first discuss briefly what may happen to the exchange rate of those countries who do join EMU at the outset. There is a serious, though somewhat technical, problem for the Ins. Their exchange rates have to be irrevocably fixed at the starting date, 1 January 1999; none the less, between the moment of their selection as Ins and the starting date for Stage Three, their currencies could fluctuate against each other, and even have their central parities revised, for example in order to try to establish a more user-friendly set of cross-rates against the Euro. If such rate revisions were, however, to be left until the very last moment, for example in December 1998, this would be liable to encourage intense efforts by private-sector agents to anticipate the possible final rate alignments, and this could generate really massive speculative capital flows in response to any rumours or information. It is unlikely that official discussions on such a sensitive topic could be kept hermetically secret for long, and any perceived leak could lead to most disorderly market conditions.

One alternative that has been canvassed would be to seek to fix both the identity of the participants in the core and the exchange rates that would be adopted amongst them at the same moment, possibly in March 1998. It is unlikely, however, that the time and energy available for the European Council would suffice to allow both complex sets of questions to be resolved simultaneously. More important, the institutional arrangements, for example, the ECB itself and the central linking electronic payment system, known as TARGET, necessary to sustain such completely fixed parities would not be in place. So long as the national monetary authorities remain independently responsible for setting interest rates in their own money markets, which is supposed to be the case until January 1999, exchange rates could diverge from their proclaimed final alignment. Would that matter? If the divergence from the announced final values became at all large, it might throw some doubt on the credibility of the announced set of future exchange rates. My own view, however, is that the ECB, together with the national central banks of the participating countries, will have the technical ability and market power to enforce whatever set of fixed exchange rates is chosen, so long as the essential political and public support for that exercise is maintained. Sensing this, I would expect any interim speculation to be stabilising, in the sense that it would drive the exchange rates of the participating Member States towards their final announced values, unless the policies adopted in the meantime by these states were patently inconsistent with the achievement of EMU.

There have been various other alternatives proposed.[12] The Executive Board of the ECB has to be established immediately after the final possible date for choosing which countries are to participate in Stage Three, that is, by 1 July 1998. Decisions on the selection and introduction of the irrevocably fixed exchange rates could be delegated to the Governing Council and Executive Board of the ECB as one of its first main tasks. Another rather neat idea, that I heard from a colleague, was that the final exchange rate should be established as the average rate over, for example, the previous three years up till 1 January 1999. That would give the market a degree of certainty from the outset, while allowing some flexibility in the run-up to the starting date. As that date grew closer, the ultimate value would become ever more firmly established, which should again lead to stabilising speculation.

The disadvantage of the latter approach would be that the final exchange rate would result from market happenstance rather than from any conscious choice. Whether either the market or a political choice would result in exchange rates near to those that economists might estimate, uncertainly, as being near 'equilibrium' is equally dubious. In particular, market outcomes would not result, except by pure chance, in any user-friendly set of cross-rates, for example with the Euro, but in some horrible fraction, to seven or so places of decimals. Since I view the key to the whole exercise as being its public acceptability, the choice of a set of user-friendly cross-rates strikes me as important. Consequently, I would argue for the earliest possible announcement of such final rates, preferably involving a proposed final realignment to a user-friendly set of cross-rates; I would expect speculation then to force the spot exchange rates in markets towards such final announced values, subject to any remaining interest differentials.

---

12. Indeed, the whole exercise of setting exchange rates for the Ins may be further inextricably complicated, depending on the interpretation to be given to the EC Treaty's requirement that such irrevocable fixing 'shall not by itself modify the external value of the ECU'. Given that only a subset of EU countries whose currencies are now part of the ECU will join Stage 3A at the outset, and that some of the Outs may have to devalue at that time, the meaning of this requirement has become opaque, but it might further hinder any planned final parity readjustments. I am grateful to John Arrowsmith for reminding me of this problem.

Some fear that any attempt to have a final chosen realignment among the Ins would open up a Pandora's box, whereby each nation would seek to achieve a more competitive parity. Whether the final group of participating countries could achieve a set of user-friendly cross-rates without any of them having to undergo a major adjustment in parities, will remain uncertain until we know the identity of the Ins, and can do the accompanying exercise. Experience suggests that it is rarely easy to produce round conversion factors by 'small' realignments, even with only a few currencies. If there should be, for example, two or more alternative ways of achieving a set of user-friendly parities, with differing implications for real exchange rates, there could be dissension and political deadlock over which to choose.

Such is the fear that each participating country would seek its own competitive advantage through a final devaluation, that the Ins may become paralysed and unable to make any conscious choice of parity realignment. Then the final parity would have to be some measure of the rates set by the happenstance of the market. My own view is that this fear (*ie,* that any opportunity for a final realignment would give occasion for selfish and conflicting national behaviour) is exaggerated. With the participating countries embarking on what would be seen, and treated, as the outset of a grand European design, clearly intended to develop further, the idea that they would run the danger of getting this underway in a fractious spirit of search for narrow national advantage seems to me unlikely, though clearly not impossible.

3.3 Relationships between the Ins and Outs?

However, concern about such 'competitive devaluation' does play a large, though again exaggerated, role in discussions about exchange-rate relationships between the Ins and the Outs. 'Competitive devaluation' is to EMU what fundamental disequilibrium was to Bretton Woods: that is, a key, central concept, but one whose meaning is somewhat hard to define. In one sense, of course, any devaluation must improve the competitive position of the relevant country, but the Outs can hardly be expected to maintain a completely fixed exchange rate against the core group of Ins, especially when they have just been publicly designated as too weak, inflationary and fiscally profligate to join the Ins. Indeed, the very fact of being ruled Out might spark off a speculative attack.

What is becoming clearer, is that the positions and objectives of the Outs will be varied. Rather than having a common purpose, the Outs might each engage in bilateral negotiations with the core group of Ins. There may be at least three alternative positions taken by the various Outs. Some might wish to mimic as far as possible the exchange-rate conditions that would have pertained had they been participating as Ins. Austria, Belgium, Denmark, and perhaps Finland, should they be Outs, might choose this route. They could aim to do so by tying their own currencies rigidly to the Euro through a currency-board system. The question would then arise whether they would have to do so absolutely on their own, relying purely on their own reserves of Euros (and other foreign-exchange reserves) to see themselves through external speculative attack or internal financial crisis, or whether they could expect assistance from the Ins. Unlimited assistance from the Ins must surely be ruled out, since that would be tantamount to contradicting the decision to keep them out in the first place. But absolute refusal of any assistance would be niggardly and hardly *communautaire*. As in other areas of central banking, constructive ambiguity on a case-by-case basis may be necessary.

At the other extreme, some countries may either be unable or unwilling to enter into a standard ERM-type relationship with the central core group. This group might comprise Greece, Italy and the UK. If Prime Minister Major is correct in stating that ERM membership is not a necessary condition for initial entry in 1999, there would seem no rationale for it to be subsequently re-established as such. Such countries would presumably continue to float. I would presume that the European bodies, the Council, Ecofin and the Commission, would press them to establish some nominal anchor, or objective; this could be a direct inflation or nominal-income target,[13] or an intermediate monetary target. In this case, a competitive devaluation would presumably be defined as a devaluation accompanying a clear failure to abide by the chosen nominal anchor. I would assume that the European bodies would feel that Article 109m of the EC Treaty would give them a legal basis for expressing an opinion on the suitability and prospective quantification of the nominal objective chosen in each case.

The third group of countries would presumably seek to establish some pegged, but adjustable, exchange-rate relationship with the core Ins. Niels Thygesen has argued that the disparity of size and weight between the core Ins and the peripheral Outs, and the absolute priority that must be given by the ECB to achieving price stability among the Ins, would probably rule out a simple continuation of the existing EMS.[14] Instead of a bilateral grid parity, this group of countries would peg directly to the Euro; what the prospective exchange-rate margins would be, and what mutual assistance, if any, from

---

13. A contemporaneous paper by T. Persson and G. Tabellini, 'Monetary Cohabitation in Europe', presented at the American Economic Association Conference (Jan. 1996), argues that an inflation target should have better characteristics for non-participating Member States than would an exchange-rate peg to the Euro.
14. N. Thygesen, 'The Prospects for EMU by 1999 – and Reflections on Arrangements for the Outsiders', inaugural lecture organised by the University of Manchester's European Policy Unit, Edinburgh University's Europe Institute and the Royal Bank of Scotland, Manchester (Nov. 1995).

the core Ins to the peripheral Outs might be expected, remains uncertain. The Iberian and Nordic countries might be in this group. There would, however, be a serious initial problem for them. As already noted, they would have just been publicly designated as weak; the ECB and the core Ins may be too preoccupied with achieving counter-inflationary credibility to offer much, if any, assistance on the exchange market; and the European authorities might attempt to seize the occasion to re-establish narrower margins. If so, peripheral Outs adopting such pegged exchange rates would be especially vulnerable to speculative attacks at the outset. If they were overwhelmed by such attacks, a small parity devaluation might not be credible; if, however, a large devaluation were regarded as 'competitive', and hence unacceptable, they would presumably then be forced to float their currencies. Only in the case of a chosen preemptive parity adjustment can one make much sense of the term 'competitive devaluation'. In this latter context, it could be defined as a devaluation which establishes a more competitive real exchange rate than that which had existed at some base date, though the difficulties of agreeing on an appropriate base date and on a way of adjusting from a nominal on to a comparable real basis are only too obvious.

The more one looks at the term 'competitive devaluation', the more slippery and difficult it becomes. For example, a nominal devaluation that is accompanied by expansionary monetary policy is unlikely to make the devaluing country excessively competitive for long, since the resulting faster domestic inflation is likely to bring the real exchange rate back to its predevaluation level rather quickly. Whereas a nominal devaluation that is not accompanied by more expansionary monetary policy is unlikely to be driven by a conscious attempt to gain a trading advantage, but, like Italy's recent experience, may be due to speculative attacks based on political, or other non-economic, concerns. It takes a rare combination of circumstances to achieve a purposeful, consciously-chosen devaluation that succeeds in achieving any medium or longer-term competitive advantage in the real exchange rate.

Besides these three alternatives for the Outs, that is, mimicry through a currency board, a revised ERM and a float with a nominal objective, there may be yet others. One suggestion that has been made is that in some countries the private sector might spontaneously shift from the national currency to using Euros. I regard this as fanciful and implausible for ordinary retail business. Everything that we know about network externalities[15] and the difficulty of getting the general public to shift to new currencies and coins so long as they have the option of sticking with the familiar old

---

15. See Dowd and Greenaway, loc. cit., n.2.

currencies, suggests that any widespread shift to using Euros by the general public will have to be enforced, by removing any alternative.

The situation may well be different for wholesale, especially multinational, business. Here the hope must be that, so long as they were prepared to deal, pay and settle in Euros, the commercial and central banks among the Outs would be encouraged to participate in the TARGET trans-European electronic real-time gross-payment system. That would help to provide the momentum and experience for subsequent accession to EMU itself.

4.   THINKING THE UNTHINKABLE

My last topic involves trying to think through the unthinkable, what to do if the transition process breaks down, either because France, and even perhaps now Germany, cannot meet the criteria, or can only meet them at an unacceptable political and social cost, or because German public and political opinion turns decisively against it. Obviously, the response should depend on the exact circumstances. If the circumstances of the failure reflected primarily the adverse economic conjuncture, then the best response would probably be simply to defer and delay the starting date. Several commentators have argued that this could irreparably damage the perceived commitment to, and credibility of, EMU. I do not share that view. Whereas a pegged, but adjustable, exchange regime is a fragile system that does rely on confidence, an irrevocably fixed system should be technically solid and secure, relatively impervious to speculative attack, as much in Stage 3A as in Stage 3B. Its weakness lies not in its technical structure, but potentially in its lack of political and public support, though that in turn depends on the overall economic success of the venture.

The current transition process was not, as I outlined back at the start of this chapter, designed primarily to minimise political and public opposition. If the exercise were to break down because of such opposition, the correct course in my view would be to analyse the wellsprings of such opposition, and then plan how to proceed in order to neutralise them.

As noted at the outset, there are three such sources of opposition. First, EMU will reduce the ability of national politicians to use the levers of monetary policy. While this loss of power disturbs some politicians, the transfer of power may disturb the public rather less; they worry more about the outcome of those decisions, and not so much about who makes them – although, as Scots know very well, any region or nation which feels that its voice or wishes are being disregarded on a long-standing basis by a quasi-permanent majority resident elsewhere is likely to become increasingly aggrieved. Be that as it may, the first step should have been the establishment of an independent central bank in each country. If the present EMU transition should irreparably break down, it should, as soon as possible, be restarted on this basis. Each central bank should choose its own nominal objective; this could be an exchange-rate target; the Commission and Council should have the right to comment on all such chosen targets. No central bank should take instructions from its government, *except* to agree the quantified nominal objective. All government debt should be accorded a risk-weighting, which should rise incrementally as its percentage in banks' portfolios increases. The achievement of the nominal objective should be reinforced by (pecuniary) sanctions and incentives on the governor and executive board of each national central bank.

After a number of years in which the independent national nominal targets are met, succeeding in reducing inflation to, for example, below 3 per cent, with unemployment no higher than, for example, 7.5 per cent or than the average of the five previous years, those Member States meeting such criteria would move to EMU, in which the exchange rates would be irrevocably fixed, preferably at user-friendly cross-rates, and the ECB would set the common nominal objective. There would be no fiscal criteria; these would be, in effect, replaced by the incremental risk-weightings for financial intermediaries wishing to hold public-debt instruments as assets.

Second, the remaining problem, and main source of public opposition in this context, would be that asymmetric shocks could still cause lengthy periods of recession and unemployment in some region or nation. While this could, to a large extent, probably be relieved by intra-national fiscal transfers, it remains necessary for political and presentational reasons for those who happen to feel themselves losers because of EMU to see that they are, nevertheless, getting some recompense from the exercise. For such political reasons, it is to my mind highly desirable, if not essential, to accompany EMU with some purpose-built federal stabilisation scheme, such as advocated by myself and Stephen Smith,[16] with an example worked out by Italianer and Vanheukelen.[17] The lack of political willingness to support monetary unification with even some strictly limited fiscal federalism is a symptom of the weakness of EMU's current political support and under-pinning.

Third, the irrevocable fixing of currencies in Stage 3A should be technically robust, and should deliver virtually all the economic benefits available in EMU. There is no need to rush on to Stage 3B and the Euro. The transition from phase A to B here will be both expensive in real resources

16. C. A. E. Goodhart and S. Smith, 'Stabilization' [1993] 5 *European Economy, Reports and Studies* 417.
17. A. Italianer and M. Vanheukelen, 'Proposals for Community Stabilization Mechanisms: Some Historical Applications' [1993] 5 *European Economy, Reports and Studies* 493.

and highly unpopular. The idea that Stage 3B is somehow much more permanent and irreversible than Stage 3A, is not correct. Once Stage 3A has been shown to work well enough, for long enough, there could be increasing enthusiasm for moving from national currencies to the Euro. Should it be agreed now that the Euro would not be introduced until a majority of the people in a majority of the participating countries wanted this to happen, most of the present opposition to the exercise would be removed at a stroke.

Chapter Two

LEGAL ASPECTS OF THE CHANGEOVER TO A SINGLE CURRENCY

Helmut Wittelsberger

Chapter Outline

1. Introduction

2. Legal Status of the Euro

3. Continuity of Contracts

European Economic and Monetary Union: The Institutional Framework (M. Andenas, L. Gormley, C. Hadjiemmanuil, I. Harden, eds.: 90-411-0687-1: © Kluwer Law International: pub. Kluwer Law International, 1997: printed in Great Britain)

1.   INTRODUCTION

The Treaty establishing the European Community specifies in some detail the steps to be taken in order to achieve Economic and Monetary Union in the sense of common economic and monetary policy-making. This stage is reached when exchange rates among participating countries are irrevocably fixed, and the responsibility for monetary policy is transferred from national authorities to the European Central Bank. In contrast, the provisions on the following steps are extremely concise: the Treaty simply states that the Council, acting according to the same procedure that applies to the decision on the conversion rates, that is, with the unanimity of the Member States participating in Stage Three, on a proposal from the Commission and after consulting the ECB, shall also take the other measures necessary for the rapid introduction of the ECU as the single currency of the participating Member States.[1]

The fact that the EC Treaty limits itself to devoting one single sentence to a subject which proves to be full of complex issues calls for an explanation.

One factor which might be cited is that the practical questions of the changeover were simply not at the centre of interest during the Maastricht Treaty negotiations. In fact, the third stage of EMU was expected to start only five to seven years after the conclusion of the negotiations in late 1991. Besides, the need for taking the phrase 'rapid introduction of the ECU as the single currency' literally may have been perceived as being less urgent five years ago. Indeed, the Maastricht Treaty was drafted at a time when the European Monetary System with narrow exchange-rate bands seemed to function smoothly in a world free of capital movements. The crisis of 1992–93 has not only damaged the convergence criterion on exchange rates, but has also raised questions about the functioning of a monetary union without a single currency. Despite the fact that EMU is fundamentally different from a system of fixed exchange rates, the experience of 1992–93 has undoubtedly reinforced the consensus that the transitional period between the start of the third stage and the completion of the changeover should be kept as short as possible.

Above all, the steps to be taken for the introduction of the single currency have not been specified in the Treaty, thus allowing for flexibility. Rightly so, the negotiators have abstained from limiting the choice. As we know today, the systematic investigation of possible strategies for the changeover only started some years after the meeting of Maastricht. With a more limiting text, it would not have been possible to have a debate about scenarios as broad as we have experienced since 1994. The reference scenario which was agreed by the European Council of Madrid in December 1995 is the

---

1.   EC Treaty, Art. 1091 (4), third sentence.

result of substantial preparatory work including the consultations of currency users. The future legal framework has now been defined more specifically.

The Green Paper of the European Commission, published in May 1995, marked an important step in the public debate about the practical questions of the changeover to the single currency.[2] As stated in the Green Paper, the easiest course of action would be to introduce the single currency in full, which would include putting banknotes and coins into circulation, from the beginning of Stage Three, that is, as soon as conversion rates are irrevocably fixed. This approach would offer considerable practical advantages and would, of course, also avoid a number of legal questions that arise in the transitional period. Because of the necessary technical preparations, however, such a period is indispensable. Its maximum length has been fixed at $3\frac{1}{2}$ years by the European Council – from 1 January 1999 to 30 June 2002, at the latest. It will be characterised in particular by the absence of banknotes and coins denominated in the single currency, a situation which gives rise to specific legal questions. In fact, such a situation is unprecedented in monetary history. Legislation must provide for specific rules which apply during this period only, a fact which may occasionally give the impression that the changeover is more complex than it basically is. The fact that these transitory provisions will apply for a short period only – hopefully for less than $3\frac{1}{2}$ years – should be kept in mind. Besides, any such provisions will undoubtedly apply only to those Member States which enter into monetary union in 1999. Whether any States joining later would be confronted with similar transitory provisions, is an open question. In any case, the timely supply of sufficient quantities of banknotes and coins denominated in Euro would present less problems once their circulation in the initial group of countries is completed.

The European economies are highly integrated open markets with well-developed legal systems. Efficient credit markets have bound households and businesses closely together via their respective financial claims and liabilities. Today's complex financial instruments were able to develop only in a climate of legal clarity and certainty. If the new currency is to be introduced smoothly, all those involved, that is, the entire population, must be afforded legal certainty ahead of the changeover. This is on the whole not a difficult task, since EMU is a well-thought-out and long-fought-for plan for progressing resolutely towards a single currency through 'convergence'. The process was not triggered, nor has it been accompanied, by political or economic upheaval. It is fundamentally different from past currency reforms, which usually marked the end of political and economic chaos.

2. European Commission, 'One Currency for Europe – Green Paper on the Practical Arrangements for the Introduction of the Single Currency' (31 May 1995), COM (95) 333 final.

For this very reason, any arguments about the legal situation in the EMU changeover which are derived from court rulings in the context of past changes in monetary regimes are of little relevance. The stable economic framework of EMU does not, however, relieve the national and European legislators from the obligation of taking painstaking, detailed steps to preserve legal clarity and certainty.

Monetary union will inevitably raise many specific legal questions in different areas. Two topics deserve special consideration: the legal status of the new currency during the period between the beginning of Stage Three and the definitive changeover; and the continuity of private-law contracts.

2.   LEGAL STATUS OF THE EURO

Once the rates of conversion of the national currencies have been irrevocably fixed between each other and *vis-à-vis* the Euro at the beginning of Stage Three, the single currency can be said to have come into existence economically. The single monetary policy will be formulated by the European Central Bank, and money will be issued under its sole authority. The national monetary units will then constitute merely different symbols representing the economic reality of the single currency. The task is to make the legal situation correspond to this economic reality. Measures will have to be taken to ensure that, from the legal viewpoint too, the national units are simply different symbols for the single currency. The EC Treaty does not produce this legal effect directly.

In fact, the Treaty includes only a few provisions which relate to currency law: issuance and legal-tender status of bank-notes (Article 105a (1)), issuance of coins (Article 105a (2)), exchange of banknotes in national denominations (Article 52 of the Statute of the ESCB), the ECU becoming a currency in its own right on the first day of Stage Three (Article 109l (4), first sentence). Any further rules will have to be established under the general mandate of taking the other necessary measures according to the third sentence of Article 109l (4).

The European Council has specified this mandate: a Council Regulation entering into force on 1 January 1999 will provide the legal framework for the use of the Euro.[3] The Regulation will ensure that the national currencies and the Euro will become different expressions of what is economically the same currency; it will establish a 'legally enforceable equivalence' between

---

3. 'The Scenario for the Changeover to the Single Currency', Annex I to the Conclusions of the European Council meeting held at Madrid, 15–16 Dec. 1995, (1996) OJ C 22/2.

the Euro and the national currency units.[4] 'Legally enforceable equivalence' means that each monetary amount is assigned, in a legally enforceable way, an unchangeable countervalue in term of the Euro unit as the official exchange rate, and vice versa. Private economic agents will be free to use the Euro; at the same time, they should not be obliged to do so. National banknotes will continue to remain legal tender within the boundaries of the respective national territories until the completion of the changeover. The technical preparatory work for this Regulation shall be completed at the latest by the end of 1996.

One way of meeting the guidelines from the European Council would be to introduce the Euro as the single currency from the very beginning of Stage Three: the Euro would not only become a currency in its own right, as stipulated by the EC Treaty, but at the same time acquire the status of the single currency. As such, the period during which the Euro would be a currency in its own right without being the single currency, would be skipped. The national currencies would, simultaneously, cease to be lawful currencies. But account would have to be taken of the fact that, until banknotes and coins are exchanged, it must still be possible to use national notes and coins. Since national notes and coins will continue to circulate, it must also be possible to use the 'old' denominations in non-cash transactions and as units of account. The continuing use of the national units would, therefore, have to be explicitly provided for. This could be achieved by legally defining them as divisions or expressions of the single currency until national notes and coins are withdrawn and replaced by notes and coins denominated in Euro and its divisions.

The approach described above would ensure that the Euro is substituted for the participating currencies at the beginning of Stage Three. This is of relevance for the questions related to the continuity of contracts which will be discussed below. The alternatives would be to postpone substitution until Euro notes and coins are in circulation. National currencies would continue to exist under national law until that date. The Euro would coexist as a currency in its own right. Its status would have to be specified further. It would be necessary to address the question of legally enforceable equivalence between the Euro and national currencies.

In all Member States, legal tender is limited to national banknotes and to coins up to certain amounts.[5] As long as the status of legal tender is not

---

4. The term 'legally enforceable equivalence' and its definition were first used by the European Monetary Institute in its report, 'The Changeover to the Single Currency' (Nov. 1995), p.20.
5. In some countries (Italy, France), specific limits for using cash for payments are in force. In the Netherlands, a debtor can validly discharge a monetary obligation by a transfer of a claim on a bank, unless the creditor has expressly opted for cash. However, these provisions do not formally affect the legal-tender status of banknotes.

extended, means of payment denominated in Euro and enjoying this quality will, therefore, not be available in the transitory period. However, in case the substitution were to occur on the first day of Stage Three, it would be incorrect to conclude that the Euro would not be endowed with legal-tender status. In fact, banknotes and coins expressed in national denominations would be legal tender of the single currency by definition.

3.   CONTINUITY OF CONTRACTS

Replacement of the national currencies by the Euro raises the question of the continuing validity of contracts which have been made in national currency and have not been fully performed at the time of the changeover. It must first be acknowledged that the relevant monetary obligations expressed in today's currencies cannot objectively be settled in the currency agreed in the contract. According to an established principle of law, contracting parties are deemed to have agreed that in such a case the monetary obligations are carried over into the successor currency introduced by the entity exercising monetary sovereignty. This is the principle of *lex monetae*, which is generally recognised in the European Community. The Council Regulation stipulating the substitution will have direct effect in the participating Member States. It has the quality of law established by the national legislator and renders any incompatible national legislative provisions inapplicable. The Regulation will have to stipulate that with effect from a given date, the currency of country A will be the Euro, and that the former currency is replaced by the Euro at a certain rate. In this way, the Euro will be defined in terms of its predecessor, and the recurrent link will be established. This, together with the recognition of the principle of nominalism, will ensure that monetary obligations will remain unaffected by the changeover.

Apart from this formal aspect, a second question concerns the substance of contracts. Provisions exist in all national jurisdictions which allow one contractual party to terminate or to modify the terms of a contract without the consent of the other contractual party in case of a fundamental disruption in economic factors. Inspection of legal systems of Member States suggests that the conditions under which contracts can successfully be challenged are quite similar (doctrine of frustration under English law, *théorie de l'imprévision* under French law, *Wegfall der Geschäftsgrundlage* under German law, *eccesiva onerosità* under Italian law, etc). In any case, EMU is far from providing such conditions. Since the changeover to the single currency is a political objective that has long been public knowledge and has been thoroughly prepared, it cannot be deemed to constitute an unforeseeable or disruptive change in economic conditions that would justify unilaterally cancelling contracts made in national currency or renegotiating their terms. Smoothness of the process is ensured, *inter alia*, by the convergence criterion relating to long-term interest rates. Price stability has become an objective of economic and monetary policies and is resolutely and successfully pursued in all Member States. The concomitant decline in long-term interest rates towards the level of the countries with the best stability record is indistinguishable from the effects of EMU. Sharp fluctuations in long-term rates have occurred repeatedly in the past; for instance, such rates declined in France from around 16 per cent in 1981 to 8.5 per cent in 1986, and from 20 per cent to below 12 per cent in Italy over the same period.

The European Council of Madrid has concluded as follows:

The substitution of the Euro for national currencies should not of itself alter the continuity of contracts; amounts expressed in national currency will be converted into Euro at the rate of conversion laid down by the Council. In the case of fixed interest rate securities and loans, this substitution will not of itself alter the normal interest rate payable by the debtor unless otherwise provided in the contract.[6]

Following the publication of the Green Paper of the European Commission in May 1995,[7] numerous business associations and advisory bodies have expressed views on continuity.[8] The general tone of these reactions was that, in principle, contracts could not be challenged in the wake of the changeover. However, many respondents called for explicit confirmation of continuity by EC legislation; in their view, limiting the Regulation to the statement that the Euro replaces national currencies at the fixed rates, while theoretically appealing, would not be sufficient in practice. In fact, these commentators seem to be looking for a translation into a legally binding form of a statement similar to that of the European Council cited above.

Regardless of whether or not such a confirmation of continuity will be enacted, the changeover to the Euro will generally just require a simple

---

6. 'The Scenario for the Changeover to the Single Currency', loc. cit., n.3.
7. Loc. cit., n.2.
8. See, *inter alia*, Financial Law Panel, *Response to the European Commission's Green Paper dated 31 May 1995 on the Practical Arrangements for the Introduction of the Single Currency* (Oct. 1995); idem, *The Need for the ECU: Supplementary Response to the Green Paper* (Dec. 1995); City of London Law Society, Banking Law Sub-Committee, *Response to the European Commission's Green Paper dated 31 May 1995 on the Practical Arrangements for the Introduction of the Single Currency* (1995); idem, *Supplemental Response to the Commission's Green Paper: The Need for Legislation to Ensure Continuity of Contracts* (Jan. 1996); Paribas Capital Markets, *Legal Implications of European Monetary Union* (Nov. 1995); Banking Federation of the European Union, *Introduction of the Single Currency: The Views of the Banking Federation of the European Union* (Nov. 1995), annex D, 'Legal Issues'.

recalculation of currency amounts, with all the other terms of the contract unaltered. However, this is not to deny that there are certain categories of contracts which raise particular questions. These include contracts denominated in the basket-ECU, contracts referring to indices, currency swaps, and contracts governed by the law of third countries.

Much attention has been drawn recently to contracts denominated in the basket-ECU. The above considerations concern national currencies only, and do not automatically apply to ECU contracts. The EC Treaty has settled the question of continuity between the basket-ECU and the single-currency-ECU in the realm of public law. On the first day of Stage Three, the nature of the ECU changes from a basket of currencies into a currency in its own right, issued by the European System of Central Banks. The conversion rate is 1:1. This occurs directly be virtue of primary law (Articles 109g and 109l (4) of the EC Treaty); no secondary legislation is required to achieve this effect.[9] The existing stock of 'official' ECUs will disappear.[10] As for continuity of ECU contracts under private law, the European Council of Madrid has provided the following clarification: 'In the case of contracts denominated by reference to the official ECU basket of the European Community, in accordance with the Treaty, substitution by the Euro will be at the 1:1 rate, subject to particular terms of individual contracts.'[11]

Contracts referring to indices which will no longer exist in the monetary union or which no longer serve the same purpose will need to be adapted. Such indices include certain types of interest or financial ratios (like a discount rate or reserve requirements, in case these facilities are discontinued). The need for such adaptations is not peculiar to the changeover to the Euro; in fact, financial indices occasionally lose their initial meaning in the process of economic and institutional developments. Reliance on case-by-case solutions may perhaps be preferable to attempts to catch all possible solutions by legislation.

Another category of contracts raising specific questions are currency swaps. Such contracts may involve participating national currencies whose delivery date falls after the start of the third stage. Obviously, volatility between these currencies will be removed from this date onwards. However, it would appear that the performance of the parties' contractual obligations would still be possible. As long as the national currencies still exist, the contract will, in the absence of netting provisions, require both parties to deliver the initially agreed amounts of currencies. After the

---

9. It will, however, be desirable to repeal Regulation No. 3320/94, which defines the ECU as a basket of currencies.
10. According to Art. 23 (2) of the Statute of the EMI, the mechanism for the creation of ECUs against gold and US dollars, as provided for by Art. 17 of the EMS Agreement, shall be unwound by the first day of the third stage.
11. 'The Scenario for the Changeover to the Single Currency', loc. cit., n.3.

completion of the changeover, settlement would result in the exchange of Euro amounts or, with netting, in a one-way delivery of Euros.

Finally, there is the question of what happens to contracts involving EMU currencies which are governed by the law of third countries. Courts outside the European Union may be expected to respect the universal principle of *lex monetae*, that is, to follow the principle of law whereby contracting parties are deemed to have agreed that the law of the country whose currency has been chosen as the currency of the contract shall determine what constitutes that currency. As for the other terms of a contract, the outcome evidently depends on whether the changeover to the Euro is seen as an event which entitles a party to challenge a contract according to the respective state's principles of contract law. In addition to safeguarding continuity within the jurisdiction of the European Union, it is essential to prepare the changeover in a stable economic environment and within a transparent legal framework in order to ensure continuity of contracts worldwide.

Chapter Three

INS AND OUTS OF EMU:
NO GROUNDS FOR DISCRIMINATION

C. S. Kerse

Chapter Outline

1. Introduction

2. Ins and Outs

3. Scope of the Select Committee's Enquiry

4. The Single Market

5. Financial Services: Special Problems
    5.1 Second Banking Directive
        5.1.1 Article 14 (2) – Monetary policy
        5.1.2 Article 19 (4) – The general good
    5.2 Investment Services Directive
        5.2.1 Article 1 (13) – Definition of regulated markets
        5.2.2 Article 15 (5) – Access to new markets

6. Conclusion

European Economic and Monetary Union: The Institutional Framework (M. Andenas, L. Gormley, C. Hadjiemmanuil, I. Harden, eds.: 90-411-0687-1: © Kluwer Law International: pub. Kluwer Law International, 1997: printed in Great Britain)

1.   INTRODUCTION

As the deadline for the commencement of the next stage of European monetary union gets ever closer, much greater attention is being given to the consideration of the question of the United Kingdom's participation. It is not proposed, in this brief chapter, to try to explain all the practical implications of a partial monetary union, that is, a monetary union to which not all the Member States are party (at least at the outset). What will be attempted is an answer to those concerned about the threat of retaliation should the UK decide to stay out of Stage Three of EMU. This question is one of a number addressed in a recent Report of the House of Lords Select Committee on the European Communities, 'An EMU of Ins and Outs'.[1]

If monetary union goes ahead, with Stage Three commencing on 1 January 1999 or shortly thereafter, one thing seems fairly clear. Not all Member States will satisfy the necessary criteria and therefore be eligible to be parties. This does not mean that EMU cannot or will not happen. Under Article 109j (4) of the EC Treaty, the third stage of EMU must go ahead, and this is so even if not all, or even a majority of, Member States are ready to join. Hence, some will be 'Ins', and the rest will be 'Outs'. It is possible to subdivide these categories, in legal terms and also politically.

2.   INS AND OUTS

The Maastricht Treaty on European Union added to the EC Treaty the necessary provisions for monetary union.[2] Member States must meet certain criteria, the so-called convergence criteria. These relate to four principal matters:

(i)   *Inflation*: the achievement of a high degree of price stability – a Member State's inflation rate must be close to that of the three best performing Member States;

(ii)   *Public finances*: the sustainability of the government financial position – a Member State must have a government budgetary position without an 'excessive deficit' as defined in the Treaty;

(iii)   *Exchange rates*: the observance of the normal fluctuation margins provided for by the Exchange Rate Mechanism of the European Monetary System for at least two years, without devaluing against the currency of any other Member State; and

1. House of Lords Select Committee on the European Communities, Eleventh Report: 'An EMU of Ins and Outs', HL (1995–96) 86.
2. EC Treaty, new Title VI of Part Three (Arts 102a–109m), as inserted by Art. G (25) of the Maastricht Treaty.

(iv) *Interest rates*: the durability of convergence achieved by the Member State, reflected in its long-term interest levels.

While the necessary amendments were prepared on the basis that all Member States would participate in the monetary union, the draftsmen of the Maastricht Treaty foresaw that provisions would be necessary to deal with those Member States whose entry would be delayed because of their failure to meet the entry criteria at the outset of EMU. It is important to note that the Maastricht Treaty does not envisage the possibility that those Member States will never join, merely that there will be a delay in their admission. The Treaty talks of these Member States having a 'derogation'. In legal terms at least, this is not the same as having an 'opt-out'. It will be recalled that in the late stages of the Maastricht intergovernmental conference Protocols were added to the proposed text, allowing the UK and Denmark to opt-out of Stage Three, if they so wished.

It follows, therefore, that the Treaty contemplates two basic categories. In the first are the 'Ins', those Member States who meet the convergence criteria and become members of the single-currency area. The second category comprises the 'Outs'. This category can be subdivided into those Member States who are not participants because they have not yet satisfied the convergence criteria and those, namely, the UK and Denmark, who choose not to participate in Stage Three. States in the first category of 'Out' are, no doubt for political reasons, sometimes referred to as the 'Pre-Ins'.

3.   SCOPE OF THE SELECT COMMITTEE'S ENQUIRY

So much for classification. What are the implications of a partial monetary union or, as the Select Committee's Report is entitled, of an EMU of Ins and Outs? The Committee received evidence and looked at a wide variety of matters including:

- the implications for the single market;
- the implications for exchange-rate arrangements;
- the implications for the European Union's Budget;
- the implications for national fiscal policy;
- the relationship with the enlargement of the EU to the East; and
- the technical preparations required in the UK.

This chapter will concentrate on the single-market issues and will address specifically certain concerns which have been raised in banking and other financial circles.

4. THE SINGLE MARKET

Access to the single market, as the Select Committee's Report acknowledges, is arguably the main economic benefit to the United Kingdom of EU membership. The single market is one of the largest markets in the world It is thus a matter of critical importance that, if the UK stays out of the monetary union, this access will not be restricted. London is also one of the key operational centres in what is now a 24-hour non-stop global financial market. If the UK, for whatever reason, were outside the single-currency area, what would be the implications for the UK as a place from which to conduct business and, in particular, for the position of the City as a financial centre? It is noteworthy that firms, including foreign banks, continue to set up in, and trade from, the UK. There may be many and various reasons for this. They do not all prefer the British weather! The Select Committee found that the UK's direct inward investment would be influenced by the perceived stability of its economic environment compared with that of the Euro area. One factor influencing this perception will be the assessment by investors of the likelihood of barriers and obstacles in the single market against the UK. The Committee was not confident that there would be no such obstacles and barriers. Particular concern was expressed by a number of those who gave evidence to the Select Committee that the UK could and would be discriminated against if it stayed out.

Overt discrimination is, it is submitted, unlikely, and not every apparently discriminatory act might be illegal or, even if so, capable of being proven to be so. There might, for example, be 'cultural' changes – other things being equal, firms might prefer to do business with others in the 'In' club, using the Euro as their common currency. Such changes are most unlikely to be challengeable, either by the Member State concerned or by its nationals. However, where a Member State or its nationals suffer discrimination as a result of a regulatory measure of, or at the direction of, or with encouragement by, another Member State, a legal remedy should be available, as it would be at present.

The Select Committee concluded that the UK's legal position in the single market should not be affected. Discrimination in the single market is illegal, and the Commission will strive to prevent it. The Commission confirmed this, at the highest level. Lord Barnett (the Chairman of Sub-Committee A, which conducted the detailed enquiry) put this question to Sir Leon Brittan:

Do you think there could be discrimination by the ins of the outs, not of those who are out because they do not meet the convergence criteria, but the outs who do meet the convergence criteria, but choose not to join?

Sir Leon replied:

Well, there is no basis whatever for such discrimination because those who are out and decide not to join because they have the right not to join are exercising a Treaty right. . . . There is, therefore, no justification for any kind of discrimination or sanction against them, however much those who are in may prefer that they had not exercised that option in that direction.

Earlier in his evidence, in response to a question from Lord Haslam on the ability of other Member States to impose trade sanctions against non-participants in Stage Three of EMU (and in the Social Chapter), Sir Leon said:

[I]t is inevitable that people on the Continent . . . will press for action which will be inconsistent with the single market in order to obtain redress against the advantage they think Britain will have. I think that those who say that will be wrong, objectively wrong and unfair and incorrect, but politically that will be a pressure which exists. The Commission will . . . as guardian of the single market resolutely oppose pressures which seek under that pretext to permit or to encourage measures that are inconsistent with the single market. Of that I can assure you.

Sir Leon, however, added: 'I cannot deny the fact there will be strong pressures in that direction.'

5.   FINANCIAL SERVICES: SPECIAL PROBLEMS

In the evidence given by a number of witnesses,[3] it was suggested that existing single-market measures might provide means for discrimination or retaliation against Outs (*eg*, in the event of a competitive devaluation). It was suggested that there were 'loopholes' in existing Community legislation which other Member States could exploit. Again the Commission firmly rejected such ideas: a specific memorandum on the issue was submitted by DG XV of the European Commission, and is reproduced as Appendix 6 to the Select Committee's Report.

Particular concern was expressed that the notion of the 'general good' might be invoked in order to take allegedly defensive (in effect, discriminatory) measures against undertakings from a non-participating Member State. Perhaps the most often referred-to provision in this context is

---

3. See, *eg*, the evidence of Mr Levitt, House of Lords Select Committee on the European Communities, loc. cit., n.1, Vol.2, p.221 (q.620).

that in Article 19 (4) of the Second Banking Directive,[4] which permits a Member State to apply, within its own territory, its domestic rules adopted in the interest of the 'general good' to the activities of an incoming undertaking based in another Member State. It is well-established[5] in Community law that a Member State may, in the absence of Community rules, apply national laws (*eg*, local marketing laws designed to protect consumers) in the 'general good'. Concern was also expressed about other measures. Reference was made to Article 14 (2) of the Second Banking Directive, concerning measures adopted in pursuance of monetary policy, and to Articles 1 (13) and 15 (5) of the Investment Services Directive,[6] concerning the definition of regulated markets and the powers of host Member States as regards the creation of new markets, respectively.

It may be helpful to consider these provisions individually. But before doing so two points should be made. First, it is worth recalling that the general scheme under the Directives is that banks and other undertakings providing financial services are subject to authorisation and prudential supervision in their 'home' Member State against agreed regulatory standards and with the benefit of that are permitted (or have, as it is said, a 'passport') to carry on the relevant business in other Member States, without need of further local authorisation. A second general point which should be made is that the financial services directives should be applied by Member States and their supervisory and regulatory authorities in a manner which does not discriminate between locally-based undertakings and those coming from other Member States. Non-discrimination is a general principle of Community law, which is expressly set out in the Treaty. The application of the principle in the present context is also made clear by provisions such as Article 28 of the Investment Services Directive.

With these points in mind, one can turn to the detailed provisions to which reference has been made.

5.1 Second Banking Directive

5.1.1 *Article 14 (2) – Monetary policy*

Article 14 (2) of the Second Banking Directive enables Member States to continue to take measures in pursuance of monetary policy. But a very large question mark must exist over whether this gives other Member States the

---

4. Second Council Directive 89/646/EEC of 15.12.89 on the co-ordination of laws, regulations and administrative provisions relating to the taking up and pursuit of the business of credit institutions and amending Directive 77/780/EEC.
5. See, generally, Usher, *The Law of Money and Financial Services in the European Community* (1994), pp.77–83. Usher traces the notion back to the *Van Binsbergen* case, Case 37/74 [1974] ECR 1229.
6. Council Directive 93/22/EEC of 10.5.93 on investment services in the securities field.

41

ability to discriminate against, for example, UK banks. This is because the Directive expressly provides that such measures 'may not provide for discriminatory or restrictive treatment based on the fact that a credit institution is authorised in another Member State'.

5.1.2 Article 19 (4) – The general good

The Second Banking Directive contains a number of references to the general good, the purpose being to confirm that a credit institution operating under a single licence (granted by its own home state) complies with host-country rules adopted in the interest of the general good. Such compliance is required both in the specific context of freedom of establishment (Article 19 (4)) and more generally (Article 21 (5)), including the provision of services. Similar provisions exist in other single-market directives relating to financial and insurance services. The important issue remains the extent of the ability of a Member State to impose restrictions in the interest of the 'general good', a term and concept derived from the case-law of the European Court of Justice. As a limitation on the exercise of the right of establishment and/or provision of services (to which this and other financial services directives give effect) the notion of the 'general good' has traditionally been narrowly construed by the European Court. A variety of national measures have, however, been held to be justified, including professional rules aimed at the protections of the recipients of services,[7] the protection of consumers,[8] the preservation of the good reputation of the national financial sector[9] and the prevention of fraud.[10] What is clear, is that for a national measure to be upheld, it must not only be in the interest of the general good (that is, justifiable by imperative requirements in the general interest) but also be non-discriminatory, objectively necessary and proportionate to the objective pursued.[11] The domestic rule must also relate to a field which has not been harmonised under Community law.[12] So, for example, with regard to banks and certain other financial institutions, national provisions concerning own funds, solvency ratios, deposit guarantees and large exposures would no longer be justifiable on grounds

7. Cases 110 and 111/78, *Ministère Public and ASBL v Van Wesemael* [1979] ECR 35, para. 28 (Belgian rules on employment agencies for entertainers).
8. Case 205/84, *Commission v Germany* [1986] ECR 3755, paras 30, 33 and 41 (German rules relating to the provision of insurance and insurance contracts).
9. Case C-384/93, *Alpine Investments BV v Minister van Financien* [1995] ECR I-1141, para. 44 (Dutch rules on cold-calling).
10. Case C-275/92, *HM Customs and Excise v Gerhart Schindler and Jorg Schindler* [1994] ECR I-1039, para. 60 (UK rules on lotteries).
11. See, *eg*, the judgment of the Court of Justice in Case C-76/90, *Sager v Dennemeyer* [1991] ECR I-4221, para. 15; and, more recently, Case C-55/94, *Gebhard v Consiglio dell' Ordine degli Avvocati e Procuratori di Milano* [1996] 1 CMLR 603, para. 37.
12. Unless the Community measure itself provides a basis for the general-good exception.

of the general good. As the Commission has put it, the level of harmonisation achieved by the Directives determines what one might call the 'Community general good'.[13] As mentioned, the key point in the present context is that any such domestic rule must be non-discriminatory as between local and incoming undertakings.

5.2 Investment Services Directive

5.2.1 Article 1 (13) – Definition of regulated markets

Article 1 (13) of the Investment Services Directive defines a 'regulated market' as a market for the instruments listed in the Annex to the Directive (which includes transferable securities, money-market instruments, financial futures contracts and forward interest-rate agreements), which must appear in a list to be drawn up by the relevant Member State, which must function regularly, and which is subject to certain operational requirements. The purpose of this provision is, not to restrict, but, as the Commission explained to the Select Committee, to open up exchange membership to investment firms and credit institutions authorised in any Member State.

5.2.2 Article 15 (5) – Access to new markets

The purpose of Article 15 (5) of the Directive is to require Member States to ensure that investment firms which are authorised in their home Member State can become members of, or have access to, regulated markets and settlement systems in other (host) Member States, whilst recognising that the structure of regulated markets should continue to be governed by national law. Article 15 (5) maintains the power of the authorities of Member States to authorise or prohibit the creation of new markets. It does not, however, permit Member States to restrict access to such markets. Article 15 (5), the Commission says, has to be read in conjunction with Article 15 (4), which allows investment firms and banks to be members of existing regulated markets in other Member States operating without any requirement for a physical presence, for example, on a remote-screen basis. Article 15 (5) merely states that Article 15 (4) does not alter the existing right of Member States to decide whether new markets may be set up in their territories for the first time.

---

13. Draft Commission Communication on the freedom to provide services and the interest of the general good in the Second Banking Directive, (1995) OJ C 291/7, p.15.

6. CONCLUSION

Whether the above quoted statements and explanations will entirely satisfy those who have raised concerns and arguments over possible discrimination, it is difficult to predict. Readers whose task it is to advise financial undertakings will know that one hundred per cent certainty is often not enough. In any event, it is in the UK's interest to participate in, and proceed with, the necessary preparations for EMU, watching out for anything which might prejudice existing rights under the Treaty and, in particular, subordinate single-market legislation. The Community is founded on the rule of law; and where the law prevails, the Commission, it will be recalled, has given the clearest indications that non-participation in Stage Three of EMU may not justify any form of discrimination and that it will itself remain the guardian of the single market.

Chapter Four

THE TRANSITION TO STAGE THREE:
IMPACT ON THE FINANCIAL MARKETS

D. R. R. Dunnett

Chapter Outline

1. Methodological Reflections

2. EMU for the Financial Markets: Credibility of Price Objective
    2.1 Why to seek it and how?
    2.2 Treaty provisions to ensure stability policy
    2.3 Further means to induce price-stability policy
    2.4 Link to fiscal policy

3. EMU through the Financial Markets: Market Integration
    3.1 ECU financial markets
    3.2 Potential new market instruments
         3.2.1 ECU-linked national-currency debt
         3.2.2 ECU-convertible option

4. EMU with the Financial Markets: Continuity of Contractual Debt
    Obligations
    4.1 The scope of the question
    4.2 Continuity in national currencies
    4.3 Continuity in ECU
    4.4 Legislative action required

5. Conclusion

European Economic and Monetary Union: The Institutional Framework (M. Andenas, L. Gormley, C. Hadjiemmanuil, I. Harden, eds.: 90-411-0687-1: © Kluwer Law International: pub. Kluwer Law International, 1997: printed in Great Britain)

1. METHODOLOGICAL REFLECTIONS

Plato, in *The Laws*,[1] relegates monetary questions to third place in order of importance, after questions of the soul and questions of the body. In a chapter on Economic and Monetary Union it is as well to remember the true order of values. Perhaps the cause of some public reserve in the face of monetary union is that, indeed, a natural order appears to have been disturbed. We are preoccupied by the question of national money; we fear to lose the symbol of sovereignty. If we devoted more thought and debate in Europe to the questions that Plato ranked of higher importance, that is to say, the soul and the body, we might dispel the sense that our inner selves are being neglected and that we have been inveigled into policies which may have their monetary justification but which, we feel, touch our collective national soul.[2] Such an apprehension, for those who hold it, is in no way allayed by the rhetoric of the last months and years,[3] telling us that a

1. Plato, *The Laws* V, 743:
    'There are in all three things about which every man has an interest, and the interest about money, when rightly regarded, is the third and lowest of them; midway comes the interest of the body and, first of all, that of the soul; and the state, which we are describing, will be rightly constituted if it distributes honours according to this scale.'
2. No good European or democrat would wish to follow the monetary system of Plato, since that involved one legal tender for the ordinary citizen, valid only in his own country, and another legal tender, a common Hellenic currency, enjoying international acceptance, for use by the state and meted out to private citizens only as and when needed by them for foreign journeys and embassies. Nevertheless, we may accept Plato's scale of civic values while rejecting his monetary system.
3. The aspect of political union that directly affects monetary policy is fiscal policy. The Maastricht Treaty provides little reinforcement to the economic institutions of the Community.
    The Member States could accept the transfer to a common European body of powers which theory and experience show are better entrusted to an autonomous body. If the body responsible for the exercise of particular powers is anyhow to be independent of the national government, it costs little in terms of loss of sovereignty to allow those powers to be shared at Community level. Indeed, where the actions and policies of the central bank of one nation clearly affect the economic conditions of another, the second country will perceive the creation of a common monetary authority as a way of regaining control.
    The same is less true of economic institutions. The decisions of a body with economic power on matters that directly and visibly affect the people, especially the level and pattern of taxation, are less easily surrendered. As Alexandre Lamfalussy concluded in his submission to the Delors Committee, 'Macro-coordination of Fiscal Policies in an Economic and Monetary Union in Europe' (Jan. 1989), in Committee for the Study of Economic and Monetary Union, 'Report on Economic and Monetary Union in the European Community' (1989) ('Delors Report'), pt.2, p.101:
    'The combination of small Community budget with large, independently determined national budgets leads to the conclusion that, in the absence of fiscal co-ordination, the global fiscal policy of the EMU would be the accidental outcome of decisions taken by

monetary union requires political union.[4] The discussion in the present chapter tends to support the opposite view. Within the modest scope of its themes, it will tend to show that technical means exist to solve the problems posed by monetary union, without any considerable transfer of political control.

This chapter is an attempt to consider certain transitional problems presented by EMU and to endeavour to solve them in a piecemeal manner. Karl Popper, who in an interview shortly before his death in 1994 expressed a sceptical view of monetary union, is associated with this methodology. Popper did not discern a problem great enough to require such a radical and utopian step as the creation of an economic and monetary union. Nevertheless, the political method that he advocated finds its role in the study of these monetary problems.

Indeed, for all the rhetoric, the monetary provisions of the Maastricht Treaty on European Union are concrete solutions to a series of known and foreseen objectives and problems. The chief problem to be addressed was, for some observers, the instability resulting from cross-border flows of funds[5] and, for others, the dominance of one country's monetary policy over the others'.[6] If the Euro-sceptics could view EMU in these terms, the debate could be more objective and less clouded by unease for the future. It would be more pragmatic, since it would be concerned with solving the problems of the present.

It is also pleaded in the cause of EMU that the union will be a platform for a coherent European voice in the international monetary sphere. In other words, monetary union addresses the fear that the economic interest of the US does not coincide with that of the world economic order or, more to the point, with the European interest.[7] In these terms, the Union helps preserve

(continued)
Member States. . . . It would imply a serious danger of an inappropriate fiscal/monetary policy mix and pressures tending to divert monetary policy from the longer-run objective of pursuing price stability . . . Consequently fiscal policy co-ordination would appear to be a vital element of a European EMU and of the process towards it of monetary policy.'

4. See, for instance, K. Pöhl, 'Economic and Monetary Union and Relaunching the Construction of Europe', in Delors Report, ibid., p.150; and J. Delors, interview given on 15 Oct. 1995 and reported in (1995) 70 *Deutsche Bundesbank Auszüge aus Presseartikeln*.
5. Long-term as well as short-term flows; see, eg, G. Bishop, speech at the 7th European Finance Convention, Brussels (Nov.–Dec. 1993).
6. For a review of the dominance of the DM, see Michele Fratianni and Jürgen von Hagen, 'Asymmetries and Realignments in the EMS', in P. de Grauwe and L. Papademos (eds), *The EMS in the 1990s* (1990), p.87.
7. A point pursued in public especially by M. de Silguy, Vice-President of the Commission.

national economic autonomy. It is an instance of power sharing for the sake of a gain in real influence. Today this motive remains powerful.[8]

This chapter will study the building of the tools that will help achieve these purposes. In particular, it will examine from a legal and institutional angle the interaction between EMU and the financial markets in these simple terms:

(i)   *EMU for the markets*: The success of EMU depends on the credibility of the new currency and the strictness of the monetarist credentials of the European Central Bank. In other words, the monetary union must be created for the markets. This chapter explores some features of the system that are designed to make the goal of price stability a credible goal and proposes some technical means to enhance the search for credibility. This matter is vital. It is said that markets have long memories. In other words, credibility, once lost, is with difficulty regained.

(ii) *EMU through the markets*: The chapter considers how EMU, by stimulating competition between European financial markets, promotes their efficiency and liquidity.

(iii) *EMU with the markets*: Stretching the use of the preposition, the chapter considers the uncertainties affecting the legal basis of traded and non-traded debt obligations denominated in national currencies and ECUs in the face of their conversion into the Euro.

2.   EMU FOR THE FINANCIAL MARKETS: CREDIBILITY OF PRICE OBJECTIVE

2.1   Why to seek it and how?

Price stability is the entrenched objective of the monetary policy of the European System of Central Banks. Price stability is desirable because it avoids the hidden taxation, the insidious depreciation of monetary savings, the consequential discouragement of saving and the partial disincentive to invest, all resulting from price inflation.

The attainment of this objective depends on the credibility of official policies, that is, a belief that the policies will be maintained in a consistent manner and that there will be continuity in the institutions determining and

---

8. See, for instance, J.-C. Trichet, 'La Monnaie Unique et la Politique Monétaire Européenne' (July 1995) 19 *Bulletin de la Banque de France* 97.

The potential political gains for the European Union from its greater influence on the international monetary system are set out in B. Thygesen (ed.), *International Currency Competition and the Future Role of the Single European Currency* (1995), pp.117 *et seq.*

applying the policies.[9] The great mobility of money in the financial markets makes credibility all the more vital an issue.

In the case of the EU, therefore, a dominant motive for the decision to merge the monetary authorities of the Member States is to increase the credibility of those policies, thereby encouraging savings and lowering the cost of funds to government and industry. For this reason, central bankers and economists emphasise the importance of this fragile and sometimes intangible quality of credibility.

This quality is especially important in the delicate phase of transition to EMU. It cannot be taken for granted. The credibility of the common monetary policy may prove to be lower than that of the monetary policies of individual Member States prior to the foundation of the union. The credibility of the policies of the stronger currencies could be damaged, while the credibility of the policies of the weaker currencies could remain unimproved.[10] Indeed, from a German perspective the writing is already on the wall.[11]

The financial markets are the zone where credibility counts. In discussing the impact of EMU on the financial markets it is, therefore, essential to consider this quality. To this end, this chapter reviews the legal provisions of the Treaty that affect credibility. It makes some suggestions designed to increase the credibility of the ESCB's price objective. Finally, under this head, it considers mechanisms by which monetary policy might encourage the co-ordination of fiscal policy, which is the weak link of monetary union and is a *sine qua non* for price stability.

2.2 Treaty provisions to ensure stability policy

The general economic objective of non-inflationary growth is stated in Article 2 of the EC Treaty. More precisely, price stability is laid down, both in the EC Treaty[12] and in the Statute of the ESCB,[13] as the primary objective. That objective prevails over any other objective set by any common

---

9. This is not a new problem: 'It would be unfortunate (at best) and disastrous (at worst) if a new Community central banking institution was required from its inception to play a critical role in the Community, without having established counter-inflationary credentials'; Robin Leigh-Pemberton, speaking in Berlin in Oct. 1900, reported in *BIS Review*, 31 Oct. 1990.

10. P. Krugman in de Grauwe and Papademos (eds), op. cit., n.6, p.61.

11. Since DM-denominated bonds maturing post-1999 are standing at a discount to those maturing earlier; in other terms, the market assumes German interest rates will rise in the third stage of EMU.

12. EC Treaty, Art. 105.

13. Statute of the ESCB, Art. 2.

international exchange-rate agreement or by any exchange policy that may be adopted by the Council.[14]

It is also an objective to be independently pursued by all the Member States.[15] The states are to provide multiannual programmes consistent with that objective, and will be assessed for their compliance with the convergence criteria. The price-stability criterion is not an absolute, but a relative test. The yardstick is the average rate of inflation of the three Member States whose rates of inflation are the lowest, and the permitted deviation is 1.5 per cent per annum.

The objective of price stability is thus imposed on both the ESCB and the Member States. The common institutional provisions likely to ensure that the objective is interpreted strictly are, however, relatively weak. The Governing Council of the ESCB will lay down the guidelines for the performance of the tasks entrusted to the ESCB.[16] This body comprises the Governors of the central banks of the participating Member States and the six members of the Executive Board.[17] The Council adopts guidelines by a simple majority vote.[18] With this allocation of responsibilities and with this voting arrangement, it is possible that nominees of the more inflation-prone economies of the European Union may command a majority. One might fear that they may be guided by the interests of their own countries. This fear might be relieved by the strict provision that no member of the Governing Council may seek or take instruction from any national government or EC institution.[19] Moreover, the national central banks must all be regulated in a manner consistent with the Statute of the ESCB.[20] In other words, they must be independent of governmental control in the setting and implementation of policy.

2.3   Further means to induce price-stability policy

Nevertheless, these provisions fail to give full assurance that the objectives of the ESCB will be pursued as strictly as its founders intended. Some legal measures and devices that might better ensure strict compliance would be:

- a legal obligation to publish a formal inflation target;

- the establishment of the independence of the national central banks early

---

14. Under the EC Treaty, Art. 109.
15. By virtue of the EC Treaty, Arts 109e (2) and 109j.
16. Statute of the ESCB, Art. 12.1.
17. Ibid., Art. 10.1.
18. Ibid., Art. 10.2. The voting rule follows that of the US Federal Reserve System and of the Bundesbank.
19. EC Treaty, Art. 107.
20. Ibid., Art. 108.

in Stage Two, rather than at the start of Stage Three, so that a practice of independence would become entrenched before it comes to be exercised in Stage Three;

- the adoption of clearer rules to balance exchange-rate policy with price-stability policy;

- a judicial process to ensure respect for the principle of impartiality that is peremptorily laid down by Article 108 of the EC Treaty.

All these measures are palliatives. Perhaps a more stringent measure would be a voting rule that gave weight to the ESCB governors' votes according to the stability of prices in the Member States by whom they are respectively nominated. Regrettably, however, since such a measure would imply public acceptance of the probable partiality on the part of the members of the Council, it should not usefully be explored further.

A measure that would have an effect on Member States that are tempted to deviate from the common policy on prices and from fiscal prudence, would be to provide a scheme of penalties and rewards.[21] This scheme would provide that all government debt be index-linked.[22] The index would be the price index of the country concerned.

A further element of credibility on which German officials in particular insist,[23] is the power, as they understand it, of a Member State to withdraw from the single currency, if the currency should cease to be managed according to the principles of the Treaty. The Bundestag, relying on the German Constitutional Court's qualified endorsement of the ratification of the Maastricht Treaty, has imposed on the German government an obligation to withdraw from the EMU, if the rules should not, in the German view, be respected. Without amendment of the Treaty, however, no party may withdraw from its obligations. The Maastricht Treaty cannot be viewed as a contract that is revocable by one party, even if the terms are not respected by the others.[24]

Finally, as a means of encouraging sound policies, the governors of the ESCB could be rewarded according to an index of their success.[25] This

---

21. Policy is deemed the more credible, the more evidently it is in the interest of the policy-maker to pursue it.
22. One would limit the measure to government debt, since, if it were extended to all debt, it might, on the contrary, provoke popular acquiescence in inflation, and even public support for it.
23. See, for instance, Stark, 'The EMU – A German View', (1995) 39 *Deutsche Bundesbank Auszüge aus Presseartikeln.*
24. Except if and where the opinion of the German Constitutional Court applies, whereby a Member State may request renegotiation of the Treaty in case of a fundamental change in circumstances; see Pipkörn, 'Legal Arrangements in the Treaty of Maastricht for the Effectiveness of EMU' (1994) 31 *CML Rev.* 210.
25. This suggestion follows the measure of credibility proposed by M. King, 'Credibility and Monetary Policy: Theory and Evidence' (1995) 35 *BEQB* 84.

success could be measured in terms of the market expectation for inflation. That expectation may be ascertained in terms of changes in the premium for inflation in the yield on the Euro bonds of EU institutions.[26] A fall in this premium for inflation would imply a gain in credibility. This premium would be compared with the level of the previous year and with the price expectations in countries outside the EMU. A combination of the two comparisons would determine the remuneration of the makers of monetary policy.

This approach to incentives has two drawbacks. Firstly, however appealing it may be as a method of instilling a sense of collective responsibility among the governors of the ESCB, and however much credibility it will impart to a conservative monetary policy, it is far from compatible with commonly held notions of the dignity of the office of a central banker. Secondly, it is a less powerful influence than an annual public defence of policy by the President of the European Central Bank before the European Parliament, even if the direction of that influence is more predictable than the variable political thrust of the Parliament.

2.4   Link to fiscal policy

Since under the Maastricht Treaty there is to be no common Union fiscal policy, it is worth enquiring how the common monetary policy could be used to influence national fiscal policies. A tight fiscal policy is vital to the credibility of the monetary system. The following questions seem to be pertinent: How could a given monetary policy make it more or less easy for a national government to fund its budget deficit on the market in Euros? Could disciplinary measures taken by the ESCB influence national fiscal policies?

Two opposing hypotheses may be considered. The first is that the ESCB would be constrained to assist the country that is under fiscal stress. Some

---

26. The calculation could be made by the following steps:
- (i)   Calculate the nominal yield on a notional synthetic zero-coupon Euro bond of any maturity. Do this by extracting the yields on coupon-bearing bonds for all maturities up to the maturity of the notional Euro bond.
- (ii)   Plot on a graph the nominal yield curve for a series of notional zero-coupon Euro bonds.
- (iii) Calculate the implied nominal forward interest rate from the height and gradient of the nominal yield curve.
- (iv)   Calculate the inflation premium demanded by the investor, as modelled by the implied nominal forward interest rate less the real rate of return on an index-linked bond.

This inflation premium represents the expectation of inflation plus a factor for policy risk.

authors believe that the self-interest of the Community and the need for cohesion would often outweigh the principle of monetary rigour.[27] The 'no-bail-out' provisions of Article 104 of the EC Treaty still leave room for certain forms of support, such as secondary-market purchases of debt. The second is that, on the contrary, the ESCB could and should exercise pressure on the recalcitrant state. It could do this in at least three ways, subject to due respect for the general principles of non-discrimination laid down in the Treaty: it could refuse to accept the debt instruments of the country concerned as collateral for money-market loans; it could put a limit on the level of debt that it would permit the central bank of the country to build up against it; or, finally, it could announce an intention to sell its holdings of debt of the country in question. These measures would tend to lower the price of the country's debt and to increase the cost of funding its budgetary deficit.

In short, the ESCB monetary policy could affect the ability of Member States to fund their deficits, and could thereby influence their fiscal policies through the institutional arrangements of the Treaty.

3. EMU THROUGH THE FINANCIAL MARKETS: MARKET INTEGRATION

3.1 ECU financial markets

Having looked at the market credibility of the central banker, it is appropriate to look at the markets themselves and consider the instruments that the authorities are using or might use in pursuit of their monetary policy. The instruments that the markets now deal in are worth attention. Those which the markets have not found useful are also worth a speculative look. Some of them may provide subtle but previously unworkable solutions to the problem of co-ordination between the 'Ins' and the 'Outs', that is, between the Member States that participate in the monetary union and those that do not.

One characteristic of the ECU market is the amicable rivalry between the two leading financial centres for the unit. The business of the market is actively solicited. The competition could be intense, since, in the one world of financial markets, the two chief European centres, namely Paris and London, are near-perfect substitutes. Both centres have developed different techniques for encouraging and protecting their respective markets. Legal

---

27. See, for instance, J. Siebke, 'Implications of Monetary Policy for Fiscal Policy', in Institut Universitaire International Luxembourg, *EMU: Legal Foundations and Economic Implications* (1993), p.158.

reform is one such technique. An important amendment, namely in relation to the law on netting (*ie*, setting off mutual claims and debts) on current dealings and in insolvency, has been necessary in France. In England, other legal uncertainties or inadequacies may have affected some activities in the market. The authorities have sponsored market-based methods for identifying and solving them. These changes, which would be justified even in the absence of EMU, have been advanced through efforts to achieve transparency and to identify the risks present in different markets.[28]

These markets will be the spheres of intervention of the ESCB. Consequently, the authorities regulating the two financial centres will no doubt zealously seek to ensure that the instruments of monetary policy adopted by the ESCB will not create an advantage in favour of one centre to the detriment of the other.

It is still open to decision to what extent the ECB will conduct itself the ESCB's money-market operations and to what extent it will delegate them to the national central banks. The principle of subsidiarity and the proper concern not to favour one financial centre over another are likely to lead to a bias in favour of decentralised intervention.

The emphasis put by the Commission[29] on the legal status of the ECU is largely irrelevant to the market place. In London, the ECU has no official status as a currency. That does not prevent an active trade in ECU debt instruments. To adopt the words of one Thomas Smith in evidence given in 1819 to the UK bullion committee, in the course of its investigation of the strange phenomenon of a pound note issue not backed by gold, that is, the fiduciary note issue, 'it was difficult to explain it, but every gentleman in England knows it'.[30]

The instruments established in London for trading in the ECU market are the following[31]:

---

28. For instance, certain leading banks have set up special-purpose subsidiaries to trade in swaps and options. The best terms in the derivatives markets can be obtained by parties allocated a shadow AAA rating by the US and international debt-rating agencies. The coveted, indeed indispensable, AAA rating depends on the agencies' view on the possibility of netting. In jurisdictions where netting on insolvency is not assured, the agencies require, as a condition of the allocation of the highest rating, that the special-purpose company observe procedures to mimic netting. These procedures entail cost. Consequently, any legal uncertainty is immediately passed through into transactional cost. If one legal regime entails greater risk than another, parties operating under that regime will tend to lose business.
29. And in ECU Institute, *The Legal and Practical Guide for the Use of the ECU* (1995).
30. Quoted by F. A. Mann, *The Legal Aspect of Money* (4th edn, 1990), p.43.
31. As described, for instance, by I. Plenderleith, Associate Director of the Bank of England, speech at the 7th European Finance Convention, Brussels (Nov.–Dec. 1993).

- ECU Treasury bills, issued by monthly tenders at maturities of one, three and six months;

- ECU Treasury notes of three-year maturity, issued by quarterly tender; and

- ECU Treasury benchmark bonds.

Liquidity of the market is facilitated by establishing a list of accredited market-makers and by making available a 'repo', or repurchase, facility, that is, a commitment to buy back Treasury ECU bills, notes and bonds on demand. This facility is made efficient by use of a real-time electronic settlement office (ESO) to supplement other settlement systems. Finally, the London International Financial Futures and Options Exchange (LIFFE) trades in future short-term ECU interest rates, contributing thereby to liquidity.

In similar terms, the Governor of the Bank of France expounds the range of instruments issued by the French government in ECUs, the range of financial products traded on the French financial futures market, known as the MATIF, the controls on credit standing of the participants and the solidity of the legal framework.[32] He concludes reasonably by lauding the merits of the Paris market for ECUs in the following terms:

Grâce à son infrastructure juridique,[33] à ses pôles d'efficience, à sa liquidité et à la qualité de ses intervenants, la place de Paris devrait être en mesure de s'engager sans difficulté dans le nouvel univers qui sera celui de la monnaie unique.

In view of the range and depth of the markets, one may conclude that, when the ESCB takes over the conduct of EMU monetary policy, it will find markets that will respond to its intervention.

3.2 Potential new market instruments

The instruments that merit examination are inspired by the same concepts that led the UK Treasury to propose a dual currency mechanism as an alternative route to an eventual single currency. They merit mention in this chapter as much for their analytical value as for their likely use in practice.

In the negotiations that led up to the signing of the Maastricht Treaty various dual or parallel currency schemes were proposed. The common intention behind such schemes was to create a competition in currency management. They were attempts to bring the discipline of the market to bear on monetary policy, or to create a new market in prudence. The currency that was best managed would be most widely used in the form of

---

32. J.-C. Trichet, (Oct. 1995) 22 *Bulletin de la Banque de France* 90.
33. Which three years ago admitted netting upon insolvency; and is even now in the process of introducing a simple system of registration of charges over securities, to match the English floating charge.

bank notes and current deposits. As a result, there would be greater monetary autonomy and greater seignorage income accruing to the issuer of the dominant currency. There would be an incentive to maintain price stability.

Such an idea was set aside in the negotiation of the Maastricht Treaty. It might, nevertheless, be revived in those Member States that do not qualify for full membership of the monetary union, where dual currencies could well coexist. Since that idea has not been raised in the context of Member States with a derogation from full membership, this chapter confines itself to exploring a less radical idea, and one that forms a bridge between a single currency and a dual currency. The idea may offer the benefit of smoothing the transition to full EMU. It would have only a limited relevance thereafter.

The following two proposals are a converse of the hard-ECU proposal of the UK Treasury and of certain economists. Instead of linking the common currency unit to the strongest national currency of the time, one would link the official debt in the national currency to some external, and presumptively strong, currency measure. The link would be either automatic or exercisable at the option of the holder.

3.2.1 ECU-linked national-currency debt

The first proposal is to create a debt instrument denominated in a national currency but linked in value initially to the ECU and ultimately to the Euro. It might be a short, medium or long-term instrument. It would be issued by the country of the currency of denomination. It would be designed to be bought by residents of that country who wish to hold assets in Euros but are deterred by (i) the residual uncertainty as to the reality and the timing of the start of the third stage of EMU and by (ii) the cost of purchase of ECUs with which to fund the subscription price. The issue would be of benefit to the government, because: (i) if the national currency is weak, the bond would carry a lower interest rate than a straight issue in the national currency; (ii) as compared with a straight ECU issue, it would save the government the cost of converting the ECU proceeds of the issue into its own currency;[34] (iii) it would tend to boost the volume of trade in the ECU money market, because the instrument would be used for hedging purposes; (iv) its premium over the straight issue would provide an index of the markets' expectation for the future of the national currency; and (v) it would help ease the pressure on the currency, since persons wishing to hedge against the currency could, instead of going short in the currency, switch from a

---

34. EC governments still have rather little expenditure in ECUs. Transfers to the EC budget are still mostly made in national currencies.

straight debt security denominated in that currency into an ECU-linked security; the transaction would not pass through the foreign exchanges.[35]

From the Community's point of view, such instruments could have a certain attraction. They would allow a market, a kind of 'grey' market, to develop in the Euro before the Euro exists; this would help build up experience in the management of the market. They might generate an immediate net inflow of investment funds seeking to acquire assets in the European currency. They would, thereby, help smooth the flow of funds that might accompany the start of Stage Three and dampen exchange-rate fluctuations.[36] This benefit would accrue as soon as the composition of the Euro is known. According to the Treaty, the deadline for making that decision is 1 July 1998. The Madrid European Council summit of 15–16 December 1995 concluded that the precise date for determining whether to launch Stage Three, and the determination of the currencies that should move to Euros, would be decided in 1998 itself. A major uncertainty, however, will remain even after that determination is made. This uncertainty is that the external value of the Euro will remain temporarily unsettled, since one or more component currencies could still be devalued between 1 July 1998 and 1 January 1999; for the Treaty does not prohibit a country[37] from playing an end-game tactic of seeking a competitive price advantage over other participating countries.[38]

3.2.2 ECU-convertible option

There is a second market instrument that might assist a smooth transition to full EMU. It is a bond issued in the national currency of the issuing government and bearing a holder's option to convert into Euros or, until Stage Three proceeds, into ECUs. The bond would naturally carry a lower yield than a comparable straight bond, and the immediate funding costs to government would be reduced. However, if the government failed to keep its currency pegged to the ECU and failed to achieve the standards set for entry into EMU, the bond would ultimately cost the government more than

---

35. The transaction would tend to give rise to knock-on transactions that would pass through the exchanges, but perhaps not to the full extent of a currency exchange and perhaps only after a lag.
36. Which may be a matter for concern; see Peter Kenen, *Economic and Monetary Union in Europe* (1995), pp.108 *et seq.*; and Barry Eichengreen and Fabio Ghironi, *European Monetary Unification: The Challenges Ahead*, Centre for Economic Policy Research Discussion Paper No. 1217 (1995), p.38.
37. Whether it has a derogation or not; but *quaere* whether Art. 5 of the EC Treaty would prohibit it.
38. See Fratianni and von Hagen, op. cit., n.6, p.7.

the initial saving. The issue of such a bond would be a spur to the pursuit of convergence and to adherence to sound fiscal policies. It would by itself add credibility to the government's pursuit of those goals and, in the event of the occurrence of an asymmetric economic shock (*ie*, an event that affects one currency more than others) prior to accession of the currency to Stage Three of EMU, it would provide a buffer against speculative attack on the currency.

4. EMU WITH THE FINANCIAL MARKETS: CONTINUITY OF CONTRACTUAL DEBT OBLIGATIONS

4.1 The scope of the question

The definition of continuity of contractual obligations depends on whether an obligation is denominated in a national currency or in ECUs. For the former, the broad problem is to ensure a seamless transition from long-term obligations denominated in national currencies into equivalent obligations denominated in Euros. The problem has two aspects as regards private-law contracts: the first aspect concerns interest rates after conversion of national currencies to Euros; the second relates to the value of the obligation upon conversion. For the latter, the problem is the continuity of obligations denominated in ECUs.

The problems are alike in that they both have at once a political and a technical aspect. They are political in the following senses. Firstly, it is not evident to all that an obligation in, for example, French francs should without more become an obligation in Euros. Secondly, it is not clear that the financial gain for the holder of an ECU obligation that results from the conversion of the ECU into a stronger currency, that is, the Euro, is worthy of protection. The holder assumes voluntarily the risk that ECU claims will not become Euro claims. Why should he be protected? The ECU is not the same as the Euro. The 'recurrent link',[39] if it ever existed in the past history of the ECU, is broken. In other words, the historical principle that the nominal value of an obligation in a national currency should be unaffected by changes in the external value of the currency, does not apply to the ECU, since the ECU is not currency. The ECU started life in 1973 as a unit of account equal to some 0.828 ounces of gold. It became a variable 'basket' of EC currencies in 1978, and became a 'fixed basket' in December 1994. It remains a unit of account, and not a currency. It cannot be transformed into a currency any more than any unit of measure may be converted into the

---

39. The term for the chain by which money claims under one denomination of the currency are recurrently converted into claims in the successor denominations at the conversion rates recurrently set by the monetary authority.

thing it measures. If this argument is correct, some radical redesign of the transition from the ECU to the Euro is needed. I first consider the conversion of national currencies, and then the ECU.

4.2 Continuity in national currencies

Once it has been decided that certain national currencies will be supplanted by the Euro, the practical implications must be faced. The chief one is the need to ensure that legal certainty is preserved. One may put the point also in enigmatic terms, namely that there must be certainty of certainty. In other words, it is inadequate to dismiss as absurd the idea that the conversion to a single currency could reopen any private-law contractual relations. On this point, there seems to have been a gap between the needs of the financial markets and the early perceptions of the Community and national authorities. There exists a concept, more or less widely held in the legal tradition of civil law and in other legal systems, of *rebus sic stantibus*, that is, that contractual obligations are binding only so long as the circumstances foreseen by the parties continue to prevail. To the extent that the concept is true, the following question arises: Does the conversion of national currencies into Euros entail such a *fundamental change* to the circumstances contemplated by the parties to a contract as to permit either of them to resile from the contract?

The concept that unforeseen events may cause a judge to modify the contractual obligations of a party is accepted to a greater or lesser degree in most of the legal systems of the Community.[40] Nevertheless, originally the Commission's experts stated confidently that:

. . . the move to monetary union will not constitute either in the legal nor [*sic*] economic sense, a fundamental disruption. Therefore, variations in the value of claims and liabilities stemming from increased monetary stability do not give rise to continuity questions.[41]

This statement begs two questions:

- Although increased monetary stability is the aim of the policy, is its achievement certain?

- Since legal theory does not require a disruption, may not even a gradual transition, if it goes beyond the contemplation of the parties, justify a *revision* of contractual terms?

---

40. A thorough study is F. Mazzaferro, 'On the Continuity of Contracts in the Process of the European Monetary Union' (1994) 6:1 *De Pecunia* 123.
41. European Commission, 'One Currency for Europe – Green Paper on the Practical Arrangements for the Introduction of the Single Currency' (31 May 1995), COM (95) 333 final, para. 130.

This pronouncement of the Commission went in the face of views of the market place that greater certainty was required. Several studies by individual banks have concluded that legislation is needed. The ECU Banking Association recommended it.[42] In the UK, the Financial Law Panel has recommended it, as has the City of London Law Society.[43] Indeed, legislation is currently drafted at the European level for this purpose, although it remains to be seen whether it will be able to address all the relevant questions.

The viewpoint represented by the Commission's experts was that the only matter for concern is the continuity of the nominal value of the contractual obligation. If this were the only aspect of the matter, the widely accepted *nominalist* principle would suffice.[44] However, that is only one of the questions.

The deeper question relates to the continuity of the interest rate. A long-term loan involving a commitment to pay a given fixed rate of interest in, for example, Italian lire is arguably a materially different obligation to that of paying the same rate of interest in Euros after the lira has been converted into the Euro. It may well depend on the circumstances of each contract to ascertain whether the parties foresaw an economic change as profound as EMU. The Italian judge, for example, has power to examine whether an extraordinary and unexpected event has occurred such as to so modify the environment in which the parties contracted as to make respect for the original terms of the contract 'excessively onerous' for one of the parties.[45] Indeed, there are instances in recent history where a national legislature has introduced a currency reform that has entailed a rewriting of debt obligations,[46] on the equitable principle that the benefit and burden of a

---

42. Ad-hoc working group set up by the ECU Banking Association, 'Legal Aspects of the Transition to the Single Currency' (1995) 7:2 *De Pecunia*, p.74.

43. See G. Yeowart, 'Legal Repercussions of a Single European Currency' [Dec. 1995] *International Financial Law Review* 44.

44. The nominalist principle is a principle of conflict of laws, as well as of national law. It provides that obligations denominated in any currency unit are to be redeemed in that currency, whatever the real value of the currency. In other words, whether the currency is the national currency of the parties or is a foreign currency, the obligation is defined in nominal, not in real terms. The opposite principle is the *valoristic* principle, maintaining that references, at least to foreign currencies, are to be taken as references to the real value of those currencies at the date of creation of the obligation. The nominalist principle is widely accepted; see Mann, op. cit., n.30, pp.80 *et seq*. It is, nevertheless, increasingly challenged on grounds of justice and efficiency; see F. A. Hayek, *Denationalisation of Money* (1990); and M. Allais, *L'Europe Face à son Avenir* (1991), p.87. Indeed the lack of a valoristic principle may still be a factor damaging the credibility of the EMU.

45. Codice Civile, Arts 1467-9. See Mazzaferro, loc. cit., n.40, p.139.

46. Two examples may be cited:
    (i) the German currency reform of 1948; see, for instance, C. Kindleberger, *A Financial History of Western Europe* (1990); and T. Mayer and G. Thumann, *The German Currency Reform of 1948*, mimeo (1989); and

radical currency reform should be shared as fairly as possible across all sections of the population. It would be consistent with that principle for an Italian judge to invoke the relevant provision of the Civil Code and invite the parties to seek to agree upon a revision of their contract, upon pain of a declaration of nullity if they should fail.

The alternative view, and one that until recently the Commission expressed, is that the fundamental changes that take place in the creation of greater price stability and lower interest rates are within the range of variations that national governments are capable of bringing about by the normal political processes. In any case, the nominalist principle recognises the power of states to determine the real value of contractual obligations denominated in the national currency, including their own such obligations. In other words, the economic effect of EMU is no greater on the parties than effects which are part and parcel of the normal uncertainties incident upon any long-term financial commitment. The fact that changes have been brought about by the imposition of the convergence criteria set out in the Maastricht Treaty, rather than by the discretionary action of a national government, is, according to this line of reasoning, beside the point.

This line of reasoning is too simple. The progressive impact on the citizen and on commercial entities of the process of EMU should be seen in its entirety and over time. The entire process is designed to create an economic revolution.

The argument also neglects the political dimension. In political terms, the move towards EMU should be free of the taint of unfairness. Where the long-term debt is governmental debt, taxpayers may well argue that they should not bear the brunt of paying for the service of the high nominal, but low real, interest rates of the past that have now become high real interest rates, through the effects of the decline in the inflation rate and the resultant convergence of real and nominal interest rates.[47] The maintenance of the high rates on old long-term debt represents a transfer of national income from labour to capital. It entails a benefit to savers. Indeed, this would exacerbate a trend of recent years by which national budget deficits of the

(continued)

(ii)   the merger of the East and West-German Mark in 1990, and the subsequent German law that gave debtors of certain long-term bank loans the choice either to bear an increase in interest rate or to repay the loan early.

47.   The convergence criteria of the Maastricht Treaty can be reconciled only on the basis that there is a 5 per cent per annum growth in nominal GNP. The reconciliation is as follows: the maximum allowed annual budget deficit is 3 per cent of GNP, while the maximum allowed debt is 60 per cent of GNP, as laid down in the Protocol on the excessive deficit procedure; to maintain the ratio of debt to GNP constant at 60 per cent while running an annual deficit of 3 per cent, presupposes that GNP rises proportionately to debt, *ie* by 3/0.60, or 5 per cent per annum. Since real growth is of the order of 2.5 per cent, that assumption implies an inflation rate of 2.5 per cent.

Member States have caused an increase in the share of capital in the division of the national revenue. The trend is likely to continue for so long as the ratio of retired persons to working population grows. It affects the volume of savings and the rate of return on past savings. The preservation of the high interest rates on past savings diminishes the individual's need to accumulate further savings.

The adjustment of parties' rights, if it is in the end to be done, might be achieved in two ways. The first would be to provide for an adjustment in the contractual rate of interest. The law would provide that, in the absence of a clear intention of the parties, the long-term interest rate would be adjusted to the currently prevailing level for comparable obligations. Where such a provision creates a windfall gain or loss, the burden of taxation would be adjusted in compensation. The second way would be to leave the parties' obligations intact, but to restore the equitable position by imposing an extraordinary tax on the beneficiary of the preserved high rate of interest, while allowing the interest-payer to establish his net taxable income after deduction of the excess interest charge. This deductibility would apply even where the interest paid would not normally be treated as a deductible expense.[48]

The problem of continuity is not limited to fixed-rate loans. It could affect a variety of instruments other than loans.[49] The complexity of the adjustment process may be a severe disincentive to tackling the matter.

4.3   Continuity in ECU

The problem with the ECU is different. It is to determine whether private-law obligations in ECUs should be simply converted at par into obligations in Euros. In other words, it concerns the 'private' ECU, and whether it should be treated in the same terms as the 'official' ECU, that is, ECU-denominated

---

48. Something of the kind was done on the occasion of the German currency reform of 1948; see Mayer and Thumann, op. cit., n.46.

49. For example:

   • Should annuity contracts be adjusted?

   • Should deep-discount bonds be treated like full-coupon bonds?

   In the case of floating-rate loans, there may arise questions of the following character:

   • Is it clear that the new benchmark, such as LIBOR, for the newly-converted Euro obligation is correct?

   • Does an escape clause permit the lender to redefine the benchmark?

   • Does the switch to Euro entail a change in bank reserve-asset requirements and, if so, is it provided that these are passed on to the borrower?

   • Is there, in fact, a public interest in regulating such matters?

claims and liabilities between Member States and European Community institutions and agencies.

The question is more material than it might seem. It is not enough merely to ensure conversion of the ECU unit into the Euro currency at par, as the Treaty provides. If the spot exchange rate is parity, the forward rate will not be. Although there will be no actual forward market rate, one may compose a theoretical rate on the basis of interest-rate differentials. The forward exchange rate is a better yardstick for equivalence of value of 'forward' obligations, such as short-term notes or medium-term bonds. This is because the forward exchange rates reflect the difference between, on the one hand, the average interest rates on the currencies comprised in the basket-ECU and, on the other hand, the interest rates on those currencies that will convert into the nascent Euro. Since the ECU is composed of certain weaker currencies, which will not initially be converted into Euros, the Euro will be a stronger currency than the ECU. In equivalent terms, the average medium-term interest rate of the basket-ECU is higher than the Euro medium-term interest rate will be.

This fact is disregarded in the proposal to convert ECU obligations into Euros at par. Holders of ECU assets will be asked to take the spot conversion rate, instead of the forward conversion rate. There is no indication that the authorities are proposing a more equitable set of conversion rules. The authorities take comfort from the effect of the markets. They claim to observe, and reason, that ECU-market bond prices already reflect, and will progressively ever more closely reflect, the prospect of the upgrading of ECU assets into Euro assets. Consequently, on this reasoning, there is no need to make an adjustment. This argument is true in theory, but not borne out in practice. Indeed, the ECU is at a discount to its theoretical value, whereas on the theory of the market's expectation of conversion to the Euro it should be at a premium. Furthermore, it does not take into account those ECU assets that are not tradable and are not realisable at their theoretical, free-market price. Finally, it is an argument against the necessity of a fairer legislative rule, but not against its merits. We are in the presence of a dilemma. It is a question of balancing theoretical equity against complexity and uncertainty. Nevertheless, if analysis would show it to be feasible, there would still be time to draft a set of legal rules that would ensure a better approximation to perfect equity under Community law.

The principle that the conversion between ECU and the single currency will be at par was reaffirmed at the Madrid European Council summit. The Council asserted that this rule would apply to the private ECU as well as the official ECU, and declared that, if necessary, legislation would be introduced to ensure that this principle be given effect. Furthermore, the chief public issuers of ECU obligations subsequently announced that they would honour those obligations in Euros at par. This might have been thought to dispose of the matter. Nevertheless, it does not answer the question stated above and does not address the case where the parties have not defined the ECU that they have used.[50] Moreover, it denies all difference between the private and the official ECU.[51]

4.4 Legislative action required

In conclusion, there may be social reasons for adopting national legislation to compensate for gains and losses resulting from the policy of convergence and the transition to a single currency. Any such legislation would be complex and could not remove all inequality of treatment. Consequently, it is unlikely that there will be a political will to legislate. The pressure will be rather in favour of legal certainty and uniformity throughout the Community, that is, in favour of simplicity at the expense of equity.

Whatever the choice made, the Community should legislate one shape or another. Legislation should implement the following principles and matters:

- primacy of the common contractual intention of the private-law parties;
- affirmation of the principle that the passage to EMU is not to be deemed a fundamental change of economic conditions affecting a contract;
- continuity of contracts in national currencies;
- maintenance of the contractual interest rate and other financial terms;[52]

---

50. The continuity problem is illustrated by the conditions of ECU long-term obligations. A typical definition currently used in ECU bond issues by Community institutions provides that:
   'The value of the ECU as referred to in Article 109g and Article 109l (4) of the EC Treaty is equal to the value of the ECU that is at present used as the unit of account of the European Communities that is from time to time valued on the basis of specified amounts of the currencies of the member countries of the European Community as shown below . . .
   Changes as to the nature or composition of the ECU may be made by the EC in conformity with the provisions of the Treaty. References herein to the ECU shall be deemed to be references to the ECU as so changed.'
   These terms could imply that the issuer of the bond assures the holder of the bond that the value of his asset is the official value. Where the market value of the private ECU is at a discount, the investor may demand a premium to compensate for the shortfall.
51. For the official ECU there is no conceptual difficulty. As regards obligations as between national central banks and the European Monetary Co-operation Fund, which is the source of official ECUs, the transition is straightforward. Mutual claims in national currency and ECUs will be netted at the conversion rate, and the Fund, ending up with no assets or liabilities, will be wound up. There will also be a netting as between the national central banks' mutual holdings of each other's currencies. There will be a one-off reduction in reserves. A certain proportion of the reserves will be transferred to the European Central Bank. No conceptual problems of a legal character seem to arise.

- implementation of needed technical changes resulting from the switch to Euros;[53]

- one-to-one equivalence of the ECU and the Euro for 'spot', that is, currently due and payable, obligations;

- conversion of forward ECU obligations into forward Euro obligations on the basis of the true forward rate of equivalence;[54] and

- equivalent rules for situations where a Member State with a derogation later joins the single-currency area, upon the abrogation of its derogation.

Relevant rules of law could be adopted country by country or at the level of the Community. Countries that are not members of the Community might be invited to legislate in the same terms, so as to ensure that continuity in the widest sense is achieved, whichever legal system the parties have adopted.

5. CONCLUSION

This chapter reviewed the interaction between the Community institutions and the financial markets in terms of credibility in the making and implementation of monetary policy. It examined the market conditions propitious for intervention by the monetary authorities. The chapter has considered the types of debt contract that the national and Community institutions should promote. Finally, the chapter explored the political and technical questions that arise when the ECU and national currencies are converted into the Euro, especially if fewer than all 12 currencies comprising the ECU were to convert.

The analysis has been of matters of special importance at the start of Stage Three of EMU. It has shown that there are weaknesses in the system but that, at the same time, certain devices are at hand to strengthen the weak links.

To revert to the quotation from Plato that was the starting point of the chapter, how should the monetary system treat questions of body and soul? As for the body, the term may be transposed in the context of EMU into the economic means of life, that is, jobs. Today's order of political priorities is not that of 1990, the year in which EMU was launched. The current Intergovernmental Conference must, if it is to ensure the maintenance of a minimum of popular support for EMU, demonstrate that the spirit that

---

52. Unless there is a political will to change them in any country.
53. Such as the calculation of the daily accrual of interest, the definition of reserve-asset costs and the definition of non-business days in floating-rate loan agreements.
54. But only if the argument set out in this chapter in favour of the use of forward rates of conversion prevails. If it does not, the 'spot' rate should be adopted.

inspired the monetary union will create demand for labour. The Conference could also with benefit consider ways to build up the institutional credibility of monetary policy. Despite the benefits, this matter is not on the agenda.

As for the national soul, the provisions of the Maastricht Treaty have not struck a just balance between the values with which, according to Plato, a state should concern itself. This question, like the first, goes beyond the goals set for the Intergovernmental Conference.

Chapter Five

THE CHANGE TO A SINGLE CURRENCY: LEGAL PROBLEMS AND SOLUTIONS

Colin Bamford

Chapter Outline

1. Introduction

2. Note Issuing in Euros
    2.1   Unitary issue
    2.2   Joint issue
    2.3   Fungible issue

3. Legal Equivalence

4. Continuity of Contracts
    4.1   Long-term cross-currency swaps and forward currency contracts
    4.2   Fixed-interest contracts
    4.3   Loan agreements and bond issues denominated in ECUs

5. Conclusion

European Economic and Monetary Union: The Institutional Framework (M. Andenas, L. Gormley, C. Hadjiemmanuil, I. Harden, eds.: 90-411-0687-1: © Kluwer Law International: pub. Kluwer Law International, 1997: printed in Great Britain)

1. INTRODUCTION

Following the signing of the Maastricht Treaty, the European Commission published in May 1995 a Green Paper discussing the practical arrangements to be made for the introduction of a single currency in the European Union.[1] The Green Paper prompted lawyers to focus on the proposals. Lawyers in London have been most active in examining the legal issues raised by the proposals and in suggesting solutions. Much work has also been done elsewhere in the Union, particularly in Germany, with the result that most of the principal legal issues have now been identified. Further investigatory work is planned, notably by the Commission itself, but it is unlikely that major new problems will be discovered.

Some of the issues can be regarded as technical: they represent changes which need to be accommodated and provided for, rather than problems which need to be solved. An example is the question of rounding. The conversion values for national currencies against the Euro will inevitably produce extremely awkward fractions. Legislation will need to provide for the basis on which these figures are rounded so as to produce the fairest and smoothest transition. Quite intricate questions arise in relation to rounding when converting legal requirements relating to the authorised and issued capital of companies. They do not, however, raise issues of principle.

There are three issues which are more problematical, and which involve the Community in making choices between different ways of addressing them. Those choices may have quite significant economic effects, particularly in the wholesale financial markets.

2. NOTE ISSUING IN EUROS

It is surprising that there should be any questions at all surrounding the way in which payments in the single currency will be settled, and clearance effected. However, the EC Treaty is not explicit on the mechanics of the operation, and leaves considerable latitude for different methods to be adopted.

The Treaty establishes a structure for the Community central banking system, comprising a European Central Bank to be based in Frankfurt and a wider structure, the European System of Central Banks, consisting of the ECB and the national central banks of the states which adopt the single

---

1. European Commission, 'One Currency for Europe – Green Paper on the Practical Arrangements for the Introduction of the Single Currency' (31 May 1995), COM (95) 333 final.

currency.[2] To complete the circle, the capital of the ECB is to be subscribed by the central banks of the participating states.

The EC Treaty does not deal in detail with the legal framework of the Euro. It does not address the question of the issuance of the currency as such, but deals explicitly only with the issue of one particular evidentiary form of currency, banknotes. On this subject, Article 105a stipulates that '[t]he ECB shall have the exclusive right to authorise the issue of banknotes within the Community. The ECB and the national central banks may issue such notes.' The Treaty does not say on what legal basis the notes are to be issued. The Statute of the ESCB deals at several points with the question of management of the reserves of the Member States and the pooling of positions with the IMF. Again, very little detail is given, although it is clearly envisaged that (as one would expect) these matters are to be dealt with on a centralised basis, under the instruction of the ECB.

The Treaty provisions give no clear guidance on the legal mechanics of the structure to be adopted by the regulation which creates the Euro. There appear to be three possible situations: unitary issue; joint issue; or fungible issue.

2.1 Unitary issue

Under a unitary-issue structure, all issues of Euros would be by, or on behalf of, the ECB. Any issue by the central bank of a participating state would be in the capacity of that bank as agent for the ECB. The individual issuing central bank would have no liability in respect of the obligation evidenced by the instrument concerned.

This has the one very great advantage that the legal status would be absolutely clear. Moreover, it would be conceptually impossible for the markets to speculate between the Euros issued by different national central banks. Since those central banks would have no personal interest in the notes issued, all Euros issued by the ESCB would be exactly the same in their nature (*ie,* they would all represent the obligation of the ECB). There would, therefore, be no way of differentiating between their economic value.

The disadvantage of the method is that it might give the impression to national populations that their individual central banks have ceded a greater degree of control over their currency than was anticipated. This system would also require the transfer of very large reserves to the ECB and the subscription of large amounts of capital. Further, in the early years one might anticipate that issues of Euros might relate more heavily to some

---

2. EC Treaty, Art. 4a.

national economies than to others, although the basis of subscription to capital and provision of reserves is on a pro-rata basis.[3]

These disadvantages are, in my view, largely a matter of presentation. The question of the apparent degree of control of a national central bank may be largely addressed in the design of the banknotes and the content of their wording. With regard to the transfer of reserves, there appears to be considerable flexibility in how this can be arranged. Article 105 of the EC Treaty declares it to be a 'basic task' of the ESCB 'to hold and manage the official foreign reserves of the Member States'. Article 30 of the Statute of the ESCB provides that the ECB 'shall be provided' with foreign-reserve assets, etc, and shall 'have the full right to hold and manage the foreign reserves that are transferred to it'. It does not seem to be a requirement that the ECB must hold and manage foreign-reserve assets in its own name. It may be in practice that the assets and positions concerned might be transferred from national central banks to the ECB by book entry, but would remain with the original holder under the control of the ECB. From the point of view of the national central banks themselves, their balance sheets would show, in effect, the conversion of those reserves into the Euro equivalent. From an external viewpoint, the change would be highly technical, to the extent that it were visible at all.

2.2 Joint issue

Under a system of joint issue, each national central bank would issue currency in its own name. A regulation at Community level would provide, however, that all issues (whether by a national central bank or by the ECB itself) amounted to the joint liability of all members of the ESCB.

This system does provide, in legal terms, a very clear framework. However, it has a number of significant disadvantages. It could easily be misunderstood as a system under which each participating state assumed responsibility for the financial obligations of each other participating state, as opposed to the obligations on the single currency issued by the other central banks. It does not follow that, because two central banks issue the same currency, each has assumed liability for all borrowings denominated in that currency incurred by the other bank.

The system has the greater disadvantage that it does not eradicate completely the possibility of speculation between the different issues of Euros. Although all issues of Euros would involve the same ultimate obligation, the individual issues would be separately identifiable. Notwith-standing the legal structure, the market might envisage the possibility that, at a time of crisis, one participating state might simply repudiate its obligations,

---

3. See Statute of the ESCB, Arts 28 and 29.

and declare that its central bank would thereafter regard Euros issued by itself as being a separate currency from those issued by others. Although this would be unlawful, it is politically possible. In a time of crisis and instability, it would be very unhelpful if the markets began to speculate between the obligations of the central banks of different Member States.

2.3 Fungible issue

The third model, that is, fungible issue, follows broadly the system adopted in the United States. Each of the national central banks and the ECB would issue notes in its own name. The enabling regulation would not make any member of the ESCB formally liable in respect of the issues by any other member. However, each member of the ESCB would be obliged by law to exchange any Euro note for one of its own. It would also presumably be necessary to require that any commercial bank which is a member of the clearing system managed by a national central bank should be obliged to accept any deposit in Euros, whether or not the funds deposited came from within the same national clearing system.

As a matter of law, this system appears to achieve the desired effect, whilst involving very little change so far as public perceptions are concerned. However, its strengths are also its weaknesses. The legal nature of the link between the obligations of the different central banks is perhaps too subtle. The markets may see the possibility of disengagement by one as easy to achieve. All that would be required would be for the state concerned to renege on its central bank's obligation to exchange currencies. The markets may remember the unilateral decision by the United States to repudiate its treaty obligation to convert US dollars into gold at the option of the holder. This apparent lack of finality might allow speculation to develop. In addition, an obligation which requires commercial banks to accept deposits from any holder of Euros appears to conflict with basic concepts of freedom of contract. Without such a provision, however, it is hard to see how the linkage is properly achieved.

The problem is a simple one: if issues of Euros are separately identified and are thought by the markets to be different from each other, there must inevitably exist the possibility of speculation. As long as the possibility exists that EMU may be dismantled, the individual identifiable components of the currency structure may be seen as potential future individual currencies. This points very clearly to the first structure (unitary issue) as being the most appropriate.

As far as financial markets and private users of the single currency are concerned, the issue is of considerable practical interest. Not only is it in their interest, as well as that of governments, that the single currency should be as stable as possible, but the market needs to know with certainty the

74

route by which currency payments settle and clear, and the timing of the stages in the process. The Bank Herstatt and BCCI collapses both illustrate that the precise point of settlement may have fundamental consequences to commercial payments in the wholesale markets. A great deal of work is currently being carried out, not least by the Commission, in order to achieve greater certainty on the question of finality of payments and the consequences of it. In this context it is important that the mechanics of the systems dealing with clearance and settlement of payments in Euros should be absolutely clear.

3. LEGAL EQUIVALENCE

A different, but closely associated question is the irrevocable fixing of values between the Euro and national currencies after 1 January 1999. Article 109l (4) of the EC Treaty reads:

. . . and the ECU [*sic*] will become a currency in its own right. . . . The Council shall, acting according to the same procedure, also take the other measures necessary for the rapid introduction of the ECU [*sic*] as the single currency of those Member States.

And the Presidency Conclusions published after the Madrid European Council meeting of 15–16 December 1995 state, in para. 9 of Annex 1:

As long as different monetary units still exist, the Council Regulation will establish a legally enforceable equivalence between the Euro and the national currency units . . . For the period before the deadline set for the completion of the changeover, the Regulation will ensure that private economic agents will be free to use the Euro; at the same time they should not be obliged to do so.

There are two ways in which the changeover might be reflected:

(i)   The 'Big Bang' approach, under which the Euro would be introduced as a single currency on 1 January 1999, completely replacing the national currencies. The old national currency banknotes would remain in circulation for a period, and it would be possible to refer to monetary obligations in the 'old' currencies. The national currencies and banknotes would, however, merely be ways of describing Euro obligations.

   Perhaps another way to describe the process would be to say that, for example, sterling ceased to be a currency, but remained in use as a unit of account, describing currency obligations which were obligations in Euros. The use of sterling as a unit of account would gradually be phased out, and would come to an end in 2002, when all sterling banknotes had been replaced by new ones which used the word 'Euro'.

(ii)   A gradual introduction, under which the national currencies would continue to exist as currencies for a period of three years. The Euro would be introduced as a parallel currency. The 'old' currencies would remain in existence during the transitional period, although their use would decline. At the end of the three-year period, notes in the 'old' currencies would be replaced by Euro notes, and the 'old' currencies would cease to exist, either as currencies or as units of account.

From a legal point of view, the Big Bang approach has very clear advantages. The position is much clearer if there is a single currency, rather than one currency which is a currency in all of the participating states, and a number of other currencies, each of which is a currency in one participating state. The gradual introduction process has one great danger which does not exist, under Big Bang: for the three years during which the national currencies exist, it will be open to private individuals to hold individual national currencies. If there is any doubt at all that EMU might fall apart, individuals might feel inclined to hold assets in national currencies, rather than in Euros, and especially in those national currencies which are thought most likely to be robust internationally, should EMU be reversed. For example, the Deutsche Mark might be much more popular as a savings medium than the Euro or the national currencies of other participating states. If this were the case, market forces might attribute different values to individual national currencies and the Euro, notwithstanding their legal equivalence.

However, there are also matters of public confidence and politics which affect the decision, and the terms of paragraph 9 of the Presidency Conclusions, quoted above, seem to indicate a clear wish to preserve the national currencies during the three-year transition period. In particular, it is stated that during this period the private sector will not be obliged to use the Euro. It must follow that it may 'use' something else. If the national currencies had been reduced to the status of units of account, which were merely alternative ways of describing Euros, this possibility would not be available. One must accept, therefore, that the gradual approach has been adopted, and look for a legal method which, so far as possible, will inhibit speculation between the currencies. In particular, one must find a device which is more effective than merely locking exchange rates by law. The normal mechanism adopted for fixing exchange rates is that the central banks of the relevant states undertake to exchange the other currency for their own currency at an agreed and immutable parity. This mechanism would not be satisfactory here, because it does not remove the possibility that, at some future stage, the fixed exchange rates might once again be severed.

The solution might lie in moving the point at which currencies are locked from the level of the central bank to the retail level. The purpose would be to ensure that any private-sector holder of an individual currency could never derive any additional value from holding that currency, as opposed to one of the other participating currencies or the Euro. Thus, as a matter of law, anyone who owed an obligation in one of the currencies concerned (and this would include all banks in respect of balances on bank accounts) would be entitled to discharge that obligation, notwithstanding anything to the contrary in any agreement, in Euros or (until 2002) in any other participating currency, in each case at the predetermined conversion rates. If this mechanism works, it will make it pointless to hold one currency rather than another.

To take account of the fact that for some time there will not be enough Euro notes and coins to be able to implement this fully, the legal principle might have to be restricted to payments above a specified level, being the level at which it is reasonable to expect recipients to accept payment by cheque, credit or bank transfer. A cut-off point of, say, 100 Euros might be appropriate.

4. CONTINUITY OF CONTRACTS

The 1995 Green Paper identifies the need to ensure continuity of contracts following the introduction of the single currency as the most significant private-law issue. It treats the issue of continuity of contracts as presenting a one-off problem. However, if not all Member States participate in the single currency at the outset, continuity of contracts could prove to be a recurring issue which arises each time an additional Member State joins in the single currency (since the accession of any new Member State may change the international view of the value of the single currency). In the Green Paper, the Commission invites Member States to review their national laws in order to identify changes which are needed to guarantee continuity of contractual obligations, or what it describes as 'the principle of non-revocability'.

The principle of non-revocability is intended to prevent contractual parties who find themselves disadvantaged by the introduction of the single currency (or perhaps by factors unrelated to the single currency) citing the introduction of the single currency as an event entitling them unilaterally to terminate or vary their contractual obligations. As a matter of English law, in the absence of express provision in the contract, the only circumstances in which one contractual party might behave as envisaged is where the doctrine of frustration operates. This doctrine enables one contractual party unilaterally to treat his contractual obligations as terminated in circumstances where, because of a supervening event, the contract has become impossible to perform or where it has been transformed into a radically different obligation from that envisaged when the contract was entered into.

It is difficult to see situations where the doctrine would apply in practice, and it is not clear that statutory change in English law is required. However, the consensus view of lawyers in London is that it may be desirable to pass legislation at the European Union level to ensure uniformity and to remove any doubt.[4]

Care needs to be taken in drafting any such legislation to ensure that it does not interfere unnecessarily with principles of freedom of contract, or produce uncertainty where none existed. The Commission does not intend the principle of non-revocability to apply to contracts which provide for termination in the event of the introduction of the single currency, nor in circumstances where, following the introduction of the single currency, the parties agree that the contract should terminate. However, the legal procedures which establish legal equivalence may involve the nullification of negotiated rights of contracting parties. The extent to which the principle of non-revocability should interfere with freedom of contract (*eg*, by overriding *force majeure* clauses) needs to be considered carefully.

It has been suggested that the issue of continuity of contracts may be of particular relevance in relation to certain particular types of contract.

4.1 Long-term cross-currency swaps and forward currency contracts

There may be circumstances where contractual parties have entered into long-term cross-currency swaps and forward currency contracts involving national currencies within the European Union some years before the values of those currencies are fixed in relation to the single currency (and thereby in relation to each other). The contractual delivery date may fall some considerable time after the date of fixing of currency values.

In many cases, the irrevocable fixing of currency values will remove the commercial rationale for entering into such contracts (*ie*, to hedge against, or to speculate on, currency volatilities). Where both contractual currencies are replaced by the single currency, the contract will, in the absence of netting provisions, require both parties to deliver amounts denominated in the single currency.

---

4. See, *eg*, City of London Law Society, Banking Law Sub-Committee, *Response to the European Commission's Green Paper dated 31 May 1995 on the Practical Arrangements for the Introduction of the Single Currency* (1995); and idem, *Supplemental Response to the Commission's Green Paper: The Need for Legislation to Ensure Continuity of Contracts* (Jan. 1996).

The question arises whether, as a matter of English law, such contracts would be regarded as frustrated by the introduction of the single currency. It would appear that the performance of the parties' contractual obligations would still be possible, by delivery by one party to the other of a net amount of the single currency. One of the parties to such a contract might argue, however, that the contract has been frustrated, on the ground that the fixing of national currencies against the single currency has, by removing the volatility between currencies at some point in the life of the contract, transformed the contract into something radically different from that which was envisaged when the contract was entered into.

4.2   Fixed-interest contracts

There are concerns about the treatment of contractual parties who have committed themselves to fixed-interest contracts based on the prevailing rates for a particular national currency of obligation and who find that, following the conversion of that currency into the single currency, the contractual rate of interest by which they are bound is considerably higher than that which then prevails in the market for new obligations denominated in the single currency. Clearly, this will work to the advantage or disadvantage of the parties, depending on whether they are lenders or borrowers. The English legal issues raised by such a scenario seem to be unproblematical; it is unlikely that the doctrine of frustration would operate in such circumstances to release a contractual party from the consequences of what proves to be a bad bargain, and it is also unlikely that English law would interfere with fixed-rate contracts merely because one party claims to have been disadvantaged by the introduction of the single currency.

It has been suggested that consumers who are parties to fixed-interest contracts where the contractual rate of interest proves to be higher than the then prevailing market rate might be treated differently and that legislation should perhaps be introduced permitting such consumers to prepay their loans. This is an issue of policy, rather than a legal issue. In any event, levels of interest rates in Europe are such that any differential is likely to be relatively small, and it is to be hoped that the convergence of economic conditions throughout the European Union will operate to reduce the practical significance of this issue by further removing marked differentials between the interest rates payable on national currencies.

4.3   Loan agreements and bond issues denominated in ECUs

Contracts denominated in ECUs present a different legal problem. The intention is that, at the inception of Stage Three of EMU, the ECU should cease to exist. The Euro will fulfil all of the functions of the ECU as a unit of account within the Communities, and the ECU will, therefore, be unnecessary. This is expressed in Article 109l (4) of the EC Treaty as follows:

At the starting date of the third stage, the Council shall, acting with the unanimity of the Member States without a derogation, on a proposal from the Commission and after consulting the ECB, adopt the conversion rates at which their currencies shall be irrevocably fixed and at which irrevocably fixed rate the ECU shall be substituted for these currencies, and the ECU will become a currency in its own right. This measure shall by itself not modify the external value of the ECU. The Council shall, acting according to the same procedure, also take the other measures necessary for the rapid introduction of the ECU as the single currency of those Member States.

The text is unclear whether the entity which is the ECU until the starting date of Stage Three then changes its nature and becomes a currency, or whether the Euro is a new concept. While this is a highly technical point, it has a very important practical effect.

The documentation for ECU bonds, notes and loans invariably contains provisions dealing with the possibility that the ECU ceases to exist before repayment. These provisions usually call for the calculation of a theoretical equivalent amount, based on the constituent currencies of the ECU. That amount is then paid in an available currency. The provisions are not in exactly the same form, but typically the language describing the trigger mechanism for the alternative-currency procedure would be as follows:

In the event that the ECU is neither used as the unit of account of the European Communities, nor as the currency of the European Union . . . [5]

If the ECU 'becomes' the Euro (in the sense that the same conceptual entity is transubstantiated), then the clause will not be triggered, because the ECU (in its new form) will still be the unit of account of the Communities. If, however, the ECU is abolished at the start of the third stage, it will clearly not then be used as the unit of account of the European Communities. Nor will replacement of the currencies of the Member States who participate in EMU at the beginning of Stage Three by the Euro satisfy the second limb of the test. There are two reasons for this:

(i)   the Euro would not be the same thing as the ECU and, accordingly, the ECU could not be said to be the 'currency of the European Union'; and

(ii)   in any event, it is extremely unlikely that the single currency will be adopted throughout the whole of the Union at the same time.

---

5. Offering circular for issue of 200 million ECU 7.25 per cent notes due 2001 by the European Community, 11 Aug. 1994, clause 7.

Article 1091 (4) of the EC Treaty speaks of the introduction of the Euro by the participating states and describes it as 'the single currency of those Member States'. It is arguable whether the currency used by Community institutions and issued by only some of the Member States would be 'the currency of the European Union'.

It would seem, then, that the alternative-currency mechanism in many market documents may be triggered if the ECU is abolished and replaced by the ECU, rather than 'becoming' the ECU. It is, therefore, important to establish the nature of the transformation process. There are logical arguments supporting both possible views.

For the first view, it can be said that, since the ECU is the creation of Community legislation, there is no reason at all why such legislation should not endow it with the characteristics required for it to be a currency. If it acquires those characteristics during the course of its life, it will 'become a currency'. The change of name is irrelevant, and the Euro will 'be' the ECU.

The contrary view is that it is conceptually impossible for the ECU literally to 'become' the Euro. This reasoning is as follows:

(i)   The basket-ECU was created by Regulation No. 3180/78, dealing with the operations of the European Monetary Co-operation Fund. Up to that point, the operations of the Fund had been described in terms of a unit whose value was equivalent to that of a stated quantity of gold. Article 1 of the Regulation stated that 'the Fund's operations shall be expressed in a unit of account known as the ecu which is defined as the sum of the following amounts of the currencies of the Member States: . . .'. There then followed a list of names of the Member States' currencies, and a fixed amount of each such currency.

(ii)   Alterations have been made to the definition, by amending the list of the currencies involved and altering the amounts of the currencies. The current instrument is Regulation No. 3320/94. Unfortunately, this Regulation appears to suffer from some unfortunate drafting. Article 1 (definition of the ECU) provides as follows: 'The composition of the ECU basket in terms of the currencies of the Member States shall be the following: . . .'. It then sets out a list of Member States' currencies, and an amount next to each.

The Regulation goes on to say that Regulation No. 3180/78 is repealed. Unfortunately, the repeal does not only sweep away the list of currencies and the amounts set out in the earlier Regulation. It also repeals the words: 'the Fund's operations shall be expressed in a unit of account known as the ecu which is defined as the sum of the following amounts of the currencies of the Member States'. It has not been suggested that Regulation No. 3320/94 intended to change fundamentally the nature of the basket-ECU. The repeal of the words concerned must have been an oversight. In order to make sense of the current Regulation, the above words need to be read into it in any event.

(iii) On this basis one can analyse the nature of the basket-ECU. It is the sum of stated amounts of a number of different currencies. The intention is, obviously, to produce a figure (the sum). This can only be produced if the constituent items of the sum (the stated amounts in individual currencies) are first rendered into the same unit, so as to be capable of being added together. Thus, for example, the amounts of stated currencies could each be translated into equivalent amounts of US dollars. Those figures, when added together, would then give a sum, which would be also a figure of US dollars. That figure would represent the value of one ECU in US dollar terms. The same calculation can, of course, be carried out in relation to any other traded currency. Thus, as the Green Paper says, the ECU calculation produces a value figure 'in terms of the currencies of the Member States'. The calculation does not produce any figure which has a meaning independent of the currency to which it relates. It is, for example, impossible to produce a calculation of the value of the ECU which results in the conclusion 'one ECU = x'. The only possible result of the application of the definition is the conclusion that 'one ECU = \$____' or 'one ECU = £____'.

(iv) The nature of the ECU is thus clear. It is a method of calculating value in terms of something else (*ie,* a currency). It is a measuring stick, by which the value of an obligation can be ascertained and stated in relation to a specific currency.

(v) In this area, analogies are dangerous, since they are never exactly congruent. However, it might be helpful to compare the use of the ECU with the way in which the centigrade scale is used to measure amounts of heat: in similar manner, the ECU calculation allows one to measure an obligation by giving it a value which can be stated as an amount of an individual currency.

The conceptual point is an essentially simple one. The ECU is a figure produced as a result of a calculation which represents a value in relation to something other than itself. It is a way of measuring currencies. It cannot itself 'become' a currency, any more than the centigrade scale can become heat.

It is, of course, perfectly possible conceptually to create a currency, each unit of which will have the same value, expressed in terms of any other currency, as that which is produced in terms of that other currency by the ECU calculation. In truncated terms, the new currency can be said to have the same value as the ECU. That is what is proposed by the introduction of the Euro. The conceptual point is that the Euro cannot *be* the ECU, even though it can have the same value.

The only safe conclusion to be drawn from this is that the exact nature of the relationship between the ECU and the Euro is unclear; it is at least possible that the change might involve the ECU ceasing to exist and, accordingly, that the alternative-currency (and possibly acceleration) clauses in ECU documentation may be triggered. The best way to avoid this is for issue documentation to provide specifically that the introduction of the Euro will not have this effect and (if this is what the parties wish) that ECU debt will be repaid after 1999 on the basis of one Euro for each ECU. The European Investment Bank has now begun to adopt this approach in its issue documentation.

With regard to the documentation already in existence, the only safe approach is for a Council regulation to provide specifically that an obligation to pay ECUs shall become an obligation to pay Euros. Whether this is to the economic advantage or disadvantage of particular parties, cannot be assessed with certainty. What is known, however, is that it is not certain that existing ECU debt must necessarily be repaid in Euros, unless legislation is introduced to make that happen.

5. CONCLUSION

These are the main legal issues which arise out of the introduction of the single currency. As far as the position within the European Union is concerned, the solutions are comparatively easy to see and to put into effect. What is required, is appropriate Community legislation. Much more difficult is the question of the effect in jurisdictions outside the European Union. To take just one example, if a US bank and an Australian bank enter into a swap, under which one bank agrees to pay ECUs and the other to pay US dollars, the agreement to be governed by New York law, what will be the approach of a New York court? Will it give effect to Community legislation which requires that ECU obligations be satisfied by payment in Euros, if the value of the Euro-denominated sum is significantly different from that which would have been payable if the ECU had still existed?

Such examples give rise to complex questions of conflicts of laws in a number of overseas jurisdictions. There is no alternative but to investigate each of the jurisdictions in turn. This is a time-consuming task, upon which the Financial Law Panel has already embarked, setting the wheels in motion. The position outside the European Union will soon become clearer, at least so far as it concerns major overseas financial centres.

Chapter Six

THE IMPROVEMENT OF THE EUROPEAN PAYMENT SYSTEMS: CRUCIAL TOOL FOR THE ACHIEVEMENT OF THE SINGLE CURRENCY

Paolo Clarotti

Chapter Outline

1. Introduction

2. Proposed Directive on Cross-border Credit Transfers

3. Proposed Directive on the Reorganisation Measures and the Winding-up of Credit Institutions

4. Proposed Directive on Settlement Finality and Collateral Security

European Economic and Monetary Union: The Institutional Framework (M. Andenas, L. Gormley, C. Hadjiemmanuil, I. Harden, eds.: 90-411-0687-1: © Kluwer Law International: pub. Kluwer Law International, 1997: printed in Great Britain)

1. INTRODUCTION

No one may dispute the crucial role payment systems will play in the progressive achievement of the single currency.

It is absolutely clear that, if the single currency, the Euro, had to become legal tender today, given the present state of the payment systems in Europe, its credibility would be very strongly contested, not least because of the incumbency of systemic risk. As a matter of fact, today retail cross-border payments may take weeks before being completed. Furthermore, commission fees are very high, with both the payer (the originator) and the beneficiary of the payment having to pay charges, even if the other party has already paid them. In case of crisis or default of the counterparty, the non-defaulting party has in certain cases to pay twice, and so on. The European Commission, aware of all these problems, has taken a certain number of initiatives in order to improve the functioning of payment systems in the wake of Economic and Monetary Union and the single currency.

Some of these initiatives have already taken the form of proposals for directives, and are now in an advanced stage of discussion in the Council of Ministers and the European Parliament. Further, the Commission has officially adopted another draft directive in this area on 30 May 1996.

In the following pages, I will comment on all these initiatives in the order of their expected adoption by the Council and the European Parliament.

2. PROPOSED DIRECTIVE ON CROSS-BORDER CREDIT TRANSFERS

The proposal on *cross-border credit transfers* is the one which has the best chance to be adopted by the two co-deciding bodies in the near future. The common position of the Council was adopted on 4 December 1995, and since then the European Parliament has had its second reading.

The purpose of this directive is to improve cross-border credit transfer services, and thus to assist the European Monetary Institute in its task of promoting the efficiency of cross-border payments with a view to the preparation of the third stage of Economic and Monetary Union which will start, as it has been confirmed in December 1995 in the European summit of Madrid, on 1 January 1999.

In order to achieve this goal, the directive will contain four important provisions. The first is the fixing of a ceiling for its scope: according to the text of the common position, it would apply to any credit transfer of an amount of less than 25,000 ECU (or Euros), with an increase in the limit to 30,000 ECU two years after the implementation of the directive.

The second is aimed at ensuring sufficient transparency in the relevant transfers. The draft directive lays down the minimum requirements needed to ensure an adequate level of customer information both before and after the execution of a cross-border credit transfer, in particular in terms of performance. It creates an obligation to indicate the time needed for the operation to be completed, the norms of calculation of any commission fees and charges payable by the customer, the reference exchange rate used, the value date, if any, applicable by the institution, etc.

The third will contribute to a reduction in the maximum time taken to execute a cross-border credit transfer and encourage those institutions which already take a very short time to do so to maintain that practice. The provision maintains the right for the parties involved to agree on the time limit within which a transfer should be completed. In addition, it stipulates that, in the absence of any agreement on such time limit, the transfer should be performed before the end of the fifth banking business day following the date of acceptance of the order given by the originator. The beneficiary's institution must credit to him the relevant amount at the latest at the end of the banking business day following the day on which the funds were credited to such institution. This means that a credit transfer should not take more than six business days to be executed. If there are intermediary institutions, each of them must not take more than one business day to execute its performance.

The fourth important provision stipulates that, where the originator has specified that the charges for the cross-border credit transfer are to be wholly borne by him, nothing has to be paid by the beneficiary.

It is equally important to stress that if the above obligations of the relevant institutions are not observed, that is, if the transfer is not executed within the specified time limits, or if charges are paid, either wholly or partially, twice, both by the originator and the beneficiary, when the originator had specified that they had to be borne by him, etc, the originator's bank shall credit the originator within a certain time limit with the amount of the cross-border credit plus an interest and plus other charges up to a ceiling of 10,000 ECU.

The European Parliament has amended the text of the common position, in particular as regards the amounts mentioned above, thus creating the need for a conciliation procedure with the Council. As a matter of fact, the conciliation procedure has now taken place, and the relevant figures have been increased to 50,000 and 12,500 ECU, respectively. However, the substance of the directive has not changed significantly.

3. PROPOSED DIRECTIVE ON THE REORGANISATION MEASURES AND THE WINDING-UP OF CREDIT INSTITUTIONS

Another important proposal for a directive, which is still discussed at the Council of Ministers' level, is that concerning the *reorganisation measures and the winding-up of credit institutions*. This is a very old proposal, dating back to 1985, which was amended by the Commission in 1988 after its first reading in the European Parliament. For a number of years, the draft directive had not been considered by the Council, because certain Member States were of the opinion that credit institutions should be included within the scope of the Convention on Insolvency Proceedings (also called the Bankruptcy Convention), which was discussed at around the same time in a special working group. At the outset, this Convention, or, to be clear, the draft Convention, was based on the principle of unity and universality of insolvency proceedings, which was also the principle on which the Commission's proposal for credit institutions was based. In other words, both proposed instruments were based on the 'single-entity' principle. That was the reason why some Member States did not recognise the specificity and the peculiarities of credit institutions, and considered that insolvency proceedings had to apply to such institutions on the same basis as to companies or firms belonging to any other type of industry.

The situation changed when the group which was drafting the Convention realised, after almost thirty years of vain discussions, that it was not possible to reach a unanimous agreement (as is necessary for a convention founded on Article 220 of the EC Treaty) on a text based on the single-entity principle, and that it was advisable to switch to the so-called 'modified-universality' principle, according to which it would be possible to have as many proceedings in the Member States as the insolvent firm has offshoots or goods on their territory. In practice, a new text was drafted which was based on the 'separate-entities' principle. In that juncture, a wide majority of Member States realised that any infringement to the single-entity principle would have collided with the principle of home-country control, which is enshrined in the Second Banking Directive[1] and in the related prudential banking directives, and decided, on the one hand, that the Council should start considering with the utmost urgency the Commission's proposal on the reorganisation and winding-up of credit institutions and, on

---

1. Second Council Directive 89/646/EEC of 15.12.89 on the co-ordination of laws, regulations and administrative provisions relating to the taking up and pursuit of the business of credit institutions and amending Directive 77/780/EEC.

the other hand, that such institutions had to be left outside the scope of the Convention.[2]

What is the state of play today? As for the proposal for a directive, discussions are very advanced, and a text has been sent for consultation to the European Monetary Institute. This text may be modified, following the comments received by the EMI, but it will not be significantly changed.

A common position could be reached within 1997. It will then be up to the European Parliament to consider the text for a second reading. This text may, however, raise a number of amendments from the European Parliament, because the text proposed by the Commission has been modified significantly by the Council. The reason for the changes relates to the fact that the Convention on Insolvency Proceedings,[3] being based on a different principle than the directive, cannot be referred to for all the issues which are not dealt with in the directive (as it was proposed by the Commission), so that all the relevant issues had to be included in the directive itself. As we will see, however, especially as regards the treatment of payments, the Council has tried to avoid the inclusion in the directive and in the Convention of divergent solutions, which would have lead to inconsistencies.

The directive stipulates that, when a credit institution faces a crisis which may jeopardise its solvency, the necessary reorganisation measures have to be brought about by the competent authority (which is normally, but not always, the banking supervisory authority) of the home country, according to the regulations in force in that country. If the reorganisation measures fail to rescue the ailing institution, the winding-up, that is, the liquidation of the relevant institution, must be decided by the competent authorities (normally, but not always, the courts) of the home country, according to the regulations in force in that country. As far as the conduct of the proceedings is concerned, the above rules do not allow any exception. But as regards the substantive rules applicable to the different possible cases, there are some exceptions, where the law applicable is not that of the home country of the relevant bank, but another, determined by the directive itself. It is in this context that there are some special rules concerning either payments generally or certain particular payments.

These exceptions are the following. The first concerns contractual netting. Contractual netting between credit institutions and their creditors shall be governed by the law of the Member State whose legislation is

---

2. Only two Member States remained of the opinion that credit institutions should be brought within the scope of the convention, notwithstanding – or, I must say, because of – the new approach.

3. The text of the Convention has been in the meantime unanimously agreed and initialised by all Member States: the wide majority of them have even signed the Convention; a few, including the UK, have to consult their parliament before doing so.

applicable to such agreements. This provision must not be confused with what is provided for by the so-called 'Netting Directive', which entered into force in July 1996,[4] and which allows for the supervisory recognition of contractual netting for the purposes of the determination of the assets to be covered by own funds for the calculation of the solvency ratio, if and to the extent that the contractual netting is legally recognised by the relevant legislation. The provision of the draft directive on the reorganisation and winding-up of credit institutions determines the law applicable in such a case. As we will see later, the intention of the Commission is to change the substance of the legislation in Europe concerning contractual netting, in order to ensure its legal recognition in all Member States.

The second exception concerns rights in securities and has, of course, indirect influence on the settlement of transactions in securities. Rights in securities whose existence presupposes the registration of such securities in a register or on an account laid down by the law of a Member State shall be governed by the law of that Member State. That law should also govern the validity of an act whereby, after the opening of winding-up proceedings, the credit institution disposes for consideration such securities.

The third exception is the one which affects more directly payments and the payment systems. According to the proposed directive, the effects of the winding-up proceedings on payment transactions carried out and the procedures applicable for settlement or, in the event of default, for the unwinding of such transactions within the framework of particular payment systems and financial markets, shall be governed by the law of the Member State governing the relevant payment system or financial market. This provision reflects the need to derogate from the general rule, in order to protect the integrity of payment systems and of financial markets operating according to the law of one Member State where financial instruments, including any type of securities and commodities and their derivatives, are traded. The same rule applies to any clearing house associated to the relevant markets.

This provision calls for a certain number of comments as to the situation in the United Kingdom. In the UK, the markets whose operations are protected from the normal application of insolvency law under Part VII of the Companies Act 1989 are:

(i) the London Stock Exchange and Tradepoint (a new equities market, opened on 21 September 1995);

(ii) the futures and options exchanges, that is, the London Commodities Exchange, the London Metal Exchange, the International Petroleum

---

4. Directive 96/10/EC of the European Parliament and of the Council of 21.3.96 amending Directive 89/647/EEC as regards recognition of contractual netting by the competent authorities.

Exchange, the London Securities and Derivatives Exchange (OMLX) and the London International Financial Futures and Options Exchange (LIFFE);

(iii) the London Clearing House, which clears for a number of these markets; and

(iv) the clearing arrangements for money-market transactions operated under approval from the Bank of England (the first organisation of this type, ECHO, has started operating in August 1995).

During the discussions in the Council's working group, there was disagreement on the appropriate terminology for the identification of these markets. The UK delegation favoured 'financial markets', while some other delegations favoured 'regulated markets', as defined in Article 1 (13) of the Investment Services Directive.[5] The UK identified three problems with using the concept of 'regulated markets', as defined in Article 1 (13) of the Investment Services Directive.

First, there are markets requiring protection which, although capable of meeting the criteria in Article 1 (13), are markets for transactions or instruments not listed in section B of the Annex to the Investment Services Directive, and are therefore excluded from the term 'regulated markets'. For example, for UK commodities futures exchanges, item 3 of section B, 'financial futures contracts', would cover futures in securities or other financial instruments, but not commodities futures. Similar considerations apply to foreign-exchange transactions cleared and settled through ECHO, since these are not covered by item 5 of section B, 'currency swaps'.

Second, the term 'regulated markets' only covers markets, not clearing houses associated with those markets. Clearing houses are not markets as such, but provide settlement services for markets, thereby protecting market members in their dealings on the market. It would be odd, and potentially harmful, to leave clearing houses outside the relevant article of the directive.

Third, there may be markets requiring protection which, even though the instruments traded fall within the list of section B, do not meet all the criteria in Article 1 (13). In currency markets, the operational procedures may be agreed by the operators, or may be established by convention and applied to participants without the formal approval of the competent authorities.

That is why the UK favoured the use of the term 'financial markets' as the most satisfactory formulation. This term is deliberately broad and would cover any market within the definition of 'regulated market' in Article 1 (13) of the Investment Services Directive, and has been used before in

---

5. Council Directive 93/22/EEC of 10.5.93 on investment services in the securities field.

Community legislation. Article 12 (5) of the First Banking Directive,[6] as substituted by Article 16 of the Second Banking Directive, refers to the exchange of information between the competent authorities and the authorities responsible for the regulation of financial markets. Article 14 (3) of the Second Banking Directive also uses the term. Member States had to incorporate Article 12 (5) of the First Banking Directive into national law; it has been incorporated into UK law in the Banking Act 1987 and the Building Societies Act 1986.

The term 'financial markets' has been included in Article 9 of the Convention on Insolvency Proceedings, for the purpose of providing parallel protection for relevant markets in the insolvency of EC-based companies with assets in different Member States. Using a different term in the proposed directive could produce the highly unsatisfactory result that the extent of market protection would depend on whether a market participant being wound up was a credit institution or not.

That is why, even if some delegations found the term 'financial markets' too vague, a wide majority of them has accepted the UK position.

The last significant provision of the directive which affects payments is the one stipulating that reorganisation measures and the opening of liquidation proceedings shall not affect the right of creditors to demand legal set-off of their claims against those of the relevant credit institution, where such set-off is permitted by the law applicable to the credit institution's claims.

One has to be aware that similar provisions, applicable to all types of firms and companies (except, for the time being, insurance companies, investment firms and unit trusts, which, together with credit institutions, are excluded from the scope of the Convention), can also be found in the Convention on Insolvency Proceedings, in particular in Article 6 as regards set-off, Article 9 as regards payment systems and financial markets, and Article 14 as regards securities whose existence presupposes registration in a register laid down by law. There is nothing in the Convention concerning contractual netting, which is a type of agreement which is frequent only between financial institutions. Of course, all the different provisions I have mentioned are not yet officially finalised, but as I have explained at the outset, the relevant proposal for a directive is at an advanced stage of discussion in the European Parliament and in the Council of Ministers.

---

6. First Council Directive 77/780/EEC of 12.12.77 on the co-ordination of laws, regulations and administrative provisions relating to the taking up and pursuit of the business of credit institutions.

4. PROPOSED DIRECTIVE ON SETTLEMENT FINALITY AND COLLATERAL SECURITY

What I will discuss now is the result of reflections within the relevant Commission departments. An official proposal, corresponding to a large extent to the discussion herein, has been presented by the Commission to the Council and the European Parliament on 30 May 1996.

The proposed text concerns *settlement finality and collateral security*. As regards its content, it would contain the following provisions:

  (i)   A definition of what is a payment system. Other directives on European instruments mention payment systems without defining them; it is necessary to provide for such a definition in order to avoid different interpretations in different Member States. One could specify that a payment system means an arrangement between two or more institutions for executing payment orders and that an EU payment system is deemed to be located in the Member State where the central counterparty of that system has its registered office or, in the absence of such a counterparty, where the settlement takes place.

 (ii)   A definition of collateral security. In the future Economic and Monetary Union, the European Central Bank and the European System of Central Banks will have to implement a monetary policy at the European level, where 'collateral securities' will play a major role. A definition of such an instrument of monetary policy should avoid future problems; it should cover all assets and mechanisms, including sale-and-repurchase agreements ('repos'), provided for the purpose of securing rights and obligations potentially arising in a payment system, or provided to the European Central Bank or a national central bank.

(iii)   The legal enforceability of bilateral or multilateral payment netting, even in the event of the insolvency of an institution participating directly in a payment system, provided that the payment order was entered into the payment system before the opening of insolvency proceedings. This will facilitate the supervisory recognition of contractual netting and will clarify the implementation of the law governing such operations or applied by the directives mentioned above. In other words, netting should be valid and protected from liquidators throughout the EU, subject to usual safeguards against fraud.

(iv)   In strict connection with the previous provision, the non-retro-activity of the effects of insolvency proceedings on an institution's rights and obligations in relation to its participation in a European payment system. Any rule or practice which has such retroactive

94

effect should be superseded in this respect. This provision should abolish the 'zero-hour rule' (a rule of bankruptcy law), which is a sword of Damocles over payment systems, always threatening to prevent settlement finality by bringing the effects of an insolvency back in time. Such a provision would complement a provision in the present text of the proposal for a directive on the reorganisation measures and the winding-up of credit institutions which stipulates that the decision taken by the competent authorities to reorganise or liquidate a credit institution should not affect payments made by that credit institution, or received by it, in relation with a payment system, a settlement or a contractual interbank netting before the making of that decision.

(v) The impossibility of revocation of a payment order either by an institution participating directly in a payment system or by a third party as against the other participants in that payment system after the moment defined by the rules of that payment system. This rule should not, of course, be affected by the opening of insolvency proceedings against any institution participating in the relevant payment system.

(vi) The placement of all participants in payment systems on a level legal playing-field, by providing that, where insolvencies occur, the law of the payment system governs the participants' rights and obligations.

(vii) The ensuring that the collateral security constituted in relation to a European payment system or in connection with monetary-policy operations shall not be affected by the opening of insolvency proceedings against any institution participating directly in the payment system. This provision is, of course, strictly related to the foregoing, and the Commission is reflecting on the advisability of extending it also to third-country institutions providing collateral security in a Member State in connection with their participation in a European payment system.

The Commission's proposal has been based on background work on the above issues, which has been carried on for three years in a working party formed by Commission officials and central banks' experts. The group had to work out a legal framework for cross-border payments. The group had two different sets of issues on its original agenda, the first of which resulted in the cross-border transfers directive, which I have discussed at the outset. The second group of issues, unlike the first, concerned customers less directly, because it related more to the problems connected with systemic risks in payment systems and the ways for minimising such risks.

These are the issues which should be dealt with by the 'finality' directive. The issues were not 'discovered' by the Commission, but emerged via the

BIS in the late 1980s, when central bankers began seriously to examine the risks inherent in payment systems. The Lamfalussy Report of 1990 was, and remains, the seminal document with regard to much of this discussion. The directive should, *inter alia*, implement Principle No. 1 of the Lamfalussy Report, which states that netting agreements should have a well-founded legal basis in all relevant jurisdictions. 'Relevant' jurisdictions in the EU context has clearly meant all Member States.

The proposed directive will, therefore, be intended to contribute to the stability of payment systems (and thus, indirectly, of the economy at large) by limiting the damage which could ensue in case of the financial collapse of one participant. This aim has been a major preoccupation of central banks in recent years.

The internal-market relevance of the directive is that it will facilitate the access by banks from one EU Member State to the payment systems of other Member States (either remote access or access through a branch). This will be particularly significant in the case of high-value payment systems, where the legal status of a participant is likely to be considered crucial. In effect, the directive will give banks a minimum harmonised legal accreditation when they join payment systems in other Member States. In other words, it will not be possible for a Member State's payment-system authority to say, in effect: 'Sorry, we'd be happy to have you as a participant in our payment system, but unfortunately the laws of your home Member State are not compatible with the kind of payment-system arrangements that we have under our own laws'.

Equally, the proposed directive will facilitate the use of collateral security throughout the territory of the European Union, thus contributing to the free movement of capital and to the development of securities markets. It will do so by minimum harmonisation of the differences in those legal doctrines which currently hinder the use of cross-border collateral security.

Relevance to EMU is an important and growing consideration. Under the TARGET large-value real-time gross settlement system, which is developed by the central banks for operation from 1 January 1999, collateral will very probably be required more and more from banks (which presently does not happen very frequently). The directive should facilitate the operation of this and other collateralised systems.

Unfortunately, at the present state one cannot be much more precise. Given the sensitiveness of this subject, especially in certain Member States such as the UK, and the fact that reflection on all these issues is still going on, it is premature to take a firm position on all these still controversial matters.

What must be stated, however, is that the Commission is playing, and will continue to play, a major role, alongside the other competent institutions, such as the Council of Ministers, the European Parliament, the European Monetary Institute, the Monetary Committee, etc, in the process leading to EMU and the single currency.

96

PART TWO

MONETARY AND MACROECONOMIC POLICY IN EMU

Chapter Seven

EMU IN PERSPECTIVE

Sir Samuel Brittan

Chapter Outline

1. Personal Background

2. A Lack of Frankness

3. How Valid Are the Arguments Against Monetary Union?
   3.1 Value of the exchange-rate weapon
   3.2 Absence of fiscal federalism
   3.3 Real convergence: a red herring
   3.4 Transfers to poor countries
   3.5 Inflation policy decisive
   3.6 Interest-rate differentials

4. What Is in It for Germany?

5. The UK Outside EMU

6. Exchange-Rate Arrangements Between Core and Periphery

7. Fiscal Criteria

8. The Road Ahead
   8.1 Would a postponement help?
   8.2 The danger from the Europhobes

9. Conclusion

European Economic and Monetary Union: The Institutional Framework (M. Andenas, L. Gormley, C. Hadjiemmanuil, I. Harden, eds.: 90-411-0687-1: © Kluwer Law International: pub. Kluwer Law International, 1997: printed in Great Britain)

1.   PERSONAL BACKGROUND

The EMU question is one instance of the perennial argument over floating versus fixed exchange rates. This is an argument in which I have been associated with both sides. In the 1960s I was a strong proponent of devaluation, preferably to a floating exchange rate, for sterling. In the 1980s I became a convinced advocate of Britain accepting an exchange-rate peg via the European Monetary System. Thus some people have come almost to associate me with the exchange-rate question.

In fact, it has never been my main interest, even inside economics. In the 1960s, when I was still a pretty unreconstructed Keynesian, I did think that throwing off the exchange-rate constraint would enable the UK to achieve faster growth. In the 1980s, when I no longer believed that we could spend our way into target rates of employment and activity, I regarded the exchange-rate question as a second-order one: in other words, it was a question of the best framework for monetary stability, without profound implications for the real economy.

But my attitude on the two occasions did have a feature in common, which lay quite outside political economy. This was my ingrained hostility to one human being trying to impose his or her views by fiat over others. It is particularly strong when that power is exercised by a British Prime Minister, who is sycophantically obeyed by most of the Whitehall machine and who does not have to overcome, as in other countries, alternative contending sources of power.

In the mid-1960s, Harold Wilson tried to use his office to make all discussion of devaluation unmentionable. Indeed, he made the sterling parity his flagship and his test of loyalty. In the 1980s, Margaret Thatcher tried to do the same thing with all mention of the opposite course of abandoning the floating exchange rate and moving into the ERM. She was determined to have her way at all costs, and only gave in when the best time to enter had long passed, but she felt cornered politically. It was the obstinate authoritarianism from 'Number 10' which I could not stomach on either occasion, and which does not seem any more attractive in retrospect.

2.   A LACK OF FRANKNESS

It so happens that I am mildly in favour both of EMU as a project and of British membership. But I do not support it with anything like the fervour with which many of the opponents oppose it. This is not a personal matter. The most sensible economic supporters of EMU believe it might do a moderate amount of good eventually, but they do not suppose that it will have a decisive effect on the European unemployment problem or any of our other main concerns. On the other hand – leaving aside those who agonise most about national sovereignty – even the purely economic opponents of EMU sincerely worry that it will check economic growth, worsen unemployment and be a force for social disharmony in many countries, including Britain. Thus, when I try to work myself up on the subject, my strongest feelings are directed, not towards the benefits of EMU, but towards the more outrageous claims made by some of its opponents and the contradictions with some of their other professed attitudes.

The most important single thing to say about EMU is that its motivation is primarily political. It would be absurd to suppose that the German Chancellor, Dr. Helmut Kohl, has spent many hours weighing up the benefits of a single currency against the costs of abandoning the exchange-rate weapon. His motive is to bind Germany more closely to its European neighbours and in particular to France.

There is nothing wrong with that motive. What however has been misguided, has been the attempt to use EMU, like other technical arrangements, as an indirect step to political union. Kohl is not guilty here, as he is crystal-clear about his motives. But I have the impression that some enthusiasts for European Union believed that governments would sign up to a single currency in the belief that it was something technical that they did not understand and then find themselves part of a larger political unit.

This game well and truly ended with the anti-Maastricht vote in the first Danish referendum of 1992 and the wafer-thin majority for Maastricht in the French vote of that year. If anything, public debate now attributes more political content to monetary union than it is likely to have.

This lack of frankness about EMU is part of a larger attempt by many politicians to deceive the public, and sometimes themselves, about the wider implications first of the European Community and more recently of the European Union. The original Treaty of Rome of 1956, and the Coal and Steel Community which went before it, were quite conscious attempts to link the states of Western Europe, and particularly France and Germany, so closely together that war between them would be unthinkable. The Macmillan memoirs and many other documents make clear that the British government's objective in seeking membership in the 1960s was primarily political. Macmillan's fear, in particular, was the historical one of Britain being isolated against a combined continental bloc. The French motive was and is to harness German energies to a greater European design. The motives of the German political classes have been the mirror-image of this: to achieve respectability by establishing a 'European Germany', rather than a 'German Europe'.

The Treaty of Rome already spoke of the goal of 'an ever-closer union'. And there were even tentative references to monetary union. The first project for European monetary union was the Werner Plan of 1970, which came to grief with the oil-price explosion at the time of the Yom Kippur war of 1973. But the idea lived on in embryonic form in the European Monetary System, even though the latter became in practice a DM zone; and there was a more explicit commitment to Monetary Union in the Single European Act, which the British government chose to pretend did not exist.

A little while ago the political goals could have been dismissed as obsolete. No-one believes that another Franco–German war threatens mankind. With the fall of the Iron Curtain, the threat from the eastern half of the continent also seemed to have vanished. We cannot be as sanguine today. The war in former Yugoslavia brought armed hostilities to within 100 miles of the border of Italy, a founding member of the Community. Nor can anyone, looking at political developments in Russia, be sure that that there will never again be a threat from that country.

One can hardly claim that EMU is the most important need from a wider foreign-policy point of view. Far more important here is the enlargement of the European Union to include some of the former Communist countries. Even among existing Member States, the development of a more impressive common approach to foreign policy and defence, by whatever method, would achieve more than a single currency on its own.

Where the sceptics go wrong is to suppose that EMU is incompatible either with enlargement or with the development of a common foreign or defence policy. Any general knows that you can advance on more than one front at the same time. If five, six or seven countries embark on EMU in 1999 or 2000, why on earth should this stop the Visegrad countries from participating in the wider union? A community of 30 countries is bound to go forward at different speeds and with different degrees of integration. We shall just have to live with this prospect – although I will offer a prize to anyone who can think of a name less hideous than 'variable geometry'.

3.   HOW VALID ARE THE ARGUMENTS AGAINST MONETARY UNION?

3.1   Value of the exchange-rate weapon

By far the most important argument against monetary union is that its existence deprives member countries of the use of the exchange-rate weapon. If countries are not allowed to devalue, it is said, the alternative is likely to be stagnation, unemployment and even depression.

The response to this argument depends critically on whether or not one believes that there is a long-term trade-off between unemployment and inflation. For devaluation is only a back-door way of reducing a country's prices and costs relative to its trading partners. The front-door method of reducing domestic inflation would have the same effect in increasing the competitiveness of a country or region that is finding difficulty in paying its way in the world.

The traditional belief was encapsulated in the Phillips curve. This said that, if a country wanted low inflation, a price had to be paid in higher unemployment. If it wanted low unemployment, a price had to be paid in higher inflation. This view should not be caricatured. It could not be rebutted simply by saying that Latin American countries with double or treble-digit inflation had no better an employment performance than Germany or Japan. Inflation could be high, it was said, for historical, institutional or structural reasons, and could not be reduced without moving to permanently higher unemployment. In other words, each country might have its own distinct Phillips curve.[1]

This approach has been superseded by the view that there is no long-term trade-off between unemployment and inflation. (There might even be a trade-off the other way, but there is no need to go into this controversial territory.) The revisionist case was formulated in the doctrine of the Natural Rate of Unemployment. A better but clumsier name is the Non-Accelerating-Inflation Rate of Unemployment (NAIRU). This second name emphasises that there is nothing natural or incurable about high unemployment, but that

1. Some such assumption must be behind Peter Jay's advocacy of the smallest feasible size for a currency area. For instance, Scotland qualifies, and the northeast of England only just fails to do so; P. Jay, *Employment, Regions and Currencies* (1995). This is not easy to reconcile with Jay's earlier acceptance of the NAIRU in other publications; see, *eg*, idem, *The Crisis for Western Political Economy* (1985).

   His criterion for the smallest feasible currency area is one in which pay and prices are fixed 'without automatic or continuous comparison back to external reference standards'. This may not be as small an area as he supposes. It is difficult to imagine that pay and prices in an independent Scotland would be set without reference to England. (The issue is open to empirical investigation, for instance, by examining Latin American countries with diverse currency regimes.)

   The Jay case is at its strongest if bouts of uncompetitiveness last only a few years and alternate with periods of overcompetitiveness, when market forces drive the currency up. It is then possible for countries to have at times real interest rates lower than the going international rate, because of market expectations that the exchange rate will recover.

   The Jay case is at its weakest when the competitiveness trend (at given exchange rates) is downwards because of domestic inflation. Then wage bargainers add on an implicit devaluation premium to the settlements they make. The US South might have been given a kick-start if it could have devalued after the Civil War, as might the Mezzogiorno in Italy after unification in 1859. But it is difficult to believe that a century-long depreciation of their currencies would have made much difference to real wages or employment in either the American or the Italian south.

   It is a serious question whether nominal rigidities are just facts of life or whether they depend on the exchange-rate regime in operation. Are they not made much worse when everyone knows that the government can always devalue? The slide of sterling from DM 12 in the early 1950s to just over DM 2 is surely relevant.

it could not be tackled by governments trying to spend their way into target rates of employment or growth.

There are, as always, some sceptics. But I must for the purpose of this chapter treat the near-vertical long-run Phillips curve as established. The problem with the old-style Phillips curve is that it assumed that workers and employers could be indefinitely fooled by inflation into accepting lower pay and prices than the state of the market really allowed. It came to grief in the simultaneous explosion of inflation and unemployment in the 1970s.[2]

Most mainstream economists believe – and I would not dispute it – that there is still a short-term Phillips trade-off, that is, a temporary unemployment cost in reducing the rate of inflation, which may be quite severe. It would, thus, be mad to enter a currency area at a conversion rate which rendered whole swathes of national industry uncompetitive, as was the case with east Germany in 1990 and, to a lesser extent, with Britain when it rejoined the gold standard at the pre-war parity after both the Napoleonic War and the First World War. But the recessionary cost does not persist once lower inflation is attained and expected.

If this were all to the argument, the costs of joining EMU would be basically transitional ones for countries running relatively high inflation rates. There would be no reason why low-inflation states, such as France, Benelux, Austria and Sweden, as well as the UK, should not join with Germany in establishing EMU tomorrow.

It is, therefore, tempting to argue that EMU and its logical culmination of a single currency do no harm, provided that the member countries have converged to common low inflation rates. But will it bring any benefit?

On the face of it, money is a public good, and the wider the area in which it circulates and in which people can be spared the costs and uncertainties of conversion to other currencies, the better. (Money, it is said, confers 'network externalities', the size of which depends on how many people use it.) But a problem that EMU supporters have is the lack of feel of economists, or anyone else, for the size of the advantages from using one money. The 0.5 per cent savings in transaction costs estimated by the Brussels Commission is

---

2. The extraordinary thing is that many of the economists who pioneered the idea that there was no lasting trade-off between unemployment and inflation are among the strongest opponents of monetary union. This includes Milton Friedman himself and followers such as Alan Walters.

   On the political side the contradiction is quite shameless. You hear British politicians in one and the same speech thumping the table and saying that excessive labour costs, tight regulations and other rigidities are responsible for high continental unemployment. Yet they then go on to say that the *franc fort* is preventing the French government from expanding the economy, and a similar policy would do the same for Britain. But my theme now is not the intellectual bankruptcy of the Radical Right; and I must go on to ask why serious economists of a free-market and classical bent are such strong opponents of EMU. They do not always make it very clear.

not of a scale sufficient to justify a large venture into the political and economic unknown. In any case, a large portion of these gains could ultimately be reaped by improvements in the bank transmission mechanism. The main gains would come from escaping the volatility and unpredictability of separate national exchange rates.

What, then, is the drawback? Is it, as opponents say, that of giving up the exchange-rate weapon? I have already noted that a long-term, continuing currency depreciation is associated with a more rapid inflation in the prices of traded products than that experienced by partner countries; and I have already argued that this brings no advantages. The economic argument of the Eurosceptics must then boil down to saying that there are advantages in temporary periods of depreciation and appreciation. A purely temporary depreciation, later offset by temporary appreciation, need not do much damage to the financial stability of the UK, or even an independent Scotland. It is then, indeed, possible for such countries to have real interest rates temporarily different from the going international rate, because of market expectations that the exchange rate will recover.

An optimal currency area can be defined as one where the advantages of a single currency just outweigh the disadvantages of not being able to make temporary adjustments in exchange rates, and of not being able to engage in a monetary policy which is *temporarily* different from the international norm. The case for a single currency is supposed to be strongest when prices and wages are flexible, when there is a high degree of openness to trade and, if possible, some mobility of labour.

Most examinations, according to such yardsticks, show an inner core of France, Germany, the Benelux countries and Austria, which enjoy a degree of integration comparable to that of the US, and a periphery of countries, such as Finland and Greece, which move in a very different way. In between come countries such as Italy, Spain and the UK.

In practice, the biggest costs of a large currency area come, not from differences in trading structure, but from the occurrence of *asymmetric shocks*. These are events like German unification, oil-price explosions or the discovery of North Sea oil, which have a different impact on the various members of the European Union. (German unification was financed by an increase in the German budget deficit and offset by a tightening of monetary policy, which was not required in neighbouring countries.) Also important are differences in financial structure which affect the transmission mechanism of monetary policy. The impact of interest-rate variations differs between countries such as the UK, where home borrowing is typically made at short-term variable rates, and continental countries, where most of such borrowing is on a medium or long-term basis.

3.2   Absence of fiscal federalism

Arguments about differential shocks are often coupled with references to the absence of a large EU budget, comparable to the US Federal Budget, to act as a shock-absorber. Suppose that there is a fall in the price of oil in the US. The shock to Texas is partly absorbed by a reduction of tax payments to Washington and partly by an increase of federal transfers to that state. It used to be said that some 40 per cent of the income loss was absorbed in this way. More recent estimates have put the proportion at more like 20 or even 14 per cent.[3] In any case, such automatic cushioning will never occur with an EU budget of only 1 per cent of the area's GDP.

I suspect, however, that the actual sums involved in US federal cushioning are much less than often supposed. There is a confusion between transfers from rich to poor states and differential payments to states – rich or poor – which are hit by localised shocks. Such payments are likely to be quite modest in relation to overall GDP both in the US and in the EU.

In many years EU states will have much the same conjunctural experience, and there will be no case for transfers. Moreover, a country that is on the receiving end in one year is likely to be a net payer another year. (If it is not, then it is not receiving a cushion but extracting a permanent subsidy.) All that is required on an EU basis is an insurance arrangement for temporary net transfers automatically related to differential changes in unemployment or GDP. Some prototype schemes talk of a fraction of 1 per cent of Community GDP.[4]

Purists will say that sums of this magnitude could be raised readily by the countries affected on the capital markets (thus justifying a temporary abrogation of the deficit criteria). But a formal insurance arrangement would be a small price to pay to meet a debating objection which turns up not only in the political context but in almost every economic gathering.

3.3   Real convergence: a red herring

Another set of debating points relate to so-called real convergence. The Maastricht criteria cover nominal indicators such as inflation rates, interest rates, exchange rates and budget deficits. Sceptics argue that this is not enough, and that they should also cover real performance in matters such as output, employment and productivity. This line of argument surfaces from time to time from the Labour Party. Prime Minister Major uses it; and even the Chancellor of the Exchequer, Kenneth Clarke, who is sympathetic to

3. D. Gros, *Towards European Economic and Monetary Union* (1996).
4. See, *eg*, C. Taylor, *EMU 2000? Prospects for European Monetary Union* (1995), pp.63-4.

EMU, has paid lip service to it. But its most articulate proponent has been the Governor of the Bank of England, Eddie George.[5]

But however eminent the proponent, the argument remains a howler. Areas with very different output levels, growth rates, real wages and unemployment rates have long benefited from trading with each other, both at flexible and at fixed exchange rates and within and across national frontiers. The expression 'level playing field' may be a natural cliché for a British spokesman, but it is in danger of ruling out all the conditions under which international, or even interregional, trade is possible. Fortunately, there is not the slightest chance of revising the Maastricht Treaty to add such 'real criteria'.

For what it is worth, the financial firm of Goldman Sachs set out in its April 1995 *Economics Analyst* four possible real convergence criteria, including a growth rate within 1 per cent of the EU average, unemployment of no more than 2 per cent above it, a current-account deficit no greater than 2 per cent of GDP, and trade competitiveness against Germany within 10 per cent of the 1987 level.

Not surprisingly, it found that the countries nearest to qualifying on the nominal Maastricht criteria qualified on most of the real criteria as well. Only Finland and Ireland looked as if they might meet the nominal, but not the real ones, because of high unemployment. Countries which were on the borderline on one set were on the borderline on the other.

There is indeed something very peculiar about British demands for convergence of unemployment rates. The old argument, formerly very popular on the left, was that Britain would be unable to use devaluation to mitigate its unemployment problems in a monetary union. Now that British labour markets are more flexible and unemployment is well below the EU average, the argument has been stood on its head. Britain, it is implied, should hesitate to join EMU because of inflexible labour markets in other countries. But if anything, Britain gains relative to its partners from labour markets that can adapt more quickly to real and monetary shocks.

3.4 Transfers to poor countries

Another dubious anti-EMU argument relates to the picture of huge transfers to poor or high-unemployment countries which an EMU is supposed to make necessary. Transfers to poorer regions may be a good or bad idea. Attitudes will depend on the extent of pan-European solidarity and on the quality of the likely transfers. The experience of regional policies within EU

---

5. *Eg*, Eddie George, Churchill Memorial Lecture (Feb. 1995).

countries is not too encouraging, *vide* the 'cathedrals in the desert', as some of the heavy industry ventures in southern Italy have been called.

Extra regional transfers are no part of Maastricht, and would have to be agreed separately and unanimously by governments. The point at issue is: will monetary union increase the pressure for such transfers by further depressing the relative position of areas such as Spain, Portugal or southern Italy? (I assume that Greece will not meet the membership criteria for the foreseeable future.)

There is a school of thought that holds that increased economic integration will benefit the prosperous core areas at the expense of the weaker peripheral ones. This argument relates, when examined, to the establishment of the single market itself. It is for such reasons that increased Structural Funds within the EU were approved by a summit attended by Lady Thatcher. Such transfers can easily get out of hand, but this is a battle that will have to be fought in any case, EMU or no EMU.

Why should the institution of a single currency add to the pressures on the weaker countries, assuming that they have come in at a realistic exchange rate and with low inflation, and have converged with the core members as laid down in the Maastricht Treaty? If anything, the ending of the downward exchange risk may be an encouragement to investment in such countries.

Should the Mediterranean countries receive extra transfers simply because of the loss of the right to devalue? Devaluation does not bring a single Euro of extra resources, so there is no obvious loss requiring compensation. It is far from obvious that the 'losses' from being deprived of the right to devalue are greater for the poorer or peripheral countries than for others, once the former have well and truly met the convergence conditions. Countries that want to join the monetary union must consider the advantages of lower transactions costs, the ending of exchange-rate uncertainty and the added counterinflationary credibility greater than any disadvantage from not being able to follow an 'independent' monetary and exchange-rate policy. Otherwise why should they wish to join?

The fear seems to be that peripheral countries with excessive underlying rates of inflation will somehow get into EMU by stretching the Maastricht criteria or by some form of political deal. The implication is that the German government, for instance, will agree to stretching the rules to allow in countries which are in no fit condition to participate; and, having done so, will vote them huge sums at the expense of the German taxpayer.

This is difficult to credit from everything that is known of German public and political opinion. In any case, the way to meet this fear is by strict insistence on the spirit of the Maastricht criteria, which is quite compatible with flexibility in their year-to-year interpretation.   •

3.5   Inflation policy decisive

If it were only a matter of balancing the gains from using one money against the costs of losing some temporary flexibility in national policy, it would be tempting to conclude that it is a question of 'half-a-dozen of one and six of the other'. To my mind, the decisive consideration for countries like Britain and France, which have lacked a tradition of stable prices, lies in the potential benefits of EMU for counter-inflation in the longer term. In principle, such benefits could be gained by pegging sterling (or the French franc) to the DM. But, after everything that has happened, a mere exchange-rate peg would lack credibility when the going became hard and would be highly vulnerable to speculative attack. If one is looking for an anchor for price stability, the best bet is a European currency based on a European central bank modelled on the Bundesbank and constitutionally insulated from national pressures.

The losses from giving up the national exchange-rate weapon should be assessed, not against some ideal vision of how a floating currency ought to behave, but on actual market experience. Since Italy was forced out of the ERM in 1992 to the end of 1995, the lira depreciated by about 35 per cent against the DM, far more than any deterioration in relative cost levels. And it was only a decade ago that the dollar first doubled and then halved against the German currency. This is not to speak of the recent over-shooting of the yen, from which the Japanese economy is only just beginning to recover. Of course, a European currency would not insulate member countries from world gyrations, but it would create an area of stability comprising well over half their trade.

Outside EMU, it would be all too easy for one temporary depreciation to be succeeded by another and become part of a long-term downward drift in sterling (see Figure 1). Such a drift would be associated with faster inflation, and would not, after the transition was over, promote growth or jobs. An independent national policy would then simply permit a higher rate of inflation, which it is hardly worth fighting to preserve.[6]

Milton Friedman once compared the case for floating exchange rates with the case for daylight-saving time in summer. The argument is that it is more convenient than asking everyone to get up an hour earlier. But the same argument tells against the wrong sort of depreciating exchange rate – which would be like a continuing adjustment of the clock in one direction, without any reversal at the onset of winter. This would surely be seen through and lead more and more people to disregard the official time in favour of making their own arrangements for rising and retiring.

---

6. I have tried to illustrate the difference between these two kinds of exchange rate fluctuation in a chapter of my last book, *Capitalism With a Human Face* (1995), p.183, which received scant attention.

Figure 1

An anchor versus a floating or sinking exchange rate

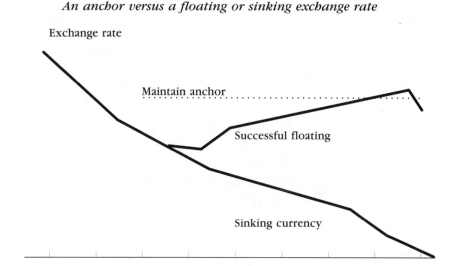

In the British case, independent national monetary policy has brought mainly faster rates of inflation than in partner countries, without any benefits to employment. The experience of the period since departing from the ERM in September 1992 is in my view the exception that proves the rule. The UK was able to devalue without the usual knock-on effect on inflation because of the depth of the recession at the time when the country left the ERM. It is too short and untypical a period on which to base a reputation of long-established experience.

The right balance is struck in my view by Christopher Taylor. He is impressed by the fragility of the purely domestic post-1992 UK framework for holding inflation down. This 'depends heavily on the will and priorities of the government of the day, as well as on the personalities of the Chancellor and Bank Governor . . . The new policy approach has not yet been put to a severe test'.[7] These points are made with the tact appropriate to a former Bank of England adviser. I would buy these arguments, even though they do not make as much noise as the dire warnings of EMU's opponents.

7. Op. cit., n.4, p.140.

3.6 Interest-rate differentials

The lack of credibility attaching to sterling outside the EMU is not a matter of conjecture. It is already being paid for in the present pattern of interest rates. In March 1996, for instance, UK rates were higher than those of any of the Group of Five leading industrial countries for all maturities (see Table 1).

Table 1

Interest-rate differentials

Tuesday, 5 March 1996
World Yields in Local Native Terms

	US	Jap	UK	Ger	Fr	Can	Itl	Aus	Switz**
O/N	5.19	0.38	6.75	3.25	4.00	5.13	9.62	7.18	
3MO	5.03	0.44	6.03	3.22	4.12	5.10	9.42	7.43	
1-year	5.09	0.66	5.72	3.28	4.25	5.41	9.18	7.70	
20-year	5.31	1.01	6.47	3.81	4.71	5.62	9.25	7.75	
5-year	5.62	1.88	7.28	4.87	5.69	6.65	9.74	8.07	4.00***
10-year	5.98	3.03*	7.83	6.34	6.57	7.38	10.34	8.43	4.11
30-year	6.40	N/A	N/A	7.16	7.42	7.98	10.60	N/A	
Disc	5.00	0.50	N/A	3.00	N/A	5.50	9.00	N/A	
Prime	8.25	3.00	6.25	N/A	7.00	7.00	N/A	10.75	
CPI	2.70	−0.20	3.10	1.50	2.00	1.60	5.50	N/A	

Notes:
*   9-year Japanese issue
**   4 March 1996
*** 3-to-7-year high-coupon

The ones most relevant to EMU are probably the yields on 5- and 10-year bonds. There was a premium on UK 5-year yields of about 2.4 percentage points relative to German yields, and one of 1.5 percentage points for 10-year bonds. By contrast, the French premium was only 0.8 points on 5-year bonds, and was down to 0.3 points for 10-year ones.

The UK premium at the very least shows that sterling's trend against the DM (and its Euro successor) is expected to be downwards. In view of the high level of the DM relative to German costs, the differential is more likely to reflect inflation-related fears than a belief in a further real devaluation of sterling relative to the DM.

The matter bears a little elaboration. Let us take 2 percentage points as a representative number for the differential between UK and German bond yields. If the market correctly expects UK inflation to be 2 percentage points above Germany's, then Britain's real interest rate is no higher, and the greater nominal rate simply offsets expected inflation. Suppose, however, that the expected differential is only 1 per cent. The other percentage point represents a risk-premium – an insurance against UK inflation being higher than the market's central estimate. It is this premium that reflects the real cost of giving the impression that the UK is likely to opt-out of EMU, at least in the initial years.

One can go just a little further. The 2.8 per cent yield on UK 5-year index-linked bonds can be taken as a rough approximation to the real rate of interest. On top of this, there might be a 1 per cent risk-premium. This leaves 3.5 per cent as the expected inflation rate. This is just within the wider version of the government's target, but does not prevent from there being a penalty for staying outside EMU.

Some of the other differentials are also enlightening, particularly the 1 to 2 percentage points by which German bond yields exceeded Swiss ones. This is often said to reflect the fears, especially of German investors, that the Euro will not be as good as the DM and the consequent desire to find a refuge in Switzerland. Thus, Germany has higher rates than Switzerland because of the suspicion regarding the Euro; and the UK has higher rates still because of a fear that sterling will not even be as good as the still-to-be-proven Euro.

Other differentials are outside the scope of this chapter, but worth a mention. Averaging over periods, US yields are about the same as German ones. In principle, this could reflect a belief that US inflation will be down to German levels. But it is more likely to reflect an expectation that any continuing German inflation advantage will be offset by a real depreciation of the dollar against the DM. The very low Japanese bond yields are a reflection of recent deflationary conditions, when prices have actually been falling. Even if this period is over, the market clearly expects Japanese inflation to be negligible over the medium to long-term.

4. WHAT IS IN IT FOR GERMANY?

The monetary-stability arguments I have given apply to more inflation-prone potential members of EMU. But EMU will not happen without Germany. Until recently Germany's likely gain from EMU was purely political. Nobody expected the Euro to be more stable than the DM; rather, a risk was being run for a broader European objective. Now, however, an economic case is emerging for German participation. This results from the growing uncompetitiveness of the German traded-goods sector both in Europe and in the wider world (see Table 2).

Table 2

Unit labour costs in manufacturing[1]

Country	1990	Oct 1993	Oct 1995
France	100.3	103.9	102.4
Germany	107.3	125.1	124.6
Italy	93.7	78.5	77.6
UK	101.5	92.3	92.6
Belgium	93.4	91.5	89.3
Netherlands	84.3	94.4	1.5
Sweden	102.4	77.5	79.8
Europe[2]	100.0	100.0	100.0
US	69.9	73.1	
Japan	77.3	121.3	
South Korea	32.3	34.4	
Taiwan	54.9	59.4	

Notes:
1   Average hourly compensation in manufacturing industry divided by output per man hour, valued in a common currency at purchasing power parity exchange rates. Relative to average for Europe.
2   Weighted average of above seven countries

Source: C. Taylor, *EMU 2000? Prospects for European Monetary Union* (1995)

Eurosceptics might answer that in that case the Bundesbank should simply loosen monetary policy enough to cause the DM to depreciate. Bernard Connolly makes the interesting point that there is nothing wrong with competitive devaluation, as it simply causes countries to loosen monetary policy in the face of a deflationary threat.[8] This might be true in a 1930s-type depression. But in today's conditions uncoordinated national policies aimed at depreciation might well create too much money world-wide and renew the inflationary danger.

Moreover, it is unlikely that retaliatory actions, taken by countries who fear that their competitors are undercutting them unfairly by currency depreciation, would stop on the monetary side. Currency wars have usually been an aspect of trade wars, in which restrictions on trade and capital movements have been imposed through the front door or back entrance.

If German industry fears competitive depreciation, its safest course would be to join the largest attainable 'zone of monetary stability'. Italy and Spain are unlikely to meet the stability conditions by 1999. But if EMU is postponed too long, the momentum could be lost to such a degree that there would be nothing for them to join later.

8. B. Connolly, *The Rotten Heart of Europe: The Dirty War for Europe's Money* (1995).

5. THE UK OUTSIDE EMU

Quite a lot of, admittedly inconclusive, academic work has been done on the consequences of establishing EMU, and even on the countries most likely to benefit from joining. But almost nothing has been done on the consequences for the countries which stay aside if EMU goes ahead. Nor is it easy to see how one could do research into the question.

It would be quite wrong to try to make people's flesh creep with the consequences of being left outside. Before the event there were numerous prophecies of the doom that would result if countries moved onto floating exchange rates. Yet after the collapse of Bretton Woods in 1973, world trade continued to flourish, and a truly international system of finance and investment was established for the first time since the First World War. Admittedly, growth in the Western industrial countries slowed down and unemployment exploded. But it would be hazardous to attribute these adverse developments to the end of Bretton Woods. It is more likely that the same underlying forces which destroyed Bretton Woods also destroyed the painless approach to full employment which prevailed after the Second World War.

But without being alarmist, some dangers can be spotted. It is difficult to believe that the existence of a single money in a core region – where guesses do not have to be made about exchange rates, nor complicated hedging arrangements entered into – will not affect some location decisions at the margin. The division between participating and non-participating Member States is likely to mark a wider division between core and peripheral EU countries; and the core is likely to attract some business which might otherwise have come to the periphery.

It is often pointed out that the members of the North American Free Trade Agreement do not envisage any currency link and that the most successful Far Eastern economic 'tigers' do not belong to any currency bloc. But these facts can be interpreted in different ways. A Japanese investor in the Far East or North America does not have the option of investing in a single currency area (apart, of course, from the United States). But he will have the choice of serving European markets from outside or inside such a bloc. It would be foolhardy to suppose that the English language and the presence of numerous golf courses will always be decisive for Japanese inward investment.

The effect on the City of London's business is one of the biggest unknowns. It does not help very much to ask one's City friends, as the response they give is usually predictable from their political and economic attitudes. The most detailed analysis I have seen is Christopher Taylor's.[9] He makes a distinction between relatively short-term institutions, such as banks

9. Op. cit., n.4.

and security houses, and long-term ones, such as insurance companies and pension funds. The latter would be likely to gain from EMU membership, because the international integration of capital markets would be boosted if exchange-rate risks were eliminated. The pressures on pension funds and insurance companies to match assets and liabilities in particular countries would diminish, and continental investors might feel less inhibited about taking advantage of British expertise. On the other hand, the case may be less strong and perhaps negative for short-term institutions, such as foreign-exchange dealers and those dealing in futures and options. It is, however, unlikely that large financial institutions such as banks would move to Frankfurt just to be near the European Central Bank. They do not move to Washington to hear the thoughts of Chairman Greenspan, who has been known to travel in other parts of the US. It has already been made clear that, although there will be a single monetary policy, the ECB's money-market operations will be decentralised through the national central banks.

6. EXCHANGE-RATE ARRANGEMENTS BETWEEN CORE AND PERIPHERY

It is a myth to suppose that there is some wonderful new exchange-rate arrangement between the single-currency area and the non-participating Member States waiting to be found. The options are very few, and are very well known. Those who propose high-level international study of the subject are open to the suspicion of a desire to delay the start of EMU.

A clear distinction should be made between countries that eventually aspire to join the monetary union, but who do not yet fulfil the criteria, and countries that already qualify, but have decided to opt out.

Aspirant members will naturally want to minimise exchange-rate fluctuations against the Euro, especially downward ones. They might or might not find it convenient to formalise these arrangements in something like an Exchange Rate Mechanism. But they cannot expect, so long as they are outside, unlimited help if there is a run on their currency. Some of the most advanced of the aspirant members might be able to fix their currencies *de facto* against the Euro, as Austria and Belgium already do against the DM. Daniel Gros has suggested recognising the achievements of such countries by giving them associate status, in which they will be able to participate in all EMU activities but without having any vote in the decisions which are made.[10]

For countries that have opted out of membership in principle, there seems little point in going for ERM status. For this would bring all the

10. Gros, op. cit., n.3.

constraints of a currency link without any say in how the arrangement is to be run. And as there would be no currency merger, there could always be a confidence crisis of the kind Britain experienced in 1992 and France in 1993.

It would, however, be a legitimate option to 'shadow' the Euro. By this I mean that the Bank of England could run a monetary policy designed to prevent any massive depreciation or appreciation against the European unit. In any case, the idea that the behaviour of sterling could be ignored either by an ultra-free-market government or one of the ultra-left, is just a pipe dream. The trend of sterling is an indication of how inflationary pressures are moving in Britain, relative to those elsewhere. And governments will not be able to prevent their economic advisers from taking a squint at the sterling charts, whether they admit it or not.

In addition, the movement of sterling is one of the transmission channels by which an inflationary or deflationary domestic monetary policy affects the British price level. Some of us may have exaggerated the strength of these linkages in the short term in a depressed economy. But the depreciation of sterling in 1992–95 has probably gone as far as it could without inflationary implications; and, if very low inflation is really here to stay, some improvement in the external value of the pound must also be expected.

This, however, is crystal-gazing. What can be said much more firmly is that any impression of deliberately engineering a sterling depreciation to steal a competitive march on European partners must be avoided like the plague. For if this were suspected, there really would be a threat of discrimination against British goods, and therefore a threat to the single market.

Admittedly, a sovereign country must have the right to relax its monetary policy and take an inflationary risk, if it so wishes. The distinction is between a general relaxation all round, which aims to stimulate home consumer and investment demand and which may also stimulate exports along with imports, and a deliberate beggar-my-neighbour policy, aimed primarily at increasing British export penetration. The distinction might not be easy to make in mutual surveillance exercises. But there would not be much inclination to give the UK the benefit of the doubt, if it also exhibited a generalised hostility to the EMU and other EU institutions.

7.   FISCAL CRITERIA

As every schoolboy knows, the main economic problem facing the establishment of EMU in 1999 lies in the fiscal criteria. According to Article 104C of the EC Treaty, two criteria have to be fulfilled: first, either the government-deficit-to-GDP ratio must be below the reference value (established in a Protocol attached to the Maastricht Treaty as 3 per cent) or the excess must be 'only exceptional and temporary' and still 'close to the reference value'; and second, the debt-to-GDP ratio must not exceed a reference value (60 per cent) or, if it does, it must be diminishing towards that reference value at a satisfactory pace.

Strictly speaking, a monetary union does not need fiscal criteria. The no bail-out rule and the desire of governments to avoid a risk premium on their bonds should be sufficient to avoid excessive deficits. The world's most successful monetary union was known as the gold standard, and had no fiscal criteria or common institutions whatever. Indeed, gold-standard countries were sometimes at war with each other. It must be admitted, however, that 19th-century governments believed in the balanced budget, as they did in gold, as an unquestioned dogma, whereas today governments have to discover the cost of fiscal excess from hard experience. Maybe, without some Treaty commitments, fiscal policy would be too loose and would put too heavy a burden on interest rates, as occurred in the US in the early 1980s.

There is, however, no need to adjudicate. Fiscal criteria are the German price for EMU. The justification goes beyond monetary technicalities. Without fiscal criteria, some countries, especially in southern Europe, may be tempted to run deficits, which they will, however wrongly, blame on EMU and in practice expect Germany to finance.

The criteria have been much criticised by economists, some of whom seek an unobtainable perfection. The second, debt-ratio criterion is indeed a mess. Most EU countries have debt ratios above 60 per cent. But, as Daniel Gros points out, if Member States concentrate on reducing their budget deficit below 3 per cent – which will have favourable effects on confidence and nominal interest rates – there will be an automatic reduction of debt ratios.[11] The main requirement is some formula to indicate the minimum normal speed of reduction.

Thus, in practice the first criterion, the budget-deficit ratio, is the crucial one. As is all too well known, not only is France having to struggle to reach that level by 1997 (after which decisions on membership will be made), but even Germany exceeded the target deficit in 1995. Everything depends in practice on the meanings attached to 'exceptional and temporary' and on how close to the reference value of 3 per cent is 'close'.

The main criticism by economists of the budget-deficit ratio is that it does not explicitly allow for the business cycle. It would, indeed, be absurd to go ahead with EMU if France and Germany can achieve deficit ratios of 2.9 per cent, but postpone the project if, because of a disappointing cyclical upturn, they come to 3.1 per cent.

11. Ibid.

Even hardline German officials are aware of the business cycle. But they are understandably afraid that, if they started talking about flexibility now, this could lead to the complete erosion of the criteria. They are also suspicious of the realism of the cyclical adjustments to deficit figures, and believe that most European unemployment is structural. In fact, German attention has now switched from the Maastricht criteria to the idea of a 'stability pact', to ensure that fiscal stability is not forgotten once EMU has come into force.

It should surely be possible to do a deal by which the normal aim is a budget deficit of well below 3 per cent of GDP, but more explicit allowance is made for the cyclical factor. (The British Treasury estimates that the swing from recession to boom can cause a swing of up to 5 per cent in the deficit ratio.)

The budgetary targets and the proposed fines for violators in the German proposal for a stability pact are opening positions, which are subject to negotiation. The non-negotiable aspect, which a British government will find more difficult to swallow, is that of a supranational and automatic aspect to the fiscal procedures.

German officials are well aware that a judgment will be required on whether an apparently excessive deficit needs censure or might be justified by exceptional economic circumstances or by remedial measures that have been put in train. The supranational element will come through majority voting by European finance ministers and through the automatic application of penalties once a decision is made.

8.   THE ROAD AHEAD

8.1   Would a postponement help?

It is sensible to expect France and other countries to tackle the structural elements, such as the social-security imbalances, in their budgets. But it would be folly to expect them to go all out for a headline budget-deficit figure of 3 per cent, if the business slowdown persists. My own advice to European governments would be to concentrate on the stability pact and really mean it, rather than endanger recovery by making short-term cuts in the face of depressed business conditions.

A postponement of the January 1999 deadlines is highly probable for technical reasons alone. This is not important so long as it of, say, 6 to 18 months, rather than several years. For example, EU government heads may need to wait longer than the beginning of 1998 for worthwhile figures on which to rationalise a decision on which countries qualify for EMU.

Moreover, there will have to be a trial run of machinery such as the interbank settlement system, on which snags are possible the first time round. The European Monetary System did not start at the beginning of 1979 as planned, but was delayed into the spring of that year.

But a longer postponement would be a much bigger blow. Momentum would be lost, recriminations would occur and – most important – the political leaders most keen on the project would have departed from the scene. There are also some of us who would find a continuation of the EMU arguments into the next century pretty unbearable.

8.2   The danger from the Europhobes

Those opponents of EMU who merely wish Britain to stay outside may be misguided, but do little harm in the wider world. They become, however, a positive menace when they try to put a spanner in the whole project. Some of them are trying to do so by undermining the *franc fort* policy in France. They assert that, if only the Chirac government would stop shadowing the DM and encourage a depreciation of the franc, the country would experience an economic renaissance, which might spread to the rest of Europe.

This is wishful thinking. For it presupposes that the French franc is overvalued against the DM, for which there is little real evidence. French inflation has been below German for most of the last five years. More recently the inflation rates in the two countries have been fluctuating around a common rate of 1.5 to 2 per cent.

France has been running a current-payments surplus for several years, while reunited Germany has been running a moderate deficit. Much more important: French unit labour costs have increased by less than German unit costs over the last 10 years. The interest-rate premium on the franc reflects, not the realities of recent cost performance, but a fear that a French government will be panicked into a 'dash for growth' of a kind which really would put the French back into the high-inflation league.

The behaviour of labour costs does suggest that there is something wrong. But the currency which is overvalued is the DM relative to the other main currencies of the world. Germany has, in fact, done well through product and process innovation and vigorous overseas selling to keep the payments deficit as low as it is. But both Chancellor Helmut Kohl and leading German industrialists have warned about the problem of high labour costs, and there are frequent reports of household-name firms shifting their new investments to the former Communist countries or further afield. The French competitive situation has deteriorated just to the extent that the franc has been pulled up with the DM.

Currencies can only be under- or overvalued in relation to each other. The yen is overvalued (although less than before) in relation to the dollar; and the DM is overvalued both in relation to the dollar and to Gemany's southern neighbours, and perhaps also the UK. If, as a result of the Paris government accepting Eurosceptic advice, the German currency also became heavily overvalued in relation to France and its other northern European trading partners, something would be liable to snap. For it would then be extremely difficult for a German government to hold the line against demands for retaliation or countervailing action of some kind. So far from having a White Wednesday, France would find itself threatened with retaliation; and it is doubtful whether it would be allowed to get away with an uncontrolled downward float of the franc.

The UK and the Mediterranean countries were sufficiently peripheral to get away with 'independent' policies conducted in their supposed national interest after the 1992–93 crises of the ERM. This would not apply if Germany's more immediate neighbours joined the game; and a currency war would be more likely than a genuinely freely floating foreign-exchange market, if the deepest wishes of Eurosceptics were granted.

So far the British government has been sensible enough not to associate itself with attempts to destabilise the French franc. But, on a lesser plane of stupidity, its efforts to insinuate that EMU will not begin until well after the announced date in 1999 are highly misguided. Unfortunately, Prime Minister Major associated himself with this campaign when he said in the House of Commons on 27 February 1995: 'I believe that the time scales currently set out cannot safely be met'.

This is putting party management above all else. Of course, if EMU were postponed beyond even the next parliament, the Conservatives would not have to say what they would do in their next election manifesto. They could even avoid a cabinet split on whether there should be a referendum. (Am I alone among the supporters of EMU in also supporting a referendum? A major quasi-constitutional change such as the abolition of the pound requires a direct popular mandate. To introduce it without one, would be asking for trouble.)

But on every other count the campaign is badly misguided. If, indeed, the EMU project were be derailed, few European leaders would be grateful to Britain, however tiny its actual role in the derailment; and the British government's influence would be negligible in any negotiations to pick up the pieces. If, as is more likely, the spoiling campaign fails, Britain's reputation and influence in Europe would be even lower than they are already; and a future British government could not expect much notice to be taken of its opinions, either in discussions on the links between EMU members and the peripheral outsiders or in discussions for later entry. Nor would I wish it otherwise. For who can admire a spoiler?

9.   CONCLUSION

The most tempting conclusion is that EMU could go ahead as near to 1999 as possible, but that Britain should not join immediately. The reason why this is tempting, is the climate of extreme hostility to all European financial arrangements, not merely among the tabloids, but among vociferous English-language analysts and journalists in the City of London and other financial centres – not to speak of Conservative backbenchers. The first law of economics is known as Murphy's Law, and says that, if anything can go wrong, it will. So it is likely that all the troubles and disappointments which are probable early in the next century (as in every other period) will be blamed on EMU, and an extremely nasty atmosphere will be kindled by the xenophobes whom we always have with us.

The temptation is therefore to say: let EMU start, and let Britain apply to join a few years later, as it has done with almost every other European venture. But it would be cowardly for me to cast my vote – if I am to have one – for such a course, both because I think that EMU would bring modest benefits and even more because of the antics of the more vociferous Eurosceptics, which do not deserve to prevail.

Chapter Eight

MONETARY-POLICY STRATEGIES FOR THE EUROPEAN CENTRAL BANK AND THEIR IMPLEMENTATION

*Claes Berg**

Chapter Outline

1. Introduction

2. The Incentive Problem, Inflation Contracts, Inflation Targets and Intermediate Targets
    2.1 The incentive problem
    2.2 Delegation of monetary policy
    2.3 Inflation contracts
    2.4 Inflation targets
    2.5 Intermediate monetary targets
    2.6 Concluding remarks on the incentive problem

3. Some Problems Related to a Strategy Based on Monetary Targets or Other Intermediate Targets

4. Monetary Policy Co-ordination Between the ECB and the Central Banks of the Non-Participating Member States

5. Conclusions

European Economic and Monetary Union: The Institutional Framework (M. Andenas, L. Gormley, C. Hadjiemmanuil, I. Harden, eds.: 90-411-0687-1: © Kluwer Law International: pub. Kluwer Law International, 1997: printed in Great Britain)

1. INTRODUCTION

According to the Maastricht Treaty on European Union, the European Monetary Institute is responsible for preparing the instruments and procedures required for the implementation of the single monetary policy in Stage Three of EMU. Although the ultimate decisions will be taken by the European Central Bank's Governing Council, the EMI shall specify the regulatory, organisational and logistical framework necessary for the European System of Central Banks to perform its tasks.

The primary objective of the ESCB shall be to maintain price stability. Without prejudice to the objective of price stability, the ESCB shall support the general economic policies in the Community with a view to contributing to the achievement of the objectives of the Community, for example, to promote a harmonious and balanced development of economic activities and sustainable and non-inflationary growth.

The Statute of the ESCB, however, offers no guidance on the strategy the ESCB should follow in attaining the price-stability objective, and it describes only in very general terms the means and procedures for policy implementation.

The President of the EMI, Alexandre Lamfalussy, has suggested that, for Stage Three, the most promising candidates for monetary-policy strategy are monetary targeting and direct inflation targeting.[1] The actual choice between these strategies will depend on two factors. The first factor is empirical evidence regarding the approaches, which will have to take into account, in particular, that since the exchange-rate crises of 1992 and 1993 several central banks have adjusted their monetary-policy strategies. The second factor which will determine the choice between monetary targeting and direct inflation targeting is an analytical discussion, based on key issues such as credibility, accountability, rules versus discretion, and central bank independence. Practical lessons for monetary policy can be drawn from the ongoing academic analysis. One important issue, which is not dealt with explicitly in the Maastricht Treaty but which has a bearing on the decision on monetary-policy strategy, is the monetary-policy co-ordination between the countries participating in the EMU and the other Member States of the European Union.

This chapter discusses some of the issues relating to monetary-policy strategy and its implementation in Stage Three of EMU. It is structured as follows. Section 2 discusses the incentive problem facing a central bank, in

---

* I am grateful for comments given by Gustaf Adlercreutz, Krister Andersson, Richard Gröttheim, Hans Lindberg, Lars Hörngren and Christina Lindenius, Torsten Persson and Lars Svensson.

1. See A. Lamfalussy, *The Harmonisation of Monetary Policy in Europe: What Steps and When?* (1995).

particular the tension between the direct benefits of lower inflation and the benefits of surprise inflation, and various possible solutions to this problem: inflation contracts, inflation targets and intermediate targets. Section 3 examines some problems related to a strategy based on monetary targets or other intermediate targets. Section 4 discusses the problem of co-ordinating monetary policy between those countries participating in the single-currency area and other EU countries. The final section concludes with some recommendations for the monetary-policy strategy of the ESCB in Stage Three.

2. THE INCENTIVE PROBLEM, INFLATION CONTRACTS, INFLATION TARGETS AND INTERMEDIATE TARGETS

In this section, the incentive problem facing a central bank will be discussed. The incentive problem arises if the private sector responds to an anti-inflationary policy by signing contracts that embody a low expected rate of inflation. The central bank might in such cases be tempted to produce higher output through surprise inflation. Rational private agents anticipate, however, what the central bank is tempted to do, and in equilibrium inflation will be higher than it needs to be; there is an inflation bias inherent in monetary policy. Actual inflation, therefore, can be analysed as being composed of two separate terms, besides any influence from demand and supply shocks: the inflation target and the inflation bias.

Various solutions to the incentive problem put forward in the theoretical literature must be considered, for example: the appointment of central bankers who give a higher weight to inflation stabilisation than society as a whole; the introduction of an inflation contract between the government and the central bankers in which the central bankers' remuneration declines in proportion to inflation; the delegation of monetary policy to a central bank with an inflation target lower than society's; and lastly, a contract based on an intermediate monetary target.

All strategies aim to anchor monetary policy, and thus the inflation rate, by increasing the cost of inflation for the central bank. They differ with respect to the way in which they reduce the inflation bias and with respect to their consequences for output stabilisation.

2.1 The incentive problem

Recent models of central bank independence are based on the inconsistency between the optimal policies that the authorities would announce if their announcements were believed by the public and the actual policies that they

126

would carry out once the public had acted on the basis of such belief.[2] Two important motives for an inflationary bias are the fiscal-revenue motive and the employment, or short-run Phillips curve, motive.

As an illustration of the first motive, a revenue-seeking government may find it attractive to acquire resources from the private sector by a levy in the form of an unanticipated increase in the price level, when government debt and government expenditures are nominally denominated.[3] Since the revenue from monetary expansion can be used to lower distortionary fiscal taxes, the incentive to increase the inflation tax may become very strong. A promise to keep inflation low may therefore not be credible. In a rational world, the private sector will understand the temptations that face the monetary authority. In equilibrium, inflation is above its target.

An illustration of the second motive is given by the inflation-bias result in aggregate demand management.[4] If the employment rate is given by an expectations-augmented Phillips curve and the central bank controls the inflation via aggregate demand, surprise inflation generates unemployment below the natural rate when prices and wages are set before agents observe aggregate demand. Once inflationary expectations have been incorporated into wages and prices, the central bank can expand the economy towards a lower unemployment rate along the short-run Phillips curve by creating unexpected inflation. The short-run incentives to expand the economy drive up the inflation rate to the point where the cost of higher inflation balances the benefit of lower unemployment. In equilibrium, monetary policy is biased towards inflation; inflation is above its target, but there is no long-term gain in unemployment. Thus, in principle, monetary policy can stabilise or destabilise output or employment, but it cannot increase the average level of these variables.

In these two examples, the incentive constraints emanate from the sequential nature of policy-making, particularly from the possibility of deviation from announced policy rules. The tension between the direct benefits of lower inflation and the potential benefits of surprise inflation is fundamental to the analysis.

It is also clear that the importance of the incentive problem and of the benefit from surprise inflation is state-contingent. The benefit from unanticipated monetary expansion increases with the level of the nominal

---

2. An excellent survey of this literature is given in the introduction to T. Persson and G. Tabellini (eds), *Monetary and Fiscal Policy – Volume 1: Credibility* (1994).

3. See, *eg*, G. Calvo, 'On the Time Consistency of Optimal Policy in a Monetary Economy' (1978) 46 *Econometrica* 1411.

4. F. Kydland and E. S. Prescott, 'Rules Rather Than Discretion: The Inconsistency of Optimal Plans' (1977) 85 *Journal of Political Economy* 473; and R. J. Barro and D. Gordon, 'A Positive Theory of Monetary Policy in a Natural Rate Model' (1983) 91 *Journal of Political Economy* 589.

government debt, and the political pressure to inflate the economy rises when the natural level of unemployment is high. With persistence in output or unemployment the inflation bias is on average larger than without persistence.

2.2 Delegation of monetary policy

Theoretical considerations and empirical evidence suggest that the incentive problem can be solved or reduced by delegating monetary policy to an independent central bank, which is held accountable for the fulfilment of a statutory objective, defined by parliament, which can be considered to be the central bank's principal.

In order to counteract the discretionary inflation bias, due to the incentive problem discussed above, the central bank is motivated to put more weight on inflation stabilisation than society does. This can be accomplished, for example, by delegating monetary policy to an independent, inflation-averse central banker.[5] The central banker and society are both assumed to have preferences for the inflation-rate and output levels, but the central banker weighs deviations of inflation from the target relative to output deviations more heavily than society does. In this model, there is a trade-off between the reduction of the average inflation rate and the increase in the variability of output. Therefore, the appointment of a conservative central banker reduces the inflation bias, but brings higher than optimal variability in output.

This is, however, only the third-best equilibrium, according to Kenneth Rogoff's terminology. The first-best equilibrium requires elimination of the distortions which are the ultimate cause behind the incentive problem, for example, distortions of the labour market or the tax system. The second-best equilibrium refers to a commitment, given the distortion, to an optimal rule, which can reduce the inflation bias without increasing the variability in the development of economic activities. The third-best equilibrium refers to the example above. Delegation of monetary policy to a central bank which puts more weight on inflation stabilisation than society does will reduce the inflation bias at the expense of more variability in output.

2.3 Inflation contracts

However, it is possible to eliminate the incentive problem without increasing output variability by imposing a simple performance contract

---

5. K. Rogoff, 'The Optimal Degree of Commitment to an Intermediate Monetary Target' (1985) 100 *Quarterly Journal of Economics* 1169.

with a linear penalty for inflation, as suggested by Carl Walsh[6] and Torsten Persson and Guido Tabellini.[7] In their analyses, which apply recent findings in contracts theory, a principal (society) with well-defined goals has to design a contract that will motivate an agent (the central bank) to act in the principal's interests. The optimal contract can be interpreted as a mandate to achieve price stability. The central bank is punished for any percentage point of inflation (or remunerated for attaining low inflation). The key distortion is that, without the contract, the central bank does not internalise the effects of its monetary-policy decisions on expected inflation. By punishing the central bank for excessive inflation in relation to the principal's interest, this contract adds the cost of higher expected inflation to the central bank's loss function, effectively causing the internalisation by the central bank of the cost of inflation.[8]

2.4 Inflation targets

The contracting approach, however, while analytically attractive, has not yet been implemented in any country.[9] In contrast, inflation targeting is becoming widely used, as several countries, including New Zealand, Canada,

6. C. Walsh, 'Optimal Contracts for Central Bankers' (1995) 85 *American Economic Review* 150.
7. T. Persson and G. Tabellini, 'Designing Institutions for Monetary Stability' (Dec. 1993) 39 *Carnegie-Rochester Conference Series on Public Policy* 53.
8. When the benefit from surprise inflation is state-contingent, due to, *eg*, unemployment persistence, a simple linear inflation contract can eliminate the average inflation bias, but cannot achieve the optimal rule. The inflation bias will be state-dependent, and the inflation response to the supply shock will be stronger than the optimal rule. A state-contingent inflation contract can achieve the second best equilibrium; see B. Lockwood, M. Miller and L. Zhang, *Designing Monetary Policy When Unemployment Persists*, mimeo, Department of Economics, University of Exeter (1995); L. E. O. Svensson, *Optimal Inflation Targets, 'Conservative' Central Banks and Linear Inflation Contracts*, mimeo, Institute for International Economic Studies, Stockholm University (1995). Another possibility to attain the second best is by combining a state-contingent inflation target with a strategy where the central bank is putting more weight on inflation stabilisation in relation to output stabilisation; see Svensson, ibid.
9. New Zealand's Reserve Bank Act of 1989 makes inflation control the sole objective of the central bank. The Act also requires the Governor of the Reserve Bank to sign an agreement with the government establishing a target rate of inflation and a date on which the target will be achieved. Failure to meet this target can then provide grounds for the government to dismiss the Governor. As part of its central bank reform, the New Zealand government actually considered including a financial incentive in the contract for the head of the central bank that would have resulted in a bonus payment if the bank's inflation target were achieved. As ultimately passed by New Zealand's parliament, the Reserve Bank Act of 1989 did not include such an incentive. See C. Walsh, *Is New Zealand's Reserve Bank Act of 1989 an Optimal Central Bank Contract?*, mimeo, University of California, Santa Cruz (Jan. 1994).

the UK, Finland and Sweden, have recently introduced explicit inflation targets. When discussing inflation targets, it is important to bear in mind that there are two possibilities for a 'conservative' central banker to put more weight on inflation stabilisation than society does.

The first possibility, discussed above in the section on delegation, is to put more weight on inflation stabilisation *in relation* to output stabilisation. In a stylised model, the decision rule applied by the central bank implies that actual inflation, besides a supply or demand-shock component, is composed of two terms: the socially desirable inflation rate and the inflation bias. This inflation-bias component is smaller than under discretion, but does not disappear unless the central bank puts zero weight on output stabilisation. The inflation-bias component thus reflects the fact that the central bank still does not totally internalise the effects of its monetary policy on expected inflation.

The second possibility for a central bank to put more weight on inflation stabilisation is to adopt a *lower* inflation *target* than society does. Then, it is also possible to completely neutralise the inflation bias resulting under discretion, without increasing output variability and without putting zero weight on output stabilisation. Actual inflation, besides a demand or supply-shock component, in this case is composed of the following two terms: the central bank's inflation target and the inflation bias. Therefore, it is possible to adopt an optimal inflation target which is sufficiently low to offset the inflation bias. The inflation target adopted by the central bank should be chosen so as to equal the socially desirable inflation rate less the inflation bias under discretion. Svensson[10] suggests that it is better to delegate monetary policy to a central bank with an inflation target lower than society's than to delegate monetary policy to a central bank with increased weight on inflation stabilisation.[11]

The advantage of an appropriately chosen inflation target is that it is easier to implement than an inflation contract, especially when it is difficult to identify the principal of the central bank.[12] However, there has to be a legal mandate for price stability in order to make explicit the responsibility for fulfilling the inflation target. If the target is imposed upon the central bank by a principal who also has the power to punish the central bank when inflation is above the target, the distinction between an inflation target and an inflation contract will not be important. Furthermore, an inflation

---

10. Loc. cit., n.8.
11. When the benefit from surprise inflation is state-contingent, a constant inflation target can eliminate the average inflation bias, but not the state-contingent inflation bias. A state-contingent inflation target can remove all inflation bias, but leaves inflation variability higher than a state-contingent inflation contract. Ibid.
12. A political problem when adopting an inflation contract would be the possible public debate when the central bank is rewarded for imposing a restrictive monetary policy.

contract or an inflation target can both be interpreted as a general mandate to achieve price stability. The penalty on the central bank for allowing high inflation would then take the form of a general loss of prestige for the institution.

2.5 Intermediate monetary targets

As emphasised by Persson and Tabellini,[13] it is also possible to interpret nominal targets such as intermediate monetary aggregates as performing a function similar to the inflation contract, by increasing the marginal cost of inflation for the central bank. These authors show that, in principle, a contract based on an intermediate target is equivalent to a contract based on an inflation target, in the sense that both can be used to implement the optimal monetary policy when the equilibrium inflation rate under discretion is too high compared to the *ex ante* optimal rate. However, the inflation contract is more direct and simpler to enforce than an intermediate monetary target.

A central bank contract based on an intermediate monetary target is much more demanding on the principal's information, and depends on shocks not known to wage-setters (*eg*, sudden changes in oil prices) and possible velocity shocks, whereas inflation contracts only depend on easily observable shocks, known to wage-setters (*eg*, the degree of wage indexation). In fact, a monetary target can be seen as a special case of an inflation target when the velocity of money is completely predictable, as noted by King.[14] Generally, it is easier to monitor the outcome – the inflation rate – than a monetary aggregate. An inflation contract or an inflation target minimises the informational requirement of the principal, and thus generally dominates contracts based on intermediate monetary targets.

2.6 Concluding remarks on the incentive problem

We have studied four possible solutions to the incentive problem facing a central bank. When the central bank puts more weight on inflation stabilisation in relation to output stabilisation, the inflation-bias component is reduced, but does not disappear unless the central bank puts a zero weight on output stabilisation. The inflation bias is reduced at the expense of more variability in output. When the central bank is punished for excessive inflation in a specific contract, the inflation-bias component can be

---

13. Persson and Tabellini, loc. cit., n.7.
14. M. King, 'Mr. King Wonders Whether Inflation Targets Work' (1995) 165 *BIS Review*.

completely neutralised without increasing output variability. A contract based on an intermediate monetary target can perform a similar function, but it is more demanding on information about, for example, velocity shocks.

If the central bank adopts a lower inflation target than society, it is also possible to completely neutralise the inflation bias. As the inflation target focuses directly on the ultimate objective of monetary policy, it may provide a clearer and more transparent framework than an intermediate target. A direct inflation target is also easier to implement than an inflation contract.

3. SOME PROBLEMS RELATED TO A STRATEGY BASED ON MONETARY TARGETS OR OTHER INTERMEDIATE TARGETS

The effectiveness of a strategy based on an intermediate target relies on the fulfilment of certain conditions: a reasonably stable and predictable relationship between the final target and the intermediate variable; and a sufficient degree of controllability of the latter by monetary-policy instruments. There are three groups of issues which are important to discuss in relation to the possible option of adopting an intermediate monetary target for the ESCB.

The first group of issues regards the controllability of the money supply, which in some studies is considered to be, most likely, higher at the level of a single-currency area than it is now for individual countries.[15] The evidence available in these studies suggests that the EC-wide money-demand functions are at least as stable and predictable as those of the best-performing countries.

However, the grounds for using this point as an argument for an intermediate monetary target can be called in question. The implications of the empirical results for the conduct of monetary policy in Stage Three are tenuous, because the inception of Stage Three is relatively far in the future, and the stability of monetary relationships may be impaired in the meantime.

A second reservation is that the important change in policy regime entailed by the beginning of Stage Three could itself impair the stability of the monetary relationships, even if at the end of Stage Two these were considered reliable on the basis of empirical evidence. The effectiveness of a monetary-targeting strategy will be negatively influenced by difficulties in

---

15. See, *eg*, A. G. van Riet, 'European Integration and the Demand for Money in the EC' [1992] 3 *De Nederlandsche Bank Quarterly Bulletin* 33; idem, 'Studies of EC Money Demand: Survey and Assessment' [1992] 4 *De Nederlandsche Bank Quarterly Bulletin.*

forecasting the velocity of money demand and potential GDP at the beginning of Stage Three. Furthermore, the aggregate money stock is a function of two components, the monetary base and the money multiplier, which both will be more difficult to control in Stage Three. Even if it were possible for a central bank to control the money supply, this does not imply that the primary objective of price stability would be attained if there is an unstable relation between money supply and inflation. A further argument regards the assessment of the relevance of econometric research. If an aggregate ERM-wide money-demand function is found to be structurally stable, in contrast to money-demand equations estimated for individual countries, this may simply reflect aggregation bias. Artis, Bladen-Hovell and Zhang,[16] for example, find that the stability of French monetary relationships exerts a powerful influence on the form and stability of the aggregate European money-demand function.

The second group of issues is related to the transfer of credibility to the future ESCB. It is very important for the ESCB to inherit from the national central banks as much of their existing reputation as possible. Adherence to an existing successful monetary-policy concept could reduce uncertainty due to the creation of monetary union for the financial market participants. For reasons of continuity, the adoption of an intermediate target for money supply could be advisable, since such a target is currently used, by and large with success, by several central banks, including the Deutsche Bundesbank.

However, the transfer of credibility from national central banks to the future ESCB is not straightforward. The ESCB will be a new institution with no track-record. Therefore, building a reputation will take time. The Governing Council will comprise members of the Executive Board and the Governors of those national central banks which participate in the single currency area. The track-records of these national central banks are different, and it is not evident that the Bundesbank's impressive track-record reflects its use of monetary targets. Therefore, it is not clear why the adoption of a strategy based on intermediate monetary targets should enhance *per se* the credibility of the ESCB.

A third group of issues influencing the analysis of a monetary-targeting strategy relates to the fact that some central banks recently have adapted their monetary-policy strategies to the deregulation of financial markets, the liberalisation of international capital flows and the increasing economic and financial integration. While the monetary policy in Germany has continued to be guided by an intermediate money-supply target for M3, the behaviour of other variables – such as wage formation, fiscal policy, exchange-rate developments and cyclical positions – are also monitored to ensure that the

16. M. J. Artis, R. Bladen-Hovell and W. Zhang, 'A European Money Demand Function', in P. R. Masson and M. P. Taylor (eds), *Policy Issues in the Operation of Currency Unions* (1993).

message coming from monetary aggregates is not misleading as an indication of inflation prospects. Thus, in 1993 and in the first half of 1994 interest rates were reduced, notwithstanding the fact that the monetary aggregate was growing at rates significantly in excess of the target range.[17] Other countries within the ERM are giving less emphasis to monetary targeting.[18]

Some central banks in countries outside the ERM, for example, the Bank of England, Sveriges Riksbank and Suomen Pankki, have adopted the mechanism of inflation targeting. The money stock is here used as an indicator variable, among several others.[19]

In conclusion, these changes in the way central banks are using monetary aggregates indicate that the effectiveness of a strategy based on an intermediate monetary target has been reduced in many European countries. The European monetary union will be a change in regime that can be expected to have important implications for the stability of all monetary relationships. However, if and when a stable relation between monetary aggregates and prices can be identified within EMU, as the new structure is established, monetary targeting may be considered more important.

4. MONETARY POLICY CO-ORDINATION BETWEEN THE ECB AND THE CENTRAL BANKS OF THE NON-PARTICIPATING MEMBER STATES

The Maastricht Treaty offers little guidance on policy co-ordination between those countries which will join the single-currency area and the other Member States of the EU. Externalities (competitive devaluations and cross-border transmissions of financial crises) may arise between the two groups of countries.

The liberalisation of capital movements has made intermediate exchange-rate arrangements like the narrow-band EMS more difficult to sustain, as self-fulfilling speculative attacks might be induced on those currencies which

17. M3 was referred to as a key benchmark variable when Bundesbank announced its monetary-policy target for 1996.
18. From 1994, the Banque de France placed its M3 target in a medium-term context and supplemented it with total domestic debt as an important indicator of financial conditions. Central banks in Denmark, the Netherlands and Portugal chose to abandon their respective intermediate targets for monetary expansion in 1993. Spain has introduced an inflation target, without giving up its exchange-rate target within the ERM.
19. Against the background of unstable M2 growth, the Banca d'Italia has announced a central reference target for M2 and decided to use a variety of indicators of future inflationary pressures. Following the gradual liberalisation of capital movements in Greece, the exchange-rate target was given more weight by the Bank of Greece, while less emphasis was placed on the monetary target.

will not take part in the monetary union from the start of Stage Three.[20] Governments in countries outside the single-currency area may not be able (or willing, given the contractionary effects on the domestic economy) to increase interest rates sufficiently to defend fixed parities, if overall macroeconomic balance is not attained.

On the other hand, if outside countries adhere to some form of floating exchange rates, persistent movements in the exchange rates away from equilibrium may trigger protectionist pressures, which would undermine the cohesiveness of the single market. The more integrated the European economies become, the more pronounced are the distributional consequences of intra-EU currency swings. With the perfection of the single market, EU Member States which depreciate their currencies may be accused of boosting exports to other Member States. Resistance to accepting this state of affairs will grow as integration proceeds. A situation where some Member States remain outside the single-currency area for a longer period may aggravate strains among the insiders, as trade flows between countries differ, as well as between insiders and outsiders. This potential conflict between countries joining the single-currency area from the start of Stage Three and countries with a derogation or an exercised opt-out calls for a co-ordinating device which will not give currency markets incentives for speculative attacks.

One solution is to create a new exchange-rate arrangement, with the single currency at the centre and the other currencies fluctuating within bands *vis-à-vis* the single currency. Such an arrangement would also allow for different national solutions within a common institutional framework. As restrictions on the movement of capital within the single market are ruled out, narrow bands around the single currency would be hard to maintain. If automatic intervention would be considered by the ECB as a risk to its commitment to price stability, the new arrangement would be similar to a unilateral peg to the common currency. In that case, there would still be a risk of speculative attacks on outside currencies. Countries outside the single-currency area would risk bearing all of the real economic costs of such currency speculation.[21]

A more symmetric co-ordination mechanism would involve the adoption of (common) inflation targets in both groups of countries. Inflation targets would reinforce the commitment to low inflation, and could prevent the use of monetary policy for pursuing competitive devaluations. Inflation targets would also reduce the volatility of nominal exchange rates, and long-term

20. B. Eichengreen and F. Ghironi, *European Monetary Unification: The Challenges Ahead*, Centre for Economic Policy Research Discussion Paper No. 1217 (1995).
21. See T. Persson and G. Tabellini, *Monetary Cohabitation in Europe*, mimeo, Institute for International Economic Studies, Stockholm (1995).

135

swings in real exchange rates would be significantly dampened.[22] The adoption of inflation targets in all EU states would also imply a more symmetric risk-sharing of the real economic costs of currency speculation between countries participating in monetary union and the other Member States of the European Union.[23]

The inflation target for a country that does not participate in the single-currency area could be announced by its national central bank or government independently, or by its national central bank or government in consultation with the ECB. Monitoring of the individual targets should be delegated to the ESCB, making it clear that even for Member States outside the single-currency area the commitment to the inflation target is a duty owed, not just to the domestic public and national legislature, but also to the EU. Opting out of the inflation target could be considered as not being in accordance with the Treaty.[24]

5. CONCLUSIONS

The ECB will formulate and implement a monetary policy whose primary objective will be to maintain price stability. The ECB's monetary policy must support the general economic policies of the Community, but only insofar as this is compatible with the final target of price stability.

Various solutions to the incentive problem facing a central bank with an explicit objective to maintain price stability have been discussed. A strategy based on inflation targeting can eliminate the inflation bias emanating from the sequential nature of monetary policy-making. Inflation contracts or nominal monetary targets can also be interpreted as performing a function similar to that of an inflation target. By increasing the marginal cost of inflation for the central bank, they can be used to secure the implementation of the optimal monetary policy. However, inflation targets are more direct, and may be easier to implement, than inflation contracts or intermediate targets. An inflation target focuses directly on the ultimate objective of

22. This is pointed out by M. Dewatripont, F. Giavazzi, J. von Hagen, I. Harden, T. Persson, G. Roland, H. Rosenthal, A. Sapir and G. Tabellini, *Flexible Integration: Towards a More Effective and Democratic Europe*, Monitoring European Integration No. 6, Centre for Economic Policy Research (1995). These authors also underline that one of the advantages of the ERM is that it dampened the fluctuations in Germany's competitiveness between 1979 and 1992. In contrast, Germany's competitiveness during the 1970s was negatively affected by the fact that the European currencies did not follow the DM in its large appreciation against the dollar, after the collapse of Bretton Woods.
23. See Persson and Tabellini, op. cit., n.21.
24. As suggested by Dewatripont *et al.*, op. cit., n.22.

monetary policy, and may provide a more transparent framework than an intermediate target.

It should be added, however, that the two strategies, based on inflation targets and monetary targets, respectively, are not mutually exclusive. Countries using an intermediate target have not done so mechanically, as they also take into account other inflation indicators when assessing monetary conditions. Similarly, the money supply can serve as an important source of information in a country using an inflation target. In fact, a monetary target can be seen as a special case of an inflation target when the velocity of money is completely predictable.

An evaluation of empirical and conceptual factors leads one to conclude that a stable relationship between the final inflation target and an intermediate monetary aggregate may not exist at the start of Stage Three. This would complicate the use of a monetary-targeting strategy. If the ECB launches monetary targeting as its preferred policy approach and it turns out that the relations are not stable, the ESCB's credibility may be jeopardised. However, monetary aggregates can be used as important indicators for the conduct of monetary policy. Furthermore, if and when a stable relation between monetary aggregates and prices can be identified within the single-currency area, as the new structure is established, monetary targeting may be considered more important.

Arrangements will also have to be made to co-ordinate the conduct of monetary policy and to establish appropriate foreign-exchange relations between the countries participating in the EMU and the other EU Member States. Inflation targets would facilitate the co-ordination of monetary policy between the two groups, as they can prevent the use of monetary policy for pursuing competitive devaluations. Inflation targets would also dampen speculative movements of capital and reduce exchange-rate volatility. Finally, the adoption of an inflation-targeting strategy would increase the accountability of the ECB and the national central banks in Member States with a derogation or an exercised opt-out.

Chapter Nine

THE EUROPEAN CONSTITUTIONAL FRAMEWORK FOR MEMBER STATES' PUBLIC FINANCES

Ian Harden, Jürgen von Hagen and Robert Brookes*

Chapter Outline

1. Introduction

2. Public Finances in Economic and Monetary Union
    2.1   No fiscal union
    2.2   The Community budget

3. The Economic Policies of the Member States and of the Community
    3.1   The objectives of economic policy
    3.2   Economic policy and public finance

4. The Community Interest in Member States' Public Finances
    4.1   Convergence
    4.2   Tendencies to fiscal laxity
    4.3   Fiscal policy co-ordination

5. Procedures Under the Treaty on European Union
    5.1   Convergence programmes
    5.2   Multilateral surveillance
    5.3   The excessive deficit procedure

6. 'Autonomy, Discipline and Co-ordination'
    6.1   Sanctions and commitment
    6.2   'Process bail-out'

—Cont'd.

European Economic and Monetary Union: The Institutional Framework (M. Andenas, L. Gormley, C. Hadjiemmanuil, I. Harden, eds.: 90-411-0687-1: © Kluwer Law International: pub. Kluwer Law International, 1997: printed in Great Britain)

1.   INTRODUCTION

A 'constitution' defines, allocates and limits public authority. That is, it contains rules about who does what, and how they are to do it. It also contains (or is based on) principles that explain the legitimacy of the who, the what and the how. A constitution usually makes explicit provision for its own amendment and, typically, some of the rules and principles it contains are harder to change than others. A constitution will also normally provide for ways in which disputes about its own meaning and application are to be resolved.

The European Union has no founding document headed 'Constitution'. However, public authority within the Union is established and governed by laws and principles, some of which are more resistant to change than others. There is an allocation of decision-making authority between Member States and the Community, and between different Community institutions. There are also rules and principles about how the allocation of authority may be changed and about how disputes are to be resolved. In this sense, the Union has a constitution. Its provisions are embodied in the Treaties, in decisions of the Court of Justice and in customs and practices that have evolved over time.[1]

Unwillingness to acknowledge the existence of a European constitution has its source in two related beliefs:

(i)   that only states have constitutions; *and*

(ii)   that a constitution necessarily involves a founding act by the people, or legitimately in their name.

This chapter assumes that neither belief is true, and the second plays no further part in the discussion.[2] Public finance, however, is highly relevant to constitutional questions about what sort of political entity the EU is now, and what it might become.

Public finance involves decisions of various kinds: about aggregate government spending, revenue and borrowing; about who is to bear the burden of taxation, and when; and about how total public expenditure is to be divided between competing claims. The economic literature identifies three functions of public finance: the allocation of productive resources; the (re)distribution of wealth and income; and the stabilisation of the economy. In practice, these three functions are highly interdependent, so that a

---

*   The research on which this chapter is based was conducted under Phase 2 of the Economic and Social Research Council's Single Market Programme (Grant No. L113251037). The chapter was completed in June 1996.

1. See, generally, I. Harden, 'The Constitution of the European Union' [1994] *Public Law* 609.

2. See I. Harden, 'Democracy and the European Union' (1996) 67 *Political Quarterly*.

decision involving one also has implications for the others. In particular, all public-finance decisions have distributional consequences and potentially involve conflicts between different groups.[3]

So important are decisions about public finance, that the institutions and processes through which these are made are at the heart of the structure of public authority in every state. The European dimension of public finance is, therefore, of fundamental importance in analysing both the extent and the constitutional forms of political integration in the EU and the constitutional implications of such integration for the location and accountability of public power. At least four possible objects of inquiry can be identified:

(i) the relative significance of Community public finance *vis-à-vis* that of the Member States;

(ii) the relationship between fiscal-policy actors and central bankers;

(iii) the Union's machinery for making and implementing decisions about the public finances of the Member States;

(iv) the impact of (iii) on the constitutional framework of public-finance decisions within the different Member States.

The main focus of this chapter is on (iii). Necessarily, however, there are some spillovers into (i), (ii) and (iv).

2. PUBLIC FINANCES IN ECONOMIC AND MONETARY UNION

The Maastricht Treaty on European Union[4] provides for 'economic and monetary union'.[5] The verbal symmetry between 'economic' and 'monetary' is misleading, however. Monetary union necessarily involves a single monetary policy and a single exchange-rate policy for those states that are part of the monetary union. The language of the Treaty reflects this. It provides for 'the monetary policy of the Community' to be formulated by the Governing Council of a single Community body: the European Central Bank.[6] 'Economic' union has no such precise contours. Indeed, under the influence of American economists 'EMU' is often thought to be an acronym

---

3. See J. von Hagen and I. Harden, 'National Budgetary Processes and Fiscal Performance' [1994] 3 *European Economy, Reports and Studies* 311.
4. Most of the relevant provisions of the Maastricht Treaty amended the Treaty establishing the European Community.
5. See, in particular, Maastricht Treaty, Art. B, and EC Treaty, Arts 2, 109e and 109j.
6. EC Treaty, Art. 3a ('single monetary policy and exchange-rate policy'); Art. 105 (2); and Statute of the ESCB, Art. 12. See, generally, I. Harden, 'The European Central Bank and the Role of National Central Banks in Economic and Monetary Union', in K. Gretschmann (ed.), *Economic and Monetary Union: Implications for National Policy-Makers* (1993).

for 'European monetary union'. Here, however, EMU stands for 'economic and monetary union'.

A fundamental aspect of economic union is the integration of markets. This is a continuing process, not a 'Big Bang' as with monetary union. Its essential element is the single market, completion of which was the principal objective of the 1986 Single European Act. The Maastricht Treaty's contribution to economic union in this sense is limited. The Treaty constitutionalises the abolition of restrictions on movement of capital and payments, but a legal basis for free movement of capital within the Union had already been largely achieved within the previous EEC Treaty framework.[7]

2.1 No fiscal union

The economic part of EMU does not involve a 'public-finance union',[8] or fiscal union. Arguably, that step would require the EU to become a state. In the scheme established by the Maastricht Treaty, spending, taxing and borrowing remain primarily the responsibility of the Member States.

The Union has no explicit mechanism for providing general revenues to support the public spending of a state, either through state-to-state or Community-to-state transfers. Both the Structural Funds and the Cohesion Fund[9] are for defined purposes, although the aggregate amount received is an important component of the overall public-finance position of some of the 'cohesion' states.

From the beginning of the third stage of EMU, there will be provision for Community financial assistance to a state that 'is in difficulties or is seriously threatened with *severe* difficulties *caused by exceptional occurrences beyond its control*'.[10] 'Financial assistance' is not defined, but would appear to allow the making of grants as well as loans. The conditions of eligibility are considerably more restrictive than under Article 109h of the EC Treaty, which allows assistance to a state with balance of payments difficulties. This Article has applied since the Maastricht Treaty came into effect, and will continue to apply in the third stage to states with a

---

7. See EEC Treaty, Art. 67; and Council Directive 88/361/EEC.
8. A term used by Dieter Biehl, 'A Federalist Budget Strategy for European Union' (1985) 6 *Policy Studies* 67.
9. EC Treaty, Art. 130d. The Protocol on economic and social cohesion provides for Community financial contributions to projects in the fields of environment and trans-European networks in Member States with a per capita GNP of less than 90 per cent of the Community average. See also Council Regulation (EC) No. 1164/94.
10. EC Treaty, Art. 103a (2) (emphasis added). Unless the severe difficulties are caused by a natural disaster, the Council must act unanimously. This provision will apply to the United Kingdom and Denmark, even if they exercise their rights not to move to the third stage of EMU.

derogation.[11] However, it is doubtful whether the 'mutual assistance' under Article 109h could include grants.

2.2 The Community budget

The Maastricht Treaty made little change to the constitutional framework of the Community's own budget. Budgetary authority in the Community is shared between the Council and Parliament.[12] The Community has no power to borrow to finance its current expenditure, so the budget must balance. Community revenue ('own resources') is governed by a Council Decision, taken by unanimity, which requires adoption by all Member States in accordance with their respective constitutional requirements.[13] The Maastricht Treaty recognised the principle that the growth of Community expenditure should be limited by available revenue.[14] To give effect to the principle as a constraint on spending, the European Council establishes a financial perspective, subsequently embodied in an interinstitutional agreement between the Commission, Council and Parliament.[15] The financial perspective imposes multiannual ceilings on Community revenue, and hence on the growth of budgetary expenditure. The current own-resources decision includes the ceilings agreed by the European Council in the 1992 financial perspective.[16] To date, these ceilings have accommodated the continued growth of expenditure.

Community spending is significant, even in large and relatively prosperous Member States.[17] However, the present Community budget is very much smaller than that of the federal government in states such as Australia, Canada, Switzerland and the USA. In those four countries, the ratio of federal government spending to GDP is about 20 per cent, representing

---

11. In substance, Art. 109h of the EC Treaty is the same as Art. 108 of the EEC Treaty before the amendments made by the Maastricht Treaty. See also Council Regulation (EEC) No. 1969/88 establishing a single facility providing medium-term financial assistance for Member States' balances of payments.
12. EC Treaty, Art. 203.
13. Ibid., Art. 201.
14. Ibid., Art. 201a. There is a rather similar provision in Art. 81 (4) of the Italian Constitution, which has not, however, proved a great success.
15. The first financial perspective covered the period 1988–92 ('Delors I') and the second, the period 1993-99. The current interinstitutional agreement (of 29 Oct. 1993) has been published in (1993) OJ C 331/1.
16. Council Decision of 31.10.94 on the system of the European Communities' own resources.
17. 'The EC constitutes a supranational element within the German public sector', and is a 'fourth budgetary level in Germany alongside the federal, Länder and local governments'; (Nov. 1993) Deutsche Bundesbank, *Monatsbericht*, pp.63-4.

between two fifths and two thirds of all public expenditure.[18] Community spending is about 1.2 per cent of Community GNP,[19] and is permitted to rise to 1.27 per cent by 1999 under the current financial perspective. This compares with an average ratio of public expenditure to GDP for the EUR-12 of about 50 per cent. Even increased Union spending on infrastructure investment and education, together with expansion of the Union to include the Central and Eastern European states, might be accommodated within a relatively small budget of around 2 per cent of Community GDP.[20]

To get a true picture of the scale of the Community's public finances, borrowing and lending activities must also be considered. As already noted, the Community does not have authority to borrow to finance its current expenditure. Its borrowing is mainly for purposes of on-lending, mostly carried out through the European Investment Bank, often in conjunction with grants from the Structural Funds.[21] Legally, lending and borrowing by the Community do not constitute 'revenue and expenditure'. They do not form part of the Community budget, and so are largely excluded from the supervisory remit of the European Parliament and the Court of Auditors.[22]

However, even taking these off-budget activities into account, Community public finance remains small in comparison with the aggregate public finances of the states. Hence, the provisions of the Maastricht Treaty concerned with public finance are designed to have an impact on the states' decision-making. The provisions that have received the most attention are those concerned with 'excessive deficits'. However, they cannot be fully understood without first considering what the Treaty says about economic policy.

18. See 'Stable Money – Sound Finances: Community Public Finance in the Perspective of EMU' (1993) 53 *European Economy*, p.36, table 6, which is based on IMF data.
19. For present purposes, the distinction between GDP and GNP is not significant. For an explanation of different definitions, see B. W. Hogwood, *Trends in British Public Policy* (1992).
20. See 'Stable Money – Sound Finances . . .', loc. cit., n.18. This figure should be contrasted with the 7.5 per cent of Community GDP, which the MacDougall Report had suggested as necessary to support EMU; 'Report of the Study Group on the Role of Public Finance in European Integration' (2 vols, 1977).
21. As envisaged by the MacDougall Report, ibid. The Report also proposed analogous arrangements for a 'small public sector federation', the budget of which could be 'high-powered' by providing subsidies that were 'designed to have a high leverage effect on national expenditures and on capital flows'; ibid., Vol. I, pp.67, 69–70.
22. See, generally, D. Strasser, *The Finances of Europe* (3rd edn, 1991). The EIB comes within the remit of the European Ombudsman, however.

3. THE ECONOMIC POLICIES OF THE MEMBER STATES AND OF THE COMMUNITY

Given the constitutional significance of controls over public finances, it is perhaps not surprising to find some ambiguity in the Maastricht Treaty about how many economic policies are supposed to exist in the Union. Member States have economic policies, as is recognised by Articles 102a and 103 (1). They are to regard such economic policies, however, as a matter of common concern. Furthermore, 'the activities of the Member States and the Community' include 'the adoption of *an* economic policy'. This economic policy is to be based on 'the close coordination of Member States' economic policies' and on 'the definition of common objectives'.[23]

3.1 The objectives of economic policy

The monetary policy and exchange-rate policy of the Community are to have 'price stability' as their primary objective. An additional objective of such policies is to provide support for 'the general economic policies [*sic*] in the Community', but this is expressed to be without prejudice to the objective of price stability.[24] Price stability is thus supposed to have 'lexical priority'.[25] There can be no question of a trade-off with the other objective.

This principle is put into effect through a substantive rule forbidding the 'monetisation' of public debt; that is, the financing of public expenditure by creating new money. Community institutions, governments (central, regional and local) and other public authorities of the Member States are forbidden to borrow directly from a central bank, or to have privileged access to financial institutions.[26]

The principle is also embedded in the constitutional position of the European Central Bank. The ECB is to be an independent body and its mandate repeats the lexical priority of price stability.[27] Correspondingly, the ECB is not an 'institution' of the Community under Article 4 of the EC Treaty. Within the limits of their powers under the Treaties, the institutions have a general responsibility for all the tasks entrusted to the Community.[28] The ECB's responsibility is more limited. It is bound by its own specific mandate to give lexical priority to price stability. It is for the ECB itself to determine what price stability is, and how best to exercise its powers to

23. EC Treaty, Art. 3a (emphasis added).
24. Ibid., Arts 3a and 105.
25. See J. Rawls, *A Theory of Justice* (1971), pp.42–3.
26. EC Treaty, Arts 104, 104a and 104b. See also Council Regulations (EC) No. 3603/93 and (EC) No. 3604/93 of 13.12.1993.
27. EC Treaty, Art. 105 (1).
28. See ibid., Art. 4.

achieve it. Its duty to 'support the general economic policies in the Community' does not, therefore, provide any basis for other public authorities to seek to limit its discretion. In fact, the ECB is protected by a rather more tightly-drafted version of the legal provisions that apply to the Bundesbank.[29]

'Economic policy' has broader objectives than monetary policy and exchange-rate policy. According to Article 3a of the EC Treaty, the adoption of an economic policy is to be 'for the purposes set out in Article 2'. Those purposes are:

... to promote throughout the Community a harmonious and balanced development of economic activities, sustainable and non-inflationary growth respecting the environment, a high degree of convergence of economic performance, a high level of employment and of social protection, the raising of the standard of living and quality of life, and economic and social cohesion and solidarity among Member States.

Article 102a requires states to conduct their economic policies with a view to contributing to the achievement of these aims. It also requires the Community and the Member States to act in accordance with the principle of an open market economy with free competition, favouring an efficient allocation of resources and in compliance with the principles set out in Article 3a. The latter are: 'stable prices, sound public finances and monetary conditions and a sustainable balance of payments'. Clearly, the purposes of Article 2 are not intended to derogate in any way from the more concrete principles of Article 3a. On the contrary, the assumption is that the purposes are to be realised through application of the principles.

Article 130b requires the states to conduct their economic policies and to co-ordinate them in such a way as, in addition, to attain the economic and social cohesion objectives set out in Article 130a.[30] Paragraph 2 of the latter Article explains in slightly more detail, but does not add to, the cohesion objective expressed in Article 2. The words 'in addition' in Article 130b are presumably intended to indicate that pursuit of the cohesion objective should not involve any departure from the principles of Articles 3a and 102a.

29. The Bundesbankgesetz of 1957 provides that:
    'Without prejudice to the performance of its functions, the Deutsche Bundesbank shall be required to support the general economic policies of the Federal Government. In exercising the powers conferred on it by this Act it shall be independent of instructions from the Federal Government.'
30. That is, reducing the disparities between the levels of development of the various regions and the backwardness of the least-favoured regions, including rural areas.

3.2 Economic policy and public finance

The term 'economic policy' has no precise meaning in ordinary usage, nor is it defined in the EC Treaty. At its broadest, it embraces all government actions intended to affect the economy,[31] including monetary and exchange-rate policies, labour-market policy, industrial policy, etc. It also includes decisions about the total of government spending, about total revenue and about the balance between them.

The latter decisions are usually labelled 'fiscal' or 'budgetary' policy. These expressions denote the same field of government decision-making. The difference between them is a matter of the targets at which government aims. It is a pity that the word 'policy' can hardly be avoided. Analysis needs to distinguish between:

(i)   the *objectives* that government might wish to pursue;
(ii) the *instruments* that are available for the purpose; and
(iii) the *outcomes* of what government does.

Unfortunately, the word 'policy' straddles these distinctions in a way that tends to credit government with more control over both its own activities – and those of others – than it may actually possess.

The term 'budgetary policy' tends to be used when government's targets relate to levels of public debt, deficit and spending. 'Fiscal policy' focuses attention on the effects of public-finance decisions on the broader economy. The nature of such effects, the extent to which government can control them to achieve economic objectives and over what time-scale, are matters of dispute amongst economists and politicians. There is broad agreement, however, that decisions about public finance may, under some circumstances, have beneficial macroeconomic effects in stabilising price and employment levels in the economy and/or in adjusting to economic changes.

Broadly two (or perhaps three) versions of fiscal policy in this sense may be distinguished:

(i)   'discretionary' fiscal policy, in which government takes positive measures to respond to the effects of economic changes of various kinds;
(ia) a version of (i) consisting of the 'fine-tuning' approach, which seeks (or sought, since it has now fallen into general discredit) to use discretionary fiscal policy to counteract the effects of business cycles by timely measures intended to expand, or contract, aggregate demand;

31. Cf. T. Daintith's definition of economic policy as comprising 'all purposeful governmental action whose actual or professed primary objective is the improvement of the economic welfare of the whole population for which the government is responsible or of some segment of that population'; T. Daintith (ed.), *Law as an Instrument of Economic Policy: Comparative and Critical Approaches* (1988), p.6.

(ii)   'automatic' stabilisation, in which government takes no action to offset the tendency of public expenditure to rise and tax revenue to fall in recessions (and *vice versa* in cyclical upswings).

Article 103 of the original EEC Treaty referred to 'conjunctural policy'. This term is happier in the original French, which is perhaps better translated by 'short-term economic policy'. This tends to imply the 'fine-tuning' approach,[32] and was not used in the Maastricht Treaty. Given the theory-laden and controversial nature of the terms 'fiscal policy' and 'budgetary policy', neither would have been a suitable replacement. Hence, perhaps, the more neutral and vague 'economic policy'. However, it is clear from the history and context of the relevant provisions that 'co-ordination of economic policies' includes decisions about the Member States' public finances, although the 'broad guidelines of the economic policies of the Member States and of the Community' for which Article 103 provides may also cover other matters.

4.   THE COMMUNITY INTEREST IN MEMBER STATES' PUBLIC FINANCES

Although there are no specific provisions about the matter in the Maastricht Treaty, the planning for EMU assumed that fiscal policy may be used in response to economic changes that have different effects on different states ('asymmetric shocks'). Since there is no automatic Community mechanism to achieve this, however, states' own fiscal policies must be used.[33]

In principle, the use of fiscal policy for this purpose could be considered as each state's own business. The reasons for the Union to be interested in Member States' fiscal and budgetary policies can be grouped under three broad headings:[34]

(i)   to achieve economic convergence during the second stage of EMU;

(ii)   to counteract the possibility of excessive debt and deficits by states taking part in the monetary union;

32. This was even clearer in the implementing Decision; Council Decision 74/120/EEC of 18.2.1974 on the attainment of a high degree of convergence of economic policies and performance. See T. Padoa-Schioppa, *Efficiency, Stability and Equity* (1987).

33. M. Emerson *et al.*, *One Market, One Money* (1992) (1990) 44 *European Economy*), ch.5.

34. See A. Lamfalussy, 'Macro-economic Co-ordination of Fiscal Policies in an Economic and Monetary Union in Europe', in Committee for the Study of Economic and Monetary Union, 'Report on Economic and Monetary Union in the European Community' (June 1989) (the 'Delors Report').

   (iii) to ensure co-ordination of fiscal policies in the interests of the Union as a whole.

Each of these requires explanation and comment.

4.1 Convergence

The Maastricht Treaty envisages the achievement of a 'high degree of sustainable convergence' between Member States before the beginning of the third stage of EMU. The Treaty's provisions about convergence have two objectives. To understand the first objective, it is necessary to recognise that monetary union means monetary union with Germany. Without Germany, monetary union is pointless. However, most Germans are unwilling to give up the low-inflation Deutsche Mark for a Euro-currency if the latter would be significantly less stable than the DM. Guaranteeing the stability of the Euro-currency, requires more than just an independent European Central Bank to decide monetary policy. It also requires that the states participating in the monetary union must share the German commitment to sound public finances.

A state's budget deficit may be too large because too great a proportion of government spending is financed by borrowing, or because total government spending is too large. How large is 'too large' is, in general, a matter of judgement. The only clear criterion is the sustainability or otherwise of the build-up of public debt.[35] However, no one argues that it makes sense always to borrow up to the limit of sustainability.

A simple way to provide reassurance on this question would have been to allow Germany to determine which states should join the monetary union and which should not. However, the only acceptable way of making distinctions between Member States is through an objective test, that can be seen to apply fairly and without discrimination.[36] One objective of the Treaty provisions about convergence is, therefore, to provide such a test. The second objective is actively to promote the goals of low inflation and sound public finance, even in states that might not meet the convergence test when the third stage of EMU begins.

The test prescribed by the EC Treaty is contained in Article 109j and the Protocol on the convergence criteria. Its four elements relate to inflation,

---

35. See Emerson *et al.*, op. cit., n.33, p.108, for a formal presentation of sustainability in terms of the intertemporal budget constraint and comment on the adequacy of the debt-to-GDP ratio as a surrogate.

36. See M. Dewatripont, F. Giavazzi, J. von Hagen, I. Harden, T. Persson, G. Roland, H. Rosenthal, A. Sapir and G. Tabellini, *Flexible Integration: Towards a More Effective and Democratic Europe*, Monitoring European Integration No. 6, Centre for Economic Policy Research (1995).

long-term interest rates, exchange-rate stability and public finance. The purpose of these provisions is not just to measure nominal convergence at a particular moment. The Treaty refers to *sustainable* and *durable* convergence. This implies that the criteria are intended to function as a proxy for measuring long-term commitment to low inflation and sound public finance.

Unlike the other three criteria, the part of the test that looks directly at public finance is clear and unambiguous.[37] However, its content is purely formal. At the time of the test, either the state concerned is the subject of an 'excessive deficit decision', or it is not. In the former case, it fails the test. In the latter, it passes. Excessive deficit decisions are made by Ecofin, through the procedure set down in Article 104c.[38]

Let us now consider the other objective of convergence. This is to promote the goals of low inflation and sound public finance in Member States where these goals are not already, or not durably, established. There is no necessary conflict between the promotional objective and convergence as a test. If low inflation and sound public finance are goals worth pursuing at all, then they are as important for states outside the monetary union as for those inside. The orthodox view of the construction of Europe, however, is that all states take part equally in any moves towards further integration. This made the framers of the Maastricht Treaty reluctant to acknowledge that the beginning of the monetary union would result in two separate groups of states – 'Ins' and 'Outs' –, possibly for the foreseeable future. The insistence of the UK and Denmark on having the right to opt out made the subject even more sensitive. Moreover, the prospect of everyone joining the monetary union at the beginning was intended to be of practical help to the weaker states, particularly those with high levels of debt. It would enhance the credibility of their policies, and so relieve some of the interest-rate burden the markets would otherwise have imposed. This, in turn, would make it less painful to reduce deficit and debt levels. The drafting of the Treaty was therefore based on the idea that success in achieving the 'promotional' objective of convergence should enable all states to pass the convergence test before the beginning of Stage Three. The main mechanism for putting this idea into effect was to be the adoption of convergence programmes.[39]

37. In so far as public finance has an indirect impact on the likelihood of fulfilment of the other convergence criteria, it is also through debt and deficits, though the size and direction of possible effects is uncertain; Lamfalussy, loc. cit., n.34.
38. See *infra*, 5.3.
39. See *infra*, 5.1.

4.2 Tendencies to fiscal laxity

For states that pass the convergence test, the question arises of what difference the fact of entry into the monetary union makes to the Union's interest in the soundness of their public finances. The literature divides this question into two:

(i)   Would monetary union increase the extent to which states' debt and deficits affect the Union as a whole?

(ii) Would it tend to encourage states to have bigger debt and deficits than they would otherwise have had?

As regards (i), the answer is clearly 'yes'. An unsustainable budgetary position in one participating state could lead to pressure on the ECB to loosen monetary policy, thus threatening price stability. The reason is simple. By definition, an unsustainable budgetary position cannot continue indefinitely. One possibility is to make painful policy adjustments (reducing spending, increasing revenue) to reduce the deficit. Another is explicitly to default on the state's debt. The third is to repudiate the debt implicitly through inflation. The constitutional position of the ECB is designed to insulate it from pressures to help a state in budgetary difficulties by loosening its monetary policy. If it appears, however, that a choice may have to be made between the second and third outcomes (financial markets may not wait for the first), the ECB might find itself under strong pressure to accommodate the state in difficulties.

It has also been argued that increases in government borrowing tend to lead to a rise in interest rates and that, within a monetary union, the economic cost of such an interest-rate rise would be spread across the Union as a whole, rather than being confined to the state in which the increase in government borrowing occurred.[40] This argument assumes that all states draw from the same limited pool of European savings. (The commonality of the pool results from the integration of capital markets, not from monetary union.) However, with modern capital markets, any borrower draws from the pool of world savings. Even the Union as a whole, and *a fortiori* the individual states, may not be large enough to affect the world level of interest rates.

As regards (ii), the answer is less clearcut. In principle, monetary union should make unsustainable budgetary positions less attractive, by denying governments the possibility of monetising their debt through direct borrowing from public financial institutions. Unsustainability would therefore necessarily lead either to default, or to expenditure cuts and/or tax increases; prospects that should encourage both governments and lenders to

---

40. Lamfalussy, loc. cit., n.34.

exercise caution. However, this effect might be offset by an assumption that the state concerned would be 'bailed out' by others in the Union.

The possibility of a bail-out is not dependent on the existence of a monetary union, but rather on the degree of solidarity amongst Member States. States forming a monetary union are likely to possess, or to develop, a greater degree of solidarity than those which do not participate.[41] It seems reasonable to suppose that such solidarity might go beyond the limited provisions of Article 103a (2).[42] Furthermore, the possible threat to financial stability in the monetary union might provide an additional incentive for a bail-out. Hence the 'no-bail-out' provision of Article 104b, which forbids the Community to assume the commitments of governments (central, regional or local) or of other public authorities, other bodies governed by public law, or public undertakings of any Member State. States are similarly prohibited from assuming each other's commitments.[43]

Despite its apparently uncompromising terms, Article 104b would not prevent the bail-out of a Member State, if that is what the Community and the other Member States wish to do. In particular, the prohibition on 'assuming commitments' would not seem to cover direct loans or grants to the state concerned.[44] This does not mean, however, that the provision is ineffective. On the contrary, it states a clear principle and at the same time raises the political cost of departure from that principle.

States might be encouraged to have larger deficits than would otherwise be the case by the fact that, with free capital movements, fiscal policy tends to be more effective under a regime of fixed exchange rates than with floating ones.[45] This increases the potential short-term pay-off to a government of a fiscal boost to its economy. A countervailing factor is that economic integration tends to reduce the effectiveness of a state's fiscal policy, as a higher proportion of domestic demand is met by suppliers in other states. (This, of course, is an effect of economic, not of monetary, union.) Perhaps more significantly, the high levels of debt and deficits that exist in nearly all Member States, combined with freedom of movement of capital, require states to ensure the credibility of their policies in the financial markets.

41. Cf. the CDU/CSU paper by W. Schäuble, 'Reflections on European Policy' (Sept. 1994).
42. See *supra*, n.10.
43. See also Council Regulation (EC) No. 3604/93 of 13.12.93.
44. By other states; see *supra*, discussion of EC Treaty, Art. 103a (2).
45. M. Fratianni and J. von Hagen, *The European Monetary System and European Monetary Union* (1992), pp.200–1.

4.3 Fiscal policy co-ordination

It is generally accepted that the Community's own budget is too small to function as a mechanism of automatic stabilisation, or to be used as an instrument of discretionary fiscal policy. Fiscal policy in the Union is, therefore, necessarily the outcome of decisions about the public finances of the Member States.

In the third stage of EMU, the states participating in the monetary union will share a common interest rate and will all be affected by the exchange rate *vis-à-vis* other currencies, such as the US dollar. Any fiscal-policy action intended to affect the external trade balance or the exchange rate of the Euro would require co-ordinated action by the states belonging to the monetary union.

How far co-ordination of fiscal policy might be needed or desired for other purposes, is open to debate.[46] If a Union fiscal policy were required, however, either for domestic or international purposes, it could only be the result of co-ordination of the Member States' policies.

5. PROCEDURES UNDER THE TREATY ON EUROPEAN UNION

5.1 Convergence programmes

Convergence programmes derive from a suggestion made by the Monetary Committee to Ecofin in spring 1991, before completion of the Maastricht negotiations, for 'crash programmes'. These were intended to go 'beyond all that had so far been possible and conceivable under co-ordination'.[47] It was agreed that Member States would draw up 'convergence programmes', setting out multiannual paths for inflation, debt and deficits and describing their policy measures for achieving them. The Maastricht Treaty subsequently provided a legal basis for these programmes, requiring states to adopt, if necessary, 'multiannual programmes intended to ensure the lasting convergence necessary for the achievement of economic and monetary union, in particular with regard to price stability and sound public finances';

---

46. 'To a large extent fiscal policy discussions have been dominated, and still are, by the need for an adjustment in high-deficit and high-debt countries. Due to this priority for convergence, genuine co-ordination issues have so far been left in the shade. However, it remains an important topic that could come to the forefront in the years ahead'; Emerson *et al.*, op. cit., n.33, p.113.
47. A. Kees, 'The Monetary Committee as a Promoter of European Integration', in A. F. P. Bakker *et al.* (eds), *Monetary Stability Through International Co-operation: Essays in Honour of André Szász* (1994), p.131.

this was to be done before the beginning of the second stage of EMU, on 1 January 1994.[48]

Convergence programmes were clearly conceived as transitional measures, with a short life-expectancy geared to monetary union in 1997. This explains why the Treaty makes no provision for them to be submitted or revised after the beginning of the second stage. In practice, the convergence-programme exercise has become a key part of the preparations for the third stage of EMU. Ten of the EUR-12 states had submitted a programme by the end of 1993, while Denmark submitted one in February 1994. Luxembourg, with consistently low inflation, debt and deficits, did not need a programme. Austria, Finland and Sweden submitted programmes during 1995, having joined the Union at the beginning of that year. Most of the original eleven programmes have subsequently been revised or updated.

Convergence programmes are officially regarded as the responsibility of the state concerned. The Commission makes an assessment of each new and revised programme as it has been presented. This assessment is sent to the Monetary Committee, which prepares the work of Ecofin. There is no formal process of approval of convergence programmes by Ecofin. Access to the Cohesion Fund,[49] however, is dependent on the state concerned 'having a programme leading to the fulfilment of the conditions of economic convergence as set out in Article 104c'. In practice, the convergence programmes submitted under Article 109e of the EC Treaty have been treated as fulfilling this purpose. An (unpublished) code of conduct for convergence programmes was drawn up by the Monetary Committee and endorsed by Ecofin in February 1994.

5.2 Multilateral surveillance

'Multilateral surveillance' was initiated by the Monetary Committee in 1987, and received a legal basis in Council Decision 90/141/EEC.[50] This decision replaced a 1974 decision that had also provided for the Council to establish economic-policy guidelines and for permanent consultation and monitoring in a co-ordinating group.[51]

Multilateral surveillance under Article 103 of the EC Treaty began with the second stage, and is a permanent feature of EMU. It has three main elements:

---

48. EC Treaty, Art. 109e.
49. See *supra*, n.9.
50. See 29th Report of the Monetary Committee, p.18; and Council Decision 90/141/EEC of 12.3.90 on the attainment of progressive convergence of economic policies and performance during Stage One of economic and monetary union.
51. Council Decision 74/120/EEC of 18.2.74.

(i)   the adoption of broad guidelines by the Council;[52]
(ii)   monitoring by the Council of economic developments in each of the Member States and in the Community as a whole and of the consistency of economic policies with the broad guidelines; and
(iii)   the issuing by the Council of recommendations to a Member State, if its economic policies are not consistent with the broad guidelines, or if they risk jeopardising the proper functioning of economic and monetary union.

Article 103 (5) provides for the Council to adopt detailed rules for the second and third elements of multilateral surveillance, but this has not yet been done. The adoption of the broad guidelines involves a complex procedure, comprising four stages:

(i)   the Commission makes a recommendation;
(ii)   acting on this recommendation and acting by qualified majority, Ecofin formulates a draft of the guidelines and reports its findings to the European Council;
(iii)   acting on the basis of the Ecofin report, the European Council is to 'discuss a conclusion';
(iv)   on the basis of this conclusion and acting by qualified majority, Ecofin adopts a recommendation.[53]

Multilateral surveillance under Article 103 allows for country-specific recommendations, as did the 1990 decision. However, no such recommendations have yet been made. In its draft of the 1990 decision, the Commission had proposed that, following a review of state budget policies, the co-ordination procedure should include 'analysis of medium-term budgetary policy trends and their implications for overall economic policy'.[54] That is, there should be explicit recognition that the aggregate of state policies constitutes a Union fiscal or budgetary policy. This suggestion was rejected by the Council in the 1990 decision, and did not find a place in the Maastricht Treaty either.

The multilateral surveillance procedure has been criticised on the grounds that it is likely to be too drawn out to allow Ecofin, or the Commission, any handle over the aggregate Community fiscal position on a year-by-year basis. Furthermore, there are only limited incentives for states to co-operate.[55]

---

52. The first broad guidelines were adopted in late 1993; Council Recommendation 94/7 of 22.12.93.
53. F. Colasanti, 'Economic Policy Co-ordination in Stage II of Economic and Monetary Union' (1994) 27 *ECU* 17.
54. COM (89) 466 final.
55. C. A. E. Goodhart, *National Fiscal Policy within EMU: The Fiscal Implications of Maastricht*, LSE Financial Markets Group, Working Paper No. 45 (1992).

5.3 The excessive deficit procedure[56]

During the second stage of economic and monetary union, states must 'endeavour to avoid excessive government deficits'. At the beginning of the third stage, this becomes an unqualified duty to avoid excessive government deficits.[57] 'Excessive deficit' is a term of art. It refers not only to the size of the annual budget deficit, but also to the size of the stock of government debt. 'Excessive deficits' are identified by Ecofin, through the excessive deficit procedure.

The consequences of a decision by Ecofin that a Member State has an excessive deficit are different in the second and third stages. A state which during the second stage becomes the subject of an Ecofin decision that it has an excessive deficit will not be able to enter the third stage, unless and until the decision is abrogated. When the third stage begins, states within the monetary union will be liable to a graduated range of sanctions, imposed by Ecofin.[58]

The gatekeeper of the excessive deficit procedure is the Commission. It monitors the development of deficits and the stock of debt in the Member States, 'with a view to identifying gross errors'. The Maastricht Treaty establishes two criteria, which in turn are linked to two 'reference values'. The reference values are an annual budget deficit (planned or actual) of more than 3 per cent of GDP and a government-debt-to-GDP ratio of more than 60 per cent.[59] There is provision in the Treaty for Ecofin, acting by unanimity, to replace the Protocol on the excessive deficit procedure.[60] This could involve setting new reference values, to replace the 3 per cent and 60 per cent figures.

Legally, the reference values are not a definition of the term 'excessive deficit'. Under the Treaty, they have two functions. The first concerns the triggering of the excessive deficit procedure. If the 60 per cent debt-to-GDP ratio is exceeded, the Commission has a duty to prepare a report unless it decides that 'the ratio is sufficiently diminishing and approaching the reference value at a satisfactory pace'. The terms 'sufficiently' and 'satisfactory' confer a fairly broad discretion on the Commission to decide that the requirements of the criterion are met, even if the reference value is exceeded.

---

56. See, generally, A. Italianer, 'The Excessive Deficit Procedure: A Legal Description', ch.11 of this volume.
57. EC Treaty, Arts 109e (4) and 104c (1).
58. See ibid., Art. 104c (9) and (11).
59. EDP Protocol.
60. EC Treaty, Art. 104c (14). Ecofin is to act unanimously on a proposal from the Commission and after consulting the European Parliament and the ECB (or the EMI, if Ecofin decides to replace the EDP Protocol during the second stage; Art. 109f (8)).

If the 3 per cent annual deficit-to-GDP ratio is exceeded, the Commission has a duty to prepare a report unless: '– either the ratio has declined substantially and continuously and reached a level that comes close to the reference value; – or, alternatively, the excess over the reference value is only exceptional and temporary and the ratio remains close to the reference value.' 'Substantially', 'close' and 'exceptional and temporary' are not further defined, and clearly require the exercise of judgment by the Commission.

If the Commission decides that a Member State does not fulfil the requirements under one or both of the criteria, it must prepare a report. The two reference values then play a part in the substantive judgment as to whether or not there is an 'excessive deficit'. However, the Commission's report 'shall also take into account whether the government deficit exceeds government investment expenditure and take into account all other relevant factors, including the medium-term economic and budgetary position of the Member State'. This provision expressly identifies the so-called 'golden rule' ('only borrow to finance investment expenditure'[61]) as a relevant factor. No limit is placed, however, on what other factors may be relevant. The Commission's report must certainly look beyond the current budgetary year, but no specific criteria for appraising the medium-term economic and budgetary position are laid down. Key issues of fiscal and budgetary policy are at stake here, in so far as the size of budget deficits may tend to vary automatically with the stage of the economic cycle.[62]

The Commission's report then goes to the Monetary Committee, which gives an opinion. At this stage, if the Commission thinks that an excessive deficit exists, or may occur, it must address an opinion to Ecofin. Ecofin has the power to make a formal decision that an excessive deficit exists. It acts on a recommendation from the Commission after 'an overall assessment', the factors relevant to which are not specified in the Treaty. Once an excessive deficit decision has been made, it remains in effect unless and until it is abrogated by Ecofin under Article 104c (12).

If it decides that an excessive deficit exists, Ecofin makes recommendations to the state concerned. These may subsequently be made public, if there is no effective action in response. Until the beginning of the third stage (and for those states which do not participate to the monetary union even after the third stage has begun), Article 104c does not provide for any other sanctions against a state with an excessive deficit.

---

61. Cf. Art. 115 (1) of the German Basic Law, setting out the principle that net borrowing by the Federal government shall not exceed the total of Federal investment expenditures.
62. But see Goodhart, op. cit., n.55, for an analysis of eight EC countries, showing that only in the UK did the main determinants of movements in the deficit ratio appear to be cyclical, rather than structural.

Once the third stage begins, paragraphs 9 and 11 of Article 104c will apply to those states that belong to the monetary union. If a participating Member State persists in failing to put Ecofin recommendations into practice, Ecofin may decide what deficit reduction is necessary and give notice to the state to take measures within a specified time limit. It may also request the state to submit reports in accordance with a specific timetable, in order to examine its adjustment efforts.[63]

Paragraph 11 of Article 104c provides for sanctions against a state which fails to comply with an Ecofin decision taken in accordance with paragraph 9. Ecofin may decide to apply the following measures:

– to require the Member State concerned to publish additional information, to be specified by the Council, before issuing bonds and securities;
– to invite the European Investment Bank to reconsider its lending policy towards the Member State concerned;
– to require the Member State concerned to make a non-interest-bearing deposit of an appropriate size with the Community until the excessive deficit has, in the view of the Council, been corrected;
– to impose fines of an appropriate size.

The initial decision that a state has an excessive deficit is made by qualified majority, and the state concerned is not excluded from the vote. However, *abrogation* of an excessive deficit decision is governed by a special voting rule.[64] This requires a qualified majority of two thirds, excluding the votes of the state concerned. The same voting rule applies to: the making of recommendations under paragraph 7; decisions to make recommendations public under paragraph 8; the *mise en demeure* and *tutelle* provisions of paragraphs 8 and 9; and the imposition of sanctions under paragraph 11.

In practice, the EDP operates on an annual cycle. It begins in March, when the Member States make reports to the Commission. These cover planned debt and deficits for the current year, the estimated outcome for the previous year and the actual levels for the three years before that.[65] The Commission then decides whether to make a report about any state that is not currently subject to an excessive deficit decision and whether to propose the abrogation of any existing decisions. In 1994, the Commission made reports, and Ecofin made excessive deficit decisions against all Member States except Luxembourg and Ireland. In the 1995 round, excessive deficit decisions, were made against the three new members – Austria, Finland and Sweden – and the decision against Germany was abrogated.

---

63. EC Treaty, Art. 104c (9).
64. Ibid., Art. 104c (13).
65. See Council Regulation (EC) No. 3605/93 of 22.11.93.

As has been shown above, the criteria to be used in the EDP are complex and rather vague. The 3 per cent and 60 per cent figures are merely the starting point. They have no particular economic significance.[66] The decision that a state has an excessive deficit is a matter for discretionary judgment by Ecofin. The Commission's role as gatekeeper also involves discretion. In 1994 and 1995, for example, Ecofin had no formal opportunity to discuss the Irish case, because the Commission decided not to initiate the EDP against Ireland.

The Treaty did not, therefore, establish a clear test for the public-finance aspect of convergence. Rather, it left it up to the Commission and Ecofin to decide precisely what the test should be, through successive rounds of the EDP. For the 1999 starting date for the third stage of EMU, the 1998 round of the procedure is likely to be crucial. It will establish the final pattern of excessive deficit decisions and abrogations, using data on the estimated debt and deficit outcomes for 1997. This will determine which states pass, and which fail, the public-finance part of the convergence test. The timing of the 1998 round of the EDP may be brought forward, so that the composition of the European Central Bank can be determined well before the Treaty deadline of 1 July 1998.

6. 'AUTONOMY, DISCIPLINE AND CO-ORDINATION'

The Commission's pre-Maastricht analysis defined the requirements of the fiscal regime of EMU as being to provide an adequate mix of autonomy, discipline and co-ordination.[67] Autonomy is required because, for states within the monetary union, fiscal policy is the only macroeconomic instrument available to deal with 'asymmetric shocks'. Discipline is required to avoid threats to price stability and/or the 'no-bail-out' principle. Finally, fiscal co-ordination may enable the monetary union to have a better mix of macroeconomic policy instruments available than if it had to rely solely on monetary policy.

On paper, the structure of the Treaty appears to fit this division. States remain responsible for their own fiscal policies. The two Community

---

66. The reference values were added to the Treaty draft at a relatively late stage: they did not appear in the Luxembourg presidency draft of June 1991; see Alexander Italianer, 'Mastering Maastricht: EMU Issues and How They Were Settled', in Gretschmann (ed.), op. cit., n.6. The 3 per cent and 60 per cent ratios have been much criticised for their apparent arbitrariness. The Commission figures for the ratios for the EUR-12 in 1990 were 4 per cent and 59.5 per cent, which suggests that this may have been the starting point.
67. See Emerson *et al.*, op. cit., n.33.

instruments of the EDP and multilateral surveillance are legally quite distinct. The EDP is compulsory and has two kinds of sanction attached to it. The first is not being allowed to join the monetary union. For states in the monetary union, there will be the possibility of further measures and sanctions under paragraphs 9 to 11 of Article 104c of the EC Treaty. In contrast, multilateral surveillance is voluntary. It can lead only to recommendations. Under Community law, these have no binding force.[68]

Thus, the EDP embodies discipline, whilst multilateral surveillance provides a mechanism for voluntary co-ordination. None the less, there is the potential for a degree of overlap and interaction between the two procedures. Ecofin's power of monitoring under multilateral surveillance is not restricted to examining conformity with the broad guidelines. Furthermore, recommendations under multilateral surveillance may be made, not only where a state's policies are inconsistent with the guidelines, but more generally if those policies 'risk jeopardising the proper functioning of economic and monetary union'. Article 103 (3) appears to put the states very much in control in deciding what information to supply to the Commission.[69] However, under the EDP, there are detailed and extensive reporting requirements for debt and deficit levels, investment expenditure, interest expenditure and levels of GDP.[70] Country-specific recommendations may be made by Ecofin under both procedures. Recommendations under the EDP are in principle confidential, unless Ecofin decides that there has been no effective action within the period of time laid down, whilst recommendations based on multilateral surveillance may be made public immediately.[71]

Despite the potential overlap, the multilateral surveillance exercise has, in practice, come to focus mainly on the broad guidelines. Although country examinations have continued, they have been very much overshadowed by the EDP. Furthermore, the convergence-programme exercise has become much more important than the text of the Treaty would suggest. There are two reasons for the latter development. The first is the partial breakdown of the ERM in 1992–93 and the associated widening of its bands. This meant loss of the anti-inflationary anchor and credibility which the narrow bands had provided. Possession of a strong convergence programme, endorsed by Ecofin, offered the possibility of an alternative source of credibility. The

---

68. EC Treaty, Arts 103a and 189. See also A. Italianer, 'Convergence in Europe: State of Affairs', in A. Wildavsky and E. Zapico (eds), *National Budgeting for Economic and Monetary Union* (1993).

69. Art. 103 (3) provides that, '[f]or the purpose of . . . multilateral surveillance, Member States shall forward information to the Commission about important measures taken by them in the field of their economic policy and such other information as they deem necessary'.

70. See Council Regulation (EC) No. 3605/93, Arts 4 and 5.

71. EC Treaty, Arts 103 (4) and 104c (8).

second reason connects to the first. When Ecofin decides that a state has an excessive deficit, it makes recommendations on how to bring that situation to an end. Where the state has a current convergence programme, the recommendations have been based on the state's own targets and policies as set out in the programme.[72] This means that convergence programmes benefit from the extra credibility provided by the 'disciplinary' aspect of the EDP. The boundaries of 'discipline' are further extended by the fact that access to the Cohesion Fund is dependent on the state concerned 'having a programme leading to the fulfilment of the conditions of economic convergence as set out in Article 104c'.[73]

Member States have used convergence programmes in different ways for domestic purposes. Portugal, Ireland and Belgium have used their programmes either to provide a multiannual framework for budget planning or to strengthen the existing framework by making deviations from target variables subject to automatic adjustment. Portugal, for example, uses the multiannual targets from its convergence programme to derive the total expenditure figure for the annual budget. In general, however, where convergence has had a publicly visible impact, it has been through emphasising a simple message that both politicians and the public have found easy to understand: 3 per cent and 60 per cent.

6.1 Sanctions and commitment

Many states can reasonably be expected to avoid public-finance risks out of self-interest. For states that are not self-policing in this way, however, it is doubtful whether the threat of sanctions will prove effective. One of the basic axioms of regulation is the compliance principle, that is, that regulation will not be effective unless the person regulated is able to control his own behaviour. If this condition is satisfied, the problem becomes one of creating an appropriate pattern of incentives.

The EDP is designed to affect the incentive structure for states, both directly and indirectly. Directly, there is the possibility of failing to qualify for the monetary union and also the specific sanctions provided for by Article 104c. Indirectly, the EDP gives political signals to the financial markets, which can be expected to influence the cost of borrowing. This provides a dual incentive to states, in the form of the budgetary cost of an

---

72. Although the recommendations in 1994 were not formally published, they appeared in *Agence Europe*. In 1995, the recommendations were kept confidential by Ecofin, perhaps in order to preserve the potential effectiveness of a decision to publish under Art. 104c (8) of the EC Treaty.
73. See *supra*, text to n.49.

interest-rate penalty and of the fact that one of the convergence criteria concerns the long-term interest rate on government bonds.

This incentive structure could work if the compliance principle were satisfied. For this to be case, the state concerned must already have a budget process that is able to resolve conflicts of interest in matters of public finance. This cannot be taken for granted. National budget processes involve different actors, with competing interests and agendas. Sometimes one party wins, sometimes there is a genuine compromise, and sometimes the result is the mutual ruin of the contending parties. The development of convergence programmes can be understood as an attempt to enhance states' ability to control their own fiscal behaviour. Although voluntary, the convergence programmes involve a commitment at Community level made by each Member State's government. Such a commitment could reasonably be expected to strengthen the bargaining position of those actors in the national budget process (typically finance ministers) who favour fiscal prudence. However, this is likely to be effective only at the margin, in states where the budget process is fundamentally sound.

A similar logic applies to another commitment device: the attachment of conditions to a Community balance-of-payments loan to Italy of 8 billion ECU, made in 1993. The loan decision contained specific targets (in lire) for the Italian public-sector borrowing requirement. The loan was to be released in four tranches over six years, each dependent on the Commission being satisfied (after consultation with the Monetary Committee and Ecofin) that satisfactory progress was being made. The recitals to the decision also stated that, 'in accordance with this decision, developments in the Italian economy and in Italian economic policy will be reviewed twice a year in the framework of multilateral surveillance or more frequently if required'.[74]

The loan and especially its conditions were intended to help the Italian government bind its own hands. The existence of the loan and the associated monitoring processes were cited in offer documents for foreign-currency borrowings in international financial markets. However, the loan did not succeed in achieving its intended purpose. Council approval of disbursal of the second tranche of the loan was given on 13 September 1993, and Italy's intention was to take up the third tranche in April 1994. However, the fiscal targets were clearly not being met, and Italy did not even request the third tranche.

---

74. Decision 93/67/EEC of 18.1.93, made under Council Regulation (EEC) No. 1969/88 (see *supra*, n.11).

6.2 'Process bail-out'

The 'magic numbers' 3 per cent and 60 per cent have increasingly come to be seen as fiscal targets for the Member States, rather than, as originally intended, triggers for the process of identifying 'gross errors'. This development is not surprising. In order to minimise the risk of having to accept inflation-prone states into the monetary union, the reference values have been presented as rules that must be strictly interpreted. Strict interpretation, however, cuts both ways. Once an activity is governed by externally-imposed rules, why should one do more than the minimum necessary to comply?

This means, however, that the 'rules' are hardly likely to be very effective as a test. How durable is a state's commitment to sound public finances and price stability, if its drive towards these goals is based mainly on the desire to pass a 'snapshot' test in 1998? When the third stage begins, states that become part of the monetary union will no longer have to worry about meeting the convergence criteria.

Furthermore, strict application of the 'rules' may make monetary union impossible. Perhaps only Luxembourg will meet them. If the claim that the reference values are rules is abandoned, however, then there is likely to be an open process of political bargaining, in which the whole idea of an objective test of which states are committed to sound public finance and low inflation will disappear.

It is perhaps in response to such considerations that the German Finance Minister, Theo Waigel, put forward proposals in 1995 for a 'stability pact' to enforce much lower numerical targets for average deficit levels, particularly for states with a high level of debt. The idea of a stability pact goes further along the road already signposted by the interpretation of the reference values as rules. That road leads towards a 'command-and-control' regulatory structure for the budgetary policy of states in the monetary union. It requires an EU institution with authority to prescribe maximum debt and deficit levels for each state, together with an effective enforcement mechanism.

Whether such a system could work, is open to question. For those states that do not meet the compliance principle, it amounts to the promise of a 'process bail-out'. If a state's own budget process is unable to deliver sound public finances, then the Union will come to the rescue. Could such a promise be kept?

An alternative approach, avoiding the need for a 'command-and-control' structure, would be to aim, not for 'process bail-out', but 'process convergence', that is, convergence between states in terms of the institutions and procedures through which budgetary decisions are made. This idea is discussed in detail elsewhere in this volume.[75]

---

75. See J. von Hagen and I. Harden, ch. 14 of this volume.

7. THE INSTITUTIONAL ACTORS

The pre-Maastricht arrangements for co-ordination of states' public-finance decisions were criticised on constitutional grounds: Ecofin, consisting of the various finance ministers, could not be expected to take a different view of states' economic policies.[76] Under the Maastricht Treaty, Ecofin remains a central actor. However, the EDP considerably strengthens the role of the Commission by making it the gatekeeper of the procedure. Unless the Commission decides to make the initial report on a Member State, Ecofin has no power to decide that the latter has an excessive deficit. The normal route by which one Member State may bring another before the European Court of Justice is specifically barred.[77] Although the Commission could in principle be challenged under Article 175 of the EC Treaty for failure to act, the criteria in the Treaty and the EDP Protocol give it a wide margin of appreciation. Abrogation of a decision that a Member State has an excessive deficit also requires Ecofin to act on a recommendation from the Commission.

The Treaty also gives a specific role to the Monetary Committee in the EDP, as well as recognising that its normal responsibilities involve preparing the work of Ecofin (including its work on multilateral surveillance and in relation to convergence programmes).[78] The Monetary Committee is a unique body. It functions as a kind of 'monetary COREPER' for Ecofin, which – according to one authority – has never taken a decision that goes against an orientation expressed by the Committee.[79] Its Rules provide that members are appointed in their personal capacity and shall, in the general interests of the Community, be completely independent in the performance of their duties.[80] Each state appoints two members of the Committee, one from its central bank and the other an official from the ministry of its Ecofin minister.[81] Two additional members are appointed by the Commission. Appointments are for a period of two years, but reappointment is common.

---

76. Padoa-Schioppa, op. cit., n.32.
77. EC Treaty, Art. 104c (10).
78. Ibid., Art. 109c.
79. A. F. P. Bakker, *The Liberalization of Capital Movements in Europe: The Monetary Committee and Financial Integration, 1958–1994* (1995).
80. In relation to the key EMS realignment decisions, however, the members of the Monetary Committee act not as independent experts, but as representatives of their countries.
81. Usually the finance ministry, or an equivalent. In Denmark, it is the Ministry of Economic Affairs.

With few exceptions, chairmen of the Monetary Committee have been from finance ministries rather than central banks, but chairmen such as Karl-Otto Pöhl, Hans Tietmeyer and Jean-Claude Trichet subsequently moved from their national finance ministries to the central bank.

Members of the Monetary Committee meet also in other contexts. The central bank members are part of the 'European monetary fraternity',[82] and meet regularly in Basle (where the Bank for International Settlements is located) and in the context of the EMI. Finance ministry members meet in other international fora, such as the G7 and the OECD.[83]

The Monetary Committee has succeeded in defining a consensual 'problem-solving' approach in its EMS role and has extended this policy style to the other areas of its work.[84] This means that the Committee cannot be understood in terms of a simple model of intergovernmental decision-making as bargaining between predetermined national interests. Rather, the Committee contributes to the making of Community and national policy at one and the same time. Its ability to do this, however, is dependent on the almost total secrecy in which its operations are shrouded. It is hard to imagine a less transparent body. Whilst the reasons for this are so obvious as not to need stating, it is equally obvious that the institutional requirements for a 'process bail-out' would need a much greater degree of legitimacy than the Monetary Committee could provide.

At the beginning of the third stage of EMU, the Monetary Committee is to be replaced by an Economic and Financial Committee. The composition of this body will be different from that of the Monetary Committee, since the ECB will appoint two members. Also, it seems unlikely that Member States that are part of the monetary union will continue to send a central bank member, who would probably be unable to say anything different from the ECB members.

8. CONCLUSION

If and when the third stage of EMU begins, the major influences on the medium-term development of the European constitutional framework for Member States' public finances are likely to come from the interaction between Ecofin and the new Economic and Financial Committee and from the character of the EDP. The latter seems likely to develop in the direction

---

82. Kees, loc. cit., n.47, p.144.
83. Bakker, *The Liberalization* . . . , op. cit., n.79, p.10.
84. Kees, loc. cit., n.47, p.127; see also Bakker, *The Liberalization* . . . , op. cit., n.79.

of the proposed stability pact. If this is combined with abandonment of the idea that membership of the monetary union should be restricted to states committed to sound public finances, then much work will be required to make 'process bail-out' work.

Even if membership of the monetary union is more restricted, it is possible, at the very least, that many of the states of the single-currency area will struggle to achieve average budget deficits of less than 1 per cent of GDP. If this is so, then a stability pact that promised such low deficits would probably not actually deliver them. Instead, its effect would be to subject Member States' budget planning for the public-finance aggregates (total spending, taxing and borrowing) to prior approval by Ecofin and the Commission. This could, in turn, provide the opportunity for making fiscal policy co-ordination a rather less voluntary exercise than is currently the case for multilateral surveillance. There is at present, however, no mechanism for injecting any democratic legitimacy – or even transparency – into such a process.

Chapter Ten

THE SEPARATION OF MONETARY AND FISCAL POLICY IN STAGE THREE OF EMU

*Christopher Taylor**

Chapter Outline

1. Introduction
   1.1 The Maastricht blueprint
   1.2 The limits on deficits
   1.3 Why separation will matter

2. What Could Go Wrong in Stage Three?
   2.1 'Fiscal free-loading'
   2.2 Weak fiscal stabilisation
   2.3 Lack of a redistributive mechanism

3. Some Feasible Remedies
   3.1 The fiscal limits
      3.1.1 The medium-term dimension
      3.1.2 The 'golden rule'
      3.1.3 An aggregate limit?
      3.1.4 Debt ratios
   3.2 Observance of the limits: carrots or sticks?
   3.3 A Financial Council for EMU?

4. Conclusions

European Economic and Monetary Union: The Institutional Framework (M. Andenas, L. Gormley, C. Hadjiemmanuil, I. Harden, eds.: 90-411-0687-1: © Kluwer Law International: pub. Kluwer Law International, 1997: printed in Great Britain)

1. INTRODUCTION

This chapter considers the problems that could arise as a result of the separation of responsibility for monetary and fiscal policy in EMU. Are they likely to be serious and, if so, what changes should be made in the Maastricht blueprint to avoid them?

1.1 The Maastricht blueprint

The model for full-scale EMU (Stage Three) agreed at Maastricht assigns exclusive responsibility for the monetary policy of participating Member States to the European Central Bank, but leaves fiscal policy in the hands of national authorities, subject to the constraints of the excessive deficit procedure. There is thus to be a major separation of authority over these two key areas of macroeconomic policy. Admittedly, there will be some arrangements for policy consultation between the ECB and the Council (in this case, in its composition of economics and finance ministers, or Ecofin). The President of the Council and a member of the Commission may participate in meetings of the ECB Governing Council, but not vote;[1] and the President of the ECB will be invited to Council meetings when matters relating to the ECB's objectives and tasks are discussed.[2] Moreover, the ECB may submit opinions to the 'appropriate Community institutions or bodies or to national authorities' on matters within its competence, and publish them.[3] But its opinions will have no binding force; while, within its own field of competence, the ECB will be totally independent of interference from outsiders, as is well known.

This separation of responsibilities will be a fairly novel experience for most participants, with certain notable exceptions. The usual situation in developed economies has been that decision-making authority over both fiscal and monetary policy has resided with governments, as has ultimate control over all key policy levers. The most important exception since the war has been Germany, where the Bundesbank is independent in its pursuit of monetary policy, in accordance with the Bundesbank Act (Bundesbankgesetz) – although the Act itself could, of course, be amended by the German parliament. There are traditions of central bank independence in some small European countries, most notably Switzerland but also

---

* This chapter develops themes from the author's Chatham House paper, *EMU 2000? Prospects for European Monetary Union* (1995), ch.8, where an extensive bibliography can be found.
1. EC Treaty, Art. 109b (1).
2. Ibid., Art. 109b (2).
3. Ibid., Arts 105 (4) and 108a (2).

the Nordic countries, and the Netherlands' central bank has considerable policy autonomy. However, until quite recently the central banks of most of the larger EU Member States, including France, Italy, Spain and the UK, have been subject to government direction or influence. The situation is now changing, not only in Europe but also globally, as discontent with the seeming inability of elected governments to maintain price stability has become widespread. In Europe, the imminence of EMU has become a catalyst in persuading many governments to make their central banks independent for policy purposes – this being one of the convergence criteria for joining Stage Three.[4]

The separation of policy responsibilities will have an additional dimension within EMU, in the dichotomy between the *singleness* of monetary policy, administered centrally by the ECB, and the *multiplicity* of fiscal policies, run separately for each participant. This feature, reflecting the multicountry character of EMU, could create further problems, as will be explained.

1.2   The limits on deficits

The freedom of EU Member States to pursue independent fiscal policies will be limited by the excessive deficit procedure, which already operates in Stage Two but which will be strengthened in Stage Three. Its essential requirements are that government deficits are to be limited to no more than 3 per cent of GDP and that, where the ratios of government debt to GDP exceed 60 per cent, these are to be brought down 'at a satisfactory pace'. Assessments are made twice annually by the Commission; if the Commission finds that the requirements are not met, it must send a report to the Council, which has some latitude in making a judgement. In Stage Three as in Stage Two, observance of the procedure will be a legal obligation for *all* Member States (except the UK, if it opts out); and in Stage Three there are to be sanctions for excessive deficits by participating countries, which could include fines or deposits.

The likely effectiveness of the EDP in Stage Three remains, nevertheless, a matter for debate. Part of the uncertainty arises because the details of the sanctions have still to be decided, and part reflects scepticism about the ability of feasible sanctions to deter governments from running large deficits, if they are subject to strong domestic political pressures. There is a body of opinion which believes that peer-group pressure in Ecofin will be

4. The Treaty requirements and the latest situation regarding progress towards making EU central banks independent are described in the EMI's second convergence report, prepared in accordance with Art. 7 of the Statute of the EMI; European Monetary Institute, 'Progress Towards Convergence 1996' (Nov. 1996), ch.2 with Annex.

influential in securing low deficits in cases where governments are inclined to play by the rules; and market discipline, bolstered by the 'no-monetary-financing' and 'no-bail-out' rules of EMU, may limit debt accumulation in less malleable cases, although some commentators are sceptical about this. It seems widely accepted that the procedure will not be watertight, and there is a risk that it will be persistently infringed if Member States with serious structural problems enter Stage Three.

Concerns of this kind have led the German government to seek reinforcement of the EDP for countries participating in Stage Three. Ecofin agreed in October 1995 to examine proposals by the German Finance Minister, Theo Waigel, for a 'stability pact' among prospective participants, designed to keep deficits well within the Treaty limits.[5] The proposals seek governmental prior commitment to payment of substantial deposits and fines for deficits in excess of the reference values, with more automaticity than in the Maastricht Treaty. The German government has pressed for agreement on the stability pact well before the key decisions on the start of Stage Three are due (in 'early' 1998). However, the proposals have had a mixed reception from states keen on retaining fiscal flexibility while supporting a responsible approach, like the UK, and few governments have found it easy to accept automatic penalties. Moreover, one could question how effective an intergovernmental agreement of such kind could be, since, without Treaty backing, governments cannot bind their successors. None the less, on 13 December 1996 the Dublin European Council summit reached a compromise on the issue, accepting the need for binding limits on deficits, but allowing for excesses in certain cases and introducing elements of discretionary political control by the Council in the proposed procedure. It remains to be seen what form the procedure may take in practice.

1.3   Why separation will matter

There are two broad sets of reasons why the split between monetary and fiscal policy in EMU could lead to problems. Firstly, it is a commonplace of macroeconomics that monetary and fiscal policies are highly interconnected, even when viewed in a single-economy context. Monetary and fiscal instruments are both capable of exerting considerable effects on aggregate demand, and thence on activity (at least in the short term) and the general price level. (They may also have different effects on the composition of demand, but that is a subsidiary point here, although important in other contexts.) It follows that the impact of fiscal policy on demand and inflation may conflict with that of monetary policy, if they are aimed at different objectives. Clearly, the ECB could find itself in considerable difficulty, if

5. *Financial Times*, 2 Oct. 1995, p.2.

national governments pursue fiscal policies which are inconsistent with its objective of maintaining price stability.

Secondly, it is accepted by economists that fiscal policy may have important external, or 'spillover', effects in a multicountry context (as, indeed, may monetary policy, when conducted nationally). For example, fiscal expansion in one country is likely to boost demand among its major trading partners, and could in due course raise activity, tighten credit and add to inflation there, as well as at home, depending on the state of capacity utilisation. These spillovers will be greater among countries that are highly integrated in trade and investment, and among which there is virtually complete freedom of international trade and capital movements, as in the single market. Moreover, the interest-rate spillovers are likely to be larger, *ceteris paribus*, under fixed exchange rates (as in EMU) than under a flexible-rate regime, for reasons developed in the literature based on the well-known Mundell–Fleming model during the 1960s.[6] Thus, in general, nationally-determined fiscal policies will have a greater potential for creating tensions within EMU, with monetary policy set centrally, than outside it.

2. WHAT COULD GO WRONG IN STAGE THREE?

2.1 'Fiscal free-loading'

Early in the EMU debate, before it became clear that the ECB would be given a strong price-stability mandate, a principal worry in this field was that the new central bank's efforts to maintain stable prices would be frustrated by fiscally-based efforts to expand activity in economies with high unemployment; these economies might secure at least short-term benefits from generating 'surprise inflation' (in the language of rational-expectations economics). Their ability to do so would be greater once in EMU, because of the relaxation of the external financing constraint normally facing free-spending governments, whether from balance-of-payments or exchange-rate pressures.[7] This has sometimes been characterised as the threat from 'fiscal free-loading'. In that event, an ECB which focused on achieving constant (nominal or real) interest rates, or 'monetary conditions' more generally, would find itself failing to maintain stable prices, and the integrity of EMU

---

6. See, *eg*, J. A. Frenkel and A. Raisin, *Fiscal Policies and the World Economy* (1987).
7. The removal of exchange-rate risk as a result of the introduction of the single currency means that the bonds issued by participating Member States will become closer substitutes for one another and there will be more inertia in the interest rates confronting individual governments – subject, however, to the likely operation of stronger credit-risk constraints associated with the 'no-monetary-financing' and 'no-bail-out' rules.

could be threatened. Fears of this kind explain the insistence by Germany and other low-inflation economies on fiscal ceilings, not only as tests of eligibility for EMU, but also as permanent mandatory limits in Stage Three.

Agreement at Maastricht that price stability will be the ECB's primary objective, so that the ECB must tighten monetary policy if its inflation objective is threatened by expansionary fiscal policies (or any other source), has converted this threat into one of rising real interest rates. The main danger foreseen is that persistent fiscal expansion by a number of EMU participants, or just one large participant, could raise real interest rates across the entire group, in the face of non-accommodation by the ECB. The multiplicity of national fiscal authorities in EMU and the absence of effective policy co-ordination between them, and with the ECB, intensifies the threat.[8] Since one of the main economic benefits from EMU is held to be a significant lowering of real interest rates for most participants, boosting investment and growth in the longer run, and since Germany views its low real interest rates (aside from the post-reunification phase) as one of the main benefits from having a strong currency, failure in this respect would be almost as bad for EMU as failure on price stability.

2.2 Weak fiscal stabilisation

Although persistent fiscal expansion, leading to high real interest rates, crowding-out of private investment and eventual economic stagnation, is seen by Germany and like-minded states as the main economic threat to EMU, it is by no means the only one in the fiscal sphere. Some economists have seen lack of co-ordination between the new central bank and national treasuries leading to a process of 'retaliatory' policy adjustments, which could mean large fluctuations of demand and activity.[9] Others have stressed the problem in EMU of *asymmetric shocks* (*ie*, economic disturbances which either are country-specific or have country-specific effects).[10] Ordinarily, the impact of such shocks can be cushioned by exchange-rate adjustment, assuming the existence of rigidities in goods and labour markets which otherwise make real-economy adjustments painful. Exchange-rate adjust-

8. P. Levine, 'Fiscal Policy Co-ordination Under EMU and the Choice of Monetary Instrument' (June 1993) 61 *The Manchester School of Economic and Social Studies*, Supplement.

9. J. Meade and M. Weale, *On the Stability of Monetary and Fiscal Policy*, Discussion Paper, Department of Applied Economics, University of Cambridge (revised Jan. 1992).

10. Among a prolific literature, the studies by D. Cohen and C. Wyplosz, *The European Monetary Union: An Agnostic Evaluation*, Centre for Economic Policy Research Discussion Paper No. 306 (Apr. 1989), T. Bayoumi and B. Eichengreen, *Shocking Aspects of European Monetary Integration,* Centre for Economic Policy Research Discussion Paper No. 643 (1992), and L. Bini-Smaghi and S. Vori, 'Rating the EC as an Optimal Currency Area' (1992) 6 *Finance and the International Economy*, have been influential.

ment cannot take place within monetary unions, but in federal economies like the USA there are typically central budgets which automatically cushion part of the effects of regional shocks through variations in taxes and transfer payments – although how far they do so is disputed.[11] However, the central budget of the EU, at around 1 per cent of Community GDP, is not large enough to play a significant stabilising role. The onus under EMU will therefore be very much on participants' national budgets to provide the necessary stabilisation.

The absence of a self-stabilising fiscal system in EMU should not be a serious problem if the asymmetric shocks are temporary and randomly distributed. National fiscal systems ought to be able to cope adequately with the effects of local business cycles, for example. Moreover, there are reasons for hoping that some types of country-specific shocks will diminish or disappear under EMU – for example, shocks that result from national monetary policy 'mistakes', or from exchange-rate instability. It is hoped, too, that labour-market flexibility will increase through greater competitiveness and wage-transparency in EMU, although that may take time. On the other hand, new kinds of asymmetries could emerge under EMU, and others could be magnified. For example, the local effects of the single monetary policy may well differ between participating economies, owing to differences in their financial structures, depending on which countries take part. A given change in the short-term interest rates that the ECB will manipulate for monetary-control purposes is likely to have a larger effect on lending rates and credit conditions in an economy with a liberalised banking system and much lending at variable rates, as in the UK, than in one where banks are still relatively cartelised and lending is typically at fixed rates, as in Germany.

There is also evidence from existing monetary unions with a far-flung internal market, such as the USA, that economic integration tends to promote regional specialisation of industry in the long run, rather than diminishing it.[12] If so, shocks that affect particular industries differently may

---

11. The seminal article was by J. Sachs and X. Sala-i-Martin, 'Fiscal Federalism and Optimum Currency Areas: Evidence for Europe from the United States' (1989), reprinted in M. Canzoneri, V. Grilli and P. R. Masson (eds), *Establishing a Central Bank: Issues in Europe and Lessons from the US* (1992). Counterarguments have been put forward by J. von Hagen, 'Fiscal Arrangements in a Monetary Union: Evidence from the US', in C. de Boissieu and D. Fair (eds), *Fiscal Policy, Taxes, and the Financial System in an Increasingly Integrating Europe* (1992), and D. Gros and E. Jones, *Fiscal Stabilisers in the US Monetary Union*, Centre for European Policy Studies Working Document No. 83 (Jan. 1994).

12. P. R. Krugman, 'Integration, Specialisation, and Regional Growth: Notes on 1992, EMU and Stabilization', paper presented at the International Conference on the Transition to Economic and Monetary Union in Europe, Banco do Portugal and Centre for Economic Policy Research (Jan. 1992).

ultimately become an increasing problem in EMU, assuming it continues to lack an effective central stabilisation mechanism.

For these reasons, it would be unwise to count on independent national fiscal policies coping smoothly with the shocks and disturbances encountered in Stage Three, even if countries were entirely free to adjust their fiscal instruments to local economic conditions. The existence of mandatory fiscal limits which make little allowance for cycles and shocks adds further to these worries, however justifiable the principle of fiscal constraint may be in the special context of EMU.

2.3 Lack of a redistributive mechanism

Finally, there is a parallel set of concerns relating to fiscal redistribution in EMU. According to one school of thought, EMU will tend to widen income differentials between participating states, although not all economists accept this. It depends on whether 'centripetal' or 'centrifugal' forces will predominate in the course of the levelling of the playing field that EMU allied to the single market will bring in time; there is still a considerable debate on this issue, with neoclassical economists arguing that EMU will mean a levelling-up of productivity through competition and the spread of technology, and others pointing to wider inequalities as scale-economies and transport costs promote concentration in the EU's main industrial centres. In most federal states the central budget plays a major role in offsetting regional income differentials, but the EU budget is unlikely to do so, except perhaps for the very poorest regions.[13] In time, this could lead to damaging political stresses in Stage Three.

A more immediate concern relates to the particular difficulties that poorer EU Member States face in the *transition* to EMU. They tend to have high inflation, fiscal deficits and unemployment, and so face more serious convergence problems than the richer Member States. This was recognised in principle at Maastricht by the setting up of the Cohesion Fund, which is intended to help the poorest states meet the costs of adjusting to EMU, but the Fund is modest in size and not intended to provide permanent support. The worry is that some poorer states will make exceptional efforts to meet the Maastricht criteria but be only partially successful, meeting the criteria but failing to eradicate their deep-rooted structural problems. This could generate greater social stresses in EMU than now, because international competition will be more intense then and the exchange rate will not be available as a safety valve to adjust real wages.

13. The literature is summarised in Commission of the European Communities, 'Stable Money – Sound Finances' (1993) 53 *European Economy*. Bini-Smaghi and Vori, loc. cit., n.10, point out that the poorer EU States do benefit substantially from transfers through the EU Budget.

However, the arguments are not all on one side for, if their efforts are successful, the less-developed Member States stand to gain most from joining EMU: if they can manage to reduce inflation lastingly with the help of the ECB's policies, their interest rates will be much reduced, as will, accordingly, their fiscal deficits and debt burdens; while their competitive wages should attract inward investment, which should raise average productivity faster than in the more mature economies. They, nevertheless, face a particularly difficult balancing act between success and failure, both before and after joining Stage Three.

3. SOME FEASIBLE REMEDIES

In considering ways of avoiding these problems, two caveats should be borne in mind. Firstly, it is not realistic to seek radical change in the blueprint, short of a complete breakdown of the EMU process: few EU governments will risk unravelling the Treaty package by pressing for amendments that would be unacceptable to the German government and the Bundestag, without whose assent EMU will not proceed.

Secondly, little comfort can be drawn from the expectation that EMU will start, if it starts at all, as a small group of prosperous and highly-integrated states, which may be less prone to the policy tensions described above. Other states, less integrated with the core and more diverse in their objectives, will join in time, although not without considerable hardships along the way. Although refinements may be possible as experience of Stage Three grows, changing the policy rules to accommodate a wide variety of members will be even more difficult after EMU has started. If modifications are to be made, they should be considered now.

3.1 The fiscal limits

3.1.1 The medium-term dimension

Although the principle of fiscal constraints can be defended in the context of the policy split in EMU, the actual limits specified in the Treaty are unduly rigid and inappropriately focused. As experience in the Community in the past few years has shown, 3 per cent is too low to be accepted as a universal *ceiling* on the deficit-to-GDP ratio; by 1993, recession had driven government deficits well above 3 per cent in over half of the Member States, as can be seen in Table 1, and determined efforts to get deficits down quickly within the limit risk generating new recession. Yet the scope under the EDP for deficits to exceed the reference value is comparatively limited: a

Table 1

Net lending (+) or borrowing (–) of general government
(as a percentage of GDP)

	1989		1991		1993		1995	
	a	b	a	b	a	b	a	b, c
Belgium	−6.2	−6.4	−6.5	−6.3	−6.6	−6.0	−4.5	−4.6
Denmark	−0.5	−0.2	−2.1	−2.2	−4.4	−3.3	−2.0	−2.4
Germany*	−0.1	−1.9	−3.3	−2.1	−3.3	−3.0	−2.9	−2.8
Greece	−14.7	−12.8	−13.0	−13.3	−13.3	−13.1	−9.3	−9.7
Spain	−2.8	−3.6	−4.9	−4.5	−7.5	−5.9	−5.9	−5.7
France	−1.2	−1.7	−2.2	−2.9	−5.8	−4.5	−5.0	−4.8
Ireland	−1.7	−3.8	−2.1	−2.1	−2.5	−2.2	−2.7	−2.1
Italy	−9.9	−10.5	−10.2	−10.0	−9.5	−9.5	−7.4	−7.4
Luxembourg	–	–	2.3	–	1.1	1.3	0.4	1.1
Netherlands	−4.7	−4.6	−2.9	−4.0	−3.3	−3.5	−3.1	−2.9
Portugal	−3.4	−5.5	−6.6	−5.2	−7.2	−5.8	−5.4	−5.4
UK	−0.1	−1.1	−2.6	−3.6	−7.7	−5.5	−5.1	−5.2
EUR−12**	−2.9	−3.8	−4.6	−4.5	−6.0	−5.2	−4.7	−4.7

Notes:
a   Actual.
b   Five-year average, centred on the year shown.
c   Includes Commission forecasts for 1996 and 1997.
*   West Germany, 1989 and 1991.
** Excludes Luxembourg, 1989 and 1991.

Sources:
1989, 1991, 1993: Commission of the EC, 'Annual Report for 1995', (1995) 59 *European Economy*; 1995: (Dec. 1995) 12 *European Economy, Supp. A - Economic Trends*; and author's calculations.

deficit is excessive unless 'the excess over the reference value is only exceptional and temporary and the deficit remains close to the reference value'.[14] It is hard to see how deficits of more than 3.5 per cent of GDP, lasting a year or two at most, could be accepted under this rubric, given that the German Parliament and Constitutional Court will be, in effect, influential arbiters.

14. EC Treaty, Art. 104c (2).

European Economic and Monetary Union: The Institutional Framework

The challenge is to find a way of allowing for the effects of shocks and cycles on government budget balances without unduly relaxing the Maastricht rules. There is some recognition of the problem in the Treaty, where it is said that the Commission should take account of 'the medium-term economic and budgetary position of the Member State' in reporting under the procedure.[15] A thoroughgoing approach would give the reference value itself a medium-term dimension. One way of doing this would be to apply recognised techniques of 'cyclical adjustment' based on econometric models, but although this approach should certainly have a role in informing the technical assessments, and is firmly established in Commission analysis, it is too arcane to be useful as a Treaty criterion.

A less sophisticated but more transparent approach would be to express the reference value as a simple arithmetic average of annual deficits over the medium term. Table 1 shows five-year averages for government net lending or borrowing for the Europe of 12 Member States, centred on selected years which span the prolonged cycle of boom and recession dating from the late 1980s.[16] 1989 was the year of peak activity for most Member States, and 1993 was generally the trough, although the cycle was not perfectly synchronised. Divergences between actual and medium-term ('smoothed') versions of the deficit display the expected cyclical pattern: for most Member States the actual deficit in 1989 was less than the smoothed version, in some cases by at least 1 per cent of GDP (Germany, Spain, Ireland, Portugal, UK); in 1993 the converse was true, by a wide margin in some cases (Spain, France, Portugal, UK).

It is evident that divergences between actual and smoothed deficits of the order of 1–2 per cent of GDP are common at peaks and troughs, and they tend to be even larger in some states. This partly reflects larger activity variations there, and partly a greater elasticity of the deficit to activity variations. On this reckoning, a 'medium-term' reference value of 3 per cent for the deficit would be consistent with actual deficits of 4–5 per cent in recession troughs.

It might be objected that giving the Treaty reference value a medium-term dimension would represent an undue weakening in the constraint. The issue is not easy to resolve analytically, because it is hard to lay down what, if any, magnitude for the deficit would be universally consistent with price stability in this context. The Treaty figure of 3 per cent was somewhat arbitrary, having little economic logic to support it.[17] Some economists have suggested a reference value of 2 per cent, or even zero, if averaging were

15. Ibid., Art. 104c (3).
16. The averages centred on 1995 include Commission forecasts for 1996 and 1997.
17. See W. Buiter, G. Corsetti and N. Roubini, 'Excessive Deficits: Sense and Nonsense in the Treaty of Maastricht' (Apr. 1993) 16 *Economic Policy* 57; and C. T. Taylor, *EMU 2000? Prospects for European Monetary Union* (1995), p.75.

adopted, and 1 per cent appears to be implied in the German proposals for a stability pact. In fact, on the record of the past decade, adopting a smoothed value of 3 per cent would represent only a minor overall relaxation of the criterion. It can be seen from Table 1 that only three out of the EUR-12 states had deficits averaging 3 per cent per annum or less in the five-year period centred on 1993, implying only a slight relaxation of the existing criterion. According to the Commission's forecasts, five out of the EUR-12 states shown will have deficits averaging less than 3 per cent per annum in the period centred on 1995, and the same five will have an actual deficit of around 3 per cent or less in 1995 (including the Netherlands, with 3.1 per cent). Again, smoothing the deficit implies little relaxation of the criterion.

3.1.2 The 'golden rule'

Introducing a medium-term dimension would not address a different issue – that government borrowing may be sustainable and non-inflationary, if it finances capital accumulation which adds to the economy's productive capacity. This is particularly relevant to less-developed Member States, where local capital markets cannot generate adequate funds for large infrastructure projects or for privatisation of utilities, etc, and inward investment may not be prepared to take the risk. As it stands, the EDP may penalise such economies.

This kind of problem could be tackled by giving greater prominence to government deficits on *current account*, that is, government *saving*, rather than to the overall financial positions. There is a respectable economic case for the proposition that governments should balance their current income and expenditure over time, meaning that they should not borrow to finance public consumption, or transfers which finance private consumption; this is sometimes known as the 'golden rule' of public finance. It attracted some support during the EMU negotiations, not least from German representatives, and, like the medium-term dimension, is already recognised in the Treaty as a factor to be taken into account by the Commission.[18]

Table 2 gives data on government gross saving (current receipts less current expenditure) for the EUR-12 states. It can be seen that deficits measured on this basis have typically been consistently lower than on the overall basis shown in Table 1, by the order of 3–4 per cent of GDP, reflecting the propensity of most governments to finance investment from borrowing. It can also be seen that the cyclical behaviour of government saving, as shown by deviations from 'smoothed' saving, parallels that of the overall deficit in Table 1 fairly closely. This is not surprising, given that the

---

18. EC Treaty, Art. 104c (3).

Table 2

Gross saving of general government (as a percentage of GDP)

	1989		1991		1993		1995
	a	b	a	b	a	b	a
Belgium	−4.3	−4.3	−4.4	−4.3	−4.8	−4.0	−2.9
Denmark	1.8	1.8	−0.7	−0.1	−1.7	−1.0	−1.0
Germany*	3.6	1.8	1.1	1.7	0.9	1.2	1.4
Greece	−10.3	−8.8	−8.9	−9.5	−10.1	−9.6	−10.1
Spain	2.9	1.9	0.9	0.8	−2.4	−1.0	−1.7
France	2.4	1.9	1.4	0.8	−1.8	−0.8	−1.3
Ireland	−0.1	−2.0	−1.1	−0.8	−0.9	−0.7	0.1
Italy	−5.5	−6.0	−6.1	−6.2	−5.9	−6.2	−5.4
Luxembourg	−	−	−	−	7.9	−	7.9
Netherlands	−1.0	−0.7	0.3	−0.6	−0.1	−0.2	−0.2
Portugal	0.9	−1.2	−2.0	−1.0	−3.0	−1.7	−1.4
UK	2.7	1.5	0.3	−0.6	−5.0	−2.9	−2.4
EUR-12***	0.6	−0.3	−0.9	−1.0	−2.3	−1.8	−1.4

Notes:
Commission forecasts for saving of general government are not published.
***Excludes Luxembourg and Spain, 1989, 1991 and 1993.
For other notes, see Table 1.

Sources:
Commission of the EC, 'Annual Report for 1995' (1996); (1995) 59 *European Economy*; and author's calculations.

cyclical pattern largely reflects the income and activity elasticities operating in the (current) tax and benefit systems.

It appears from Table 2 that in 1993 the governments of only three of the EUR-12 states were in 'actual' saving balance (if the Netherlands, with a deficit of 0.1 per cent, is included), and the same three were in balance on a smoothed basis (it is safe to assume than Luxembourg was in balance on that basis). However, seven of the EUR-12 had governments in, or close to, saving balance on the smoothed basis, if 'close' means within 1 per cent of GDP, which seems not unreasonable, given the margins of error in the figures. In 1995 the governments of three of the EUR-12 countries were in actual saving balance, and five were in balance or 'close'. On a reasonable interpretation of the criterion, the 'golden rule', with or without smoothing, would imply some moderate relaxation of the EDP constraint.

This particular test is not equally favourable to all Member States. For example, the UK government's current account deficit has recently been comparatively close to its overall deficit, whereas France and Germany both tend to be considerably closer to balance on current than on overall account.

It may be objected that there are deficiencies in the saving measure which detract from its usefulness. The borderline between current and capital expenditure is sometimes rather arbitrary. Most economists would regard *net* saving as a preferable concept, but capital consumption in the government sector is notoriously hard to measure. More fundamentally, some public current expenditure, for example, on technical and scientific education and training, is partly in the nature of investment. This is further illustration of the intrinsic difficulty of fiscal assessment; but the 'overall' measure of the deficit is also subject to some of these drawbacks, among others.

Other versions of the deficit have their supporters. For example, the Commission attaches weight to the 'primary deficit' (*ie*, the government's overall deficit excluding net interest payments). There is an economic case for looking at this measure too, because it may reveal more about a government's current underlying fiscal position, abstracting from the burden of past deficits, and illustrates the consequences of a possible fall in the long-term real interest rate, such as might be expected from joining EMU. However, there are also rather compelling objections to focusing on a measure that excludes interest: interest payments have to be financed, and borrowing in order to do so suggests an unsustainable position and is potentially inflationary; moreover, EMU will not necessarily deliver a fall in a government's interest costs if this is seen to be less creditworthy owing to the prohibitions on monetary financing and government bail-outs.

3.1.3 An aggregate limit?

Focusing attention exclusively on individual country deficits risks ignoring the aggregate fiscal position, yet it will be the aggregate among EMU participants that matters most for the determination of the single monetary policy – as opposed to the solvency and inflationary situation of an individual state. Moreover, the aggregate position may shed light on the fiscal positions of individual states; it would be hard to attribute deficits to an asymmetric shock, if the entire EU moves simultaneously into deficit.

Arguments of this kind were recognised by the Delors Committee and led it to recommend, along with mandatory individual fiscal limits, 'the definition of the overall stance of fiscal policy over the medium term, including the size and financing of the aggregate budgetary balance'.[19] In the

19. Committee for the Study of Economic and Monetary Union, 'Report on Economic and Monetary Union in the European Community' (June 1989), p.28.

event, this recommendation was not taken up, and the Maastricht Treaty made no mention of the aggregate fiscal position. Yet, there is a good case for supplementing the national reference values with a corresponding aggregate value, which in principle should be of the same magnitude. Then, performance in relation to the aggregate should be used to inform assessments of individual deficits. If the aggregate deficit is within its reference value, there is a prima facie case for judging that national deficits above the reference value are 'exceptional', 'temporary' or 'asymmetric' in character; whereas, if the aggregate deficit is above its reference value, while individual deficits show a high dispersion, there is prima facie evidence of excess in at least some cases. However, careful judgment of individual cases would still be necessary, lest high-spending governments were tempted to take advantage of headroom offered by more disciplined neighbours. Nevertheless, augmentation of the reference values with an EMU aggregate, suitably defined, would add a useful incentive to fiscal co-operation, since governments would see that others' fiscal positions affected their own scope under the EDP.

The behaviour of the aggregate deficit suggests that, abstracting from the effects of the cycle, there was a greater degree of fiscal 'excess' in 1993 than in 1989. The smoothed deficit for the EUR-12 in 1993 was well above 3 per cent, while the dispersion of national deficits then was also high; whereas the smoothed aggregate deficit in 1989 was within 1 per cent of the reference value. A similar impression emerges from Table 2. Any such interpretation should, nevertheless, be treated with caution, being just one element in a complex picture.

3.1.4 Debt ratios

In principle, many of the above considerations apply to the assessment of debt ratios. For example, it can be argued that government debt is likely to be more sustainable if it is counterbalanced by productive assets, and on that ground the outstanding stock of assets owned by general government, suitably valued (*ie*, at net replacement cost), should be deducted in assessing the debt burden.[20] The matter is, however, complicated by the severity of measurement problems in this field, both in determining what are productive assets in this context, and estimating their depreciated value.

In practice, the need to refine the formal constraints relating to debt is less acute, because the Treaty provides a lot more room for judgement on debt ratios, which are not required to be 'close' to the reference value, but merely to be 'sufficiently diminishing and approaching the reference value at

---

20. Moreover, consistency with the deficit ratio, which is measured *net*, suggests that debt should also be measured net of financial assets at least.

a satisfactory pace'.[21] There is admittedly a danger that this large element of flexibility will be used by the Council to make purely political judgements of debt ratios, as commentators have pointed out. The case for specifying supplementary economic factors to govern debt judgements is that this would reduce the large scope for political deals. But, since it might well be extremely difficult to reach agreement on such factors, it will probably have to be left to the stern scrutiny of the German authorities to ensure that the debt criteria are not applied in an unduly permissive way.

3.2   Observance of the limits: carrots or sticks?

As noted above, the sanctions provided under the EDP will have to be specified in more detail before Stage Three starts. The European Council is now facing up to this task, prompted by the proposal for a stability pact, which relies on prior agreement on deposits and fines for excessive deficits (of the order of $\frac{1}{4}$ per cent of GDP for every percentage point by which the 3 per cent limit is exceeded).

Such penalties are open to a number of criticisms. They will add to the deficit in question, without making any contribution to its solution; they are large enough to antagonise the affected government, but may not be enough to persuade it to change course, if it is under strong domestic pressure for fiscal expansion, however misguided; and however strong the prior commitment to automaticity, penalties may in the event be disputed, perhaps before the European Court, if only to win time.[22]

The challenge in this area is to find a more constructive and reliable way of securing observance of the fiscal rules, modified along lines suggested above. Such modification itself should assist reinforcement, since rules that are regarded as transparent and sensible are more likely to be respected. One possibility worth considering would be to combine the penalties with a system of conditional loans, somewhat as follows. A country found to have an excessive deficit would be presented formally with policy recommendations by the Council, as the Treaty provides.[23] These would take the form of a package of adjustment measures, somewhat on the lines of an IMF programme but mainly in the fiscal field, with a target for reduction of the deficit and a time-path for reaching it, which might extend over three or five years. If the country failed to adopt the programme and to begin implementing it within a prescribed interval, it would be required to pay the fine. If it agreed to implement the programme, it would immediately be

---

21. EC Treaty, Art. 104c (2) (b).
22. Presumably, non-participants in Stage Three will not be parties to a pact that provides automatic penalties (from which they are exempt under the Treaty).
23. EC Treaty, Art. 104c (7)–(9).

offered a loan from other governments participating in Stage Three at a favourable rate of interest, which would reduce the recipient's debt costs. Loans would be repayable at the end of the programme period, except that, if by that time the country surpassed its targets, it might be forgiven some or all of the repayment. The loans would be financed through market borrowing by participating governments under collective guarantee.[24]

A conditional medium-term loan facility on these lines could help cushion the effects of deeper-than-usual cycles and temporary disturbances, more particularly in cases of governments with an unfavourable credit rating in EMU. It would be less appropriate for coping with major permanent shocks, for which longer-term structural measures would be necessary. It would combine a 'carrot-and-stick' approach to observance of the EDP, involving the Council in policy design as well as surveillance, and offering financial benefits to governments under pressure which could help them win domestic support for unpopular measures. Although having limited applicability in a small-group EMU, it could have a larger part to play both in helping less-converged economies to manage the transition to Stage Three and in assisting them to observe the fiscal rules once they have joined.

3.3 A Financial Council for EMU?

As outlined earlier, fiscal policy in the Maastricht Treaty is left to the Ecofin Council, which conducts regular economic surveillance over all EU Member States. This reflects the dominant vision during the EMU IGC, which saw the Community moving towards EMU more or less together, and which sought to retain fiscal sovereignty in national hands.

The reality now is somewhat different. Stage Three of EMU is likely to start with a fairly small group of participating states. It will grow in time as more states converge, but there will always be a significant number outside, fed by newcomers as the EU grows to include eventually perhaps 30 or more countries. Councils and committees comprising such numbers are almost certainly too large to cope effectively with fiscal co-ordination, yet this will be at a premium in EMU.

Policy co-ordination in Stage Three seems likely to call for a new body in the form of a ministerial Council for EMU. It would be a counterweight to the ECB, albeit without the latter's collective authority over policy within its field of competence. It might be called the 'Financial Council', to distinguish it from Ecofin, and to signify that its competence lies mainly in the fiscal

---

24. Secondary legislation might be needed to exempt such lending from the 'no-bail-out' rule. There is a precedent for this, in that lending under the Community's Medium-Term Financial Support scheme is exempted from the Treaty prohibitions on government bail-outs and ECB credits to governments.

field, rather than other economic policy areas. Its tasks would be: (i) to co-ordinate the stance of national fiscal policies within EMU; in this, its role would be essentially advisory, but its advice would carry weight because of authority in relation to the EDP; (ii) to decide whether individual deficits are excessive under that procedure, which would entail setting and monitoring the aggregate fiscal ceiling described above, as well as the ceilings on individual budgets, modified as suggested earlier; and (iii) to decide penalties and conditional lending policies under the EDP, as also described above. Additionally, it should (iv) decide the external regime or guidelines for the single currency, a competence retained for ministers in the Maastricht Treaty.[25] This is to be a subject for close consultation with the ECB, the Commission and the European Parliament, and the ECB's view on it is likely to be highly influential. It will hardly be possible to undertake such consultations with the necessary speed and secrecy in an Ecofin that includes a substantial number of Member States not participating in the single currency. Along with this, the Financial Council's president should (v) represent the group of participating Member States on international fora such as the G7, which will almost certainly need to be revamped in Stage Three.[26]

Finally, the new Council could be given a new task: (vi) to decide periodically, in co-operation with the ECB, an explicit target for price stability. At present, interpretation of this objective is left to the ECB's discretion, but a number of economists have suggested that transparency and accountability would be improved if there were an explicit target, in the selection of which ministers would have a voice. This should be medium-term in character, and subject to annual review. The monetary policy needed for its achievement would be solely a matter for the ECB, but involving finance ministers in setting the precise inflation target would recognise that fiscal policy may have considerable effects on inflation.

Decisions in the Financial Council would be by weighted majority voting among ministers representing the participating Member States. Given its competence and the links with monetary policy, the President of the ECB should be an *ex officio* member, but not vote (mirroring the arrangement in the ECB's Governing Council). The Financial Council would be supported by an officials' committee, analogous to the prospective Economic and Financial Committee provided by the Maastricht Treaty for Stage Three.[27] The Council would normally meet less frequently than either Ecofin or the ECB's Governing Council; fiscal policy, unlike monetary policy, does not

---

25. EC Treaty, Art. 109.
26. The president of the Financial Council should be invited to attend the ECB Governing Council, on the same basis as the president of Ecofin, when the latter is drawn from a non-participating Member State.
27. EC Treaty, Art. 109c (2).

need continuous monitoring, and the burdens of meetings on finance ministers are already heavy.

This innovation would free Ecofin to concentrate on other economic policies, including the EU budget, etc, and on macropolicy links between participants in Stage Three and the other Member States, which could become an ongoing source of tension in Stage Three. These will include decisions under the EDP for non-participating Member States and the conduct of exchange-rate arrangements between the single-currency area and the rest of the EU, including a possible successor to the ERM.

4. CONCLUSIONS

The problems threatened by the split between monetary and fiscal policy in Stage Three should be addressed by making the fiscal ceilings in the Treaty more flexible while preserving their general thrust; and by strengthening the provisions for fiscal-policy co-operation among participating Member States, and between them and the rest of the EU. The former could be done by giving the fiscal limits a medium-term and collective dimension and, ideally, by changing their focus to government saving. The latter could be achieved by supplementing the sanctions under the EDP with a conditional lending facility and creating a finance ministers' Council for EMU, which would be a counterpart to the ECB and facilitate consultation with it, including consultation on a price-stability target. This would leave Ecofin more time to cope with the other economic policy matters within its competence, and with macropolicy links between states inside and outside the single-currency area.

Even with these innovations, no EMU will be immune from inappropriate fiscal policies. If some participants are intent on using fiscal policy to achieve objectives which conflict with those of the ECB, the only effective remedies are likely to be more drastic ones, not excluding dismantling the project in the event of serious and persistent rule-breaking. But assuming willingness on the part of governments to pursue supportive policies within EMU, it would be sensible to modify the Maastricht blueprint now, in order to give more substance to macroeconomic policy co-ordination and enable ministers and the ECB to work in harmony, without sacrificing the independence of either group in their respective fields of competence.

Chapter Eleven

THE EXCESSIVE DEFICIT PROCEDURE: A LEGAL DESCRIPTION

Alexander Italianer

Chapter Outline

1. Introduction
   1.1 Explanation of the provisions
   1.2 Origins of the excessive deficit procedure
   1.3 Dates of applicability of the provisions

2. Principles

3. Identification of an Excessive Deficit
   3.1 Monitoring by the Commission
   3.2 The deficit criterion
   3.3 The debt criterion
   3.4 The report of the Commission
   3.5 The opinion of the Committee provided for in Article 109c
   3.6 The opinion of the Commission
   3.7 The Council decision on the existence of an excessive deficit

4. Actions Taken by the Council
   4.1 The confidential recommendation by the Council
   4.2 The public recommendation by the Council
   4.3 The possibility for the Council to give notice to a Member State

5. Sanctions

—Cont'd.

European Economic and Monetary Union: The Institutional Framework (M. Andenas, L. Gormley, C. Hadjiemmanuil, I. Harden, eds.: 90-411-0687-1: © Kluwer Law International: pub. Kluwer Law International, 1997: printed in Great Britain)

1. INTRODUCTION

1.1 Explanation of the provisions

The excessive deficit procedure is a new procedure in the Treaty establishing the European Community, which was introduced through Article G (25) of the Maastricht Treaty on European Union. The EDP introduces the legally binding principle that Member States shall avoid excessive government deficits, a procedure which permits the identification of such excessive deficits, a number of measures of increasing strength which the Council may apply in order to remedy the situation, the decision-making rules for the application and abrogation of such measures, several further provisions and the legal basis for modifying or detailing these provisions. The EDP is constituted by the provisions of Article 104c of the EC Treaty. The new Article 104c forms part of Chapter 1, 'Economic Policy', of the new Title VI, 'Economic and Monetary Policy', which, following the Maastricht Treaty, replaces Title II, Chapters 1, 2 and 3, of Part Three of the Treaty establishing the European Economic Community, as last amended by the Single European Act.

In accordance with Article 104c (14), first subparagraph, further provisions relating to the implementation of the procedure are set out in the Protocol on the excessive deficit procedure annexed to the EC Treaty. Since the EDP Protocol forms an integral part of the EC Treaty in accordance with Article 239, it has the same legal rank as Article 104c and is therefore also an integral part of the EDP. The fact that the EDP Protocol can be replaced by other provisions, in accordance with the provisions of Article 104c (14), does not reduce its legal rank. It means that the authors of the Treaty considered that any modification to these provisions, which do not constitute the core of the EDP, would not need to be adopted via the heavy procedure of Article N of the Maastricht Treaty.[1]

The name 'excessive deficit procedure' does not appear in Article 104c, but it is clear from the recital in the EDP Protocol and the first subparagraph of paragraph 14 that the procedure described in Article 104c is the excessive deficit procedure.

The EDP is a separate procedure compared to the multilateral surveillance procedure contained in Article 103. Although the multilateral surveillance procedure can, by its nature, address the issue of budgetary policy, the scope of the EDP and its arrangements are clearly distinct.[2]

Although Article 104c and the EDP Protocol constitute the EDP as such, the EDP gets a wider meaning through the provisions of Article 109e (4),[3]

---

1. See also *infra*, section 7.3.
2. See also *infra*, section 8.
3. See *infra*, sections 1.3 and 2.

Article 109j (1) and the Protocol on economic and social cohesion annexed to the EC Treaty.[4]

1.2 Origins of the excessive deficit procedure

The first thoughts about Community involvement in national budgetary policies in the context of an economic and monetary union were contained in the Werner Report on the establishment of an Economic and Monetary Union, which was presented by Luxembourg Prime Minister Pierre Werner in 1970,[5] after a request made by the Heads of State and Government at the summit in The Hague in 1969. According to this report, the Community should set quantitative guidelines for national budgetary policies: '[T]he essential features of the whole of the public budgets, and in particular variations in their volume, the size of balances and the methods of financing or utilising them, will be decided at Community level.'[6] Also the Delors Report, written in preparation for the negotiations which led to the Maastricht Treaty,[7] foresaw a high degree of Community involvement in national budgetary policies: '[T]he Council of Ministers, in cooperation with the European Parliament, would have the authority to take directly enforceable decisions, *ie*: – to impose constraints on national budgets to the extent to which this was necessary to prevent imbalances that might threaten monetary stability; ...'[8] The Delors Report also advocated that binding rules and procedures should be developed in order to impose effective upper limits on budget deficits of individual member countries.[9]

In the opinion which the Monetary Committee delivered in accordance with the provisions of Article 102a of the EEC Treaty prior to the start of the intergovernmental conference which negotiated the Maastricht Treaty,[10] the Committee advocated a number of elements which later found their way into the Maastricht Treaty. For instance, the Committee stated that it should be laid down in the Treaty that 'excessive deficits must be avoided',[11] and that

4. See also *infra*, section 8.
5. 'Report to the Council and the Commission on the Realisation by Stages of Economic and Monetary Union in the Community', (1970) 11 EC Bull., Supp.
6. Ibid., p.12.
7. Committee for the Study of Economic and Monetary Union, 'Report on Economic and Monetary Union in the Community' (1989).
8. Ibid., pp.39–40.
9. Ibid., p.28.
10. Monetary Committee of the European Community, 'Economic and Monetary Union Beyond Stage 1. Orientations for the Preparation of the Intergovernmental Conference' (July 1990). The report was confidential, but was published as an annex to a letter from the Netherlands Minister of Finance, Tweede Kamer der Staten-Generaal, Vergaderjaar 1990–1991, Vergaderstuk 21501/07.
11. Ibid., p.8.

[t]he Council should have the duty of forming an opinion as to whether any planned or actual deficit is excessive ... Whether or not a budget deficit is excessive must remain a matter of judgement based on objective criteria ... They will relate, *inter alia*, to levels and trends of public indebtedness ... in relation to GDP, as well as to the sustainability of deficits; ...[12]

Once the Council would be of the opinion that a deficit is excessive, the Committee recommended that the Council

... should be in a position to bring pressure for compliance ... This process should start with an attempt to reach agreement in a context of confidential peer-group pressure. Beyond that, the Council should be able to make recommendations by majority vote which would be published. If these recommendations were ineffective, the Council should be enabled to take a legally binding position by majority vote that a given deficit is or would be excessive. The Treaty would have to provide an appropriate decision-making and enforcement procedure.[13]

The Commission, in accordance with Article 236 of the EEC Treaty, also delivered an opinion on economic and monetary union prior to the start of the intergovernmental conference.[14] In its opinion, the Commission also advocated that the Treaty should state that excessive deficits must be avoided. Contrary to the Monetary Committee, which advocated the use of a 'formal Community procedure designed to ensure that excessive deficits do not arise',[15] the Commission recommended[16] that the judgement whether a deficit is excessive should be an integral part of the multilateral surveillance procedure, that is, the procedure defined under the 1990 Convergence Decision,[17] which should be extended with additional provisions for that purpose. As a yardstick for the identification of excessive deficits, the Commission proposed to use the 'golden rule of public finance', that is, that public borrowing should not exceed investment expenditure. Complementary to this rule, other objective criteria, such as the deficit and debt-to-GDP ratios were to be used. In the draft Treaty which the Commission submitted prior to the start of the intergovernmental conference,[18] it was proposed to introduce an article laying down that

12. Ibid., p.9.
13. Ibid., pp.9–10. The Committee members from one country expressed a reservation regarding the recommendation that a position taken by the Council that a budget deficit is excessive should be legally binding; cf. ibid., p.10.
14. Commission of the European Communities, 'Economic and Monetary Union' (21 Aug. 1989).
15. Ibid., p.8.
16. Ibid., p.25.
17. Council Decision 90/141/EEC of 12.3.90.
18. Commission of the European Communities, 'Intergovernemental Conferences: Contribution by the Commission', (1991) EC Bull., Supp. 2/91.

'[e]xcessive deficits shall be avoided'. In addition, this article empowered the Council to adopt appropriate measures pursuant to the provisions of the chapter on economic policy. This would allow the Council to adopt specific recommendations for a Member State or to modify the secondary legislation concerning the multilateral surveillance procedure.[19] It may be concluded from this overview that Article 104c has a long history, which goes back to the Werner Report.

The reason behind Article 104c being one of the longest articles in the EC Treaty must be seen to lie in the concern of the authors to lay down in stone a guarantee for sound public finances in the context of Economic and Monetary Union. Leaving the provisions of the EDP as a subject for secondary legislation, in particular if it could be adopted by a qualified majority, was thought to be an insufficient safeguard against the potential threat for stable monetary policy that could arise from a budgetary policy which was not subject to strong Community pressure.

1.3   Dates of applicability of the provisions

The excessive deficit procedure was specifically designed to operate in the third stage of EMU. It is therefore only in that stage of EMU that the procedure will be fully operational. For two reasons it was, however, considered to be useful that important parts of the procedure would already apply before the start of the third stage. The first is that is was decided that all other provisions concerning Chapter 1, 'Economic policy', should enter into force as early as possible in order to contribute to the process of convergence which is necessary during the first and second stage of EMU. It is obvious that by identifying and endeavouring to avoid excessive deficits, the EDP could contribute significantly to the process of achieving a high degree of convergence. A second reason for bringing forward in time the application of parts of the EDP resides in the fact that, according to Article 109j (1), the absence of a Council decision on the existence of an excessive deficit is one of the four convergence criteria on the basis of which the Commission and the EMI will report on the achievement of a high degree of sustainable convergence. In order to know whether there exists an excessive deficit, it is therefore necessary that the procedure is at least partially operational.

19. See L. Bini-Smaghi, T. Padoa-Schioppa and F. Papadia, *The Transition to EMU in the Maastricht Treaty*, Essays in International Finance No. 194, International Finance Section, Princeton University (Nov. 1994), and A. Italianer, 'Mastering Maastricht: EMU Issues and How They Were Settled', in K. Gretschmann (ed.), *Economic and Monetary Union: Implications for National Policy-Makers* (1993), for an account of the history of Art. 104c during the Intergovernmental Conference.

The dates of entry into force of the provisions regarding EMU in Title VI, and in particular of those regarding the EDP, are determined by Articles 109e (3) and 109k (3). Other relevant provisions are contained in Article 109e (4) and in the Protocols which allow Denmark and the United Kingdom to have an exemption as regards participation in the third stage of EMU. According to the first subparagraph of Article 109e (3), the provisions of Article 104c, with the exception of paragraphs 1, 9, 11 and 14, shall apply from the beginning of the second stage. According to the second subparagraph of Article 109e (3), the provisions of Articles 104c (1), (9) and (11) shall apply from the beginning of the third stage. According to Article 109k (3), however, Articles 104c (9) and (11) do not apply to a Member State with a derogation, that is, a derogation as regards participation in the third stage of EMU in the sense of Article 109k (1). From these different provisions it follows that the EDP enters into force according to the following scheme:

Table 1

Applicability of provisions excessive deficit procedure

At the entry into force of Treaty (1 November 1993)	104c (14) EDP Protocol	All Member States
At the start of Stage Two (1 January 1994)	104c (2)–(8) 104c (10) 104c (12) + (13) 109e (4)	All Member States
At the start of Stage Three	104c (1)	All Member States*
	104c (9) + (11)	Only Member States participating in Stage Three

Note:
* Excluding the United Kingdom unless it enters the third Stage Three.

Upon entry into force of the Maastricht Treaty (*ie*, on 1 November 1993), only Article 104c (14) and the EDP Protocol entered into force. The entry into force of Article 104c (14) follows from the fact that all provisions of the Treaty, unless otherwise mentioned, enter into force upon the date of entry into force of the Treaty itself. Since paragraph 14 of Article 104c is excluded from the list of paragraphs which, according to Article 109e (3), enters into force at the beginning of the second stage or even at the beginning of the third stage, it follows that Article 104c (14) entered into force at the same time as the Treaty. The entry into force of the EDP Protocol at the same time as Article 104c (14) follows from the fact that the Protocol is mentioned in Article 104c (14) and therefore logically should enter into force at the same date. Since the EDP Protocol is an integral part of the Treaty, however, and since Article 109e (3) or any other Treaty provision does not mention otherwise, the EDP Protocol should be deemed to fall under the general rule regarding entry into force of Treaty provisions.[20] The entry into force of Article 104c (14) at the same date as the entry into force of the Maastricht Treaty allowed the Council to adopt the necessary secondary legislation before the start of the second stage of EMU.[21]

Upon the start of Stage Two of EMU (*ie*, on 1 January 1994), Articles 104c (2)–(8), (10), (12) and (13) entered into force in addition to Article 104c (14) and the EDP Protocol. Furthermore, according to the provisions of Article 109e (4), in the second stage Member States have to endeavour to avoid excessive deficits. The latter provision must be assumed to take the place, during the second stage, of Article 104c (1), which only becomes applicable from the start of the third stage. The result is that the EDP is fully operational during the second stage with the exception of the measures foreseen in paragraphs 9 and 11, and with the legal obligation from paragraph 1 to avoid excessive deficits replaced by the obligation to 'endeavour' to avoid excessive deficits during Stage Two.

Several reasons can be advanced for having a 'political', rather than legal, commitment to avoid excessive deficits during Stage Two. First, the non-applicability of the measures of Articles 104c (9) and (11) during Stage Two makes it less necessary that there be a legal obligation to avoid excessive deficits during that stage. Indeed, a Council decision in the third stage giving notice to a Member State to take measures under Article 104c (9) would constitute a binding act according to Article 189 (contrary to the recommendations under Articles 104c (7) or (8), which are not binding), and could only be taken if there is a counterpart in terms of an obligation which is violated.[22] Second, an obligation to avoid excessive deficits during Stage Two would be contrary to the nature of the second stage, which is a stage of preparation for Stage Three during which Member States should improve upon their performance with regard to the convergence criteria of

---

20. Another example is the Protocol on the Statute of the EMI. According to Art. 109f (1), the impression might be given that the Statute of the EMI would apply only from the start of Stage Two. Provisions from the Statute of the EMI were however used as legal basis for Council Decisions 93/716/EC and 93/717/EC of 22.11.93, *ie*, the Statute of the EMI was deemed to be applicable immediately upon entry into force of the Treaty rather than after the start of Stage Two.

21. See *infra*, section 7.3.

22. This case is similar, but not completely equal to, the procedure under Art. 93 (2), for which Art. 92 serves as the legal obligation to be respected.

Article 109j (1), and which could therefore imply that several Member States start Stage Two with an excessive deficit which is eliminated in the course of that stage prior to their participation in the third stage. It would indeed be inconsistent to impose, on the one hand, obligations in terms of (budgetary) convergence while, on the other hand, granting Member States a period during which they can improve on the same convergence. Thirdly, the legislator may also have borne in mind the fact that a Council decision on the existence of an excessive deficit in accordance with Article 104c (6) in combination with the legal obligation of Article 104c (1) to avoid excessive deficits but without the binding legal instruments of Articles 104c (9) and, (11), could induce natural or legal persons to seek to obtain, through legal proceedings or otherwise, the elimination of the excessive deficit. Such a case again would be contrary to the nature of Stage Two, which implicitly allows for the existence of an excessive deficit in any Member State.

Upon the start of the third stage, Article 104c (1) becomes applicable both for Member States participating in the third stage as well as for Member States with a derogation in the sense of Article 109k (1). In addition, but only for those Member States participating in the third stage, Articles 104c (9) and (11) enter into force. Therefore, in the third stage the full EDP only applies to those Member States which participate in the single monetary policy. The question arises, why the legislator has foreseen the applicability of Article 104c (1) to Member States with a derogation in Stage Three, given that in Stage Two there is no such obligation. In principle, it could be argued that the situation for Member States with a derogation in Stage Three is the same as for Member States in Stage Two, in the sense that both do not participate yet in the single monetary policy, so that it would seem inconsistent to have two different situations as regards the obligation to avoid excessive deficits in the second and third stage.

The situation in Stage Three is, however, different from that in Stage Two. First, it is desirable that the Member States with a derogation participate as much as possible in the economic policy of the third stage. Since the obligation to avoid an excessive deficit is part of this policy, the extension of this obligation to Member States with a derogation is a symbol for the desire that they participate as much as possible in the policies of the third stage. At the same time, it would go too far to apply to them the measures foreseen in Articles 104c (9) and (11), since the latter were introduced having in mind a situation in the third stage where an excessive deficit of one participating Member State could pose a threat for the monetary stability for all participants, justifying the use of strong measures *vis-à-vis* the Member State with the excessive deficit. Second, after the second stage it is reasonable to expect that all Member States, including those with a derogation, have made progress towards reaching the sustainable financial position mentioned in Article 109j (1). Imposing an obligation to avoid excessive deficits is therefore at the same time reasonable (since the progress made, even if it is insufficient with regard to the obligations for participating in a single currency, should allow the Member States with a derogation to eliminate the excessive deficit within a reasonable delay), as well as a justified incentive in order to prepare for future participation in the third stage. Finally, a sustainable financial position of the governments of the Member States with a derogation can be seen as comparable to the requirement that the central banks of the Member States with a derogation should respect Article 107, that is, have to be made independent. These can be seen as conditions which the legislator desired to impose for participation of the central banks of Member States with a derogation in the General Council of the ECB.

The United Kingdom and Denmark, in accordance with, respectively, the Protocol on certain provisions relating to the United Kingdom of Great Britain and Northern Ireland and the Protocol on certain provisions relating to Denmark, have the possibility of an exemption regarding their participation in the third stage of EMU.[23]

In the case of an exemption for the UK, its position as regards the EDP will be different from that of a Member State with a derogation, since paragraph 5 of the UK Protocol lays down that in such a case not only Articles 104c (9) and (11), but also Article 104c (1), that is, the obligation to avoid excessive deficits, will not apply to the UK. Instead, as laid down in paragraph 6 of the UK Protocol, Article 109e (4), that is, the obligation to endeavour to avoid excessive deficits, will continue to apply to the UK. If, after the start of the third stage, the UK should, in accordance with paragraph 10 of the UK Protocol, change its earlier notification according to which it did not intend to move to the third stage, the situation regarding the EDP as foreseen in paragraphs 5 and 6 of the UK Protocol does not change until the UK moves to the third stage. The latter follows from the last subparagraph of paragraph 10 of the UK Protocol, according to which paragraphs 3 to 9 of the said Protocol cease to have effect if the UK moves to the third stage. One of the implications of this construction is that, if the UK changes its intention in order to participate in the third stage, but if the Council decides in accordance with the procedure of Article 109k (2) that the United Kingdom does not fulfil the necessary conditions, Article 104c (1) will continue not to apply until the United Kingdom moves effectively to the third stage. Instead, Article 109e (4) will continue to apply.

In the case of an exemption for Denmark, paragraph 2 of the Denmark Protocol lays down, *inter alia*, that all provisions of the Treaty referring to a

23. Pursuant to the 'Decision of the Heads of State and Government, meeting within the European Council, concerning certain problems raised by Denmark on the Treaty on European Union', (1992) OJ C 348/2, Denmark has notified upon the coming into effect of the Treaty on European Union that it will not participate in the third stage of EMU.

derogation shall be applicable to Denmark. This implies that, as regards the EDP, Denmark will be in the same situation as a Member State with a derogation. In particular, Article 104c (1) will apply to Denmark, while Articles 104c (9) and (11), which only apply to Member States participating in the third stage, will not apply. This conclusion is confirmed in the decision of the Heads of States and Government adopted at the Edinburgh European Council,[24] of which paragraph 2 of section B reads that '[a]s a consequence, Denmark ... will not be bound by the rules concerning economic policy which apply only to the Member States participating in the third stage of Economic and Monetary Union...' In this context, the rules which apply only to the participants in the third stage are Articles 104c (9) and (11), but not Article 104c (1), since the latter applies also to the Member States with a derogation.

2.   PRINCIPLES

The formulation of paragraph 1 reflects the legal obligation for Member States, in the third stage of EMU and subject to the possible exception for the United Kingdom discussed above,[25] to avoid excessive government deficits.

The economic reasons for such a provision in a monetary union arise from the negative impact which a non-sustainable government financial position in one or more participating Member States could exercise on monetary stability in the whole union. The existence of such a negative externality can arise through different channels. High government deficits may increase final demand in the economy and thereby lead to inflationary pressures, which would need to be counteracted by the central bank through a more restrictive monetary policy in order to contain the inflationary pressure. Although the inflationary pressure might originate in only one Member State, the restrictive monetary policy would naturally affect all members of the union through a rise in short-term interest rates.

Secondly, high deficits and/or high levels of public debt could lead to a demand for financial capital which could, through higher long-term interest rates, crowd out the demand for financial capital arising from the private sector. The effect on long-term interest rates in the Union may be mitigated in a world with perfect capital mobility, but nevertheless there may remain *de facto* obstacles to such a perfect mobility in the form of different fiscal incentives, differences in prudential regulation affecting investment behaviour, and exchange-rate uncertainty between the single currency and other

24.   Ibid., p.2.
25.   See *supra*, section 1.3.

currencies. These obstacles, as well as the fact that the weight of EMU in world capital markets will be considerable, could have the effect that the additional demand for capital is not absorbed completely by world capital markets without raising long-term interest rates.

Thirdly, if the sustainability of a Member State government's financial position is at stake, so that there is the threat of imminent default, even more severe risks for the other participants in the monetary union could arise. The presence of systemic risks for the financial system could exert a pressure on the central bank to buy more government bonds than it would like to for monetary-policy purposes, thus making room for inflationary pressure. There could also be pressure on other Member States to come to the rescue of the defaulting Member State, despite of the provisions of Article 104b, for instance, if there is the risk that the defaulting Member State would leave the monetary union in order to finance its deficits through inflationary policies, such as a surprise devaluation or monetary financing.

The presence of the possible negative externalities described above justifies Community involvement in the budgetary policies of the Member States participating in the monetary union. However, in accordance with Article 3b, third subparagraph, any action by the Community should not go beyond what is necessary to achieve the objectives of the EC Treaty. In particular, this implies that the EDP should only address budgetary situations which are non-sustainable in the sense of the convergence criterion of Article 109j (1), second indent, and not issues of budgetary policy that go beyond the minimum requirements for participation in a monetary union. These other issues fall under the multilateral surveillance procedure of Article 103. This limitation of the action by the Community to what is strictly necessary for the functioning of a monetary union is also reflected in paragraph 2, which restricts the purpose of the monitoring by the Commission to the identification of what are called 'gross errors'.

In addressing non-sustainable budgetary situations, the authors of the Treaty do not make a distinction between the size of the Member State concerned, although this would have made sense economically in some cases. For instance, the inflationary pressure that a small Member State would exert throughout the Union is evidently smaller than that of a large Member State. In other cases, however, such as the threat that a Member State might leave the monetary union, the negative externality in terms of the credibility of the monetary union and its monetary policies is the same for all. Indeed, a differential treatment in the context of the EDP according to the size of the Member State concerned would be a discrimination in the sense of Article 6 of the EC Treaty. The non-discrimination according to size of the Member State for the EDP does not exclude that the ECB would react differently as regards its monetary policy in order to counteract inflationary pressures coming from a smaller or a larger Member State, since the ECB is concerned with price stability in the Union as a whole.

An inherent difficulty lies in the definition of a sustainable government financial position, and therefore in defining what should be understood as 'avoiding excessive government deficits'. Although these concepts are frequently used in the context of economic theory and in discussions of economic policies, the operational meaning given to them is either difficult to measure or devoid of unanimous agreement, and therefore would inevitably bear a judgmental, if not political, character. As a result of this difficulty, the 'avoidance of excessive government deficits' has been made a Treaty obligation the infringement of which by a Member State, following paragraph 10, can be brought before the Court of Justice neither by the Commission nor by any other Member State.[26]

It must therefore be understood that the EDP has a double purpose in this context. First, it defines more precisely what is meant by the obligation of paragraph 1, and thereby gives content to the meaning of the words 'avoid', 'government' and 'excessive deficits'. Second, it institutes a procedure which bears some similarity to infringement proceedings before the Court of Justice, with the ultimate possibility to use financial or other sanctions. The meaning given in the EDP provisions to the words 'avoid', 'government' and 'excessive deficits' is either explicit or implicit.

The concept of 'government' is given an explicit meaning in Article 2 of the EDP Protocol, and has been further defined in the secondary legislation[27] that has been adopted on the basis of Article 104c (14). Its meaning, which comprises not only central government (or federal government and Länder governments combined, in the case of federal Member States), but also regional or local government and the social-security sector, is wider than the concept of government which figures in Article 146. On the one hand, this wider concept of 'general government' has a statistical meaning, since it is used to define the coverage of the economic variables that are being used in the EDP. For instance, it implies that the deficits of regional or local governments or of the social-security funds have to be included in the definition of deficit that is being used as a reference for the procedures of the EDP.

On the other hand, the fact that the wider concept of 'general government' is used implies that the Treaty obligation to avoid excessive deficits extends beyond central (or federal/Länder) government. Since the EDP foresees that the budgetary situation of a Member State in case of an excessive deficit is discussed in the Council, the use of the concept of 'general government' raises the question whether the representative of the Member State, in the Council, who, in accordance with Article 146, should be authorised to commit the government of that Member State, can also commit the 'general government'. Since the representative in the Council

26. See *infra*, section 7.2.
27. Council Regulation (EC) No 3605/93 of 22.11.93.

represents the Member State, and therefore also 'general government', the answer to this question is unequivocal: any commitment by the government is a commitment which covers whatever subjects of that Member State, including regional or local governments and social-security funds. How the government ensures the commitment, is an internal matter for the Member State. The fact that it is the government which should speak for the 'general government' in the Council is confirmed by the first sentence of Article 3 of the EDP Protocol, which, referring to the need to ensure the effectiveness of the EDP, lays down that the governments of the Member States are responsible under the procedure for the deficits of 'general government'. This provision emphasises that each Member State should ensure that its representatives in the Council can talk also on behalf of 'general government'.[28]

The meaning of the concept 'excessive deficit' appears implicitly from paragraphs 2 to 6, which lay down the procedure to be followed which leads to a Council decision that an excessive deficits exists in a particular Member State. The decision that there exists an excessive deficit is, accordingly, a discretionary decision by the Council, which is obliged to take this decision after an overall assessment. The first step of the EDP is therefore the identification of the excessive deficit. The political nature of such a decision confirms the difficulty in circumscribing precisely and objectively what an excessive deficit is.

The meaning of the concept 'avoid' is even more implicit than that of the concept 'excessive deficit'. The word 'avoid' contrasts with an outright prohibition on the existence of an excessive deficit. In fact, it suggests that excessive deficits are not completely prohibited, and could be allowed to exist for a given period without entailing sanctions other than a confidential recommendation from the Council, provided that effective action is taken to remedy the situation. This difference with an outright prohibition arises from the fact that an excessive deficit situation is a reversible one: although the fact that an excessive deficit situation has existed in a particular year is not reversible, the situation can be remedied in a future year. Second, due to the existence of annualised budgetary processes and procedures, it takes time to bring down a deficit. Also this aspect must be deemed to be contained in the word 'avoid'.

During Stage Two,[29] the legal obligation to avoid excessive government deficits contained in Article 104c (1) does not apply. On the other hand,

---

28. A more far-reaching interpretation of this provision would be that, in the case of the existence of an excessive deficit, the (central or federal) government would have to compensate, by reducing its own deficit, any contribution to the excessive deficit from other sectors of 'general government'. It should, however, not be up to the Union to determine in a binding manner which sectors of 'general government' should contribute to the reduction of the deficit.

29. And possibly in Stage Three for the UK; see *supra*, section 1.3.

Article 109e (4) applies, according to which Member States should endeavour during the second stage to avoid excessive deficits. This provision imposes on Member States the obligation to make an effort during the second stage to avoid excessive deficits, without representing an outright obligation. In order to comply with this provision, Member States have to demonstrate that they are indeed endeavouring to avoid excessive government deficits. The counterpart of this weaker condition is that the legally binding measures of Articles 104c (9) and (11) do not apply during Stage Two. As a result, the difference with the third stage as regards the application of the EDP lies in the reduced possibility for Council measures, and not in the fact that an excessive deficit should be defined differently in the second stage compared to the third stage, or should be defined differently at the beginning of the second stage compared to later in the second stage, when decisions on the start of the third stage have to be taken. The fact that Article 109e (4) applies instead of Article 104c (1) during the second stage should therefore not influence the identification of an excessive deficit in the sense of paragraphs 2 to 6. As will be seen below,[30] however, there may be an impact on the recommendations foreseen in paragraphs 7 and 8.

3. IDENTIFICATION OF AN EXCESSIVE DEFICIT

The identification of an excessive deficit is the subject of a number of different steps, which are described in paragraphs 2–6, and which involve the Commission, the Council and the Committee provided for in Article 109c of the Treaty.[31] The philosophy behind these steps is that, once the procedure is initiated through a report by the Commission as foreseen in paragraph 3, there is a presumption of an excessive deficit. After different steps, which involve notably the judgment of the Commission, it is, however, up to the Council to decide whether an excessive deficit really exists. It is therefore not the case, in particular, that the non-fulfilment of the requirements under the criteria of paragraph 2 is tantamount to the existence of an excessive deficit, the latter fact having to be decided separately by the Council.[32]

---

30. See *infra*, sections 4.1 and 4.2.
31. In the second stage of EMU, this is the Monetary Committee; in the third stage, this is the Economic and Financial Committee.
32. J. Pipkorn, 'Legal Arrangements in the Treaty of Maastricht for the Effectiveness of the Economic and Monetary Union' (1994) 31 *C.M.L. Rev.* 278.

3.1 Monitoring by the Commission

Paragraph 2 gives the Commission the task of monitoring the development of the budgetary situation and of the stock of government debt in the Member States with a view to identifying gross errors. In particular, the Commission has to examine compliance with two criteria, one for the government deficit and one for the government debt.

This paragraph makes clear, first, that an 'excessive deficit' applies, not only to a Member State's government deficit, but to its complete budgetary situation and to the situation regarding the stock of government debt. The word 'deficit' is therefore a *pars pro toto* in this context. Secondly, it appears from the text that an 'excessive' deficit can only correspond to a gross error in a Member State's budgetary policy. Budgetary policies which are not optimal from an economic viewpoint or from the viewpoint of policy co-ordination inside the Community can therefore not be qualified as 'excessive'. The yardstick must be the minimum requirements to be imposed on the budgetary situation for the functioning of a monetary union, even if this monetary union is not present during the second stage. A reference in this context is the second convergence criterion from Article 109j (1), which refers to the 'sustainability' of the government financial position. The word 'sustainability' in this context is used in the economic literature to indicate a budgetary situation which prevents the government debt from exploding, that is, from entering into a vicious circle in which high levels of accumulated debt caused by high deficits lead to high interest payments, which in their turn lead again to even higher deficits, and so on.[33] Such an evolution depends clearly on both the size of the deficit and the size of the government debt in relation to GDP.

The monitoring by the Commission is, in principle, a continuous one. Budgetary data and data on GDP become, however, only available at regular time intervals. The continuous monitoring may therefore be constrained by discontinuities in data availability. Council Regulation (EC) No. 3605/93 of 22 November 1993[34] has recognised this by imposing on the Member States the obligation to report their data to the Commission twice a year, before 1 March and 1 September.

---

33. This phenomenon is commonly referred to as the 'snowball effect'. There are different formal conditions for sustainability. A strong form is the respect by the government of the so-called intertemporal budget constraint, which states that, at any point in time, the sum of a government's future revenues (discounted at an appropriate rate of interest) should be sufficient to cover all future government expenditure (also discounted) and to pay back any debt outstanding at that time. A less strong condition is to require that the ratio of debt to GDP should stabilise at an arbitrary value. The weakest condition for sustainability is simply that there is no debt explosion, *ie*, that the ratio of debt to GDP does not move towards infinity.
34. (1992) OJ L332/7.

The Commission should in particular examine compliance with budgetary discipline on the basis of the two criteria specified in subparagraphs (a) and (b). This formulation allows the Commission also to monitor, in addition to the two criteria, other elements of the budgetary situation which could constitute a gross error. The most important example of such an element can be derived from the Treaty itself. Since the Commission also has to prepare a report under paragraph 3 if, notwithstanding the fulfilment of the requirements under the two criteria, it is of the opinion that there is a risk of an excessive deficit, it follows that the Commission has to monitor whether such a risk is present. The latter could arise if there is a possibility that the requirements under the two criteria will not be fulfilled after the period under examination. This is relevant because the deficit criterion, according to Council Regulation No. 3605/93, is not examined for any year later than the year of examination itself, while the debt criterion is only examined for the period until the year preceding the examination.[35] The risk could also arise from the possibility that the data in accordance with the definitions of the Treaty exclude contingent liabilities, that is, factors which contain the risk of influencing the deficit and/or the deficit at a later stage. Examples of such contingent liabilities are state guarantees, off-budget items or preannounced financial commitments (*eg*, debt takeovers, or pensions in some cases).

3.2   The deficit criterion

Subparagraph (a) of paragraph 2 defines the first criterion on the basis of which the Commission has to examine compliance with budgetary discipline. This criterion is usually referred to as the 'deficit criterion', and relates to the government deficit *stricto sensu*, as opposed to the wider notion of deficit contained in the expression 'excessive deficit'. The deficit criterion is formulated negatively, implying that, if the criterion is satisfied, this gives rise to a report by the Commission. The negative formulation explains why paragraph 3 is not formulated in terms of 'fulfilling the criteria', but in terms of fulfilling *the requirements* under the criteria, that is, the requirements that follow logically from not meeting the criteria.

The central variable under consideration in the deficit criterion is not the deficit itself, that is, the nominal value of the deficit expressed in national currency, but the ratio of the planned or actual government deficit to gross

---

35. This is related to the fact that, according to Art. 2 of the EDP Protocol, the debt is measured as the debt outstanding at the end of the year. Since, contrary to the deficit, it is difficult to *plan* a debt-to-GDP ratio for the end of the year, due to the fact that the evolution of the debt-to-GDP ratio is influenced by several factors outside the control of the government, only the debt-to-GDP ratio until the year preceding the examination is examined.

domestic product (*'deficit ratio'*). By thus scaling the deficit, a measure is obtained which is comparable among the Member States, assuming that the definitions of the numerator – the deficit – and the denominator – GDP – are sufficiently harmonised. A comparable measure, in turn, allows for the use of a common benchmark for the evolution of this measure. In the case of the deficit criterion, the common benchmark is whether the deficit ratio exceeds a reference value.

The deficit ratio can be the actual or planned deficit. The meaning of the notions 'planned' and 'actual' has been defined in Article 3 of Council Regulation No. 3605/93. The definitions contained in this Council Regulation are given with respect to the particular point in time at which one looks at the deficit. This is clear from the fact that the notion 'planned' is defined as referring to 'the current year', and the notion 'actual' as referring to any 'past year'. The notion 'actual', in this context, therefore means in most cases that one refers to the realisation of a deficit after the budget year has elapsed, while, *mutatis mutandis*, the notion 'planned' refers in most cases to the budget which is in the process of being executed.[36] The definitions of 'planned' and 'actual' have been used in Council Regulation No. 3605/93 to define the reporting requirements by the Member States, referring to specific years relative to the year ('year n') in which the reporting takes place. The examination of the criteria is, however, not restricted to these years. For instance, the Council Regulation requires the reporting on the 'actual' deficit (or debt, for that matter) to go back to the year $n-4$, but the examination of the criteria could cover a longer time span. Similarly, a special case arises if data reporting takes place in any year n, but the examination in the following year $n+1$. In such a case, what was still a 'planned' deficit during the reporting year n, has become the 'actual' deficit when viewed from the year $n+1$. For the latter year itself, until a new reporting round has taken place, no 'planned' deficit will have been reported.[37]

The notion 'government deficit' which is used in this criterion is made more explicit in Article 2 of the EDP Protocol. The notion 'government' refers to 'general government', that is, central government, regional or local government and social-security funds with the exclusion of commercial operations as described in the European System of Integrated Economic Accounts (ESA).[38]

---

36. An exception in both cases is the UK, for which the budget year runs from April 1 to March 31, and is therefore not equivalent to the calendar year.
37. This situation is not purely hypothetical. In many countries, the budget for the year $n+1$ is only presented by the government after the reporting date of 1 Sept. in the year n as defined in Council Regulation No. 3605/93. Such a budget, even if not reported to the Commission, could give rise to a Commission report early in year $n+1$, but before the next reporting which has to take place before 1 March of year $n+1$.
38. Eurostat, *European System of Integrated Economic Accounts* (2nd edn, 1979).

The notion 'deficit' is defined as net borrowing as defined in ESA. The main implication of this definition is that the notion of government deficit does not have the same content which it usually has in national policy discussions, or national public accounts, where 'government deficit' usually refers to the net balance to be financed by the central government. Apart from the distinction between general and central government, the main difference between the Treaty definition and the usual national definition resides in the fact that 'net borrowing' is based on an accruals basis and excludes financial operations, while the net balance to be financed is on a cash basis and includes financial operations (for example, the proceeds from privatisations by the government).

Article 2 of the EDP Protocol also defines 'gross domestic product' with reference to ESA, thus ensuring that the definition for the denominator of the deficit ratio is comparable among Member States. As with the notion 'government deficit', this implies in some Member States that a denominator is used which is different from that which is used for domestic purposes, for example, 'national income' or 'gross national product'.

Subparagraph (a) of paragraph 2 only refers to a 'reference value' as regards the benchmark for the deficit criterion. The reference value itself is defined in Article 1 of the EDP Protocol as being equal to 3 per cent. The difference between defining the reference value in paragraph 2 or in the EDP Protocol is that, in accordance with the second subparagraph of paragraph 14, the EDP Protocol can be replaced by new provisions, including a new reference value, without following the amendment procedure of Article N (1) of the Maastricht Treaty.[39]

Subparagraph (a) contains two exceptions; either[40] may justify that the deficit ratio exceeds the reference value. In order for either to apply, the deficit ratio should at least be close to the reference value. The interpretation of the word 'close' in this context is left to the Commission, which has to judge whether the requirements under the criterion are fulfilled. The two exceptions clearly aim at two different cases.

The first applies to the case where initially the deficit ratio has been considerably above the reference value. If, in such circumstances, the deficit ratio has declined substantially and continuously, and has reached a value close to the reference value, the exception applies. This exception clearly is most relevant in the second stage, because the EDP should in the third stage

---

39. Other examples of such a simplified Treaty amendment are contained in Article 6 of the Protocol concerning the convergence criteria of Art. 109j of the Treaty, Art. 106 (5) of the Treaty, Art. 165, fourth subpara., of the Treaty and Art. 45 of the Protocol covering the Statutes of the European Court of Justice and, to some extent, subpara. 2 of Art. 1 (2) of the Protocol concerning the Grand Duchy of Luxembourg.

40. They are formulated in such a way that it is virtually excluded that they occur at the same time.

prevent deficit ratios from ever exceeding considerably the reference value. For Member States which start the second stage with a high deficit ratio and which have made appreciable efforts such that the ratio has almost attained the reference value, this exception, *inter alia*, allows them to meet the budgetary convergence criterion of Article 109j (1). Again, the judgment on the interpretation of the words 'substantially' and 'continuously' is left to the Commission.

The second exception could logically occur both in the second stage and in the third stage. It allows the deficit ratio to exceed the reference value if this excess is exceptional and temporary, provided the deficit ratio stays close to the reference value. The exceptional nature of the excess over the reference value must be seen as being opposed to 'normal' fluctuations in the deficit ratio. Such fluctuations are usually understood to be those resulting from cyclical variations in government revenue and expenditure, without the underlying policy being changed. It follows that, in order to be considered as an exception, the excess over the reference value should be due, not to normal, but to exceptional cyclical variations. For instance, this exception is important in the context of so-called 'asymmetric shocks'.[41] These are events of an unpredictable nature which are normally outside the control of the government and which lead the economy of a Member State to undergo a downturn relative to other Member States. If such effects are strong, they may pose a more than normal burden on the budget, possibly leading to the excess of the deficit ratio above the reference value. Examples of such asymmetric shocks which could be considered exceptional are a major natural disaster, the sudden disappearance of export markets as in the case of the export market in the former Soviet Union for Finland, or a major geopolitical event such as German reunification in 1990.

Even if the excess of the deficit ratio above the reference value can be qualified as 'exceptional' and if the deficit ratio stays close to the reference value, the excess over the reference value has to be temporary. This implies, first, that it should arise starting from a situation where the deficit ratio was effectively below the reference value and, second, that the excess should not be maintained any longer than what can be qualified as being 'temporary'. For example, if the other requirements for the exception are fulfilled and the actual deficit ratio for year $n-1$ is above the reference value, but the planned deficit ratio for year n is below the reference value, the situation could fall under this exception.

---

41. See M. Emerson, D. Gros, A. Italianer, J. Pisani-Ferry and H. Reichenbach, *One Market, One Money* (1992), ch. 6.

3.3 The debt criterion

Subparagraph (b) of paragraph 2 defines the second criterion on the basis of which the Commission has to examine compliance with budgetary discipline. This criterion is usually referred to as the 'debt criterion'. As with the deficit criterion, the debt criterion is formulated negatively, implying that if the criterion is satisfied, it gives rise to a report by the Commission.

For the same reasons as for the deficit criterion,[42] the central variable under consideration in the debt criterion is not the debt itself, that is, the value of the debt expressed in national currency, but the ratio of government debt to GDP ('debt ratio'). Since this is a measure which is comparable among Member States, it allows for the use of a common benchmark for its evaluation. In the case of the debt criterion, the common benchmark is whether the debt ratio exceeds a reference value. Contrary to the case of the deficit criterion, where the notions 'actual' and 'planned' are used in relation to the deficit ratio, subparagraph (b) does not use these notions for the debt ratio. One reason for this is that one cannot properly speak of a 'planned' debt ratio, since the debt ratio at the end of any particular year is equal to the sum of the debt ratio at the end of the previous year, the deficit ratio and a number of other factors over which the government has no direct control, such as changes in the valuation of foreign debt expressed in national currency. Figures for the debt ratio are, contrary to the deficit ratio, not reported for the 'current year', but only for past years according to Council Regulation No. 3605/93. This does not imply, however, that the Commission cannot take account of the forecasted debt ratio at the end of the year of examination.

As with the deficit criterion, the value of the reference value for the debt criterion is not mentioned in the definition of the criterion, but in Article 1 of the EDP Protocol, and has been set at 60 per cent. This figure could therefore be changed through the amendment procedure of the second subparagraph of paragraph 14.

Subparagraph (b) allows one exception in case the debt ratio exceeds the reference value. Contrary to the deficit criterion, this exception does not require that the debt ratio be close to the reference value. Instead, in order to apply, the exception specifies that the debt ratio should be sufficiently diminishing and approaching the reference value at a satisfactory pace. It is to be noted that the exception does not require the debt ratio to decline continuously, contrary to what is required for the first exception under the deficit criteria. The notion 'sufficiently' under this exception means at least that the debt ratio should not decline by minimal amounts. Together with the notion 'approaching the reference value at a satisfactory pace', it also

---

42. See *supra*, section 3.2.

means that the required size and pace of the decline in the debt ratio are not independent from the debt level relative to the reference value. The more the debt level exceeds the reference value, the bigger should be the size and pace of decline. A judgment on these notions is, again, left to the Commission when it assesses whether the requirements under the debt criterion are fulfilled. It is clear, however, that the exception under the debt criterion can apply at any level of the debt ratio, provided that it is judged that the conditions for the exception are fulfilled. In this respect, the debt criterion differs considerably from the deficit criterion, as to which both exceptions require the deficit in any case to stay close to the reference value.

3.4 The report of the Commission

According to paragraph 3, the Commission has the obligation to prepare a report if a Member State does not fulfil the requirements under one or both of the two criteria under paragraph 2. In addition, the Commission is obliged to prepare such a report if, notwithstanding the fulfilment of the criteria, it is of the opinion that there is a risk of an excessive deficit.[43] The Treaty leaves it therefore to the Commission to assess whether the requirements under the criteria are fulfilled. This, in turn, implies that the Commission has to exercise judgment, because exceptions under both the deficit criterion and the debt criterion contain elements that are not precisely circumscribed,[44] either elsewhere in the Treaty or in secondary legislation. The Treaty does not specify explicitly to whom the report from the Commission should be addressed. It follows from paragraph 4, however, that the report should be discussed by the Committee provided for in Article 109c, and this Committee should therefore receive the report.

If the Commission judges that the requirements under the criteria are fulfilled and that there is no risk of an excessive deficit, it may happen that one or more Member States have a judgment which is different from that of the Commission. In such a case, they could not invoke Article 109d (which refers to recommendations or proposals) or, through their participation in the Council, Article 152 (which refers to studies or proposals) in order to request that the Commission write the report under paragraph 3. The only way to obtain this would be through the procedure for failure to act under Article 175, according to which the Commission should, however, first be invited to act.

On the other hand, if the Commission judges that the requirements under the criteria are not fulfilled or that there is a risk of an excessive deficit, it may happen that a Member State or the Council has a judgement which is

43. See *supra*, section 3.1.
44. See *supra*, sections 3.2 and 3.3.

different from that of the Commission. In such a case, they cannot stop the Commission from preparing the report. The Commission's report is, however, only sent to the Committee provided for in Article 109c and has no other direct implications. Moreover, within the Committee provided for in Article 109c, the members nominated by the Member States in question can express whatever judgment through the opinion which this Committee has to formulate under paragraph 4.

Paragraph 3 requires the Commission, in its report, to take account of all factors which are relevant in judging whether the presumption underlying the existence of the report, namely, that there could exist an excessive deficit, is confirmed. Two such factors are mentioned in paragraph 2: whether the government deficit exceeds government investment expenditure; and the medium term economic and budgetary position of the Member State concerned.

The first of these factors relates to what is known as the 'golden rule of public finance'. Indeed, for instance in a country such as Germany, the federal government and the governments of the Länder are obliged, except in special circumstances, to ensure that the deficit does not exceed investment expenditure.[45] In the context of the EDP, a situation in which a deficit exceeds the reference value, but not the amount of investment expenditure, may be a mitigating factor in evaluating whether an excessive deficit exists. Vice versa, if the deficit exceeds both the reference value and the amount of investment expenditure, this may be an aggravating factor.

The second relevant factor, that is, the medium-term economic and budgetary situation in the Member State, serves several purposes. For instance, it allows analysis of the impact of cyclical factors on the evolution of the deficit: this may give an indication whether the underlying deficit is lower than the effective deficit. It also allows one to look at the medium-term prospects for the evolution of the debt ratio or for the evolution of those non-budgetary variables which are indirectly related to the budgetary situation. For example, the situation on the balance of payments can indicate to what extent dissaving by the government has a negative impact on the balance between savings and investment.[46] Finally, at least in the second stage, the objectives of the convergence programme[47] of the Member State can be provided as an indication of the Member State's medium-term economic and budgetary policy intentions.

45. Art. 115 of the German Grundgesetz (Basic Law).
46. For this reason, the situation on the balance of payments figures among the additional variables to be examined in the reports of the Commission and the EMI in accordance with the last subpara. of Art. 109j (1).
47. Art. 109e (2)(a) of the EC Treaty only requires Member States, if necessary, to adopt a 'convergence programme' before the start of the second stage. In practice, however, such programmes have also been continued to be presented by Member States during the second stage in the context of the multilateral surveillance procedure of Art. 103.

The report of the Commission should indicate the Commission's motivation for establishing the report in terms of fulfilment of the requirements under the criteria of paragraph 2 or in terms of the existence of a risk of an excessive deficit. Beyond providing all relevant factors, however, the report should abstain from a final judgment on the question whether the presumption underlying the existence of the report, namely, that there could exist an excessive deficit, is confirmed. Such a final judgment by the Commission should only be made during the further steps under the EDP, in particular under paragraphs 5 and 6.

3.5 The opinion of the Committee provided for in Article 109c

According to paragraph 4, the Committee provided for in Article 109c (Monetary Committee in the second stage, Economic and Financial Committee after the start of the third stage) should formulate an opinion on the report of the Commission. Since the Commission has the initiative, it follows that the Committee's opinion on whether to take the next step of the EDP under paragraph 5 should be addressed to the Commission such that it can decide whether or not to take this next step.

The opinion of the Committee can logically apply to two elements contained in the report of the Commission. First, it can confirm the grounds on the basis of which the Commission has decided to prepare a report. The Committee can therefore give its opinion on the way in which the Commission has applied the two criteria under paragraph 2 or, as the case may be, on the reasons given by the Commission for the existence of a risk of an excessive deficit. Second, the Committee can give a judgment on the question whether the presumption underlying the existence of the report, namely that there could exist an excessive deficit, is confirmed. The Committee can do so on the basis of an examination of all relevant factors contained in the Commission's report.

Upon receiving the opinion from the Committee, the Commission can decide to proceed with the case, or to drop it. The latter possibility could be relevant if the opinion from the Committee provides convincing arguments that there is no excessive deficit or that there does not exist a risk of an excessive deficit.

3.6 The opinion of the Commission

Should the Commission consider, on the basis of an examination of all relevant factors and after taking into account the opinion from the Committee provided for under Article 109c, that an excessive deficit in a Member State exists or may occur, then it is obliged under paragraph 5 to address an opinion to the Council. The difference between the formulation that an excessive deficit 'exists' or that it 'may occur' corresponds to the difference between not fulfilling the requirements under the criteria of paragraph 2 and the situation where there is a risk of an excessive deficit in the sense of the second subparagraph of paragraph 3. As long as there is a risk, the excessive deficit by definition has not yet occurred. In this context, it should be noted that the existence of an excessive deficit is not a situation which is restricted exclusively to a deficit for any past budget year. The formulation of paragraph 2, for instance, allows explicitly for the existence of a gross error, that is an excessive deficit, on the basis of the planned deficit.

Article 104c does not explicitly provide the obligation for the Commission to wait, or to wait for a reasonable period, for the opinion of the Committee provided for in Article 109c. Nevertheless, given the order of the paragraphs, it would seem logical for the Commission to take account of the opinion of the Committee, also given the fact that the Committee contributes, in accordance with Article 109c (1), second indent, to the preparation of the work of the Council under Article 104c. Should the Committee for one reason or another not be able to formulate an opinion on the report of the Commission under paragraph 4 within a reasonable period of time, then there is no formal reason for the Commission to wait any longer before addressing its opinion under paragraph 5 to the Council.

The opinion addressed by the Commission to the Council under paragraph 5 must be seen in conjunction with the recommendation from the Commission to the Council under paragraph 6. In practice, the opinion under paragraph 5 and the recommendation under paragraph 6 are addressed to the Council at the same moment. Since the opinion under paragraph 5 is the first official signal from the Commission to the Council with regard to the existence of an excessive deficit, the Commission will, in its opinion, duly explain why it considers that an excessive deficit exists or may occur. After having presented all relevant factors, but not a final judgment, in its report under paragraph 3, the opinion therefore constitutes the operative part of the Commission's contribution to the process of identification of an excessive deficit.

3.7 The Council decision on the existence of an excessive deficit

When the Commission addresses its opinion under paragraph 5 to the Council, it will at the same time make a recommendation to the Council inviting it to decide that an excessive deficit exists under paragraph 6.

For the Council decision under paragraph 6, the Treaty departs from the usual practice according to which the Council decides on a proposal from the Commission, rather than on a recommendation. The only difference between the two decision-taking procedures resides here in the type of majority which is required in the Council to amend the recommendation put forward by the Commission.[48]

Before the Council decides on the existence of an excessive deficit in a Member State, it has the obligation to take into consideration any observations which the Member State concerned may wish to make. This requirement bears similarity to a legal proceeding before a court, where the defendant is given the right to defend himself before the court makes its verdict.[49] Secondly, the Council has to take its decision after an overall assessment. This implies that a decision on the existence of an excessive deficit is far from being an automatic decision. Otherwise, a separate assessment by the Council would not be necessary. In particular, the Council should weigh in its assessment the arguments contained in the Commission's opinion against any observations made by the Member State in its 'defence', as well as adding its own overall judgment on the case in question.

If the Commission, in its opinion under paragraph 5 concludes for a Member State that an excessive deficit 'may occur' (as opposed to the conclusion that an excessive deficit 'exists'), the question arises whether the Council can decide under paragraph 6 that an excessive deficit 'exists'. One reason for answering this question negatively would be to say that as long as the excessive deficit has not occurred, there are no grounds for concluding that the excessive deficit has materialised, and that one should wait for this materialisation before deciding that an excessive deficit effectively exists.

The notion 'existence of an excessive deficit' is, however, not confined to past events, as witnessed by the fact that the deficit criterion also applies to 'planned' deficits. Also other, clearly identifiable, factors that bear on the budgetary situation in any year beyond the year of examination by the Commission could lead to the existence of an excessive deficit, even if the latter has not yet materialised. Examples of such factors are budgets which have been formally proposed by a Member State government for any year later than the year of examination, or contingent liabilities which are known, or are highly likely, to fall due in such a later year.[50] By identifying an excessive deficit which could materialise in a future year, the Council contributes to the purpose of 'avoiding' 'excessive deficits, even more so because the first actions which the Council undertakes after identifying the excessive deficit consist of measures which are not legally binding, *in casu* the recommendations under paragraphs 7 or 8.

---

48. See *infra*, section 7.1.
49. See *infra*, section 7.2.
50. Examples of contingent liabilities which may fall due are preannounced takeovers by the central or federal government of debts of those public bodies which do not fall under the definition of 'general government' which is relevant for the EDP. In Germany, the preannounced takeover of the Treuhand debt by the federal government in 1995 constitutes a case of a preannounced debt takeover.

In its decision, the Council should, for legal clarity, indicate the reasons for the existence of an excessive deficit. It can refer to the opinion of the Commission. By indicating the reasons for the existence of an excessive deficit, the Council defines implicitly under which conditions the excessive deficit would no longer exist, *ceteris paribus*. The speed at which to return to these conditions should, however, form the subject of the recommendations under paragraph 7.

4.   ACTIONS TAKEN BY THE COUNCIL

Upon the identification of the existence of an excessive deficit by the Council under paragraph 6, the Council is obliged to undertake action with a view to ensuring that the Member State concerned corrects the situation. In a first instance, these actions by the Council do not yet have the character of outright sanctions, even though they could have an impact on the assessment by financial markets of the creditworthiness of the government of the Member State concerned, and thus result in sanctions by the market. The Council actions prior to the use of sanctions (which are however only possible in Stage Three) consist of recommendations that are not made public under paragraph 7, recommendations that are made public under paragraph 8, and, for Member States participating in Stage Three, the use of a formal notice to the Member State concerned to take measures for the necessary deficit reduction under paragraph 9.

4.1   The confidential recommendation by the Council

The recommendations by the Council under paragraph 7 are the only action which the Council is obliged to undertake once it has decided under paragraph 6 that an excessive deficit exists. The recommendations, however, do not necessarily have to be adopted at the same time as the decision under paragraph 6.[51]

Paragraph 7 requires that the recommendations are made with a view to bringing the situation of an excessive deficit to an end within a given period. This requirement must be interpreted differently, on the one hand, for Member States participating in the third stage and, on the other hand, for Member States not participating in the third stage, or during the second

---

51. The first time the EDP was applied, was when the Council made its decisions on 19 Sept. 1994 on the existence of an excessive deficit for 10 Member States (at that time, all Member States excluding Ireland and Luxembourg). The Council then only adopted the recommendations under para. 7 on 7 Nov. 1994.

stage. For Member States participating in the third stage, it may be assumed that they are not in the situation of an excessive deficit at the time they join in the third stage. When they switch from a situation of not having an excessive deficit to one where they have one, it must be possible, in all likelihood, to take measures to reverse this situation within a relatively short period of, say, one or two years. In those circumstances, and due to the fact that the presence of an excessive deficit for a Member State participating in the third stage constitutes a greater negative externality for other Member States than during the second stage or in case that Member State does not participate in the third stage, it seems natural to lay down precisely the period within which the excessive deficit situation has to be brought to an end.

In other cases, that is during the second stage or in the case of a Member State which does not participate in the third stage, there is *a priori* no reason to assume that the period within which the situation of an excessive deficit has to be brought to an end is as short as one or two years. Indeed, the question of whether the Council can lay down a period within which the Member State concerned should bring the situation to an end is unlikely to be answered positively during Stage Two or for Member States not participating in Stage Three. This follows from the fact that one cannot oblige Member States to pursue the abrogation of their excessive deficit according to any particular schedule as long as they do not participate in the third stage. At most, there are the deadlines laid down in the Treaty for the decisions as regards the start of, and participation in, the third stage that could provide an incentive to the Member States (excluding those exercising their right for an exemption). To the extent that these, or other, considerations result in medium-term objectives for budgetary policy, such objectives provide an indication of the period over which the excessive deficit is intended to be corrected by the Member States. Indeed, the practice developed by Member States under the multilateral surveillance procedure of Article 103 to continue to present and update 'convergence programmes' (as originally only required by Article 109e (2)(a), second indent, prior to the start of the third stage) will add to the availability of such medium-term objectives.

Given the uncertainty about the year-to-year evolution of medium-term economic and budgetary objectives, the recommendations during Stage Two or for Member States not participating in Stage Three can only refer to precise objectives for a short period, for example not going beyond the year following the year of adoption of the recommendations by the Council. Paragraph 7 provides the basis for thus adopting several consecutive recommendations which refer to precise objectives for the short-term. This possibility has the advantage that each consecutive recommendation can be adapted to the latest evolution of the economic and budgetary situation, and would continue to be a relevant input into a Member State's budgetary policy process. Moreover, if the period laid down in the consecutive precise recommendations is short, this allows the Council to take further steps under paragraph 8 if there is no effective action in that period in response to the recommendations under paragraph 7.

4.2 The public recommendation by the Council

Paragraph 8 gives the Council the possibility, where it establishes that there has been no effective action in response to its recommendations under paragraph 7 within the period laid down, to make its recommendations public. The Council, however, has no obligation to do so.

The possibility to make a public recommendation is meant to bring into the open the Council's finding that a Member State is not following up on the Council's recommendations in an effective way. The relevant finding is not that the recommendations have not been followed, but that no effective action has resulted, that is action with the effect of bringing the excessive deficit situation to an end within a given period. This leaves it up to the Member States to decide by which means to achieve this objective. The publication of the recommendations gives financial markets a visible signal that the Council is discontent with the action of the Member State concerned, which could therefore lead to stronger market pressure in the form of, for instance, lower credit ratings. By rendering the recommendations public, the Council also opens up the opportunity for the public to scrutinise whether the subsequent results in the budgetary area for the Member State concerned are in line with the recommendations from the Council. This transparency again could sharpen or at least accelerate market pressure on the Member State concerned.

Paragraph 8 can only be invoked by the Council if the 'period laid down' under paragraph 7 has expired. However, this period is not necessarily the same period as the 'given period' under paragraph 7. The 'period laid down' may very well correspond to a shorter period for which the Council has given a precise recommendation. The possibility to make recommendations public after a shorter period than the 'given period' within which to bring the excessive deficit situation to an end is especially relevant during the second stage or for Member States not participating in the third stage. In case a Member State needs a long period to correct the situation, it would make little sense, if there is no effective action towards the correction of the situation in accordance with precise recommendations for a shorter time horizon, to wait any longer with stepping up the pressure on the Member State through a recommendation that is made public.

The content of the public recommendation is not necessarily equal to that under paragraph 7. First, since time has elapsed between the two recommendations, it may be necessary to update the recommendation in

217

accordance with the most recent information. Second, the Council may not want to disclose confidential information or other information which goes beyond what is needed to display publicly that the Member State's action is insufficient. Third, a public recommendation under paragraph 8 has to be formulated such that when the Member State concerned puts it into practice, the abrogation, under paragraph 12, of the public recommendation should automatically entail the abrogation of the Council decision under paragraph 6 on the existence of an excessive deficit. The latter follows from the formulation under paragraph 12, which states that as soon as the Council has abrogated the public recommendations made under paragraph 8, it has to make a public statement that an excessive deficit in the Member State concerned no longer exists. For the content of the public recommendation, the need for joint abrogation of the decisions under paragraphs 6 and 7 implies that it should lay down the period within which to bring the excessive deficit situation to an end. The possibility is left open, however, to make precise recommendations for several consecutive shorter time periods, as long as they cover the whole period within which to bring the excessive deficit situation to an end.

If neither the recommendations for a consecutive short time period are put into practice nor the excessive deficit has been eliminated after the expiry of the whole given period, the Council can use paragraph 8 as a legal basis to make other public recommendations. During the second stage, or concerning Member States which do not participate in the third stage, this is obvious because paragraph 9 cannot be applied. But even for Member States participating in the third stage, the Council is not obliged to apply paragraph 9, although this is suggested by the order of the paragraphs 7, 8 and 9. The reason for this conclusion derives, on the one hand, from the fact that the Council has no obligation to apply paragraph 9 if a Member State fails to put into practice the recommendations of the Council and, on the other hand, from the fact that the requirement for the application of paragraph 8 is only that there has not been effective action in response to 'its recommendations', without specifying that these recommendations are exclusively the recommendations under paragraph 7.

4.3   The possibility for the Council to give notice to a Member State

Paragraph 9 can only be applied to Member States participating in the third stage. It gives the Council the possibility (but not the obligation) to give notice to a Member State which persists in failing to put into practice the Council's recommendations; the notice is a request to the Member State to take, within a specified time limit, measures for the deficit reduction which is judged necessary by the Council in order to remedy the situation. It is presumably the legally binding character of this Council measure which has made the legislator decide to apply it only to Member States participating in the third stage. The legally binding character derives from the sanctions which failure to comply with the notice may entail under paragraph 11. In this respect, even though the expression 'giving notice' has a certain connotation because it appears elsewhere in the Treaty (Article 93), this step must be considered to be the counterpart of the 'reasoned opinion' under Article 171 which, in cases brought before the Court of Justice may also, after several steps, lead to (financial) sanctions.

Although it is not said explicitly, the presumption before applying paragraph 9 is that recommendations have first been made not only under paragraph 7 but also under paragraph 8. This follows from the condition specified in paragraph 9 that a Member State 'persists' in failing to put into practice the Council's recommendations. In particular, it is not possible to apply paragraph 9 without having applied paragraph 8. On the other hand, a repeated application of paragraph 8 without applying paragraph 9 is not ruled out by the Treaty.[52]

The notice to the Member State should concentrate on the specific deficit reduction which is judged necessary by the Council in order to remedy the situation rather than on the measures to achieve this objective. Furthermore, the Council should specify a time limit within which the measures need to be taken.

The expression 'deficit reduction' which is referred to in this paragraph must, as in the expression 'excessive deficit', be interpreted as a *pars pro toto*. It may very well be that the deficit *per se* fulfils the requirements under the deficit criteria, but that the requirements under the debt criterion are not fulfilled. In such a case, the notice to the Member State may concern a given reduction in the debt ratio rather than in the deficit. Although a reduction of the former generally requires a reduction in the latter, the debt ratio may also be reduced by other means, notably by liquidation of government assets. Such financial operations, for example, privatisations, will reduce the stock of debt while generally not affecting the deficit.

In case the Council gives a notice to a Member State under paragraph 9, it may in accordance with the second subparagraph, also request the Member State concerned to submit reports in accordance with a specific timetable in order to examine the adjustment efforts of that Member State. In case the adjustment efforts of the Member States are not commensurate with the necessary reduction, but the specified time limit has not yet been reached, the Council can renew its notice to the Member State concerned, including the specification of a new time limit if this is judged necessary by the Council. The possibility for renewal follows from the fact that in case of non-compliance with the deficit reduction imposed under the Council

---

52. See *supra*, section 4.2.

notice, the Council has no obligation to pursue the next step, that is the imposition of sanctions under paragraph 11.

There is a possible incoherence between the fact that under paragraph 9 the Council can request reports to be submitted by a Member State and Articles 3 and 4 of the EDP protocol which lay down that, for the normal reporting under EDP, the Member States report to the Commission, which in turn provides the data for the application of the EDP Protocol. The role of the Commission in normal reporting is to ensure that the data are in conformity with the definitions. Furthermore, in the case of overly optimistic – or pessimistic – assumptions by the Member States concerning the evolution of variables for the year in which the reporting takes place, the Commission can replace the reported data by what it considers to be more realistic figures. This particular role of the Commission may get lost if the information which is reported by the Member States following a Council request under paragraph 9 is used without further scrutiny. It must therefore be assumed that the information requested by the Council is distinct from that reported under the rules of Articles 3 and 4 of the EDP Protocol.

5.   SANCTIONS

As long as the Member State with an excessive deficit fails to comply with the decision taken by the Council under paragraph 9, the Council has the possibility, under paragraph 11, to apply or intensify one or more of four measures. If there is no compliance with the Council decision under paragraph 9, this means that the Member State concerned has not taken measures, within a specified time-period, for the necessary deficit reduction. Measures under paragraph 11 can therefore only be decided if the Council has previously taken a decision under paragraph 9 and after the expiration of the specified time period.

The measures which the Council, without having an obligation, may impose are intended to serve as sanctions which should give a maximum incentive to the Member State concerned to correct the situation. As long as the Member State concerned does not comply with the decision under paragraph 9, the Council has a large degree of freedom in imposing the sanctions. It may apply, as it sees fit, one or more of them without respecting any particular order or being restricted as regards the combination. It may also restrict the sanctions under the first and second indent over time beforehand, although it can only abrogate a sanction which is in force in accordance with paragraph 12, that is, if there is partial or complete correction of the excessive deficit. Furthermore, it may renew an existing sanction upon expiry, or add a sanction to one or more existing sanctions.

The intensification of a sanction, which is explicitly mentioned in the first subparagraph of paragraph 11, is possible because the formulation of some of the sanctions, in particular the sanctions specified in the third and fourth indent of paragraph 11, leaves the Council the choice to determine their severity.

Although the Council has complete freedom to choose any combination of one or more from the list of four sanctions, it is clear that the order of the sanctions is intended to be one of progressive strength.

The first sanction allows the Council to impose on the Member State the publication of additional information before issuing bonds and securities. The purpose of this sanction is, first, to render the issuing of debt for the Member State more expensive through the obligation to publish additional information and, second, to increase awareness of the markets of the fragile budgetary situation in the Member State, such that more market pressure will be exerted towards the elimination of the excessive deficit. This sanction should be seen in relation to the Prospectus Directive[53] which imposes certain obligations on issuers of transferable securities in terms of the information they have to provide to potential buyers, and of which public authorities are excluded in accordance with Article 2, subparagraph 2(c) of the Prospectus Directive. Although information on a Member State's budgetary situation is usually well known, the Council may impose the publication of additional information which could provide the public with the means to make a more complete risk assessment of buying government debt paper.

The second sanction gives the Council the possibility to invite the European Investment Bank to reconsider its lending policy towards the Member State concerned. At first sight, this sanction may only seem to entail a general signal to the EIB that it should be careful in its lending to the Member State concerned. However, since the Board of Governors, which decides on the general directives for the credit policy of the EIB by majority,[54] consists of the ministers designated by the Member States,[55] the implication of this sanction is more far-reaching because the EIB would in practice be under strong pressure to execute that which the Council would consider as an appropriate change in the EIB's lending policy. The Council is therefore, if it invokes this sanction, not restricted to a general invitation to the EIB: it could suggest concrete measures regarding changes in the lending policy. Ultimately, such changes could lead to complete suspension of loans

---

53. Council Directive 89/298/EEC of 17.4.89 co-ordinating the requirements for the drawing up, scrutiny and distribution of the prospectus to be published when transferable securities are offered to the public.
54. Art. 10 of the EIB Statutes. In addition, the majority should represent at least 50 per cent of the subscribed capital to the EIB.
55. Art. 9 of the EIB Statutes.

from the EIB in the Member State concerned. In such a case, the cost of borrowing would increase because the borrowers affected in the Member State would in general need to go to commercial banks which usually charge higher interest rates.

The third sanction which the Council can apply consists of the requirement for the Member State concerned to make a non-interest-bearing deposit of an appropriate size with the Community until the excessive deficit has, in the view of the Council, been corrected. This sanction can therefore not be restricted over time beforehand, because the return of the deposit to the Member State can only take place once the excessive deficit has been corrected. The latter, in its turn, requires the abrogation, under paragraph 12, of the Council decision under paragraph 6. The fact that the non-interest-bearing deposit has to be of an appropriate size reflects the idea that the sanction needs to be in proportion with the size of the gross error committed by having an excessive deficit and failing to remedy the situation in accordance with the Council's decision. Thus, all other things being equal, a larger Member State (in economic terms, *eg*, gross domestic product) will have to make a larger deposit than a smaller Member State. Similarly, all other things being equal, a Member State with a big excessive deficit will have to deposit more than a Member State with a small excessive deficit. The deposit itself has to be made with the Community and any interest on the deposit would constitute revenue for the Community.[56]

The sanctions foreseen in the first three indents of paragraph 11 are all reversible in the sense that they can be abrogated under paragraph 12. The sanction foreseen under the fourth indent of paragraph 11, that is, the imposition by the Council of fines of appropriate size, is, however, not reversible. This sanction is therefore to be considered as the strictest of the four sanctions. The fact that such fines should be of appropriate size has the same interpretation as in the sanction under the third indent: the size should relate to the economic size of the Member State (*eg*, gross domestic product) and to the extent to which the deficit is excessive. The fine has to be paid to the Community and constitutes revenue of the Community in the same way as, for instance, financial penalties in respect of firms as foreseen under Article 87 and Article 88 of the ECSC Treaty or in respect of Member States under Article 171. In fact, in the same way as the Council decision under paragraph 9 resembles the procedure under Article 171 (2), first subparagraph, the imposition of a fine under paragraph 11 is considered as the equivalent of the imposition of a lump sum or penalty payment on a Member State under the fourth subparagraph of Article 171 (2).

---

56. Since the Commission implements the budget of the Community, the deposit has to be made with the Commission. Contrary to what has been proposed by R. Smits, 'De Monetaire Unie van Maastricht' (1992) 8/9 *SEW* 702, p.713, it is therefore not possible that the deposit be made with the European Central Bank.

The President of the Council has to inform the European Parliament of the decisions taken under paragraph 11. This is the only moment during the EDP where the European Parliament is informed of any of the results of the EDP (except for the role of the European Parliament in the secondary legislation under paragraph 14). The reason for this must mainly[57] be seen, on the one hand, in the confidential nature of most of the proceedings under the EDP and, on the other hand, in the fact that the European Parliament, together with the Council, makes up the budgetary authority of the Community.

6.   ABROGATION OF COUNCIL DECISIONS

Paragraph 12 foresees an explicit procedure for the abrogation of the Council decisions under paragraphs 6, 7, 8, 9 or 11 of the EDP. There are three reasons for having an explicit abrogation procedure. First, in the context of the procedure of Article 109j for transition to the third stage, the criterion under the second indent of Article 109j (1) refers to the requirement of a 'government budgetary position without a deficit that is excessive as determined in accordance with Article 104c (6)'. In case the Council has decided on the existence of an excessive deficit in accordance with paragraph 6, this requirement is therefore only fulfilled if any previous decision under paragraph 6 is explicitly abrogated. Second, since the EDP is a procedure of graduated response, it is appropriate that if a Member State with an excessive deficit is making progress in correcting this situation, the Council decisions constituting the graduated response, in particular some of the sanctions, are also gradually abrogated in line with the progress made by the Member State. Third, in its original conception, the Council decisions under paragraphs 6 and 7 were supposed to be confidential,[58] while only a Council decision under paragraph 8, by definition, would be made public. Only in the latter case would the public know that a Member State had an excessive deficit. In such a case, as long as the Council did not explicitly state the contrary, the public would therefore have no reason to believe that the excessive deficit had disappeared. For this reason, paragraph 12 requires a public statement to be made as soon as the decision under paragraph 8 has been abrogated.

---

57. In addition to the value deriving, in the context of transparency, from informing the European Parliament of the Council's decisions.
58. Already in its first application of the EDP, the Council made a statement announcing for which Member States it had taken decisions under para. 6 (Council meeting of 19 Sept. 1994) and under para. 7 (Council meeting of 7 Nov. 1994).

The graduated abrogation of Council decisions under the EDP is reflected in the first sentence of paragraph 12, which obliges the Council to abrogate some or all of its decisions under paragraphs 6–9 and 11 to the extent that the excessive deficit has, in the view of the Council, been corrected. The idea reflected in this provision is not only that all relevant Council decisions are to be abrogated once the excessive deficit has been completely corrected, but also that abrogation of a limited number of decisions should already take place once sufficient progress with the correction of the excessive deficit has been made, even if the excessive deficit has not yet been completely corrected.

Although partial abrogation (*ie*, abrogation of some decisions without abrogation of the decision on the existence of an excessive deficit under paragraph 6) in principle is possible for all Council decisions under paragraphs 7 to 9 and 11, the possibilities are in practice limited to abrogation of the decisions under paragraph 9 and under paragraph 11, first and second indent. This follows from: (i) the fact that the imposition of a fine under the fourth indent of paragraph 11 is not a reversible decision;[59] (ii) the fact that the non-interest bearing deposit under the third indent of paragraph 11, once decided, is not returned until the excessive deficit has been corrected; (iii) the requirement from the second sentence of paragraph 12 that the abrogation of a public recommendation made under paragraph 8 has to be accompanied by a public statement that the excessive deficit in the Member State no longer exists, that is, that the Council decision under paragraph 6 is also abrogated; (iv) the fact that the compulsory joint abrogation of decisions under paragraphs 8 and 6 which follows from (iii) also implies the abrogation of decisions under paragraph 7 at the same time; and (v) the fact that decisions under paragraph 7 cannot be abrogated separately from paragraph 6, since the existence of a decision under paragraph 6 always implies the existence of a decision under paragraph 7.

7.   INSTITUTIONAL PROVISIONS

7.1   The rules for decision-taking by the Council

In the context of the EDP, decisions by the Council are foreseen under paragraphs 6 to 9, 11 and 14. In accordance with the Declaration on Part

---

59. This would be different in the case of a periodic penalty payment of the type foreseen, for instance, under Art. 87. In such a case, the periodic penalty payment could be installed until sufficient progress with the correction of the excessive deficit would have been made.

Three, Titles III and VI, of the Treaty establishing the European Community added to the final Act of the Maastricht Treaty, this will normally be the Council in the composition of economic and finance ministers. Whereas the Council acts under paragraph 14 constitute Community legislation in the classical sense,[60] those under the other paragraphs have a special character which is reflected in the rules for decision-taking. For paragraph 6, this rule is spelled out explicitly in the paragraph itself. It lays down that the Council acts by a qualified majority on a recommendation from the Commission. For paragraphs 7–9 and 11, there is a common decision rule which is spelled out in paragraph 13, and which lays down that the Council acts on a recommendation from the Commission by a majority of two thirds of the votes of its members weighted in accordance with Article 148 (2), excluding the votes of the representative of the Member State concerned.[61]

The common feature of these rules is that the Council acts on a recommendation from the Commission instead of on a proposal, as is the usual practice for Council acts.[62] The difference between the two cases rests on the fact that, whereas the Council can, under Article 189a (1) only amend a Commission proposal with unanimity, it can amend a Commission recommendation for a particular Council act by the same majority as whereby it has to adopt the act itself. This difference does not affect the Commission's right of initiative: it can always withdraw its recommendation such that the Council cannot act.[63] In the case of a Council act which is directed at a particular Member State, such as the acts under paragraphs 6–9 and 11, the rule according to which the Council acts on a recommendation from the Commission implies that the Member State concerned cannot block any amendment to the Commission's recommendations, as long as their exists the necessary majority for the amendment in the Council. Whereas this reasoning makes sense for the Council decision under paragraph 6, it cannot be applied to the decisions under paragraphs 7–9 and 11, because in those cases the votes from the Member State concerned are excluded. Indeed, for decisions under those paragraphs, the only effect from deciding on a recommendation rather than on a proposal from the Commission is to make it easier for the Council to amend the Commission's recommendation.

It is an innovative feature of the Maastricht Treaty that according to the decision rules under paragraphs 7–9 and 11 the votes from the Member State

---

60. See *infra*, section 7.3.
61. Although this voting rule is close to that of a qualified majority in the sense of Art. 148 (2), the provision of the second indent of Art. 148 (2) concerning the minimum number of votes cast in favour must be deemed not to be applicable here.
62. The recommendation of the Commission in such a case is not related to a recommendation in the sense of Art. 189.
63. Under Art. 109d, however, the Council or a Member State can request the Commission to make a recommendation under paras. 6–9 or 11. The Commission has to examine this request and submit its conclusions to the Council without delay.

concerned are excluded. The effect of this exclusion is that the Member State concerned is not given an unequal advantage as regards the number of votes needed for a minority that can block the decision on the Council act. In other words, it is not made easier for Member States with a relatively large number of votes to block a Council act under paragraphs 7–9 or 11 that concerns them, than for Member States with a relatively small number of votes.

The committee referred to in Article 109c is involved in the EDP not only explicitly through paragraph 4, but also because of the role assigned to it in Article 109c (1), third indent and Article 109 (c), third indent, according to which the committee contributes, without prejudice to Article 151, to the preparations for the work of the Council.

7.2 The role of the Court of Justice

Paragraph 10 lays down that the rights to bring actions provided for in Articles 169 and 170 may not be exercised within the framework of paragraphs 1–9. Concretely, this means that neither the Commission, nor any member State can obtain through the Court of Justice that influence is exercised on a Member State's public finances without the political legitimacy of a decision by the Council. In particular, this provision precludes the application of any sanction by the Court of Justice in accordance with Article 171. Whereas this provision excludes an 'active' role for the Court of Justice in these paragraphs of the EDP, its 'passive' role in terms of, for instance, annulment procedures under Article 173 against Council decisions taken under paragraphs 6–9 is not affected. Similarly, procedures for failure to act under Article 175 could be started, but these would be directed at the Commission or the Council in this context, and not at any Member State.[64]

Although the restriction of the role of the Court of Justice applies to all paragraphs 1–9, it has particular significance for paragraphs 1, 6 and 9 individually. In the context of paragraph 1, it implies that the Commission or the Member States cannot use the Court of Justice to enforce the avoidance of excessive deficits by a Member State, thereby emphasising that paragraph 1 is not directly applicable. Without the restrictions, the Court of Justice could have been asked to pronounce itself on whether a particular Member State has an excessive deficit and, if so, to impose on the Member State measures which it should take to correct the excessive deficit situation, failing which financial sanctions could be imposed. The Court of Justice, for instance, would in such a case be given the responsibility to interpret the

---

64. J. Pipkorn, 'Der Rechtliche Rahmen der Wirtschafts- und Währungsunion' [1994] *EuR*, Beiheft 1, pp.85–95.

two criteria of paragraph 2 or even to apply the relevant factors mentioned in paragraph 3.[65] Even if the Court of Justice were not to be given the possibility to rule on the existence or not of an excessive deficit, the application of Articles 169 or 170, once an excessive deficit would have been decided under paragraph 6, could have led to the imposition of the Court of Justice of measures or sanctions on the Member State concerned. For paragraphs 7 and 8 the non-applicability of Articles 169 or 170 is less relevant, since Council recommendations are not binding, and their non-respect could therefore not be challenged under those Articles. The Council decision under paragraph 9, however, is legally binding, so that its non-respect could have been challenged under Articles 169 and 170 if it had been made applicable, again possibly leading to sanctions. In this case, it is not only the verification by the Court of Justice of the fact whether the Member State has complied with the notice under paragraph 9 which is the object of exclusion, but also the nature of the sanctions which can be given in the case of non-compliance. The determination of sanctions is left to the Council in paragraph 11.

The application of Articles 169 and 170 is not suppressed for paragraph 11. Indeed, an infringement procedure by the Commission or a Member State against another Member State is in this case restricted to non-compliance with the sanctions which the Council can impose under paragraph 11.[66] The establishment of non-compliance with the sanctions does not carry the degree of judgment involved in the paragraphs for which Articles 169 and 170 do not apply: it is therefore normal that an infringement procedure could be invoked against a Member State which does not comply with any of the sanctions imposed on it.

7.3 Secondary legislation

Paragraph 14, second and third subparagraphs, allows the Council to lay down two types of additional legislation. In the first place, there is the obligation for the Council, in accordance with the third subparagraph, to lay down, before 1 January 1994, detailed rules and definitions for the application of the EDP Protocol. The Council complied with this obligation through adoption of Council Regulation No. 3605/93. This Regulation lays down a number of definitions for the application of the EDP Protocol, as well as the rules and coverage for the reporting by the Member States of data

---

65. The Court of Justice would still have to make such interpretations under the procedures of Art. 173, but in this case it would, in all likelihood, allow a margin of interpretation by the Council.

66. R. Geiger, *EG-Vertrag, Kommentar zu dem Vertrag zur Gründung der Europäischen Gemeinschaft* (1993).

relevant for the EDP. It is clear that without such definitions and rules, the direct applicability of the EDP Protocol would be difficult to impose.

The fact that paragraph 14 specifies that the Council has to adopt this legislation before 1 January 1994 does not preclude that the Council could adopt such legislation also after that date. This could be necessary, for instance, if the EDP Protocol were to be modified in accordance with the second subparagraph of paragraph 14. Indeed, the provisions of this subparagraph allow the Council to adopt, by unanimity, on a proposal from the Commission and after consulting the European Parliament and the ECB,[67] appropriate provisions which would replace the EDP Protocol. Since the EDP Protocol is an integral part of the Treaty, this would mean a modification of the Treaty without applying the procedure of Article N of the Maastricht Treaty.[68] The modifications which could be introduced in any new EDP Protocol could be wide-ranging: the only constraint is that the new EDP Protocol would comply with paragraph 14, first subparagraph, according to which it could contain further provisions relating to the implementation of the procedure described in Article 104c.

On the one hand, a new EDP Protocol could be used to introduce additional provisions regarding the implementation of the EDP to the extent that the existing provisions were judged insufficient.[69] For instance, such new provisions could specify in more detail the meaning or definition of certain concepts used in Article 104c, such as the meaning of 'all other relevant factors' in paragraph 3. On the other hand, a new EDP Protocol could be used to modify the existing provisions if they were no longer judged to be satisfactory. In particular, a new EDP Protocol could modify upward or downward the reference values for the two criteria of paragraph 2. This would, however, have important implications for the results of the procedure and therefore the contribution of the EDP to a high degree of convergence. These implications for convergence also explain why a new EDP Protocol has to be adopted by unanimity and why the ECB has to be consulted.

---

67. As a result of Art. 109f (8), the consultative tasks of the ECB are undertaken by the EMI prior to the establishment of the ECB. Following the same Article, the consultative tasks of the EMI were undertaken by the Committee of Governors prior to 1 Jan. 1994.
68. See *supra*, n.39.
69. Further detailed rules and definitions of the existing provisions of the EDP Protocol would not need to be laid down in a new EDP Protocol, since they can be specified in secondary legislation under para. 14, subpara. 3.

8. RELATIONSHIP WITH OTHER PROVISIONS

Through the numbering of the article, the legislator has indicated that Article 104c bears a certain relationship with the other Articles of which the number starts with '104'. Indeed, Articles 104, 104a, 104b and 104c constitute together the provisions which should, first, ensure that governments are obliged to finance their deficits and debts under market conditions and, second, to the extent that market pressure is insufficient to bring governments to avoid excessive deficits, exert sufficient pressure on them with a view to re-establishing sound public finances. In doing so, these Articles therefore support, and give meaning to, the general principles of Articles 3a and 102a.

The existence of a separate procedure in the case of excessive deficits raises the question to which extent the multilateral surveillance procedure of Article 103 can also address the budgetary situation in the Member States. In this respect, it is important to note that, according to paragraph 2, the EDP is limited to situations which constitute a 'gross error'. In other words, the application of the EDP is restricted to the minimum requirements on the budgetary situation that are compatible with participation in a monetary union. This is quite distinct from the co-ordination of economic policies that takes place under the multilateral surveillance procedure of Article 103 which could, in principle, go much further as regards the desirable features of budgetary policy,[70] albeit it in a less binding way than the EDP, at least in the third stage. During the second stage, or in the case of Member States not participating in the third stage, there is however a certain parallel between the two procedures because they each allow for confidential recommendations or recommendations which can be made public.[71]

Theoretically, for instance in the case of broad guidelines which recommend that the budget deficit should be close to zero, a Member State could be the subject of two recommendations: one under the EDP, in case it

---

70. In the broad guidelines of the economic policies of the Member States and of the Community of 22 Dec. 1993, the Council recommends, for instance, that government budgets of the Member States should perhaps be close to balance by the year 2000; (1994) OJ L7/9.

71. The decision procedures, however, are not the same in the two cases. A confidential recommendation under Art. 103 (4) of the EC Treaty is adopted by the Council *including* the votes of the Member State concerned, while these votes are *excluded* for a confidential recommendation under Art. 104c (7). The same difference also holds when the Council makes its recommendations public under Art. 103 (4) or under Art. 104c (8). Finally, recommendations could, in theory, be made public directly under Art. 103 (4), while this is only possible under Art. 104c (8) if there has not been any effective action in pursuance of the confidential recommendations of Art. 104c (7). For other differences in these procedures, see A. Italianer, 'Convergence in Europe, State of Affairs', in A. Wildavsky and E. Zapico-Goni (eds), *National Budgeting for Economic and Monetary Union* (1993), pp.13–31.

has an excessive deficit and another under the multilateral surveillance procedure, because its budget deficit is also not consistent with the broad guidelines. For Member States participating in the third stage, the EDP could then become more binding by involving paragraphs 9 and 11 in the case of non-compliance with the recommendations under paragraph 8, while the multilateral surveillance procedure has no other means to exert pressure beyond confidential or public recommendations. Member states participating in the third stage could thus be faced with sanctions imposed by the Council under the EDP for that part of their budget deficit which is excessive, while they could receive a Council recommendation under the multilateral surveillance procedure for the remaining part of the deficit to the extent that it deviates from the broad guidelines.

The Council is not the only Community body which can address recommendations to the Member States regarding their budgetary situation. In accordance with Article 109f (4), second indent, the EMI can issue opinions or recommendations to governments and to the Council on policies which might affect the internal or external monetary situation in the Community and, in particular, the functioning of the EMS. Clearly, sound public finances are important for monetary stability. The EMI could therefore issue opinions or make recommendations to governments of the Member States regarding their budgetary policy. In doing so, the EMI should, however, respect the competences of the other Community institutions in the context of the EDP. The limited stature of the EMI in this area is also illustrated by the fact that the advisory functions of the ECB with respect to national authorities, in accordance with Article 105 (4), are much more circumscribed, and limited exclusively to matters falling under the ECB's competence.

The EDP has special significance in the context of the process of convergence that is relevant for the transition to, and participation in, the third stage of EMU. Article 109j (1), second indent, and Article 2 of the Protocol on the convergence criteria referred to in Article 109j Treaty specify as one of the convergence criteria the sustainability of the government financial position, which should be apparent from the absence of a Council decision on the existence of an excessive deficit under paragraph 6. In order to comply with this criterion, a Member State should therefore not have been the subject of a Council decision under paragraph 6, or if it has been, this decision should have been abrogated in accordance with paragraph 12. From the way this convergence criterion has been formulated, it appears that the relevant criterion is not whether the requirements under the deficit criterion and the debt criterion of paragraph 2 are fulfilled, but whether the Council has decided on the existence of an excessive deficit. This makes the compliance with this convergence criterion a fact which is simple to verify.

Related to the process of convergence is also a provision in the Protocol on economic and social cohesion annexed to the Treaty ('Cohesion Protocol'), 15th paragraph, according to which a Cohesion Fund has to be established for which Member States are eligible which, *inter alia*, meet the requirement that they have a programme leading to the fulfilment of the conditions of for economic convergence as set out in Article 104c. The underlying idea behind this provision is that, in support of the efforts by such Member States to achieve and maintain a situation without an excessive deficit, they receive financial transfers as a contribution to their process of economic development. Given this underlying idea of a *quid pro quo*, it is not surprising to find in the Council Regulation establishing the Cohesion Fund[72] not only the formal eligibility criterion of the existence of a programme leading to the fulfilment of the conditions of economic convergence, but also, in Article 6, a conditionality provision. This provision lays down that the financing of new projects or, in the case of large multi-stage projects, no new stages of a project shall be suspended if the Council decision under paragraph 6 has not been abrogated in accordance with the provision of paragraph 12 within one year or any other period laid down for correcting the deficit in a recommendation under paragraph 7.[73] As long as the Member State concerned complies with the recommendations under paragraph 7, it will therefore not see its financing suspended.

9.   THE PROTOCOL ON THE EXCESSIVE DEFICIT PROCEDURE

The Protocol on the excessive deficit procedure has been annexed to Treaty and therefore, in accordance with Article 239, forms an integral part of it. The EDP Protocol may, however, in accordance with paragraph 14, second subparagraph, be replaced by new provisions by the Council, acting unanimously on a proposal from the Commission, and after consulting the European Parliament and the European Central Bank.[74] The purpose of the EDP Protocol is defined in paragraph 14, first subparagraph as containing further provisions relating to the implementation of the EDP. The provisions

---

72. Council Regulation No. 1164/94.
73. A further condition is that the suspension shall not take effect less than two years after the entry into force of the Maastricht Treaty. Furthermore, the Council is allowed, acting by a qualified majority on a proposal from the Commission, to defer the suspension of financing exceptionally in the case of projects directly affecting more than one Member State.
74. See *supra*, section 7.3.

may be divided into definitions, reporting obligations and other obligations. Detailed rules and definitions concerning the application of these provisions of the EDP Protocol are given in Council Regulation No. 3605/93.

9.1 Definitions

The most important definitions of the EDP Protocol are undoubtedly those given in its Article 1, which lay down the reference values for the deficit criterion and the debt criterion of paragraph 2 as being equal to 3 per cent for the deficit criterion and being equal to 60 per cent for the debt criterion. By defining these reference values in the EDP Protocol rather than in the main body of Article 104c, and by giving the possibility to modify the EDP Protocol – including the reference values – by a more simple procedure than that of Article N of the Maastricht Treaty, the legislator has admitted that there may be circumstances under which, albeit by unanimity, the Council could need to modify the reference values without going through the heavy process of Treaty modification through ratification by the Member States. One of the reasons underlying this possibility was the desire to strengthen the criteria of paragraph 2 in the course of Stage Three: in this way, budgetary performance could gradually be improved and deficits and debts be kept below lower and lower ceilings. On the other hand, it cannot be denied that the possibility offered by paragraph 14 to replace the EDP Protocol could also be used to weaken the criteria of paragraph 2. There are however two factors which guard against this possibility. The first is that the reference values can only be modified by unanimity in the Council, so that all Member States need to agree. Secondly, such a modification should in any case not be contrary to the principles of the Community as contained in Article 3a (3), such as stable prices and sound public finances.

Article 2 of the EDP Protocol contains the definitions of the concepts that are of relevance for the application of the EDP:[75] government, deficit, investment and debt. These definitions are given with reference to the European System of Integrated Economic Accounts (ESA). This is a system of statistical concepts which is used for the harmonised presentation of statistical data in the Community.[76] The reference to such a text must be understood as pointing to concepts which are well-known and accepted for statistical purposes. The legislator has, however, sought protection against undesirable revisions in ESA by specifying in Article 7 of Council Regulation No. 3605/93 that '[i]n the event of a revision of ESA to be decided on by the Council ... the Commission shall introduce the new references to ESA in Articles 1 and 4 [of the Council Regulation]'. This provision obliges any

---

75. See also *supra*, section 3.2.
76. Eurostat, op. cit., n.38.

revision in ESA to be adopted formally by the Council such that the latter can exercise control over possible changes that could affect the way in which the data for the EDP are to be calculated.

Article 2, first indent, of the EDP Protocol defines 'government', with reference to ESA, as 'general government', that is central government, regional or local government and social-security funds, to the exclusion of commercial operations. These definitions are repeated in Article 1 (2) of Council Regulation No. 3605/93 with reference to their ESA codes, specifying that 'the exclusion of commercial operations' means that the sector of general government only comprises institutional units producing non-market services as their main activity. The broad definition of 'government' implies that a wide concept of government is used for the EDP, thereby not discriminating in favour of Member States which have a large degree of local autonomy in raising and spending public money, nor against Member States which have no separate sector for social-security funds. On the other hand, the definition of government implicitly and explicitly excludes public enterprises. If the latter had been included, discrimination could take place against Member States, depending on the degree of state-ownership of enterprises and the financial situation of such enterprises.

Article 2, second indent, of the EDP Protocol defines 'deficit' as net borrowing as defined in ESA. Article 1 (3) of Council Regulation No. 3605/93 specifies, in addition to providing the ESA code, that this is the net lending of 'general government' and that the interest comprised in the government deficit is the sum of interest as defined in ESA. In the second edition of ESA, interest as defined in ESA (code R41) comprises interest payments. The formulation in Council Regulation No. 3605/93, by not referring to 'payments' leaves open possibilities for revision of ESA where R41 would not only cover interest payments, but also other forms of interest, such as accrued interest on liabilities on which no annual interest is paid. The concept of 'net borrowing' which is used as definition for the deficit implies, in accordance with the definitions of ESA, that the deficit equals the difference between general-government total (current and capital) expenditure and revenue on an accruals basis and excluding the results from financial operations on loans, advances and equities. In particular, the proceeds from privatisations by the government are not included in this definition of deficit.

Article 2, third indent, of the EDP Protocol defines 'investment' as gross fixed capital formation as defined in ESA. This definition implies that government investment as referred to in paragraph 3 is confined to physical investment. This narrowly circumscribed definition therefore excludes investment in other than physical assets, such as investment in human capital in the form of expenditure on education or health. This restrictive interpretation is due to the fact that, during the Treaty negotiations, the 'golden rule of public finance' figured for some time among the criteria on the basis on which the EDP could be triggered, before it was relegated to the status of auxiliary criterion in paragraph 3. The legislator wanted to prevent that a wide definition of government investment could be used to circumvent a strict interpretation of fiscal discipline. With a criterion according to which the deficit would be allowed to be equal to the size of investment expenditure, a more or less arbitrary definition of investment could have led to exceedingly high admissible levels of the deficit.

Article 2, fourth indent, of the EDP Protocol defines 'debt' as the total gross debt at nominal value outstanding at the end of the year and consolidated between and within the sectors of general government as defined in the first indent of the same Article. This definition, as it stands, has a number of notable features. First, it concerns total debt, that is all forms of debt. Council Regulation No. 3605/93 has, however, in Article 1 (5) defined these forms of debt with reference to ESA in a limitative way as consisting of currency and deposits, bills and short-term bonds, long term bonds, other short-term loans and other medium and long-term loans. This limitative list excludes, for instance, a form of debt such as trade credits and is therefore not completely exhaustive. A second feature of the definition of debt is that it concerns gross debt as opposed to net debt whereby assets would be deducted from liabilities. A concept of net debt would, however, have met with considerable difficulties as regards the valuation of certain assets such as shares in public enterprises, and has therefore not been retained. This does not exclude that certain assets which considerably influence the gross debt position of a Member State could not be taken into account as 'relevant factor' under paragraph 3, such as very liquid assets (*eg*, holdings of the government with the central bank), holdings of fully funded pension schemes or loans to public enterprises for which the government, has borrowed on the capital market. A third feature of the definition of debt is that it is consolidated between and within sectors of general government that is that liabilities of general government are excluded for which the corresponding assets are also held by one of the sectors of general government. A fourth feature of the definition of debt is that it has to be valued at nominal value as opposed to, for instance, market value. Article 1 (5) of Council Regulation No. 3605/93 stipulates that the nominal value for a liability outstanding at the end of the year is the face value, except for index-linked liabilities for which the face value has to be adjusted by the index-related capital uplift accrued to the end of the year. Furthermore, liabilities denominated in foreign currencies have to be converted into the national currency at the representative market exchange rate prevailing on the last working day of each year.

In addition to the definitions given in Article 2 of the EDP Protocol, Council Regulation No. 3605/93 also gives, in Article 3, the definitions of 'planned' government deficit, 'actual' government deficit and government debt 'level',[77] as well as, in Article 2, the definition of gross domestic product (GDP). The latter, which is the denominator for both the deficit ratio and the debt ratio, is defined by reference to Article 2 of Council Directive 89/130/EEC, Euratom, where GDP is defined with reference to ESA for the purpose of the calculation of gross national product (GNP) which is the basis for the Community's fourth own resource.[78]

9.2 Reporting obligations

Article 3 of the EDP Protocol obliges the Member States to report promptly and regularly to the Commission their planned and actual deficits as well as the levels of their debt. Further rules concerning this reporting obligation have been specified in Articles 4, 5 and 6 of Council Regulation No. 3605/93. According to these rules, the Member States have to report data twice a year to the Commission, the first time before 1 March of each year, and the second time before 1 September of each year. The data to be reported concern the government deficit (both according to the definition of the Treaty and according to the corresponding national public accounts), the government debt and the figures explaining the variation in the level of government debt. In addition to these data which have to be 'reported', and which therefore derive directly from the obligation under Article 3 of the EDP Protocol, Articles 4 and 5 of Council Regulation No. 3605/93 also foresee that the Member States have to 'provide' a certain number of additional figures, concerning respectively government investment expenditure, interest expenditure and gross domestic product. The need to provide these data for GDP derives from the fact that GDP is used as the denominator for the deficit ratio and the debt ratio; for government investment expenditure, from the fact that it is one of the relevant factors of which the Commission has to take account in its reports under paragraph 3; and for interest expenditure (which is largely extent outside the control of the government), from the fact that the deficit excluding interest expenditure is an important indicator of the budgetary adjustment effort which a government is making.

Despite these reporting obligations for the Member States, it is in the end the Commission which, under Article 4 of the EDP Protocol, has to provide the statistical data for the application of the Protocol and therefore for the EDP. The Commission is therefore allowed to correct data reported by the Member States to the extent that this is needed (i) in order to apply correctly

---

77. See *supra*, sections 3.2 and 3.3.
78. Council Decision 88/376/EEC, ECSC, Euratom.

the common definitions or (ii), in the case of data which concern current or future years, in order to introduce assumptions concerning the future evolution of the data which are considered to be more realistic. In this way, any biases or unduly optimistic (or pessimistic) data introduced by the Member States can be adjusted by the Commission.

9.3 Other obligations

In addition to the reporting obligations, Article 3 of the EDP Protocol imposes two other obligations on the Member States. The first of these obligations is that, in the context of the EDP, governments of the Member States are responsible for the deficits of general government.[79] This obligation seeks to confirm that, when a Member State speaks in the Council through its government, the government is able to speak on behalf of all sectors of general government, including in particular regional or local government. For example, in Member States where there exist shared budgetary competences between the central government on the one hand and regional or local government on the other hand, the Treaty therefore gives the central government the obligation to ensure that it is also responsible for these other sectors in the context of the EDP. This responsibility holds with regard to the Member State's representatives in the Council when that Member State's budgetary situation is discussed in the context of the EDP, as well as with regard to the recommendations, notices or sanctions addressed to that Member State under paragraphs 7, 8, 9 or 11.

The second obligation for the Member States in addition to the reporting requirements, under Article 3 of the EDP Protocol, requires the Member States to ensure that their national procedures in the budgetary area enable them to meet their obligations from the Treaty in this area. The most direct application of this obligation concerns the reporting requirements for the Member States for which national procedures may need to be adapted, for instance to ensure that there exist planned figures for the deficit in accordance with the definition from Treaty. A second, less obvious obligation, concerns the relationship between national budgetary procedures and budgetary performance.[80] In many Member States, for instance, the national parliament is the budgetary authority. If a government budget proposal is in line with the requirements under the EDP, but if the national parliament either modifies the government's proposal or authorises supplementary budgets such that the budgetary outcome is no longer in conformity with the requirements from the EDP, the representatives from

---

79. See *supra*, section 2.
80. See J. von Hagen and I. Harden, 'National budget processes and budgetary procedures' [1993] 3 *European Economy, Reports and Studies* 311.

the Member State in the Council could claim that the budgetary outcome is not their responsibility but imposed on them by the national parliament. The obligation of Article 3 of the EDP Protocol seeks to avoid such situations, by requiring Member States to ensure that their national procedures take proper account of the EDP. The implication of this obligation is, however, less far-reaching than it may seem at first sight. Member States already have a general obligation under Article 5 of the EC Treaty to take all general or specific measures to ensure fulfilment of the obligations arising from the Treaty.

Chapter Twelve

TOWARDS A CREDIBLE EXCESSIVE DEFICIT PROCEDURE

Daniel Gros*

Chapter Outline

1. Introduction

2. Why Limits on Excessive Deficits?

3. The Existing Enforcement Mechanism

4. A Concrete Proposal
    4.1   A last chance
    4.2   For persistent offenders: suspension!
    4.3   Who decides?

5. The 'Stability Pact'

6. Concluding Remarks

Annex: Summary of Proposed Additions to Article 104c

European Economic and Monetary Union: The Institutional Framework (M. Andenas, L. Gormley, C. Hadjiemmanuil, I. Harden, eds.: 90-411-0687-1: © Kluwer Law International: pub. Kluwer Law International, 1997: printed in Great Britain)

1.   INTRODUCTION

Although the officials preparing the current Intergovernmental Conference on the revision of the Maastricht Treaty would appear to be in full agreement that the EMU chapter of the Treaty should not be reopened, there is growing unease among policy analysts and financial authorities with one key aspect of the system as it was designed in 1991.

The most important cause for concern, at least in some countries, is that the enforcement of the prohibition of excessive deficits is assigned to the Ecofin Council, which has never taken any real decision in the sense that it has never imposed any tough measures on countries that systematically flout the basic rules of the Union. In the case of Greece, it has not even been able to impose a conditionality such as that used by the IMF.

It is symptomatic that there has been no public discussion of the fact that the prohibition of excessive deficits cannot be enforced by the Court of Justice as other provisions because paragraph 10 of Article 104c of the EC Treaty explicitly rules out this. This is the fundamental reason why the Maastricht Treaty had to contain a special procedure to enforce the prohibition of excessive deficits.

This chapter addresses this strategic issue. The concrete proposal is to make the excessive deficit procedure much more automatic and based on firm rules, thereby reducing the room for discretion exercised by Ecofin. The rationale for the limits on excessive deficits in the Maastricht Treaty has been hotly debated among economists. Some maintain that in an ideal world there is no need for special rules on excessive deficits, since it would be out of the question that the Union would ever bail out a Member State and the European Central Bank would ever be deflected from its anti-inflationary stance by fiscal policy problems. Others argue that in reality the no-bail-out rule cannot be enforced under all circumstances, and therefore a public debt crisis in any one Member State would affect the others and would likely make it more difficult for the ECB to pursue a tough anti-inflationary policy.

There is little disagreement, however, that the Maastricht Treaty lacks a credible mechanism to enforce the fiscal criteria (maximum deficit of 3 per cent of GDP and a debt level converging towards 60 per cent of GDP). The main purpose of this chapter is to discuss a way to make the EDP more credible by making it more automatic. The only sign that this might be happening in reality is that the regulations concerning the Cohesion Funds contain a provision that implies that they can be curtailed or cut in the case

*   The author wishes to thank Erik Jones and Peter Ludlow for fruitful discussions and comments. Research for this chapter was done in connection with the Centre for European Policy Studies' Economic Policy Group project which has received financial support from the Bundesbank, Banco d'España, Sveriges Riksbank and the German Marshall Fund (Grant No. B-0119).

of countries that do not follow their own convergence programme. A first step towards more automaticity has thus been taken. But only four countries are recipients of the Cohesion Funds (which are much smaller than the Structural Funds). This provision thus does not concern most members of the EU. But what other sanctions could one apply?

The solution proposed below is to exclude (or rather suspend) countries with persistent excessive deficits from the decision-making process in the ECB and Ecofin. The purpose of this measure would not be to 'punish' the country, but rather to ensure that its problems do not affect the stability of the common currency. If the ECB perceives that there is a danger for the Euro, it would be empowered to bar banks from the problem country from the common payment system. This would be equivalent to a full exclusion from EMU.

This chapter is organised as follows: Section 2 recapitulates briefly the main arguments for limits on deficits. Section 3 provides a critique of the enforcement mechanism in the Maastricht Treaty, and Section 4 offers a concrete counter-proposal. Section 5 discusses briefly the so-called 'stability pact', originally presented by the German Minister of Finance, Theo Waigel, in late 1995. Section 6 presents conclusions.

2.   WHY LIMITS ON EXCESSIVE DEFICITS?

Before going into a discussion of how to enforce the excessive deficit limits, it is useful to recall briefly the reason why limits on excessive deficits are needed. There are two main arguments that speak in favour of limits on excessive deficits. The first argument is that the accommodation of large public debt might lead to instability in financial markets, which in turn would make it difficult for the ECB to follow a tough anti-inflationary policy. The second argument is simply that large public-sector deficits take up private-sector savings that would otherwise go to investment. Hence, large deficits lower growth prospects in the medium-to-long term.[1]

The first argument is based on the way financial markets work. Experience shows that financial markets do not work with smooth supply curves of credit. If the creditworthiness of a borrower deteriorates, interest rates increase at first; but once a certain threshold has been passed, credit is just cut off. Furthermore, theoretical considerations and experience suggest that a slight change in overall financial market conditions can trigger a run on weak creditors, who are then at least temporarily excluded from further

---

1. For an elaboration of these ideas, see D. Gros and N. Thygesen, *European Monetary Integration* (1992).

access to financial markets. This threat of exclusion explains why 'junk-bond' markets are highly vulnerable. If a run on the public debt of a Member State were to occur, the ECB would be under immense pressure to lower interest rates. Under these circumstances, a number of large banks might become illiquid and require emergency credits to convince the banking system that it is safe to deal with them. For these reasons, the ECB would be hard pressed in such a situation not to loosen its anti-inflationary policy stance in general. The result could be an increase in the European rate of inflation.

The counter-argument is that this danger to price stability could be eliminated by building the appropriate early warning signals to financial markets through a regular rating of public debt and by forcing banks to recognise that, in EMU, national debt carries a similar default risk as local debt does at present. Banks would then be required to hold the appropriate reserves against this risk. Even an appropriate risk-rating of public debt, however, will never be sufficient to eliminate the problem entirely.

The second argument is less technical. It is actually similar to the line of thinking that led to the European Monetary System and the idea that an independent central bank is useful. This approach, pioneered by James Buchanan,[2] starts from the fact that in most cases the benefits of a given fiscal measure, *eg*, a transfer or expenditure programme, accrue to a well-defined group, that will thus have an incentive to lobby for it. The cost has to be borne by all taxpayers and contributors to social security, who will find it more difficult to organise opposition to spending decisions, because their interests are more dispersed. Hence, the process by which fiscal decisions are taken in a democracy entails a 'deficit bias'. On average special interest groups win, although the cost of the overall set of all these decisions has to be paid by everybody, including these interest groups. The outcome, then, is a public sector that is too large and a tendency to let future generations, who constitute the least effective lobby, pay for the debt that has been accumulated in the meantime.

The most important consideration might thus be that, even if the monetary policy of the ECB could be protected in other ways against the inflationary fall-out from excessive deficits, little is lost by introducing additional safeguards against policies that are in any event not in the long-term interest of any country.

These two arguments suggest potentially valid economic reasons for rules against excessive deficits that lead to an unsustainable build-up of public debt. In addition to these economic arguments, one must also take account of the fact that the German Constitutional Court decided in a landmark ruling that strict observance of the convergence criteria is a condition for

2. J. Buchanan, *Democracy in Deficit: The Political Legacy of Lord Keynes* (1977).

German participation in EMU.[3] The ruling implies that any German government would be entitled (and maybe required) to pull out from EMU when a danger to the stability of the common currency arises.[4] This provides an additional reason why it is important to have an enforcement mechanism that works. The threat of German withdrawal will act as a deterrent, but it cannot be the sole sanction, because the costs of German withdrawal (implying effectively a dissolution of EMU) would be borne by all countries, not just the one that has the excessive deficit and caused the upheaval.

For the discussion below, the main point to keep in mind is that the EDP should have an exceptional character: it should be used only if the fiscal situation in a country becomes unsustainable to the point that the danger of a fiscal crisis exists. Practical examples of this include the present situation in Italy and the 'mini' debt crisis in Sweden in 1994.

3. THE EXISTING ENFORCEMENT MECHANISM

How credible is the enforcement mechanism provided for in the Maastricht Treaty? The Treaty of Rome already had a strong enforcement mechanism, namely the Court of Justice, that applies in principle for all provisions, including the chapter on EMU that was added in Maastricht. However, it has been little noticed so far that the article dealing with the EDP excludes specifically in its paragraph 10 the normal enforcement mechanism of the Treaty via the Court of Justice.[5] This is why Article 104c had to contain a new enforcement mechanism specifically designed to overcome the problem that it would be impossible to make member countries obey the prohibition of excessive deficits if there were no sanctions. It is strange that this fundamental reason for the existence of the complicated EDP is seldom mentioned in public.

The EDP detailed in Article 104c of the EC Treaty starts with a recommendation and could finally entail sanctions. These sanctions can,

---

3. *Brunner v The European Union Treaty*, Cases 2 BvR 2134/92 & 2159/92, Bundesverfassungsgericht, Judgment of 12 Oct. 1993, BVerGE 89, 155 (1993), English translation published in [1994] 1 CMLR 57.
4. Statements by politicians from all the major parties continue to underline that strict observance of the fiscal criteria is a *conditio sine qua non* for German participation in EMU. All this risks leading to the typical situation where 'irresistible force meets immoveable object'. Special domestic interest groups represent the irresistible force that drives deficits against the immoveable object in the form of the judgment of the German Constitutional Court.
5. Art. 104c (10) reads as follows: 'The rights to bring actions provided for in Articles 169 and 170 may not be exercised within the framework of paragraphs 1 to 9 of this Article.'

however, only be imposed after a complicated procedure. A closer look at the graduated response set forth in this article suggests that it does not constitute a credible threat. Paragraph 11 is the key provision, which reads as follows:

As long as a Member State fails to comply with a decision taken in accordance with paragraph 9 [*ie*, notification by Ecofin of a time-limit and measures to eliminate the excessive deficit], the Council may decide to apply or, as the case may be, intensify one or more of the following measures:
– to require the Member State concerned to publish additional information, to be specified by the Council, before issuing bonds and securities;
– to invite the European Investment Bank to reconsider its lending policy towards the Member State concerned;
– to require the Member State concerned to make a non-interest-bearing deposit of an appropriate size with the Community until the excessive deficit has, in the view of the Council, been corrected;
– to impose fines of an appropriate size.

Until now, no Member State has openly defied the legal and judicial system of the Community (for example, by refusing to implement a directive). This might be the reason why the Maastricht Treaty does not contemplate the possibility that a state would not heed the requests for fiscal adjustment addressed to it. Fiscal criteria, however, are a different matter, since fiscal policy remains fully under national control, even under EMU. Hence, the effectiveness of the EDP will depend on the sanctions that underpin it.

How should one evaluate the sanctions listed above? They seem to consist mainly of peer pressure. Their direct deterrent effect would be minor, and hence they would do little to resolve the problem, as spelled out below.

(i)   Requiring a state to publish additional information would not seem to be a very strong deterrent. What information that is not already widely known could be revealed in this way?

(ii) The EIB finances long-term investment projects at market rates of interest. It cannot hold up work on projects already begun and, at any rate, there is almost no subsidy element in its lending. The threat of withholding Structural Funds would probably have a strong impact in the four main recipient countries, but this sanction has not been retained, probably because it would appear unjust to subject only poorer countries to this discipline.

(iii) What would be the appropriate size of the non-interest-bearing deposit? 1 per cent of GDP (about 10 billion ECU at current exchange rates for Italy)? At interest rates of 8 per cent, this would amount to an annual cost (in terms of interest foregone) of 0.08 per cent of GDP, hardly a strong deterrent.

(iv) What would be the appropriate size of the fines? In the hundreds of millions or in the billions of ECUs? A large fine (say, 1 per cent of GDP) would only increase the deficit and make it even more difficult to get it below 3 per cent of GDP. What should the money be used for?

Another drawback of this approach is that enforcement is discretionary (sanctions *may* be imposed), requiring a decision by Ecofin for each specific step. This body has not even been able to impose IMF-type conditionality towards Greece in the context of large support programmes. Thus, sanctions need to be made not only more concrete, but also more automatic. Some action or decision needs to be triggered automatically once a certain threshold has been passed. Moreover, the purpose of the EDP should not be to 'punish' the offending state, but to help it get its fiscal accounts under control.

In this context, one must keep in mind that a likely circumstance under which a country does not follow the recommendations of the Council is when the national government concerned is weak, or when there is no working majority in parliament that is willing to take the unpopular decisions needed to redress the budgetary problem. It is unlikely that a Member State's government possessing a clear majority in the national parliament will openly defy the EU by acting against the letter and the spirit of the Maastricht Treaty. Recent events in Italy show that it is precisely the lack of a clear majority that might make fiscal consolidation difficult. Although no significant political group denies the urgent need for drastic action, very little can be done until the domestic political situation has been clarified.

Automatic emergency measures proposed in a concrete form by a neutral body would have a much higher probability of being accepted in such a situation, since they would actually allow politicians to avoid taking some unpopular decisions. By contrast, 'fines' imposed by the Council might not be enough to produce the working majority necessary to increase taxes or reduce expenditure. A government that has only a very limited time horizon would not be impressed by fines, nor by a higher interest-rate premium imposed on public debt.

One has to recognise that fiscal 'sovereignty' ultimately remains in national hands, even after the third stage of EMU has begun. If a country is really determined to accumulate excessive deficits, the EU will not be able to stop it. Nevertheless, the Union also has the right to say that, under such circumstances, a country that continues to flout its basic rules cannot continue to be part of EMU. The ultimate sanction must thus be exclusion. This means that member countries retain their fiscal sovereignty, but they pay a price for clearly deviant behaviour. In the final analysis, member countries retain a clear choice: participation in the common currency area or the freedom to pursue irresponsible fiscal policies.

Moreover, given that satisfying the Maastricht fiscal criteria has been made a condition for entering EMU, it is only logical that a blatant violation of these criteria should also be ground for expulsion from EMU.

One might object to the sort of interference in national economic policy-making proposed here, on the ground that it constitutes 'process bail-out'. According to this view, the underlying problem is that the process by which budgetary decisions are taken at the national level produces a systematic bias towards deficits. What needs to be changed is the constitutional set-up that determines budgets at the national level.[6] One could argue that the EU should not take these fundamental decisions, which need to be taken at the national level. Various arguments from the field of political science have been used in opposition to the idea that external constraints can actually be beneficial.

The view that process bail-out is not desirable loses much of its force if one considers that, in a certain sense, one of the main features of the European integration process has always been to constrain the freedom of Member States in their own long-term interest. The customs union is the first example of this approach, but the best-known example of governments willing to have their hands tied is the EMS. Upon entering the EMS, participating countries did not agree to alter the constitutional procedures that determined national monetary policy; they only introduced an external constraint. The system turned out to be useful because the external constraint was a shield against domestic political pressures. Only with the Maastricht Treaty did Member States agree to modify their constitutional set-up in the monetary area. This was possible because a consensus existed that only an independent central bank can deliver price stability in the long run.

Requiring constitutional changes in all Member States is not appropriate in the fiscal area, since there is no similar consensus that only one particular set-up will deliver a sensible fiscal policy. Moreover, fiscal policy involves incomparably more political decisions about redistribution than does monetary policy. Hence, it is much more difficult to design a mechanism that channels the political pressures acting on fiscal policy into a process that will give the desired result, namely, a reduction in the fiscal bias.

6. The term 'process bail-out' was suggested by Ian Harden. See J. von Hagen and I. Harden, 'National Budget Processes and Fiscal Performance' [1994] 3 *European Economy, Reports and Studies* 311, for a concrete proposal; see also I. Harden, J. von Hagen and R. Brookes, 'The European Constitutional Framework for Member States' Public Finances', ch.9 of this volume, section 6.2.

4.   A CONCRETE PROPOSAL

How can one make the EDP more credible? This section proposes three small amendments to the Maastricht Treaty. The point of the first two proposed amendments is that a country with an excessive deficit should be given a last chance before it is excluded from EMU. In order to put this idea into practice, the existing version of paragraph 11 of Article 104c should be eliminated and substituted by the provisions proposed here.

4.1   A last chance

Paragraph 11 of Article 104c should begin with the following text:

Once a Member State has become subject to a decision under paragraph 9 [*ie*, notification by Ecofin of a time-limit and measures to eliminate an excessive deficit], the ECB and the Commission will report on compliance every three months. If the compliance reports of the ECB and the Commission indicate that a Member State has failed to comply with a decision taken under paragraph 9,[7] the Council will request the Member State concerned to limit spending by the national government on a monthly basis to the same amounts as in the previous year and to increase the rate of value-added tax by an amount sufficient to eliminate the excessive deficit within one year.

The advantage of such a formulation is that it gives the government a precise indication of the provisions it must propose to its national parliament. These emergency measures would therefore be removed from the domestic political debate, because they would be seen as coming from a neutral authority. This would serve to galvanise the sort of bipartisan support that can only be mobilised under extreme circumstances. It should be stressed that there is no presumption that sequestering expenditure and raising VAT is the optimal way to reduce the deficit. These measures are proposed only because they are relatively transparent and easy to implement and monitor.[8]

4.2   For persistent offenders: suspension!

If the provision proposed above is followed, there should be no need for further sanctions. In order to clarify in advance the consequences of

---

7. The procedure leading up to the decision in para. 9 could be shortened by eliminating the step foreseen in para. 8, but this a question of detail in this context.
8. A temporary surcharge on income tax (like the German *Solidaritätszuschlag*) might also be useful. The Commission's services would work out the details of the package necessary to redress the situation.

declining to take advantage of this last chance, however, the Treaty should also specify the ultimate sanction: exclusion. This would further increase the likelihood that the national parliament will not torpedo the measures prescribed above. Thus, the second recommendation is that the new text proposed above for the opening of paragraph 11 of Article 104c should continue as follows:

If the Council finds, acting on a proposal from the ECB and after consulting with the European Parliament, that a Member State has failed to comply within three months with the obligations foreseen in the previous indent, the Member State concerned shall have a derogation as defined in Article 109k (3).

Receiving a derogation would effectively relegate a persistent offender to the ranks of those who do not participate in EMU. The automatic element in this provision is essential. The Ecofin should not be given the opportunity to 'go soft'.

What happens 'the day after'? In legal terms, what happens in the monetary area is determined by Article 109k (3), which implies that the governor of the national central bank of the country that has been given a derogation (ie, has been excluded) would no longer participate in the decisions concerning the common monetary policy.[9] Furthermore, the decisions of the ECB would no longer automatically apply to the country concerned (Article 105), and the national central bank would regain its freedom to set monetary policy independently. If the third recommendation presented below is also implemented, an additional (and logical) consequence would be that the country that had been given a derogation would no longer participate in Ecofin decisions concerning the EDP.

The EU can not force the country concerned to reintroduce a national currency. One has to distinguish here between two possible scenarios.

Let us assume, in the first instance, that expulsion takes place before the common currency is introduced in the form of banknotes (*ie*, before 2002). The national currency in physical form would still exist, whether or not the country is in EMU. Under this scenario, then, the main decision to be taken by the authorities of the excluded country would be whether to de-link their currency from the ECU or whether to continue 'as if' they were still

9. Art. 109k (3) of the EC Treaty specifies that the following provisions do not apply to a country with a derogation:
   - 104c (9) and (11) (excessive deficit procedure);
   - 105 (1), (2), (3) and (5) (monetary policy);
   - 105a (notes and coins);
   - 108a (empowering the ESCB);
   - 109 (exchange-rate system with rest of world);
   - 109a (2) (b) (membership of the Executive Board of the ESCB); and
   - Chapter IX of Statute of the ESCB.

members of EMU, that is, to peg unilaterally and without any margins of fluctuation to the currencies of the remaining 'core'. Any country with a derogation could thus chose to maintain a sort of 'associated membership' of EMU. However, this would require a decision by the government and by the national central bank. The government would have to be involved because it is responsible for exchange-rate policy, and the central bank would have to 'bind its hands'.

If expulsion (suspension) comes at a time when the common currency is already in circulation, separation would be more difficult. Continued unilateral participation in the common-currency area would then actually be easier. The country concerned would just have to maintain the common currency of the EMU as the national currency, and the national central bank would have to continue following the decisions of the ECB.

At present, one of the main problems for Europe are the so-called 'competitive devaluations', which are perceived as giving industry in some member countries a larger competitive advantage. Would a country that is excluded from (the decision-making structures of) EMU not be tempted to take the occasion to obtain a competitive advantage (boost to employment and production) by (re)introducing a national currency and devaluing it? This is unlikely to be the case in reality. A country that is excluded because of a serious fiscal problem would have to pay such a large price in terms of higher interest rates if it did follow the devaluation route, that this option is not likely to be attractive. Moreover, it would mean that re-entering EMU would become impossible for a long time. Since most countries attach a high priority to participating in EMU, this is likely to be the ultimate deterrent to the reintroduction of a national currency.

The crucial question is to what extent a unilateral participation in EMU is credible with financial markets. If this sort of 'currency board' were credible, interest rates in the country concerned would remain very close to those of the rest of the EMU. Given that the country concerned was excluded on grounds of accumulating an excessive fiscal deficit, however, it is likely that financial markets would add a risk-premium to the interest on its public debt. If there were serious doubts about the solvency of a government, its continued unilateral participation in the common-currency area would lack credibility, with the likely result that interest rates on all instruments issued domestically would increase. Domestic interest rates would increase even more if the country concerned signalled its unwillingness to return to sound fiscal management in the near future by reintroducing a national currency, which thus might not be an attractive policy.

Reintroducing a national currency would not be easy. It is possible, as demonstrated by the separation of the Czech and Slovak currencies. But in that case the financial markets were rather rudimentary, so that all bank deposits could be nationalised according to the bank at which they were held. In the EU, separation would be incomparably more complicated, given the large volume of cross-border activity. Moreover, households and enterprises would start to shift their deposits massively towards other EU countries in anticipation of such a move.

Countries that have been excluded (suspended) would thus have a strong incentive to continue to behave as if they were still in the currency area[10] until they have eliminated their excessive deficit and can be readmitted. Expulsion would thus, *de facto*, directly imply *only* that the governor of the national central bank no longer has a vote on the Council of the ECB. While this might not appear to be a strong sanction, it would fulfil the more important aim of protecting the rest of the Union from being influenced by this Member State.

Excluding (suspending) a country would potentially imply much more than merely excluding the governor of the national central bank. First of all, the government and the national central bank would have to take an explicit decision to stay unilaterally in the common-currency area, with all the political upheaval that this would involve. Secondly, if the deficits continued and threatened to ignite a financial crisis, the ECB would be forced to exclude banks located in the problem country from participation in the common large-value payments system. This would really force the country out of the common-currency area. It would be likely to lead to a discount on deposits in this country, and people would try to convert their deposits into Euro cash at par. However, this would force the national central bank to get more Euro cash, which it could obtain only if it still had enough foreign-exchange reserves and the ECB were willing to co-operate. If the markets perceived that the ECB would not provide more cash, a financial crisis would be likely to follow immediately.

Exclusion from the common payments system is thus a very strong weapon. If a country does not care about the exclusion of its governor from the Council of the ECB and continues with large deficits, there are thus other means the Union can use to call it to order.

4.3   Who decides?

Another important point related to the enforcement of the limits on deficits concerns the composition of the (Ecofin) Council when it has to decide on these matters. Paragraph 13 of Article 104c specifies that the country concerned does not vote on an action involving itself. Moreover, paragraphs 3 and 5 of Article 109k imply that countries with a derogation do not participate in the decisions on the (weak) sanctions foreseen in the current

---

10.   This would also imply that they would share in the profits of the ECB according to Art. 32 of the Statute of the ESCB.

version of Article 104c. Article 109k (4), however, does not state that a country with a derogation cannot participate in the voting (with weighted two-thirds majority) under paragraph 13 of Article 104c, which determines how decisions under the EDP are taken. This is a mistake that should be rectified. There is no reason why countries that do not participate in EMU should have a voice in deciding whether a country that is in EMU has an excessive deficit, or whether a country should be excluded from EMU. This is a matter that affects primarily the interests of participating countries of EMU. Countries that do not participate in the third stage of EMU have only a limited interest in protecting the monetary policy of the ECB from the danger of financial market crises, and could be influenced in their position by other issues. Moreover, it is conceivable that in the beginning a majority will be composed primarily of countries that do not participate in EMU.

In the long run, when all countries participate in EMU, this problem will disappear. However, it is now likely that it will be several decades before all present and future Member States will participate in EMU. This issue will thus remain important for some time to come.

As a consequence, it is further recommended that the expression 'without a derogation' should be inserted in paragraph 13 of Article 104c as follows (with emphasis on the proposed change):

When taking the decisions referred to in paragraphs 7 to 9, 11 and 12, the Council shall act on a recommendation from the Commission by a majority of two thirds of the votes of its members *representing Member States without a derogation as defined in Article 109k (3)* weighted in accordance with Article 148 (2), excluding the votes of the representative of the Member State concerned.

5.   THE 'STABILITY PACT'

The main argument against the proposal of this chapter is that it would be unprecedented for the EU to exclude a Member State from part of its business because it has not followed the Treaty. Many would argue that this is not really necessary, since a country that followed a clearly deviant fiscal policy that endangered price stability for the entire EMU would be subject to immense pressure by the rest of the EU. Moreover, there would also be the threat of an action before the German Constitutional Court, which could order Germany to leave EMU. The importance of the ruling by the German Constitutional Court can be debated, but it is clear that even the mere potential for a ruling against EMU will unsettle financial markets. One can only hope that this will be sufficient to prevent large deficits under EMU. This indirect enforcement mechanism has the disadvantage that the consequence would be a break-up of EMU, so that the cost of deviant fiscal behaviour by any one country would have to be borne by the rest of the EU as well. Such a negative externality is clearly undesirable.

The potential conflict between the prohibition of excessive deficits and the principle that fiscal sovereignty remains at the national level cannot be resolved short of a Treaty revision that makes the continuation of excessive deficits incompatible with full membership in EMU. Since there is a general unwillingness to change any part in the chapter on EMU, one is forced to think about other ways to reinforce the EDP. One way to reduce its weakest points might be through an intergovernmental agreement that would be signed by all EMU participants. In such an agreement, the participating governments would precommit their voting behaviour in Ecofin. For example, they could agree to always vote for sanctions once a country has failed to implement the recommendation to eliminate an excessive deficit. Moreover, the sanctions (*ie*, the size of the fines) themselves could be specified in advance.

The 'stability pact', originally proposed by the German Finance Minister, Theo Waigel, in November 1995, goes in this direction. The essence of this proposal is that those governments that participate in the third stage would agree among themselves that the sanctions foreseen in the Treaty should be specified as follows:

(i)   The reference value of a 3 per cent deficit would hold also under unfavourable economic conditions. Exemptions from this rule could be approved only in exceptional circumstances with a qualified majority vote (of the participants in EMU).

(ii) If a country were found (during the semi-annual evaluation performed by the Commission) to have a deficit in excess of 3 per cent of GDP, it would have to immediately make a non-interest-bearing deposit equivalent to 0.25 per cent of GDP for each point of additional deficit.

(iii) The deposit would be returned as soon as the deficit goes below 3 per cent; if the excess deficit persists for over two years, the deposit would become a fine.

These specifications would not require a change in the Treaty, if they are just intended as 'guidelines' for Ecofin. However, this approach begs the question of how one can ensure that ministers will actually follow these guidelines and vote for these type of sanctions. If governments are not bound by a separate treaty, but just by a 'gentlemen's agreement', there is very little that, for example, the German authorities could do if some governments decide not to follow this approach when sanctions are discussed in Ecofin. Some governments might find valid reasons in future not to vote for sanctions after all, fearing that they might be the next victim. If the stability pact were to be embedded in an international treaty, it would be equivalent to a change in the Maastricht Treaty. Moreover, Ecofin has to vote on a recommendation from the Commission. It would thus be important that the Commission also takes part in this agreement.

The implications of the stability pact would be far-reaching. Large deviations from the 3 per cent deficit rule would clearly become very expensive. For example, a country that ran a deficit of 7 per cent for over two years would have to pay a fine (or, more precisely, forfeit deposits) equivalent to 1 per cent of GDP for each following year. This would be comparable to an average country's annual contribution to the EU budget. But it would be substantially larger than the average *net* contribution. Payments of this size would certainly have a large political impact, since they would require a substantial increase in taxes and/or reduction in expenditure, unless they are financed by issuing more debt.

In principle, large budgetary overruns should no longer occur under EMU; hence, this problem should not arise. The main problem for EMU, however, is not deficits slightly above the 3 per cent limit, which are actually allowed for in Article 104c; but substantial excessive deficits (caused possibly by a combination of unfavourable economic circumstances and weak governments). EMU, and by extension the entire EU construction, might become deeply unpopular if citizens had to pay substantially higher taxes in order to finance the relevant fines.

One consequence of tighter sanctions would be that member countries would have an even stronger incentive to keep items off-budget in order to produce better deficit numbers. The services of the Commission, which compile the official deficit measures, would only partially be able to correct for such actions. It would probably be impossible to hide deficits forever; they would have to show up sooner or later in the debt figures as a 'stock-flow adjustment', implying that a specification of the debt criterion becomes even more important.

A concrete example can illustrate the problems that could arise in this situation. In a member country, the pressure for spending mounts, but given the 3 per cent limit and the fines that might follow quickly, the government prefers to deflect this pressure into a special agency. The official deficit could thus be kept below 3 per cent for some time. After a number of years, however, the government has to recognise the accumulated deficits, for example, by taking over the special agency. The debt figures would rise suddenly when this happens (there would be a 'stock-flow adjustment'). If the debt ratio was clearly below 60 per cent to begin with, Ecofin could do little. However, if the debt ratio was already above 60 per cent, Ecofin could still make a finding that an excessive deficit exists (long after the deficit had actually occurred). How would one then calculate the size of the fine?

This problem would arise under any enforcement mechanism. But by linking the size of the fine to the size of the excess deficit, the incentive to 'massage' the deficit numbers is much increased, because the stability pact introduces an asymmetry between the enforcement mechanism of the deficit and the debt criterion.

Another drawback of large fines paid into the EU budget is that they are not directly linked to EMU. All the other countries, even those not participating in EMU, would benefit.

6. CONCLUDING REMARKS

The current debate on sanctions in the EDP revolves essentially around one key issue: Is it necessary for the EU to take a specific decision to impose certain sanctions each time a particular country has an excessive deficit? Or should there be a presumption that the same type of sanctions will be imposed automatically, unless Ecofin actively decides otherwise? Each of these two approaches would impart a completely different dynamic to the EDP. Under the first approach a small group of countries that do not strongly feel the need for fiscal discipline could block the imposition of sanctions. Under the second approach the countries that care more about fiscal discipline would probably usually have enough votes to make sure that sanctions are actually imposed.

The argument in favour of automaticity is based on the observation that Ecofin is different from other specialised Councils in that it has never had to take concrete decisions against a Member State. The nature of Ecofin has to change if it is to implement the key role it has been assigned in the EDP. The argument against automaticity is that it could involve excessive rigidity, and could lead to conflicts between a state in distress and the Council.

A legal automaticity is difficult to achieve, because the Treaty stipulates explicitly that sanctions can only be imposed after a decision of Ecofin that requires a majority of two thirds. The challenge to those who favour more automaticity is to devise a political mechanism or understanding that yields a presumption that sanctions will be imposed.

The basic idea presented in this chapter is that national governments might stand to gain from tying their hands in the area of fiscal policy. This could be achieved through a credible EDP whose consequences are triggered automatically if an excessive deficit persists. At first the national parliament would have to consider automatic proposals to cut expenditure and/or increase taxes. The ultimate sanction would be expulsion from (the decision-making mechanism of) EMU.[11]

It is highly unlikely that the threat of expulsion will ever have to be carried out. The mere existence of such an 'ultimate weapon' will already

---

11. See the Annex to this chapter, for a summary of the proposed additions to the text in Art. 104c.

impose a strong disciplinary effect. Moreover, it is likely that, once expelled from EMU, a country would try to maintain the common currency on an unilateral basis.

ANNEX
Summary of Proposed Additions to Article 104c

Paragraph 11 of Article 104c should begin with the following text:

Once a Member State has become subject to a decision under paragraph 9 [*ie*, notification by Ecofin of a time-limit and measures to eliminate an excessive deficit], the ECB and the Commission will report on compliance every three months. If the compliance reports of the ECB and the Commission indicate that a Member State has failed to comply with a decision taken under paragraph 9, the Council will request the Member State concerned to limit spending by the national government on a monthly basis to the same amounts as in the previous year and to increase the rate of value-added tax by an amount sufficient to eliminate the excessive deficit within one year.

Following the new text proposed above, paragraph 11 of Article 104c should continue as follows:

If the Council finds, acting on a proposal from the ECB and after consulting with the European Parliament, that a Member State has failed to comply within three months with the obligations foreseen in the previous indent, the Member State concerned shall have a derogation as defined in Article 109k (3).

The expression 'without a derogation' should be inserted in paragraph 13 of Article 104c as follows (with emphasis on the proposed change):

When taking the decisions referred to in paragraphs 7 to 9, 11 and 12, the Council shall act on a recommendation from the Commission by a majority of two thirds of the votes of its members *representing Member States without a derogation as defined in Article 109k (3)* weighted in accordance with Article 148 (2), excluding the votes of the representative of the Member State concerned.

Chapter Thirteen

SOUND PUBLIC FINANCES AND FISCAL TARGETS

Stephen Matthews

Chapter Outline

1. Introduction

2. The Question of Sound Public Finances
   2.1 Debt sustainability
   2.2 The public sector's balance sheet and the 'golden rule'
   2.3 Demographic trends and other factors

3. Fiscal Objectives
   3.1 The medium-term fiscal objective
   3.2 Implementing fiscal policy: the effects of the cycle

4. Fiscal Policy in a Single-Currency Area

5. Concluding Remarks

European Economic and Monetary Union: The Institutional Framework (M. Andenas, L. Gormley, C. Hadjiemmanuil, I. Harden, eds.: 90-411-0687-1: © Kluwer Law International: pub. Kluwer Law International, 1997: printed in Great Britain)

1.   INTRODUCTION

All governments are in principle in favour of maintaining sound public finances, but how much in practice can they safely borrow? This chapter explores this issue, with a view to casting some light on the wider question of the institutional arrangements that should govern fiscal policy – and ensure sound public finances – in EMU.

This chapter first looks at various approaches to judging whether the public finances are 'sound' and at what they imply for the budget balance that the government ought to run in normal times. In particular, the chapter looks at:

- debt sustainability;

- the 'golden rule' and the public-sector balance sheet; and

- demographic trends, state pension liabilities, the level of national saving and related factors.

The broad conclusion of this discussion is that the economic analysis points to aiming for budget balance or only a very small deficit, but suggests that we can not be very precise in defining objectives in the budgetary area. It is, for instance, easier to quantify what constitutes permanently low inflation than sound public finances.

The chapter then discusses what variation in the budget balance around a given fiscal objective should be permitted. This involves an assessment of such factors as:

- the effects of variations in output growth on the budget balance (*ie*, the impact of the automatic stabilisers);

- whether fiscal policy should play a role in managing nominal demand; and

- the appropriate balance of rules and discretion.

The final section of the chapter looks at how things might change in a monetary union. The common monetary policy would naturally be the main instrument for maintaining price stability and, whatever else it did, fiscal policy would have to continue to maintain sound public finances.

While the authorities would (as now) not be able to raise output and employment permanently through demand management policy, there could be a role for macroeconomic policy to help stabilise output and employment in response to short-term or transitory shocks. In particular, national *fiscal* policies could play a useful role when there are country-specific shocks. This could have implications for how tightly constraints over national fiscal policy should be drawn.

2. THE QUESTION OF SOUND PUBLIC FINANCES

2.1 Debt sustainability

One answer to the question of how much it is safe for a government to borrow is that, at the very least, governments should avoid getting into a situation where the ratio of public debt to GDP rises without limit and the public finances become unsustainable.

There is a much greater risk of this occurring when interest rates exceed GDP-growth rates, as in recent years. This is essentially a matter of arithmetic, as the numerator of the debt ratio then tends to rise faster than the denominator. Stabilising the debt ratio then requires the government to run a primary surplus. (The primary surplus or deficit is the budget balance when net debt interest payments are excluded.) This primary surplus will need to be larger, the higher the initial debt ratio. It will also have to be larger the greater the excess of interest rates over GDP-growth rates.

However, stabilising the ratio of public sector debt to GDP could be a rather arbitrary objective. In particular, why should the initial debt ratio be regarded as the right level? It will reflect a country's history of budget deficits, and it seems unlikely in the real world that this will have been optimal. Similarly, if one country's initial debt-to-GDP ratio is 100 per cent while another's is 40 per cent, should they both seek to stabilise their respective ratios?

In the case of the UK, the national debt in relation to GDP has tended to rise sharply to high levels during major wars and to fall in peacetime. This experience suggests that it is not impossible to operate sound policies in the face of a high public-sector debt ratio, as in the 1950s and 1960s. Nevertheless, reducing the ratio over time gives the government much more room for manoeuvre to respond to any future adverse shocks (which would not necessarily have to be so dramatic as a war). Such arguments for a falling debt ratio are, though, inevitably stronger when the ratio is of the order of, say, 100 per cent of GDP than, say, 40 per cent.

Some simple arithmetic can give an indication of the sort of public-sector budget deficits needed to achieve a low debt ratio in a period of low inflation. With money-GDP growth of, say, 5 per cent a year (2.5 per cent inflation, 2.5 per cent trend real growth) the deficit ratio would need to be 2 per cent to stabilise the debt ratio at 40 per cent. A deficit ratio of 1 per cent would put the debt ratio on a declining trend, but the decline would be only gradual (about 1 percentage point a year), if the debt ratio were already 40 per cent. This declining trend would be faster if the debt ratio were higher (*eg*, nearly 4 percentage points a year, if the initial debt ratio were 100 per cent), but this is essentially a statistical phenomenon.

The Maastricht Treaty established reference values of 3 per cent of GDP for budget deficits and 60 per cent of GDP for public-sector debt as part of the procedure for identifying whether a Member State has an 'excessive deficit'. If one assumes a growth rate of money-GDP of 5 per cent a year (as in the previous paragraph), there is an arithmetic link between these two ratios. Ignoring complications about gross/net debt, running budget deficits of 3 per cent of GDP would lead the debt ratio to converge on 60 per cent (from wherever it started).

2.2 The public sector's balance sheet and the 'golden rule'

However, arithmetical neatness does not tell us what the optimum public-sector debt ratio might be. One factor relevant to determining the desired debt ratio is the amount of assets that the public sector also has in its balance sheet, for example, transport infrastructure, hospitals, schools, public corporations' investments, etc.

But how should we decide the appropriate level of net assets? Reformulation of the 'golden rule' (*ie*, that governments should borrow only to finance investment) in stock terms (*ie*, zero net assets) might provide one possible answer. However, there are both conceptual and statistical difficulties with such a principle.

First, it may not be consistent with sustainable tax rates. Many public assets do not generate a pecuniary return. Thus, an increase in capital spending financed by borrowing will sooner or later require tax increases to finance the higher debt interest costs. Concern about the implications for the future tax burden might point to financing some capital expenditure from current tax receipts and to aiming for positive net public-sector assets.

Secondly, data on public-sector net worth are not particularly reliable. Statistical problems include the difficulty of valuing assets where there is no ready market price: written-down book values can only be approximate, and in some past instances seem to have represented a considerable overstatement of market values.

2.3 Demographic trends and other factors

Other factors that might be relevant to determining a prudent level of public borrowing include demographic trends, prospective productivity growth, future state pension liabilities and other influences on intergenerational equity. For instance, if future generations of working age are likely to have to pay more taxes to finance state pensions on a pay-as-you-go basis (*eg*, because of population ageing), it may be sensible to run smaller budget deficits now, so that they do not also inherit a high public-sector-debt ratio.

But while looking at the public-sector balance sheet, demographic trends, the future cost of state pension liabilities, etc, is undoubtedly interesting, it is unlikely to give us any clear rules for the budget balance. For instance, prospective demographic developments point to running low budget deficits now, with a view to ensuring relatively low debt ratios in the medium term, but, since we do not know how much better off future generations will be than ourselves, it is difficult to draw any clear-cut conclusions.

Another (related) set of arguments for aiming for budget balance or only a small deficit is that otherwise aggregate national saving may be lower than is desirable (*eg*, because of disincentives to save arising from the tax and social security systems). Moreover, as the G-10 study on 'Saving, Investment and Real Interest Rates' of October 1995 noted, budget deficits appear to have played a significant part in the trend decline in national saving rates in many developed countries.

3. FISCAL OBJECTIVES

3.1 The medium-term fiscal objective

Thus far I have deliberately avoided considering the relationship between the budget deficit and the state of the economy by focusing on what the deficit ought to be in the medium term, when the economy is on trend. However, even holding other things constant in this way, there is no simple or unique way of defining either how much debt it is appropriate for the public sector to have in relation to GDP or how much it is prudent to borrow in a normal year. A budget deficit which delivers a stable debt ratio and/or meets the 'golden rule' would be a possible benchmark, but it may be desirable to aim for smaller budget deficits than these imply or for budget balance (*eg*, to take account of future pension liabilities, or to put the debt ratio on a stronger downward trend).

Looking across the EU as a whole, it is difficult to see how any single fiscal objective could be right for all Member States, given their different initial debt ratios, public-sector balance sheets, contingent future liabilities, etc.

3.2 Implementing fiscal policy: the effects of the cycle

Even if a government can devise a suitable medium-term fiscal objective, delivering it may not be straightforward because of fluctuations in the economy.

The path of the economy clearly has a major influence on the size of the budget deficit. Most tax receipts vary broadly in line with money-GDP, and some (notably corporation tax) more than proportionately (so that they are higher in relation to GDP in a boom than in a recession). On the expenditure side, planning and control procedures in the UK generally mean that most items of spending remain fixed in the short term as the path of output varies, so that the ratio of spending to GDP varies over the cycle; and this variation is enhanced by the fact that unemployment-related spending will rise and fall over the cycle and so, to some extent, will debt interest payments.

These automatic variations in tax and spending should help to stabilise the economy in the event of shocks to the path of output. But they may make it more difficult to maintain sound public finances, since they may obscure the underlying budgetary picture. However, estimating the underlying deficit may not be easy.

In the first place, even if we can make a fair stab at de-trending the path of output in the past to distinguish between trend and cycle, there are obvious problems in doing this *ex ante*. Projecting trend output is difficult, because we cannot be sure of the true process behind the evolution of potential (*ie*, trend) output, or about the extent of mean reversion likely after economic disturbances. Similarly, it is difficult to be sure of the nature of shocks and whether they are permanent or transitory until one has the benefit of hindsight. For instance, a slowdown in growth might initially be regarded as temporary, but it might prove in practice to be a more permanent slowdown in the growth of potential output. Estimates of the underlying level of GDP are thus subject to uncertainty.

So are estimates of what the budget deficit would be if output were at this trend level of GDP (assuming current tax and spending policies). Experience suggests that there is not a simple arithmetic relationship between money-GDP, on the one hand, and tax receipts and unemployment-related spending, on the other. Relationships estimated on past data are always vulnerable to the fact that one cycle is never the same as the last. There is always a range of special factors, including changes to the tax/benefit regime, to be taken into account.

These analytical problems may make it tempting not to bother about the 'underlying' deficit, and just focus on the actual deficit. But pursuing a rule for the actual budget balance, irrespective of the cycle, could well be a costly policy.

We are not in practice completely agnostic about the causes of the business cycle. Despite the theoretical attractions of real-business-cycle models, they do not appear to explain very well the magnitude of actual cycles. In practice, there is a form of 'natural-rate' model underlying the approach to macroeconomic policy adopted in most countries, implying that a distinction between cyclical and trend elements is valid and giving a significant role to transitory, demand-side factors in explaining economic fluctuations.

On such a view of the world, overriding the automatic stabilisers (when a shock is transitory) is likely to be destabilising, making recessions worse and accentuating booms. It is, accordingly, not something which a government would generally wish to do, unless it is clear that such a tightening/easing of policy would be desirable on other grounds, for example, to support monetary policy.

More frequent variations in tax rates to offset the effects of cyclical variations in the budget deficit have supply-side costs. In-year changes to spending plans may also harm the efficient delivery of public services.

Creative accounting wheezes and delaying or accelerating the payment of bills might avoid some of the costs associated with more substantive measures to offset the effects of cyclical variations in budget deficits, but obviously raise questions about the point of sticking to a target for the actual budget deficit in such circumstances (as well as about the government's commitment to maintaining sound public finances).

Assuming, then, that there is a presumption that the in-built stabilisers should be allowed to operate, how large might we expect them to be? Research at the Treasury[1] suggests that in the UK a 1 per cent increase in output relative to trend would after two years reduce the ratio of the budget deficit to GDP by about 0.75 per cent.

This study used an eclectic approach to trend estimation, drawing upon both statistical trend extraction and productive-potential approaches. The result is in effect a split, 'deterministic' trend (with the timing and magnitude of breaks informed by a Kalman filter analysis); IMF and OECD analyses use much the same sort of approach.

An important aspect of the study is a careful attempt to adjust for the effects of discretionary tax changes on receipts. Failure to remove these effects can easily bias econometric estimates of the true cyclical responsiveness of tax receipts. To estimate the cyclical component of tax receipts, the adjusted receipts series were regressed on the output gap. This was done for aggregate and individual tax receipts. The results were broadly consistent and indicated that receipts vary significantly in relation to GDP over the cycle: a 1 per cent rise in output relative to trend increasing the ratio of aggregate receipts to GDP by 0.25 per cent after two years, with corporation-tax receipts showing a particularly marked cyclical pattern.

These estimates of the cyclical responsiveness of the budget deficit are a little above the more broad-brush estimates produced by the OECD and IMF. But even on the OECD estimation, the cyclical component of the UK budget deficit has on occasion been as large as 3 per cent of GDP, with a swing over the latest cycle of some 5 per cent of GDP. In short, this essentially passive response of the budget deficit to the cycle is clearly far from trivial.

To conclude this section, output variations clearly present a significant operational problem for fiscal policy, even when governments are directing policy primarily at maintaining sound public finances. Past experience

---

1. S. Virley and M. Hurst, *Public Finances and the Cycle*, Treasury Occasional Paper No. 4 (1995).

suggests that cyclical variations in output can have significant automatic effects on the budget balance. On conventional views about the causes of output variations, governments would not generally wish to override these automatic effects by making discretionary policy changes. But there could be exceptions to such a rule – for example, where the authorities wanted a discretionary tightening of fiscal policy to reinforce the effects of a monetary-policy tightening, or where the output variation had been caused by permanent (particularly supply-side) disturbances. Attempting to use fiscal policy to offset the effects of permanent shocks could put sound public finances at risk. (Slower growth in trend output would mean that tax receipts would be permanently lower than previously expected, producing persistently bigger budget deficits, if no action is taken.) The problem is that it may take some time before one can reasonably gauge whether a shock is temporary or permanent.

There may be a case for setting some ceiling on the actual budget deficit, as a fail-safe against mistakenly identifying a period of weak growth as cyclical (and thus justifying an automatic rise in budget deficits) when it is actually a slowdown in trend growth. But the level at which that ceiling should be set (and the rigidity with which it should be applied) will depend on the appropriate level of the budget deficit when the economy is operating at trend levels (*ie*, the medium-term fiscal objective) and the cyclical variability in output and public finances that might normally be expected.

4. FISCAL POLICY IN A SINGLE-CURRENCY AREA

Maintaining sound public financing is an essentially timeless objective. Aiming for budget balance or only a small deficit in normal times would continue to be appropriate in a monetary union. The problem is how much variation about that norm to allow and in what circumstances.

Moving to a single-currency area means that an individual country cannot use monetary policy for country-specific stabilisation purposes. It should, though, continue to be practicable and desirable (especially given wage/price stickiness) to allow national fiscal policies to cushion the effects of transitory shocks to national output. The efficacy of fiscal policy might even increase, for example, because a national fiscal expansion might be expected to push up a country's interest rate and exchange rate to a lesser extent in a single-currency area.

But not all shocks are transitory and as I have discussed, it may not be easy at the time to judge whether a shock is temporary or permanent. Permanent shocks are likely to require some adjustment in domestic absorption and in the allocation of resources. Unless there was some discretionary fiscal tightening in response to a shock which reduced trend output, the structural budget deficit would rise, since tax receipts would be lower on a permanent basis, while public expenditure would, if anything, be higher. This would pose a threat to sound public finances.

Permanent shocks which are country-specific may well require changes in *real* exchange rates between the participants of the single-currency area for successful adjustment. By definition, these can no longer take place through changes in nominal exchange rates. This points to a need for greater flexibility in real wages and increased labour mobility, responses which the use of fiscal policy to offset the demand effects of shocks could tend to slow down.

The conclusion is perhaps that the role of fiscal policy would not fundamentally change in a single-currency area, nor would the main operational concerns. Maintaining sound public finances would remain the prime objective, but fiscal policy would continue to have a useful role to play when transitory shocks hit an economy (particularly where they are country-specific and where real exchange adjustment would not necessarily have been an optimal response even under floating exchange rates).

If anything, the importance of successfully distinguishing between permanent and temporary shocks would tend to increase (if sound public finances are not to be put at risk), and so might the importance of being prepared to resist the temptation to delay action (*eg*, because adjustment to an adverse permanent shock by reducing real wages would be painful).

This may reinforce the case for setting some form of ceiling on actual budget deficits. As we have seen, though, the analytical basis for quantifying such a rule does not give clearcut answers. Economic analysis points to aiming to balance the budget or run only very small budget deficits in normal times, but it does not give any clear guidance on quantifying this norm, or on whether the same norm would be appropriate for all countries.

Given this, and the inevitable uncertainty about how great cyclical variability in budget deficits will be in a new single-currency area, economic analysis can also not give any clear-cut answers on the level of a ceiling on budget deficits that would be consistent with achieving the medium-term fiscal objective. This may point to allowing some discretion, as an unduly rigid ceiling could impose costs. However, since we cannot be sure what the scale or frequency of asymmetric, country-specific shocks will be, it is difficult to tell in advance of forming a single-currency area how great these costs might be.

5.   CONCLUDING REMARKS

This chapter has reviewed some of the main economic factors relevant to the setting of medium-term fiscal objectives and ceilings for budget deficits. Both could play an important role in ensuring that sound public finances are maintained, but economic analysis does not suggest any clear conclusions on the parameters that should be chosen. In a world of permanently low inflation, budget deficits in normal times need to be very small or close to balance (especially given prospective demographic developments, the relatively low levels of national saving at present, and so on). However, there may be costs in terms of a single monetary area's ability to take adverse (country-specific) shocks in its stride, if a ceiling linked to this medium-term objective is implemented in an unduly restricted manner.

Chapter Fourteen

NATIONAL DEBT BOARDS: AN INSTITUTIONAL ROUTE TO FISCAL DISCIPLINE

Ian Harden and Jürgen von Hagen *

Chapter Outline

1. Introduction

2. Why the Excessive Deficit Procedure Will Not Work

3. Budget Processes and Fiscal Performance

4. Reform of the Budget Process
   4.1 The debt-change limit
   4.2 National Debt Boards
       4.2.1 The independence of the National Debt Boards
   4.3 Enforcement of the debt-change limit

5. National Debt Boards and the Excessive Deficit Procedure

6. National Debt Boards and Democracy

European Economic and Monetary Union: The Institutional Framework (M. Andenas, L. Gormley, C. Hadjiemmanuil, I. Harden, eds.: 90-411-0687-1: © Kluwer Law International: pub. Kluwer Law International, 1997: printed in Great Britain)

1.   INTRODUCTION

High and rising levels of public debt and large and persistent government deficits are matters of concern in most OECD countries. In some countries, they have reached levels high enough to raise doubts about the soundness of their currencies. Debt-service obligations have reduced the governments' ability to serve more pressing social needs. In Europe, high and rising deficits and debts raise additional concerns as the EU Member States have committed themselves to avoiding 'excessive government deficits' in the upcoming Economic and Monetary Union.[1]

The EU has sought to assure the fulfilment of this commitment by including the excessive deficit procedure in the Maastricht Treaty. The EDP defines what excessive deficits are on the basis of numerical criteria and provides a catalogue of actions that ought to be taken when a country has an excessive deficit. In this chapter, we argue that the EDP is not a promising approach to guarantee fiscal stability in the Member States of the European monetary union. In view of that, we propose an alternative that, in our opinion, promises better results than the EDP. The essence of our approach is to rely on procedural reform of budgeting at the national level, rather than on a numerical criterion to be enforced in intergovernmental co-operation. To make our point, we begin by explaining why we expect the EDP not to work.

2.   WHY THE EXCESSIVE DEFICIT PROCEDURE WILL NOT WORK

There are, at least, four reasons why the EDP will not work. First of all, the EDP promises political and economic sanctions for countries violating the numerical criteria defined in the Protocol on the excessive deficit procedure. Such a promise can only be credible if there is an objective basis for these criteria. Otherwise, countries subject to sanctions would find the procedure unfair and would not comply with the requirements imposed on them. In democratic countries, it must be possible to explain to the public why cutting public spending and raising taxes to meet a numerical criterion is a sensible thing to do. Yet, the numerology of the EDP criteria is

---

*   The research on which this chapter was based was conducted under Phase 2 of the Economic and Social Research Council's Single Market Programme (Grant No: L 113251037). The chapter was completed in June 1996.
1. This commitment is contained in the new Art. 104c of the EC Treaty, as inserted by the Maastricht Treaty.

almost completely arbitrary.[2] It is probably possible to make the public agree that 10 per cent inflation is worse than 3 per cent, but how should we tell the public that a deficit of 3 per cent of GDP is worse than a deficit of 4 per cent? Many fast-growing countries have larger deficits than that, others have smaller ones. Economic theory tells us preciously little about the correct size of the deficit, other than that public debt cannot grow faster than GDP forever.

Second, the numerical criteria must be enforceable. Experience with numerical criteria in the US suggests that they induce substitution into non-regulated forms of state debt and encourage creative accounting.[3] Apart from that, the member governments of the EU have a questionable track record when it comes to enforcing policies that require tough domestic policies – see the experience with state subsidies for airlines and other projects.[4]

Furthermore, experience shows that numerical limits on deficits established by law are not an effective incentive to changes in behaviour. This is because they tend to lack credibility: people do not believe that they will be enforced. Credibility problems are made worse if there are potential discretionary let-outs in the text of the law itself. This was the case, for example, with the Gramm-Rudman-Hollings Deficit Reduction Act in the USA in the mid-1980s.[5] The legislation contained annual deficit targets that declined each year to reach a balanced budget in 1991. The targets were subsequently raised, and the goal of a balanced budget deferred to 1993, but the revised targets were not met either. The Maastricht reference values could also be ignored in practice if it were politically convenient to do so, and their lack of economic justification makes this outcome more probable.

Third, one of the main axioms of regulatory theory, the compliance principle, which holds that regulation will not be effective unless the person regulated is able to control his own behaviour, suggests that performance-oriented criteria such as those of the EDP must be imposed on the political body responsible for the relevant decisions. The assumption underlying the

2. The only objective link in these criteria is that, with an assumed nominal-GDP-growth rate of 5 per cent and an assumed deficit-to-GDP ratio of 3 per cent, the debt-to-GDP ratio must eventually stabilize at 60 per cent.

3. See J. von Hagen, 'A Note on the Empirical Effectiveness of Formal Fiscal Restraints' (1991) 44 *Journal of Public Economics* 99.

4. See, *eg*, M. Dewatripont, F. Giavazzi, J. von Hagen, I. Harden, T. Persson, G. Roland, H. Rosenthal, A. Sapir and G. Tabellini, *Flexible Integration: Towards a More Effective and Democratic Europe*, Monitoring European Integration No. 6, Centre for Economic Policy Research (1995).

5. Balanced Budget and Emergency Deficit Control Act 1985, Public Law 99–177; Balanced Budget and Emergency Deficit Control Reaffirmation Act 1987, Public Law 100–119. See, generally, J. White and A. Wildavsky, *The Deficit and the Public Interest: The Search for Responsible Budgeting in the 1980s* (1989); and A. Wildavsky, *The New Politics of the Budgetary Process* (2nd edn, 1992).

EDP is that national governments are responsible for general-government budget deficits. A review of government budgeting in the EU shows, however, that this is not generally true, because the national frameworks of budgeting do not always give the governments sufficient power.[6]

Finally, the EDP as laid out in the Maastricht Treaty seems much too complicated and cumbersome a procedure to work in practice. The multitude of conditionalities and shared responsibilities makes the process too complex to be practicable.

We conclude, therefore, that the EDP is doomed to fail. The same fear clearly lurks behind Mr Waigel's proposal of a stability pact. But Waigel's hope that, by toughening the process, it can be made to work is misguided. Instead, a workable institutional solution to the problem of excessive deficits must meet three important requirements. First, it must attack the problem at the national level in order to assure democratic acceptability and enforceability. Since the EU will not be, for the foreseeable future, a fiscal union, choices about the relative size of the public sector, about spending priorities and about the distribution of the tax burden will have to be made, legitimated and enforced at the state level. Decisions about borrowing belong at the same level, because they are logically bound up with the other public-finance decisions and need to be legitimated within the same political context. Second, it must be sufficiently flexible to avoid the main weakness of numerical criteria, namely, the lack of responsiveness to changing economic and political conditions. Third, it must be based on reasonable economic and political judgment to avoid the impression of arbitrariness and unfairness.

Such a solution can be sought by institutional reform of the national budget process. The basic idea here is to force political decision-makers to apply certain decision-making procedures, rather than to impose exact standards of performance. The underlying idea is known from other areas of public policy: from regulatory policy, where regulatory agencies are often required to follow specific rules of judgment, rather than to impose product or other standards; and, not least, from monetary policy, where central bank independence, that is, isolating monetary-policy decisions from the government's daily political business, has proven a successful way of achieving low-inflation policies.

Empirical evidence suggests that government deficits and debts are, to a large extent, determined by the quality of the national budget process. Reform of the budget process is, therefore, an important alternative to the EDP. In the next section, we briefly review the role of national budget processes for the government's fiscal performance.

---

6. See J. von Hagen and I. J. Harden, 'National Budget Processes and Fiscal Performance' [1994] 3 *European Economy, Reports and Studies* 311.

3. BUDGET PROCESSES AND FISCAL PERFORMANCE

Political economy views the budget process as a mechanism through which political interest groups 'bargain over conflicting goals, make side-payments, and try to motivate one another to accomplish their objectives'.[7] In the broadest sense, the budget process is a system of rules, both formal and informal, governing the decision-making process that leads to the formulation of a budget by the executive, its passage through the legislature and its implementation. These rules divide this process into steps and determine which steps are taken when. The rules also assign roles and responsibilities to the participants and regulate the flow of information among them, thus distributing strategic influence and creating or destroying opportunities for collusion. Interest in the budget process derives from the widespread belief that the process itself can shape the decisions made according to its rules.[8] In particular, by changing the institutional rules that form the budget process, a government's fiscal performance can be changed in a predictable way.[9]

How can the budget process influence the budget and, most importantly, the budget deficit? A general characteristic of modern public finances is that government activities tend to be targeted at specific groups while being paid for by the general taxpayer.[10] The incongruence between those who benefit and those who pay implies that policy-makers representing spending agencies or groups benefiting from particular public activities take into account the full benefit from expanding the programmes with which they are concerned, but recognise only that part of the costs that falls on their constituencies. As a result, policy-makers systematically overestimate the net marginal benefit of increasing public spending and, hence, use their political clout to increase spending beyond the level that would equate social marginal costs and benefits. For example, a member of parliament representing a particular electoral district will appreciate the full value of road improvements for the local economy. But since his district pays only a small portion of the central government's tax revenues, he will ask for more road improvements when the central government pays for them than when they have to be paid for by local taxes. As all policy-makers have reasons to behave in the same way, the result is excessive spending. We call this the 'common-pool problem' of government budgeting, because the nature of

7. A. Wildavsky, *Budgeting* (1975), p.4.
8. I. Rubin, *The Politics of Public Budgeting: Getting and Spending, Borrowing and Balancing* (1993).
9. Note that this belief has also found its way into the Maastricht Treaty: Art. 3 of the EDP Protocol commits the Member States to putting in place 'national procedures in the budgetary area' that 'enable them to meet their obligations in this area deriving from this Treaty'.
10. See, *eg*, J. M. Buchanan and G. W. Tullock, *The Calculus of Consent* (1962); and M. Olson, *The Logic of Collective Action* (1965).

the problem is not unlike that of a common resource exploited by unco-ordinated private parties.

From the point of view of political economy, the question then is, how can the common-pool problem be mitigated by institutional structures that correct the flawed incentives. The key to an answer is in the introduction of elements of *centralisation* into the budget process, that is, institutional provisions that promote a comprehensive view of the marginal costs and benefits of public activities and diminish the power of special interests. Such elements can be sought at all levels of the budget process.[11] At the executive planning stage, giving the finance minister and/or the prime minister special strategic powers over the spending ministers is important. Examples of this are the strong agenda-setting powers of the French Finance Minister in the budget process or the veto power of the German Finance Minister. Alternatively, the common-pool problem at this stage can be addressed by forcing the cabinet members to reach a collective agreement on the main budget parameters early on in the process. At the level of the legislative process, the strength of the government relative to the legislature is the critical variable. The more limited the scope for amendments, the less important the common-pool problem will be at this stage. At the implementation stage, finally, the power of the finance minister to make the budget binding for the spending departments clearly matters.

Looking across the EU countries, one can easily see that there is a fair degree of institutional variation in the budget processes. This allows us to consider the link between the institutional design of the budget process and fiscal performance empirically. For this purpose, von Hagen has developed a numerical *index of centralisation of the budget process*, a gauge of how strong elements of centralisation are in different countries.[12] A high score on the index indicates the following characteristics in a country's budget process:

(i) a strong position of the prime minister or finance minister in government, or government negotiations evolving under a binding general constraint on the size of the budget, imposed early on in the process;

(ii) a parliamentary process with strong limits on amendments, with votes proceeding item-by-item on expenditures, and with a global vote on the total size of the budget preceding the parliamentary debate;

(iii) a large degree of transparency of the budget; and

(iv) an execution process with limited flexibility and a strong position of the finance minister *vis-à-vis* the spending ministers.

11. See J. von Hagen and I. Harden, loc. cit., n.6, for details.
12. J. von Hagen, *Budgeting Procedures and Fiscal Performance*, European Commission DG-II, Economic Papers No. 96 (Oct. 1992).

Figure 1 shows the performance on this index together with the average deficit ratios for the first and the second half of the 1980s of the 12 Member States. The upper half of the graph charts performance on the index, the bottom half the deficit ratios (negative numbers for deficits). France, Luxembourg and Britain rank highest on the index. Elements of centralisation are strongest in these three countries. In contrast, the index shows that Italy and Belgium have the lowest degrees of centralisation in their budget processes. The relationship between centralisation of the budget process and fiscal performance is clearly visible in the figure: countries ranking high on the index have relatively small deficits, while countries ranking low on the index come out with large deficits. Figure 2 provides the same impression for the government debt ratios. Again, we see that countries ranking high on the index have much better fiscal performance in the 1980s than countries ranking low.

In a recent study of budget processes in 28 Latin American states, Alesina *et al.* present evidence similar in spirit and methodology to ours.[13] They, too, find that cross-country differences in public-sector deficits can be

Figure 1

Centralisation of budget process and public-deficit performance

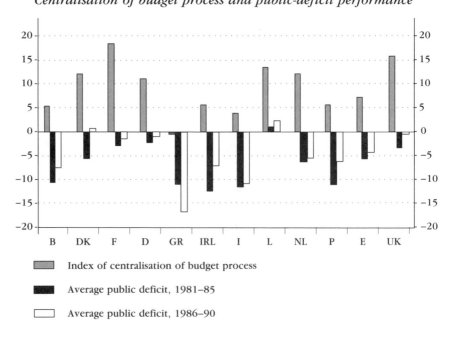

■■■ Index of centralisation of budget process

■ Average public deficit, 1981–85

☐ Average public deficit, 1986–90

13. A. Alesina, R. Hausmann, R. Hommes and E. Stein, *Budget Institutions and Fiscal Performance in Latin America*, mimeo, Interamerican Development Bank (1995).

Figure 2

Centralisation of budget process and public-debt ratios

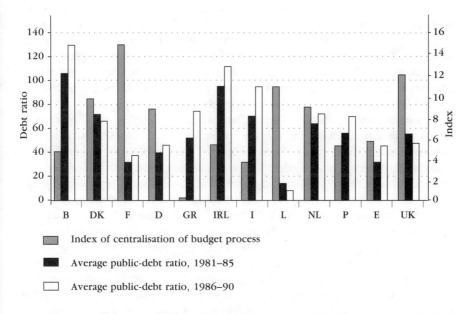

☐ Index of centralisation of budget process

■ Average public-debt ratio, 1981–85

☐ Average public-debt ratio, 1986–90

explained by differences in the degree of centralisation of the budget process. In sum, the empirical evidence strongly suggests that reform of the budget process is a promising way to enable governments to comply with the commitment to sound public finances embodied in the Maastricht Treaty. With this in mind, we now turn to a specific reform proposal.

4. REFORM OF THE BUDGET PROCESS

The first part of this chapter has explained that there is a link between the process through which budgetary decisions are made and the budgetary outcomes in terms of levels of debt and deficits. This part outlines how reform of the budget process can improve the outcomes. The term 'budget process' refers to two main elements: the participants, and what they do. The participants are the range of actors involved in making budgetary decisions and putting them into effect. They have defined institutional roles, and there is a division of authority and responsibility between them. What they do also has a strong institutional dimension in the form of procedures; that is to say, of a defined set of activities carried out in a particular sequence. Institutional roles and procedures are partly laid down by formal rules and principles, but are also partly matters of administrative practice.

Reform of the budget process may involve either the institutional or procedural dimensions, or both. An example of procedural change is the New Zealand Fiscal Responsibility Act 1994.[14] The Act sets out principles of responsible fiscal management. It requires the government to publish an annual budget-policy statement three months before the budget is presented to Parliament. The budget-policy statement must specify the government's long-term objectives for fiscal policy and its objectives for the coming year's budget. The statement must also explain how the objectives accord with the principles set out in the Act. The legislation does not oblige the government to pursue a particular budgetary policy, but it does structure the government's discretion. The government must address the question of what its long-term fiscal objectives should be, and consider how its annual budget choices relate to those objectives. Furthermore, it must publish an explanation of its reasoning on these matters. As a result, it must take into account – though not necessarily act upon – a long-term fiscal perspective.

Analogous arrangements in the field of monetary policy have been put in place in the United Kingdom following sterling's ejection from the Exchange Rate Mechanism in 1992. Unlike the New Zealand Fiscal Responsibility Act, however, the changes to UK monetary policy are a matter of administrative practice, not law. Monetary-policy decisions continue to be made by the Chancellor of the Exchequer. The government publishes a target range for inflation, while the Bank of England publishes an inflation forecast, without prior vetting by the Treasury.[15] There are monthly meetings between the Governor of the Bank and the Chancellor, at which the Governor advises on the interest-rate changes that he judges necessary to stay within the target inflation range. Since 1994, the minutes of the meetings have been published after a six-week delay.[16]

The procedural changes outlined above improve the transparency of decision-making. This is valuable for democracy; what government is doing is more visible and understandable to citizens. The gain in transparency is greater in the New Zealand case, because the reforms are embodied in legislation. This means that any further change to the procedures would also have to be transparent. In contrast, there is no such guarantee of transparency if there were to be further shifts of administrative practice in UK monetary-policy decision-making.

---

14. 1994, No. 17. For commentary, see G. Scott, 'New Zealand's Fiscal Responsibility Act' (1995) 2 *Agenda* 3.
15. See Treasury and Civil Service Committee, First Report: 'The Role of the Bank of England', HC (1993–94) 98, paras 20–21.
16. HC Deb. (6th Ser.), Vol. 241, col. W170, written answers, 13 April 1994.

Greater transparency may also result in substantive changes; that is, in decisions different from those that would otherwise have been made. Forcing government to reflect on the long-term consequences of its choices may bring about changes in its behaviour. But procedural change of this kind has a general weakness. That is, decision-makers may continue to behave in fundamentally the same way and merely put a new gloss on what they are doing. This is likely to be the case if the problem is not ignorance, but distorted incentives. As we have seen in the first part of this chapter, the 'common-pool problem' and 'deficit bias' do indeed distort the pattern of incentives for the actors in the budget process. Greater transparency can alter the incentive structure by making criticism of the government more likely and more effective. By itself, however, this is insufficient to counteract the common-pool problem and deficit bias.

The second and more far-reaching type of reform is institutional. This involves changing the structure of authority and responsibility in the budget process; that is, either reallocating decision-making powers between existing actors, or creating a new actor. The analogy in monetary policy is central bank independence.

4.1   The debt-change limit

Our proposal for reform of the budget process involves both procedural and institutional reform.[17] The basic idea is that in each country there should be a legally binding decision about the maximum permissible change in the total stock of public debt during the forthcoming budget year. We call this the 'debt-change limit' ('DCL'). The DCL would be fixed at the beginning of the planning process for the following year's budget. Typically, in most European countries this is six to nine months before the beginning of the budget year. The DCL would be determined by a new institution, called the 'National Debt Board' ('NDB').

Once announced, the DCL would be binding on the government and the parliament and could not be changed, even by the NDB. There would be only two exceptions. First, the government could suspend the DCL if it declared war against another state. Second, the NDB could revise the DCL if it made a formal determination that it was necessary to do so because of a natural disaster.

Fixing the DCL at the very beginning of the budget round means that, at every stage of the budget process, the participants face an upper constraint on possible borrowing. Spending agencies would know of the constraint when submitting their budget bids. The government and cabinet would be

---

17.   First set out in J. von Hagen and I. Harden, loc. cit., n.6.

bound by the constraint in preparing the budget, and parliament would be bound by it in debating and amending the government's budget proposal.

Each state would enact legislation setting up its own National Debt Board. The precise details of the legislation would have to vary according to the legal and constitutional system of the particular state concerned. In what follows, we set out the results that need to be achieved by the legislation in order to implement the NDB scheme.

4.2 National Debt Boards

The NDB would be established by ordinary legislation, without any constitutional entrenchment. The primary objective of the NDB, set out in the legislation, would be to safeguard the soundness and stability of the country's public finances. Without prejudice to that objective, it would support the general economic policies of the government. The intention of the latter formula is that the NDB should itself make the economic judgments concerned: even in relation to the second part of its mandate, it should not be subject to instruction by the government. Equally, however, the NDB would not have a mandate to define an agenda of fiscal policy of its own. The NDB's mandate and the interpretation of the second part of the mandate are based on the analogy of the German Bundesbank.

The process change involved in creating a NDB has a family resemblance to that involved in creating an independent central bank. But the NDB's range of powers and responsibilities would be much more limited. An independent central bank has responsibility for determining and executing monetary policy. The NDB would have no such broad authority over public-finance issues. It would have no role to play in determining expenditure priorities, nor in allocating the tax burden between different sources of revenue. It would have no mandate to develop its own fiscal or budgetary policy. Its task would be to set the annual DCL with the objective of safeguarding the soundness of the public finances. The job of determining spending and taxing levels within the overall constraint imposed by the DCL would be left to the government and the parliament. There is no reason why they should plan to borrow up to the limit. It would make more sense to leave room for the unexpected. But that would be a judgment for government and parliament to make.

An important feature of the proposal is that the NDB would be accountable to the parliament, but its accountability would be separate from that of the government. The reasons for having separate account-ability, and the details of how to achieve it, are discussed below. To maintain the separation, the NDB must be independent of government. The next section discusses how to achieve such independence.

4.2.1   The independence of the National Debt Boards

The independence of the NDB has two dimensions. The first is institutional, and consists of ensuring that the NDB has the organisational structure and resources needed to carry out its mandate. The second is the personal independence of its members. This requires minimisation of potential incentives to depart from the NDB's mandate, or to defer to the judgment of others in carrying it out.

We envisage that the institutional home of the NDB would be a 'National Debt Institute' ('NDI'). The NDI would be headed by a chairperson and a vice-chairperson in charge of administration. It would have two branches: a small permanent staff working for the NDB and a Debt-Monitoring Commission, whose role is described in the next section. It is important that the NDI should have full budgetary autonomy. In some states, the method of determining the budget of the supreme audit institution offers an appropriate model.[18] Alternatively, the NDI could be entrusted with the management of the central government's debt. In the latter case, it could charge a fee to cover its total expenditure, thus removing the need for annual appropriation of its budget by parliament.

The NDB and its members would be forbidden to accept instructions from government, parliament, or anyone else. The NDB would be entitled to receive information or advice from any person, but information or advice given by, or on behalf of, government, a non-independent agency of government or a political party would be required to be placed in a public record. The requirement of transparency is designed to minimise the risk of undue pressure being put on the NDB and its members and to allow critical scrutiny of information supplied by governmental and political sources.

NDBs need have only a small number of members, for instance, between three and seven. They would be persons of recognised standing and professional expertise in matters of public finance or public audit. Appointments would be made by government, from a list of names submitted by the NDB itself, and subject to hearing and approval by the parliament. To promote their personal independence, NDB members would not be allowed to work for the government and would be ineligible for such work for five years following the end of their terms. They would be appointed for long non-renewable terms (for instance, eight years – the period chosen for members of the Executive Board of the European Central Bank[19]). Appointments would be staggered, with one member retiring each year, to minimise the force of partisanship in appointments. Salaries of the members of the NDB would be determined by a formula, laid down by law, linking them to ministerial salaries.

18. In the UK, *eg*, consider the role of the Public Accounts Commission in relation to the National Audit Office; see National Audit Act 1983, s.4.
19. EC Treaty, Art. 109a (2).

4.3   Enforcement of the debt-change limit

To ensure compliance with the DCL, there would need to be a rule (either a rule of law or a parliamentary standing order) that no budget legislation could be proposed or enacted, in which the planned level of borrowing would cause the DCL to be exceeded. The rule would apply to the main budget legislation and to any supplementary budgets. There would also have to be independent monitoring of compliance with the DCL during the budget year. This would be the task of the other part of the NDI, the Debt-Monitoring Commission.

If the Debt-Monitoring Commission's projections showed that the DCL was likely to be exceeded, it would make a public report to that effect. The government would then have one month in which to bring before parliament measures to prevent breach of the DCL. If such measures were not proposed, or not enacted within a further month, spending for the remainder of the budget year would be restricted by an across-the-board spending limit. The finance minister (or another appropriate body, depending on the state concerned) would have both a legal power and a duty to enforce the spending limit by imposing a block on expenditures.

As with all forms of regulation, there would undoubtedly be changes of behaviour designed to circumvent the DCL. An obvious danger is manipulation of accounting techniques. To make this more difficult, there should be independent audit of the government's financial reporting. This would in turn require the establishment of generally accepted accounting principles and standards to be used in the preparation of government financial reports.[20]

Some other possible techniques of evasion are caught by using a debt-change limit, rather than a deficit limit. For example, many states have off-budget public entities, whose debt and deficits do not count as part of the national definitions of public or state debt and deficits. Such bodies may be created for legitimate reasons, as is recognised by the Maastricht Treaty, whose definitions exclude public commercial bodies.[21] In some countries, however, the debt of certain off-budget entities is regularly taken over by

20. Cf. the New Zealand Fiscal Responsibility Act 1994, s.5.
21. Public commercial enterprises are excluded from privileged access to financial institutions, but their deficits and debt are not counted for purposes of the excessive deficit procedure; see EC Treaty, Art. 104a; and Council Regulations (EC) No. 3604/93 of 13.12.93 and (EC) No. 3605/93 of 22.11.93, Art. 1 (2) ('The exclusion of commercial operations means that the sector of general government (S60) comprises only institutional units producing non-market services as their main activity'). The German agency charged with privatising the industry of former East Germany (the Treuhand) fell within this exemption, so that its borrowing was excluded from Commission figures for German budget deficits.

the state. In effect, this is a way of disguising the extent of annual public deficits. Such debt takeovers would be caught by the DCL.[22]

There would also need to be close monitoring of the activities of government-owned financial institutions and of the use of loan-guarantees by government as an alternative to direct spending or borrowing for on-lending. The Debt-Monitoring Commission and the state's supreme audit institution would need to work together to ensure that the effectiveness of the debt constraint was not undermined by creative accounting or other techniques of evasion.

A related danger is what is known in the United States as the 'Rosy Scenario'; that is, relying on macroeconomic forecasts and projections that are unduly optimistic. Both the National Debt Board and the Debt-Monitoring Commission must have the right to make their own determinations of the data on which their decisions are based.

5.   NATIONAL DEBT BOARDS AND THE EXCESSIVE DEFICIT PROCEDURE

The provisions of the Maastricht Treaty about 'excessive deficits' have a number of overlapping objectives. The first objective is to provide a test: only those states which do not have an 'excessive deficit' are to be allowed to join the monetary union when the third stage of EMU begins. Second, the provisions are intended to promote sound public finances in all states, whether or not they pass the test for joining the monetary union from the beginning. Finally, they are intended to provide a way of dealing with a state that passes the test, joins the monetary union, but subsequently fails to observe budgetary discipline.

Underlying all three objectives is a general principle: the desirability of sound public finances. Excessive government borrowing is a threat to price stability. Maintenance of price stability and of sound public finances go together as fundamental principles of the EC Treaty.[23] The logic of the Treaty's provisions is that each Member State is responsible for ensuring the soundness of its own public finances. The EDP should not therefore be regarded as a substitute for states making their own fiscal-policy decisions. The responsibility of Member States is emphasised by the 'no bail-out rule', which forbids the Community to assume the commitments of governments

---

22. This is also the position as regards the Maastricht definitions. Hence, when the German federal government took over Treuhand's stock of debt in 1995, this was reflected in a sudden jump in the Maastricht debt figures for Germany. Note that debt takeovers may also require approval by the Commission under the Community state-aids regime.
23. See, in particular, EC Treaty, Arts 3a and 105.

or other public bodies of any Member State.[24] Furthermore, the Treaty provides for the Commission to monitor debt and deficits 'with a view to identifying *gross errors*'.[25]

However, despite the wording of the EC Treaty, the EDP has come to be seen in terms of fixed rules: that is, the 'reference values' of 3 per cent of GDP for deficits and 60 per cent for the debt-to-GDP ratio. Increasingly too, these numbers have been treated as budgetary targets for the Member States, particularly for those which have high debt and deficit levels. A full analysis of why the EDP has come to be seen in this way is beyond the scope of the present chapter. One contributory factor is probably the multiple objectives of the procedure. Another is that both politicians and the public have found the numbers easy to understand. Whatever the causes, the EDP is now widely perceived as consisting of fixed numerical rules imposed by the Union. The numbers are treated as a definition of sound and stable public finances, and the procedure itself is discussed as if it could, or should, be a sufficient mechanism to ensure sound and stable public finances in the Member States. The proposal by the German Finance Minister for a 'stability pact' between those states that join the monetary union has confirmed this approach.

For the reasons discussed in section 2 above, the EDP is unlikely to bring about sustained improvement in the budget-deficit and debt levels of states in which the budget process is weak and conducive to excessive deficits. Nor can the EDP become a substitute for an effective national budget process; that is, it cannot be a kind of 'process bail-out', since it does not attack the problem at the national level. An NDB is likely to be more effective in improving budget outcomes than the EDP. In contrast to the rigidity of numerical limits fixed in law, the NDB could adopt a long-term perspective. In times of recession, it could set annual DCLs so as to take account of automatic stabilisers and discretionary macroeconomic stabilisation, confident in the knowledge that it could cancel these out over the course of the business cycle. Furthermore, the NDB accords with the principle of subsidiarity. Instead of external policing and enforcement by the Commission and Ecofin, National Debt Boards would work within each Member State, relying on local knowledge and expertise about domestic fiscal conditions. This represents institutional and procedural reform at the right level. If the NDB scheme were implemented, the EDP could become what the Treaty's reference to 'gross errors' suggests it should be; that is, a long-stop mechanism that would rarely, if ever, need to be invoked.

---

24. Ibid., Art. 104b; see also Council Regulation (EC) No. 3604/93. States are similarly prohibited from assuming one another's commitments.
25. EC Treaty, Art. 104c (2) (emphasis added).

6. NATIONAL DEBT BOARDS AND DEMOCRACY

The NDB and its members would be independent from the government. In the Anglo-American world, the idea of independent institutions has traditionally had an uneasy relationship with democratic beliefs. In Britain, for example, criticism of 'quangos' often assumes that any public institution that is not directly controlled by government ministers is 'unaccountable and undemocratic'. This approach oversimplifies the position.

An institution may be made accountable by giving it a clear legal mandate and requiring it to explain and justify its actions. An independent central bank can be made accountable in this way.[26] An independent central bank, however, is a 'non-majoritarian' institution.[27] That is to say, it does not have to defer to the judgment of democratically-elected officials in carrying out its legal mandate. An elected body can make its will prevail only if parliament amends or repeals the law under which the central bank operates.

The NDB would, of course, be an accountable institution. Its announcement of the DCL would have to be accompanied by a statement of reasons, explaining and justifying the figure that had been determined. The NDB would also have to provide a retrospective commentary on its decision, which would be submitted to parliament at the same time as the final accounts of the relevant budget year. At this point, parliament would have the opportunity to dismiss the members of the NDB, if the government so recommended. However, if the NDB were dismissed, any DCL already announced would remain in force. Neither the new Board nor anyone else could alter it, except for the two cases already specified (natural disaster or declaration of war).

Its democratic accountability to the parliament means that, although independent of government, the NDB should not be thought of as a 'non-majoritarian' institution. It would be democratically accountable, but separately from government. The justification for the NDB scheme is, not that decisions about public borrowing should be removed from the process of democratic politics, but that institutional reform can help the democratic process to function more effectively. In other words, the NDB is about improving democracy, not limiting its scope.

The budget document authorises taxes and establishes priorities between competing claims on public resources. The total expenditure for which it

---

26. Centre for Economic Policy Research, Report of an independent panel chaired by E. Roll, *Independent and Accountable: A New Mandate for the Bank of England* (Oct. 1993); I. Harden, 'Regulating Government' (1995) 66 *Political Quarterly* 299.

27. G. Majone, *Independence vs. Accountability? Non-Majoritarian Institutions and Democratic Government in Europe*, EUI Working Paper, SPS No. 94/3, European University Institute (1994).

provides implies an overall division of national resources between private and public spending. These are political choices, for which there should be effective democratic accountability. An essential component of such accountability is that the budget must reflect choices that can be explained and defended, rather than merely the results of a process for which no one has overall responsibility.

In all European states, the budget is authorised by a democratically-elected parliament. A parliament, however, cannot function as a collective actor, on whom voters can deliver a judgment through the ballot box. This is why, in practice, the budget is usually the government's budget, and the role of parliament is to hold government to account for the budget. The NDB is also democratically accountable, but separately from the government and over a longer time-scale than the annual budget process. For same states, this amounts to making more transparent conflicts that, at present, take place within the executive branch of government. Finance ministers, for example, typically have a different institutional role from spending ministers. The NDB scheme gives a clearer institutional shape to the role of those whose responsibility is to maintain sound public finance. It also strengthens their role, so as to avoid the foreseeable systematic distortions in the process of making collective choices represented by the common-pool problem and deficit bias.

Why not go further and make the NDB a 'non-majoritarian institution', like a central bank? The justification of central bank independence is a consensus that the primary objective of monetary policy should be price stability – including consensus, within a relatively narrow range, about what 'price stability' means. There is no similar consensus about what constitute prudent levels of deficit and debt. But although different political communities may differ in their views on these questions, every such community needs to articulate a view to guide its budget process. Otherwise, the common-pool problem and deficit bias will run unchecked. Because the NDB must explain its judgment and because it can be dismissed by the parliament, the likely outcome is greater political debate and discussion about the medium and long-term consequences of budgetary decisions.

A similar improvement could also occur in political debate about the total size of public expenditure. Although the NDB would not have authority to prescribe the total amount of public expenditure, its determination of the DCL would have to be based on a view of how large the public sector should be. That view would have to be made clear in the explanation of the DCL. If governments chose to do so, they could ensure that the NDB's decisions were linked to choices made at elections by announcing a multiannual target for the ratio of public expenditures to GDP. This target would be announced by a government upon coming into office. If the target were made valid for the lifetime of the parliament and could be changed only under the same conditions as the DCL, then it would probably become part of each political party's electoral platform.

PART THREE

THE EUROPEAN CENTRAL BANK

Chapter Fifteen

EUROPEAN MONETARY UNION AND CENTRAL BANK INDEPENDENCE

Rosa María Lastra*

Chapter Outline

1. Introduction

2. The Process Leading Towards the Setting Up of the ESCB in Stage Three of EMU

3. Steps Already Taken in Implementation of the Maastricht Treaty

4. Central Bank Independence
   4.1 Central bank independence as a political decision
   4.2 Arguments for and against central bank independence
       4.2.1 The arguments for independence
       4.2.2 The arguments against independence
       4.2.3 Conclusion: accountable independence
   4.3 The legal articulation of independence
   4.4 Organic safeguards of independence
       4.4.1 Appointment
       4.4.2 Terms of office
       4.4.3 Dismissal
       4.4.4 Suitability and salary
       4.4.5 Prohibitions applicable to central bank officials while in office
       4.4.6 Restrictions on central bank officials after they leave office
       4.4.7 Liaisons with Treasury or minister of finance
   4.5 Functional safeguards of independence

—Cont'd.

European Economic and Monetary Union: The Institutional Framework (M. Andenas, L. Gormley, C. Hadjiemmanuil, I. Harden, eds.: 90-411-0687-1: © Kluwer Law International: pub. Kluwer Law International, 1997: printed in Great Britain)

1. INTRODUCTION

The establishment of the European Central Bank and the European System of Central Banks as envisioned in the Treaty on European Union, commonly referred to as the Maastricht Treaty, is an important step in the transformation of the European Union into a fully functioning, integrated financial market. The effectiveness of the ESCB depends in large part to the independence with which it will be allowed to operate. The structuring of this independence will depend upon both theoretical and political decisions, and it promises to involve many interesting (if not controversial) questions. In this chapter, my discussion of the ESCB will proceed along the lines of three different issues:

(i)   the process leading towards the setting up of the ESCB in Stage Three of EMU;
(ii) the steps already taken in the implementation of the Maastricht Treaty; and
(iii) central bank independence.

The first two issues are of particular interest for Europeans, and offer a general backdrop for the discussion of central bank independence. I approach the third issue by laying out a general discussion that is structured in such a manner as to illuminate the major considerations that must go into the framing of a central bank's independence. Specific examples of the devices that have been employed by both the individual Member States and the Community as such via the Maastricht Treaty are offered in an attempt to place the discussion in a European context, so that the issue of central bank independence can be examined as it directly affects EMU and the establishment of the ESCB. Crucial at the level of the European Union, the independence issue is also key for other nations in the developed world and for developing countries.

2.   THE PROCESS LEADING TOWARDS THE SETTING UP OF THE ESCB IN STAGE THREE OF EMU

Though the Maastricht Treaty partially addresses the challenges of the 1990s, it fails to provide an adequate solution to some of the concerns of Member States and prospective applicants. There are also constitutional constraints in the realisation of the goals agreed upon in Maastricht. The EU

*   The author is grateful to Sam Cross, Hans Decker, Charles Goodhart, Manuel Guitián, Peter Kenen and Etienne de Lhoneux for helpful comments, and to Matthew Morgan for editorial assistance.

is not a federation. Neither the Maastricht Treaty nor the founding treaties of the European Communities provide a formal 'Constitution' to the Union. Moreover, the non-exclusive transfer of sovereign powers from the Member States to the EU institutions in Stage Three of EMU will result in a dual responsibility, divided between EU institutions and national authorities.

It should be noted that the Maastricht Treaty is a rather complex legal document. Amendments to the Treaty establishing the European Economic Community – pertaining, *inter alia*, to monetary union – comprise Article G of the Maastricht Treaty. The European Union is formed of the three existing European Communities, that is, the European Coal and Steel Community, the European Economic Community – now the European Community[1] – and the European Atomic Energy Community (Euratom), and is supplemented by two forms of co-operation established by the Maastricht Treaty, the common foreign and security policy and the co-operation in the areas of justice and home affairs.[2]

While the Single European Act captured the momentum gained in the launching of the internal-market programme, establishing an '[area] without internal frontiers in which the free movement of goods, persons, services and capital is ensured',[3] and prepared the way for further monetary co-operation,[4] the Maastricht Treaty tried to capitalise on the momentum gained in the road towards EMU. However, its drafting, signature, ratification and implementation provide a good example of the ups and downs of the history of EC integration. The Treaty finally came into force on 1 November 1993, opening the way towards the future establishment of the ESCB. Its forerunner, the European Monetary Institute, started

1. Art. G.A of the Maastricht Treaty states that, throughout the Treaty of Rome, the term 'European Economic Community' shall be replaced by the term 'European Community'.
2. See Art. A of the Maastricht Treaty; and the Judgment of the German Federal Constitutional Court (Bundesverfassungsgericht) of 12 Oct. 1993 in the case of *Brunner v The European Union Treaty*, Cases 2 BvR 2134/92 and 2159/92, BVerGE 89, 155 (1993), English translation published in [1994] 1 CMLR 57.
3. See EEC Treaty, Art. 8a, as revised by the SEA.
4. With the insertion in Part Three, Title II, of the EEC Treaty of a new Chapter 1, entitled 'Cooperation in Economic and Monetary Policy (Economic and Monetary Union)'. Art. 102a, which was the only provision in that chapter, read as follows:
    '1. In order to ensure the convergence of economic and monetary policies which is necessary for the further development of the Community, Member States shall cooperate in accordance with the objectives of Article 104. In so doing, they shall take account of the experience acquired in cooperation within the framework of the European Monetary System (EMS) and in developing the ECU, and shall respect existing powers in this field.
    2. Insofar as further development in the field of economic and monetary policy necessitates institutional changes, the provisions of Article 236 shall be applicable. The Monetary Committee and the Committee of Governors of the Central Banks shall also be consulted regarding institutional changes in the monetary area.'

operations in January 1994, at the start of Stage Two of EMU, which is conceived as a transitional and preparatory phase for entry into Stage Three. The EMI is a rather weak institution, whose operations display a continuity with the Committee of EEC Central Bank Governors which it replaced,[5] rather than a substantial new approach to the realisation of EMU. More monetary stability seems to be necessary in order to move ahead with the EMU plan and – as the Member States retain their monetary-policy responsibilities in Stage Two – it is contested whether the EMI has the powers to achieve this goal.[6]

Paradoxically, the Maastricht Treaty gained binding legal force at a time when some Member States were more preoccupied about their growth prospects and their unemployment problems than they were about the pursuit of price stability. The economic slowdown in many European countries and the historical events that have changed the shape of Europe at the beginning of the 1990s, namely, German reunification, the break-up of the former Soviet Union, the transition in Eastern Europe and the former Soviet Union from centrally planned economies to market economies, and the break-up and war in Yugoslavia, have signified a change of priorities in the European continent.

Arguably, the supranational objectives agreed in Maastricht are out of touch with European citizens and their expectations. The latter criticism was evidenced during the period of ratification of the Maastricht Treaty. The Danish and French referenda, the British opposition to the Treaty, the legal challenges presented to the German Constitutional Court,[7] the strength of popular opinion in Germany against the disappearance of the Deutsche Mark and a general disenchantment across Europe, with a Community perceived as distant from its citizens, were some of the difficulties Member States faced during this period.

Following the September 1992 currency crisis and the speculative movements in the ensuing months, the Exchange Rate Mechanism of the European Monetary System was reformed in August 1993. The widening of

---

5. The EMI also replaced the European Monetary Cooperation Fund (EMCF). See EC Treaty, Art. 109f.
6. An article published in the *Financial Times*, 31 Jan. 1994, reported that Mr Tietmeyer, the Bundesbank's President, speaking at the annual meeting of the World Economic Forum in Davos, had ruled out transferring any of its currency reserves to the newly established EMI. Mr Tietmeyer had stressed the *advisory* role of the EMI, and had also said that he did not believe lasting monetary union could be achieved without a parallel political union of EU countries.
7. Though the Bundesrat and the Bundestag approved the Maastricht Treaty in Dec. 1992, full ratification only came after the favourable ruling of the German Constitutional Court of 12 Oct. 1993 in *Brunner* [1994] 1 CMLR 57. Germany was the last country to ratify the Maastricht Treaty, even though the ESCB has been largely patterned upon the Bundesbank model.

the bilateral bands to plus or minus 15 per cent (except for the bilateral relationship between the DM and the Dutch guilder, where the previous + / − 2.25 per cent band still applies) has been characterised by some economists as a virtual breakdown of the system.[8]

With regard to the future of the ERM there are in theory several options,[9] besides the present *status quo*: reintroduction of exchange controls, accelerated move to EMU in a subset of core countries, alternative route to EMU, and reversion to narrow bands. The last option seems to be rejected as an official solution by the ministers of finance of the Member States and by the President of the EMI, since it would require a credible commitment to intervene to defend a currency that is about to move outside those bands (*ie*, a commitment of the central bank of the strongest currency to support the weak currency).[10] Unofficially, however, some Member States (such as Benelux, Denmark and Ireland) have been trying to operate within a fuzzy + / − 2.25 per cent narrow band, and the ERM has been relatively stable since its reformation.

The 'convergence criteria' which Member States must meet in order to qualify for monetary union, defined in Article 109j[11] and further elaborated in the Protocol on the convergence criteria referred to in Article 109j of the Treaty establishing the European Community, which is annexed to the Treaty, refer to price stability, non-excessive government budgetary deficits, stability within the ERM and low long-term interest-rate levels.

According to the letter of the law, stability within the ERM (one of the four criteria of economic convergence) can be understood as stability within the wide bands and, therefore, can be managed in the context of Article 109j. But the spirit of the law when the Maastricht Treaty was signed in February 1992 was different.

---

8. See*, eg,* C. Goodhart, *ERM and EMU*, mimeo (1993).
9. Ibid.
10. An article published in the *Financial Times*, 7 Sept. 1994, p.16, reported that Mr Lamfalussy, the EMI's President, had said that wider ERM bands should be preserved 'in order to defend currencies against speculative attacks'.
11. Art. 109j (l) spells out the following criteria of economic convergence:
    - the achievement of a high degree of price stability; this will be apparent from a rate of inflation which is close to that of, at most, the three best performing Member States in terms of price stability;
    - the sustainability of the government financial position; this will be apparent from having achieved a government budgetary position without a deficit that is excessive as determined in accordance with Art. 104c (6);
    - the observance of the normal fluctuation margins provided for by the exchange-rate mechanism of the European Monetary System, for at least two years, without devaluing against the currency of any other Member State;
    - the durability of convergence achieved by the Member State and of its participation in the exchange-rate mechanism of the European Monetary System being reflected in the long-term interest rate levels.'

The main problem regarding the achievement of economic convergence lies in the size of government deficits, as most of the Member States, including Germany, would not pass today the test of having a 'sustainable government financial position', strictly read. However, the language of Article 104c of the EC Treaty, in combination with the Protocol on the excessive deficit procedure annexed to the Treaty, provides some room for interpretation. Thus, the sustainability of the government financial position is defined by reference to the following criteria:

(a) whether the ratio of planned or actual government deficit to gross domestic product exceeds a reference value [of 3 per cent[12]], unless
 – either the ratio has declined substantially and continuously and reached a level that comes close to the reference value;
 – or, alternatively, the excess over the reference value is only exceptional and temporary and the ratio remains close to the reference value;
(b) whether the ratio of government debt to gross domestic product exceeds a reference value [of 60 per cent[13]], unless the ratio is sufficiently diminishing and approaching the reference value at a satisfactory pace.[14]

Therefore, a country (*eg*, Ireland) whose debt-to-GDP ratio considerably exceeds the 60 per cent reference value, would still be able to qualify for EMU if that ratio is considered to be 'sufficiently diminishing' at a 'satisfactory pace'. The Council, acting on a recommendation from the Commission, will decide whether an excessive deficit exists or not.[15]

The criteria of economic convergence have been regarded by Germany as a *conditio sine qua non* in order to move ahead with EMU. The ruling of the German Constitutional Court of 12 October 1993 clearly reaffirmed:

[T]he convergence criteria cannot be relaxed . . . [T]he Federal Republic of Germany by ratification of the Union Treaty is not subjecting itself to an 'automatic' progress to a monetary union, which is unsupervisable and the momentum of which puts it beyond control . . .[16]

The wording of the Court's ruling is consistent with previous and subsequent declarations of the Bundesbank:

The key to further advance in monetary integration is a sufficient degree of convergence in economic development and economic policy between the member countries of the union . . . [T]he Treaty stipulates that the European economic and monetary union shall enter its third stage on January 1, 1999. However, even then only those countries that meet the convergence criteria can participate.[17]

12. See EDP Protocol, Art. 1.
13. Ibid.
14. EC Treaty, Art. 104c (2).
15. Ibid., Art. 104c (6).
16. [1994] 1 CMLR, pp. 100–1.
17. See [Jan 1994] *Deutsche Bundesbank Monthly Report*, pp.23–4. For previous declarations on this issue, see also the *Monthly Reports* of Aug. 1993, p.27, and February 1992, p.52.

The scepticism reigning in the debate about Maastricht will probably pose difficulties in the fulfilment of the EMU timetable. According to Article 109j of the EC Treaty, not later than 31 December 1996, the Council (meeting in the composition of Heads of State or Government) 'taking due account'[18] of the reports prepared by the Commission and the EMI on the progress made by Member States regarding the convergence criteria, and the opinion of the European Parliament, should decide, acting by a qualified majority, whether a majority of the Member States fulfil the necessary conditions for the adoption of a single currency (*ie*, the convergence criteria) and whether it is appropriate for the Community to enter the third stage; if so, it should set the date for the beginning of Stage Three of EMU. If by the end of 1997 the date for the beginning of the third stage has not been set, Stage Three shall start on 1 January 1999. Despite the latter Treaty provision, the ruling of the German Constitutional Court firmly declared:

Given th[e] conditional nature of the content of the Treaty and the factual convergences it presupposes, the time for the commencement of the third stage of economic and monetary union must also be understood as a target rather than as a legally enforceable date.[19]

The EU is currently holding an intergovernmental conference, for the purpose of revising the Maastricht Treaty as far as seems desirable in the light of experience.[20] Any change in the EMU provisions in the IGC would probably open up a 'Pandora's box': a revision of the timetable for EMU is in fact a revision of the Treaty, and a new ratification by all the Member States in accordance with their respective constitutional requirements[21] would probably mean years of discussion. The Maastricht Treaty represents a compromise between those who favour a federal Europe and those who oppose it. Its ambiguity in many provisions is rooted in this difficult balance. Should the provisions on monetary union be revised in the IGC, EMU might be postponed *sine die*. Seemingly, the only way to go ahead is to respect the principle: '*pacta sunt servanda*', perhaps through a creative reinterpretation of the language of the Treaty pertaining to EMU. A consolidation of the incipient economic recovery in Europe may rekindle enthusiasm for EU integration and should help Governments to streamline their budget deficits, hence facilitating compliance with the Maastricht requirements.

18. A vague expression from a legal point of view.
19. [1994] 1 CMLR, p. 99.
20. Art. N (2) of the Maastricht Treaty reads as follows:
    'A conference of representatives of the governments of the Member States shall be convened in 1996 to examine those provisions of this Treaty for which revision is provided, in accordance with the objectives set out in Articles A and B.'
21. According to Art. N of the Maastricht Treaty.

The real challenge for the IGC lies upon the institutional reform of the European Union, and particularly the future structure of the Parliament to accommodate both the needs of a Community of 15 or more members, and the new responsibilities entrusted to it in the monetary area and, eventually, in the political area. The roles of the Parliament, Commission and Council, as well as the representation and voting powers of the Member States, need to be redefined. Moreover, with a free flow of capital, a new policy on the fiscal means of the Community needs to be adopted.

Together with the debate about the deepening of the institutions of the European Union, the debate about its widening poses much controversy. The EU has only recently opened its doors to Austria, Finland, and Sweden, and several Eastern European countries have already applied or intend to apply.

3. STEPS ALREADY TAKEN IN IMPLEMENTATION OF THE MAASTRICHT TREATY

The implementation of the requirements imposed by the Maastricht Treaty is on course both at the level of the Member States and also at the level of the EU institutions, in the form of secondary Community law. As regards the latter, three EC regulations came into force on 1 January 1994. Two of them specify definitions for the application of the prohibitions contained in Articles 104 and 104a of the EC Treaty, that refer respectively to the prohibition of the financing of government deficits via central bank credit and to the prohibition of privileged access by public authorities to financial institutions.[22] Another regulation concerns the application of the controversial Protocol on the excessive deficit procedure, which requires Member States to report to the Commission their planned and actual government deficits and levels of government debt twice a year.[23] The procedure for avoiding excessive deficits is triggered whenever one of the reference values (3 per cent of government deficit to GDP and 60 per cent of public debt to GDP) is exceeded or threatens to be exceeded.

Furthermore, there are also EC decisions on the functioning of the EMI. One of them refers to the calculation – in terms of population and gross domestic product at market prices – of the Member States' contributions to the financial resources of the EMI.[24] Another important EC decision refers to

---

22. See Council Regulation (EC) No. 3603/93 of 13.12.93, which also specifies definitions for the application of the prohibition referred to in Art. 104b(1); and Council Regulation (EC) No. 3604/93 of 13.12.93.
23. See Art. 4 of the Council Regulation (EC) No. 3065/93 of 22.11.93 on the application of the Protocol on the excessive deficit procedure.
24. See Council Decision 93/716/EC of 22.11.93 on the statistical data to be used for the determination of the key for the financial resources of the European Monetary Institute.

the consultation of the EMI by the Member States on draft legislation relating, *inter alia*, to currency legislation, the status and powers of national central banks, clearing and payment systems and rules applicable to financial institutions.[25]

At the level of the Member States, some of them, such as Italy, France and Belgium, already introduced legislation in compliance with the requirements of Article 108 of the EC Treaty in the course of 1993.[26] Spain and Germany have introduced legislation in 1994, and Greece is expected to enact its legislative proposals soon. The Bank of Spain Autonomy Law was finally enacted in June 1994,[27] following a period of amendments to address some of the concerns posed by the corruption charges faced by the former Governor of the Bank of Spain. In Germany, the Bundesbank Act was amended in July 1994,[28] in order to comply with Article 104 of the EC Treaty and the regulation implementing it. In particular, the authorisation contained in Section 20.1 of the Bundesbank Act, which permitted the Bank to grant short-term cash advances to the Federal and Länder Governments, has been revoked. In connection with the ban on cash advances, Section 17 of the Act, requiring public authorities to deposit their liquid resources with the Bundesbank, has also been repealed.

The United Kingdom, whose central bank recently celebrated its tercentenary anniversary, is considering the idea of central bank independence, without necessarily linking it to the compliance of the Maastricht requirements (Articles 109e (5) and 108 of the EC Treaty). Two relatively recent reports on the independence of the Bank of England, the so-called Roll Report and the report prepared by the House of Commons Treasury and Civil Service Select Committee,[29] have not given rise to any legislative

---

25. Council Decision 93/717/EC of 22.11.93 on the consultation of the European Monetary Institute by the authorities of the Member States on draft legislative provisions.

 In a paper on 'European Monetary Union and the European System of Central Banks', presented in the 4th seminar sponsored by the Legal Department of the IMF (1994), Cynthia C. Lichtenstein points out that 'the EMI may have some *real* power' as regards this review of Member States' draft legislation. 'One can speculate that if a Member State were to exempt its large financial houses from, say, prudential supervision of participants in the derivative markets without consulting the EMI, the EMI might very well have a *judiciable* complaint' (her italics).

26. See R. C. Effros, 'The Maastricht Treaty: Independence of the Central Bank and Implementing Legislation', in T. J. Balino and C. Cottarelli (eds), *Frameworks for Monetary Stability: Policy Issues and Country Experiences* (1994).

27. Law 13/1994, published in the Spanish Official Journal of 2 June 1994.

28. See German Federal Law Gazette of 8 July 1994.

29. See Centre for Economic Policy Research, Report of an independent panel chaired by Eric Roll, *Independent and Accountable: A New Mandate for the Bank of England* (1993); and Treasury and Civil Service Committee, First Report: 'The Role of the Bank of England', HC (1993–94) 98.

initatives so far. Those two reports propose a middle way between the German Bundesbank model and the New Zealand Reserve Bank model for an independent Bank of England.

4. CENTRAL BANK INDEPENDENCE

For central banks in Europe and in other parts of the world, there is a wave of change towards greater independence. It has become more widely accepted that the central bank should be committed to price stability and that, in order to control inflation, the central bank should be independent from political interference. In this section, I would like to point out a few controversial points in the debate about independence.[30]

4.1 Central bank independence as a political decision

Despite the economic merits of central bank independence, the actual decision to grant independence is a political one. Relations between central banks and governments are not easy at all times. The link between economics and politics is a difficult and complex one, which changes across countries and over time. This is true both for European countries and other developed nations, and also for the developing world.

Central bank independence is advocated mainly in the conduct of monetary policy, as a way of accomplishing a partial depolitisation of the money-supply process. In this respect, central bank independence provides an intermediate solution between full depolitisation, as advocated in the free-banking proposals, and politisation, in which all economic policy is under governmental control.

Though independent central banks are generally free to formulate and implement monetary policy, they remain constrained by their statutory objective, which in many cases is price stability.[31] Sometimes the objective is

---

30. Further elaboration on the legal aspects of central bank independence in the context of the EMU proposals can be found, *inter alia*, in R. M. Lastra, 'The Independence of the European System of Central Banks', (1992) 33 *Harv. Int'l L.J. 475.*

31. S. Fischer, 'Modern Central Banking', paper presented at the Bank of England's Tercentenary Celebration, London (June 1994), p.41. Fischer distinguishes between 'goal independence' and 'instrument independence'. See also C. Goodhart and D. Schoenmaker, *Institutional Separation Between Supervisory and Monetary Agencies*, LSE Financial Markets Group (April 1993), p.5; and R. Caesar, 'A European Central Bank: The Issue of Independence', – paper presented at a meeting of the Confederation of European Economic Association (CEEA) on Exchange Rate Regimes and Currency Union, Frankfurt (Feb. 1990), p.3.

defined in narrow terms (*eg*, in New Zealand, where a numerical target is imposed) and some others in broad terms (*eg*, in Germany, where the Bundesbank can flexibly interpret its legal duty of securing the value of the currency). The central bank's mandate may encompass several objectives, rather than a single or primary goal. This is the case, for instance, in the US, where the Federal Reserve System (the Fed) is required by law to pay attention to a variety of unranked targets, including stable prices, growth and employment. As independent central banks can seldom choose their final goal(s), the discussion about central bank independence mainly focuses on the scope of powers delegated to central banks for the achievement of their statutorily defined objectives.

In a democracy there is no real case for a central bank which is totally independent from government. The increasing complexities of monetary and financial management imply an expanding two-way flow of consultation and co-operation between the central bank and the government. There do remain, however, strong reasons for maintaining within government an independent central bank as a widely knowledgeable and expert source of advice and information which can contribute to, and implement, monetary and banking policy.[32]

Central bank independence manifests itself in three ways. It can be organic, functional and professional. The first two dimensions require the protection of a binding legal framework. 'Organic' legal safeguards are directed towards the organisation of the central bank and its institutional relationships with the government; whereas 'functional' or 'operational' guarantees legally define both the functions of the central bank and the scope of powers entrusted to it.[33] The third dimension, 'professional',[34] is part of the *de facto* independence, which, in my opinion, is determined by: the personalities of the governor of the central bank and the minister of finance (and in some countries of other high officials); the political and economic circumstances (*eg*, economic expansion or recession); the history and national priorities of the country concerned; the depth and quality of monetary analysis; the rate of turnover of central bank governors; and other factors.[35]

---

32. See D. Fair, 'The Independence of the Central Bank' (1979) 129 *The Banker* 37.
33. If we dissected central bank independence into political and economic central bank independence, we could argue that political central bank independence depends upon the organic guarantees, and economic central bank independence upon the functional guarantees.
34. O. Pöhl, 'Towards Monetary Union in Europe', in *Europe's Constitutional Future* (1990), emphasised the importance of the 'personal and professional independence of the governing bodies' of the central bank.
35. The measurement of central bank independence generally focuses on the legal framework, though some studies also take into account elements of the *de facto* dimension of central bank independence. See A. Cukierman, S. Webb and B. Neyapti, 'Measuring the Independence of Central Banks and Its Effect on Policy Outcomes' (Sep. 1992) 6:3 *World Bank Economic Review*; and A. Cukierman, *Central Bank Strategy, Credibility, and Independence: Theory and Practice* (1992).

4.2 Arguments for and against central bank independence

4.2.1 The arguments for independence

One of the most common arguments advocating central bank independence is the fear that governments and parliaments will be tempted to succumb to monetary expansions to meet their financial needs, hereby neglecting the risks and detriments of inflation. This problem of so-called 'fiscal inflation' is illustrated in references to historical examples and economic literature. As Keynes eloquently stated:

> The power of taxation by currency depreciation is one which has been inherent to the State since Rome discovered it. The creation of legal tender has been and is a government's ultimate reserve.[36]

Inflation is a non-legislated tax, not subject to parliamentary approval. In order to prevent the monetary financing of government deficits, the central bank should be granted independence.[37]

A variation of this argument maintains that the separation of powers between the legislative and executive branches of the state has a different meaning now than it did in the 19th century. Although parliaments once exercised effective control of government budgets, today parliamentary control and approval of a government's budget can be more of a 'formality' than a real check,[38] at least in some European countries (though certainly not in the US). In this respect, the independence of the central bank could operate like a check on the government, particularly over its fiscal policies, and prohibit monetary financing of government deficits.

Central bank independence is seen as a means of achieving the goal of price stability. Analysis of the costs of inflation (particularly if unanticipated),[39] as well as a general acceptance of the vertical longer-term Phillips

---

36. J. M. Keynes, *A Tract on Monetary Reform* (1923), pp.8–9.
37. A. Posen, 'Why Central Bank Independence Does Not Cause Low Inflation: There Is No Institutional Fix For Politics', in R. O'Brien (ed.), *Finance and the International Economy: The Annex Bank Review Prize Essays* (1993), p.45, downgrades the importance of this argument: 'Since seigniorage is far more an issue for developing countries than for countries with . . . functioning tax collections systems, the empirical relevance of this factor to a discussion of inflation in industrialised democracies is questionable'. C. Goodhart, *Game Theory for Central Bankers: A Report to the Governor of the Bank of England*, mimeo (1993), p.23, points out: 'Weak governments without the ability to raise taxes or bond revenues have to turn to the printing press'.
38. See C. Holtferich, 'La Evoluzione del Grado di Autonomia dalla Deutsche Reichsbank alla Deutsche Bundesbank', in D. Masciandaro and S. Ristuccia (eds), *L'Autonomia delle Banche Centrali* (1988), p. 130.
39. See S. Fischer, *Indexing, Inflation and Economic Policy* (1986); idem, 'Modern Central Banking', loc.cit., n. 31.

curve,[40] have contributed to the priority given by economists and policy-makers to price stability in the last two decades. Inflation is considered a grave disease for the economic well-being of a country; it increases uncertainty, discourages investment and brings conflict into industrial relations. It also has pernicious social effects, including the arbitrary redistribution of income and wealth, and the erosion of and disincentive to savings. Much of the theoretical and empirical justification for central bank independence is rooted in the conviction that the conduct of monetary policy should be aimed primarily at controlling inflation.

The 'time-inconsistency' or 'dynamic-inconsistency' literature,[41] which explains the inflationary bias of the political authorities, provides a theoretical economic rationale for central bank independence. This literature brings the debate on central bank independence back to a key discussion in monetary policy: the issue of rules versus discretion. Time-inconsistency emphasises the need for a credible and binding precommitment to a particular mandate that effectively prevents violations *ex post*. Without such precommitment, rational agents will disbelieve the authorities and behave in ways that prevent them from achieving their original goals. Central bank independence is one way (though not the only way) of formulating a credible and binding commitment to price stability. Other ways include legislated monetary rules, an exchange-rate peg, a currency board, or a constitutional amendment binding the government to price stability.

The empirical evidence – attained through a series of econometric and statistical tests – appears to confirm a negative correlation between legal central bank independence and inflation.[42] Alas, a number of qualifications should be made.

40. Goodhart argues that the current enthusiasm for central bank independence rests importantly on general acceptance of the vertical longer-term Phillips curve; see C. Goodhart, F. Capie and N. Schnadt, *The Development of Central Banking*, paper presented at the Bank of England's Tercentenary Celebration, London, (June 1994). I would claim that the unexploitable trade-off between inflation and unemployment in the medium or longer term has instead ignited support for a monetary policy directed towards price stability, with or without central bank independence. Friedman, for instance, has opposed the independence of the Fed, favouring legislated monetary rules to achieve price stability; see, *eg,* M. Friedman, 'Should There Be an Independent Monetary Authority?', in L. Yeager (ed.), *In Search of a Monetary Constitution* (1962).

41. Most of the recent economic literature on central bank independence has followed the time-inconsistency argument, first formulated by F. Kydland and E. Prescott, 'Rules Rather than Discretion: The Inconsistency of Optimal Plans' (June 1977) 85:3 *Journal of Political Economy*, and further developed by R. Barro and D. Gordon, 'Rules, Discretion and Reputation in a Model of Monetary Policy' (July 1983) 12:1 *Journal of Monetary Economics.*

42. See M. Parkin and R. Bade, *Central Bank Laws and Monetary Policies: A Preliminary Investigation*, typescript (unpublished), Research Report No. 7804, University of

(1) The conclusiveness of the evidence on this issue is limited by the fact that until 1989 only three central banks had legal independence: the Federal Reserve System, the Bundesbank and the Swiss National Bank. Only in these three cases is the time period long enough to draw relevant conclusions. Chile and New Zealand acquired legal central bank independence in 1989; Argentina and Venezuela in 1992; Mexico, Philippines and France in 1993. With time, the analysis of the relation between central bank independence and inflation will acquire more relevance, as the sample of legally independent central banks, both in the developed and in the developing world, expands.

Early indications of the relation between price stability and legal central bank independence appear to provide encouraging signs in the cases of Chile, New Zealand and Argentina, but less optimistic results in Venezuela. It can be argued, however, that the 'success' stories are contingent on other economic reforms adopted concomitantly with legal central bank independence (*eg*, radical labour-market deregulation and fiscal prudence in New Zealand).[43] Such reforms enhance the credibility of the country's commitment to fighting inflation. But that credibility is often fragile, hard to gain, easy to lose, and very sensitive to economic and political uncertainty. The Venezuelan case clearly exemplifies the threats faced by newly independent central banks; the former Governor, Ruth de Krivoy, resigned in April 1994, citing government actions which compromised central bank independence.

(2) Cukierman, Webb and Neyapti argue that legal independence is inversely related to inflation in industrial countries, but not in developing economies.[44] In developing countries, the turnover rate of central bank governors is a better proxy for central bank independence. Yet, this statement overlooks two facts:

(i)   Until 1989, no developing country had passed legislation granting independence to its central bank; Chile, considered the 'pioneer'

(continued)

Western Ontario (1977); K. Banaian, L. Laney and T. Willet, 'Central Bank Independence: An International Comparison' [1983] *Economic Review*, Federal Reserve Bank of Dallas, reprinted in E. Toma and M. Toma (eds), *Central Bankers, Bureaucratic Incentives and Monetary Policy* (1986); A. Alesina, 'Macroeconomics and Politics', [1988] *NBER Macroeconomics Annuals*; idem, 'Politics and Business Cycles in Industrial Democracies' (April 1989) *Economic Policy*; idem and L. Summers, 'Central Bank Independence and Macroeconomic Performance: Some Comparative Evidence' (May 1992) *Journal of Money, Credit, and Banking*; V. Grilli, D. Masciandaro and G. Tabellini, 'Political and Monetary Institutions and Public Financial Policies in the Industrial Countries' (Oct. 1991) 13 *Economic Policy*; A. Cukierman, *Central Bank Strategy, Credibility, and Independence: Theory and Evidence* (1992); and Cukierman, Webb and Neyapti, loc.cit., n.35.

43. See 'Monday Interview' with Donald Brash, Governor of the Reserve Bank of New Zealand, *Financial Times*, 14 June 1993.

44. Cukierman, Webb and Neyapti, loc. cit., n.35.

among developing countries in enacting legal central bank independence, only did so in 1989.[45]

(ii)   Law enactment always needs to be accompanied by an effective system of law enforcement. The level of compliance with the law affects the success or failure of legislative provisions. The foundations of the rule of law (division of powers, independence of the judiciary, recognition and protection of human rights) are often less established and respected in developing countries than in the developed world. The frequency of change of central bank governors is an element of the *de facto* independence, generally related to a poor level of compliance with the law.

(3) Correlation does not imply causation.[46] Japan's inflationary record in recent years has been excellent, despite the political dependence of its central bank. Christopher Fildes wrote in 1990: 'The trouble with a mandate is that with a good government it might not be needed and with a bad government it might not be worth having'.[47] If the government itself were credibly committed to the goal of price stability, there would be no need to delegate this function to a central bank.[48]

(4) Independence alone does not guarantee price stability.[49] Other factors and institutional arrangements are required in order to make independence effective in controlling inflation. These include: fiscal restraint and a credible programme of economic stabilisation; labour market discipline;[50] the support of the financial and non-financial community to anti-inflationary measures; the political stability of the country.

In addition to arguments of primarily economic nature, there are also political arguments supporting the independence of central banks. Painful

45. The literature on central bank independence in developing countries is relatively scarce. For a recent study, see, eg, S. Maxfield, *Gatekeepers of Growth: The International Political Economy of Central Banking in Developing Countries* (1996).
46. Goodhart argues that the true underlying correlations may be between the priorities of the electorate and the economic outcome; C. Goodhart, 'Central Bank Independence', The A. C. Goode Address to CEDA (Nov. 1993), p.12. Posen argues that both central bank independence and low rates of inflation are determined by national differences in the political efficacy of financial opposition to inflation; Posen, loc. cit., n. 37.
47. See *The Daily Telegraph,* 23 April 1990.
48. See 'Monday Interview' with the then Deputy Governor of the Bank of England, George Blunden, *Financial Times,* 5 March 1990.
49. Furthermore, the experience of inflation rarely comes in isolation from other economic problems. As Fischer points out, it is usually associated with other problems, supply shocks or a lack of fiscal control; Fischer, 'Modern Central Banking', loc. cit., n.31.
50. Hall argues that the institutional structures underpinning wage bargaining affect rates of inflation and economic performance as much as central bank independence does. In his opinion, Germany's system of co-ordinated (and centralised) wage bargaining has contributed to its success in controlling inflation; P. Hall, 'Central Bank Independence and Coordinated Wage Bargaining: Their Interaction in Germany and Europe' (Spring 1994) 31 *German Politics and Society.*

experience with the manipulation of monetary policy for short-term political ends, such as the hyperinflation in Germany during the Weimar Republic, and in Argentina in the 1980s, highlights the importance of monetary stability as a common ground which should be endorsed by different political parties, rather than an object of their political struggle. Some German economists have argued that non-political money should be considered an essential, quasi-constitutional part of the general economic order, and not just one of several objectives of economic policy.[51] Thus, an independent central bank, operating without regard to the day-to-day business of politics, can be a guarantor of continuous stabilisation policy.

This argument is rooted in the belief that central bankers, because of their specialisation and relative insulation from political pressures, are more prepared than politicians to pursue the objective of price stability. The skills, expertise and superior qualifications of central bankers compared to politicians recommend an independent central bank, better able to guarantee a more objective, more 'neutral' and faster decision-making process. This 'technical' argument assumes that the slow and heavy machinery of the government lacks the necessary flexibility and swiftness to adapt to changing circumstances.

Politicians tend to focus on the near future, and are susceptible to command extensive monetary accommodation in the short term, risking the long-run destabilisation of the economy. Politicians are likely to be subject to the pressures of public opinion and special interest groups and tend to exhibit an inflationary bias when elections approach.

One problem with this political argument is that its logic could theoretically justify the 'depolitisation' of other economic policies, converting a democracy into a technocracy. G. Holtham claims:

If monetary policy can be taken out of politics, why not take fiscal policy, too? In fact, there is much more international evidence of fiscal policy being manipulated for electoral ends than is the case with monetary policy. Yet, no one proposes that fiscal policy should be put in the hands of independent functionaries.[52]

---

51. See Caesar, loc. cit., n.31, p.2; H. Ungerer *et al.*, *The European Monetary System: Developments and Perspectives*, Occasional Paper No. 73, International Monetary Fund (Nov. 1990), p.46. The concept of *Ordnungspolitik* used by these authors can be defined as the underlying basic policy aimed at establishing and maintaining a certain economic order characterised by free markets, unrestricted competition, free international trade and what has sometimes been called 'non-political money'.

52. G. Holtham, 'No Case for Independent Central Bank', *Financial Times*, Jan. 22, 1993. Hopkin and Wass also maintain that, if monetary policy is to be taken out of the hands of politicians, because they cannot be trusted to give inflation the priority that it deserves, then other instruments of policy which have a bearing on inflation (they cite government borrowing, taxation, competition policy and public-sector pay) should also be taken out of their hands; B. Hopkin and D. Wass, 'The Flows in Central Bank Freedom', *Financial Times*, Sept. 3, 1993.

Additionally, there are other political counter arguments. To begin with, despite the economic merits of central bank independence, the actual decision to grant independence is a political one. Furthermore, as M. Toma and others have pointed out, the political authorities may have an interest in maintaining central bank independence, as it allows them to blame the central bank for unpopular policies.[53] Following this line of thought, the Fed may often be portrayed as the villain and used as a scapegoat by the US government. Goodhart argues that central bank independence actually throws the central bank back into the political arena, for an independent central bank in fact becomes another political actor, who needs to justify its actions 'with the full gamut of political and presentational skills'.[54]

The political and economic arguments really collapse into one. Today's discussions on central bank independence centre on how the central bank's non-political, non-partisan positions can contribute to the credibility and long-sightedness of a monetary policy geared towards price stability.

4.2.2 The arguments against independence

The dominant argument against central bank independence is that an institution which is free from the direct effect of political control lacks democratic legitimacy.[55] Concern about the so-called 'democratic deficit', which is often raised about the actual organisation and powers of institutions of the European Union, is also present in the debates about the yet-to-be-created European System of Central Banks.[56]

Yet, arguments about democratic legitimacy overlook several points about institutional independence. To begin with, legal independence is not absolute. One statute may be removed by another, and parliament is entitled to modify existing legislation and change the contents of the central bank's governing statutes. Moreover, a potential democratic deficit can be prevented by providing adequate sources of accountability.[57]

---

53. See, *eg*, M. Toma, 'Inflationary Bias of the Federal Reserve System', in Toma and Toma (eds), op. cit., n. 42.

54. Goodhart, 'Central Bank Independence', loc.cit., n.46.

55. See G. Blunden, 'The Role of the Central Bank', Julian Hodge Annual Lecture, University of Wales, College of Cardiff (1990); Friedman, loc.cit., n.40;; C. Samm, *Die Stellung der Deutschen Bundesbank in Verfassungsgefüge* (1967); D. Uhlenbruck, *Die Verfassungsmässige Unabhängigkeit der Deutschen Bundesbank und ihrer Grenzen*, Bankrecht Schriften des Instituts für Bankwirtschaft und Bankrecht a.d. Universität zu Köln, Band 4 (1968).

56. Lastra, loc. cit., n.30.

57. Though central bank independence in terms of instruments ('instrument' independence) does not necessarily conflict with the notion of democratic legitimacy, central bank independence in terms of goals ('goal' independence) may conflict with such notion. Nevertheless, as noted above, independent central banks can seldom choose their own objectives, which are generally statutorily defined.

The legitimacy of independent institutions may also be understood by reference to the 'Robinson Crusoe' paradigm.[58] Just as an individual – recognising his own imperfection in the face of possible temptations – imposes constraints upon himself, in order 'to channel his own expedient behaviour toward rationally selected norms', a government, recognising its own weakness in the face of 'temptations, limits itself by allowing or creating autonomous or independent bodies'. Parliament's willingness to submit itself to restrictions – by legislating on central bank independence – provides a considerable degree of democratic control.

The state's exemption of an institution from the usual mechanisms of a democracy (most typically the majority voting rules) can be justified either by the need to protect the very existence of democracy (*eg*, protection of human rights, or prohibition of the suppression of democracy) or by the need to maintain the stability of the existent democratic system. Monetary stability, it is argued, is a necessary condition for a working market economy. Pöhl, in debates about European monetary union, raised the question of whether politically managed money is an essential democratic principle.[59]

The second major objection to the independence of central banks is that it hinders the maintenance of a consistent economic policy. Some economists fear that 'friction losses' would result from unco-ordinated monetary and fiscal policy.[60] They argue that the formulation of the guidelines of general economic policy should be entrusted to a single decision-making body, with one comprehensive political direction. Consequently, they favour the subordination of the central bank to the government.

Goodhart qualifies this argument, stating that the concern is not really about co-ordination, but rather about which policy instrument should have priority.[61] Under the Keynesian policy modalities of the 1950s and 1960s, fiscal policy had primacy, whereas with an independent central bank, priority is given to a monetary policy aimed at achieving price stability.

The discussion about consistency in economic policy-making relates to the debate about the conflicting or complementary character of the various macroeconomic goals, in particular, whether the strict pursuit of price stability implies a sacrifice in attaining growth and employment objectives. Acceptance of the vertical Phillips curve suggests that there is no exploitable trade-off between inflation and unemployment in the long run. In the short run, however, there is a trade-off, which may explain why central bank independence, as a means of achieving price stability, may seem more attractive and 'popular' when a country is concerned with inflation than

58. See J. Buchanan, *The Limits of Liberty: Between Anarchy and Leviathan* (1975), p.93.
59. O. Pöhl, 'Prospects of European Monetary Union', in *Britain and EMU* (1990).
60. See, *eg*, Caesar, loc. cit., n.31, p.6.
61. Loc. cit., n.46, pp.15–16.

when it is trying to fight recession and unemployment. For instance, the high-interest-rate policy of the Bundesbank in the aftermath of German reunification was criticised in the rest of Europe, which was suffering from an economic slowdown, as well as by some in Germany. Parkin and Bade concluded in their study of central bank institutional arrangements:

The fully independent central bank pursues anti-inflationary policies to the exclusion of concern for macroeconomic stability more broadly defined, whilst those which are pursuing monetary policies dictated by their governments are much more concerned in the formulation of those policies with broader macroeconomic objectives and, in particular, with real output and employment fluctuations.[62]

While it has become widely accepted that central bank independence promotes price stability, there is still little evidence to support that it has a significant impact on other macroeconomic goals.[63] Nevertheless, if, as Barro hints in a recent study,[64] there is a causal relationship between higher long-term inflation and reduced economic growth and investment, then we could infer that, in the long run, the monetary discipline associated with central bank independence will also benefit growth and employment.

Consistency is needed between interest-rate policy and exchange-rate policy (which is almost invariably in the hands of the Treasury and the minister of finance), between domestic and international considerations. As Fischer contends,[65] the very effectiveness of central bank independence will depend on the government's choice of exchange regime. Under floating rates, monetary policy affects the exchange rate; whereas a system of fixed exchange rates greatly curtails an independent central bank's room for manoeuvre in the conduct of monetary policy.

A third argument against central bank independence is a product of the 'bureaucratic theory', which (in line with public-choice theory) suggests that the central bank will further its own benefit and prestige instead of the

---

62. Parkin and Bade, op. cit., n. 42, p.29.
   Rogoff suggests that though an independent central bank reduces average inflation, it increases output variability. K. Rogoff, 'The Optimal Degree of Commitment to an Intermediate Monetary Target' (Nov. 1985) 100:4 *Quarterly Journal of Economics*.
63. See, *eg*, Alesina and Summers, loc. cit., n. 42.
64. See R. Barro, 'Inflation and Economic Growth' (1995) 35 *BEQB*. Barro carries out a statistical analysis of the effects of inflation on growth, drawn from the experience of more than 100 countries, which concludes that an increase of 10 per centage points in the average annual inflation rate from 1960 to 1990 reduced the long-term growth rate of real gross domestic product by 0.2 to 0.3 percentage points. Barro's preliminary results on this issue further strengthen the case for price stability. They should, however, be interpreted with a few grains of salt. Barro recognises (p.171) that some omitted variable may be correlated with growth and inflation; *eg*, the degree of maintenance of the rule of law. See also 'Personal View', *Financial Times*, 17 May 1995.
65. Fischer, 'Modern Central Banking', loc. cit., n. 31, p.55.

general welfare.[66] This argument can be reversed, however, if the prevention of inflation is the central bank's primary task, for in this case central bankers will maximise their reputation by striving for price stability.

The New Zealand contractual approach offers the central bank's governor a great incentive to achieve the policy target fixed by the minister of finance; if he fails to meet the target, he loses his job.[67] The introduction of a monetary reward would further reinforce the governor's incentive to attain his target.

4.2.3 Conclusion: accountable independence

In my opinion, the arguments in favour of central bank independence outweigh those against it. Central bank independence provides monetary policy with the credibility required to achieve price stability. The dominant argument against independence is the concern with the democratic legitimacy of such an institution free from political control. Nevertheless, adequate sources of accountability can counteract the possibility of a democratic deficit.

4.3 The legal articulation of independence

Despite the importance of *de facto* independence, central bank independence requires the protection of a binding legal and institutional framework as a source of political legitimacy and credibility. As was pointed out in section 4.1, 'organic' safeguards are legal provisions regulating the organisation of the central bank and its institutional relationships with the government; whereas I call provisions legislating both the functions of the central bank and the scope of its powers 'functional' or 'operational' guarantees. Legal provisions should also refer to the different ways in which central banks can be held accountable for their actions.[68]

---

66. Toma and Toma (eds), op. cit., n. 42.
67. The New Zealand contractual approach to central bank independence, whereby the governor and the minister of finance sign a contract, has been the object of recent game-theory studies under the principal–agent model. The governor is seen as an agent of the political principals. See C. Walsh, 'Optimal Contracts for Independent Central Bankers: Private Information, Performance Measures and Reappointment', Working Paper 93-02, Federal Reserve Bank of San Francisco (May 1993); T. Persson and G. Tabellini, 'Designing Institutions for Monetary Stability', (Dec. 1993) 39 *Carnegie Rochester Conference Series on Public Policy* 53; Annex 2 provides a copy of New Zealand's 'Policy Targets Agreement' (the 'contract') signed by the Governor and the Minister of Finance in Dec. 1992.
68. See *infra*, section 5.

The formal declaration of central bank independence can be contained in a constitution, in a law or in a contract. Chile (1980) and the Philippines (1987) are among the very few countries to have 'constitutionalised' the independence of their central banks. Most countries choose to grant independence to their central banks through a law. This is the case, for instance, in Germany,[69] the US and Switzerland. Statutory independence is preferred for it grants parliament the right to amend or repeal the law at any time. While a constitution can also be amended, this is generally a lengthy and complex procedure. Even those countries, which follow the 'constitutional' path, such as Chile and the Philippines, or the 'contractual' path, such as New Zealand, also proceed through a 'statutory' path. New Zealand and Chile enacted legislation in 1989; the Philippines passed its law in 1993.

Legal central bank independence can, in principle, be more easily embraced in those countries where constitutions have been drafted trying to curb the central government's power than in unitary states. Germany has historically favoured decentralisation, both territorially ('Bundesrepublik', or Federal Republic) and functionally ('Selbstverwaltung', or self-administration). The concentration of power in the US, especially economic power, has been prevented or mitigated by the existence of a federal structure and by the administrative design of its central government, where Congress has delegated powers over important sectors of economic activity (money, securities, energy, telecommunications, and so on) to independent regulatory commissions. Conversely, France and other civil-law countries, which follow a Napoleonic model of 'Administration', have traditionally favoured centralisation and a hierarchical structure of the central government. Though recent developments in central banking tend to show unitary states moving in the same direction as federal states (*eg*, New Zealand, Chile, and even France), the constitutional structure of the state will continue to play a differential role in the design of central bank independence. Unitary

---

69. The only reference to the Central Bank in the German Grundgesetz – Art. 88 – 'constitutionalises' the existence of the Bundesbank, not its independence. Nevertheless, the legal independence of the Bundesbank was to some extent strengthened through the process of German reunification. The Treaty of 18 May 1990 between the Federal Republic of Germany and the German Democratic Republic establishing a Monetary, Economic and Social Union stated in its Art. 10 (3): 'The Deutsche Bundesbank . . . independent of instructions from the Governments of the Contracting Parties, shall regulate the circulation of money and credit supply in the entire currency area with the aim of safeguarding the currency'. The German Unification Treaty (Treaty of 31 August 1990 between the Federal Republic of Germany and the German Democratic Republic on the establishment of German Unity) confirmed the validity of the previous Treaty of May. One legal implication of the provision mentioned above is the 'formal' strengthening of the Bundesbank's independence, as it is not only recognised in an Act, but also in a Treaty, whose greater binding force and more difficult procedures for revision suggest a stronger formal commitment to independence than that contained in the 1957 Bundesbank Act.

states, because of their traditional centralised system of checks and balances, will tend to exhibit greater concern with accountability than federal states, where the rule of law has been articulated in response to a decentralised geographic and functional structure of government.

Though there is no magic formula for 'perfect' central bank independence, a law granting independence to a central bank should take into account the different categories (comprising 'organic' and 'functional' guarantees) analysed in the remainder of this section, and the mechanisms of accountability surveyed in section 5. As examples, I cite provisions of the Maastricht Treaty, of the German Bundesbank Act, of the US Federal Reserve Act, of the New Zealand Reserve Bank Act, and of other central bank laws.

4.4 Organic safeguards of independence

4.4.1 Appointment

The central bank appointment process should be pluralistic.[70] This implies the participation of bodies or economic agents besides the government: officials of the central bank itself; other representatives from the regions, member states or geographic areas of the country; representatives of the regulated sectors of the economy (*eg*, banking and financial institutions); interest groups (*eg*, consumers, farmers, workers employed in different sectors of the economy); the shareholders in those central banks in which ownership is, either completely or partially, private. The particular nature of such non-governmental participation will vary from country to country.

One might even consider the appointment by parliament of some of the members of the board of directors.[71] This proposal, which addresses the 'democratic deficit' concern, might, however, lead to undesirable results in some cases: if, for instance, the parliament is dominated by the executive (*ie*,

---

70. Typically a central bank may have up to two or three tiers of governing bodies. One level is generally a supervisory level (in the US the Board of Governors, in Germany the Central Bank Council) and the other level is generally a regular decision-making or executive body (in the US the Federal Open Market Committee, in Germany the Directorate). The president, chairman or governor of the central bank generally chairs the governing bodies.

71. This is the case in Denmark, where eight members of the Board of Directors are appointed by Parliament. In Sweden, all members of the Riksbank's Governing Board, except for the Governor, are appointed by Parliament. R. Sparve, 'The Independence of Central Banks', mimeo, Sveriges Riksbank (June 1992). Sweden is the only OECD country where membership to the central bank's board is divided along political party lines. After each general election to Parliament, the members of the Governing Board are appointed. In this manner, changes in public opinion are immediately reflected in the make-up of the Governing Board. It is usually argued in Sweden that the desire for change should be reflected, not only in fiscal policy, but also in monetary and exchange-rate policy (both of which are the responsibility of the Riksbank).

by the political party in power), it might be tempted to make appointments purely on the basis of political patronage or on the willingness to support the government's economic policy, hereby undermining the purpose of independence.

A good example of a pluralistic structure is given by the new French Monetary Policy Council. The French law on central bank independence (1993) prescribes that the Governor and other members of the Monetary Policy Council will be appointed by the Council of Ministers, and shall be selected from a list of three candidates for each member to be appointed. The list is to be jointly proposed by the President of the Senate, the President of the National Assembly and the President of the Economic and Social Council.[72]

In Germany, according to the Bundesbank Law (Article 7), the President of the Bundesbank and its Directorate are appointed by the President of the Federal Republic, on nomination by the federal government, which in turn consults the Central Bank Council. The Central Bank Council consists of the Directorate and the presidents of the central banks of the Länder. The latter are nominated by the Bundesrat (Parliament) and appointed by the government, based on proposals from an appropriate authority of the Land concerned, pursuant to consultations with the Central Bank Council.

Under the Maastricht Treaty, the Council of the European Union will, after consultation with the European Parliament and the Governing Council of the European Central Bank, recommend candidates for President, Vice-President and other members of the Executive Board of the ECB. These officers shall be appointed by common accord of the governments of the Member States at the level of the heads of state or government.[73]

4.4.2 Terms of office

Central bankers should have a sufficiently long term of office to safeguard independence and prevent politisation and short-term perspectives. A tenure longer than that held by legislators serves these ends; a shorter term of office could make central bankers vulnerable to political pressures and electoral cycles.

In the Bundesbank, the President, the Directorate and the presidents of the central banks of the Länder are appointed for a term of eight years (which is renewable).[74] Within the Federal Reserve System, the members of the Board of Governors are appointed for fixed terms of 14 years. The Chairman and Vice-Chairman are appointed for four-year terms. The nine

---

72. See Art. 8 of the Loi No. 93-980 of 4 Aug. 1993, on the statutes of the Bank of France.
73. Statute of the ESCB, Art. 11.2.
74. Bundesbank Law, Arts 7 (3), 8 (4).

members of the Board of Directors of the Federal Reserve Banks hold office for three years.[75]

In the ESCB, the President, the Vice-President and the other members of the Executive Board shall be appointed for a period of eight years, and their terms will be non-renewable. The governors of the national central banks shall have a term of office of not less than five years.[76] Some Member States, such as Spain and France, have already amended their legislation to comply with this requirement.

4.4.3 Dismissal

Central bank independence is enhanced if the governor and other members of the governing bodies can not be dismissed by the political authorities in the event of discontent with the bank's policies. Grounds for dismissal should be clearly defined and may include criminal offences or serious misconduct, permanent incapability, or serious lack of fulfilment of their obligations (to be judged by independent courts of justice, not by the government).

The members of the Bundesbank Directorate may not be removed from office before the end of their term except for reasons which lie in their person (interpreted as being guilty of crime or serious misconduct) and if the initiative comes from themselves or the Central Bank Council.[77] Under the Federal Reserve System, each member is subject to removal 'for cause' by the President.[78]

Article 14.2 of the Statute of the ESCB provides that '[a] Governor [of a national central bank] may be relieved from office only if he no longer fulfils the conditions required for the performance of his duties or if he has been guilty of serious misconduct'. Likewise, Article 11.4 of the Statute of the ESCB provides that, '[i]f a member of the Executive Board no longer fulfils the conditions required for the performance of his duties or if he has been guilty of serious misconduct, the Court of Justice may, on application by the Governing Council or the Executive Board, compulsorily retire him'. It strikes me as unsatisfactory that these provisions address the issue of serious misconduct, but fail to address instances of poor performance *vis-à-vis* the tasks and goals of the ESCB.

---

75. 12 USC 241, 242 and 302.
76. Statute of the ESCB, Arts 11.2, 21, 14.1 and 14.2.
77. See *The Deutsche Bundesbank: Its Monetary Policy Instruments and Functions*, Deutsche Bundesbank Special Series No 7 (1987), pp.7–8.
78. 12 USC 241, 242.

4.4.4 Suitability and salary

Central bankers should have professional skills that correspond to their functions (*eg*, monetary policy and banking supervision) and should also demonstrate 'professional independence'. The 'suitability' of candidates would be heightened by adequate tests of their experience, knowledge and ability to accomplish central bank policies.

In Germany, the Bundesbank requires 'special professional qualifications' for members of the Directorate as well as members of the Boards of Management of the central banks of the Länder.[79] Similarly, in the Federal Reserve System, the Chairman of each of the Federal Reserve Banks has to be a person 'of tested banking experience'.[80] *A fortiori*, members of the Board of Governors, and particularly the Chairman of the Federal Reserve Board, must have suitable qualifications. As for the ECB, Article 11.2 of the Statute of the ESCB stipulates that the members of the Executive Board shall be selected among 'persons of recognised standing and professional experience in monetary or banking matters'.

Monetary incentives can be used to attract talented candidates to a central bank, reward strong performance and foster dedication. A monetary incentive mechanism acts, in this way, both as an 'organic' and as a 'functional' guarantee of central bank independence. Such a mechanism would require high initial salaries, which are then increased or decreased according to the individual's ability to adequately perform tasks and achieve stipulated goals. The governor's success in controlling inflation, for instance, would be rewarded with a bonus or salary increase. Conversely, should the governor fail to achieve price stability, he or she would somehow be 'penalised'.[81] The governor and other central bank officials would certainly be inflation-averse if their salaries were set in nominal terms and fixed during their tenure.

The President of the Bundesbank earns a high salary.[82] The salaries of the members of the Directorate and of the presidents of the central banks of the Länder 'shall be provided by agreements with the Central Bank Council. Such agreements are subject to the approval of the Federal Government'.[83]

79. Bundesbank Law, Arts 7 (2), 8 (3).
80. 12 USC 305.
81. Goodhart points out that, as an external advisor to the Reserve Bank of New Zealand before the 1989 Act, he advocated relating bonus to senior officials to the outcome, relative to the target; C. Goodhart, 'What Should the Central Banks Do? What Should Be Their Macroeconomic Objectives and Operations?' (1994) 104 *The Economic Journal* 1442.
82. The annual salary of the President of the Bundesbank in 1993 was estimated to be about $420,000, according to *Business Week*, 15 Nov. 1993.
83. Bundesbank Law, Arts 7 (4), 8 (5). There are, in addition, 'non-monetary' incentives. 'The Deutsche Bundesbank and its staff shall enjoy the privileges granted to the federal government and its staff in the fields of construction, housing and rent'; ibid., Art. 29 (2).

In the US, the salaries of the members of the Fed Board of Governors are regulated pursuant to the Federal Reserve Act, and have been adjusted many times.[84]

In the ECB, the salaries of the individual members of the Executive Board are governed by the Statute of the ESCB. Article 11.3 provides that such salaries and other conditions of employment 'shall be the subject of contracts with the ECB and shall be fixed by the Governing Council on a proposal from a Committee comprising three members appointed by the Governing Council and three members appointed by the Council'. The members of the Executive Board will not have the right to vote on salary issues.

4.4.5 Prohibitions applicable to central bank officials while in office

To avoid conflicts of interest, central bankers must not be diverted from their professional responsibilities during their terms of office. To ensure full-time dedication, a list of incompatible or disqualifying activities should be established. For example, a central banker should not simultaneously be a financial adviser to a private company, an employee or shareholder of a bank, or a member of parliament.

In Germany, Bundesbank directors 'hold office under public law' and therefore are precluded from simultaneously holding private-sector jobs.[85] Within the Federal Reserve System, 'members of the Board shall devote their entire time to the business of the Board'.[86] In addition, the Federal Reserve Act provides that '[n]o member of the Board of Governors of the Federal Reserve System shall be an officer or director of any bank, banking institution or trust company; and before entering upon his duties as a member of the Board he shall certify under oath that he has complied with this requirement'.[87]

The Statute of the ESCB provides similar restrictions. Article 11.1 stipulates that: 'The members shall perform their duties on a full-time basis. No member shall engage in any occupation, whether gainful or not, unless exemption is exceptionally granted by the Governing Council.'

4.4.6 Restrictions on central bank officials after they leave office

Central bank officials should also be limited in their ability to pursue private employment in credit and financial institutions for a reasonable period

---

84. See, *eg*, 12 USC 241, 5313, 5314. As of 1 Jan. 1994, the Chairman earned $133,600, and the other members of the Board earned $123,100.
85. Bundesbank Law, Art. 7 (4).
86. 12 USC 241.
87. 12 USC 244.

following their term of office. These restrictions are designed to preclude their susceptibility to 'private' incentives while in office. Such provisions are particularly necessary for central banks responsible for regulating the banking industry, so as to avoid the 'capture' of the regulator by the regulated institutions.

Central bankers should also be temporarily ineligible to become government officials after their term in office. This limitation is aimed at avoiding or mitigating political influence during their tenure with the central bank.

Yet if central bankers are temporarily barred from government positions and posts in financial institutions, how are they to make a living upon leaving office? One possible solution is given by the Bank of Spain Autonomy Law, which entitles central bankers to receive 80 per cent of their salary for two years after they leave office, 'unless the individual holds a paying post or activity in the public or private sector, except for teaching' (Article 26). The only such restriction in the Statute of the ESCB is found in Article 38.1, which calls for professional secrecy 'even after . . . duties have ceased'. The Statute does, however, not specify what central bankers should not do after their terms expire.

4.4.7 Liaisons with Treasury or minister of finance

There is a trade-off between, on the one hand, consistency in the conduct of general economic policy and the need for co-operation between the central bank and the government and, on the other hand, some of the guarantees protecting central bank independence. Thus, by preventing a member of the government from being at the same time a member of the central bank's governing body, we sacrifice greater co-operation to achieve a higher degree of independence. This quandary over restrictions on the interchange and liaison of staff is one of the most difficult and controversial issues in the discussions about guarantees of central bank independence.

In Germany, according to Article 13 (2) of the Bundesbank Law, '[t]he members of the Federal Government shall be entitled to attend meetings of the Central Bank Council. They shall have no right to vote, but may propose motions. At their request decisions shall be deferred for up to two weeks.' And Article 13 (3) states that '[t]he Federal Government should invite the President of the Deutsche Bundesbank to attend its discussions on important monetary-policy matters'. Although there is no formal liaison or interchange of staff members, the Bundesbank and the Ministry of Finance work closely together in national and international bodies such as the IMF. This right to attend meetings, but not to vote, has also been adopted by the new central bank laws in Spain and France.

Because of the EU's unique structure, the ESCB will have to maintain liaison with public authorities on two levels.

(1) *Liaison with Community institutions.* According to Article 109b of the EC Treaty, the President of the Council of the European Communities and a member of the Commission may participate, without having the right to vote, in meetings of the Governing Council of the ECB. The President of the Council may submit a motion for deliberation to the Governing Council of the ECB.

Furthermore, Article 109b stipulates that the President of the ECB shall be invited to participate in Council meetings when the Council is discussing matters relating to the objectives and tasks of the ESCB.

Under Article 107 of the EC Treaty, the ESCB cannot seek or take any instructions from Community institutions. The Community institutions may not seek to influence the ECB or the national central banks. One implication of this Article is that the ESCB will be independent in performing all its tasks and duties, and not only in its monetary-policy functions.

(2) *Liaison with national governments.* Because the independence of the ESCB has to be based upon the independence of the ECB and of each of the participating national central banks, the Treaty requires the Member States of the European Union to change their legislation and make their central banks independent from their correspondent national governments (Articles 108 and 109e (5)).

Under Article 107 of the EC Treaty, neither the ECB nor any national central bank may seek or take any instructions from governments of Member States. In turn, the Member States cannot seek to influence the ECB or the national central banks.

4.5 Functional safeguards of independence

4.5.1 Limitations on lending to the public sector

The government's access to borrowing from the central bank is governed by central bank laws and their implementing regulations. A prohibition or limitation on financing the public sector's deficits or monetising public debt is a classic indication of central bank economic independence. This prohibition refers both to:

(i)   direct credit to the government; if such credit were to be allowed, it should only be: (i) of a limited amount; (ii) subject to the discretion of the central bank (*ie*, not automatic); (iii) at a market interest rate (discount rate); and (iv) explicitly temporary;[88] and

(ii)   purchases of government securities directly from the issuer (in the

---

88. See Grilli, Masciandaro and Tabellini, loc. cit., n. 42.

primary market); the prohibition does not generally extend to purchases of public-sector debt in the secondary market.

Some authors[89] argue that the notion of central bank independence has practical meaning primarily for institutions in industrialised countries with developed capital markets, as these private sources of financing provide an additional source of government finance. In developing countries, governments must rely on their own central banks and foreign capital markets for debt financing. Therefore, developing countries wishing to grant independence to their central banks – thus, prohibiting the financing of government deficits via central bank credit – should aim at a parallel development of their government-securities markets, generating funds to meet the government needs.[90]

The Maastricht Treaty prohibits the financing of government deficits via central bank credit (through both direct overdrafts and purchases of public-debt instruments in the primary market). This ban on deficit monetisation is already binding in Stage Two of EMU (which started on 1 January 1994).[91] The Maastricht Treaty contains other measures to promote fiscal restraint, such as the prohibition of privileged access by the governments to financial institutions. Moreover, according to the Maastricht Treaty, a country needs to have a sustainable government financial position – among other convergence criteria – in order to be considered fit for EMU. Such sustainability is defined as 3 per cent of government deficit to GDP and 60 per cent of government debt to GDP.

German legislation on the monetary system includes decisive measures that forbid the access by the state to central bank credit.[92] In the US, because the Fed enjoys independence from the Treasury Department, it is not compelled to monetise the government's budget deficits.

---

89. See Banaian, Laney and Willet, loc. cit., n. 42, pp.201–2.
90. The Chilean case represents one of the strictest prohibitions on central bank financing of government expenditures. Such prohibition has even been 'constitutionalised'. Art. 98 of the 1980 Constitution says that no public expenditure or loan can be financed with direct or indirect credit from the central bank, except in case of war or threat of war.
91. See EC Treaty, Art. 104, in combination with Art. 109e. In accordance with Art. 104 of this Treaty, overdrafts or any other type of credit facility with the ECB or with the national central banks in favour of Community institutions or bodies, central governments, regional, local or other public authorities, other bodies governed by public law or public undertakings of Member States shall be prohibited, as shall be the purchase directly from them by the ECB or national central banks of debt instruments.
92. Following the Maastricht requirements, the authorisation which permitted the Bundesbank to grant short-term cash advances to public authorities (Bundesbank Law, Art. 20 (1)) has been revoked. See Bundesbank, 'The Monetary Policy of the Bundesbank' (1994).

4.5.2   Conduct of monetary policy

An independent central bank should be responsible for implementing monetary policy, as well as for determining or formulating its content. This requires freedom to use a sufficient array of market instruments, whose application is not restricted by administrative regulations or political interference.

The Bundesbank is responsible for the formulation and implementation of monetary policy, 'with the aim of safeguarding the currency' (Article 3 of the Bundesbank Law). The Bundesbank's independence in the conduct of monetary policy – proclaimed in Article 12 of the Bundesbank Law – has become the epitome of what central bank independence represents for controlling inflation.

The ESCB shall 'define and implement the monetary policy of the Community' (Article 3 of the Statute of the ESCB). One of the principles embodied in the Statute of the ESCB is that responsibility for monetary policy is indivisible. Monetary policy will be a single unity, 'one piece' that cannot be shared. Thus, with the goal of achieving price stability, the ESCB will be responsible for both the formulation and implementation of monetary policy.[93]

4.5.3   Other central bank functions

Though central bank independence is generally confined to the domain of monetary policy, it can be expanded or contained by the extent of autonomy enjoyed by the central bank in the execution of other responsibilities,[94] particularly as regards the implementation of exchange-rate policy. As was noted above, the choice of exchange regime made by the government will influence the very effectiveness of central bank independence.

Exchange-rate policy in Germany is the responsibility of the Ministry of Finance. Potential conflicts between interest-rate and exchange-rate policy tend to be resolved favouring the government's objectives, as was shown in the case of German reunification, when the Bundesbank opposed the proposed one-to-one conversion rate of the Ost-Mark *vis-à-vis* the Deutsche Mark, and in the dispute over the setting up of the European Monetary System in 1978.[95]

---

93. Statute of the ESCB, Art. 12.1. Art. 18 refers to open-market and credit operations and Art. 19 refers to minimum reserve requirements; no other instruments of monetary policy are specifically mentioned.
94. On the issue of central bank independence in banking supervision, see R. M. Lastra, *Central Banking and Banking Regulation* (1996), pp.151–6.
95. See 'Bundesbank's Record in Standing Up to Bonn Government', *Financial Times*, 1 Oct. 1993.

Article 107 of the EC Treaty declares that the ESCB will be independent in performing all its tasks and duties, and not only in its monetary-policy function. Nevertheless, as the Maastricht provisions on the conduct of foreign-exchange policy remain unclear, and as other functions, such as prudential supervision, are not included among the 'basic tasks' of the ESCB, the independence of the ESCB will mainly affect the conduct of monetary policy.

The new central bank laws in Spain and France were careful to circumscribe the independence of their central banks to monetary policy, clearly stating that exchange-rate policy is to be determined by the government.[96]

The Swedish Riksbank is one of the few central banks in the world responsible for the conduct of exchange-rate policy. Though the Riksbank remains under political control, the Swedish Government will be required to grant it independence in compliance with the Maastricht requirements (Article 108 of the EC Treaty).

4.5.4 Regulatory powers

The legitimacy of statutory instruments and regulations issued by the central bank, as opposed to those issued by the government, is especially contentious in some civil-law countries. Nevertheless, if we are to entrust an independent central bank with powers and responsibilities, it seems logical to accord it a rule-making role. In particular, the central bank should be permitted to issue regulations as part of both its banking supervisory and its monetary-policy functions.

In Germany, the Bundesbank Law provides that '[t]he by-laws of the Deutsche Bundesbank shall be resolved by the Central Bank Council. They shall be subject to the approval of the Federal Government and shall be published in the Federal Gazette.' In the US, because the Fed is an independent agency, the Board of Governors of the Federal Reserve System may issue rules and regulations.[97]

Article 108a of the EC Treaty refers to the adoption of regulations, decisions, recommendations and opinions by the ECB 'in accordance with the provisions of this Treaty and under the conditions laid down in the Statute of the ESCB'. As regards the binding force and applicability of each of these regulatory instruments, Article 108a (2) provides that an ECB regulation 'shall have general application' and 'shall be binding in its entirety and directly applicable in all Member States'; an ECB decision 'shall

---

96. See Arts 3, 11 and 12 of the Bank of Spain Autonomy Law; and Art. 2 of the 1993 Bank of France Law.

97. Regulations are published in the Federal Register and codified in the Code of Federal Regulations (CFR).

be binding in its entirety upon those to whom it is addressed'; and ECB recommendations and ECB opinions 'shall have no binding force'.

4.5.5 Financial autonomy

The powers of the governing bodies of a central bank independent from the Treasury or ministry of finance may be extended through the provision of financial and budgetary autonomy to the bank. Most central banks have power over their own resources, even if they lack monetary-policy independence. Unlike other public institutions, central banks in developed countries often generate considerable profits. (The situation is, however, different in developing countries, where central bank losses, rather than profits, often present difficult problems.) In the US, the Fed enjoys full financial and budgetary autonomy;[98] whereas in Germany, the Bundesbank has the power to prepare and approve its own accounts.[99]

The provisions of Chapter VI, Articles 26–33, of the Statute of the ESCB provide a framework for safeguarding the financial autonomy of the ESCB. Articles 29 and 30 mandate the endowment of the ECB with capital and foreign-reserve assets. These provisions do not necessarily strip the national central banks of all of their foreign reserves. Thus, Article 31 states that those operations involving foreign-reserve assets can be carried out by the national central banks only with the approval of the ECB, thereby ensuring consistency with the exchange-rate and monetary policies of the Community.

4.5.6 Decisional autonomy

The powers of the governor and board of directors *vis-à-vis* the ministry of finance or Treasury are also defined by the decision-making processes of the central bank's governing bodies. A dependent central bank is by law typically required to secure prior government approval of its policies, particularly monetary policy. An independent central bank, on the other hand, should be subject only to non-binding consultations with the government in the carrying out of its policies. In terms of the extent of government intervention in central bank activities, I consider 'non-binding consultations' to be a middle ground between a requirement of prior approval (the most intrusive) and a requirement simply to maintain 'informal contacts' (the least intrusive). Subjecting the central bank to such consultations would require greater co-operation, and hence more

---

98. Indeed, the stock of the twelve Federal Reserve Banks is privately held by Federal Reserve member banks. However, stock ownership by member banks does not carry with it the usual attributes of control and financial interest.
99. Bundesbank Law, Art. 26.

accountability, than simply allowing the bank to proceed on the basis of informal contacts with the government.

Although the Bundesbank is independent from the government in the conduct of monetary policy, it must co-operate with it. Article 12 of the Bundesbank Law states that, 'without prejudice to the performance of its functions, the Bundesbank is required to support the general economic policy of the Federal Cabinet'.[100] The Bundesbank needs the federal government's approval to participate in institutions serving the purposes of supranational monetary policy or international payments and lending.[101]

In theory, an independent central bank should be able to pursue objectives potentially conflicting with those of the government. This is particularly true if the bank is the only authority responsible for monetary policy. Nevertheless, in order to avoid the debilitating emergence of a 'state within the state', the laws should clearly define the circumstances and conditions under which such conflict and disagreement is permissible.

In principle, the Bundesbank can act contrary to the government's economic objectives.[102] In practice, however, the conflict may be resolved in favour of the government's goals, as was shown by the process of German reunification when the government's decision prevailed over the Bundesbank's recommendation, giving rise to an expansion of government expenditure that threatened price stability.[103] The Bundesbank Law contains no provisions for cases where serious differences of opinion and tensions may arise between the government and the central bank, but it does include regulations committing both sides to co-operation and mutual consultation.[104]

The Maastricht Treaty does not require the formal approval of the ESCB's monetary policy, or any other decisions taken in the execution of the ESCB's tasks, by either the Community institutions or national governments. Article 107 of the EC Treaty explicitly forbids the members of the ECB and the national central banks from receiving any instructions from either the Community or national political institutions.

Article 4 of the Statute of the ESCB requires that Community and national authorities consult the ECB in relation to any proposed Community act or

---

100. K. Stern, *Das Staatsrecht der Bundesrepublik Deutschland*, Vol. II (1980), pp.463–508, refers to Art. 12 of the Bundesbank Law – under which the Bundesbank should be independent from the government in the conduct of monetary policy, but supporting the general economic policy of it – as the 'squaring of the circle'.
101. Bundesbank Law, Art. 4.
102. Ibid., Art. 13 (2).
103. Nevertheless, it can be argued that, had the Bundesbank been legally dependent upon the Government, it would not have fought the inflationary pressures produced by reunification as tenaciously as it did.
104. See *The Deutsche Bundesbank: Its Monetary Policy Instruments and Functions*, loc. cit., n. 77, p.5.

any draft national legislative provision within its field of competence. It also provides that the ECB may frame opinions for submission to the appropriate Community institutions and bodies or national authorities on matters within its field of competence, and that it may publish its decisions.

Article 25.1 of the Statute of the ESCB proclaims that the ECB shall be entitled to offer advice and to be consulted on 'Community legislation relating to the prudential supervision of credit institutions and to the stability of the financial system'. Article 25.2 further provides that, '[i]n accordance with any decision of the Council under Article 105 (6) of [the EC] Treaty, the ECB may perform specific tasks concerning policies relating to the prudential supervision of credit institutions and other financial institutions with the exception of insurance undertakings'.

5. CENTRAL BANK ACCOUNTABILITY

5.1 Forms of accountability

Accountability requires that the central bank, at the very least, explain and justify its policies or actions, and give account for the decisions made in the execution of its responsibilities. An independent central bank needs to be accountable to another authority. This authority may be executive, legislative or judicial, as I explain below. Accountability should be 'diversified', that is, dispersed through the three branches of the state, through institutions with differing obligations to the electorate, to provide the democratic legitimacy that an independent central bank would otherwise lack. In addition to this institutional articulation of accountability, which aims to ensure the legality of the central bank's actions and decisions, there is an important factual dimension: the support of public opinion. In order to maintain its long-term status of independence, the central bank needs the support of the financial and non-financial community.[105] A country like Germany – in which the population retains bitter memories of the painful experience of hyperinflation – experiences a close affinity between the public's dislike of inflation and support for central bank independence. Conversely, nations such as the US – where the deflationary episode of the 1930s bears heavily on people's memories – may support central bank independence, but not necessarily the anti-inflationary policies that could cause higher interest rates and higher unemployment in the short term. Because of this less cohesive public support for price stability, legislation has provided for institutional mechanisms of accountability for

---

105. See J. Goodman, *Monetary Sovereignty: The Politics of Central Banking in Western Europe* (1992).

the Fed, as I explain later in this section. The possibility of a break in the link between fear of inflation and support for central bank independence within a future independent ESCB raises questions of democratic legitimacy in some European countries, where public support for low inflation is lower than in Germany.

Disclosure, that is, transparency in the operation of monetary policy, is another form of accountability, generally supported by countries, such as the US or the UK, which encourage strong financial-market discipline and transparency. In the US, the minutes of the Federal Open Market Committee meetings are published with a six-week delay. In the UK, which still lacks a legally independent central bank, there has been a recent change in the relationship between the Treasury and the Bank of England, providing for more accountability in terms of monetary disclosure. The decisions on interest rates are now regularly taken at monthly meetings, and the minutes of these monthly monetary meetings between the Bank of England and the Treasury are published after a six-week interval.[106] Germany, whose model of corporate governance fosters close ties between banks and corporations, with a corresponding flow of confidential information, does not display such a strong tradition of transparency and disclosure.[107] The secrecy surrounding the Bundesbank's interest-rate decisions may be understood in this context. Prompt publication of the minutes of the Bundesbank's meetings might also go against the traditional German consensus-seeking approach, as dissensions among the members of the Central Bank Council could become apparent. The Bundesbank has, however, since the mid-1970s, published in a monthly report its aggregate monetary targets.

Another key form of accountability is performance.[108] Performance is generally measured with relation to the statutory goal(s) to be achieved. The governing bodies of the central bank, particularly the governor, should be held accountable for failing to achieve such objectives. Performance control is facilitated, first, by the existence of one goal, rather than multiple ones (or by their unambiguous ranking), and secondly, by the existence of a clearly stated and narrowly defined statutory goal.

The announcement of a single goal (or a primary goal), rather than several unranked goals,[109] enables authorities and public opinion to control

106. See *Financial Times*, 21 Apr. 1994; and (1995) 35 *BEQB*, p.103.

107. Though some important reforms have been undertaken in the last few years in order to ensure greater financial disclosure. In July 1994, the Second Financial Markets Promotion Act was adopted, providing, among other things, for the prohibition of insider trading.

108. Fischer defines accountability as 'adverse consequences for the central bank or the central banker of not meeting targets'; loc. cit., n. 31, p.41.

109. It is also argued that, since monetary policy is essentially a single instrument, it cannot simultaneously be assigned to more than one objective. Monetary tools are best suited to achieve price stability, while other policies and mechanisms should be applied to other objectives; M. Castello-Branco and M. Swinburne, *Central Bank Independence: Issues and Experience*, IMF Working Paper 91/58 (1991).

performance more effectively. It is easier to control a narrowly defined target than a broadly defined objective; performance in the case of New Zealand, with an inflation target of 0–2 per cent annual increase in the consumer-price index,[110] is easier to monitor than in Germany, where the Bundesbank's broad statutory mandate is to secure the value of the currency.[111] The Bundesbank is also required to support the general economic policy of the government, without prejudice to the primary objective of price stability. This secondary objective of supporting the general economic policy of the government can, under certain circumstances, prevail over the primary goal, as happened for instance in the case of German reunification.[112] None the less, under 'normal' conditions, inflation-averse Germans will not challenge the Bundesbank on accountability grounds, as long as inflation control is in place; the courts will not challenge the Bundesbank either, as long as its decisions and operations are in accordance with its mandate to achieve monetary stability.[113]

The listing of the statutory goals of the future ESCB follows the Bundesbank pattern. Nevertheless, to support the general economic policies of the Community without prejudice to price stability (Article 105(1) of the EC Treaty) may prove to be the squaring of the circle.[114] Member States of the EU, such as France (1993) and Spain (1994), also refer to the primary goal of price stability and to the secondary goal of supporting the general economic policy of the government.

Multiple objectives or vaguely defined ones, as well as the absence of any explicit statutory objective,[115] not only hinder the control of central bank independence, but also undermine the credibility of the central bank's policies, which is, after all, an important rationale underlying central bank independence.

110. Though, in the case of New Zealand, such a single objective *need not be price stability*. S. 12 of the 1989 Act states that the Bank may be directed to formulate and implement monetary policy for different economic objective than the one specified in s. 8, *ie*, stability in the general level of prices.
111. 'The Bundesbank regulates the amount of money in circulation ... with the aim of safeguarding the currency'; Bundesbank Law, Art. 3.
112. '[T]here is a thing that Germans care about even more than inflation: reunification'; C. Fildes, 'Old Lady Spurns the If Onlysts', *Daily Telegraph*, 23 Apr. 1990.
113. However, there was a legal debate in Germany in the 1960s about the constitutionality of *Ministerialfreien Raums*, and more specifically about the constitutionality of the independence of the Bundesbank. See, *eg*, C. Samm, *Die Stellung der Deutschen Bundesbank in Verfassungsgefüge* (1967); and D. Uhlenbruck, op. cit., n.55.
114. Stern, op. cit., n.100, pp.463–508.
115. This is the case, for instance, in Belgium (1993).

5.2 Institutional accountability

Having defined the different forms of accountability, in the ensuing paragraphs I proceed to elaborate on the institutional mechanisms that help independent central banks remain accountable to executive, legislative and judicial bodies.

5.2.1 Accountability to executive bodies

To avoid an undemocratic 'state within the state', the central bank should upon demand provide the government with certain information, reports and advice.[116] This is particularly necessary when co-operation between the central bank and the government is weak, when there are only informal contacts, when there is no interchange of staff between the Treasury and the central bank, and when no member of the government is part of the central bank's board of directors.

In Germany, the Bundesbank Law (Article 13(1)) provides that '[t]he Deutsche Bundesbank shall advise the Federal Government in monetary-policy matters of major importance and provide it with information on request'. Article 109b (3) of the EC Treaty stipulates that the ESCB shall provide an annual report to the Community institutions (European Parliament Council, Commission, European Council).

5.2.2 Accountability to legislative bodies

Making a central bank accountable to the legislature could mean one of two things: either (i) direct control by parliament, if we exempt the central bank from the government's general responsibility; or (ii) reporting requirements to parliament, both on a periodic (ordinary) and on an extraordinary basis. But, if parliament is dominated by the executive, as it is often the case in the UK and in Spain, this source of accountability may in fact make the central bank responsive to the ruling party exclusively. Such a result would directly contradict the goal of insulating the central bank from pressures inherent in partisan politics.

The solution to this problem is not readily apparent, since it would imply a change in the current functioning of the democratic state in many countries. There are, however, mechanisms to alleviate this problem. One such mechanism is the strengthening of the role of minorities in parliament, by requiring, for instance, that a member of the opposition be chairman of the relevant parliamentary committee or subcommittee that is in charge of

---

116. Furthermore, the central bank should also be able to take the initiative to provide advice to the government.

reviewing the central bank's performance.[117] More radical proposals include proportional representation or other methods for greater direct participation by citizens in the governance of a country.

Nevertheless, accountability does not necessarily politicise a central bank; rather it means that the central bank should provide a justification of its actions. Parliament would not be allowed to change legally made decisions; the central bank's supervision would mean that it would be required to account for its actions, before both parliament and the public. The central bank would thus be judged for the reasonableness of its actions, by the parliament, by the executive, as well as by public opinion.

The Bundesbank publishes an annual report, which is presented to Parliament (though the Bundesbank does not have a formal accountability to the Bundestag and Bundesrat). Yet Parliament is always empowered to change the legislation, remove its independence, and even dissolve the Bundesbank.[118]

Under Article 109b (3) of the EC Treaty, the ESCB will be somewhat accountable to the European Parliament. The ECB will be required to present an annual report on the activities of the ESCB and on the monetary policy of the previous and current years to the European Parliament. The same paragraph also states that, '[t]he President of the ECB shall present this report to the Council and to the European Parliament; the latter might hold a general debate on that basis'. In addition, '[t]he President of the ECB and the other members of the Executive Board may, at the request of the European Parliament or on their own initiative, be heard by the competent Committees of the European Parliament'.

If the main source of democratic accountability is parliamentary control, the ESCB would clearly suffer from a 'democratic deficit', if the role of the European Parliament remained insignificant. But the Maastricht Treaty strengthens the role of the European Parliament, diminishing the extent of such a 'deficit'.

It is also argued that the existence of the ESCB would be democratic, legitimate and accountable once the Maastricht Treaty were approved by the Member States and ratified by their national parliaments. In my opinion, however, accountability cannot be guaranteed by the fact that the initial stage of a central bank's creation is democratic. It is in its continuing operations and policies, in the 'life' of the ESCB, that the system must be subject to democratic control.

---

117. See T. Congdon, 'Monetary Policy in the Nineties – Part 2. The Case for an Independent, but Accountable Bank of England' (July 1991) 25 *Gerrard & National Monthly Economic Review* 2.
118. Bundesbank Law, Art. 44.

5.2.3 *Accountability to judicial bodies*

The judiciary should control the lawfulness of the central bank's acts and decisions in the fulfilment of its functions. The judicial review of administrative actions, to prevent an arbitrary and unreasonable exercise of discretionary authority, is an important element of the rule of law; the discretion of central bankers should never be unfettered, but should be subject to legal control.

In addition, the court of auditors should control the accounts and practices of the central bank, to ensure transparency, particularly if the bank enjoys budgetary and financial autonomy.

In Germany, the Bundesbank Act refers to jurisdictional issues and the representation of the Bundesbank in court.[119] The annual accounts are first audited by one or more auditors appointed by the Central Bank Council in agreement with the Federal Court of Auditors. The auditors' report then serves as the basis for the audit carried out by the Federal Court of Auditors. Finally, the auditors' report and the comments of the Federal Court of Auditors are communicated to the Federal Minister of Finance.[120]

Article 35 of the Statute of the ESCB ensures that the acts of the ECB are subject to the same judicial control as the acts of other Community institutions.[121] Article 35.6 refers to the jurisdiction of the European Court of Justice in disputes concerning the fulfilment of obligations by a national central bank under the Statute.

In terms of auditing and transparency, Article 27.1 of the Statute of the ESCB refers to the need for the accounts of the ECB and the national central banks to be audited by independent external auditors recommended by the Governing Council and approved by the Council. In my opinion, the EC's Court of Auditors should examine the ESCB's accounts, or at least be entitled to revise the reports of the independent external auditors.

6.   CONCLUSION: ACCOUNTABLE, YET INDEPENDENT

One problem in the design of an 'accountable independence' lies in the possible reversal of the intended objective of 'depoliticising' the institution. If too much independence may lead to the creation of a democratically unacceptable 'state within the state', too much accountability threatens the

---

119. Ibid., Art. 11.
120. Ibid., Art. 29.
121. By virtue of the Maastricht Treaty, Arts 173, 175 and 184 of the EC Treaty have been modified, to provide for the review of the legality of the decisions of the ECB by the Court of Justice.

effectiveness of independence; an independent central bank which is fully accountable to all three branches of government may be constrained in its room for manoeuvre. An optimal trade-off between independence and accountability must be attained. Independence and accountability can be seen as opposite ends of a continuum or as two sides of the same coin. To some extent, the debate about independence and accountability resembles the philosophical debate about freedom and responsibility; independence without accountability would be like freedom without responsibility.

Chapter Sixteen

INDEPENDENCE AND ACCOUNTABILITY OF THE EUROPEAN CENTRAL BANK

Jakob de Haan and Laurence Gormley*

Chapter Outline

1. Introduction

2. Accountability of National Central Banks and the ECB

3. European Central Bank

4. Independence and Political Influence: The Case of the Fed

5. Independence and Political Influence: Some European Considerations

6. Conclusions

European Economic and Monetary Union: The Institutional Framework (M. Andenas, L. Gormley, C. Hadjiemmanuil, I. Harden, eds.: 90-411-0687-1: © Kluwer Law International: pub. Kluwer Law International, 1997: printed in Great Britain)

1. INTRODUCTION

Article 105 (1) of the EC Treaty provides that the *primary* objective of the European System of Central Banks, consisting of the European Central Bank and national central banks, must be price stability.[1] Furthermore, the EC Treaty and the Protocol on the Statute of the ESCB and of the ECB annexed thereto contain various measures to ensure that the ESCB will be independent. Under Article 108 of the EC Treaty every Member State (thus also those with a derogation) must ensure, at the latest at the date of the establishment of the ESCB, that its national legislation, including the statutes of its national central bank, is compatible with the EC Treaty and the Statute of the ESCB.[2]

It is frequently argued that a high level of central bank independence coupled with some explicit mandate for the bank to aim for price stability are important institutional devices for the assurance of price stability.[3] In that context the position of the Bundesbank is often mentioned as the prime example: it is relatively autonomous; at the same time, Germany has one of the best inflation records among the OECD countries since 1945. Indeed, the Statute of the ESCB is largely modelled after the law governing the Bundesbank. It is thought that an independent central bank can give priority to a low level of inflation, whereas in countries with a more dependent central bank other considerations (such as re-election perspectives of politicians, or a low level of unemployment) may interfere with the objective of price stability. However, no matter how important central bank independence may be, it is important that in a democratic society the accountability of monetary policy is properly arranged. This chapter starts with a summary of our argument[4] that in comparison with the central banks

---

* The authors are currently supervising a research project on democratic accountability and judicial protection in relation to central banks. Jakob de Haan thanks Geert Beekhuis for research assistance.

1. See also Statute of the ESCB, Art. 2.
2. See also Statute of the ESCB, Art. 14.1. The ECB will take over from the European Monetary Institute (set up under Art. 109f of the EC Treaty and the Protocol on the Statute of the European Monetary Institute, and operating from Jan. 1, 1994) from the first day of the third stage of EMU; EC Treaty, Art. 109l (1)–(2). Art. 108 of the EC Treaty will not apply to the UK, if the UK government notifies the Council that it does not intend to proceed to the third stage of EMU.
3. See, *eg*, J. de Haan and J. E. Sturm, 'The Case for Central Bank Independence' (1992) 182 *Banca Nazionale del Lavoro Quarterly Review* 305; and A. Cukierman, *Central Bank Strategy, Credibility, and Independence* (1992). C. Goodhart, *The Central Bank and the Financial System* (1995), p.63, has observed that the case 'for an independent, more autonomous Central Bank is a highly fashionable argument, very much the flavour of the month'.
4. See L. Gormley and J. de Haan, 'The Democratic Deficit of the European Central Bank' (1996) 21 *E.L. Rev.* 95.

in three countries (Germany, the Netherlands and New Zealand)[5] the democratic accountability of the ECB is not properly provided for. Next we try to gauge the extent to which the ECB may be under political pressure despite its independence by analysing the experience of the American Federal Reserve System.

2. ACCOUNTABILITY OF NATIONAL CENTRAL BANKS AND THE ECB

Central bank independence and democratic accountability are implemented in various ways in different countries, as the examples of three relatively independent central banks, the Deutsche Bundesbank, the Nederlandsche Bank (the Dutch Central Bank) and the Reserve Bank of New Zealand, demonstrate. Five aspects of the division of responsibilities between the government and the central bank are important in this respect.[6]

First, the ultimate objective(s) of monetary policy. The Reserve Bank of New Zealand has as its primary objective the pursuit of price stability.[7] The Bundesbank has a similar primary objective which is, however, not as specific (formally referred to as defence of the value of the currency).[8] In addition, the Bundesbank has the obligation to offer general support to the government's economic policy in instances in which this does not prejudice

---

5. These three countries provide useful models of varying degrees of considerable independence. On the independence of the Bank of England, see Centre for Economic Policy Research, Report of an independent panel chaired by E. Roll, *Independent and Accountable: A New Mandate for the Bank of England* (Oct. 1993); and T. Daintith, 'Between Domestic Democracy and an Alien Rule of Law? Some Thoughts on the 'Independence' of the Bank of England', ch.17 of this volume. On the Banque de France, see G. Iacono, 'Le Nouveau Statut de la Banque de France, Une Etape vers l'Union Economique et Monétaire' [1994] *Rec. Dalloz Chron.* 89; and J.-P. Duprat, 'The Independence of the Banque de France: Constitutional and European Aspects' [1995] *Public Law* 133. See also, generally, G. Quaden, 'Indépendance et Responsabilité des Banques Centrales: L'Expérience des Banques Nationales' [1991] *Reflets Perspectives de la Vie Economique* 133; and W. L. Hoskins, 'Some Observations on Central Bank Accountability' [Oct. 1991] *Federal Reserve Bank of Cleveland, Economic Commentary*.
6. See Centre for Economic Policy Research, op. cit., n.5, pp.21 *et seq.*
7. Reserve Bank of New Zealand Act 1989, s.8: 'The primary function of the Bank is to formulate and implement monetary policy directed to the economic objective of achieving and maintaining stability in the general level of prices.'
8. Deutsche Bundesbankgesetz (hereafter, 'BbankG 1957') (BGBl. I S. 745; for the Law in the version published on 22 Oct. 1957, see BGBl. I S. 1782; the Law has been amended subsequently, but not on this point), Art. 3: 'The Bundesbank shall regulate the amount of money in circulation and of credit supplied to the economy, using the monetary powers conferred on it by this Act, with the aim of safeguarding the currency, and shall provide for the execution by banks of domestic and external payments' (our translation).

the primary objective of price stability.[9] However, this subsidiary statutory objective is in practice not very important.[10] The objective of the Dutch Central Bank is to regulate the value of the guilder in a welfare-enhancing way.[11] Nowadays, this objective is interpreted as a stable exchange rate of the guilder *vis-à-vis* the DM.[12]

The second aspect is the precision of specification of targets. The Governor of the Reserve Bank of New Zealand has to agree with the government a tight target range for inflation three years hence. The Bundesbank is under no legal obligation to agree, obey or announce any targets, although since 1974 it announces the targeted rate (or zone) for money growth, which implies a certain inflation target. The German Federal Government is responsible for decisions about the exchange rate, which has been a cause for many a conflict between the Bundesbank and the Federal Government.[13]

Third, the statutory basis for independence is a key element. Whereas the Governor of the Reserve Bank of New Zealand must agree a target range with the government,[14] the Bundesbank in Germany is completely independent of any instructions from government;[15] it may consult the government, but is under no obligation to agree with it.[16] Under Article 13 (2) of the Law on the Bundesbank, government representatives have the right to attend meetings of the Zentralbankrat (the Bundesbank Council), but not to vote. All members of the government are entitled to be present, and the Ministers of Finance and Economics are regularly invited, but in practice rarely attend (although one of them is always present when the annual money supply targets are being set); other ministers may be present if issues of concern to their departments are being discussed. In practice, ministers have never proposed motions at meetings: their standpoint is usually

---

9. BbankG 1957, Art. 12.
10. See, *eg*, O. Lampe, *Die Unabhängigkeit der Deutschen Bundesbank* (1971), pp.47–53; and E. Kennedy, *The Bundesbank* (1991), p.27.
11. Bankwet (Bank Law) 1948 (Stb. 1948 I 166), Art. 9 (1): 'The Bank's task is to regulate the value of the Dutch currency in such a manner as is most useful for the welfare of the country and thereby to stabilize that value as much as possible' (our translation).
12. See, *eg*, A. H. E. M. Wellink, 'Mogelijkheden van het Monetaire Beleid na de Liberalisering: De Visie van de Nederlandsche Bank' [1990] *Preadviezen NIBE-jaardag* 15, p.32; and Smits (1996) 45 *ICLQ* 319, p.325.
13. See, generally, D. Marsh, *The Bundesbank: The Bank that Rules Europe* (1992), pp.189–95.
14. Reserve Bank of New Zealand Act 1989, s.9.
15. BbankG 1957, Art. 12: 'Without prejudice to the performance of its functions, the Deutsche Bundesbank shall be required to support the general economic policy of the Federal government. In exercising the powers conferred on it by this Act, it shall be independent of instructions from the government' (our translation). See also Lampe, op. cit., n.10, pp.50–51.
16. BbankG 1957, Art. 13 (1): 'The Deutsche Bundesbank shall advise the government on monetary policy matters of major importance and provide it with information on request' (our translation).

explained beforehand.[17] The Dutch Bank Law contains no specific articles on the statutory basis for independence.

Fourth, the question when the bank's view can be overridden is a central measure of the degree of central bank independence. In New Zealand the Governor of the Reserve Bank can be dismissed if he fails to deliver the inflation target (obligation *ad hominem*),[18] although his contract contains some clearly identified escape clauses (such as a rise in indirect taxes, or change in exchange-rate regime). This normative control[19] of the Governor goes well beyond the control which can be exercised in Germany and the Netherlands. In Germany the government can suspend the taking of decisions by the Bundesbank for a maximum of two weeks,[20] but this temporary veto has never been formally deployed.[21] Only through a change in legislation can the Bundesbank be overruled by the government. The Zentralbankrat of the Bundesbank is responsible for monetary policy (collective responsibility). The Netherlands has a very unique central bank legislation. According to Article 26 of the Bank Law of 1948, the Minister of Finance has the right to give a so-called instruction to the bank with regard to monetary policy.[22] Through this construction the Minister is responsible to Parliament for monetary policy. The days of this construction are now numbered: by the third stage of EMU, which is planned to start no later than 1999,[23] since the right of the Minister of Finance to give instructions to the Central Bank has to be abolished.[24]

17. T. Werres, *The Deutsche Bundesbank and its Relationship with the Federal Government* in *Europe's Economy in the 1990s*, AGENOR Research Unit's European Research Project on Autonomy, Phase I, 1989–90, Vol.II (1989), p.7.

18. Reserve Bank of New Zealand Act 1989, s.9 (1): 'The Minister [of Finance (see s.2)] shall, before appointing, or reappointing, any person as Governor, fix, in agreement with that person, policy targets for the carrying out by the bank of its primary function during that person's term of office, or next term of office, as Governor'.

19. Normative control, according to Daintith, loc. cit., n.5, p.364, involves the evaluation of specific action by reference to predetermined rules of sufficient clarity to be a guide both to behaviour and censure.

20. BbankG 1957, Art. 13 (2).

21. Marsh, op. cit., n.13, p.73.

22. Bankwet 1948, Art. 26 (1). Although the Governing Board of the Bank may object within three days of having received the binding directive, the Crown (which means in practice the Minister) has the last word; ibid., Art. 26 (2). If the Crown decides to overrule the objections, they and the Crown's reasoned decision are published in the *Staatscourant*, unless the Crown deems that the national interest otherwise requires; ibid., Art. 26 (3). This right is in effect an ultimate remedy and has never been applied. In his memoirs, Zijlstra, who was President of the Dutch Central Bank between 1967 and 1981, states that Prime Minister Den Uyl (1974–77) contemplated using this instrument after the Bank had introduced credit restrictions in 1977; see J. Zijlstra, *Per Slot van Rekening* (1992), pp.215–16.

23. EC Treaty, Art. 109j (4).

24. This follows from EC Treaty, Art. 107, and Statute of the ESCB, Art. 7.

The fifth, and final aspect is the appointment of bank officials. The Governor of the Reserve Bank of New Zealand is appointed by the Minister of Finance on the recommendation of the Board of Directors[25] for a period of five years.[26] Besides the Governor, there are one or two deputies, appointed by the Board on the recommendation of the Governor.[27] The Board of Directors consists of not less than seven and not more than ten members: the Governor and the Deputy Governor(s) of the Bank and four to seven non-executive directors, appointed by the Minister of Finance for five years.[28] The governing board of the Bundesbank is the Zentralbankrat.[29] Apart from the Directorate (Direktorium) the presidents of the nine Landeszentralbanken are members of the Zentralbankrat. The Directorate comprises the President, Vice-President and a maximum of nowadays six other members, appointed by the Federal President on nomination of the Federal Government in Bonn.[30] The Zentralbankrat is consulted in this process.[31] The Presidents of the Landeszentralbanken are nominated by the Bundesrat (the upper federal chamber), based on recommendations from governments of the Länder.[32] The Zentralbankrat is again consulted.[33] In the Netherlands the President and the Secretary of the Central Bank are appointed by the Crown (in effect by the Minister of Finance), on the basis of a recommendation list containing only two names, which has been decided upon in a combined meeting of the Governing Board and the Supervisory Board of the Bank.[34] The other members of the Governing Board are also similarly appointed, on the basis of a recommendation list containing three names, again drawn up by the Governing and Supervisory Boards in a

---

25. Reserve Bank of New Zealand Act 1989, s.40 (1).
26. Ibid., s.42 (1). He may be reappointed for a further term or terms, each of up to 5 years.
27. Ibid., s.43 (1).
28. Ibid., ss.54 (1)–(2); 55 (1). As to the first non-executive directors, see ibid., s.55 (2). The non-executive directors are eligible for reappointment; ibid., s.55 (3).
29. BbankG 1957, Art. 29.
30. Ibid., Art. 7 (3). The term of office of members of the Directorate is eight years, although exceptionally appointments may be made for a shorter period, which may not, however, be less than two years; ibid. Until unification, each of the 11 western Länder had its own central bank; their presidents were members of the Zentralbankrat, as were the members of the Directorate, which could consist of up to 10 persons, including the President and the Vice-President of the Bundesbank. After unification, the number of Länder representatives was reduced to nine, and the maximum membership of the Directorate to eight; ibid., Arts 6 (2), 8 (1) and 7 (2). See E. Owen Smith, *The German Economy* (1994), p.141.
31. BbankG 1957, Art. 7 (3).
32. Ibid., Art. 8 (4).
33. Ibid.
34. Bankwet 1948, Art. 23 (1). They are appointed for a term of seven years and are eligible for reappointment; ibid., Art. 23 (1) and (3).

combined meeting and presented by the Governing Board.[35] The so-called Royal Commissioner is responsible for supervision on behalf of the government; he is also appointed by the Minister.[36] As from the start of the third stage of EMU this construction will also no longer be permitted.

Table 1 summarises the preceding analysis. It follows from this table that central bank independence in a democratic society can be implemented in different ways.

3.   EUROPEAN CENTRAL BANK

The European Central Bank will become responsible for the formulation and implementation of the monetary policy of the Community[37] and will have legal personality.[38] While its institutional autonomy is guaranteed,[39] it does not have the status of a Community institution within the meaning of Article 4 of the EC Treaty. Its statute is set out in a separate protocol, which implies a solid legislative base, since most of the provisions of the Statute of the ESCB can only be changed through an amendment of the EC Treaty itself, according to the procedure of Article N (1) of the Maastricht Treaty.[40]

35. Ibid., Art. 23 (2). The term of office is again seven years. If the Crown has not within three weeks of the date of the proposal appointed one of the candidates, a new list drawn up in the same way is submitted by the Governing Board. If within three weeks of the submission of the new list, no appointment has been made, the Crown appoints a candidate of its own choosing; ibid. All members of the Governing Board are eligible for reappointment; ibid., Art. 23 (3). The Governing Board (Directie) consists of the President, the Secretary and at least two, and at most five, directors; ibid., Art. 22 (1) (as amended by the Law of 9 Dec. 1993, Stb. 1993 676).
36. Ibid., Arts 30 and 31.
37. EC Treaty, Art. 105 (2). The Governing Council of the ECB *formulates* the monetary policy of the Community, including, as appropriate, decisions relating to intermediate monetary objectives, key interest rates and the supply of reserves in the ESCB, and establishes the necessary guidelines for their implementation. The Executive Board of the ECB *implements* monetary policy in accordance with the guidelines and decisions laid down by the Governing Council; in doing so it may give instructions to national central banks. It may also have certain powers delegated to it where the Governing Council so decides. Statute of the ESCB, Art. 12.1.
38. EC Treaty, Art. 106 (1); and Statute of the ESCB, Art. 9.1. The ESCB as such does not have legal personality; see M. Crawford, *One Money for Europe?* (1993), p.191. The shareholders in the ECB are not the Member States, but the national central banks; Statute of the ESCB, Art. 28.2.
39. EC Treaty, Art. 107; and Statute of the ESCB, Art. 7.
40. EC Treaty, Art. 106 (5), provides for a simplified amendment procedure in respect of the following Articles of the Statute of the ESCB: Arts 5.1-5.3, 17, 18, 19.1, 22, 23, 24, 26, 32.3-32.4, 32.6, 33.1 (a), and 36 – none of which are significant for present purposes; see also the parallel provision of Statute of the ESCB, Art. 41.1. A recommendation made by the ECB under the Statute of the ESCB, Art. 41, requires a unanimous decision by the

Table 1

Alternative approaches to central bank independence

	Bundesbank	Reserve Bank of New Zealand	Nederlandsche Bank	ECB
Policy objective:				
Price stability	Primary objective	Sole objective	If welfare enhancing	Primary objective
Supporting government economic policy	Secondary objective	–	–	Secondary objective
Government override	Implicit (new law)	Yes	Right to give instructions	Only via amendment of Treaty (with limited exceptions)
Policy targets:				
Obligatory	No	Yes	No	No
Agreed with government	No	Yes	No	No
Escape clauses	No	Yes	No	No
Time horizon	No	Three years	No	No
Responsibility:				
Laid upon:	Bundesbank Council (Zentralbankrat)	Governor of Reserve Bank	Implicitly with Minister	Executive Board of the ECB
Monitoring	Only implicit	Dismissal of Governor for failure to meet target	Through Royal Commissioner	No, save reporting and presence at Governing Council and General Council of the ECB

Sources: Based upon Centre for Economic Policy Research, Report of an independent panel chaired by E. Roll, *Independent and Accountable: A New Mandate for the Bank of England* (Oct. 1993); and the Dutch Bankwet (Bank Law) 1948.

(*continued*)

        Governing Council; ibid., Art. 41.2. In these cases the views of the ECB are clearly designed to carry more weight than those of the Commission: if the recommendation for amendment emanates from the ECB, the Council acts by qualified majority after consulting the Commission and obtaining the assent of the European Parliament; if the proposal is made by the Commission, the Council acts unanimously after consulting the ECB and after obtaining the assent of the European Parliament. Unlike when the Council acts on the basis of a proposal from the Commission (as to which, see EC Treaty, Art. 189a (1)), no requirement of unanimity is provided for if the Council decides to act in a manner different from that set out in the ECB's recommendation.

Although the *primary* objective of ESCB is to maintain price stability,[41] and although no other objective is expressly stated, the ESCB has also, without impairing this primary objective, to support 'the general economic policies in the Community with a view to contributing to the achievement of the objectives of the Community as laid down in Article 2 [of the EC Treaty].[42] This means that account has to be taken of the task of the Community as expressed in Article 2 of the EC Treaty. The ESCB is obliged to act 'in accordance with the principle of an open market economy with free competition, favouring an efficient allocation of resources, and in compliance with the principles set out in Article 3a [of the EC Treaty].'[43] These additional obligations effectively amount to secondary objectives for the ESCB.

The Governing Council of the ECB will comprise the members of the Executive Board and the Governors of the national central banks.[44] It will formulate the monetary policy of the Community; the Executive Board must implement monetary policy in accordance with the guidelines and decisions laid down by the Governing Council, and in doing so, the Board must give the necessary instructions to national central banks.[45] The Executive Board will comprise the President, the Vice-President and four other members,[46] all of whom must be nationals of Member States and persons of recognised standing and professional experience in monetary or banking matters; they will be appointed by common accord of the Member States at the level of the Heads of State or Government, on a recommendation from the Council after consulting the European Parliament and the Governing Council of the ECB; their term of office will be eight years and the mandate is not renewable.[47]

41. EC Treaty, Art. 105 (1); and Statute of the ESCB, Art. 2.
42. Ibid.
43. EC Treaty, Art. 105. The guiding principles for such activities of the Member States and the Community as set out in Art. 3a (1)–(2) of the EC Treaty are: stable prices, sound public finances and monetary conditions, and a sustainable balance of payments; EC Treaty, Art. 3a (3).
44. EC Treaty, Art. 109a (1); and Statute of the ESCB, Art. 10.1. This means central banks of Member States without a derogation from participation in the third stage of EMU. See I. Harden, 'The European Central Bank and the Role of National Central Banks in Economic and Monetary Union', in K. Gretschmann (ed.), *Economic and Monetary Union: Implications for National Policy-Makers* (1993), pp.149 *et seq.*
45. Statute of the ESCB, Art. 12.1.
46. EC Treaty, Art. 109a (2) (a); and Statute of the ESCB, Art. 11.1. If there are Member States enjoying a derogation at the beginning of the third stage of EMU, the number of members of the Executive Board may be less, but in no case may it be less than four people in all, the appointments being made by those Member States without a derogation; EC Treaty, Art. 109l (1); and Statute of the ESCB, Arts 43.3 and 50.
47. EC Treaty, Art. 109a (2) (b); and Statute of the ESCB, Art. 11.2. As to the initial appointment, see Statute of the ESCB, Art. 50, and *supra*, n.46. The EMI is the precursor of the ECB, and is governed by EC Treaty, Art. 109f, and the Statute of the EMI. During the second stage of EMU the term ECB used in EC Treaty, Arts 173, 175-7, 180 and 215,

This ensures the personal autonomy of the members of the Executive Board. The eight-year term is sufficiently long, and the ineligibility for renewal sufficiently disinteresting[48] to offer some realistic chance that the formal personal autonomy will be translated into functional autonomy. Both the Governing Council and the Executive Board will be limited to the relevant persons from Member States without a derogation under Article 109k (1) of the EC Treaty.[49]

Article 7 of the Statute of the ESCB provides that 'neither the ECB, nor a national central bank, nor any member of their decision-making bodies shall seek or take instructions from Community institutions or bodies, from any government of a Member State or from any other body'. This provision parallels the terms of Article 157 (2) of the EC Treaty relating to the Commission.[50] However, the President of the Council (which will be the Ecofin Council) and a representative of the Commission may participate (but not vote) in meetings of the ECB Governing Council, and the President of the Council may submit a motion for deliberation to the Governing Council.[51] Attendance, without the right to vote, but certainly with the right to speak when invited to do so, is standing practice for the Commission in Council meetings and at European Parliament sessions and committee

(*continued*)

    is to be read as referring to the EMI; EC Treaty, Art. 109f (9). In cases in which the ECB has a consultative role under the EC Treaty, the reference is to be similarly read; EC Treaty, Art. 109f (8).

48. *Ie*, the incumbents will not be people glancing over their shoulders with an eye to reappointment, so there is more likelihood that the incumbents will be at the *fin de carrière* stage than 'hotshots' seeking to make their names.

49. Statute of the ESCB, Arts 43.2 and 43.3. As to the effect of a derogation, see EC Treaty, Art. 109k (3)–(6).

50. Although, unlike Art. 157 (2) of the EC Treaty, Art. 7 of the Statute of the ESCB does not contain any provisions relating to the acceptance of positions by members of decision-making bodies on leaving office. As to the obligations on the members of the Executive Board of the ECB relating to full-time commitment and abstention from engagement in any other occupation without express permission of the Governing Council of the ECB, see Statute of the ESCB, Art. 11(1). As to the obligations of professional secrecy, see ibid., Art. 38. We return below to the parallel with the independence of the Commission.

51. A French proposal to empower the President of the Council to force the Governing Council to postpone a decision for up to a fortnight (paralleling BbankG 1957, Art. 13 (2), in relation to the Bundesbank) was not accepted by the Intergovernmental Conference which approved the Maastricht Treaty, and there was no question of giving such a power to the Commission. On the negotiations in the IGC in this field, see Alexander Italianer, 'Managing Maastricht: EMU Issues and How They Were Settled', in Gretschmann (ed.), op. cit., n.44, pp.51 *et seq.*; see also J. Kugler and J. H. P. Williams, 'The Politics Surrounding the Creation of the EC Bank: The Last Stumbling Block to Integration', in B. Bueno de Mesquita and F. N. Stokman (eds), *European Community Decision Making: Models, Applications, and Comparisons* (1994), pp.185 *et seq.* It will be recalled that German ministers have never proposed motions at meetings of the Zentralbankrat of the Bundesbank, their views being usually explained beforehand.

meetings. In the European Council the President of the Commission is a full member, assisted by a Member of the Commission.[52] However, just as representatives of the other institutions are not entitled to participate in meetings of the Commission, so too there is no entitlement for them to participate in meetings of the ECB Executive Board. The President of the ECB must be invited to participate in Council meetings when the Council is discussing matters relating to the objectives and tasks of the ESCB, but this does not, of course, give him the right to vote.[53] As an extra guarantee of its independence, the ECB has financial autonomy in that its income and expenditure do not fall under the Community budget[54]; its capital resources are dealt with in the Statute of the ESCB.[55]

In accordance with Article 108 of the EC Treaty, each Member State must ensure, at the latest at the date of the establishment of the ESCB, that its national central bank is independent.[56] This implies that the minimum term of office of a Governor has to be five years[57] and that he can only be removed from office if he no longer fulfils the conditions required for the performance of his duties or if he has been guilty of serious misconduct.[58] Such a decision is subject to appeal to the Court of Justice by the Governor concerned or by the Governing Council of the ECB on grounds of infringement of the EC Treaty or of any rule of law relating to its application.

The European Parliament mostly plays but a minor role, although its assent is essential for the use of the simplified amendment procedure for certain provisions of the Statute of the ESCB[59] and for the conferment on the ECB of specific tasks relating to prudential supervision.[60] The ECB has to present an annual report on the activities of the ESCB and on the monetary policy of both the previous and current year to the European Parliament, the

52. Maastricht Treaty, Art. D.
53. EC Treaty, Art. 109b (2). The word 'him' is in accordance with the wording of the EC Treaty.
54. Somewhat remarkably, the Statute of the ESCB does not indicate whether the Governing Council or the Executive Board is responsible for approving the budget of the ECB. It seems that this will be dealt with in the Rules of Procedure which the Governing Council will adopt under Statute of the ESCB, Art. 12.3. The accounts of the ECB and the national central banks are to be audited by independent external auditors recommended by the Governing Council and approved by the Council; Statute of the ESCB, Art. 27.1. The role of the Court of Auditors under Art. 188c EC is confined to an examination of the operational efficiency of the management of the ECB; ibid., Art. 27.2. It does not therefore cover the reliability of the ECB's accounts and the legality and regularity of the underlying transactions, nor does it cover any of the activities of the national central banks.
55. Statute of the ESCB, Arts 28, 29, 48 and 49.
56. Ibid., Art. 14.1.
57. Ibid., Art. 14.2.
58. Ibid., Art. 14.3.
59. EC Treaty, Art. 106 (5); and Statute of the ESCB, Art. 41.1.
60. EC Treaty, Art. 105 (6).

Council, the Commission and the European Council; the President of the ECB presents it to the Council and to the European Parliament, which may hold a general debate on that basis.[61] The ESCB has to publish a consolidated financial statement weekly,[62] and the ECB must draw up and publish reports on the activities of the ESCB at least quarterly.[63] The President of the ECB and the other members of the Executive Board of the ECB may, at the request of the European Parliament or on their own initiative, be heard by the competent committees of the European Parliament.[64] The European Parliament will also be consulted in appointing Executive Board members.[65] In relation to European Parliament control, the context of the annual report is the only plenary control on the activities of the ESCB: the incidental audience is with the competent committees. The democratic legitimation of European monetary policy also keeps a national dimension, since national parliaments can call on their minister of finance to explain his contribution to the deliberations between the Ecofin Council and the ECB. At best then, the control by the European Parliament is almost entirely *ex post* and non-normative[66] – *ex ante* involvement being confined to the points indicated at the beginning of this paragraph. The European Parliament does not even have the possibility of using the instrument of the budgetary procedure to encourage the ECB to toe a particular line.

It follows from the foregoing analysis that the democratic accountability of the ECB is poorly arranged in comparison with the accountability of the central banks of the countries examined in this chapter. Also in comparison with the Bundesbank there is less accountability, since the mandate of the ECB can only be changed through amendment of the Treaty, which requires unanimity. In contrast, the Bundesbank always has to take into account the possibility of a change of the law. Through this mechanism the Bundesbank will, in the long run, follow a policy which is in agreement with the wishes of democratically elected politicians. In the Netherlands this political approval is arranged differently, but in this country the Central Bank pursues policies which can count on broad political support.[67] Also from the

61. EC Treaty, Art. 109b (2); and Statute of the ESCB, Art. 15.3. The nature of the presentation is oral, whether before the relevant committee of the European Parliament or in plenary debate. The inspiration for this appears to be the American Humphrey-Hawkins procedure.
62. Statute of the ESCB, Art. 15.2.
63. Statute of the ESCB, Art. 15.1.
64. EC Treaty, Art. 109b (3).
65. EC Treaty, Art. 109 (2) (b); and Statute of the ESCB, Art. 11.2.
66. In Daintith's terms; see Daintith, loc. cit., n.5.
67. The Dutch Central Bank reports on general economic and financial developments and on the Bank's policy to an advisory Bank Council, which includes representatives of a broad cross-section of Dutch economic-interest groups; Bankwet 1948, Arts 32–3; see also the decision of 14.2.84, Stb. 1984 47. The Bank Council may give advisory opinions of its own motion; Bankwet 1948, Art. 33 (4).

343

viewpoint of economic theory, the democratic accountability of the ECB can be improved by following the Netherlands or New Zealand examples.[68] We now continue our analysis by examining whether, despite its statutory independence, there will be political pressures on the ECB. As the ECB does not yet exist, we analyse the experience of the Federal Reserve which may give some indications.

4. INDEPENDENCE AND POLITICAL INFLUENCE: THE CASE OF THE FED

In comparison with central banks in other OECD countries, the Federal Reserve has a relatively independent position. Table 2 provides the ranking of the Fed according to a number of measures of legal central bank independence, which are all based upon the charters of the central banks. Although the ranking of central bank charters by their degree of legal independence is a difficult task involving some subjective judgement, it is remarkable that all these proxies for legal independence yield a similar outcome for the Federal Reserve.[69]

Table 2

Legal central bank independence measures: the ranking of the Fed

Measure of central bank independence	Max. score	Score	Number of countries	Ranking of Fed
Alesina	4	3	17	3/4
Grilli *et al.*	13	12	18	2/3
Eijffinger-Schaling	5	3	12	4/6
Cukierman	0.68	0.51	23	5

Although the Fed has a relatively independent position, 'the contemporary view is that the Administration, while granting significant leeway to the Fed, when necessary obtains the monetary policy actions that it desires'.[70] The question which we will analyse in this part of the chapter is on which

---

68. See Gormley and de Haan, loc. cit., n.4.
69. For a review of these indicators of central bank independence, we refer to S. C. W. Eijffinger and J. de Haan, *The Political Economy of Central Bank Independence*, Princeton Special Papers in International Economics no. 1g (1996).
70. T. Havrilesky, *The Pressures on American Monetary Policy* (1993), p.30.

evidence this 'contemporary view' is based. Havrilesky's work[71] is the most extensive attempt to provide empirical underpinnings for this view. Before reviewing his findings, we will start by summarising the older literature on political business and partisan cycles in American monetary policy.

According to the political business cycle (PBC) literature – either in its original form as presented by Nordhaus, or in its more modern version as presented by, for example, Rogoff and Sibert – re-election opportunities of the incumbent President or political party are assumed to depend upon the inflation and unemployment performance of the economy.[72] Indeed, there is ample evidence that macroeconomic factors are important determinants of election outcomes. Therefore, an incumbent politician can enhance his probability of success through stimulating the economy, provided that the positive effects of increased employment are felt before the negative effects of inflation, and that the electorate fails to take into account the future consequences of such policy.

Quite a few studies have examined presidential influence on the Federal Reserve, with rather divergent outcomes. Table 3 summarises the studies of which the present authors are aware.[73] Many of these studies can be criticised on various grounds. For example, various authors analyse the influence of elections on policy outcomes, instead of policy instruments, whereas only the latter are controlled by the authorities. Furthermore, none of the studies summarised in Table 3 takes the popularity of the incumbent into account. This is unsatisfying: after all, why would the incumbent put

---

71. Ibid.
72. W. Nordhaus, 'The Political Business Cycle' (1975) 42 *Rev. Econ. Stud.* 169; K. Rogoff and A. Sibert, 'Equilibrium Political Business Cycles' (1988) 55 *Rev. Econ. Stud.* 1.
73. D. G. Luckett and G. T. Potts, 'Monetary Policy and Partisan Politics' (1980) 12 *Journal of Money, Credit, and Banking* 54; N. Beck, 'Presidential Influence on the Federal Reserve in the 1970s' (1982) 26 *Am. J. Pol. Sci.* 415; L. O. Laney and T. D. Willett, 'Presidential Politics, Budget Deficits, and Monetary Policy in the United States, 1960–1976' (1983) 40 *Public Choice* 53; M. S. Wallace and J. T. Warner, 'Fed Policy and Presidential Elections' (1984) 6 *Journal of Macroeconomics* 79; S. D. Allen, 'The Federal Reserve and the Electoral Cycle' (1986) 18 *Journal of Money, Credit, and Banking* 88; D. J. Richards, 'Unanticipated Money and the Political Business Cycle', (1986) 18 *Journal of Money, Credit, and Banking* 447; K. B. Grier, 'Presidential Elections and Federal Reserve Policy: An Empirical Test' (1987) 53 *Southern Economic Journal* 475; N. Beck, 'Elections and the Fed: Is There a Political Monetary Cycle?' (1987) 31 *Am. J. Pol. Sci.* 194; D. R. Hakes, 'Monetary Policy and Presidential Elections: A Nonpartisan Political Cycle' (1988) 57 *Public Choice* 175; K. B. Grier, 'On the Existence of a Political Monetary Cycle' (1989) 33 *Am. J. Pol. Sci.* 376; R. Renshaw and E. Trahan, 'Presidential Elections and the Federal Reserve's Interest Rate Reaction Function' (1990) 12 *Journal of Policy Modelling* 29–34; S. D. Allen and D. L. McCrickard, 'The Influence of Elections on Federal Reserve Behavior' (1991) 37 *Economics Letters* 51; N. Beck, 'The Fed and the Political Business Cycle' (1991) 9 *Contemporary Policy Issues* 25; W. J. Bettow and R. J. Cebula, 'Does the Federal Reserve Create Political Monetary Cycles?' (1994) 16 *Journal of Macroeconomics* 461.

Table 3

Political business cycles in American monetary policy: a summary

Study	Sample period	Model	Outcome
Luckett and Potts (1980)	1961–76	Model for monetary policy stance (tight/easy)	No significant influence of elections
Beck (1982)	1970–79	Reaction function with change in federal-funds rate as independent variable	No significant influence of elections
Laney and Willet (1983)	1960–76	Money-supply reaction function with election variables	No evidence of direct influence of elections on money supply, but Fed accommodates (election-induced) budget deficits
Wallace and Warner PBC(1985)	1963–80	Reaction function for various instruments and indicators of monetary policy	Except for Nixon administration, no support for PBC
Allen (1986)	1954–80	Reaction function for M1 and monetary-base growth with electoral variables	No direct impact of elections, but evidence that Fed accommodates deficits more before elections
Richards (1986)	1960–84	Effects of elections on fore-cast errors of money supply	There is some evidence for PBC for the period until 1975, but not for the entire period
Grier (1987)	1961–82	Test of the significance of electoral variables in money supply	Money-supply cycle corresponds with the PBC; the electoral variable is significant
Beck (1987)	1961–84	Models for money (M1) growth with election variables	Cycle in money supply, but this is caused by accommo-dation of fiscal policy
Grier (1989)	1961–82	Model for money (M1) growth with election variable	Support for PBC
Hakes (1988)	1953–84	Reaction function with policy indicator in which pre-election and post-election estimates are compared	Although Fed reacts differently to pre- and post-electoral conditions, this is not caused by political influence
Renshaw and Trahan (1990)	1954–88	Simulated interest rates estimated on the basis of reaction function are compared with actual rates	No evidence for PBC
Allen and McCrickard (1991)	1917–84	Monetary reaction function with election variables	Only support for PBC during the 1930s and 1940s
Beck (1991)	1961–84	Models for money growth and for instruments of Fed	A cycle is present in money growth until 1976, but not in instruments
Bettow and Cebula (1994)	1974–83	Reaction function with election variables	Only limited evidence for influence of elections

pressure on the Fed if he faces a high chance of re-election? The specifications of the models employed also show considerable diversity, while most authors do not attempt to link their own research effort with those of others. However, it is clear that there is only limited evidence that electoral considerations influence American monetary policies. Except for the work of Grier,[74] most studies find little or no support for a consistent political cycle in monetary policy. Still, there are indications that during certain periods electoral considerations have played some role in American monetary policy. An interesting issue for future research would be to examine why political influence has changed over time. Has it anything to do with the changes in the way independence and accountability have been arranged for? Or are allegations that the Fed was caught with its hands in the electoral cookie-jar, like, for instance, over the 1972 election, restraining the central bank? Another interesting conclusion following from Table 3 is that there is at least some evidence that the Fed accommodates budget deficits (*ie*, in case of federal government budget deficits money growth is higher than it would otherwise have been), also if these deficits are caused by policies aimed at increasing the chances of re-election of the incumbent administration.

Table 4 summarises some studies based on the so-called partisan approach.[75] The central hypothesis of this approach pioneered by Hibbs is that left-wing and right-wing political parties have different priorities with respect to inflation and unemployment.[76] Whereas right-wing parties give a higher priority to lower inflation, left-wing parties favour a lower level of unemployment. If governments are able to impress their views on the central bank, it is to be expected that monetary policy in the US would be different under Republican and Democratic administrations. It follows from Table 4 that there is considerable evidence in support of this view. In other words, despite its statutory independence, the Fed apparently delivers the kind of policies favoured by the incumbent administration. This conclusion also follows from recent work of Havrilesky, which will be reviewed in some more detail.

74. Grier, loc. cit., n.73.
75. R. E. Weintraub, 'Congressional Supervision on Monetary Policy' (1978) 4 *J. Mon. Econ.* 341; K. B. Grier and H. E. Neiman, 'Deficits, Politics, and Money Growth' (1987) 25 *Economic Inquiry* 201; T. Havrilesky, 'A Partisan Theory of Fiscal and Monetary Regimes' (1987) 19 *Journal of Money, Credit, and Banking* 308; A. Alesina, 'Macroeconomics and Politics' [1988] *NBER Macroeconomics Annual*; A. Alesina and J. Sachs, 'Political Parties and Business Cycles in the United States, 1948-1984', (1988) 20 *Journal of Money, Credit, and Banking* 632; G. Tabellini and V. La Via, 'Money, Deficit and Public Debt in the United States' (1989) 71 *Rev. Econ. & Stat.* 15.
76. D. Hibbs, 'Political Parties and Macroeconomic Policy' (1977) 71 *Am. Pol. Sci. Rev.* 1467; see also A. Alesina, 'Macroeconomic Policy in a Two-party System as a Repeated Game' (1987) 102 *Quart. J. Econ.* 651, in which rational expectations are included.

Table 4

Partisan effects in American monetary policy: a summary

Study	Sample period	Model	Outcome
Weintraub (1978)	1951–77	Measure of monetary policy thrust	Policy fitted with President's objectives
Beck (1982)	1970–79	Reaction function with change in federal funds rate as independent variable	No change when Carter became President, but change in policy between Nixon and Ford
Grier and Neiman (1987)	1957–83	Money growth functions with political variable	Budget deficit affects money growth; only during Democratic administrations is there an effect of business cycle on money growth
Havrilesky (1987)	1948–84	Money supply equation	Change from Republican (Democratic) to Democratic (Republican) administration leads to an increase (decrease) in money supply growth
Alesina (1988)	1949–85	Money growth equation with political variable	Money growth is lower under Republican administrations
Alesina and Sachs (1988)	1948–84	Money growth equation with political variable	Money growth is lower under Republican administrations
Tabellini and La Via (1989)	1955–85	Reaction function with political variable included	Evidence that Democratic administrations have larger money base creation than Republican administrations
Bettow and Cebula (1994)	1973–83	Reaction function with political variables	Some evidence that there is a difference in the policy path under Democratic and Republican administrations

Havrilesky examines the Fed from a public-choice perspective.[77] This perspective regards the Federal Reserve as a group of bureaucratic agents who sustain institutional reciprocity arrangements with their political principals and with private-sector constituencies. This reciprocity goes as follows. Politicians grant a certain degree of immunity from outside pressure; in exchange, they can sometimes have their way with monetary policy, if need be. The routes by which politicians attempt to influence monetary policy vary. Havrilesky distinguishes between pressures from the executive branch and those from the legislative branch. He has developed an index, called SAFER (Signalling from the Administration to the Federal Reserve), which is based upon articles in the *Wall Street Journal* from

77. Op. cit., n.70.

January 1952 to November 1991 in which members of the administration indicate a desire for a change in monetary policy. Each article is categorised as to whether it signalled a desire for monetary ease, monetary tightness, or no change. An article expressing an interest from the side of the administration in monetary ease was counted as + 1; an article expressing a desire for monetary tightness was counted as − 1; all other articles were counted as zero. The simple sum of pluses and minuses constitutes the SAFER index. Using the SAFER index, it is shown that politically inspired pressures on monetary policy began in earnest in 1961 and have continued unabated ever since. Havrilesky also shows that this index is econometrically causal on the federal-funds rate in the period 1964–91. Changes in the SAFER index result in changes in the federal-funds rate after about three weeks.[78] Before 1961, administration signalling was rare; after 1969 it was commonplace. This suggests that the 1960s were a watershed. Signalling from the Treasury and unidentified administration sources has a statistically significant impact, while signalling from the Oval Office and the Council of Economic Advisers does not. It is also shown that monetary policy only under the chairmanships of Arthur Burns during the Nixon administration and Paul Volcker during the Carter and first Reagan administrations was responsive. Under Burns the Fed only responded to signals for monetary ease.[78a]

The explanation for these differences is found by examining Congressional pressures. Until the advent of regularly scheduled hearings on monetary policy in 1975, the record shows, according to Havrilesky, that Congressional attempts to influence Fed policy were quite sporadic. It is hypothesised that only during periods in which the Fed is under attack from Congress, the Fed will cater to the desires of the administration. This hypothesis is tested by examining bills proposed in Congress which threatened or enhanced the position of the Fed. A total of 210 such bills was found. A simple ratio of net threats to the powers of the Fed was constructed (bills which threatened powers of the Fed minus bills which enhanced them, divided by the total of all such bills). It is found that the variable which measures threat-augmented signalling (THREAT*SAFER) superseded unaugmented signalling. So in the face of Congressional threats to its powers, the Fed caters to the desires of the administration in order to garner its protection from those threats.

78. In turn, the SAFER index responds to state-of-the-economy measures as well as to the partisan composition of the Federal Reserve Board. An administration that already has friendly governors apparently doesn't find it as necessary to press publicly for changes in policy.
78a Recent evidence confirms differing Fed policy under various chairs: Allew, J. et al 'A Multinominal logic analysis of the influence of policy variables and board experience on FOMC voting behaviour' (1997) 92 *Public Choice* 27.

Havrilesky has also examined whether the number of times that politicians mention certain state-of-the-economy concerns in hearings on the conduct of monetary policy has any effect on policy actions. He concludes that the federal-funds rate is affected by signals of senators, whereas the number of times representatives mention state-of-the-economy concerns has no impact on the federal-funds rate. The apparent reason for this behaviour is that senators must confirm all Board appointments, while House members have no such power.

The state of uncertainty in early 1996 about the confirmation of the renomination of Greenspan shows very clearly how the system of confirmation hearings can be used to seek more accountability of central bankers to democratic institutions. Greenspan's term of office in fact expired in March 1996 and President Clinton renominated him, but the confirmation was delayed by calls within the Senate's Banking Committee for an extensive (three-day) debate on the monetary policy pursued by the Fed before the Banking Committee sent the renomination to the full Senate with a positive recommendation. In the present political climate three days out of the legislative timetable is something the majority leaders did not desire, yet they found it difficult to muster the 60 votes in the Senate to allow the recommendation of Greenspan to proceed to the full House without unanimity in the Banking Committee (one senator, with some support from others, was blocking the recommendation). Greenspan continued to act, although it was not until July 1996 before progress was made on his confirmation. Given that a Republican Congress was out to embarrass a Democrat administration, interests of sound monetary policy seem, with the utmost possible respect, to have become secondary to considerations of political advantage. In other words, alleged considerations of clearer democratic accountability are used to mask political opportunism.

5. INDEPENDENCE AND POLITICAL INFLUENCE: SOME EUROPEAN CONSIDERATIONS

The conflict between the independent exercise of functions and the political interests of national administrations is well demonstrated in the functioning of the European Commission. As has been noted above, the Commission's independence is guaranteed in Article 157 (2) of the EC Treaty, and the independence of the ECB, national central banks and members of their governing bodies is guaranteed in Article 7 of the Statute of the ESCB. While the fact that the Commission takes its decisions by simple majority, with collegiate responsibility, affords a certain assurance that it will act exclusively in the Community interest, it is notorious that national governments constantly seek to influence 'their Commissioner(s)' in Brussels to block proposals or to fix deals. In some instances there have been blatant threats of non-renomination used in order to try to persuade Commissioners not to act on Commission decisions or to do deals to prevent decisions perceived as adverse to the national interest being taken. More common is the use of Commissioners' *cabinets* as vehicles for exerting pressure. The *cabinets* are the Commissioners' eyes and ears, often partially consisting of 'minders' detached from national administrations to ensure that the Commissioner does not 'go native'. The ultimate sanction for those who do is non-renomination, hence the membership of the Commission is sometimes a position from which a person is in effect sacked for doing rather too well (as Lord Cockfield and Ivor Richard demonstrate, to name but two instances). An additional consideration is that, as members of the Commission are eligible for reappointment (and sometimes still have an eye to national ambitions at home), the temptation to have regard to domestic interests is inherent in the position.

It would, of course, be absurd to suggest that the Commission should operate wholly in a vacuum, irrespective of what will command a political constituency in the Member States. As long as much Community legislation is adopted by the Council, or is subject to the possibility of the Council substituting its own decision for that of the Commission, the Commission will usually be inclined to look at what is politically feasible. This will still be the case if the European Parliament replaces the Council as the main legislative forum, and it is entirely right that the Commission should have regard to the wishes of the body which approves the nomination of its members and can dismiss it.[79] However, in view of the actions of national governments hitherto, it may seriously be questioned just how much confidence may be placed in the institutional guarantee of the Commission's independence.

This raises the question whether, in the light of the experience with the Commission, the equivalent guarantee of independence is likely to work with the ESCB and the ECB. A number of factors suggest that it is more likely to succeed. First, the Executive Board's term of office is longer than that of any national administration, the Commission, the European Parliament or even the Court of Justice. Secondly, it is a single-term appointment. Thirdly, the requirement of recognised standing and professional experience in monetary or banking matters would militate in favour of technocrats, rather than (retired) politicians, being appointed, although, given that on the Continent there is no tradition of prohibition of (senior) civil servants being members of political parties, political colour may not be entirely absent. Fourthly, the independence of the Governors of the national central banks

79. EC Treaty, Arts 158 (appointment) and 144 (motion of censure).

has also been assured. However, it will be recalled that politicians may be present at the meetings of the ECB Governing Council, and the President of the Council (of the European Union) may propose motions for deliberation by the Governing Council. This is at least more transparent than the behind-the-scenes activities in the Commission, although, as the example of the Bundesbank shows, it does not exclude behind-the-scenes pressure and deals in smoke-filled rooms.

Goodhart has suggested that it may be better to speak of autonomy, rather than independence,[80] and that the real benefit of an independent (or autonomous) central bank is as an incremental step with a long-term horizon, leading to a better public understanding of policy issues, and also to somewhat improved policy measures in both the monetary and fiscal areas.[81] Certainly, it is clear that a central bank will have to command a broad public consensus for its policies, if it is to remain independent.[82] To that extent, the ECB and the ESCB are subject to constraints to which the Commission is (rightly) also subject. But, given that the institutional structure of the ECB is clearly geared to medium-to-long-term interests (as is evidenced by the length of the term of office of the Executive Board), there are perhaps some indicators that the ECB and the ESCB might be less prone to political interference than is the Commission.

6. CONCLUSIONS

By now it is well-known that central bank independence may improve upon monetary policy. In that sense, the independence of the ESCB and its mandate to strive for price stability are to be applauded, given the virtues of a low and stable rate of inflation. An important problem is how central bank independence is related to democratic accountability. Some authors argue that monetary policy should be treated like other instruments of economic policy, *eg*, like fiscal policy, and should be fully decided upon by democratically elected representatives.[83] Such an approach implies, however, too much direct involvement of politicians with monetary policy, which would more likely be determined by cheap (*ie*, short-term) interests of survival, rather than serious considerations of the welfare of the economy. Nevertheless, it is respectfully submitted that monetary policy

---

80. Op. cit., n.3, p.63.
81. Ibid., p.70.
82. Ibid.
83. R. Cooper, 'Yes to European Monetary Unification, But No to the Maastricht Treaty', in A. Steinherr (ed.), *Thirty Years of European Monetary Integration* (1994), p.71, argues, *eg*, that full accountability with respect to monetary policy of government to the general public is essential in a democratic society.

ultimately must be controlled by democratically elected politicians. As has been demonstrated in this chapter, there are various methods by which this can be assured. Both the New Zealand and the Dutch methods deserve consideration as models for improvement of the ESCB arrangements. Some way or another, the central bank has to be accountable. The New Zealand model deserves particularly serious attention. As Walsh has recently pointed out, the match between the Reserve Bank Act and a central bank contract which is optimal from an economic point of view is surprisingly good.[84]

Another important conclusion which follows from this chapter is that its statutory independence is no guarantee that there will be no attempts from politicians to influence the monetary policy of the ECB, as the example of the Federal Reserve amply demonstrates. Also in this respect, the New Zealand model probably outperforms the Bundesbank/ESCB model. If there is a clear contract between the government and the central bank, in which the objectives of the central bank are clearly specified, there is hardly any possibility for politicians to interfere.

84. C. E. Walsh, 'Is New Zealand's Reserve Bank Act of 1989 an Optimal Central Bank Contract?' (1995) 27 *Journal of Money, Credit, and Banking* 1179; see also Gormley and de Haan, op. cit., n.4, and Eijffinger and de Haan, op. cit., n.69.

Chapter Seventeen

BETWEEN DOMESTIC DEMOCRACY AND AN ALIEN RULE OF LAW? SOME THOUGHTS ON THE 'INDEPENDENCE' OF THE BANK OF ENGLAND

Terence Daintith

Chapter Outline

1. Introduction

2. Monetary Policy and Central Banking Provisions of the Maastricht Treaty

3. The View from the United Kingdom and France

4. The Problem of 'Accountability'

5. Democratic Accountability and Legal Control

6. The Balanced Constitution

7. Conclusion

European Economic and Monetary Union: The Institutional Framework (M. Andenas, L. Gormley, C. Hadjiemmanuil, I. Harden, eds.: 90-411-0687-1: © Kluwer Law International: pub. Kluwer Law International, 1997: printed in Great Britain)

1.   INTRODUCTION

The Maastricht Treaty on European Union presents, in the shape of the European System of Central Banks, a vision of central banking and of the conduct of monetary policy which is alien to traditional British ways of thinking about these subjects. The idea of an independent European central bank, established as a Treaty institution and controlled principally by a legal mandate, is not best calculated to appeal to British politicians schooled in a tradition of purely political responsibility for a monetary policy in whose conduct the central bank is the intimate, but ultimately subordinate, partner of the Treasury.

The purpose of this chapter is to work out, in the United Kingdom context, some of the issues of constitutional principle raised by central bank independence as projected in the Maastricht Treaty. This does not involve a discussion of how the monetary provisions of Maastricht might work, either in general or in relation to the UK in particular. The next section gives some information about those provisions, but simply so that the European background – and perhaps future framework – of current UK policy discussion may be properly understood. That discussion, as we shall see, responds to changes in thinking about effective monetary policy which are global in their diffusion, and raises questions of constitutional ordering which are of great importance at national level, but are peculiar neither to the UK, nor indeed to Member States of the European Union.

2.   MONETARY POLICY AND CENTRAL BANKING PROVISIONS OF THE MAASTRICHT TREATY

As is well known, the Maastricht Treaty contemplates the installation of a European monetary union, moving from interlocked to fully locked parities and a single European currency.[1] In pursuance of the recommendations of the Delors Report,[2] this movement is to be accomplished in three stages, the first involving the full liberalisation of capital movements, the improvement of economic and monetary co-ordination, and the participation of all Member States in the Exchange Rate Mechanism of the European Monetary System. That first stage began on 1 July 1990 and ended, officially, on 31 December 1993, though its objectives have not been satisfied, notably in the inability to get all Member States into EMS, or keep them in, or to achieve

---

1. EC Treaty, Arts 105–109; see also Art. 104.
2. Committee for the Study of Economic and Monetary Union, 'Report on Economic and Monetary Union in the European Community' (June 1989).

convergence within EMS, where limits on exchange parities have recently widened, not narrowed. Stage Two involves the setting up of the European Monetary Institute, which is designed to prepare the way for the final stage of fixed parities and single currency, notably by setting out how the final stage institutional structure – the ESCB – is going to work.[3] Though the EMI has been duly set up and has started operations, there must, in the light of events in Stage One, be grave doubts as to whether the conditions for the coming into operation of Stage Three, notably the attainment by Member States of the conditions for adoption of a single currency set out in Article 109j (1) of the EC Treaty, will be realised by the 'final' date for its coming into operation, if at all.[4] None the less – and also despite the fact that the UK's 'opt-out' from Stage Three[5] would, if maintained, make the ESCB provisions inapplicable in relation to it – those provisions merit careful consideration, by reason of the way in which they confront us with important constitutional questions about central banking in our own jurisdictions.

The monetary policy provisions of the Maastricht Treaty set up a European Central Bank and a European System of Central Banks, comprising the ECB and the relevant national central banks.[6] The provisions are not purely constitutive: ESCB is given a clear mandate, assorted with a number of prohibitions addressed to it and to Member States, which make it clear that ESCB is to be much more 'independent' than has been traditional for the central banks of the United Kingdom and France.

The central mandate is modelled closely on that of the German Bundesbank:

The primary objective of the ESCB shall be to maintain price stability. Without prejudice to the objective of price stability, the ESCB shall support the general economic policies in the Community with a view to contributing to the objectives of the Community as laid down in Article 2. The ESCB shall act in accordance with the principle of an open market economy with free competition, favouring an efficient allocation of resources, and in accordance with the basic principles set out in Article 3a.[7]

The Bundesbankgesetz (1957) refers to a primary role of maintaining the value of the currency (Article 3), coupled, to the extent compatible with this role, with an obligation to support the economic policy of the Federal Government (Article 12).[8] It is worth noting that while this mandate is of

---

3. EC Treaty, Art. 109f (3); and Statute of the EMI, Arts 4–7.
4. This is 1 Jan. 1999; EC Treaty, Art. 109j (4).
5. Protocol on certain provisions relating to the UK, Art. 4.
6. EC Treaty, Arts 4a, 106 (1), 109a and 109b; and Statute of the ESCB.
7. EC Treaty, Art. 105 (1).
8. For English translation, see *The Deutsche Bundesbank, Its Monetary Policy Instruments and Functions*, Deutsche Bundesbank Special Series No. 7 (2nd edn, 1987), p.105.

purely statutory, not constitutional, origin – the Grundgesetz does no more than recognise the Bundesbank (Article 88) – it has since been reinforced by the German Treaty of 18 May 1990, whose Article 10 (3) states that:

The Deutsche Bundesbank, by deploying its instruments on its own responsibility and, pursuant to section 12 of the Bundesbank Act, independent of instructions from the Governments of the Contracting Parties, shall regulate the circulation of money and credit supply in the entire currency area with the aim of safeguarding the currency.[9]

This provision cannot simply be repealed by the legislature as could the 1957 Act.[10] The ESCB, of course, will enjoy Treaty status *ab initio*, and the difficulties of revision of Community Treaties mean that, regardless of whether we think and speak in terms of a European Constitution, its mandate is certainly no less well protected than that of the Bundesbank.

Complementary protection of the independence of the ESCB in the pursuit of its mandate is afforded by Article 107, which forbids not only the ESCB as a whole, but also the ECB and national central banks, to seek or take instructions from Community institutions or bodies, from any government of a Member State or from any other body. A variety of other provisions of the Treaty and Protocol also clearly contribute to ESCB independence. Implicit in Article 107, and spelled out in the succeeding Article 108, is the need for Member States to ensure that their own central banks are independent in the sense that they may not receive instructions from the Member State government.[11] Clearly this is a key issue for national constitutional law and one to which I shall revert. It reflects, again, the German law, which states simply that the Bundesbank, in the exercise of its powers, 'is independent of instructions from the Federal Government'.[12]

A further important resemblance between the ESCB and the Bundesbank lies in their federal character. This is present in the ESCB both at the institutional level, where the ECB co-operates with and directs the activity of the national central banks within the framework of the ESCB, and within

9. Treaty of 18 May 1990 between the Federal Republic of Germany and the German Democratic Republic establishing a Monetary, Economic and Social Union, 29 ILM 1108, p.1126.
10. Some commentators have argued that other provisions of the Grundgesetz protect the independence of the Bundesbank; for these arguments, see K.-H. Ladeur, 'Die Autonomie der Bundesbank – ein Beispiel für die Institutionelle Verarbeitung von Unge-wißheitsbedingungen' (1992) 3 *Staatswissenschaft und Staatspraxis* 486. I am indebted to Ian Harden for this reference.
11. See also EC Treaty, Art. 109e (5), for the explicit obligation to make national central banks independent.
12. Art. 12. The Bundesbankgesetz, Art. 13 (2), also provides for ministers to attend meetings of the Bank's Council, to propose motions, and to require the deferment of a decision for up to two weeks; but it gives them no vote.

the ECB itself, whose Governing Council comprises a full-time Executive Board of six, as well as the governors of the central banks.[13] Again there is a strong reflection, at this latter level, of the German structure, in which the Bundesbank Council is composed of its (executive) Directorate together with the presidents of the 'central banks' of the Länder.[14] This federal structure and context has important constitutional implications, which I discuss at the end of this chapter.

3. THE VIEW FROM THE UNITED KINGDOM AND FRANCE

An ESCB could hardly be other than federal in nature, but it is not just in this way that its design departs from the pattern of government–central bank relations traditional in the UK and, indeed, in France, where the central bank has likewise been seen as subordinate to ministers. The very idea of central bank independence, or indeed of a legislatively determined central bank mandate, is unfamiliar to us in the UK. The tradition is, instead, one of strong (though not necessarily consistent) political direction of monetary policy, in which the lead has been taken by the Treasury as the relevant government department. Such policy has been pursued on a unified, national basis, with no special consideration being given to regional or local interests. The Bank of England has appeared in a multitude of roles within this structure: as executant of monetary policy (enjoying varying degrees of discretion, depending on the instruments employed) as adviser, and as intermediary between the government and financial institutions.

Monetary policy in the UK has been pursued within a framework which is high on discretion, low on transparency. There is very little legal structure. Legislative provision exists for some peripheral matters like coinage,[15] and for formal aspects of major matters like exchange-rate policy: the Bank administers the Exchange Equalisation Account, which bears the risks of exchange-rate support, as agent of the Treasury, and financial provision for the Account is made by the Exchange Equalisation Account Act.[16] Only prudential bank supervision and regulation is subject to a full legislative regime, now contained in the Banking Act 1987. The central issues of

---

13. Statute of the ESCB, Art. 10, which also lays down the voting rules.
14. Bundesbankgesetz, Art. 6. For the somewhat similar United States position, see the Federal Reserve Act of 1913, as amended in 1935, 12 USC §§241–2.
15. *Eg*, Coinage Act 1971; and Currency Act 1983.
16. Draconian exchange control legislation remains on the statute book, in the shape of the Exchange Control Act 1947. It could, under its own provisions, be reactivated at any time, but its operation is likely to be substantially restricted by the United Kingdom's existing Community obligations, and even more so by its potential ones.

monetary policy are reflected only in a single section of the Bank of England Act 1946, section 4, which provides that the Treasury may give directions to the Bank and that the Bank may, with the approval of the Treasury, give directions to bankers. No directions of either kind have ever been issued nor, it is thought, could directions to bankers be issued, in that the necessary preliminary step, *ie*, the definition for the purposes of the Act of who is a 'banker', has never been taken. However, the Treasury's power to issue directions, even if never exercised, makes it the master of the Bank in monetary policy and fully answerable for such policy to Parliament.

There are no substantive constraints on the content of such policy, no legal stipulations of the kind to which the Bundesbank is, and the ESCB will be, subject. Such discretionary monetary policy now has a bad name, in that it is argued that politicians, left to themselves, will always yield to temptations to print money in difficult times, thus fuelling the inflation which – for the time being at least – we remember as an uncomfortable and debilitating feature of economic life. The Maastricht Treaty reflects the view that such discretionary monetary policy should give way to a much more structured monetary environment, in which there is a definite legislative mandate, preferably addressed, not to politicians at all, but to the central bank, which for this purpose (and in part by this means) would attain an important degree of independence from its former political masters. That this idea has obtained an important degree of acceptance in Europe is evidenced by its appearance – in regard to national central banks – in the Maastricht Treaty itself, but it is also noteworthy that it has attracted support quite independently of the European Union framework, both in France and in the UK.

In France the idea was incorporated in the Law of 4 August 1993 on the Statute of the Banque de France, notably in its Article 1, which reflects Article 108 of the EC Treaty and provides for the Banque de France to 'define and implement monetary policy with a view to assuring the stability of prices' and to perform this mission 'within the framework of the general economic policy of the Government'.[17] In the United Kingdom the position is more nuanced. The government, as noted above, has reserved its position on the monetary union provisions of the Maastricht Treaty, and has not been prepared to bring forward, or to support, legislation which would furnish a legislative mandate for monetary policy or enhance the independence of the Bank of England. At the same time, it has taken a variety of administrative steps which have enhanced the *de facto* independence of the Bank and clarified the division of responsibilities between Bank and Treasury. Most important among these is the publication, after a six-week delay, of the

---

17. On the French reforms, see generally J.-P. Duprat, 'The Independence of the Banque de France: Constitutional and European Aspects' [1995] *Public Law* 133.

minutes of the monthly meetings between the Chancellor of the Exchequer and the Governor of the Bank.[18] It has, furthermore, received in a spirit of agnosticism, rather than outright opposition,[19] two weighty requests for reform in a direction similar to that followed in France: the first formulated in a report by a panel of bankers, industrialists, and economists under the chairmanship of Lord Roll – on which I served as a provider of public law input;[20] the second a report from the House of Commons Select Committee on the Treasury and the Civil Service,[21] a bipartisan committee of senior members of the House.[22]

Each of these reports suggests a strictly defined legislative mandate for the Bank of England, namely (in the formulation of the Treasury and Civil Service Committee) 'to achieve and maintain stability in the general level of prices'.[23] Unlike the German and French formulations, this mandate makes no reference to general economic policy, as a means through which other policy concerns might be advanced, possibly so as to qualify a commitment to price stability in all circumstances. Instead, following the model developed in New Zealand,[24] the Government would be given the power temporarily to override the Bank's legislative mandate. This it would do by substituting a new mandate, for a limited period, by an order requiring the approval of Parliament.[25] As with the French and German arrangements, the Bank would acquire autonomy in its use of monetary instruments; the Treasury's power of direction would be removed. The Treasury might, however, – the proposals differ on this important point – retain an involvement in the policy process by agreeing with the Bank upon the inflation targets to be aimed at over a given period of time.[26] Recent United Kingdom practice has been for the Government to announce such targets in

18. For these arrangements, see Treasury and Civil Service Committee, 'The Government's Response to the First Report from the Committee in Session 1993-94', HC (1993–94) 338; and HC Deb. (6th Ser.), Vol.241, col. W170, written answers, 13 April 1994.
19. See the speech of the Financial Secretary to the Treasury, H.C. Deb. (6th Ser.), Vol. 236, cols 575–82, 28 Jan. 1994.
20. Centre for Economic Policy Research, Report of an independent panel chaired by E. Roll, *Independent and Accountable: A New Mandate for the Bank of England* (Oct. 1993).
21. As it then was; responsibility for the relevant issues has now passed to a successor committee, the Treasury Committee, while responsibility for the Civil Service was transferred to a new Public Service Select Committee; Standing Order No. 130, 7 Nov. 1995.
22. Treasury and Civil Service Committee, First Report: 'The Role of the Bank of England', H.C. (1993–94) 98.
23. Ibid., para. 77. Cf. Centre for Economic Policy Research, op. cit., n.20, pp.31-2.
24. See Reserve Bank of New Zealand Act 1989, s.12.
25. Treasury and Civil Service Committee, loc. cit., n.22, para. 82; and Centre for Economic Policy Research, op. cit., n.20, pp.31-2.
26. The precedent is provided by the Reserve Bank of New Zealand Act 1989, s.9. On this point, compare Treasury and Civil Service Committee, loc. cit., n.22, paras 48-50 and 78, with Centre for Economic Policy Research, op. cit., n.20, pp.32, 51-3.

Parliament. This system provides a purely political underpinning for the targets, not a legal one. It also leaves the Bank's commitment to them unclear, though this lacuna is being filled in other ways, notably by the Bank's independent preparation and publication (since 1993) of its Inflation Report, without reference to the Treasury.

Though the Government secured, in early 1994, the speedy defeat of a bill brought forward by a member of the Treasury and Civil Service Committee to implement its central recommendations,[27] it did so in terms which do not close the door to possible change. The concern that it has persistently articulated is one about accountability: in the words of the Prime Minister, '[w]ere a way to be found to get the benefits of an independent central bank without the loss of parliamentary accountability, my views would be very close to those of [a former Chancellor of the Exchequer who now favours independence]'.[28] This is the cue to turn to a consideration of the problem of accountability.

4.   THE PROBLEM OF 'ACCOUNTABILITY'

There is a tendency for us in Britain to assume that this problem of parliamentary accountability is peculiarly ours, as the result of our merger of executive and legislative powers, with executive leaders drawn from and continuing, as it were, to live in the legislature. The issue presented, however, by calls for central bank independence does not seem to be uniquely related to our peculiar parliamentary system of government; it derives rather from the threat to a broader idea of democratic responsibility, which is common to all democratic constitutions, and whose key elements the Roll Report sought to draw out.[29] We tend to view our situation as unique for the additional reason that our constitutional expression of this principle is highly informal, and reposes on understandings and expectations about what ministers should 'answer for'. The scope of these understandings and expectations is not restricted to those areas in which Parliament has created, controlled or structured executive power through legislative enactment. Foreign policy is maybe the best example of an area where such expectations exist in the absence of any legislatively attributed responsibilities.

---

27. The Bank of England (Amendment) Bill, brought forward by Nicholas Budgen MP; for debates, see HC Deb. (6th Ser.), Vol. 236, cols 524–86, 28 Jan. 1994.

28. Quoted in Treasury and Civil Service Committee, loc. cit., n.22, para. 8.

29. See Centre for Economic Policy Research, op. cit., n.20, especially pp.47–9.

The fact that democratic responsibility is a common issue is well demonstrated by the decision of the French Constitutional Council on the first (August) passage of the 1993 Law on the Banque de France,[30] holding that law unconstitutional in that the attribution to the Ban҉   ҉e France, via its new Monetary Policy Council, of the power to *define*, as well as to *implement*, monetary policy was inconsistent with the power of the government, under Article 20 of the Constitution, to 'decide and carry out the policy of the Nation', notably because of the Banque de France's immunity from governmental instruction under Article 1 (2) of the new law. The French constitution formalises, while the British does not, the attribution of policy-formulating powers to a democratically responsible body. Only the subsequent coming into operation of Article 88-2 of the French constitution, implementing the requirements of the Maastricht Treaty, could justify this derogation.[31] It does not, however, furnish an answer to the common question of how to reconcile democratic account-ability with the depoliticisation of monetary policy which is now generally – but by no means universally[32] – thought necessary to secure international confidence (especially market confidence) in national monetary stability. This question is not only common to the UK and France; it is of crucial importance at the European constitutional level also. In the remainder of this chapter, I propose to look at this from two angles: first, that of the possible complementarity of legal and democratic control; second, that of the idea of constitutional balances of power.

5. DEMOCRATIC ACCOUNTABILITY AND LEGAL CONTROL

To suggest a possible complementarity between legal and democratic control does not imply setting them up as opposites. In the states of the European Union legal control is itself a form of democratic control, in the sense that the law is made by a popular assembly or by the executive under powers conferred either by that assembly or by a democratically adopted constitution. It is more helpful to identify a conceptual contrast between two forms of control, normative control and non-normative control, and to identify the roles of our legal institutions (courts) and democratic institutions (Parliament) in relation to the two forms. Normative control involves the evaluation of specific action by reference to predetermined rules of sufficient clarity to be a guide both to behaviour and censure. Non-

---

30. Décision no. 93-324 DC, du 3 août 1993.
31. See Duprat, loc. cit., n.17.
32. For elements of the debate, in the UK context, see Treasury and Civil Service Committee, loc. cit., n.22, paras 23–39, and references there cited.

normative control involves answerability to a body (a parliamentary assembly, the electorate itself) which may examine and censure regardless of any established norms, and also regardless of their absence. In the UK, the courts only operate through normative control, whether on the basis of legislation or of common-law rules. They do not, however, have a monopoly over such control. Parliament, on the other hand, has a multiple role. It participates *ex ante* in the process of normative control, by furnishing its basis, whenever it approves legislation containing effective guides to conduct. It also, however, operates both normative and non-normative processes of control through the instruments of parliamentary accountability. In consequence, most activity by ministers and government departments in the UK is subject, in Parliament, to both types of control; that is, parliamentary accountability may make reference both to the legality of governmental conduct and to its appropriateness regardless of legality.[33]

At the moment, monetary policy departs from this normal, double pattern of parliamentary control of ministers in much the same way as foreign policy: the normative basis of control is almost non-existent. If the path of 'independence' were taken, the Bank of England would escape its subordination to Treasury direction, in return for accepting a binding legislative mandate. Parliament would, as noted above, participate *ex ante* in the new control process by defining that mandate and (under the reform proposals which have been made) approving temporary variations of that mandate. It would, however, find it more difficult to operate the *ex post* instruments of accountability, for reasons which apply whenever powers are vested in non-ministerial bodies. Those bodies are not present in Parliament as are ministers; and while they can be required to report to Parliament, or summoned to explain themselves before parliamentary Select Committees, such as the Treasury Committee, the chain of relations through which such accountability might actually be enforced passes through ministers. If therefore ministers have no control over such bodies – and this is what we postulate in relation to 'independent' central banks – the foundations of their parliamentary accountability are, to say the least, constitutionally problematic.[34]

---

33. See the parliamentary inquiries into government aid for the Pergau Dam project in Malaysia, which considered (if only to dismiss) questions of legality before moving on to questions of appropriateness and value for money; Public Accounts Committee, Seventeenth Report: 'The Pergau Hydro-Electric Project', HC (1993–94) 155, para. 30, and Minutes of Evidence, q.2; Foreign Affairs Committee, Third Report: 'Public Expenditure: The Pergau Hydro-Electric Project, Malaysia, The Aid and Trade Provision and Related Matters', HC (1993–94) 271, paras 13–17, and Minutes of Evidence, pp.5, 9–16 and 36–41. Subsequently, the High Court found the aid granted for the dam to be unlawful, because it was not covered by the terms of the Overseas Development and Co-operation Act 1980, s.1 (1); *Financial Times*, 11 Nov. 1994, p.1.
34. Cf. Centre for Economic Policy Research, op. cit., n.20, pp.53–6.

In a wide range of other cases, however, we do not worry about the fact that the constitutional foundations of *ex post* accountability to Parliament are not wholly secure. This is essentially because the functions of the relevant non-ministerial body have been legislatively defined by Parliament with sufficient clarity for its performance to be monitored by reference to legal standards and to be subject to effective judicial control. Thus the functions of regulation and supervision of the banking system are now discharged by the Bank of England under the statutory regime of the Banking Act 1987, which eliminates Treasury powers to direct the Bank in the performance of these functions.[35] The Bank is formally accountable to Parliament through the making of an annual report to the Chancellor of the Exchequer, who lays it before Parliament;[36] but the key control of the Bank's decisions is secured by the legal framework and through a procedure of appeal to a specialised tribunal instituted by the Act, and thence to the courts.[37] Despite the failures of the system as documented in the report of the inquiry into the collapse of the Bank of Credit and Commerce International,[38] there has been no suggestion that parliamentary control should play a larger part. In practice, it is clear that in this case the absence of Treasury responsibility has not inhibited thorough *ex post* parliamentary discussion, particularly through the Treasury and Civil Service Committee – and, more recently, its successor, the Treasury Committee.[39]

The worry about the 'democratic deficit' of the European Union can itself be expressed in terms of the proper balance of legal and democratic controls – or, rather, of the absence of such a balance.[40] In the early years of the European Economic Community, there was little concern about this problem, notwithstanding the fact that the European Parliament – not even called the Parliament at that time – had minimal powers and was not directly elected. The reason was that the Community had an agenda set out with a fair degree of clarity in a legally binding Treaty. There was a single objective – economic integration – and an assumption that its attainment could in large measure be legally structured by straightforward legal prohibitions

---

35. The Treasury retains certain powers to make regulations supplementing the statutory regime; see ss. 7, 30, 32, 34 and 80. Exceptionally, a specific power of the Treasury to direct the Bank is preserved, in cases involving reciprocal treatment by overseas jurisdictions, by s.23.
36. S. 1 (3).
37. Ss. 27–31.
38. See 'Inquiry into the Supervision of the Bank of Credit and Commerce International', HC (1991–92) 198 (the Bingham Report).
39. See Treasury and Civil Service Committee, Second Report: 'Banking Supervision and BCCI: The Implications of the Bingham Report', HC (1992–93) 250, paras 83–103.
40. An alternative, but not inconsistent, version of this story may be found in Weiler, 'The Transformation of Europe' (1991) 100 *Yale L.J.* 2403.

addressed mostly to Member States,[41] linked to limited collective legislative competences designed to create the essential conditions of harmonisation of policy for the prohibitions on restraints of trade to operate. The exercise of power under that system could effectively be policed by judicial means. As obvious barriers to trade and discriminatory measures have steadily been removed, however, subtler barriers and distortions have revealed themselves; and these, unlike tariffs and the grosser non-tariff barriers, appear as integral to the operation of distinctive national policies of economic regulation in pursuit of a variety of public interests. In consequence, continuing to pursue a policy of economic integration implies developing, at the European level, policies – for health and safety at work, for consumer protection, for environmental protection, for employment relations – in substitution for those which, if pursued nationally, are doomed to produce distortions of trade. It is at this point, where European policy acquires a multitude of objectives to be held in some kind of balance, and hence totally ceases to be 'programmable' through the legal structures adopted in the original ECSC and EEC Treaties, that the sense of a 'democratic deficit' becomes palpable, and the legitimacy of reliance on judicial policing becomes suspect.[42]

How does monetary policy fit into this set of ideas? Assuming (and I am well aware that this is not an uncontroversial assumption) that it is *desirable*, for the promotion of market confidence in the soundness of the national currency, to define the purposes of monetary policy in a more rigid and binding way, is it actually possible to conceive of a legislative mandate for monetary policy sufficiently narrow to justify the consequent shift away from non-normative democratic control and towards a normative control, which might rely more heavily on judicial enforcement? In particular, is a legal obligation on the central bank[43] to maintain price stability precise enough for this purpose? In the following paragraphs I offer some preliminary thoughts on this issue, which, while phrased in terms of our domestic situation, are relevant also to the way the issue presents itself on the European level.

41. Exceptionally to individuals, as in EC Treaty, Arts 85–6.
42. For its continued importance, see Snyder, 'The Effectiveness of European Community Law: Institutions, Processes, Tools and Techniques' (1993) 56 *MLR* 19.
43. It may be worth remarking *en passant* that the imposition of this obligation on ministers, rather than on the Bank of England, would wholly eliminate the problems of effective parliamentary *ex post* control to which I referred above. None of the participants in the reform debates, however, seems to think that subjecting governments, as opposed to central banks, to this legal obligation would effect the slightest improvement in market confidence. This shows very clearly what the legal obligation is really for: not to force the central bank, as obligee, to change its behaviour, but to reinforce its capacity to pursue, in the face of pressure to do otherwise, the behaviour it would have adopted anyway.

A first observation is that even precise legislative mandates may not be appropriate for *judicial* policing; and, if courts have no effective jurisdiction, Parliament may be the only available forum for *ex post facto* censure of conduct by reference to such mandates. This was clearly the assumption of the two UK inquiries into Bank of England independence, which saw the Treasury and Civil Service Committee as the necessary guarantor of the Bank's respect for its proposed statutory obligations.[44] The Maastricht Treaty likewise makes specific provision as to the accountability of the ESCB, through the ECB, to the European Parliament and its Committees,[45] though without any attempt at exclusion of the ordinary system of enforcement, involving the European Court of Justice, under Articles 169 and 170 of the EC Treaty.[46]

Secondly, if we ask why judicial control has not entered into United Kingdom thinking on this issue, at least a part of the answer must be found in the fact that the current exercise of monetary policy instruments does not involve any action capable of impairing individual legal rights, so that litigants may find it difficult – I put it no more strongly than that – to establish that they have a sufficient interest to seek judicial review.[47] Current policy relies on the control of interest rates through signalling processes backed up by open-market operations, and has abandoned 'regulatory' devices, like control, for monetary purposes, of cash or liquidity ratios, or imposition of credit ceilings. Contract, not unilateral regulation, is the legal vehicle of monetary policy,[48] and transmits its effects over an extraordinarily wide sphere through the operation of voluntary legal arrangements, such as banker–customer agreements. The individual interests which will be affected by the given use of a monetary policy instrument could scarcely be more diffuse or unpredictable. Diffuseness of the interests

---

44. Treasury and Civil Service Committee, 'The Role of the Bank of England', loc. cit., n.22, para. 79; and Centre for Economic Policy Research, op. cit., n.20, pp.59–61.
45. EC Treaty, Art. 109b (3).
46. Such enforcement is, in contrast, excluded in relation to the obligations of Member States to avoid excessive government deficits; see ibid., Art. 104c (10).
47. An attempt in 1991 to sue the Treasury for damages for the negligent conduct of economic policy apparently survived an attempt to strike the action out, but thereafter vanished from sight; see 'Treasury Sued by Troubled Builder', *Financial Times*, 1 Oct. 1991, p.11. In general, it is difficult to reconcile recent judicial decisions in this area; for general guidance, see *R v Inland Revenue Commissioners, ex p National Federation of Self-Employed and Small Businesses Ltd* [1982] AC 617; but then contrast *R v Commissioners of HM Treasury, ex p Smedley* [1985] QB. 857, or the *Pergau Dam* decision, *supra*, n.33, with *R. v Secretary of State for the Environment, ex p Rose Theatre Trust Co.* [1990] 1 QB 504.
48. It might be noted that even when 'regulatory' monetary controls *were* operative in the UK, they rested on a non-statutory basis, ultimately attributable to convention and to the Bank of England's economic power; see T. Daintith, 'The Functions of Law in the Field of Short-Term Economic Policy' (1976) 92 *LQR* 62, pp.72–8.

to be affected by a decision (as opposed to a bilateral dispute required to be decided one way or another) is, of course, one of the criteria most relevant to the cognate issue of what are appropriate decision-*making*, as opposed to decision-*policing*, methods, and has been held to argue against the use of judicial, and in favour of administrative, mechanisms.[49]

A third point: a further inhibition on judicial control stems from the nature of the legislative mandate itself. No matter how narrowly it is drawn, it remains an obligation of *result*, not of *means*. The crucial arguments in monetary policy today are not about the general direction to be taken: this is broadly agreed to be price stability. The arguments are about how fast to go, and when and for how long progress should be interrupted or even reversed out of concern for other economic policy goals – and about the relation of that progress to closely linked issues such as exchange-rate policy. Even the Roll Committee, which was prepared to be more rigorous in these respects than the French, German, American or Community legislature, excluding all considerations other than progress toward price stability from the decision-set of the Bank of England, was still bound to admit that the Bank would require some discretion both as to the rate of progress and as to the choice, timing and intensity of the monetary instruments deployed to achieve it.[50] It is hard to imagine how that discretion could be the subject of meaningful judicial review, even if the courts would recognise any individuals or organisations as having the interest to ask for it. Despite the robustness of the European Court of Justice's approach to its task, the same doubts would apply to the reviewability of ESCB decisions: *a fortiori*, in view of ESCB's broader policy concerns.

Fourthly, it may perhaps be possible to conceive of an approach to 'non-coercive' monetary instruments, such as those wielded in the UK, which is so mechanistic and non-discretionary as not to amount to a monetary policy, or to the exercise of governmental power, at all. Decisions about the coin and note issues were once the crucial expression of monetary policy. Now, the massive importance of money in other forms means that such decisions are mere reflections of movements on the larger monetary stage: if the system is to work smoothly, it is important that this legal tender be available in the right quantities and at the right places, even though monetary policy is not being made at the Royal Mint. Until governments decide that they wish to use their contemporary monetary policy instruments in this purely reactive way, the considerations I have mentioned, of diffuseness and lack of justiciability of monetary policy, at the very least cast doubt on the idea of reliance on legal control as a means for averting the problems of democratic

---

49. See L. Fuller, 'Adjudication and the Rule of Law' (1960) 54 *Proc. Am. Soc. Int'l Law* 1; idem, 'Collective Bargaining and Arbitration' (1963) *Wisconsin L.Rev.* 3, pp.30–34.
50. Centre for Economic Policy Research, op. cit., n.20, pp.31–41, 52.

responsibility which are implicit in endowing central banks with greater autonomy.

6.   THE BALANCED CONSTITUTION

This leaves us with the task of suggesting how it is that the United States and Germany, not undemocratic countries, have managed this trick. In concluding this short chapter, I can do no more, for the present, than to invoke the concept of constitutional 'balance' – as an alternative, or complement, to the democratic principle. The manifestation of balance which is most important in the structure of both the United States Federal Reserve and of the German Bundesbank is found in the importation of the federal principle, as a reflection of its presence in the constitution itself. The governing body of the Bundesbank is, as already remarked,[51] dominated by representatives of regional interests, which are likewise strongly (if not dominantly) represented in the Open Market Committee of the Federal Reserve by five governors of regional Reserve Banks. Federalism cuts both ways in democratic terms: seen from the standpoint of the nation as a whole, the entrenched and protected positions of the component units function as a major constraint on the operation of the democratic principle; seen from the standpoint of the component unit, the presence of those units as such in the national decision-making structure projects local democratic decisions onto the broader national stage. This federalist logic is clearly available within the European Community to underpin, as with the Bundesbank in Germany, the operation of an independent ESCB; but is there any alternative form of 'balance' which could function, within unitary constitutions such as ours, to buttress the legitimacy of politician-proof central banks?

There is an irony worth savouring here in the contrast between the unitary constitutions which rule on either side of the Channel. Those most centralising French found ready to hand, when considering how to constitute the new Monetary Policy Council of the Banque de France, a device which reflects subsisting balances of power within the constitution of the Fifth Republic: between presidential and parliamentary elements in government; between territorial representation in Parliament and represen-tation by *métier* in the Economic and Social Council; and between the components of Parliament itself, whose chambers are elected on different systems and for different periods. Thus the non-executive members of the Monetary Policy Council could be found by way of nomination, by

51. See *supra*, text to n.14.

consensus or in equal parts, by the presidents of the Senate, the National Assembly and the Economic and Social Council, and appointment, by decree in the Council of Ministers, from the resulting list.[52] We in Britain, by contrast, who developed the relations between King, Lords and Commons, with their differing interests, into a theory of a 'balanced constitution' long before France was experiencing its first Republic, let alone its fifth,[53] now find ourselves unable to imagine means by which any notion of balance could operate in decisions such as those for the appointment of the Court of Directors of the Bank of England.[54] The colonisation of large areas of the constitution by party politics makes it very difficult for us to utilise the formal structure of our constitution, notably the institutional distinctness of executive, Lords and Commons, for useful ends such as this. Why, however, should it be unthinkable to provide for the appointment of some members of the Court of the Bank by the Crown on the advice of the Speaker of the Commons and of the Lord Chancellor as Speaker of the Lords, while others, including the Governor and Deputy Governor, would continue to be appointed on the advice of the Prime Minister and the Chancellor, as at present? Such a procedure would seem to have stronger constitutional roots than would the employment of a regional basis for appointments to a UK equivalent of the French Monetary Policy Council, as proposed by the Liberal Democrats in their *Alternative Budget '94.*[55] Proposals of the latter type do not get round the obstacle of who (other than ministers) could effectively appoint the members. A parliamentary role in appointments would, moreover, short-circuit the difficulties already referred to of how to achieve an appropriate degree of parliamentary accountability for the Bank in respect of activities which ministers should not control.

7. CONCLUSION

There is no doubt that the desire to achieve a more stable monetary environment through the removal of political powers over central banks raises serious constitutional difficulties, in the UK as elsewhere. Nor do the

52. See Law 93-980 of 4 Aug. 1993, as amended by Law 93-1444 of 31 December 1993, Arts 8 (2) and (4); and Duprat, loc. cit., n.17. Cf. the system of appointment of members of the Constitutional Council, under Art. 58 of the Constitution (one third each by the President of the Republic, the President of the Senate and the President of the National Assembly); for commentary on the results of that system, see Bell, *French Constitutional Law* (1992), pp.34–41.
53. See generally Vile, *Constitutionalism and the Separation of Powers* (1967).
54. See Treasury and Civil Service Committee, 'The Role of the Bank of England', loc. cit., n.22, paras 69, 81; Centre for Economic Policy Research, op. cit., n.20, p.63.
55. (1994), p.7.

difficulties disappear when the problems are transposed to the European level: the issue of the constitutional legitimacy of the use of monetary instruments remains, whether or not the Bank of England (and the Banque de France) are operating within the framework of the ESCB. If this short and exploratory chapter has any single message, it is that the solution to these issues will not readily be found simply by readjusting the boundaries of the operations of courts and Parliament *vis-à-vis* ministers and Bank, or of the principles of control they employ. To the discussion of review and accountability there needs to be added, whether by way of a new exploration of the concept of constitutional 'balance' or otherwise, a consideration of the nature and articulation of the very power whose legitimate exercise is in issue.

Chapter Eighteen

BANKING SUPERVISION, THE INTERNAL MARKET AND EUROPEAN MONETARY UNION

Mads Andenas
and
Christos Hadjiemmanuil

Chapter Outline

1. Introduction

2. The Background

3. Banking and the Single Market
    3.1 Towards home-country control
    3.2 Why were banking services so difficult?
    3.3 Home-country control and minimum standards

4. Monetary Union and Centralisation of Banking Supervision

5. Banking Supervision and the Maastricht Treaty
    5.1 Advisory functions
    5.2 Supervisory tasks
    5.3 Substantive scope of the prudential functions

6. Constitutional Concerns
    6.1 Subsidiarity
    6.2 Central bank independence

7. Conclusion

European Economic and Monetary Union: The Institutional Framework (M. Andenas, L. Gormley, C. Hadjiemmanuil, I. Harden, eds.: 90-411-0687-1: © Kluwer Law International: pub. Kluwer Law International, 1997: printed in Great Britain)

1.   INTRODUCTION

Banking supervision in the Internal Market has been left to the Member States. Is this likely to continue after the establishment of the European Central Bank? That is the main question of this chapter. It is not clear whether home-state supervision will be sufficient in the future, or what the institutional factors are that will determine the development of banking supervision.

In the course of the discussion the relationship between banking services, the prudential supervision of banking, the internal market and monetary union will be examined. The internal market in banking depended on capital liberalisation, which in turn depended on the Member States abandoning certain economic policies. European monetary union with the creation of a single currency may be regarded as the ultimate internal-market measure in banking services. The advent of monetary union makes even more pressing the need for consistent and practical solutions to the institutional and policy aspects of the organisation of banking supervision in the Internal Market.

The role of the new European Central Bank will inevitably extend to important functions with implications for banking supervision, in spite of conscious efforts of the Member States to ensure that the Maastricht Treaty does not open the door for the centralisation of supervisory functions at the European level. The discussion focuses on the legal grounds for, and limitations on, possible extensions of ECB jurisdiction in matters of banking supervision.

2.   THE BACKGROUND

The signing of the Maastricht Treaty on 7 February 1992 opened a new chapter in the integration of the economies of the Member States of the European Community.[1] The provisions of the Maastricht Treaty made extensive amendments to the Treaty of Rome for the purpose of ensuring a

---

1. On the drafting efforts, negotiations and compromises leading to the final Treaty provisions on monetary union, see R. Corbett, *The Treaty of Maastricht, from Conception to Ratification: A Comprehensive Reference Guide* (1993), which reproduces the most important primary documents; L. Bini-Smaghi, T. Padoa-Schioppa and F. Papadia, *The Transition to EMU in the Maastricht Treaty*, Essays in International Finance No. 194, International Finance Section, Princeton University (Nov. 1994); A. Italianer, 'Mastering Maastricht: EMU Issues and How They Were Settled', in K. Gretschmann (ed.), *Economic and Monetary Union: Implications for National Policy-Makers* (1993); and M. Andenas 'Economic and Monetary Union: Stage Two' (1993) 14 Co. Law. 233.

gradual (phased in three stages) but irreversible movement of the Member States towards full Economic and Monetary Union, broadly in accordance with the Delors Report of June 1989.[2]

The main aim of the new arrangements is a new common currency to be adopted by a first core group of Member States by 1 January 1999 at the latest. The rest of the Member States are to follow as soon as they too have achieved a sufficient degree of economic convergence, allowing them to participate in the fully-fledged monetary union without placing it under undue strains. The preparedness of Member States for participation is to be judged by reference to a number of criteria indicated in the Maastricht Treaty. However, two Member States, the United Kingdom and Denmark, have retained the right of 'opting out' of the third, and final, stage of monetary unification.

There are several important institutional features. The first stage of the process of monetary unification began prior to the Maastricht Treaty, on 1 July 1989, and comprised increased co-ordination of the monetary and economic policies of Member States. The second, and current, stage began on 1 January 1994. Its most important feature is the establishment in Frankfurt of a transitional monetary institution. The European Monetary Institute[3] is the predecessor to a permanent institution, the European Central Bank. The latter will come into existence and take over the tasks of the EMI soon before the beginning of the third, and final, stage.[4] The ECB and the national central banks of the Member States will compose the European System of Central Banks.[5] The ESCB will have full responsibility for defining and implementing the monetary policy of the single currency area, conducting its foreign-exchange operations, holding and managing the official foreign reserves of the Member States and promoting the smooth operation of the payment system.[6]

The third stage of the process of monetary unification involves the actual replacement of the existing national currencies by the single currency. It is set to commence on 1 January 1999 at the latest, even if only a minority of Member States fulfill the conditions for participation.[7] The Council will provide for, by unanimous agreement of the Member States participating in

---

2. Committee for the Study of Economic and Monetary Union, 'Report on Economic and Monetary Union in the European Community' (June 1989), presented to the Madrid European Council meeting of 26–27 June 1989; the Chairman of the European Commission, Mr Jacques Delors, was chairman of the Committee, whose other members were the Governors of the central banks of the Member States.
3. EC Treaty, Art. 109f; and Protocol on the Statute of the European Monetary Institute.
4. EC Treaty, Arts 4a and 109l (1)–(2); and Protocol on the Statute of the European System of Central Banks and the European Central Bank, Art. 1.1.
5. EC Treaty, Art. 106 (1); and Statute of the ESCB, Art. 1.2.
6. EC Treaty, Art. 105 (2); and Statute of the ESCB, Art. 3.1.
7. EC Treaty, Art. 109j (4).

the third stage, the modalities and definitive implementation date for the transition to the single currency.[8]

The detailed provisions of the Maastricht Treaty concern almost exclusively the issues relating to the monetary responsibilities of the new central banking system, which is regarded to be required to pursue the objective of achieving price stability within the monetary union.[9] On the other hand important questions remain unresolved in relation to the non-monetary functions of the new central banking system. In particular, the Maastricht Treaty provides only limited guidance to the problem of institutional organisation of banking policy (including such matters as prudential supervision, the lender-of-last-resort function and the operation of the payment system) in the monetary union. This, however, is an area where the introduction of a new central bank, even if it were to have only limited monetary authority, at Community level will necessarily have major repercussions.

3. BANKING AND THE SINGLE MARKET

3.1 Towards home-country control

The right of establishment and the right to provide services under conditions of competitive equality are fundamental principles of EC law.[10] In the area of banking, the initial Community strategy sought to introduce a compulsory common legislative framework for all European banks. However the attempts undertaken in this direction in the early 1970s failed. The Member States were unable to reach agreement on the content of the relevant legislation. As a result, a new approach was adopted which, without abandoning the aim of substantial uniformity,[11] attempted to implement it gradually. The legal form of directives was chosen for this purpose, because directives (unlike regulations, which are legislative acts of general application whose provisions are binding in their entirety and directly applicable in all Member States) are binding only as to the result to be achieved, but leave to each Member State the choice of the form and methods for their implementation in its territory,[12] thus preserving a degree of national

---

8. Ibid., Art. 109l (4).
9. EC Treaty, Art. 105 (1); and Statute of the ESCB, Art. 2. The commitment to price stability is also binding on the Community as a whole; EC Treaty, Art. 3a (2)–(3).
10. EC Treaty, Arts 52–8 (on the right of establishment) and Arts 59–66 (on the freedom to provide services).
11. See First Council Directive 77/780/EEC of 12.12.77 on the co-ordination of laws, regulations and administrative provisions relating to the taking up and pursuit of the business of credit institutions (the 'First Banking Directive'), Preamble, eighth recital.
12. EC Treaty, Art. 189.

discretion, at least in the details. For some time, however, even this approach yielded only modest results.

A First Banking Directive was adopted in 1977 as a first measure of harmonisation. The hope was that, following further measures harmonising prudential requirements, banks with their head office in a Member State wishing to operate in another Member State through a branch would eventually be exempted from the latter's regulatory requirements.[13] In this manner, home-country supervisory control was recognised in principle as an objective of Community banking law. The Directive imposed authorisation requirements on 'credit institutions'. That is, undertakings whose business is to receive deposits or other repayable funds from the public and to grant credits for their own account.[14] It set out minimum conditions for authorisation, including the adequate and separate capitalisation of the applicant institution, the effective direction of its business by at least two persons of good repute and appropriate experience and the submission to the authorities of a programme of operations.[15] This limited harmonisation of prudential standards did not provide a sufficient basis for the operation of the principle of home-country control. The authorisation and regulation of local branches remained at the hands of the host Member State, pending further co-ordination.[16]

For a number of years, however, little additional progress was made.[17] The national approaches to a host of basic prudential issues, including solvency requirements, continued to diverge widely.

3.2 Why were banking services so difficult?

In the Commission's 1985 White Paper 'Completing the Internal Market',[18] which set out the legislative programme for the creation of a single market by the end of 1992, financial services stood out as an area where little had been achieved and where the Commission proposed many ambitious measures. One reason for the slow progress of the internal market in financial services was that it depended on capital liberalisation, that is, on the abolition of restrictions and administrative controls on cross-border

---

13. First Banking Directive, Preamble, tenth recital.
14. Ibid., Art.3 (1). The concept of 'credit institution' is defined in Art.1.
15. Ibid., Art. 3 (2) and (4).
16. Ibid., Art.4 (1).
17. However, in response to the failure of Banco Ambrosiano, the principle of consolidated supervision of banking groups was adopted by the Community; Council Directive 83/350/EEC of 13.6.83 on the supervision of credit institutions on a consolidated basis, eventually repealed by Art. 10 (1) of Directive 92/30/EEC, which introduced a reformed framework of consolidated supervision.
18. COM (85) 310.

financial transactions. Capital liberalisation would, in turn, inevitably lead to deregulation of financial markets, and the abolition or easing of rules limiting the participation in domestic financial markets of foreign institutions.

Capital restrictions were a necessary precondition for the effectiveness of the direct instruments of monetary and credit policy. The latter would impose limitations on the growth of clearing banks' assets (in some cases also their liabilities). They also usually extended to other financial institutions' assets and to markets such as those in corporate bonds. With the help of such instruments, monetary objectives could be achieved at a lower interest rate than would otherwise be possible. Capital restrictions made it possible to pursue relatively autonomous monetary and credit policies. Such policies depended on the possibility of maintaining a real interest rate different from that of neighbouring countries. Capital restrictions were instruments to limit capital inflows and outflows, the importance of which would depend on the trends in other financial markets. Restrictions on capital outflows, for instance, so that savers and investors could not go abroad, would allow, in the short term, the preservation of low interest rates and impede downward pressures on the currency exchange rate. In the long term, they would protect domestic savings and domestic capital markets. Particularly strict restrictions on pension funds and life-assurance companies in terms of their ability to diversify their investments by investing abroad would have both such short-term and long-term effects. Restrictions on capital inflows, for instance so that lenders could not go to banks or securities markets abroad to raise capital, would preserve, in the short term, price stability and avoid upward pressure on the exchange rate. In the long term, control of foreign investors would protect domestic control of key industries, and this was in several countries considered an important matter of national sovereignty. In particular, the national interest in maintaining control of financial institutions such as banks, pensions funds and insurance companies would be considered to be especially strong.

Capital controls have been applied by all countries, albeit in different ways and to different degrees. There is a tidal quality to capital controls, which rise and subside with some regularity. They have never been at a lower ebb than today in modern history. Economic policy in the 1980s became increasingly based on a doctrine of greater market orientation. The direct instruments of monetary policy were gradually replaced by indirect instruments, seeking to influence credit expansion through price mechanisms. This is what is usually described as the liberalisation in domestic economic policy and in domestic financial markets.

The final conversion to liberalisation came after the experiences of the late 1970s and the early 1980s, when sceptics had to accept that the existing controls were characterised by a low degree of effectiveness and high costs. There were costs of an administrative nature, but more importantly a macroeconomic cost in that distortions in asset prices and interest rates could lead to a suboptimal allocation of capital resources. There were also problems involved in shielding financial markets from external influences: temporary advantages could be outweighed by the cost of postponing the economic-policy and private-sector adaptation to changes in international economic circumstances.

The direct instruments of monetary and credit policy had created a close relationship between financial institutions, in particular the large clearing banks, and monetary authorities, ministries of finance and central banks. Banking supervision became subordinated to this relationship, and played a limited role. Prudential rules, for instance capital adequacy requirements, were turned into instruments of monetary policy, with a view to influencing interest rates. Competition polices were not developed, or at least not enforced with any rigour. All the parties to those close relationships had a strong interest in retaining them. None the less, the gradual deregulation in domestic credit and monetary policy, with the abolition of direct controls, spurred a strengthening of prudential requirements and supervision and of competition policies.

Some degree of internationalisation of financial markets and institutions took place despite the restrictions of direct monetary and credit policies. This clearly undermined the effectiveness of such policies. But there was no immediate link between, on the one hand, domestic deregulation and, on the other hand, the opening-up of domestic markets for financial institutions from other Member States or the development of an internal financial market in other ways. The financial services industry continued to enjoy a close relationship to the authorities. In some countries, the state would own the major clearing banks. For most Member States, retaining domestic control over the financial services industry was considered to be of vital importance; financial institutions and markets should remain in the hands of their own nationals. The prospect of clearing banks, pension-fund managers or life-assurance companies being bought up by nationals of other countries appeared distant. Any other direct access to markets for foreign institutions would be seriously curtailed.

Gradually, however, deregulation in domestic credit and monetary policy did lead to the implementation of free movement of capital from 1990 based on the Capital Liberalisation Directive,[19] which was adopted in 1988. This was the first time that all Member States agreed that the escape clause in Article 67 of the Treaty of Rome (abolishing capital-movement restrictions 'necessary to ensure the proper functioning of the common market') implied a full liberalisation.

---

19. Council Directive 88/361/EEC.

An internal financial market was now possible, and even necessary for ensuring that financial business would not drift to that Member State offering the least intensive regulatory environment and the best financial and tax incentives. The economic policies of Member States did not any longer depend on domestic markets. Most of the other obstacles just mentioned were still in place. The attempt to resolve them and to guarantee unrestricted market access was made in a series of financial-market directives, the most important of which has been the Second Banking Directive of 1989.[20]

Before the 1992 deadline of the Commission's 1985 White Paper, the major directives in this area were either adopted or going through the late stages of the legislative process, with a common position having been reached, guaranteeing their adoption. The 1992 deadline was extremely tight in an area where so little had been achieved, placing considerable pressure on both the Member States and on the Commission. This was bound to have some impact of the form of the solutions that were found, and certain issues could not be explicitly resolved in the directives.

3.3 Home-country control and minimum standards

A new emphasis on market integration followed the decision on the completion of the internal market by the end of 1992. The amendment of the Treaty of Rome by the Single European Act provided the basis for the adoption of banking directives in the Council by qualified majority voting, rather than unanimity.[21] Together this created the conditions for further harmonisation in the area of banking law as it did elsewhere. Regulatory approximation was considered to be a means of ensuring that the banks of all Member States would compete on equal terms in the single market. These terms should not be dictated by the most liberal national regime, but instead reflect the concerns of the major jurisdictions. The Community was closely involved in the efforts for the international convergence of prudential standards in the Committee on Banking Regulations and Supervisory Practices, better known as the 'Basle Committee',[22] in which seven Member

20. Second Council Directive 89/646/EEC of 15.12.89 on the co-ordination of laws, regulations and administrative provisions relating to the taking up and pursuit of the business of credit institutions and amending Directive 77/780/EEC (the 'Second Banking Directive').
21. EEC Treaty, Art. 100a, as inserted by Art. 18 of the SEA.
22. The Committee, whose full name has since been changed to the Basle Committee on Banking Supervision, is made up of representatives of the central banks and banking supervisory authorities of Belgium, Canada, France, Germany, Italy, Japan, Luxembourg, the Netherlands, Sweden, Switzerland, the UK and the US. For an introduction to the Committee's work, see A. Cornford, *The Role of the Basle Committee on Banking Supervision in the Regulation of International Banking* (Sept. 1993); J. J. Norton,

States were represented.[23] Its Capital Accord promulgated in 1988 provided the Community with commonly accepted understandings and a framework of regulatory standards on which to build.

None the less, comprehensive harmonisation appeared still to be politically unattainable. Thus, the objective of full harmonisation was abandoned in favour of the mutual recognition of the authorisation procedures and regulatory standards of the Member States. Harmonisation only covered those basic elements of prudential regulation to which convergence was accepted to be essential.[24]

The new strategy permitted the adoption in December 1989 of the Second Banking Directive. This is the main measure of Community law giving effect to the European Commission's designs for the completion of a single market in the field of banking. The Second Banking Directive established firmly the shift from host-country control of branches to the

---

(continued)

> *Devising International Bank Supervisory Standards* (1995), ch.4; and C. Hadjiemma-
> nuil, *Banking Regulation and the Bank of England* (1996), pp.55-70. On the Basle
> Committee's links with the EC, see Norton, ibid., pp.163-7.

23. As a consequence of the accession of Sweden to the EU, the Community is currently represented in the Basle Committee by eight Member States.

24. The mutual recognition of regulatory standards in matters of lesser importance or of a contentious nature was a key component of the Commission's strategy for the construction of a single market in financial services. Despite the introduction of qualified-majority voting in the Council, the traditional approach of comprehensive harmonisation had very few prospects of producing results, especially within the tight time-limits imposed by the 31 Dec. 1992 deadline. To solve this problem, the Commission abandoned the idea of uniformity in favour of the mutual recognition of national standards in non-essential matters. The concept of mutual recognition was originally developed in the jurisprudence of the European Court of Justice on the free movement of goods, most notably in Case 120/78, *Rewe-Zentral AG v Bundesmono-polverwaltung für Branntwein ('Cassis de Dijon')* [1979] ECR 649. The adaptation of this concept to the context of services provided the solution, because it simplified dramatically the negotiations and made politically feasible the harmonisation of those minimum standards, without which most Member States, fearful of the competitive advantages that would accrue to the least regulated banks in a single market but unwilling to undertake drastic deregulation of their domestic banking systems, would resist the liberalisation of banking services and the opening up of the national banking markets to direct and unrestricted competition. On the Commission's policy for the accomplishment of a single banking market, see White Paper 'Completing the Internal Market', loc. cit., n.18, paras 100–107; E. Lomnicka 'The Internal Financial Market in Investment Services' in M. Andenas and S. Kenyon-Slade *EC Financial Market Regulation and Company Law* (1993) p. 81; E. Lomnicka 'The Single European Passport in Financial Services' in B. Rider and M. Andenas *Developments in European Company Law* (1997) p. 175; G. S. Zavvos, 'Towards a European Banking Act' (1988) 25 *C.M.L. Rev.* 263; idem, 'The Integration of Banking Markets in the EEC: The Second Banking Coordination Directive' (1988) 3 *JIBL* 53; idem, 'Banking Integration and 1992: Legal Issues and Policy Implications' (1990) 31 *Harv. Int'l L. J.* 463; P. Clarotti 'The Completion of the Internal Financial Market: Current Position and Outlook' in M. Andenas and S. Kenyon-Slade *EC*

mutual recognition of national licenses. It opened the way to the Community-wide banking operations whether by means of direct cross-border provision of services or through the establishment of local branches, on the basis of a credit institution's home state authorisation (single banking license).[25] The single license is based on the model of the universal bank. Accordingly, credit institutions can carry on throughout the Community a broad range of banking activities,[26] provided that these are covered by their home authorisation. The main limitation of the single license is that it does not extend to the establishment of subsidiaries in host Member States.

The Directive allocates the responsibility for the prudential control and supervision of credit institutions to the regulatory authorities ('competent authorities') of the home Member State, with only limited exceptions.

The minimum harmonisation which was thought to be necessary for the mutual recognition of national regulatory standards was achieved in part by certain provisions in the Second Banking Directive, which set an absolute minimum capital requirement of ECU 5 million for credit institutions, required the vetting of their owners and imposed limits on their participations in non-financial undertakings. The more significant element of harmonisation, however, consisted in the formal adoption, by means of the Own Funds Directive[27] and the Solvency Ratio Directive,[28] of common risk-related capital requirements based on the Basle Committee's Accord.[29] They require that all credit institutions operating within the Community observe a minimum ratio of 8 per cent of eligible capital items ('own funds') to risk-weighted assets.

The harmonisation of a limited number of minimum rules only has been criticised by some commentators on the ground that it does not lead to a

(continued)
   Financial Market Regulation and Company Law (1993) p. 1. See also U. H. Schneider, 'The Harmonization of EC Banking Laws: The Euro-Passport to Profitability and International Competitiveness of Financial Institutions' (1991) 22 *Law & Pol'y Int'l Bus.* 261, pp.267–76.
25. Second Banking Directive, Arts 6 (1) and 18 (1).
26. These are listed in the Annex to the Second Banking Directive.
27. Council Directive 89/299/EEC of 17.4.89 on the own funds of credit institutions (the 'Own Funds Directive'). This technical directive determined the items which may be included in the calculation of a bank's capital ('own funds').
28. Council Directive 89/647/EEC of 18.12.89 on a solvency ratio for credit institutions (the 'Solvency Ratio Directive'). This establishes common rules for the risk-weighting of assets and off-balance sheet items and set the minimum ratio of 8 per cent.
29. Basle Committee, 'International Convergence of Capital Measurement and Capital Standards' ('the Accord') (July 1988). On the Accord, see J. J. Norton, 'The Work of the Basle Supervisors Committee on Bank Capital Adequacy and the July 1988 Report on 'International Convergence of Capital Measurement and Capital Standards' (1989) 23 *Int'l Law*. 245.

really unified market.[30] On this view, if there is to be a truly European market, regulation should be conducted at Community level, because the mutual recognition approach does not remove the incentives of national authorities to lower their supervisory standards for the purpose of attracting financial activity in their territory.

The single license is an attempt to circumvent the anticompetitive effects of the higher regulatory standards of certain Member States, as incoming banks can now secure access to their markets simply by conforming to their home-country rules.

Furthermore, the uniform minimum capital standards limit the extent to which individual Member States can in fact unilaterally relax their regulatory standards for competitive reasons, as the critics claim. Rather than encouraging 'competition in laxity', the capital standards can be interpreted as introducing an effective constraint on the growth of banks originating in the weaker Member States. Such banks may find it difficult to meet the standards, due to their low profitability and limited ability to raise new capital. In addition, the credible implicit safety-nets provided by the authorities of the stronger Member States in the form of lending of last resort and lifeboat practices for ailing institutions, discourages the drift of banking business to jurisdictions with low supervisory standards.[31]

The success of the mutual recognition approach is displayed by the fact that it has actually accelerated the trend of regulatory convergence, gradually levelling the remaining differences in substantive prudential standards. In 1992, directives introducing a revised framework for the consolidated supervision of banking groups[32] and setting limits on large exposures[33] were adopted. The following year, in conjunction with the application of the single license approach to the securities industry,[34] uniform capital requirements for both investment firms and credit institutions were promulgated in the Capital Adequacy Directive,[35] with the aim of covering risks arising from the securities and foreign-exchange trading activities of these institutions. In combination with the Own Funds

---

30. See, *eg*, C. Bradley, '1992: The Case of Financial Services' (1991) 12 *Nw. J. Int'l L. & Bus.* 124.
31. For a game-theoretical analysis of the effects of the mutual-recognition approach, see P. van Cayseele and D. Heremans, 'Legal Principles of Financial Market Integration in 1992: An Economic Analysis' (1991) 11 *Int. Rev. L. & Econ.* 83.
32. Council Directive 92/30/EEC of 6.4.92 on the supervision of credit institutions on a consolidated basis (the 'Second Consolidated Supervision Directive').
33. Council Directive 92/121/EEC of 21.12.92 on the monitoring and control of large exposures of credit institutions (the 'Large Exposures Directive').
34. Council Directive 93/22/EEC of 10.5.93 on investment services in the securities field (the 'Investment Services Directive').
35. Council Directive 93/6/EEC of 15.3.93 on the capital adequacy of investment firms and credit institutions (the 'Capital Adequacy Directive').

and Solvency Ratio Directives, the Capital Adequacy Directive completes the risk-related framework of capital adequacy for banks. In May 1994, the Deposit-Guarantee Directive was adopted. It requires the introduction by the Member States of deposit-guarantee schemes ensuring a minimum degree of protection for the depositors of credit institutions on a Europe-wide basis.[36] Deposit insurance under the Deposit-Guarantee Directive is based on the home-country principle. As a result, the costs of bank failures are shifted, at least in so far as formal deposit insurance is concerned, to the national authorities who are responsible for exercising supervisory control. This may be an important disincentive to competition in laxity. It may dissuade Member States which act as centres for international financial operations, such as Luxembourg, from tolerating the operation of weak banks from their jurisdiction or exercising inadequate prudential supervision, in the expectation that the costs of failure will be shouldered by other countries.

With the adoption of these measures, and in particular of the common capital rules for the securities activities of banks, the Community has achieved significant convergence in substantive regulatory standards. However, the measures have not attempted to affect the institutional organisation of the supervisory function by establishing a supra-national supervisory authority or imposing on the Member States a specific scheme of organisation of their national agencies. The institutional organisation of the supervisory function and, in particular, of the executive stage of actual exercise of supervision remains within the national discretion of the Member States.[37]

The Community regime only demands co-operation between the various 'competent authorities' to which the Member States delegate functions in the area of prudential supervision.[38] It is significant that the relevant rules

36. Directive 94/19/EC of the European Parliament and of the Council of 30 May 1994 on deposit-guarantee schemes (the 'Deposit-Guarantee Directive'). See M. Andenas 'Deposit Guarantee Schemes and Home Country Control' in R. Cranston, *The Single Market and the Law of Banking* (1995) p. 105.

37. On the allocation of responsibilities for specific tasks in the field of banking supervision to various types of competent authorities within each Member State (the central bank, a separate public agency with general supervisory responsibilities, autonomous bodies with limited tasks or other persons appointed by the primary supervisory authority, including auditors) and the total lack of uniformity in organisational structure across Member States, see T. Padoa-Schioppa, *The Road to Monetary Union in Europe: The Emperor, The Kings, and the Genies* (1994), pp.223, 229–35.

38. The First Banking Directive, Art. 7 (1), already required close collaboration between the competent national authorities regarding the supervision of institutions operating in more than one Member State and the exchange of all information likely to facilitate the monitoring of their liquidity and solvency. See currently First Banking Directive, Art. 7 (1), as amended by Art. 14 (1) of the Second Banking Directive; Second Banking Directive, Arts 7 and 15 (2); Second Consolidated Supervision Directive, Art. 7 (2)–(4), (7); Investment Services Directive, Art. 23; and Capital Adequacy Directive, Arts 7 (3), eighth indent, and 9 (4).

do not require the supervisory authorities, where these are organised as separate institutions, to co-operate with their national central banks. EC law simply qualifies the supervisory authorities' duty of secrecy by allowing them to exchange confidential information with the monetary authorities,[39] but otherwise leaves the question of their co-operation to the discretion of each Member State.

The residual discrepancies between national regulatory regimes seem to reflect, not as much conscious competitive strategies aimed at attracting banking business by manipulating the prudential standards, as more mundane differences in the quality of supervisory performance. This can be explained by the limited manpower, sophistication or resources of the national authorities of the smaller Member States. By requiring them to supervise groups headed by credit institutions authorised by them on a consolidated basis, it has been claimed, the current allocation of regulatory responsibilities increases unduly the regulatory burden on these autho-rities.[40]

4. MONETARY UNION AND CENTRALISATION OF BANKING SUPERVISION

Many commentators maintain that the present organisation of supervisory responsibilities at national level cannot be sustained in a monetary union: a much higher degree of co-ordination, and even centralisation of prudential supervision at Community level, will be required.[41] Leaving banking supervision to the Member States may create obstacles to the development of an internal market in banking. Conversely, in an internal banking market national banking supervisors may not be particularly effective with their limited jurisdiction.

One particularly compelling reason for centralisation is the growing integration of EC financial markets, characterised by the rise of large

39. See First Banking Directive, Art. 12 (6), as substituted by Art. 4 of Directive 95/26/EC.
40. M. Dassesse, S. Isaacs and G. Penn, *EC Banking Law* (2nd edn, 1994), p.107.
41. See, *eg*, P. B. Kenen, *Economic and Monetary Union in Europe: Moving Beyond Maastricht* (1995), pp.32–5; and B. Eichengreen, *Should the Maastricht Treaty be Saved?*, Princeton Studies in International Finance No. 74 (Dec. 1992), pp.42–7. R. Kinsella, 'The European Central Bank and the Emerging EC "Regulatory Deficit"', in D. Currie and J. D. Whitley (eds), *EMU After Maastricht: Transition or Revaluation?* (1995), p.103, speaks in dramatic terms about a 'regulatory gap' and a 'black hole' at the centre of Europe's emerging central banking system, as a result of the lack of a clear supervisory role for the ECB; his argument, however, rests on the questionable premise of the 'indivisibility' of monetary policy and supervisory responsibilities.

financial conglomerates operating across national borders. It has been said that:

As European financial markets become more integrated and competition increases, both externalities among countries and the potential instability of the system will increase. ... Increased cross-country external effects mean that the role for coordinating and centralising regulation and supervision will increase correspondingly. The EMI could be a natural candidate to perform this function. Indeed, ... national regulators will tend to pay insufficient attention to overseas customers of domestic banks; systemic risks in overseas countries in which domestic banks trade (both instances present in the BCCI case); systemic risks in the EC as links in interbank markets grow; and finally, risks to the EC payments system with a single currency. The solution proposed involves a European regulatory process with increasing degrees of coordination and centralisation and with a European wide deposit insurance system.[42]

Despite the reference to a prudential role for the EMI (and, presumably, in the third stage of EMU, to the ECB and the ESCB), the main thrust of this and similar arguments concerns the choice of the level of government at which the supervisory function must be located in the single market. This is a 'vertical' choice. It raises issues of subsidiarity,[43] but leaves open the question of the distribution of roles between particular institutions operating at Community level.

Assuming that the organisational centralisation of banking policy, and in particular prudential supervision, is indeed necessary, one could envisage several candidates for the role of European banking authority. Generally, the design and execution of Community policies is a matter for the various Directorates General of the Commission. Nevertheless, the allocation of executive supervisory responsibilities in the field of banking to the Commission would probably be too drastic a departure from current institutional practices. As the Commission would appear to lack the appropriate expertise and suitable institutional structure, the relevant functions could be assigned, instead, either to the ESCB or to a specially constituted agency.[44] This agency could, for instance, be based on, and

42. X. Vives, 'The Supervisory Function of the European System of Central Banks' (1992) 51 *Giornale degli Economisti e Annali di Economia* 523, pp.530–31. See also the similar remarks of M. Onado, 'Monetary Policy, Regulation and Growing Bank Risks. Comments' (1992) 51 *Giornale degli Economisti e Annali di Economia* 505, p.510.
43. See *infra*, section 6.1.
44. On the power of the Community to create agencies with distinct legal personality and entrust them with specific tasks, see K. Lenaerts, 'Regulating the Regulatory Process: "Delegation of Powers" in the European Community' (1993) 18 *ELR* 23, pp.40–49. The Community's experience in matters of delegation of powers is still limited. 'The crucial question indeed remains the political accountability for open-ended policy choices, . . . even if the exercise of such powers occurs at the "executive" level'; ibid., pp.46–7. Participation by representatives of the Member States, the Commission and sometimes

absorb, the three existing fora for supervisory co-operation at Community level, that is: (i) firstly, the Contact Group of EU Supervisory Authorities, the informal and largely autonomous forum where views are exchanged on policy matters and individual cases of supervisory concern; (ii) then the Banking Advisory Committee,[45] composed of representatives of the central banks, competent authorities and finance departments of the Member States and of the Commission, which plays an advisory role with regard to proposed EC banking legislation and also participates, in its capacity as a regulatory committee, in the making of technical amendments to the existing banking directives,[46] but does not discuss individual cases; (iii) and finally the Banking Supervisory Sub-Committee of the EMI, consisting of representatives of the central banks of the Member States or, in cases where the central banks do not have legal responsibility for banking supervision,[47] of the separate supervisory authorities, which assists the EMI in the performance of its limited consultative and advisory functions in the area of banking supervision, to be assumed in the third stage by the ECB.[48]

If it is only a question of centralising certain supervisory tasks at Community level, the involvement of the ESCB would not be necessary.[49] A

cont.

the European Parliament may contribute in taking into account the affected interests, but should not substitute the operation of the carefully balanced mechanisms of political control set out in the EC Treaty, which vary in important respects from one area to another. 'The bottom line of institutional inventiveness is probably that the margin of political discretion which might be left to a newly-established internal body may not remain unchecked before it produces rules with a Community law status, which is in the end what "balance of powers" and representative democracy are all about'; ibid., p.49.

45. Established under the First Banking Directive, Art. 11.

46. A regulatory committee is a group of officials from specialised agencies of the Member States entrusted with the task of reviewing Commission proposals for technical measures within their field. The relevant proposals become law once the regulatory committee gives the green light ('comitology procedure'); Decision 87/373/EEC of 13 July 1987 laying down the procedures for the exercise of implementing powers conferred on the Commission. If the regulatory committee withholds its concurrence, a decision may be taken by the Council.

47. See EMI, 'Annual Report 1994' (April 1995), p.70.

48. For an account of recent activities of the Banking Advisory Committee, the Contact Group of Banking Supervisory Authorities and the Banking Supervisory Sub-Committee of the EMI, see Basle Committee on Banking Supervision, 'Report on International Developments in Banking Supervision No. 10' (June 1996), pp.215–24.

These bodies do not have a hierarchical relationship, nor official lines of communication. However, their membership overlaps, and in practice there is continuous exchange of information between them, ensuring informal co-ordination and division of labour.

49. Indeed, a separate Community agency might be able to bring within its jurisdiction non-bank financial groups more easily than the ECB and would also avoid the over-concentration of powers in the hands of the Community's central bankers. See J.-V. Louis *et al.* (Working Group of the ECU Institute), *Banking Supervision in the European Community: Institutional Aspects* (1995), p.16.

related but conceptually distinct line of argument, however, insists on a direct supervisory role for the ECB and ESCB in particular. The argument is based on the ground that this is essential for the performance of their other functions, including the conduct of monetary policy. On this view, banking policy in the monetary union should not only be centralised, but also combined with the monetary policy function. This 'horizontal' choice of competent authority transforms the question from one concerning the operation of the single market to one inherently linked to the construction of a monetary union. At the same time, it raises questions of legitimation, given the ESCB's very high degree of independence from the Community's and Member States' political institutions.[50]

The combination of monetary and prudential functions is sometimes espoused on the ground that the soundness of the banking system is a prerequisite to the maintenance of monetary stability.[51] It is, indeed, the case that, in financial environments dominated by insolvent banking institutions, a number of special problems arise which put in question the effectiveness of a central bank's market-oriented instruments of monetary control.[52] This observation, however, does not have direct or immediate policy implications for the organisation of the prudential function in the Community. The banking systems of the Member States are not as fragile as to potentially impede the effective conduct of monetary policy. Furthermore, the central bank's interest in a safe and robust banking system as a condition for the performance of its monetary functions does not necessarily provide a valid justification for assigning the responsibility for prudential policy to the central bank itself. In fact, the combination of monetary and prudential functions could be counterproductive. It could create perverse incentives, leading the central bank, on occasions, to relax its monetary policy and accommodate the liquidity requirements of banking institutions in order to protect their solvency and profitability. This may be inconsistent with monetary stability.[53] At any rate, the empirical evidence

---

50. See *infra*, section 6.2.
51. See, *eg*, R. M. Lastra, *Central Banking and Banking Regulation* (1996), pp.61–2; and Kinsella, loc. cit., n.41.
52. See D. J. Mathieson and R. D. Haas, 'Establishing Monetary Control in Financial Systems with Insolvent Institutions' (1995) 42 *IMF Staff Papers* 184.
53. See D. Masciandaro, 'Monetary Policy, Banking Supervision and Inflation' (1992) 51 *Giornale degli Economisti e Annali di Economia* 533.

On the other hand, a central bank may be more resistant than a separate supervisory authority to 'capture' by private banking interests, because its reputation depends primarily in achieving its macroeconomic objectives. See Allan Greenspan, Testimony before the Committee on Banking, Housing and Urban Affairs, US Senate, 2 March 1994.

does not provide clear support either for the combination of these functions in the central bank or for their separation.[54]

In practice, even in countries as Germany and Belgium, where the two functions are separated, the central bank usually collaborates closely with the supervisory authorities in the elaboration of prudential policy and rules and in the collection and analysis of banking statistical returns, with a view to avoiding policy conflicts and ensuring the efficient sharing of information.[55] This, however, does not require the transfer of decision-making powers in the central bank.[56]

The more persuasive arguments for the allocation of supervisory responsibilities to the ESCB do not relate to the supposed complementarity of the monetary and banking policies. They relate to the need to control credit exposures that it might undertake as lender of last resort or through its involvement in the operation of European payment systems.[57]

In theory, the lender-of-last-resort function shares with banking supervision in the strict sense common objectives. That is, to ensure the smooth and continuous operation of banking markets, and thus the long-term stability of, and confidence in, the financial system.[58] Generally, however, in lending of last resort the emphasis is placed almost exclusively on macro-prudential concerns. The theoretical arguments for supervision also encompass micro-prudential objectives, such as the protection of the users of the financial system, regardless of systemic repercussions. Furthermore,

54. See C. Goodhart and D. Schoenmaker, 'Institutional Separation between Supervisory and Monetary Agencies' (1992) 51 *Giornale degli Economisti e Annali di Economia* 353; and idem, 'Should the Functions of Monetary Policy and Banking Supervision Be Separated?' (1995) 47 *Oxford Economic Papers* 539. The authors' study of 24 countries, of which 11 could be classified as following the combined system and 13 the separate one during the 1980s, did not reveal an unambiguous advantage for any of the two systems in terms of either a better inflation record or a more stable banking system.

55. See Padoa-Schioppa, *The Road to Monetary Union . . .* , op. cit., n.37, pp.230–31; Louis *et al.*, op. cit., n.49, p.69; and J. Priesemann, 'Policy Options for Prudential Supervision in Stage Three of Monetary Union', revised version of a paper presented at the Conference on Banking, International Capital Flows and Growth in Europe, University of Potsdam, Potsdam (13–14 Oct. 1995), pp.5–6.

56. The formal responsibility of a separate authority can even be seen as a means of protecting the central bank's reputation in the event of bank failures; Priesemann, ibid., p.6.

57. More generally, the active involvement of the central bank in supervision will be justified to the extent that the central bank underwrites, openly or implicitly, the operations of the private banking system, because the central bank must limit the attendant risks. In this context, Goodhart & Schoenmaker, 'Should the Functions . . . Be Separated?', loc. cit., n.54, pp.554–6, identify a tendency for decreasing central bank involvement in the organisation and funding of bank rescues, in favour of explicit deposit insurance schemes and government-financed bail-outs. This may be a major factor encouraging the separation of functions.

58. For the central bank, an operational benefit of acting as lender of last resort is that the commercial banking system becomes dependent on it for its liquidity.

supervision operates *ex ante*, while lending of last resort consists in *ex post* interventions, once problems have been identified.

As lender of last resort, the central bank can act either by standing ready to increase the liquidity of the banking system as a whole whenever there are signs of an impending system-wide liquidity crises or by providing support to individual banking institutions under pressure. Such support is often justified on the ground that the prevention of individual failures is necessary to avoid the contagion, through interbank credit exposures, of other institutions and the eruption of crises of confidence, which might potentially engulf large segments of the banking system.[59]

In a monetary union, support to individual banks may still be provided by the national central banks on a decentralised basis. System-wide problems will require ECB intervention, because the injection of liquidity has direct implications for the single monetary policy. Furthermore, with increasing integration of banking markets and the emergence of very large cross-border groups, even in the case of individual banks the initiative for lending of last resort may have to rest with the ECB (assuming, of course, that similar operations are within its legal powers[60]) and conducted on the account of the ESCB as a whole.[61] This can constitute an argument for giving supervisory responsibilities to the ESCB. The information-gathering activities which are necessary for the enforcement of prudential standards overlap with the assessment of financial soundness for the purpose of deciding whether or not to extend credit to particular institutions.

It may perhaps be possible to draw a distinction between lending of last resort to the market as a whole and support for individual institutions. One could say that only the latter type of intervention requires individualised screening of applicants for central bank credit, and thus raises directly issues of moral hazard. Similar concerns do not arise with the same force where a central bank refrains from providing support to individual institutions. In principle, the monetary authority could refuse to lend on an individual basis. It could act as lender of last resort only to the banking system as a whole, when this appears to face a generalised liquidity crisis. A crisis of this type could make necessary a rapid liquidation of bank assets at distressed prices. That could trigger a deflationary spiral, where the attempt of banks to dispose of their assets immediately and simultaneously would in itself

---

59. In truth, however, lending of last resort may be used to bail-out insolvent institutions, under the pretext of providing 'liquidity support'. In this case, it constitutes a covert form of public safety-net and a source of moral hazard, similar to a system of comprehensive deposit insurance or outright rescue operations, since the expectation of public support in times of crisis creates incentives for banking institutions to increase risk-taking.

60. See *infra*, section 5.

61. See D. Schoenmaker, 'Banking Supervision and Lender of Last Resort in EMU', ch.19 of this volume, pp.435–6.

magnify the initial fall in prices, eventually driving otherwise sound banks to insolvency. As a liquidity crisis has important implications, not only for the survival of the banking system, but also for the economy's stock of money, the intervention of the central bank in this case would constitute in essence a monetary operation. Its purpose would be to counteract the monetary contraction caused by a provisional fall in asset prices, caused by a shift to base money, until normal conditions are restored. The role of the central bank as lender of last resort in this context would simply involve indiscriminate lending to the market as a whole and the accommodation of the temporary liquidity pressures through open-market or discount operations, without need for screening the soundness of individual borrowers.[62] Accordingly, the function of the lender of last resort could be undertaken quite independently of any prudential responsibility. The only real issue in this case would be whether, in view of the prevailing monetary circumstances of the moment, a temporary expansionary intervention of the central bank is compatible with the main long-term objective of price stability.

To answer this question, however, the central bank must be able to discriminate between a temporary liquidity problem and a permanent decline of asset prices, due to a reassessment of their fundamental value. If it mistakes the latter for the former and is led to provide lending of last resort, its actions may contribute to the overexpansion of the monetary supply and create inflationary pressures in the economy. The concentration of assets of questionable long-term value at its hands as collateral for its lending may even force it to absorb part of the financial system's losses. Some authors argue that, given the high potential costs of the lack of relevant information, the attribution to the central bank of supervisory powers would increase the efficiency of the lender-of-last-resort function.[63] In a European context, in particular, the ECB needs such powers, because without them the national authorities may exploit their own superior information and misrepresent the true state of their domestic banking system. They may, the argument goes, emphasise potential threats to the stability of the financial system in order to put pressure on the ECB to provide lending-of-last-resort facilities in inappropriate cases.[64]

This may be a valid reason for giving to the ECB full access to the supervisory information gathered by the national competent authorities. It does not necessarily support a direct regulatory and supervisory role for the ECB. Moreover, it is questionable whether, in order to discriminate between true liquidity crises and fundamental shifts in asset values, a central bank

---

62. See M. Goodfriend and R. G. King, 'Financial Deregulation, Monetary Policy, and Central Banking' (May–June 1988) 74:3 *Fed. Res. B. Richmond Ec. Rev.* 3.
63. See A. Giovannini, *The Debate on Money in Europe* (1995), pp.358–61.
64. Ibid., p.360.

must have recourse to privileged supervisory information relating to the situation of individual banking institutions. The type of information required for this purpose relates primarily to the evaluation of the aggregate situation of the financial markets, which probably can be carried out on the basis of statistical information. More importantly, the combination of monetary and supervisory responsibilities in the central bank may create incentives for neglecting price stability and misusing lending of last resort not as an instrument of monetary policy but as a means of supporting the banking system and avoiding failures, which might reflect badly on the central bank as regulator.[65]

A more clear cut case for the involvement of the ESCB (or at least of the national central banks which compose it) with prudential issues can be made in the context of the operation of European payment systems. For the completion of the single market and the achievement of the attendant efficiency gains, the reform and integration of national payment systems is required. In this context, considerations of competitive equality and efficient operation dictate the need for consistent rules governing matters such as conditions of access to clearing and settlement systems, legal arrangements, technical standards, working hours, pricing of central bank services and, last but not least, risk management policies.[66] The devise of such rules comes naturally within the field of interest of the central banking authorities which operate the payment systems.

At the same time, the active involvement of national central banks in the provision of settlement services necessitates that they screen individual participants, set credit limits, impose collateral requirements, take corrective action, investigate irregularities, etc. A central bank will need privileged information, often within minutes, in which case the possibility of co-operation with non-central-bank supervisors will be narrowly limited. It may be that it can obtain such information only through supervision. As the relevant decisions must be taken within a very short time-frame and require privileged information, central bank supervision of the payment system participants may become unavoidable.

The potential introduction of an integrated European-wide payment system, managed at the centre by the ECB, would imply similar functions for the ECB itself.[67] However, the pan-European large-value payment system for the third stage of EMU, the TARGET (Trans-European Automated Real-time Gross settlement Express Transfer) system, which is currently designed by

---

65. Vives, loc. cit., n.42, pp.527–8.
66. See Committee of Governors, Ad-Hoc Working Group on EC Payment Systems, 'Issues of Common Concern to EC Central Banks in the Field of Payment Systems' (May 1992).
67. See Giovannini, op. cit., n.63, pp.361–2; and P. Angelini and F. Passacantando, 'Central Banks' Role in the Payment System and its Relationship with Banking Supervision' (1992) 51 *Giornale degli Economisti e Annali di Economia* 453, pp.475–81.

the EMI and the national central banks of the Member States,[68] does not appear to require a direct supervisory role for the ECB. It will be decentralised, with membership confined at a national level and the ECB providing only the interlinking between the national components.

At any rate, to the extent that participation to the payment system provides significant commercial benefits to the members, a central bank may not need to resort to legal regulation and administrative supervision. It can instead use its contractual capacity to ensure that members accept conditions of access which combine a high degree of safety and efficiency.[69]

5. BANKING SUPERVISION AND THE MAASTRICHT TREATY

The Maastricht Treaty assigns to the ECB and ESCB certain competences in the field of banking policy and prudential supervision, but only reluctantly and subject to considerable limitations.

The original proposals for Economic and Monetary Union in the Delors Report envisaged that, as part of its mandate and functions, the Community's future monetary institution, the European System of Central Banks, 'would participate in the co-ordination of banking supervision policies of the supervisory authorities'.[70] It did not specify in greater detail its role in this area. It was the Committee of Central Bank Governors[71] which pressed for the inclusion in the Treaty of specific provisions for this purpose. In its draft statute for a future European central bank, forming the basis of the statute of the ESCB in the Maastricht text,[72] the Committee of Governors placed prudential control within the basic tasks of the new monetary

---

68. See *infra*, n.130.
69. See Angelini and Passacantando, loc. cit., n.67, p.479. For an example of the ways in which a central bank can apply its contractual capacity to control the behaviour of its counterparties, see Hadjiemmanuil, op. cit., n.22, ch.4.
70. Delors Report, loc. cit., n.2, point 32.
71. The Committee of Governors of the Central Banks of the Member States was formed in 1964, as a forum for co-operation between the central banks of the Member States; see EEC Decision 64/300 of 8 May 1964. With the establishment of the European Monetary System in 1979, the Committee of Governors acquired new responsibilities, in particular in the management of the ERM. At the beginning of the first stage of EMU on 1 July 1990, the responsibilities of the Committee of Governors were strengthened, in order to ensure the co-ordination of monetary policies in the Member States for the purpose of promoting price stability; see Council Decision 90/142/EEC of 12 March 1990, amending the 1964 Decision. At the start of the second stage on 1 Jan. 1994, the Committee of Governors was dissolved and replaced by the transitional monetary institution, the EMI, whose responsibilities are set out in the EC Treaty, Art. 109f, and the Statute of the EMI.
72. See Corbett, op. cit., n.1, p.13; and Italianer, loc. cit., n.1, p.65.

institution.[73] It provided for specific prudential functions to be conferred to the ESCB. Not only should the latter be consulted on new prudential legislation, but it should also be given independent decision-making responsibilities.[74] The Commission endorsed the Committee of Governors' approach, including prudential supervision as one of the tasks of the proposed 'Eurofed' in its draft treaty on economic and monetary union.[75]

In the course of the Intergovernmental Conference on EMU, the Committee of Governors explained that its draft provisions relating to prudential supervision

. . . were introduced into the Statutes with three considerations in mind. Firstly, the System, even though operating strictly at the macro-economic level, will have a broad oversight of developments in financial markets and institutions and, therefore, should possess a detailed working knowledge which would be of value to the exercise of supervisory functions. Secondly, the ESCB's primary objective of price stability will be supported by the stability and soundness of the banking system in the Community as it evolves. Thirdly, measures to deal with fragility or disturbance in the banking system must take account of their effect on monetary objectives and policies.[76]

In other words, in the Governors' view the ESCB should be given a prudential role for three reasons. Firstly, because of its privileged vantage

73. Committee of Governors, 'Draft Statute of the European System of Central Banks and of the European Central Bank' (27 Nov. 1990), Art. 3.1, second indent.

74. Italianer, loc. cit., n.1, p.65, attributes to the special position of the Committee of Governors (which was not merely a contributor to the preparation of the Intergovernmental Conference but also an interested party) the inclusion in its draft Statute of
'. . . some provisions which gave particular emphasis to the responsibilities of the ESCB and the ECB. Examples are the relative autonomy created in the field of exchange rate policy, the role foreseen for the ESCB in the field of prudential supervision and the requirement that coins be put into circulation by the ECB and/or the national central banks. No related articles survived unchanged in the final text. However, the main thrust of the Committee's draft was maintained.'

75. See Commission of the European Communities, 'Proposal for a Draft Treaty Amending the Treaty Establishing the European Economic Community with a View to Achieving Economic and Monetary Union' (21 Aug. 1990), especially para. 3 of the Explanatory Memorandum, underlining the close affinity of the Commission's own views with the Governors' draft statute, and draft Art. 106b (1) (vii), providing that one of Eurofed's tasks should be 'to participate as necessary in the formulation, coordination and execution of policies relating to banking supervision and the stability of the financial system'. Draft Arts 106b (3) and 109e (2) recognised specifically the Eurofed's advisory role regarding any draft Community or national legislation or proposed international agreement on prudential supervision and banking or financial matters.

76. Copy of a letter of the President of the Committee of Governors to the President of the Intergovernmental Conference on EMU concerning the Statute of the ESCB and the ECB, dated 2 Sept. 1991 (Doc. CONF/EMU 1617/91 of 5 Sept. 1991), Pt. II, 'Prudential Supervision', pp.4–5.

point as a central bank, facilitating effective information-gathering. Secondly, because of the long-term complementarity of its monetary tasks with the aim of banking stability. Thirdly, because of the need for co-ordination of the instruments employed for the avoidance of financial fragility and crises with the objective of price stability.

This assessment was not endorsed by all Member States. There were wide differences of opinion between them on this point, explicable by a variety reasons, such as: the lack of a common concept of prudential supervision and of a consistent approach to the institutional organisation of the responsibilities for prudential policy; different expectations concerning the viability of the Second Banking Directive's system of supervision on a cross-border basis by the Member States' competent authorities coupled with national discretion in the organisation of prudential responsibilities, which at the time of the Intergovernmental Conference had not yet been tested in practice; the reluctance of certain Member States to countenance the transferral of supervisory competences to the Community; and fears of concentrating excessive power at the hands of an independent ESCB.[77] The draft provisions presented by the French Government confined the ESCB to purely monetary functions and did not envisage any participation in the exercise of prudential control.[78] Germany, which follows domestically the separate system, was also reluctant to accept a significant prudential function for the new monetary institution, for fear that this might lead to conflicts of policies and weaken its resolve to pursue its primary objective of price stability. During the Intergovernmental Conference, the relevant provisions appeared for some time in the text of the draft statute of the ESCB within brackets.[79]

The Intergovernmental Conference failed to reach agreement on the principles that might guide the allocation of supervisory responsibilities in the monetary union between the Community and the national levels ('vertical' allocation) and between different institutions (central banks or

---

77. See Louis *et al.,* op. cit., n.49, pp.14 and 42; Lastra, op. cit., n.51, pp.241-2; and Kenen, op. cit., n.41, p.34.
78. French Government, 'Proposal for a Draft Treaty on Economic and Monetary Union' (Jan. 1991). Even with regard to advisory functions, the French draft confined the ESCB's consultative function to draft legislation or international agreements 'having implications for the Community's monetary policy', but not for measures relating to prudential supervision or general banking and financial policy; see draft Art. 2-4 (4). On the other hand, the French draft left open the possibility that additional functions be delegated to the ESCB by unanimous decision of the Council; see draft Arts 2-4 (2), 7th indent, and 5-7 (2).
79. See J.-V. Louis, 'L'Union Economique et Monetaire', in *Commentaire Megret: Le Droit de la CEE,* Vol. 6 (2nd edn, 1995), p.92.

other agencies) at each level ('horizontal' allocation), or on the precise role that the ESCB might play in this area.[80]

Although the references to a prudential role for the ESCB were not eliminated altogether from the final text, the drafting of the relevant provisions of the EC Treaty and the Statute of the ESCB is characterised by considerable imprecision and a limiting spirit.[81] Instead of figuring among the basic tasks of the ESCB,[82] prudential supervision is treated as a separate, supplementary function.[83] More importantly, the wording of the relevant provisions is significantly different from the Committee of Governors' draft. The Governors had envisaged that it would be the ESCB's task 'to participate as necessary in the formulation, co-ordination and execution of policies relating to prudential supervision and the stability of the financial system'. In the final text, however, it is only a matter of the ESCB's 'contribution' to 'the smooth conduct of policies pursued by the competent authorities relating to the prudential supervision of credit institutions and the stability of the financial system'.[84]

The provisions do not clarify the nature of the expected involvement in prudential matters. Should the ECB concentrate on purely advisory, facilitating or co-ordinating tasks, or may it exercise independent functions in connection to policy or rule-making? May it be involved in the implementation of prudential policy and exercise direct supervisory functions in connection to individual institutions? Nor is any attempt made

80. In fact, several practical issues were ignored in the negotiations, in an attempt to facilitate agreement on principle on EMU. T. Congdon, 'Problems that Were Neglected at Maastricht' (Summer 1992) 3:1 *Central Banking* 54, claims that the neglect of the operational aspects of monetary and banking policies in the third stage was so thorough as to raise basic questions about the viability of the whole project. Instead, the discussions focused on the conditions for the acceptance of Member States to the third stage and on the question whether the ESCB should be created from the start of the second stage or whether a transitional monetary institution, the EMI, should be used during the second stage. See Bini-Smaghi, Padoa-Schioppa and Papadia, *The Transition to EMU . . .* , op. cit., n.1.

81. See Louis, 'L'Union Economique et Monetaire', loc. cit., n.79, pp.92–4

82. Committee of Governors, 'Draft Statute . . .', loc. cit., n.73, draft Art. 3.1, second indent.

83. EC Treaty, Art. 105 (5); and Statute of the ESCB, Art. 3.3.

84. The specific provisions of Art. 25 of the Committee of Governors' draft statute were incorporated in the final Treaty text with similar changes. While the draft statute envisaged that the ECB would be 'entitled to offer advise and to be consulted' on the interpretation and implementation of EC legislation on prudential matters, Art. 25.1 of the Statute of the ESCB provides that it 'may' do so. Furthermore, while the draft statute stated that the ECB would 'formulate, interpret and implement policies relating to the prudential supervision of credit and other financial institutions for which it is designated as competent supervisory authority', Art. 25.2 of the Statute of the ESCB provides, instead, a procedure for the attribution by unanimous decision of the Council to the ECB of specific supervisory tasks and excludes insurance undertakings from the range of institutions in connection with which such tasks may be attributed.

to define the content and outer limits of the supervisory function. Conceivably, this could include, beyond prudential regulation in a narrow sense (encompassing the adoption of standards of financial soundness for individual institutions and their enforcement through licensing, continuous supervision and the imposition of sanctions), conduct-of-business regulation, the lender-of-last-resort function, the operation of payment systems and the organisation of deposit insurance, since all of them are of potential relevance for the stability of the financial system.

Any imprecision in this area can be the source of particular legal difficulties, especially since the competence of the ESCB in matters of banking (as opposed to monetary) policy is neither complete nor exclusive. It is on the basis of the relevant Treaty provisions that the regulatory competence of the ESCB must be determined, the legitimacy of its potential interventions judged, and lines drawn, both horizontally and vertically, between its powers and those of other Community and national bodies with related legislative and administrative competencies. These provisions, however, provide only tentative guidance on the level and type of action that the ESCB and the ECB can undertake.

5.1 Advisory functions

The clearest direction in the Maastricht Treaty is given in connection to the advisory functions that the ECB is called to perform. The ECB must be consulted on any proposed Community act (regulation, directive, decision or recommendation or opinion) within its field of competence.[85] It must also be consulted by the Member States on domestic legislation falling within its fields of competence, but in this case the requirement of consultation is subject to limits and conditions set out by the Council.[86] In addition to its consultative role in the legislative process, the ECB may submit opinions to the appropriate Community institutions or bodies and to the national authorities on any matter within its field of competence.[87] This power allows the ECB to influence the performance of the administrative tasks of these bodies but also, conceivably, to take itself the initiative for changes in the law.

To the extent that prudential supervision is one of its fields of competence,[88] these provisions could in themselves justify a consultative

---

85. EC Treaty, Art. 105 (4), first indent; and Statute of the ESCB, Art. 4 (a), first indent.
86. EC Treaty, Art. 105 (4), second indent; and Statute of the ESCB, Art. 4 (a), second indent. The Council must reach its decision by qualified majority, either on a proposal by the Commission, in which case it must first consult the European Parliament, or on a recommendation from the ECB itself, in which case it must consult both the European Parliament and the Commission; EC Treaty, Art. 106 (6); and Statute of the ESCB, Art. 42.
87. EC Treaty, Art. 105 (4), *in fine*; and Statute of the ESCB, Art. 4 (b).
88. See EC Treaty, Art. 105 (5); and Statute of the ESCB, Art. 3.3.

or advisory role for the ECB in relation to legislation and other aspects of the prudential supervision of banks or the stability of the financial system. A more explicit basis for the consultation of the ECB by the institutions of the Community and the competent authorities of the Member States in matters relating to the prudential supervision of credit institutions and to the stability of the financial system is provided by Article 25.1 of the Statute of the ESCB. But this basis only reaches so far as the question concerns specifically the scope or implementation of Community (but not national) legislation in this field.[89]

During the second stage of EMU, the EMI exercises analogous consultative functions in relation to Community and national legislation within its more limited field of competence, including prudential regulation.[90] In line with the arrangements for the third stage, the relevant provisions require that the limits and conditions of the EMI's consultative role in relation to legislative activities at national level be set out by the Council. For this purpose, shortly before the establishment of the EMI, the Council, acting on a proposal of the Commission and after consultation with the Parliament and the Committee of Governors, adopted a decision,[91] which could, in the future, serve as a basis for the decision governing the consultation of the ECB.

Reflecting the formulation used in the Maastricht Treaty to describe the EMI's consultative tasks in the field of prudential policy,[92] the Council Decision recognises 'rules applicable to financial institutions in so far as they influence the stability of financial institutions and markets' to be within the EMI's field of competence.[93] The Council Decision confines the meaning of

89. Conceivably, one might argue that the limited and derivative responsibility of the ESCB to contribute to the conduct of prudential policies in accordance to Art. 105 (5) of the EC Treaty does not constitute 'a field of competence'. On this assumption, Art. 105 (4) could not provide a basis for the ECB's advisory role on questions of a prudential nature. Accordingly, Art. 25.1 of the Statute of the ESCB would need to be interpreted in the context of Art. 105 (5) of the EC Treaty, and not as a specific instance of the general advisory functions of Art. 105 (4). In this case, the ECB's advisory role in this field would be confined by the express terms of Art. 25.1 to issues concerning the enactment and implementation of legislative measures reached at the Community level, leaving outside purely national legislation and all non-legislative matters of a prudential nature. See Priesemann, loc. cit., n.55, p.12.

   Significantly, although the general provisions of Art. 105 (4) of the EC Treaty and Art. 4 of the Statute of the ESCB requiring the consultation of the ECB on draft legislation shall not apply to the United Kingdom if it does participate in the third stage of EMU, Art. 25.1 is not covered by the United Kingdom's 'opt-out' and will apply automatically; see Protocol on certain provisions relating to the United Kingdom of Great Britain and Northern Ireland, Arts 5 and 8.

90. EC Treaty, Art. 109f (6); and Statute of the EMI, Art. 5.3.

91. Council Decision 93/717/EC of 22.11.93 on the consultation of the European Monetary Institute by the authorities of the Member States on draft legislative provisions.

92. EC Treaty, Art. 109f (2), fourth indent; and Statute of the EMI, Art. 4.1, fourth indent.

93. Council Decision 93/717/EC, Art. 1 (1), fifth indent.

'draft legislative provisions', regarding which consultation is obligatory, to legally binding measures of a general character (that is, rules for an indefinite number of cases and addressed to an indefinite number of persons), excluding rules of local applicability only.[94] Measures consisting merely in the national implementation of Community directives are excluded from the requirement of consultation, because the relevant rules have already been the subject of consultation at the time of their adoption at Community level.[95] To guarantee that the consultation is not a mere formality, the decision requires from the Member States to ensure that

... the EMI is consulted at an appropriate stage enabling the authority initiating the draft legislative provision to have the EMI's opinion before taking its decision on the substance and that the opinion received by the EMI is brought to the knowledge of the adopting authority if the latter is an authority other than that which has prepared the legislative provisions concerned.[96]

Except in cases of extreme urgency, the EMI must be given at least one month to submit its opinion.[97]

In its first two years of operation, the EMI received thirty requests for consultation, nine of which originated from the Council and twenty-one from national authorities; three of the requests by the Council and eight by the national authorities involved matters of prudential interest. While the primary criterion used by the EMI for assessing the proposed legislative measures was their compatibility with the EC Treaty, their potential impact on the arrangements for the third stage of EMU and their effect on the stability of financial institutions and markets were also taken into account.[98]

5.2 Supervisory tasks

The position regarding the direct regulatory responsibilities of the ESCB in the field of prudential supervision is much less clear than that regarding its advisory functions. The Maastricht Treaty does not contemplate a general

---

94. Ibid., Art. 2 (1).
95. Ibid., Art. 2 (2). This guarantees the discretion of Member States to choose the form and method of implementation when this type of Community legislation is used; see EC Treaty, Art. 189.
96. Ibid., Art. 3.
97. Ibid., Art. 4.
98. EMI, 'Annual Report 1994', loc. cit., n.47, pp.96–7; and 'Annual Report 1995' (April 1996), p.79. In particular, the requests by the Council concerned: an amendment of the Solvency Ratio Directive, for the purpose of accepting various forms of (bilateral) contractual netting; an amendment of the Directive on Undertakings for Collective Investments in Transferable Securities ('UCITS'); and a draft directive on investors' compensation schemes.

transfer of competence to the ESCB in this field in the third stage of EMU. Instead, the responsibility for prudential supervision may remain within the hands of the competent authorities at national level, in accordance with current secondary EC banking legislation. Although the national central banks may exercise specific supervisory functions, they may do so only in their capacity as national authorities under domestic law, not as part of the ESCB.[99]

None the less, the Maastricht Treaty does not exclude altogether a role for the ESCB in matters relating to prudential supervision. In fact, the ESCB is required to 'contribute to the smooth conduct of policies pursued by the competent authorities relating to the prudential supervision of credit institutions and the stability of the financial system'.[100] During the second stage of EMU a limited consultative role with regard to matters 'within the competence of the national central bank and affecting the stability of financial institutions and markets' is given to the EMI as one of its primary tasks.[101]

The role of the ESCB under the provision quoted above can be described as consultative and co-ordinating. It is clear that the ESCB is not intended to replace the competent authorities, but only to assist in the performance of their functions. It is less evident whether the ESCB can resort to formal rule-making or decision-making for this purpose.[102] Another, very restrictive, possibility is supported by the fact that the provision does not apply to those

99. The national central banks are an integral part of the ESCB and must act in accordance with the guidelines and instructions of the ECB; Statute of the ESCB, Art.14.3. Nevertheless, they may perform additional functions on their own account and under domestic law, although the Governing Council of the ECB has a reserve power to divest them of these functions if it decides, by a majority of two thirds of the votes cast, that these functions are incompatible with the performance of the responsibilities of the ESCB; ibid., Art. 14.4.

100. EC Treaty, Art. 105 (5); and Statute of the ESCB, Art. 3.3.

101. EC Treaty, Art. 109f (2), fourth indent; and Statute of the EMI, Art. 4.1, fourth indent. On this basis, the EMI held in 1995 consultations among supervisory authorities on a number of issues, including: credit-risk management; central credit registers; internal control systems; the public disclosure of derivatives activities; and some aspects related to implementation of home country control; see EMI, 'Annual Report 1995', loc. cit., n.98, pp.74–6

102. Certain authors distinguish between an agreed minimum interpretation of the provision and a bolder, more controversial one; Louis *et al.*, op. cit., n.49, pp.45 and 54; and Priesemann, loc. cit., n.55, pp.10–11. The former interpretation holds that the drafters' intention was only to involve the ESCB in prudential policy-making in a consultative capacity, while the latter would also see a role for the ESCB in encouraging the adoption of new prudential rules and policies and taking action to ensure the proper implementation of the common framework of banking supervisory standards in the day-to-day practice of supervisory agencies. The wider interpretation emphasises that Art. 105 (5) of the EC Treaty gives to the ESCB a coordinating role in prudential matters, rather than a consultative one, which is the focus of Art. 25.1 of the Statute of the ESCB. It also discovers in the wording of the provision a flexibility appropriate for an expansive, teleological application, evolving over time in pace with the experiences of the single market and the monetary union.

Member States which do not participate in the third stage of EMU (either, in the case of UK and Denmark, because of their specific right to opt-out or because of their inability to meet the convergence criteria).[103] It is that the ESCB must contribute to the smooth conduct of prudential policies in the monetary union by factoring the likely impact of its monetary operations on such policies in its monetary decision-making, rather than by playing a direct part in the conduct of banking policy.

The Maastricht Treaty also leaves open the prospect that the ECB might be entrusted with specific tasks concerning supervisory policies by providing that the Ecofin Council

. . . may, acting unanimously on a proposal from the Commission and after consulting the ECB and after receiving the assent of the European Parliament, confer upon the ECB specific tasks concerning policies relating to the prudential supervision of credit institutions and other financial institutions with the exception of insurance undertakings.[104]

This enabling clause makes it possible – although, in view of the substantial procedural difficulties, not very probable – for the ECB to acquire direct and express European supervisory powers. The specific tasks must 'concern' prudential supervisory policies, but it is not absolutely clear whether this may include the conduct of first-line supervisory functions over individual financial institutions. It is more likely that the provision envisages the conferring of specific aspects of supervisory policy and rule-making. This is supported by the fact that the ECB is specifically authorised to issue regulations, that is, legal acts of general and direct application, for the purposes of implementing the prudential tasks that may be transferred to it.[105] According to certain interpretations, however, the provision aims to ensure the ability of the ECB to exercise supervisory duties in the event that the development of multinational financial institutions undermines the effectiveness of supervision by the national competent authorities. Accordingly, a potential delegation of tasks would confer on the ECB both rule-making powers and direct supervisory responsibilities regarding monitoring and enforcement.[106]

103. EC Treaty, Art. 109k (3); and Statute of the ESCB, Art. 43.1; and Protocol on certain provisions relating to the United Kingdom of Great Britain and Northern Ireland, Arts 4 and 8. At any rate, the exclusion of these countries reduces considerably the ability of the ESCB to coordinate prudential supervision on a pan-European manner.
104. EC Treaty, Art. 105 (6); see also Statute of the ESCB, Art. 25.2.
105. EC Treaty, Art. 108a; and Statute of the ESCB, Art. 34. However, the same provisions give to the ECB a general power to make decisions, that is, measures binding only upon those to whom they are addressed, whenever this is necessary for carrying out any of its tasks, and also to impose fines or periodic penalty payments on undertakings which fail to comply with its regulations and decisions.
106. Ian Harden, 'The European Central Bank and the Role of National Central Banks in Economic and Monetary Union', in Gretschmann (ed.), op. cit., n.1, p.161.

For the purposes of any supervisory responsibilities, the ECB may have resort to its general power to collect (through the national central banks) statistical information, either from the competent national authorities or directly from the private sector.[107] It is for the Ecofin Council to define, by qualified majority, the exact scope of the reporting requirements, including the natural and legal persons subject to them, the confidentiality regime and the means of enforcement.[108] In all cases, a duty of professional secrecy applies to all information collected by the ECB and the national central banks in the performance of their functions, including those relating to prudential supervision,[109] in line with the similar obligations imposed by secondary EC law on national competent authorities.[110]

5.3 Substantive scope of the prudential functions

Significantly, to define the limits of the ESCB's competence in matters of banking regulation, the Maastricht Treaty relies on the concept of prudential supervision, without, however, specifying further what this means. The use of the words 'prudential supervision of credit institutions' in immediate conjunction with 'the stability of the financial system'[111] leaves no doubt that the ECB's interventions in this field may be guided by concerns of both microprudential and macroprudential nature. On the other hand, it is not clear what are the outer boundaries of the supervisory function, in an exact legal sense.

The potential attribution of direct discretionary powers to the ECB for the performance of specific regulatory tasks[112] makes the lack of a precise definition particularly important. An expansive notion of prudential supervision may potentially be used as a tool for an extensive concentration of administrative powers in the hands of the ECB. It may however also result in a confused horizontal and vertical allocation of responsibilities for banking policy, with overlapping competencies and a proliferation of jurisdictional disputes.

It could be argued, for instance, that the words 'prudential supervision' are meant to cover, in addition to the definition and implementation of prudential standards intended to prevent failures of financial institutions, policies relating to deposit insurance, rules of market organisation or

---

107. Statute of the ESCB, Art. 4 (1)–(2).
108. Ibid., Art. 5.4, in conjunction with Art. 42.
109. Ibid., Art. 38. However, the duty of secrecy is not precisely defined in the relevant provision of the Statute and requires further specification for its enforcement.
110. See First Banking Directive, Art. 12, as substituted by Art. 4 of the Second Banking Directive and subsequently amended by Art. 4 of Directive 95/26/EC.
111. EC Treaty, Art. 105 (5); and Statute of the ESCB, Arts 3.3 and 25.1.
112. EC Treaty, Art. 105 (6); and Statute of the ESCB, Art. 25.2.

conduct-of-business rules, the regulation of payment systems and lending of last resort. Although all these aspects of banking policy are more or less interdependent,[113] to answer the questions concerning the constitutional limits of the ESCB's attributed powers it becomes necessary to draw some conceptual lines between them.

Existing secondary Community law can provide only limited assistance regarding the boundaries of prudential supervision for the purposes of the provisions of the Maastricht Treaty. This applies to the Second Banking Directive and the Investment Services Directive, which set out the framework for the mutual recognition of the licensing and prudential supervision systems of the Member States.[114] It is clear from the harmonised prudential rules that prudential supervision focuses on the financial soundness and, in particular, the solvency of financial institutions, the fitness of their owners and senior managers and the existence of appropriate internal administrative and accounting systems and controls, ensuring effective managerial control over their activities.

As one moves beyond these core aspects of prudential supervision, a degree of confusion appears to prevail regarding the classification of regulatory standards as prudential or otherwise. Thus, many commentators classify the provisions of the Second Banking Directive by virtue of which certain matters are specifically reserved for the authorities of the host Member State, as 'exceptions' to the principle of home-country control.[115] These so-called 'exceptions' include, beyond the supervision of liquidity, which is clearly a prudential matter,[116] the implementation of monetary policy,[117] statistical return requirements[118] and rules adopted in the interest of the general good.[119] It is very questionable whether such matters are

113. In certain ways, they also form a continuum with monetary policy. It has been shown already that this is the case with the lender-of-last-resort function. Similarly, minimum reserve requirements are an instrument of monetary policy, but they also have an impact on the liquidity of banks and thus on their prudential situation. Cf. Art. 19 of the Statute of the ESCB, conferring on the ECB the power to impose minimum reserve requirements.
114. See Second Banking Directive, Preamble, fourth recital; and Investment Services Directive, Preamble, third recital.
115. Cf. Second Banking Directive, Art. 13 (1).
116. It should be noted that the reason for maintaining host-country regulatory powers in matters of liquidity is that this aspect of prudential supervision is closely linked to the conduct of monetary policy. With the introduction of a single currency and a common monetary policy in the third stage of EMU, the need for special treatment will vanish.
117. Second Banking Directive, Art. 14 (2).
118. Ibid., Art. 21 (1).
119. Ibid., Art. 21 (5). See the discussion of the general good concept in M. Andenas 'The Interplay of the Commission and the ECJ in Giving Effect to the Right to Provide Financial Services' in P.P. Craig and C. Harlow *Lawmaking in the European Union* (1997).

indeed of prudential nature, which in the absence of express reservation for the host Member State would be the responsibility of the home country.[120]

It is true that the directives appear in certain cases to treat all regulatory measures as essentially prudential. For instance, the Investment Services Directive assumes in its Preamble an intrinsic link of rules adopted in the interest of the general good with the objective of systemic stability – a fundamental prudential concern – stating that

. . . the stability and sound operation of the financial system and the protection of investors presuppose that a host Member State has the right and responsibility both to prevent and to penalise any action within its territory by investment firms contrary to the rules of conduct and other legal or regulatory provisions it has adopted in the interest of the general good and to take action in emergencies.[121]

On the other hand, in its operative provisions, the same directive draws a sharp distinction between the prudential supervision of non-bank financial institutions, which is a matter for home-country control,[122] and conduct-of-business rules, which are applied by a Member State to all firms operating in its markets, including incoming institutions authorised and supervised by another Member State.[123] Although the classification of particular matters under each of the two general categories may display a lack of conceptual coherence under the influence of political compromises, it is significant that the Investment Services Directive entrenches a clear distinction between them as a matter of secondary Community law.

It should, indeed, be recognised that the various rules of market organisation and conduct-of-business rules are concerned primarily with the fairness of individual transactions and the orderly conduct of financial markets. But neither fall within the concept of prudential supervision nor concern the stability of the financial system as a whole and are, arguably, outside the field of competence of the ESCB. On the other hand, questions concerning deposit insurance, the operation of payment systems and lending

---

120. Indeed, even if they were not expressly reserved for the host Member State, they might still be within its competence, since the principle of home-country control should apply only to the prudential supervision of credit institutions and investment firms. See ibid., Art. 13 (1); and Investment Services Directive, Preamble, second and third recitals, as opposed to thirty-third and thirty-ninth recitals. In the earlier recitals of the Investment Services Directive's Preamble the mutual recognition of authorisation is linked to the mutual recognition of prudential supervision systems. This, however, does not seem to affect the operation of host-Member-State laws and regulations adopted for the protection of the general good or for purposes of market organisation. Such regulations appear, accordingly, to consist in independent systems of rules, outside the scope of prudential supervision.
121. Investment Services Directive, Preamble, forty-first recital.
122. Ibid., Art. 10.
123. Ibid., Art. 11.

of last resort can have major implications for the stability of the financial system. This might justify a degree of involvement of the ESCB in support of the policies of the competent national authorities in these areas or in an advisory capacity.[124] Furthermore, in the case of the lender-of-last-resort function, the responsibility will invariably belong to the national central bank of each Member State, subject possibly to the consent of the government in the case of individual rescue operations.

In the operation of payment systems, the ESCB does not need to rely on the ambiguous and limiting provisions concerning its supervisory competency. The Maastricht Treaty contains special provisions, giving it jurisdiction in this field. Likewise, its involvement in lending-of-last-resort activities does not depend primarily on the question concerning regulatory competence. It depends on the ability of the ECB and the national central banks to apply their financial resources for this purpose. It should however be asked whether the relevant operations are conducted under the authority and on account of the ESCB or by the individual national central banks as domestic institutions.

As might be expected, the Maastricht Treaty does not recognise explicitly the ESCB's role as lender of last resort, since this could create moral hazard. However, it gives to the ECB and the national central banks the power to conduct credit operations with credit institutions and other market participants as a means of furthering the ESCB's objectives.[125] The ECB is required to establish general principles for the credit operations conducted by itself or by the national central banks.[126] Although such operations will in most cases constitute an instrument for achieving the ESCB's primary objective of price stability, they can also be relied upon for the purpose of supplying liquidity to the banking system and for the conduct of rescue operations. However, a major constraint on the use of the instrument is that any lending must be based on adequate collateral. A strict insistence on high-quality collateral would prevent in many cases the exercise of the lender-of-last-resort function. Banks with a sufficient amount of high-quality, liquid collateral could sell it in the market and would not seek liquidity support from the central bank.[127] A relaxation of the rules of eligibility for paper

---

124. Under EC Treaty, Art. 105 (4) or (5); and Statute of the ESCB, Arts 3.3, 4 or 25.1.
125. Statute of the ESCB, Art. 18.1, second indent.
126. Ibid., Art. 18.2.
127. Schoenmaker, 'Banking Supervision . . .', loc. cit., n.61, p.429. In the opinion of the same author, ibid., pp.431–5, if the ECB were to devise rules or guidelines for emergency assistance, these might include: collateral requirements for lending-of-last-resort operations and specification of eligible types of collateral, subject to overriding provisions for cases where the provision of liquidity appears necessary despite the absence of eligible collateral; clear allocation of responsibilities for the decision to provide or withhold support to each institution, possibly on the basis of home central bank responsibility; and methods for the co-ordination of the decisions and for taking into account the broader, supra-national implications of action or inaction. As the

used as collateral, on the other hand, beyond a certain point would constitute a breach of the EC Treaty by the ECB.

The greatest contribution of the ESCB in terms of ensuring financial stability in the single market could concern the establishment and operation of efficient, but safe payment and settlement systems. Indeed, the build-up of settlement and counterparty risks in large-value payment and securities settlement systems can constitute a major transmission mechanism for the spreading of bank failures, raising very important systemic concerns.

The Maastricht Treaty includes the promotion of the smooth operation of payment systems within the ESCB's (and, during the second stage, of the EMI's) basic tasks.[128] It also authorises the ECB and the national central banks to provide facilities, and the ECB to issue regulations, for the purpose of ensuring efficient and sound clearing and payment systems, both within the Community and with third countries.[129] It is questionable whether this means that the ESCB can manage the payment systems directly, although in most Member States these are run by the national central banks in their capacity as national authorities.

During the second stage of EMU, the EMI is given responsibility for promoting the efficiency of cross-border payments, in preparation for the third stage,[130] and for overseeing the functioning of the ECU clearing

---

(continued)

      national central banks may be overzealous in assisting their domestic banking system, even when there is no direct systemic impact, Schoenmaker discusses the possibility of giving a power of veto to the ECB, although he accepts that, to the extent that the potential costs of the operations are borne by the lending national central bank only, a degree of rivalry between the national central banks is acceptable. However, the rescue of clearly insolvent banks would constitute a competitive distortion and should not be permitted.

128. EC Treaty, Art. 105 (2), fourth indent; and Statute of the ESCB, Art. 3.1, third indent.

129. Statute of the ESCB, Art. 22.

130. EC Treaty, Art. 109f (3), fourth indent; and Statute of the EMI, Art. 4.2, fourth indent.

      Although the EC Treaty does not distinguish between large-value and retail payments, the emphasis has been on large-value payments, which raise the main systemic concerns. Less attention has been devoted to retail payments and securities settlement systems. Analysis of the move to a single currency in connection to payment systems began under the aegis of the Committee of Governors in 1992 and was continued by the EMI, where a Working Group on EU Payment Systems, operating under the aegis of the EMI Council is responsible for co-ordinating central banks' initiatives in this area. See EMI, 'Annual Report 1994', loc. cit., n.47, p.70.

      Work is in progress with regard to establishing a large-value payment system for cross-border transactions in the area of the single currency. While today payment relations between EU countries rely on correspondent relationships between banks, it is planned that large-value payments within the EMU area should be effected through an integrated central-bank operated real-time gross payment system, which could ensure security, speed and efficiency. The EMI and the central banks of the Member States have adopted a strategy based on minimum harmonisation of national systems and a common system.[131] Finally, there is co-operation between the national central banks in this field within the EMI framework,[132] mainly concerning: (i) the co-operative oversight of payment systems; and (ii) the definition of minimum common features in domestic payment systems.[133]

6. CONSTITUTIONAL CONCERNS

6.1 Subsidiarity

Prudential supervision is evidently an area where the Community does not have exclusive competence and where, accordingly, it must respect the principle of subsidiarity.[134] The principle is enshrined in the Maastricht

(continued)

infrastructure that would allow them to implement new payment arrangements for the third stage, the TARGET system, based on the principles of efficiency, market-orientation and decentralisation. While transactions related to monetary policy will have to be processed through TARGET, the execution of other payments through the proposed system will not be compulsory, and alternative large-value payment systems may remain in operation, provided that they meet equivalent safety standards. Other systems will also be used for retail payments. To achieve decentralisation, infrastructures and payment systems will be maintained at the level of national central banks, rather than ECB level. See EMI, Working Group on Payment Systems, 'The EMI's Intentions with Regard to Cross-border Payments in Stage Three' (Nov. 1994); 'The TARGET System (Trans-European Automated Real-time Gross settlement Express Transfer System; A Payment System Arrangement for Stage Three of EMU)' (May 1995); and 'Annual Report 1995', loc. cit., n.98, pp.61-3.

131. EC Treaty, Art. 109f (2), third indent; and Statute of the EMI, Art. 4.1, sixth indent. The EMI oversees the operation of the private ECU Clearing and Settlement System, which was set up in Feb. 1986 and is fully operational since April 1987, seeking to ensure that the ECU Banking Association, which manages the System, takes action to reduce substantially the level of systemic risks involved, consistently with risk-reduction policies pursued by the national central banks with regard to their domestic payments systems. See EMI, 'Annual Report 1994', loc. cit., n.47, pp.84-6; and 'Annual Report 1995', loc. cit., n.98, p.73.

132. See EC Treaty, Art. 109f (2), first indent; and Statute of the EMI, Art. 4.1, first indent.

133. See EMI, 'Annual Report 1994', loc. cit., n.47, pp.87-90; and 'Annual Report 1995', loc. cit., n.98, pp.70-72.

134. On the concept of subsidiarity, see European Institute of Public Administration, *Subsidiarity: The Challenge of Change* (1991), reproducing the proceedings of the Jacques Delors Colloquim organised by the Institute and held in Maastricht, 21-22 March 1991; N. Emiliou, 'Subsidiarity: An Effective Barrier Against the "Enterprises of Ambition"?' (1992) 17 *ELR* 383; and D. Z. Cass, 'The Word That Saves Maastricht? The Principle of Subsidiarity and the Division of Powers within the European Community' (1992) 29 *C.M.L. Rev.* 1107, who points to the close relationship of the principle with federalist constitutional ideas and notes, at p.1108, that the principle, rather than contributing to the decentralisation of power, may in fact 'lead to a transfer

Treaty,[135] which provides that:

In areas which do not fall within its exclusive competence, the Community shall take action, in accordance with the principle of subsididiarity, only if and in so far as the objectives of the proposed action cannot be sufficiently achieved by the Member States and can therefore, by reason of the scale or effects of the proposed action, be better achieved by the Community.

This provision raises significant problems of interpretation. It appears to introduce two different, and potentially conflicting, tests: a strict one, based on the absolute necessity of the Community action for the sufficient performance of the relevant task; and a less demanding one, based on the added value of that action. What is clear, however, is that an action should not be taken at Community level if an equivalent result can be achieved by the Member States acting individually.[136]

(continued)

of power towards the Community, especially in view of there being a "centralising" and "decentralising" approach to its interpretation'. For a hostile interpretation of the principle, which is said to be totally alien to the tradition of Community law as it evolved up to the Maastricht Treaty and incompatible with the process of gradual and purpose-oriented concentration of power to the Community institutions within the field of their attributed powers, which is inherent in the project of European integration, see A.G. Toth, 'The Principle of Subsidiarity in the Maastricht Treaty' (1992) 29 *C.M.L. Rev.* 1079.

135. EC Treaty, Art. 3a, second paragraph, inserted by Art. G (5) of the Maastricht Treaty.
136. See Conclusions of the Edinburgh meeting of the European Council, 11–12 Dec. 1992, general part, Annex 1: 'Overall approach to the application by the Council of the subsidiarity principle and Article 3b of the Treaty on European Union', where it is maintained, at para. 2 (ii)–(iii), that the principle permits action by the Community only 'where an objective can better be attained at the level of the Community than at the level of the individual Member States' (value-added test) and only through means proportional to the objective pursued.

R. Dehousse, *Does Subsidiarity Really Matter?*, EUI Working Paper, Law No. 92/32, European University Institute (Jan. 1993), claims that subsidiarity is an overrated concept, because the question is not one of allocating spheres of competence among different levels of government but of managing interdependence among overlapping areas of governmental action. In the opinion of Dehousse, even if the political value of the principle as a guideline in favour of decentralisation is accepted, its direct utility as legal instrument is limited, especially because of the ambiguous drafting of the Treaty provision.

In contrast, J. P. González, 'The Principle of Subsidiarity (A Guide for Lawyers with a Particular Community Orientation)' (1995) 20 *ELR* 355, thinks that, while the principle is unsuitable for judicial review, due to its political content, it can play a significant role as a guiding principle for the relationships between the Community institutions and the Member States, providing for a division of powers consistent with a modern federal system; the principle sets the ground for a pre-federal pattern of organisation of these relationships, and as such is a factor conducive to integration.

Henning Christophersen, the former Vice-President of the Commission, has identified two sorts of circumstances in which the Community is better placed to act than the Member States. Firstly, where there are cross-border spillover effects giving rise to so-called externalities. Secondly, where a policy function is characterised by economies of scale, allowing for efficiency gains when it is performed at a higher level of government.[137]

As it is a decentralist paradigm, subsidiarity requires both these circumstances to respect a degree of *proportionality*: it is only when independent national measures lead to significant externalities or fail to harvest considerable efficiency gains that competences should be transferred to the Community level.[138]

The words 'independent national measures' are significant in the present context: the mere decentralisation of executive functions is not subsidiarity. Accordingly, the delegation by the ECB of particular actions to the national central banks, operating within the structure of the ESCB,[139] which exists at Community level, would not necessarily satisfy the requirements of subsidiarity where this dictates action at national level, that is, national choice of the institutional means and substantive content of the action.[140]

Any decision of the Council allocating specific tasks in the area of prudential supervision to the ECB,[141] aside of the procedural difficulties, could only be taken in the light of the principle of subsidiarity. The Council must be satisfied that the attribution of tasks to the ECB would present manifest advantages in comparison with action at the national level. This might be, for instance, the case if the emergence of large pan-European banking groups renders supervision by the authorities of the home countries ineffective. In practice, it is doubtful whether considerations of subsidiarity could ever present an obstacle if the Council were willing to transfer responsibility to the ECB. This would require unanimity: in practical terms the unanimous consent of all Member States would render the question of subsidiarity purely academic. On the other hand, such considerations could be precisely a factor preventing unanimous agreement. Assuming that the Council ever reaches a decision to confer responsibility, the principle of

137. 'Subsidiarity and Economic Monetary Union', in European Institute of Public Administration, op. cit., n.134, p.67.
138. Ibid. (emphasis in the original).
139. In accordance with the requirement of decentralisation of the ESCB's operations in the Statute of the ESCB, Arts 9.2 and 12.1, final paragraph.
140. Cf. Louis *et al.*, op. cit., n.49, pp.67–8, who find little difference between subsidiarity and the requirement of decentralisation. See also Padoa-Schioppa, *The Road to Monetary Union . . .* , op. cit., n.37, p.232, who notes that decentralisation within the ESCB has sometimes been confused with the retention of strong national jurisdiction in supervision and that it may not always be clear whether, in carrying out supervisory responsibilities, a national central bank is acting under national powers or as part of the ESCB.
141. EC Treaty, Art. 105 (6); and Statute of the ESCB, Art. 25.2.

subsidiarity may also be relevant in the exercise by the ECB of the transferred tasks. Conceivably, it can even play a role in determining the limits of the contribution that the ECB can already make to the conduct of the supervisory policies directly under the Maastricht Treaty.[142]

6.2 Central bank independence

The potential delegation to the ESCB of decision-making powers relating to the prudential supervision of financial institutions also raises significant questions of public control and accountability. This is a consequence of the ESCB's constitutionally guaranteed position of organic and functional independence.[143] The principle of central bank independence is expressly enshrined in the Maastricht Treaty, which provides that:

When exercising the powers and carrying out the tasks and duties conferred upon them by this Treaty and the Statute of the ESCB, neither the ECB, nor a national central bank, nor any member of their decision-making bodies shall seek or take instructions from Community institutions or bodies, from any government of a Member State or from any other body. The Community institutions and bodies and the governments of the Member States undertake to respect this principle and not to seek to influence the members of the decision-making bodies of the ECB or of the national central banks in the performance of their tasks.[144]

This provision requires total functional autonomy for the ESCB and forbids outside interventions in its decision-making processes.

Other safeguards seek to ensure the personal and professional independence of the members of the ECB's governing bodies. Overall, the relevant provisions seek to guarantee that only professionally suitable persons, enjoying the trust of all national governments, are appointed as members of the Executive Board,[145] to protect these persons from financial and other

---

142. EC Treaty, Art. 105 (5); and Statute of the ESCB, Art. 3.3.
143. See R. M. Lastra, 'The Independence of the European System of Central Banks' (1992) *Harv. Int'l L. J.* 475; and idem, ch.15 of this volume.
144. EC Treaty, Art. 107; and Statute of the ESCB, Art. 7.
145. The members of the Executive Board must be appointed among persons of recognised standing and professional experience in monetary or banking matters by common accord of the governments of the Member States at the highest level (Heads of State or Government), on a recommendation from the Council and after consultation with the European Parliament and the Governing Council of the ESCB; EC Treaty, Art. 109a (2) (b); and Statute of the ESCB, Art. 11.2.

pressures relating to their terms of employment,[146] to prevent conflicts of interest, and to ensure that the hope of reappointment will not be a factor which might lead them to accommodate political pressures in their decision-making.[147]

The independence of the ESCB is not confined to the ECB, but extends to the national central banks. During the second stage of EMU, and before the establishment of the ESCB, the Member States are required to take steps to achieve the independence of their central banks and the compatibility of their legislation to the relevant provisions of the Treaty and the Statute of the ESCB.[148]

As a result of these provisions, central banking in the EMU is removed from the ordinary mechanisms of executive and parliamentary control. The Treaty provides that the president of the Ecofin Council and a member of the Commission will have the right participate, without vote, in meetings of the ECB's Governing Council. Conversely, it requires the invitation of the President of the ECB to Ecofin meetings whenever matters relating to the ESCB's field of competence are discussed.[149] These institutional contacts are intended to provide opportunities for policy-making co-ordination through discussion between the Community institutions and the ESCB. However, the final responsibility for monetary decision-making is placed firmly in the hands of the ECB. It will have exclusive competence for the formulation and implementation of the monetary policy of the Community, without need for participation or consent by any other body.[150] Moreover, the resources (capital and foreign-reserve assets) which may be required for the effective conduct of monetary operations will be made available to the ECB. This will

---

146. The terms and conditions of employment of members of the Executive Board, including their salaries, pensions and other benefits, shall be determined by the other members of the Governing Council, that is, the Governors of the national central banks; Statute of the ESCB, Art. 11.3. Their removal from their position shall only be possible following a decision of the European Court of Justice, if they no longer fulfil the conditions required for the performance of their duties or if they have been guilty of serious misconduct; ibid., Art. 11.4.

147. Their appointment may only be for a non-renewable, eight-year term, during which they shall be required to perform their duties on a full-time basis, without being permitted to engage in any other occupation; EC Treaty, Art. 109a (2) (b); and Statute of the ESCB, Art. 11.1–2.

148. EC Treaty, Art. 108 and 109e (5); and Statute of the ESCB, Art. 14.1.
    The Governors of the national central banks must be appointed for a term of office which may not be less than five years; they may be relieved from their duties only on the same grounds as the members of the Executive Council, and the decision to remove them is subject to referral to the ECJ; Statute of the ESCB, Art. 14.2.

149. EC Treaty, Art. 109b (1).

150. EC Treaty, Art. 105 (2); and Statute of the ESCB, Arts 3.1 and 12.1.

ensure the ESCB's financial independence from the political authorities of the Community and the Member States.[151]

The elimination of political controls and influences in this area is justified on the basis that it ensures an institutional environment conducive to the attainment of the ESCB's primary objective of price stability.[152] However, the extent to which the purely instrumental consideration that an independent central bank may be more likely to achieve price stability can in itself justify the removal of monetary policy from the political arena.

Three other factors play an indispensable part in legitimising the transferral of full decision-making power in the monetary field to a politically unaccountable body. Firstly, the belief that its objective, price stability, is a fundamental economic good, which cannot be traded off against other objectives and whose superior value justifies its constitutional entrenchment and removal from the political process.[153] Secondly, the strict confinement of its mandate to the implementation of this peculiar objective, in so far as other areas of public policy should not unnecessarily be covered by the same immunity from the political process.[154] Thirdly, a sufficiently precise and transparent formulation of its mandate, providing clear legal

---

151. Statute of the ESCB, Arts 28–30.
152. EC Treaty, Art. 105 (1); and Statute of the ESCB, Art. 2.
153. It is only because price stability appears to be a fundamental longer-term precondition of any successful economic policy that its constitutional entrenchment is justified. If it were merely one of several mutually incompatible short-term economic objectives, which could be traded off for one another, the relevant decisions would clearly belong to the political arena. In signing the Maastricht Treaty, the Member States decided to vest full jurisdiction in monetary matters to the ESCB because they were convinced that this is not the case. For this reason, although it is provided that 'the ESCB shall support the general economic policies in the Community', such support is made subject to the objective of price stability; EC Treaty, Art. 105 (1).
154. Cf. *Brunner v The European Union Treaty*, Cases 2 BvR 2134/92 and 2159/92, Bundesverfassungsgericht, Judgment of 12 Oct. 1993, BVerGE 89, 155 (1993), English translation published in [1994] 1 *CMLR* 57, p.104:

    'Placing most of the tasks of monetary policy on an autonomous basis in the hands of an independent central bank releases the exercise of sovereign powers of the state from direct national or supra-national control in order to withdraw monetary matters from the reach of interest groups and holders of political office concerned about re-election.

    This restriction of the democratic legitimation which proceeds from the voters in the Member States affects the principle of democracy, but, as a modification of that principle provided for in Article 88, second sentence, of the [German Basic Law], is compatible with Article 79 (3) [which, in conjunction with Article 20 (1)–(2) of the Basic Law, declares unassailable the democratic principle, protecting it against constitutional amendments]. The supplementation of Article 88 undertaken in view of the European Union allows a transfer of powers of the Bundesbank to a European central bank if to do so accords with "the strict criteria of the Maastricht Treaty and the Statute of the European System of Central Banks regarding the independence of

---

criteria for the exercise of its discretion and a basis for the *ex post* evaluation of its conduct.[155]

It has been observed that price stability is not a precise rule, but only a principle – and a vague principle, for that matter, vesting on the ESCB a considerable margin of discretion, not only in deciding the means for its implementation, but also in interpreting its meaning.[156] None the less, while a precise definition of price stability may be lacking, changes in the rate of

(continued)

> the Central Bank and the priority of maintaining the value of the currency''. The will of the legislature in amending the [Basic Law], therefore, is clearly aimed at creating a constitutional basis for the monetary union provided for in the [Maastricht Treaty], but restricting the creation of the powers and institutions which are connected therewith and given independence in the manner explained to that case. This modification of the democratic principle for the purpose of protecting the confidence placed in the redemption value of a currency is acceptable because it takes account of the special characteristics (tested and proven – in scientific terms as well – in the German legal system) that an independent central bank is a better guarantee of the value of the currency, and thus of a generally sound economic basis for the state's budgetary policies and for private planning and transactions in the exercise of the rights of economic freedom, than state bodies, which as regards their opportunities and means for action are essentially dependent on the supply and value of the currency, and rely on the short-term consent of political forces. To that extent the placing of monetary policy on an independent footing within the sovereign jurisdiction of an independent European Central Bank (a jurisdiction not transferable to other political areas) satisfies the constitutional requirements under which a modification may be made to the principle of democracy.'

155. The EC Treaty envisages that, in the case of the ESCB, public accountability will be achieved through reporting commitments and official statements by the President and the other members of its Executive Board to the competent committees of the European Parliament; EC Treaty, Art. 109b (3); and Statute of the ESCB, Art. 15.

> The effectiveness of such mechanisms, however, depends primarily on the existence of objective criteria for assessing monetary performance. Assuming that discernible criteria do exist, the institutional prestige of the ESCB will depend primarily on the successful implementation of its mandate; without such criteria, however, moral pressure can play a very limited role in keeping the ESCB within its responsibilities.

> Nor can judicial review provide effective protection, where there are no clear standards of performance. The Statute of the ESCB, Art. 35 (1), provides that the acts and omissions of the ECB will be open to review or interpretation by the ECJ. It is doubtful, however, whether judicial review could be used to enforce the objective of price stability. See Terence Daintith, 'Between Domestic Democracy and an Alien Rule of Law? Some Thoughts on the ''Independence'' of the Bank of England', ch.17 of this volume, pp.367–70.

156. H. J. Hahn, 'The European Central Bank: Key to Monetary Union or Target?' (1991) *C.M.L. Rev.* 797–8, emphasises that the ESCB statute (which at the time of his comments existed still only in draft form)

> '. . . expressly and unequivocally commits the ESCB to maintain price stability as the primary objective of the System. However, in line with the legislative technique employed by national statutes equally devoted to the maintenance of a currency's value, the text adds that[,] without prejudice to the objective of price stability, the

inflation provide a readily observable indicator of monetary developments and a benchmark against which to evaluate the ESCB's performance.

The exceptional character, and conditional legitimacy, of the ESCB's regime of constitutionally guaranteed functional independence should be clearly recognised. The special considerations which apply to its monetary functions may not with equal force provide a justification for removing political controls in the area of banking and financial policy. However, the allocation to the ESCB of broad discretionary responsibilities in the field of prudential regulation could have precisely this effect, because its independence is not confined to monetary matters, but extends to all its activities under the Treaty.

Many commentators do not think that the ESCB's special status of independence presents an obstacle to the allocation of prudential responsibilities to it. In their opinion, banking supervision is a purely administrative matter, which (with the possible exception of rescue operations) does not justify political interventions, but only appropriate mechanisms of judicial review.[157]

The considerations providing the justification for central bank independence in the monetary field may not, with equal force, be applied to regulatory responsibilities of a prudential nature for three main

(continued)
System shall support the general economic policy of the Community. Thus monetary policy is not considered to be conducted in isolation from other aims of economic policy. Yet this also amounts to saying that the general economic policy of the EC may be supported by the ESCB only in as much as that support would not interfere with the pursuit of its primary objective, namely, the maintenance of price stability. The form of words used in the draft statute defines the objective of the ESCB even more precisely than the statute establishing the German Federal Bank (*Bundesbankgesetz*) as the latter, in its section 3, refers only to the target of safeguarding the currency and thus expresses in rather relative terms that safeguarding the currency consists in the obligation to maintain the domestic value [*ie*, not the external parity] of that currency.'

None the less, a degree of scepticism can be expressed as to the ability of the provision to provide unambiguous criteria for the ESCB's actions. As Harden, loc. cit., n.108, p.150, observes, price stability

'. . . is not a rule which tells the ECB what to do. It is a principle to guide it in deciding what to do. Furthermore, it is a vague principle. "Price stability" in not defined, either in quantitative or qualitative terms. It could mean zero inflation, though some economists have argued that a 1–2 per cent annual rate of price increases is appropriate to reflect secular improvements in the quality of goods and services. A low and non-accelerating rate of inflation might also be described as "price stability", especially if the costs of further reducing it are believed to outweigh the benefits. The ECB will thus have discretion in interpreting the meaning of price stability as well as in deciding how to achieve it.'

157. See Louis *et al.*, op. cit., n.49, pp.14 and 61.

reasons.[158] Firstly, there may be no reason to suppose that independence improves the quality of supervisory performance in the field of prudential tasks. One could even conjecture that the allocation of these tasks to an independent central bank with very close links with the banking and financial industry might facilitate the 'capture' of the regulatory process and the effective determination of supervisory policy by that industry's narrow interests. Secondly, policy trade-offs are of essence in the field of prudential supervision. As more rigorous controls on risk-taking increase the cost of financial intermediation, reduce market efficiency, impede innovation and stifle competition, the single-minded pursuance of prudential objectives cannot be the purpose of the regulatory system. Instead, by their very nature, these objectives must be constantly balanced against market efficiency and competition. However, drawing the balance between administrative intervention and market discipline is a matter, not simply of technical judgement, but of substantive political choice. Finally, the concepts of 'financial stability' and 'bank safety and soundness', which guide prudential supervision, are broad and imprecise. They do not provide operational criteria for administrative action, but require the application of discretion on an individual basis. Their operationalisation can, of course, take place through the development of general rules or prudential policies. This, however, is an essentially legislative function, and it must be asked why it should be better performed by exercise of the ECB's rule-making powers[159] than through the normal constitutional channels, which permit the appropriate representation of all affected interests.

Functional independence would not present a problem in cases involving the concrete application of Community legislation to individual institutions. This should, indeed, be considered to be a purely administrative matter, requiring detachment from political considerations and a quasi-judicial approach. Further than this, however, the delegation of decisive prudential responsibilities, especially of a rule-making nature, to an independent ESCB is more problematic.

Significantly, similar reservations may not apply to the allocation to the central banks of the Member States, in their capacity as national competent authorities, of regulatory responsibilities under their national laws. As such additional responsibilities at the national level would not be regarded as

---

158. Lastra, op. cit., n.51, pp.151–4, suggests that the independence of banking supervisors is justified as a natural extension of a central bank's independence in monetary matters. In her opinion, a sound banking system is a condition for maintaining price stability and this creates a need to distance banking policy from the political process, especially since politicians may be tempted to hijack the banking system in order to gain short-term advantage, thus undermining its soundness. This view may be questioned, for the reasons given in the text.
159. EC Treaty, Art. 108a (1); and Statute of the ESCB, Art. 34.1.

being part of the functions of the ESCB,[160] their performance may not be subject to the same requirements of functional independence.

7. CONCLUSION

Monetary Union introduces a set of institutional factors in the area of banking supervision. The analysis in this chapter shows that the concepts of banking supervision, central banking, monetary policy and payment systems – as used in the EC Treaty, directives and indeed economic and legal theory – are less than precise and with potential for overlap. The analysis also highlights some constitutional concerns going against a delegation of broad rule-making powers to the ESCB in the area of prudential banking supervision.

The case for a European financial market supervisor may not yet have been fully made out. That is not the subject of this chapter. But the regulatory pressures of the Internal Financial Market may be expected to promote a more effective coordination of prudential supervision, perhaps also moving supervision from a national up to a community level.

Member States, and their supervisors and central bankers, may be less inclined to acknowledge this. The existence of a well-funded, centrally placed institution with wide and somewhat unclear powers, may, over time, provide the answer. It may gradually take over the supervisory functions. It will be pure speculation to say anything about how far and how fast this process may be. In practical terms, it may be the only solution to the problems of the Internal Financial Market. It may also prove to be a pragmatic and flexible solution: perhaps the best possible solution.

160. Ibid., *in fine*.

Chapter Nineteen

BANKING SUPERVISION AND LENDER-OF-LAST-RESORT IN EMU

Dirk Schoenmaker *

Chapter Outline

1. Introduction

2. Need for Banking Supervision and Lender of Last Resort in EMU
   2.1 Depositor protection
   2.2 Systemic risk

3. Systems of Central Banks
   3.1 Federal Reserve System
   3.2 European System of Central Banks

4. Payment Systems in EMU

5. Lender of Last Resort in EMU
   5.1 Lender-of-last-resort support by national central banks
   5.2 Liquidity support by the European Central Bank

6. Banking Supervision in EMU

7. Conclusions

Annex: Supervisory Agencies in the EU Member States

European Economic and Monetary Union: The Institutional Framework (M. Andenas, L. Gormley, C. Hadjiemmanuil, I. Harden, eds.: 90-411-0687-1: © Kluwer Law International: pub. Kluwer Law International, 1997: printed in Great Britain)

1.   INTRODUCTION

Following closely the Bundesbank model, the provisions of the Maastricht Treaty governing the role of the European Central Bank grant the ECB independence for the execution of its monetary policy, but give it no formal supervisory powers (although, under Article 105 (6) of the EC Treaty, the ECB could be given such powers at a later point by a unanimous vote of the Council). While the prospective ECB will thus have full responsibility for a single monetary policy in Stage Three of Economic and Monetary Union, banking supervision will, almost certainly, continue to be the prerogative of the national authorities. With national supervision of banks, the ECB cannot be expected to have the information, nor the hands-on experience with banks, needed to be an effective lender of last resort. This chapter examines what role, if any, the ECB should have in banking supervision and lender-of-last-resort support.[1]

Defining the setting of EMU, Stage Three will start on 1 January 1999 at the latest according to the Maastricht Treaty. From the start of Stage Three, the exchange rates of the participating currencies would be replaced by irrevocably fixed conversion rates and the European System of Central Banks – the ECB and the national central banks – would begin to conduct monetary policy in the single currency, the Euro. Although the use of the Euro would be mandatory for monetary policy transactions from the start (during the so-called Stage 3A), the ESCB would only begin issuing Euro banknotes and coins three years later, prompting the start of Stage 3B. It is expected that transactions in the money, interbank and foreign exchange markets would be conducted in Euros, rather than in the national currencies, during Stage 3A. The establishment of an integrated money market in Euros is crucial to support a truly single monetary policy throughout EMU from the outset.

---

*   The author is grateful to Charles Goodhart and Peter Clarke for discussions on this topic. He would also like to thank members of the Centre for European Policy Studies Working Party on 'The Single Market in Banking: From 1992 to EMU' and participants at the King's College Workshop on 'Institutional Aspects of EMU' for useful comments. Any opinions expressed, as well as any errors, are those of the author.
1. See D. Folkerts-Landau and P. Garber, 'The ECB: A Bank or a Monetary Policy Rule?', in M. Canzoneri, V. Grilli and P. Masson (eds), *Establishing a Central Bank: Issues in Europe and Lessons from the US* (1992); A. Giovannini, *Central Banking in a Monetary Union: Reflections on the Proposed Statute of the European Central Bank*, Centre for Economic Policy Research Occasional Paper No. 9 (1992); and C. Monticelli and J. Vials, *European Monetary Policy in Stage Three: What are the Issues?*, Centre for Economic Policy Research Occasional Paper No. 12 (1993).

2.   NEED FOR BANKING SUPERVISION AND LENDER-OF-LAST-RESORT IN EMU

The rationale for banking regulation and supervision is twofold: it involves (i) depositor protection and (ii) the avoidance of systemic risk.

2.1   Depositor protection

Depositors are less informed than banks, and small depositors in particular are very often financially unsophisticated. As a response to this asymmetric information and lack of sophistication, banking regulation attempts to protect the banks' depositors. The recently adopted Deposit-Guarantee Directive[2] requires deposit insurance for all EU countries and introduces home-country deposit insurance. All depositors in the EU will be protected up to a minimum of 20,000 ECU, beyond which individual Member States can extend protection levels, if they so wish. Given the relatively low minimum level of protection, the primary purpose of this deposit-insurance directive is to protect small depositors and not to promote systemic stability.

Establishing the home-country principle for deposit insurance links it with the home-country regime for banking supervision embodied in the Second Banking Directive. Home countries responsible for exercising supervision will then make payments to all depositors who suffer losses as the result of the failure of a bank under their supervision. Home-country deposit insurance will thus provide a strong incentive for countries to maintain or improve the quality of their banking supervision.[3] In this way, the national authorities can continue to conduct banking supervision on a home-country basis and there seems to be no need for extra ECB involvement.

2.2   Systemic risk

Whether they supervise the commercial banks or not, central banks have a concern for the systemic stability of the financial system. Systemic issues arise when an incident at one financial institution (usually a bank) spreads to

---

2. Directive 94/19/EC of the European Parliament and of the Council of 30.5.94 on deposit-guarantee schemes.

3. See S. Key, *Deposit-Protection Schemes: Issues for an EC Directive*, Centre for European Policy Studies Research Report No. 11 (1992); M. Andenas 'Deposit Guarantee Schemes and Home Country Control' in R. Cranston *The Single Market and the Law of Banking* (1995), p. 105 and D. Schoenmaker, 'Internationalisation of Banking Supervision and Deposit Insurance' (1993) 8 *J.I.B.L.* 106.

other financial institutions and/or financial markets.[4] The nature of the financial system primarily determines the need for central bank intervention (as lender of last resort) to prevent systemic risk. With the establishment of Stage Three of EMU, there will be a single money market and the national payment systems will be integrated. Banking problems in one country are therefore likely to have a stronger cross-border impact than at present (*ie*, the risk of contagion may be less contained within domestic markets and institutions). One strategy to minimise the need for lender-of-last-resort intervention at the EU level is to promote financial stability by developing safe payment systems (*eg*, based on real-time gross settlement).

Even so, the move towards Stage Three of EMU could enhance financial fragility in certain respects. First, such a move would remove intra-European foreign-exchange activities. This would affect both the profitability of wholesale banks (which are active in the forex markets) and that of retail banks (which do forex transactions with their clients). Second, retail banking may experience some fragility in the transition period. Although wholesale banking is already fully integrated in Europe, most domestic retail banking markets are still dominated by (a few) domestic institutions. Competition in the retail area from banks from other EU Member States has not been significant so far. But with the introduction of a single currency in Stage 3B of EMU, differences between domestic banks and those originating from other EU countries may become less important in the eyes of depositors. EU banks can thus be expected to compete more effectively in each other's markets. This process of increased competition will eat into local oligopolies, and hence create more fragility in the short run. But retail banking may become more stable in the long run, if a few large European banking groups survive. Furthermore, there will be more scope for diversification of the loan book and banks may thus be less prone to idiosyncratic shocks. There is here an interesting parallel with the lifting of restrictions on interstate branching long imposed in the USA. The spread of nationwide branch banking is widely believed to foster the long-run stability of the US banking system.[5]

---

4. J. Paroush, 'The Domino Effect and the Supervision of the Banking System' (1988) 43 *Journal of Finance* 1207.
5. C. Calomiris and E. White, 'The Origins of Federal Deposit Insurance', in C. Goldin and G. Libecap (eds), *The Regulated Economy* (1994). Banks that confine their business activities to one state typically experience more difficulties than banks with a nationwide presence in the USA. An example of the 1980s is the banking sector in Texas. Texas banks were heavily exposed to the oil industry and ran into difficulties when oil prices dropped. Similarly, banks in the New England area faced a crisis when property prices collapsed in New England in the early 1990s. Recent European examples can be found in Scandinavia. See C. Goodhart and D. Schoenmaker, 'Should the Functions of Monetary Policy and Banking Supervision be Separated?' (1995) 47 *Oxford Economic Papers* 539, for a cross-country survey of bank failures.

The ECB will presumably seek to encourage liquid and well-developed trans-European markets. This is likely to provide a more competitive milieu for banks than some of the present domestic money markets. Furthermore, the range of counterparties will be far wider in an integrated European money market. Interbank linkages will then be increasingly on a European basis, rather than a domestic basis. Can the ECB still rely on the national central banks to prevent systemic risk within a developing *European* monetary system? Is such a strategy viable, or might the ECB end up as lender of last resort, especially if there were to be a few large bank failures?

Summing up, banking supervision for deposit protection reasons can continue to be done at the national level. However, some co-ordination or centralisation of central bank operations and banking supervision for systemic stability may be needed under EMU. Before exploring the appropriate division of responsibilities in this field between the ECB and the national central banks, I will briefly examine the arrangements in the USA.

3. SYSTEMS OF CENTRAL BANKS

3.1 Federal Reserve System

The Federal Reserve Board has authority over the regional Federal Reserve Banks regarding banking supervision, payment systems and the use of the discount window.[6] Using this authority, the Board has, for example, issued rules specifying under what conditions regional Federal Reserve Banks can grant discount-window loans (*ie*, Regulation A). But the operational staff and the expertise are in the regional Federal Reserve Banks: they grant discount-window loans on their own books. In practice, there is consultation with the Board for any large discount-window loan. Similarly, the Board is responsible for strategic policy-making in the area of banking supervision, and the regional Federal Reserve Banks implement the policy.[7] Staff of the regional Federal Reserve Banks are, however, heavily involved in the policy-making process both at the domestic and at the international level (*eg*, the Fed sends usually a representative from the Board and one from the Federal

6. See Board of Governors of the Federal Reserve System, *The Federal Reserve System: Purposes and Functions* (8th edn, 1994), for an overview of the Federal Reserve System.
7. It should be noted that Federal Reserve Board shares this responsibility for policy-making with other agencies, *eg*, the Federal Deposit Insurance Corporation (FDIC), the Office of the Comptroller of the Currency (OCC) and the Office of Thrift Supervision (OTS). The Federal Financial Institutions Examination Council was established in 1979 as a formal interagency body to prescribe uniform standards and report forms for the federal examination of financial institutions.

Reserve Bank of New York to the Basle Committee on Banking Supervision), because the regional Federal Reserve Banks have hands-on experience of supervising.

The 12 regional Federal Reserve Banks operate together the Fedwire funds transfer system. Commercial banks in the USA have accounts at regional Federal Reserve Banks, but funds move instantly from one bank to another, even when the accounts are held at different district Federal Reserve Banks. A technical arrangement offsets imbalances between regional Federal Reserve Banks.[8] Fedwire was, and still is, instrumental in the creation of an integrated US money market, the so-called fed-funds market. Fedwire thus contributes to an efficient redistribution of reserves within the USA.

3.2 European System of Central Banks

The European System of Central Banks will consist of the national central banks and the ECB at the centre. The main difference with the Federal Reserve System is that the Fed Board has policy-making power in the field of banking supervision and financial stability, while the ESCB may only 'contribute to the smooth conduct of policies pursued by the competent authorities relating to the prudential supervision of credit institutions and the stability of the financial system' according to Article 105 (5) of the EC Treaty. Article 105 (6) specifies that unanimity in the Council (and a majority in the European Parliament as well) is needed before any supervisory powers can be transferred to the ECB. This suggests that there will be no centralisation of prudential systems and responsibilities in Frankfurt. But some harmonisation has already been achieved through Brussels (in the form of directives, notably the Second Banking Directive,[9] formulating minimum regulatory standards) and Basle (since eight of the 15 EU Member States are represented on the Basle Committee on Banking Supervision), and further harmonisation, if needed, may be possible via these channels.

8. There is no central Federal Reserve Bank like the prospective European Central Bank, where the district Federal Reserve Banks can keep funds for interdistrict settlement. Treasury securities in an Interdistrict Settlement Fund are transferred to offset payment flow imbalances on Fedwire between regional Federal Reserve Banks. It should be noted that such an arrangement is only an internal bookkeeping issue for the Federal Reserve and has no risk implications for the participants. See P. Kenen, *EMU after Maastricht*, Group of Thirty Occasional Paper (1992).
9. Second Council Directive 89/646/EEC of 15.12.89 on the co-ordination of laws, regulations and administrative provisions relating to the taking up and pursuit of the business of credit institutions and amending Directive 77/780/EEC.

4.   PAYMENT SYSTEMS IN EMU

Notwithstanding its lack of supervisory powers, the ECB 'may make regulations to ensure efficient and sound clearing and payment systems within the Community and with other countries' according to Article 22 of the Statute of the ESCB. Moreover, Article 3.1 stipulates that one of the basic tasks of the ESCB is 'to promote the smooth operation of payment systems'. From the start of Stage Three of EMU, large-value payment systems of the participating Member States must be linked to support an integrated money market. There may be difficulties in linking net settlement systems. The Lamfalussy standards state that netting schemes should have a sound legal basis, proper risk-management procedures and arrangements to ensure settlement in case of a settlement failure.[10] The legal basis for an EMU-wide multilateral netting scheme is doubtful, because of the incompatibility of domestic insolvency laws.[11] To implement risk-control measures and loss-sharing agreements, a certain degree of cohesion and mutual trust is needed among the participating banks.[12] The granting of bilateral receiver caps, an important element of risk-management in netting schemes, may be more difficult as banks may not have sufficient information on the creditworthiness of banks located in other EU countries. Accordingly, banks may initially be reluctant to enter into loss-sharing agreements with banks located in other EU countries.

There may be a case for a small and more cohesive group of European banks to run an EMU-wide netting scheme, such as the private ECU Clearing and Settlement System. But the ECB should promote an EMU-wide payment system with a large membership for a variety of reasons. First, a large number of member banks is crucial to form an effective vehicle for cross-border transfers. Otherwise, a payment can need up to four banks before it is executed: a non-member bank has to use a domestic member bank to make a transfer to a foreign member bank, and when the beneficiary does not hold an account at the foreign member bank, this bank has to transfer the payment to the beneficiary's bank. In addition, a large membership is needed if the ESCB wishes to conduct its open-market operations with a wide, rather than narrow, range of counterparties. Furthermore, to create a deep Euro interbank market, it is useful to have an EMU-wide payment

---

10.   BIS, 'Report of the Committee on Interbank Netting Schemes of the Central Banks of the Group of Ten Countries' (1990).

11.   Netting is a legally complex issue under the national laws of most EU Member States. For an EMU-wide net settlement system to be safe, the law of each country involved has to be adequate. That is far from clear at present; see Bank of England, 'The UK Approach to Controlling Risk in Large-Value Payment Systems' (1993) 33 *B.E.Q.B.* 530.

12.   D. Folkerts-Landau, P. Garber and D. Schoenmaker, *The Impact of Payment System Reform on Financial Markets*, Group of Thirty Occasional Paper (1996).

system for the settlement of Euro-funds in which many banks can participate. But a (small) private netting scheme could run parallel with a larger system sponsored by the ECB.

The alternative is to link real-time gross settlement systems. Provided that real-time gross settlement works on collateral or reserves,[13] there will be no settlement risk for the participating banks and central banks. Banks can continue to keep accounts at their respective national central banks. The national central banks can maintain correspondent balances with each other or establish settlement accounts at the ECB to settle cross-border payment flows.[14] The main problem which may occur in such a real-time gross settlement environment is gridlock caused by insufficient settlement funds. A payment delay at one bank may lead to further payment delays at other banks as they do not receive incoming funds from the former, and may eventually lead to a gridlock situation, by which I mean a standstill of the payment system as no funds are moving.

To limit the likelihood of gridlock, it is necessary, and would be sufficient, for the ECB in conjunction with the national central banks to control the aggregate level of collateral or reserves. The introduction of real-time gross settlement based on collateralised overdrafts will not only demand active liquidity management by banks, but may also require a more frequent injection of reserves by the national central banks during the day to avoid a building-up of intraday liquidity shortfalls. At the moment, central banks generally aim to eliminate liquidity shortages in the course of the day to enable banks to square their end-of-day position or to meet reserve requirements imposed on them. An aggregate liquidity shortage in the money market during the day could cause settlement delays in real-time gross settlement systems.

Moreover, a well-functioning interbank market is needed to redistribute settlement funds from surplus banks to deficit banks. Only when a bank's solvency is put in doubt may it lose its access to the interbank market. But then it becomes a wider problem, not only restricted to the payment system. Potential problems in the interbank market are discussed in the next section on lender of last resort. The linking of real-time gross settlement systems without uncovered credit extensions will thus minimise the need for lender-of-last-resort intervention for payment-system reasons by the ECB and the national central banks.

---

13. This is called the cover principle. A bank needs either to have reserves in its account or to pledge collateral to cover an overdraft before it can make a payment. Payments are thus always prefunded (*ie*, covered) by reserves and/or collateral.
14. D. Schoenmaker, *Externalities in Payment Systems: Issues for Europe*, Centre for European Policy Studies Research Report No. 15 (1994).

In this context, the European Monetary Institute published a blueprint for the new payment system for the single currency in May 1995.[15] The new system, called TARGET, will build upon national real-time gross settlement systems and provide an interlinking mechanism. Under TARGET, bilateral links between the national central banks will be established. Each prospective participating country thus needs to have a real-time gross settlement system before it can join EMU. Banks can continue to keep their settlement accounts at the national central banks, and the role of the ECB will be limited.

The EMI proposes minimum harmonisation for payment-system features in the early stages. Aspects which affect the implementation of a single monetary policy, such as the provision of liquidity, will be harmonised, but there will be, for example, no harmonisation of queuing procedures in the individual country payment systems. This may be problematical, because systems with sufficient liquidity and no queuing will send liquid funds in real-time, while systems with low liquidity and heavy reliance on queuing will delay outgoing payments. The real-time gross settlement systems with queuing may thus be draining liquidity from other, more liquid, systems.

Although collateral will be immobile under TARGET (banks can only pledge it with their domestic payment system), liquidity will freely move across borders. Furthermore, banks can participate in the payment system of more than one country and transmit liquidity between their accounts. The TARGET blueprint stresses that a well-functioning payment system is needed as a channel for arbitrage flows to establish a single monetary policy throughout EMU. Payment transfers routed via the interlinking mechanism will be exclusively denominated in Euro, the new European currency. To create an open system, non-EMU central banks have the option to link their real-time gross settlement system to TARGET, provided they convert payments from the national currency into Euro before they are transmitted.

5. LENDER-OF-LAST-RESORT IN EMU

An illiquid bank will, almost always, be able to borrow additional liquid funds to meet a short-term liquidity problem from the interbank market,

---

15. EMI, Working Group on Payment Systems, 'The TARGET System (Trans-European Automated Real-time Gross Settlement Express Transfer System; A Payment System Arrangement for Stage Three of EMU)' (May 1995).

unless the market already suspects its solvency.[16] A bank which cannot borrow from the money market to meet its liquidity needs is, almost by definition, a bank whose solvency is suspect in that market.[17] A central bank acting as lender of last resort should therefore be in a position to supervise, in order to constrain, the use of its lender-of-last-resort function and should have the best available information on the solvency of a bank in need of liquidity support. If the central bank is not the supervisor, it will need good and fast communication links with that specialist supervisor, which is usually the case. The annex to this chapter lists the supervisory arrangements, including the links between central banks and specialist supervisors in case of separation, in EU countries.

Given the home-country regime for banking supervision in the European Union, home central banks are the natural choice to provide lender-of-last-resort support, if and when needed. The cost of lender-of-last-resort support (and deposit-insurance payouts) will then be fully internalised at the home supervisor. Note that lender-of-last-resort operations are not without credit risk, as the solvency of a bank in need of liquidity support is often suspect. Although a collateral requirement can be imposed, this cannot always be enforced in practice. Banks with a sufficient amount of high-quality, liquid, paper on their books can usually sell that paper in the market, and hence do not need liquidity support. Consequently, a lender of last resort has often to secure its loans against lower-grade paper and/or against the loanbook of the ailing banks. If the range of permissible collateral were too restrictive, a rescue would not be possible in such cases.

To avoid the moral hazard and credit risk of credit operations (*ie*, discount-window loans) with individual banks, Goodfriend and King[18] argue that central banks should only use open-market operations to stem a liquidity crisis. While the ESCB could use open-market operations, as much as possible, to stem general liquidity crises, such as a gridlock problem in the payment system or a sudden drop of prices in stock markets, open-market operations will not always suffice. In the £-crisis of September 1992, for example, payment flows in CHAPS, the UK large-value payment system, were doubled due to extra forex transactions. More payment flows imply more payment-system overdrafts to process all the payments. If banks do not have sufficient extra collateral under real-time gross settlement, payment delays or even gridlock may occur. The national central banks

---

16. C. Goodhart, 'Why Do Banks Need a Central Bank?' (1987) 39 *Oxford Economic Papers* 75.

17. There have been some exceptions, notably when some technical failing in the settlement system leads to a bank making out-payments, but unable to obtain offsetting in-payments. This occurred in the Bank of New York case in 1985.

18. M. Goodfriend and R. G. King, 'Financial Deregulation, Monetary Policy, and Central Banking' (May–June 1988) 74:3 *Federal Reserve Bank of Richmond Economic Review* 3.

may then need to accept non-eligible paper as collateral for payment-system overdrafts, or they may need to accept non-eligible paper in their open-market operations to inject extra reserves, if they want to solve the problem. Furthermore, individual loans are needed to resolve a specific crisis concerning one or more bank(s). So there is likely to be a need for credit operations by national central banks both to complement open-market operations in a general crisis and to deal with liquidity or solvency problems of individual banks.

Although liquidity support will often have to be decided upon if and when the emergency occurs, general guidelines could cover issues such as: *when* to intervene (*ie*, which contingencies require, or justify, lending of last resort); *how* to intervene (*ie*, open-market operations or credit operations); and *who* will intervene (*ie*, the national central banks or the ECB). These are essentially technical points. The underlying (political) issue is the ECB's attitude, as Folkerts-Landau and Garber[19] convincingly argue: will the ECB allow the ESCB to be an active lender of last resort (and thus support the development of deep and liquid Euromarkets), or will the ECB propagate a minimum lender-of-last-resort role (and thus risk failures with systemic impact, hampering the development of Euromarkets)? In other words, will the ECB regard monetary and financial stability as equally important, or must monetary stability take precedence over financial stability, if there is a conflict of interest, as argued by Häusler?[20] An alternative view is that official intervention in such circumstances is misguided.[21] There is a claim that lender-of-last-resort support (as well as deposit insurance) generates so much moral hazard that the need for such support is largely self-inflicted. While I appreciate this argument in theory, I believe that lender-of-last-resort support is justified if there is a systemic threat.

Two issues arise with the advance towards Stage Three of EMU: (i) will the national central banks be allowed to continue lender-of-last-resort operations at their own choice and on their own account? and (ii) is there a need for ECB involvement to preserve European-wide systemic stability?

19. D. Folkerts-Landau and P. Garber, 'What Role for the ECB in Europe's Financial Markets?', in A. Steinherr (ed.), *30 Years of European Monetary Integration from the Werner Plan to EMU* (1994).

20. G. Häusler, 'The Competitive Position of Germany as a Financial Centre as Seen by a Central Banker', in D. Fair and R. Raymond (eds), *The Competitiveness of Financial Institutions and Centres in Europe* (1994).

21. See, *eg*, G. Benston, R. Eisenbeis, P. Horvitz, E. Kane and G. Kaufman, *Perspectives on Safe and Sound Banking: Past, Present, and Future* (1986); K. Dowd, 'Competitive Banking, Bankers' Clubs, and Bank Regulation' (1994) 26 *Journal of Money, Credit, and Banking* 289; and L. White, *Free Banking in Britain: Theory, Experience and Debate* (1984).

5.1   Lender-of-last-resort support by national central banks

Does the ECB have a policy-making power (similar to the Fed Board's) to issue guidelines for the provision of lender-of-last-resort support by the national central banks and the ECB? A possible answer is given in Article 18 of the Statute of the ECB:

18.1. In order to achieve the objectives of the ESCB and to carry out its tasks, the ECB and the national central banks may . . . conduct credit operations with credit institutions and other market participants, with lending being based on adequate collateral.

18.2. The ECB shall establish general principles for . . . credit operations carried out by itself or the national central banks, including for the announcement of conditions under which they stand ready to enter into such transactions.

But it is not clear whether Article 18 covers only routine credit operations, or also credit operations in the context of lender-of-last-resort support. This ambivalence is not surprising, as most central bank charters do not explicitly specify the lender-of-last-resort function for moral hazard reasons. The ESCB is a system comprising the ECB and the national central banks. Following the principle of decentralisation, the national central banks will probably execute the single monetary policy of the ECB. Thus, the national central banks will conduct open-market operations and credit operations with banks. Moreover, these national central banks are directly or indirectly involved in banking supervision (see the next section on banking supervision). Hands-on experience with financial markets and institutions and information on market conditions and individual banks' liquidity or solvency will thus be located at the national central banks, and not at the ECB. So, if the ECB were to devise rules or guidelines for emergency assistance to individual banks, it should do so in conjunction with the national central banks. While each crisis is specific and often different form previous crises, such guidelines can only be general.

A first possible guideline is a collateral requirement for lender-of-last-resort loans and a specification of the type of collateral that is eligible.[22] Although this is appropriate as a general rule, overriding provisions are needed. As discussed above, banks in difficulties do not always have sufficient eligible collateral available. A well-known example is the Bank of New York computer failure in 1985. Although the bank's computer sold government securities, it could neither deliver them nor collect the money owed to the bank. The New York Fed made an overnight loan of $22.6 billion from the discount window, collateralised by $36 billion in securities. In this case the Fed had to discount assets other than eligible government securities.

22. Statute of the ESCB, Art. 18.1.

An interesting parallel can be drawn with the functioning of the Federal Reserve System in its early years.[23] While the Federal Reserve Banks were free to make discounts with member banks, the Federal Reserve Board had the authority to specify the terms. The Board adhered to the 'real-bills' doctrine stating that '[l]ending policy required the [Federal Reserve] banks to confine [discounts] to short-term, self-liquidating paper growing out of actual commercial, industrial and agricultural operations'.[24] Strict adherence to these eligibility criteria prevented the Federal Reserve Banks from providing sufficient accommodation to solvent member banks on several occasions.

A further possible guideline is that the home-country central bank should be responsible for lender-of-last-resort support. The Deutsche Bank branch in London, for example, will first go to Deutsche Bank HQ in Frankfurt (funds can easily be transferred from Frankfurt to London via the real-time gross settlement system) and, if the parent bank does not have sufficient funds, then the Bundesbank will be responsible. What if the Bundesbank as home-country central bank refuses to do the lender-of-last-resort operation on its own account? Note that each national central bank will naturally assess the contagion risk in its own market, rather than in the wider EMU market. The contagion risk can affect both the UK and German market: should the Bundesbank or the Bank of England do the lender-of-last-resort operation on the account of the ESCB,[25] because of the cross-border impact?

In addition, it may become more difficult to identify the home-country central bank of each bank. Emerging European banking groups may be chartered in two or more EU Member States. An example of such a multiple chartered European bank would be the merger of a Dutch and a Belgian bank on equal terms. The respective supervisors, de Nederlandsche Bank and the Belgian Banking and Finance Commission, would then have to find a *modus operandi* for joint supervision. The two central banks, de Nederlandsche Bank and the National Bank of Belgium, in their capacity as lenders of last resort, could follow the same division of responsibility as the supervisors.

Another example is the case of a large French company that issues commercial paper in London which is bought by the London branch of a Portuguese bank. Suppose the French company faces financial problems and cannot repay its commercial paper at maturity. Possible contagion effects involve uncertainty in the London commercial-paper market and uncer-

---

23. See R. Timberlake, *Monetary Policy in the United States: An Intellectual and Institutional History* (1993).

24. Ibid., p.255.

25. Art. 32.4 of the Statute of the ESCB states that '[t]he Governing Council may decide that national central banks shall be indemnified against costs incurred . . . in exceptional circumstances for specific losses arising from *monetary policy operations* undertaken for the ESCB' (emphasis added). But this clause does not seem to cover losses from lender-of-last-resort operations.

tainty about the solvency of the Portuguese bank. Which is the responsible central bank to intervene, if necessary? The Banque de France (as the French company is causing the trouble), the Bank of England (whose commercial-paper market is affected), the Banco de Portugal (one of whose banks is in difficulties), or the ECB, in order to assess the overall effects? A possible answer is that the Banco de Portugal has to deal with problems at banks under its supervisory wing, and that the ESCB (not only the Bank of England) may, or may not, choose to inject extra reserves (or to reduce its interest rate) to relieve possible strains in the commercial-paper market.

These examples highlight the following questions: who authorises support operations; and who is liable for the cost? When responsibility is not clearly allocated, there is a risk that a crisis will be exacerbated by delays in the provision of assistance. Such delays may be due to misunderstandings and disputes among potential lenders of last resort about who is responsible.[26] For moral hazard reasons, I do not argue that lender-of-last-resort support should be granted to all institutions under all circumstances. The ECB and the national central banks could preserve the central bank adagium of 'constructive ambiguity', that is, the availability of lender-of-last-resort support should remain vague and subject to the discretion of the central bank. But I argue that there should be a clear allocation of responsibility for the decision to support, or not. At the moment, there is only one central bank which can act as lender of last resort in each country. The move towards Stage Three of EMU would needlessly create an additional factor of uncertainty, if it were not clear whether the ECB or the national central banks would assume the role of lender of last resort.[27]

Although the monetary effects of lender-of-last-resort operations can be undone by open-market operations on the same day or the next morning, the ECB may wish to constrain the use of the lender-of-last-resort function by national central banks. National central banks may be overzealous in assisting their local banking system, even if there is no direct systemic impact. For the earlier mentioned moral hazard reasons, it is advisable to reserve lender-of-last-resort support only for genuine banking crises that have the potential to create a systemic crisis. But what if a national central bank wants to support one of its own national banks and that is not allowed under the rules? On the one hand, the ECB can be a useful device to

---

26. R. Herring and R. Litan, *Financial Regulation in the Global Economy* (1995).
27. Some observers have argued that it is sufficient that a small group of those involved know whether the ECB or the national central banks would assume the lender-of-last-resort function. However, markets tend to be overly sensitive during times of crisis. Decisive intervention (stating clearly it will support, or stating clearly it will not support) by the responsible central bank (either the ECB or one of the national central banks) can help to calm a crisis situation, while lingering uncertainty about which body is responsible will only amplify a crisis.

constrain the use of the lender-of-last-resort function: only when a national central bank can make a case for lender-of-last-resort support at the ECB, will this happen. On the other hand, can ECB bureaucrats, with no hands-on experience with and no direct information on individual banks, have the final say? Rivalry between national central banks seems to be acceptable, as long as it is nationally financed, that is, as long as lender-of-last-resort activities are conducted on the account of national central banks.

More generally, what should be done when a bank is clearly in solvency problems as well (*eg*, Banesto, Crédit Lyonnais)? National authorities will be under more (domestic) political pressure to come to the assistance if a local bank is in difficulties. There is an analogy with state aid for other symbols of national pride, such as airlines. It is arguable that bail-outs of banks that face a gradual erosion of their capital base are not the domain of central banks, but that of finance ministries. Only the latter have the deep pockets to finance such operations. The European Commission has the power, based on Article 92 of the EC Treaty, to investigate state aid to banks (and to other companies as well) in order to prevent competitive distortions.

Furthermore, the emergence of European banking groups makes the organisation of life-boat operations on a domestic basis more difficult, if not impossible. Examples of such lifeboats financed by the domestic banking sector are the rescues of Schröder, Münchmeyer, Hengst & Co in Germany (1983), Johnson Matthey in the UK (1984) and, more recently, Banesto in Spain (1993). In France, Article 52 of the 1984 Banking Act has given legal recognition to interbank solidarity. The procedure of Article 52, under which the Governor of the Banque de France can call upon the shareholders of an institution to provide the latter with the support it needs, was activated *inter alia* in the case of Al Saudi Bank in 1988 and the Banque de Participations et de Placements in 1989. The viability of such arrangements has run into increasing difficulties with the collapse of domestic banking clubs and is likely to do more so with further European integration.[28]

The alternative to discretion by national authorities (either national central banks or ministries of finance) might be a rule-based approach of structured early intervention and resolution, which is incorporated in the FDIC Improvement Act of 1991.[29] Under this approach, banks qualify for minimum supervision, if they are sufficiently highly capitalised. In contrast, as capital levels drop below the 8 per cent level, a bank will come under increasingly tight supervision and will be more severely restricted in its

28. Goodhart and Schoenmaker, loc. cit., n.5.
29. See G. Benston, 'The Purpose of Capital for Institutions with Government-Insured Deposits' (1992) 5 *Journal of Financial Services Research* 369; and G. Kaufman, 'Capital in Banking: Past, Present and Future' (1992) 5 *Journal of Financial Services Research* 385.

activities. Moreover, if capital falls below a 'critical' ratio, even though the bank may still be, at least nominally, solvent, prompt resolution by the authorities is required. Boot and Greenbaum[30] argue, however, that an early intervention policy imposes an unrealistic informational burden on the supervisor. Early intervention requires improved information regarding a bank's assets and liabilities, but the value of many assets (in particular loans) is difficult to establish. The question could therefore be raised whether such an early intervention approach would be appropriate under all circumstances. Moreover, would it be politically feasible in Europe?

5.2 Liquidity support by the European Central Bank

While the national central banks can deal effectively with a specific crisis at one or more banks under their control, only the ECB can formulate a response to a (general) liquidity crisis. With the establishment of Stage Three of EMU, there will be a single monetary policy and a single interest rate. There will be no scope for a national central bank to relieve monetary conditions in its local market (in so far as local markets would continue to exist within a European monetary system) during times of crisis without affecting the monetary conditions in the rest of the system. So only the ECB, or more precisely the Governing Council of the ECB,[31] can decide to relax monetary conditions by injecting extra reserves and/or reducing money-market rates during times of stress.

Examples of liquidity crises are the collapse of Penn Central in 1970 and the stock-market crash in 1987.[32] After Penn Central Railroad, a major issuer of commercial paper, had to declare bankruptcy, the Federal Reserve was concerned about the negative effects on the commercial-paper market causing problems for other companies. To prevent a crisis, the Fed encouraged banks to lend to customers who were unable to roll over their commercial paper and made the discount window available to them so that they could make such loans. The Fed provided liquidity so that the commercial-paper market would keep functioning.[33] The 1987 stock-market crash caused major problems for the clearing and settlement systems

---

30. A. Boot and S. Greenbaum, 'American Banking Legislation, Recent', in P. Newman, M. Milgate and J. Eatwell (eds), *New Palgrave Dictionary of Money and Finance* (1992).

31. The Governing Council consists of the Executive Board of the ECB and the governors of the national central banks. The Executive Board, which comprises the President, the Vice-President and four other members, must implement monetary policy in accordance with the guidelines and decisions laid down by the Governing Council. See Statute of the ESCB, Arts 10–12.

32. See, *eg*, A. Brimmer, 'Central Banking and Systemic Risks in Capital Markets' (1989) 3 *Journal of Economic Perspectives* 3.

33. F. Mishkin, 'Anatomy of a Financial Crisis' (1992) 2 *Journal of Evolutionary Economics* 115.

of the stock and future markets.[34] Brokers and securities houses needed additional funds to finance their activities and to settle margin calls for their customers. Again, the Fed encouraged banks to keep their credit lines to brokers and securities houses open and made the discount window available to them. A more recent example is the collapse of Barings. After it decided not to support Barings in the weekend of 25–26 February 1995, the Bank of England announced, before the London markets opened, that it would 'stand ready to provide liquidity to the banking system to ensure that it continues to function normally'.[35]

The crucial factor in stemming such liquidity crises is that the central bank is prepared to stand ready to provide liquidity (either by open-market operations, or by credit operations) to the banking system. With the advance towards Stage Three of EMU, only the Governing Council of the ECB can take that decision. The ECB must determine how much extra liquidity can be injected without unduly impairing the price-stability objective. Both 'monetary' and 'financial' stability concerns must be considered when such liquidity support is granted. Even if such liquidity is provided in the form of credit operations by one or more national central banks, the ECB will decide on the conditions. The ECB can, for example, choose to make liquidity available on demand at the given interest rate, that is, to furnish an elastic currency. The market can then decide how much extra reserves it needs. Alternatively, the ECB can reduce interest rates, though it is not clear why pressure in the markets should be relieved at a subsidised rate.

Without such central bank intervention money-market rates can be expected to spike during times of stress. Non-bank financial institutions rely on banks for liquidity, and make calls on the banking sector for extra liquid funds in a crisis. Banks have access to the interbank market to raise liquid funds. If liquidity is in large demand, banks will bid up the interbank rate to get the desired amount of liquidity. Only an extra injection of reserves can ease the pressure on interbank rates.

In summary, liquidity support for individual banks in difficulties can still be given on the initiative and account of the national central banks, but problems affecting EMU-wide markets will require ECB intervention to relieve pressure on the money market, the primary source of liquidity. If the cross-border impact of banking problems should increase in a developing European banking market, there may be a case for conducting lender-of-last-resort operations for individual banks on the account of the ESCB, rather than on the account of the national central banks, but it is not clear whether there would be a legal basis for such a policy.

---

34. B. Bernanke, 'Clearing and Settlement during the Crash' (1990) 3 *Review of Financial Studies* 133.
35. 'Barings Forced to Cease Trading', *Financial Times*, 27 Feb. 1995.

6. BANKING SUPERVISION IN EMU

While lender-of-last-resort activities (and deposit insurance pay-outs) may be described as *ex post* prudential policy (the lender-of-last-resort function will only be activated when a crisis is imminent or has already commenced), banking regulation and supervision are part of *ex ante* prudential policy. If national central banks have to co-operate in their lender-of-last-resort operations and/or the ECB becomes involved, there may be a case for co-ordinating policies to prevent such systemic crises occurring. Following the Federal Reserve example, it seems clear that the operational part of banking supervision will be conducted by the national central banks or relevant national authorities. The bulk of the supervisory staff is employed at this operational level, which means that there will be no massive shift of people to the ECB. As illustrated in the Annex to this chapter, 10 out of the 15 national central banks within the European Union are directly responsible for banking supervision, while most of the remaining five national central banks are indirectly involved (*eg*, collecting prudential returns on behalf of the independent supervisory agency). The question is which parts of supervision need to be co-ordinated, or centralised, at the policy-making level, and in what institutional setting (Frankfurt, Basle, Brussels).

The nature of banking supervision is to some extent dependent on the type of bank that is supervised. Broadly speaking, two types of banks can be distinguished: (i) small-to-medium-sized banks; and (ii) large banks.

Small-to-medium-sized banks have primarily a domestic presence and are retail-oriented. The focus of supervision is on traditional loan quality assessment: sufficient diversification, no large exposures, adequate provisions, etc. In so far as they engage in derivatives trading, banks of this size use such derivatives mainly to hedge their interest-rate or foreign-exchange exposure. Their limited amount of cross-border loan activities has, however, increased with the establishment of the single market in banking since January 1993 and may be expected to increase further with the move to Stage Three of EMU, and this may require some co-ordination among supervisors. But the recently adopted Memoranda Of Understanding between national authorities can serve this purpose at a bilateral level.

Large banks have an international (and EU-wide) presence and are more wholesale-oriented. They are the big players in the OTC-derivatives and forex markets. As these banks trade in several kinds of money-market and derivative instruments and rely often more on wholesale funding, they are very sensitive to liquidity shocks. These banks are the equivalent of the New York money-centre banks. In addition to loan assessment, supervision also focuses on the off-balance-sheet activities of these large banks. There is a trend from rule-based regulation (detailed capital adequacy requirements, etc) to self-regulation (reliance on internal risk measurement and control systems) for large banks. This is backed-up by regulatory efforts to increase transparency in order to facilitate monitoring by market participants. In this area co-operation at the European level is needed, because liquidity problems at any of the large EU banks will have an impact on the European-wide money market. There will be a single money market in Stage Three of EMU, and (large) banks will increasingly have interbank linkages on a European basis in such a single money market.

One proposal put forward by the Centre for European Policy Studies,[36] is to have a two-tier structure: small-to-medium-sized banks would be chartered and supervised at the national level, while large banks would be chartered and supervised by the ECB (in addition to their national supervision).[37] The latter European charter would give access to the 'European' payment system. In exchange for this charter, large banks would be subject to a certain degree of ECB supervision and to certain reserve requirements. In a similar fashion, Grüner and Hefeker[38] develop a model explaining that large banks are induced to operate internationally and gain from EMU, while small banks are likely to lose. The idea is that common regulations would make it cheaper to operate EMU-wide. Large banks would be better placed to reap the benefits of further integration (*eg*, through access to the 'European' payment system) and would increase their market share in cross-border transfers within EMU.

I see, however, two main difficulties with such a two-tier structure. First, this proposal assumes the development of a new 'European' payment system for large banks. The ESCB will presumably only conduct open-market operations with banks participating in this payment system for the settlement of Euro-funds. In contrast, the decentralised model of linking domestic payment systems will create an EMU-wide payment system with a large membership. This will support the establishment of a truly integrated and deep Euro money market, as argued in section 4. Second, a two-tier

36. Centre for European Policy Studies, 'The Single Market in Banking: From 1992 to EMU', Proposal for a CEPS Programme (1994).
37. Returning to the Federal Reserve example, it is interesting that, when the US Treasury drafted proposals for a single banking regulator in 1994 (under which the Federal Banking Commission would assume the regulatory functions of the Office of the Comptroller of the Currency, the Federal Reserve, the Federal Deposit Insurance Corporation and the Office of Thrift Supervision), Alan Greenspan clearly stated that the Fed should still be involved in supervision, and at least supervise the large money-centre banks and bank-holding companies. Greenspan argued, *inter alia*, that the Fed's role in resolving financial crises makes it imperative for it to have a close and continuous knowledge of the position and workings of banks – knowledge that can only be gained by hands-on supervision. Alan Greenspan, Testimony before the United States Senate Committee on Banking, Housing and Urban Affairs (2 March 1990).
38. H. P. Grüner and C. Hefeker, *Bank Cooperation and Banking Policy in a Monetary Union: A Political-Economy Perspective on EMU*, University of Konstanz Discussion Paper No. 238 (1994).

structure may start a process of competitive deregulation. The United States provides an instructive example with its dual banking system, in which banks had, and still have, the choice between a state and federal charter. The willingness of banks to join the federal system depends on the relative costs and benefits of membership. Examining the operation of the dual banking system from 1900 to 1929, White[39] found that, when the Federal Reserve eased its regulation to attract more banks, the states easily undermined its increased attractiveness by weakening their requirements. The Centre for European Policy Studies proposal[40] would prevent such a process of competitive deregulation, because any ECB supervision would come on top of the existing home-country supervision. But in that case it is not clear why banks would voluntarily opt for additional supervisory restrictions.

Another problem with a centralised approach is that supervisory staff located at the ECB in Frankfurt will be too far removed from the financial centres of London and Paris (though not Frankfurt). The alternative is that national central banks or supervisors continue to supervise large banks as well, but that the ECB (via the Banking Supervisory Sub-Committee) develops a leading and co-ordinating role at the policy-making level for this kind of supervisory activities. The Statute of the ESCB, however, specifies in Article 3.3 that the ECB may only 'contribute to the smooth conduct of policies pursued by the competent authorities relating to the prudential supervision of credit institutions and the stability of the financial system'. In addition, Article 25.1 states that 'the ECB may offer advice to and be consulted by the Council, the Commission and the competent authorities of the Member States on the scope and implementation of Community legislation relating to the prudential supervision of credit institutions and to the stability of the financial system'. This is far short of a co-ordinating role in policy-making. But informal discussions in the Banking Supervisory Sub-Committee[41] may be as useful as formal policy-making powers, as illustrated by the Basle Committee on Banking Supervision, which cannot issue legally binding regulations.

Furthermore, the granting of formal supervisory powers to the ECB would raise the thorny issue of accountability. In the national setting, primary banking regulation is typically drafted by the ministry of finance and approved by Parliament. National supervisors operate thus within a legal framework and are, at least to some extent, accountable to the minister of finance and/or Parliament. The equivalent institutions at the European level are not (yet) fully developed. In addition, the ECB would probably not like to compromise its hard-fought independence in the field of monetary

---

39. E. White, *The Regulation and Reform of the American Banking System* (1983).
40. Centre for European Policy Studies, loc. cit., n.36.
41. The national supervisors of the EU countries are represented in the Banking Supervisory Sub-Committee of the EMI.

policy by interventions from the European Commission or the Council in the execution of its possible supervisory responsibilities.

As the ECB is not allowed to take a formal supervisory role under the present Treaty, could co-ordination in the European Union (via the Banking Advisory Committee and/or banking directives) or the Group of Ten (G-10) countries (via the Basle Committee on Banking Supervision) be a suitable surrogate? The status of the Banking Advisory Committee (meeting in Brussels) is similar to that of the Banking Supervisory Sub-Committee (meeting in Frankfurt), in the sense that it has no formal supervisory powers. The main drawback of EC directives is that they take a long lead time (two to five years) from initiation to final form and, once in place, they are difficult to change. Because banking practices and financial markets are rapidly changing, directives may be too inflexible as an instrument of regulation-making.[42]

An alternative channel for co-ordination between supervisors of EMU participating countries is the G-10. Over the last two decades, the Basle Committee on Banking Supervision has proved to be the most effective forum for international co-ordination of regulatory and supervisory practices. The Committee's informal and depoliticised character has significantly contributed to its success. But the Basle Committee is an international, rather than a European, forum. Even so, European co-ordination of regulation and supervision (in Brussels or Frankfurt) should be in line with international developments in Basle, to prevent conflicting and accumulating regulatory burdens.

There are conflicting demands for geographical and functional co-ordination of supervision, as national and institutional boundaries between previously distinct financial sectors continue to diminish. While geographical integration between banks may suggest co-ordination at the ECB, functional integration between banks, securities houses and insurance companies may suggest an independent supervisory authority (perhaps responsible to Ecofin) for co-ordination at the EU level, if such co-ordination is desirable. This issue is related to the emerging financial conglomerates within the European Union. Closer links between banking supervision and securities and insurance supervision may be needed to supervise effectively such conglomerates.[43] If there is to be more co-operation and integration between banking, securities and insurance supervisors, the ECB, as any other central bank, may well lose its appetite for supervising banks, if only

---

42. A case in point is the recent decision of the Basle Committee to allow banks to use internal models to calculate market risks for capital adequacy purposes. It is not clear how long it will take to incorporate this proposal in the EU Capital Adequacy Directive, if the Council wishes to do so.

43. See, *eg*, Tripartite Group of Bank, Securities and Insurance Regulators, 'Supervision of Financial Conglomerates' (1995).

to avoid the impression that the public safety net (lending of last resort, deposit insurance) would be available to all parts of a financial conglomerate. A possible solution is to have separate functional regulators for the different financial activities and a single lead regulator for the whole entity.[44]

Although the ECB may leave banking supervision to national central banks or supervisors as specified in the Maastricht Treaty, it will need a capacity to assess financial stability. In section 5.2, I argued that the ECB is the only body which can alleviate a liquidity crisis within a European monetary system. The main institutional channel for the ECB to get information on financial conditions is the Banking Supervisory Sub-Committee, in which the national central banks and specialised supervisory authorities are represented. In addition, the ECB itself will need to monitor banks and financial markets to make its own independent assessment. The president of the ECB can then call upon both the national central banks[45] and its own staff in case of a liquidity crisis.

In a similar way, the ECB has to be familiar with the different financial and banking systems in the EU Member States to assess the impact of monetary policy. The potential for a conflict of interest between 'monetary' and 'supervisory' objectives is larger in some countries than in others.[46] This is, for example, illustrated by the damage that high short-term interest rates (*eg*, to support the Euro or to counter strong inflationary pressures) may do to the banking system in the different countries. This damage depends importantly on the structure of the banking system. Those banking systems which are primarily financed by a retail deposit base, whose interest rates are unlikely to follow (large) changes in money-market wholesale rates, would be better able to cope with (temporarily) tight monetary conditions. Again, where bank loans and mortgages are made on a fixed-rate basis, the system may be less sensitive, both economically and politically, to temporary periods of high rates, than when such loans are based on floating rates. Furthermore, those banking

---

44. The viability of this solution depends on close ties between the separate regulators. It has, for example, been rumoured in the City that during the recent Barings crisis the Bank of England, as lead regulator of Barings, did not call upon the Securities and Futures Authority (SFA), as functional regulator of Barings Securities (a subsidiary of Barings). While the expertise on futures exchanges was available at the SFA, it was not used by the Bank to assess the position of Barings Securities on the Singapore and Osaka futures exchanges. Furthermore, Dale has argued that the separation of banking and securities regulation between different agencies makes sense only if the risk exposures of these two businesses can also be segregated; R. Dale, 'Barings: The Regulatory Fallout' [March 1995] *Financial Regulation Report* 1.

45. The EMI is considering the implementation of advanced teleconference facilities between the ECB and the national central banks; see EMI, 'Annual Report 1994' (1995).

46. Goodhart and Schoenmaker, loc. cit., n.5.

systems which are effectively nationalised, or where the banks run a profitable cartel, will be inherently better placed to ride out such (temporary) volatility, since their solvency will be less at risk. These examples suggest that the potential for conflict between 'monetary' and 'supervisory' objectives depends to some large extent on the structure of the banking and financial system. The more such a system involves intermediaries financing maturity mismatch positions through wholesale markets in a competitive milieu, the greater such dangers of 'conflict' are likely to be.

The Bank for International Settlements[47] has quantified the role played by financial structure in the monetary policy transmission mechanism. It finds notable differences in the effects of interest-rate changes on interest payments and economic activity in France and the UK. While interest payments increase almost immediately in the UK after a rise in interest rates, there is little immediate response in France. Moreover, the ultimate effect is much smaller in France than in the UK. The impact of interest-rate changes on real GDP growth is also much more modest in France than in the UK. In setting a *single* monetary policy, the ECB would have to take into account the distinct effects on the banking and financial systems of the EMU participating countries. Failing to do so could cause undue damage to the banking sector of those countries whose financial system is more vulnerable to changes in monetary conditions.

This raises the question whether not only economic but also financial convergence is needed in the run-up to Stage Three of EMU. The debate on EMU has mainly focused on nominal versus real economic convergence between countries before they can enter the final stage of EMU, while the issue of differing financial structures has so far largely been ignored.

Summing up, the ECB may be able to avoid direct involvement in the conduct of banking supervision, but it must develop an understanding of banking and financial structures to preserve financial stability within a European monetary system.

7. CONCLUSIONS

While it may not be politically feasible for the ECB to be directly involved in banking supervision, there is a need for it to develop a capacity to understand and monitor systemic stability within a developing European monetary system. This is based on the premise that monetary stability and financial stability are mutually interdependent.

47. BIS, '64th Annual Report, 1993–94' (1994).

Microprudential control can continue to be conducted at the national level. Given the home-country regime of the Second Banking Directive, national central banks (or supervisors) are responsible for supervising the European-wide activities of banks incorporated in their country. The establishment of home-country deposit insurance has brought this area in line with banking supervision. In addition, the central bank of the home country can act as lender of last resort in case of an emergency crisis at individual banks. A separate question is how to deal with ailing banks which need a capital injection to restore their capital base, rather than a swift injection of cash. But such bail-outs are a case for the (national) ministries of finance, which have the deep pockets, and not for central banks. Responsibility for supervision and the safety net (*ie*, deposit-insurance pay-outs, lender-of-last-resort actions and bail-outs) are in the same (national) hands.[48] The single market in banking, regulated on a home-country basis, can thus, at least initially, be preserved within a European monetary system. If the cross-border impact of banking problems should increase, the balance may shift towards more ECB involvement in lender-of-last-resort operations and banking supervision.

Nevertheless, macromanagement of financial stability must be done by the ECB from the start. This includes concern for stability of trans-European payment systems and financial markets. At the outset of Stage Three of EMU, national payment systems must be linked to support an integrated money market. The development of real-time gross settlement systems that operate on a standard of permitting only collateralised overdrafts has been promoted by the EMI, the forerunner of the ECB. Real-time gross settlement without intraday credit minimises the need for lender-of-last-resort intervention.

To stem a liquidity crisis generated in *European* financial markets, only the ECB can respond by relaxing monetary conditions. While an unduly liberal policy of relaxing the monetary stance may impair the price-stability objective, a restrictive policy may exacerbate financial instability. In its decision to provide liquidity support during such liquidity crises, the ECB will need information on the causes of the disturbances and the condition of the financial sector. The ECB needs, therefore, to have good and fast communication links with national central banks and supervisors to assess the situation (*ie*, it is crucial that the ECB and the national central banks act as a system of central banks). But the ECB should not exclusively rely on national authorities. The ECB also needs its own staff to provide an independent and overall assessment of the crisis situation. Moreover, an awareness of systemic issues is indispensable, if the ECB is going to devise guidelines for the use of the lender-of-last-resort function by national central banks.

---

48. The information on individual banks is locally available and, if national authorities bear the cost of the safety net (*ie*, deposit-insurance pay-outs, lender-of-last-resort actions and bail-outs), an 'incentive compatible' supervisory system is created.

ANNEX

Supervisory Agencies in the EU Member States

Country	Supervisory Agency	Link with Central Bank
Austria	Federal Ministry of Finance	Separated[1]
Belgium (G-10)	Banking and Finance Commission	Separated[2]
Denmark	Finance Inspectorate	Separated[3]
Finland	Financial Supervision Authority	Combined[4]
France (G-10)	Banque de France (CB) Commission Bancaire	Combined[5]
Germany (G-10)	Federal Banking Supervisory Office	Separated[6]
Greece	Bank of Greece (CB)	Combined
Ireland	Central Bank of Ireland (CB)	Combined
Italy (G-10)	Banca d'Italia (CB)	Combined
Luxembourg (G-10)	Luxembourg Monetary Institute (CB)	Combined
Netherlands (G-10)	De Nederlandsche Bank (CB)	Combined
Portugal	Banco de Portugal (CB)	Combined
Spain	Banco de España (CB)	Combined
Sweden (G-10)	Financial Supervisory Authority	Separated[7]
United Kingdom (G-10)	Bank of England (CB)	Combined

Notes

CB   Central Bank

G-10 Member of the Basle Committee on Banking Supervision

1.   The Federal Ministry of Finance is the banking regulatory and supervisory authority. The Ministry of Finance has a special department, 'Bankenaufsicht', for the supervision of banks. The role of the National Bank of Austria is similar to that of the Bundesbank (see below) in so far as the Bank does statistical work for the Ministry of Finance and gives advice on supervisory matters.

2.   In June 1991, the Banking Commission changed its name to the Banking and Finance Commission (BFC). The BFC is a legally autonomous institution and has a twofold task: controlling the banks and controlling the issuing of public securities. One member of the board of the National Bank of Belgium is a member of the BFC. Because of minimal involvement of the National Bank in the management of the BFC, the BFC can be considered as autonomous from the National Bank (unlike the case of France, see below). Banks have to submit their monthly prudential returns both to the National Bank and to the BFC.

3. The Finance Inspectorate was formed at the end of 1987 as a result of the merger of the Bank Inspectorate and the Insurance Industry Inspectorate. The Finance Inspectorate is a directorate of the Ministry of Industry. The Nationalbank is the granter of liquidity support, while the Inspectorate is responsible for the supervision of banks. The Inspectorate has no formal link with the Nationalbank, although there is in practice co-operation between the two on many issues.

4. The Banking Supervision Office was responsible for the supervision of banking, securities and derivatives activities until 1993. After the Finnish banking crisis in the early 1990s, the Banking Supervision Office, as an autonomous office, was moved from the Ministry of Finance into the Bank of Finland (CB). The Financial Supervision Authority, the new name of the Banking Supervision Office, started its operations in connection with the Bank of Finland on 1 Oct. 1993. Representatives from the Ministry of Finance, the Bank of Finland and the Ministry of Health and Social Affairs (in its capacity as supervisor of insurance companies and pension funds) have seats on the Board of the Authority. The Bank of Finland representative is the chairman of the Board. The Authority acts independently in its decision-making, but its administrative operations are connected with the Bank of Finland.

5. The Banking Commission (Commission Bancaire) is a composite body chaired by the governor of the Banque de France, with representatives from the Treasury. The Banking Commission supervises compliance with the prudential regulations. The inspections and on-site examinations are carried out by the Banque de France on behalf of the Banking Commission. The Committee on Bank Regulation (Comité de la Réglementation Bancaire) establishes prudential rules. The Committee on Credit Institutions (Comité des Établissements de Crédit) is responsible for licensing new banks. In all three commissions both the Banque de France and the Treasury are represented.

6. The Federal Banking Supervisory Office (Bundesaufsichtsamt für das Kreditwesen) is entrusted with the supervision of banks. It is responsible for sovereign acts, such as licensing and issuing regulations, whereas the Bundesbank is involved in current supervision by collecting and processing bank prudential returns (certain inspections of the authorised banks are conducted by Bundesbank employees). The Banking Act provides for co-operation between the Supervisory Office and the Bundesbank (*ie* the two bodies communicate information to each other, and the Supervisory Office has to consult the Bundesbank on new regulations).

7. The Bank Inspection Board used to be responsible for the supervision of banks. Supervisors of banks, securities and insurance companies merged into the Financial Supervisory Authority in July 1991.

Source: C. Goodhart and D. Schoenmaker, 'Should the Functions of Monetary Policy and Banking Supervision be Separated?' (1995) 47 *Oxford Economic Papers* 539.

Appendix 1

TREATY ON EUROPEAN UNION ('MAASTRICHT TREATY')

(February 7, 1992)

(Extracts with relevance for EMU)

PREAMBLE

[...]

RESOLVED to achieve the strengthening and the convergence of their economies and to establish an economic and monetary union including, in accordance with the provisions of this Treaty, a single and stable currency,

[...]

TITLE 1
COMMON PROVISIONS

[...]

Article B

The Union shall set itself the following objectives:
- to promote economic and social progress which is balanced and sustainable, in particular through the creation of an area without internal frontiers, through the strengthening of economic and social cohesion and through the establishment of economic and monetary union, ultimately including a single currency in accordance with the provisions of this Treaty;

[...]

TITLE II
PROVISIONS AMENDING THE TREATY ESTABLISHING THE EUROPEAN ECONOMIC COMMUNITY WITH A VIEW TO ESTABLISHING THE EUROPEAN COMMUNITY

[Integrated into the TREATY ESTABLISHING THE EUROPEAN COMMUNITY *infra*, Appendix 2.]

[...]

449

Appendix 2

TREATY ESTABLISHING THE
EUROPEAN COMMUNITY

(Treaty establishing the European Economic
Community of March 25, 1957, as amended by the
Single European Act of February 17/28, 1986
and the Treaty on European Union of February 7,
1992)

(Extracts with relevance for EMU)

PART ONE
PRINCIPLES

[...]

Article 2

The Community shall have as its task, by establishing a common market and an economic and monetary union and by implementing the common policies or activities referred to in Articles 3 and 3a, to promote throughout the Community a harmonious and balanced development of economic activities, sustainable and non-inflationary growth respecting the environment, a high degree of convergence of economic performance, a high level of employment and of social protection, the raising of the standard of living and quality of life, and economic and social cohesion and solidarity among Member States.

[...]

Article 3a

1. For the purposes set out in Article 2, the activities of the Member States and the Community shall include, as provided in this Treaty and in accordance with the timetable set out therein, the adoption of an economic policy which is based on the close coordination of Member States' economic policies, on the internal market and on the definition of common objectives, and conducted in accordance with the principle of an open market economy with free competition.

2. Concurrently with the foregoing, and as provided in this Treaty and in accordance with the timetable and the procedures set out therein, these activities shall include the irrevocable fixing of exchange rates leading to the introduction of a single currency, the ECU, and the definition and conduct of a single monetary policy and exchange-rate policy the primary objective of both of which shall be to maintain price stability and, without prejudice to this objective, to support the general economic policies in the Community, in accordance with the principle of an open market economy with free competition.

3. These activities of the Member States and the Community shall entail compliance with the following guiding principles: stable prices, sound public finances and monetary conditions and a sustainable balance of payments.

[...]

Article 4a

A European System of Central Banks (hereinafter referred to as 'ESCB') and a European Central Bank (hereinafter referred to as 'ECB') shall be established in accordance with the procedures laid down in this Treaty; they shall act within the limits of the powers conferred upon them by this Treaty and by the Statute of the ESCB and the ECB (hereinafter referred to as 'Statute of the ESCB') annexed thereto.

[...]

PART THREE
COMMUNITY POLICIES

[...]

TITLE III
FREE MOVEMENT OF PERSONS, SERVICES AND CAPITAL

[...]

CHAPTER 4
Capital and payments

[...]

Article 73f

Where, in exceptional circumstances, movements of capital to or from third countries cause, or threaten to cause, serious difficulties for the operation of economic and monetary union, the Council, acting by a qualified majority on a proposal from the Commission and after consulting the ECB, may take safeguard measures with regard to third countries for a period not exceeding six months if such measures are strictly necessary.

[...]

TITLE VI
ECONOMIC AND MONETARY POLICY

CHAPTER 1
Economic policy

Article 102a

Member States shall conduct their economic policies with a view to contributing to the achievement of the objectives of the Community, as defined in Article 2, and in the context of the broad guidelines referred to in Article 103 (2). The Member States and the Community shall act in accordance with the principle of an open market economy with free competition, favouring an efficient allocation of resources, and in compliance with the principles set out in Article 3a.

Article 103

1. Member States shall regard their economic policies as a matter of common concern and shall coordinate them within the Council, in accordance with the provisions of Article 102a.

2. The Council shall, acting by a qualified majority on a recommendation from the Commission, formulate a draft for the broad guidelines of the economic policies of the Member States and of the Community, and shall report its findings to the European Council.

    The European Council shall, acting on the basis of the report from the Council, discuss a conclusion on the broad guidelines of the economic policies of the Member States and of the Community.

    On the basis of this conclusion, the Council shall, acting by a qualified majority, adopt a recommendation setting out these broad guidelines. The Council shall inform the European Parliament of its recommendation.

3. In order to ensure closer coordination of economic policies and sustained convergence of the economic performances of the Member States, the Council shall, on the basis of reports submitted by the Commission, monitor economic developments in each of the Member States and in the Community as well as the consistency of economic policies with the broad guidelines referred to in paragraph 2, and regularly carry out an overall assessment.

    For the purpose of this multilateral surveillance, Member States shall forward information to the Commission about important measures taken by them in the field of their economic policy and such other information as they deem necessary.

4. Where it is established, under the procedure referred to in paragraph 3, that the economic policies of a Member State are not consistent with the broad guidelines referred to in paragraph 2 or that they risk jeopardizing the proper functioning of economic and monetary union, the Council may, acting by a qualified majority on a recommendation from the Commission, make the necessary recommendations to the Member State concerned. The Council may, acting by a qualified majority on a proposal from the Commission, decide to make its recommendations public.

    The President of the Council and the Commission shall report to the European Parliament on the results of multilateral surveillance. The President of the Council may be invited to appear before the competent Committee of the European Parliament if the Council has made its recommendations public.

5. The Council, acting in accordance with the procedure referred to in Article 189c, may adopt detailed rules for the multilateral surveillance procedure referred to in paragraphs 3 and 4 of this Article.

Article 103a

1. Without prejudice to any other procedures provided for in this Treaty, the Council may, acting unanimously on a proposal from the Commission, decide upon the measures appropriate to the economic situation, in particular if severe difficulties arise in the supply of certain products.

2. Where a Member State is in difficulties or is seriously threatened with severe difficulties caused by exceptional occurrences beyond its control, the Council may, acting unanimously on a proposal from the Commission, grant, under certain conditions, Community financial assistance to the Member State concerned. Where

the severe difficulties are caused by natural disasters, the Council shall act by qualified majority. The President of the Council shall inform the European Parliament of the decision taken.

Article 104

1. Overdraft facilities or any other type of credit facility with the ECB or with the central banks of the Member States (hereinafter referred to as 'national central banks') in favour of Community institutions or bodies, central governments, regional, local or other public authorities, other bodies governed by public law, or public undertakings of Member States shall be prohibited, as shall the purchase directly from them by the ECB or national central banks of debt instruments.

2. Paragraph 1 shall not apply to publicly owned credit institutions which, in the context of the supply of reserves by central banks, shall be given the same treatment by national central banks and the ECB as private credit institutions.

Article 104a

1. Any measure, not based on prudential considerations, establishing privileged access by Community institutions or bodies, central governments, regional, local or other public authorities, other bodies governed by public law, or public undertakings of Member States to financial institutions shall be prohibited.

2. The Council, acting in accordance with the procedure referred to in Article 189c, shall, before 1 January 1994, specify definitions for the application of the prohibition referred to in paragraph 1.

Article 104b

1. The Community shall not be liable for or assume the commitments of central governments, regional, local or other public authorities, other bodies governed by public law, or public undertakings of any Member State, without prejudice to mutual financial guarantees for the joint execution of a specific project. A Member State shall not be liable for or assume the commitments of central governments, regional, local or other public authorities, other bodies governed by public law or public undertakings of another Member State, without prejudice to mutual financial guarantees for the joint execution of a specific project.

2. If necessary, the Council, acting in accordance with the procedure referred to in Article 189c, may specify definitions for the application of the prohibitions referred to in Article 104 and in this Article.

Article 104c

1. Member States shall avoid excessive government deficits.

2. The Commission shall monitor the development of the budgetary situation and of the stock of government debt in the Member States with a view to identifying gross errors. In particular it shall examine compliance with budgetary discipline on the basis of the following two criteria:

    (a) whether the ratio of the planned or actual government deficit to gross domestic product exceeds a reference value, unless

- either the ratio has declined substantially and continuously and reached a level that comes close to the reference value;
- or, alternatively, the excess over the reference value is only exceptional and temporary and the ratio remains close to the reference value;

(b) whether the ratio of government debt to gross domestic product exceeds a reference value, unless the ratio is sufficiently diminishing and approaching the reference value at a satisfactory pace.

The reference values are specified in the Protocol on the excessive deficit procedure annexed to this Treaty.

3. If a Member State does not fulfil the requirements under one or both of these criteria, the Commission shall prepare a report. The report of the Commission shall also take into account whether the government deficit exceeds government investment expenditure and take into account all other relevant factors, including the medium-term economic and budgetary position of the Member State.

   The Commission may also prepare a report if, notwithstanding the fulfilment of the requirements under the criteria, it is of the opinion that there is a risk of an excessive deficit in a Member State.

4. The Committee provided for in Article 109c shall formulate an opinion on the report of the Commission.

5. If the Commission considers that an excessive deficit in a Member State exists or may occur, the Commission shall address an opinion to the Council.

6. The Council shall, acting by a qualified majority on a recommendation from the Commission, and having considered any observations which the Member State concerned may wish to make, decide after an overall assessment whether an excessive deficit exists.

7. Where the existence of an excessive deficit is decided according to paragraph 6, the Council shall make recommendations to the Member State concerned with a view to bringing that situation to an end within a given period. Subject to the provisions of paragraph 8, these recommendations shall not be made public.

8. Where it establishes that there has been no effective action in response to its recommendations within the period laid down, the Council may make its recommendations public.

9. If a Member State persists in failing to put into practice the recommendations of the Council, the Council may decide to give notice to the Member State to take, within a specified time-limit, measures for the deficit reduction which is judged necessary by the Council in order to remedy the situation.

   In such a case, the Council may request the Member State concerned to submit reports in accordance with a specific timetable in order to examine the adjustment efforts to that Member State.

10. The rights to bring actions provided for in Articles 169 and 170 may not be exercised within the framework of paragraphs 1 to 9 of this Article.

11. As long as a Member State fails to comply with a decision taken in accordance with paragraph 9, the Council may decide to apply or, as the case may be, intensify one or more of the following measures:
    - to require the Member State concerned to publish additional information, to be specified by the Council, before issuing bonds and securities;

     –   to invite the European Investment Bank to reconsider its lending policy towards the Member State concerned;

     –   to require the Member State concerned to make a non-interest-bearing deposit of an appropriate size with the Community until the excessive deficit has, in the view of the Council, been corrected;

     –   to impose fines of an appropriate size.

The President of the Council shall inform the European Parliament of the decisions taken.

12. The Council shall abrogate some or all of its decisions referred to in paragraphs 6 to 9 and 11 to the extent that the excessive deficit in the Member State concerned has, in the view of the Council, been corrected. If the Council has previously made public recommendations, it shall, as soon as the decision under paragraph 8 has been abrogated, make a public statement that an excessive deficit in the Member State concerned no longer exists.

13. When taking the decisions referred to in paragraphs 7 to 9, 11 and 12, the Council shall act on a recommendation from the Commission by a majority of two-thirds of the votes of its members weighted in accordance with Article 148 (2), excluding the votes of the representative of the Member State concerned.

14. Further provisions relating to the implementation of the procedure described in this Article are set out in the Protocol on the excessive deficit procedure annexed to this Treaty.

The Council shall, acting unanimously on a proposal from the Commission and after consulting the European Parliament and the ECB, adopt the appropriate provisions which shall then replace the said Protocol.

Subject to the other provisions of this paragraph the Council shall, before 1 January 1994, acting by a qualified majority on a proposal from the Commission and after consulting the European Parliament, lay down detailed rules and definitions for the application of the provisions of the said Protocol.

CHAPTER 2
Monetary policy

Article 105

1. The primary objective of the ESCB shall be to maintain price stability. Without prejudice to the objective of price stability, the ESCB shall support the general economic policies in the Community with a view to contributing to the achievement of the objectives of the Community as laid down in Article 2. The ESCB shall act in accordance with the principle of an open market economy with free competition, favouring an efficient allocation of resources, and in compliance with the principles set out in Article 3a.

2. The basic tasks to be carried out through the ESCB shall be:
     –   to define and implement the monetary policy of the Community;
     –   to conduct foreign-exchange operations consistent with the provisions of Article 109;
     –   to hold and manage the official foreign reserves of the Member States;
     –   to promote the smooth operation of payment systems.

3. The third indent of paragraph 2 shall be without prejudice to the holding and management by the governments of Member States of foreign-exchange working balances.

4. The ECB shall be consulted:
   - on any proposed Community act in its fields of competence;
   - by national authorities regarding any draft legislative provision in its fields of competence, but within the limits and under the conditions set out by the Council in accordance with the procedure laid down in Article 106 (6).

   The ECB may submit opinions to the appropriate Community institutions or bodies or to national authorities on matters in its fields of competence.

5. The ESCB shall contribute to the smooth conduct of policies pursued by the competent authorities relating to the prudential supervision of credit institutions and the stability of the financial system.

6. The Council may, acting unanimously on a proposal from the Commission and after consulting the ECB and after receiving the assent of the European Parliament, confer upon the ECB specific tasks concerning policies relating to the prudential supervision of credit institutions and other financial institutions with the exception of insurance undertakings.

Article 105a

1. The ECB shall have the exclusive right to authorize the issue of banknotes within the Community. The ECB and the national central banks may issue such notes. The banknotes issued by the ECB and the national central banks shall be the only such notes to have the status of legal tender within the Community.

2. Member States may issue coins subject to approval by the ECB of the volume of the issue. The Council may, acting in accordance with the procedure referred to in Article 189c and after consulting the ECB, adopt measures to harmonize the denominations and technical specifications of all coins intended for circulation to the extent necessary to permit their smooth circulation within the Community.

Article 106

1. The ESCB shall be composed of the ECB and of the national central banks.

2. The ECB shall have legal personality.

3. The ESCB shall be governed by the decision-making bodies of the ECB which shall be the Governing Council and the Executive Board.

4. The Statute of the ESCB is laid down in a Protocol annexed to this Treaty.

5. Articles 5.1, 5.2, 5.3, 17, 18, 19.1, 22, 23, 24, 26, 32.2, 32.3, 32.4, 32.6, 33.1(a) and 36 of the Statute of the ESCB may be amended by the Council, acting either by a qualified majority on a recommendation from the ECB and after consulting the Commission or unanimously on a proposal from the Commission and after consulting the ECB. In either case, the assent of the European Parliament shall be required.

6. The Council, acting by a qualified majority either on a proposal from the Commission and after consulting the European Parliament and the ECB or on a recommendation from the ECB and after consulting the European Parliament and the Commission, shall adopt the provisions referred to in Articles 4, 5.4, 19.2, 20, 28.1, 29.2, 30.4 and 34.3 of the Statute of the ESCB.

Article 107

When exercising the powers and carrying out the tasks and duties conferred upon them by this Treaty and the Statute of the ESCB, neither the ECB, nor a national central bank, nor any member of their decision-making bodies shall seek or take instructions from Community institutions or bodies, from any government of a Member State or from any other body. The Community institutions and bodies and the governments of the Member States undertake to respect this principle and not to seek to influence the members of the decision-making bodies of the ECB or of the national central banks in the performance of their tasks.

Article 108

Each Member State shall ensure, at the latest at the date of the establishment of the ESCB, that its national legislation including the statutes of its national central bank is compatible with this Treaty and the Statute of the ESCB.

Article 108a

1. In order to carry out the tasks entrusted to the ESCB, the ECB shall, in accordance with the provisions of this Treaty and under the conditions laid down in the Statute of the ESCB:
    -   make regulations to the extent necessary to implement the tasks defined in Article 3.1, first indent, Articles 19.1, 22 and 25.2 of the Statute of the ESCB and in cases which shall be laid down in the acts of the Council referred to in Article 106 (6);
    -   take decisions necessary for carrying out the tasks entrusted to the ESCB under this Treaty and the Statute of the ESCB;
    -   make recommendations and deliver opinions.

2. A regulation shall have general application. It shall be binding in its entirety and directly applicable in all Member States.

    Recommendations and opinions shall have no binding force.

    A decision shall be binding in its entirety upon those to whom it is addressed.

    Articles 190 to 192 shall apply to regulations and decisions adopted by the ECB.

    The ECB may decide to publish its decisions, recommendations and opinions.

3. Within the limits and under the conditions adopted by the Council under the procedure laid down in Article 106 (6), the ECB shall be entitled to impose fines or periodic penalty payments on undertakings for failure to comply with obligations under its regulations and decisions.

Article 109

1. By way of derogation from Article 228, the Council may, acting unanimously on a recommendation from the ECB or from the Commission, and after consulting the ECB in an endeavour to reach a consensus consistent with the objective of price stability, after consulting the European Parliament, in accordance with the procedure in paragraph 3 for determining the arrangements, conclude formal agreements on an exchange-rate system for the ECU in relation to non-Community currencies. The Council may, acting by a qualified majority on a recommendation from the ECB or

from the Commission, and after consulting the ECB in an endeavour to reach a consensus consistent with the objective of price stability, adopt, adjust or abandon the central rates of the ECU within the exchange-rate system. The President of the Council shall inform the European Parliament of the adoption, adjustment or abandonment of the ECU central rates.

2. In the absence of an exchange-rate system in relation to one or more non-Community currencies as referred to in paragraph 1, the Council, acting by a qualified majority either on a recommendation from the Commission and after consulting the ECB or on a recommendation from the ECB, may formulate general orientations for exchange-rate policy in relation to these currencies. These general orientations shall be without prejudice to the primary objective of the ESCB to maintain price stability.

3. By way of derogation from Article 228, where agreements concerning monetary or foreign-exchange regime matters need to be negotiated by the Community with one or more States or international organizations, the Council, acting by a qualified majority on a recommendation from the Commission and after consulting the ECB, shall decide the arrangements for the negotiation and for the conclusion of such agreements. These arrangements shall ensure that the Community expresses a single position. The Commission shall be fully associated with the negotiations.

   Agreements concluded in accordance with this paragraph shall be binding on the institutions of the Community, on the ECB and on Member States.

4. Subject to paragraph 1, the Council shall, on a proposal from the Commission and after consulting the ECB, acting by a qualified majority decide on the position of the Community at international level as regards issues of particular relevance to economic and monetary union and, acting unanimously, decide its representation in compliance with the allocation of powers laid down in Articles 103 and 105.

5. Without prejudice to Community competence and Community agreements as regards economic and monetary union, Member States may negotiate in international bodies and conclude international agreements.

CHAPTER 3
Institutional provisions

Article 109a

1. The Governing Council of the ECB shall comprise the members of the Executive Board of the ECB and the Governors of the national central banks.

2. (a) The Executive Board shall comprise the President, the Vice-President and four other members.

   (b) The President, the Vice-President and the other members of the Executive Board shall be appointed from among persons of recognized standing and professional experience in monetary or banking matters by common accord of the governments of the Member States at the level of Heads of State or Government, on a recommendation from the Council, after it has consulted the European Parliament and the Governing Council of the ECB.

   Their term of office shall be eight years and shall not be renewable.

   Only nationals of Member States may be members of the Executive Board.

Article 109b

1. The President of the Council and a member of the Commission may participate, without having the right to vote, in meetings of the Governing Council of the ECB.

   The President of the Council may submit a motion for deliberation to the Governing Council of the ECB.

2. The President of the ECB shall be invited to participate in Council meetings when the Council is discussing matters relating to the objectives and tasks of the ESCB.

3. The ECB shall address an annual report on the activities of the ESCB and on the monetary policy of both the previous and current year to the European Parliament, the Council and the Commission, and also to the European Council. The President of the ECB shall present this report to the Council and to the European Parliament, which may hold a general debate on that basis.

   The President of the ECB and the other members of the Executive Board may, at the request of the European Parliament or on their own initiative, be heard by the competent Committees of the European Parliament.

Article 109c

1. In order to promote coordination of the policies of Member States to the full extent needed for the functioning of the internal market, a Monetary Committee with advisory status is hereby set up.

   It shall have the following tasks:
   - to keep under review the monetary and financial situation of the Member States and of the Community and the general payments system of the Member States and to report regularly thereon to the Council and to the Commission;
   - to deliver opinions at the request of the Council or of the Commission, or on its own initiative for submission to those institutions;
   - without prejudice to Article 151, to contribute to the preparation of the work of the Council referred to in Articles 73f, 73g, 103 (2), (3), (4) and (5), 103a, 104a, 104b, 104c, 109e (2), 109f (6), 109h, 109i, 109j (2) and 109k (1);
   - to examine, at least one a year, the situation regarding the movement of capital and the freedom of payments, as they result from the application of this Treaty and of measures adopted by the Council; the examination shall cover all measures relating to capital movements and payments; the Committee shall report to the Commission and to the Council on the outcome of this examination.

   The Member States and the Commission shall each appoint two members of the Monetary Committee.

2. At the start of the third stage, an Economic and Financial Committee shall be set up. The Monetary Committee provided for in paragraph 1 shall be dissolved.

   The Economic and Financial Committee shall have the following tasks:
   - to deliver opinions at the request of the Council or of the Commission, or on its own initiative for submission to those institutions;
   - to keep under review the economic and financial situation of the Member States and of the Community and to report regularly thereon to the Council and to the Commission, in particular on financial relations with third countries and international institutions;
   - without prejudice to Article 151, to contribute to the preparation of the work of the Council referred to in Articles 73f, 73g, 103 (2), (3), (4) and (5), 103a, 104a,

104b, 104c, 105 (6), 105a (2), 106 (5) and (6), 109, 109h, 109i (2) and (3), 109k (2), 109l (4) and (5), and to carry out other advisory and preparatory tasks assigned to it by the Council;

– to examine, at least once a year, the situation regarding the movement of capital and the freedom of payments, as they result from the application of this Treaty and of measures adopted by the Council; the examination shall cover all measures relating to capital movements and payments; the Committee shall report to the Commission and to the Council on the outcome of this examination.

The Member States, the Commission and the ECB shall each appoint no more than two members of the Committee.

3. The Council shall, acting by a qualified majority on a proposal from the Commission and after consulting the ECB and the Committee referred to in this Article, lay down detailed provisions concerning the composition of the Economic and Financial Committee. The President of the Council shall inform the European Parliament of such a decision.

4. In addition to the tasks set out in paragraph 2, if and as long as there are Member States with a derogation as referred to in Articles 109k and 109l, the Committee shall keep under review the monetary and financial situation and the general payments system of those Member States and report regularly thereon to the Council and to the Commission.

Article 109d

For matters within the scope of Articles 103 (4), 104c with the exception of paragraph 14, 109, 109j, 109k and 109l (4) and (5), the Council or a Member State may request the Commission to make a recommendation or a proposal, as appropriate. The Commission shall examine this request and submit its conclusions to the Council without delay.

CHAPTER 4
Transitional provisions

Article 109e

1. The second stage for achieving economic and monetary union shall begin on 1 January 1994.

2. Before that date:

(a) each Member State shall:
   – adopt, where necessary, appropriate measures to comply with the prohibitions laid down in Article 73b, without prejudice to Article 73e, and in Articles 104 and 104a (1);
   – adopt, if necessary, with a view to permitting the assessment provided for in subparagraph (b), multiannual programmes intended to ensure the lasting convergence necessary for the achievement of economic and monetary union, in particular with regard to price stability and sound public finances;

(b) the Council shall, on the basis of a report from the Commission, assess the progress made with regard to economic and monetary convergence, in particular with regard to price stability and sound public finances, and the progress made with the implementation of Community law concerning the internal market.

3. The provisions of Articles 104, 104a (1), 104b (1) and 104c with the exception of paragraphs 1, 9, 11 and 14 shall apply from the beginning of the second stage.

   The provisions of Articles 103a (2), 104c (1), (9) and (11), 105, 105a, 107, 109, 109a, 109b and 109c (2) and (4) shall apply from the beginning of the third stage.

4. In the second stage, Member States shall endeavour to avoid excessive government deficits.

5. During the second stage, each Member State shall, as appropriate, start the process leading to the independence of its central bank, in accordance with Article 108.

Article 109f

1. At the start of the second stage, a European Monetary Institute (hereinafter referred to as 'EMI') shall be established and take up its duties; it shall have legal personality and be directed and managed by a Council, consisting of a President and the Governors of the national central banks, one of whom shall be Vice-President.

   The President shall be appointed by common accord of the governments of the Member States at the level of Heads of State or Government, on a recommendation from, as the case may be, the Committee of Governors of the central banks of the Member States (hereinafter referred to as 'Committee of Governors') or the Council of the EMI, and after consulting the European Parliament and the Council. The President shall be selected from among persons of recognized standing and professional experience in monetary or banking matters. Only nationals of Member States may be President of EMI. The Council of the EMI shall appoint the Vice-President.

   The Statute of the EMI is laid down in a Protocol annexed to this Treaty.

   The Committee of Governors shall be dissolved at the start of the second stage.

2. The EMI shall:
   - strengthen cooperation between the national central banks;
   - strengthen the coordination of the monetary policies of the Member States, with the aim of ensuring price stability;
   - monitor the functioning of the European Monetary System;
   - hold consultations concerning issues falling within the competence of the national central banks and affecting the stability of financial institutions and markets;
   - take over the tasks of the European Monetary Cooperation Fund, which shall be dissolved; the modalities of dissolution are laid down in the Statute of the EMI;
   - facilitate the use of the ECU and oversee its development, including the smooth functioning of the ECU clearing system.

3. For the preparation of the third stage, the EMI shall:
   - prepare the instruments and the procedures necessary for carrying out a single monetary policy in the third stage;
   - promote the harmonization, where necessary, of the rules and practices governing the collection, compilation and distribution of statistics in the areas within its field of competence;
   - prepare the rules for operations to be undertaken by the national central banks within the framework of the ESCB;
   - promote the efficiency of cross-border payments;
   - supervise the technical preparation of ECU banknotes.

At the latest by 31 December 1996, the EMI shall specify the regulatory, organizational and logistical framework for the ESCB to perform its tasks in the third stage. This framework shall be submitted for decision to the ECB at the date of its establishment.

4. The EMI, acting by a majority of two-thirds of the members of its Council, may:
   - formulate opinions or recommendations on the overall orientation of monetary policy and exchange-rate policy as well as on related measures introduced in each Member State;
   - submit opinions or recommendations to governments and to the Council on policies which might affect the internal or external monetary situation in the Community and, in particular, the functioning of the European Monetary System;
   - make recommendations to the monetary authorities of the Member States concerning the conduct of their monetary policy.

5. The EMI, acting unanimously, may decide to publish its opinions and its recommendations.

6. The EMI shall be consulted by the Council regarding any proposed Community act within its field of competence.

   Within the limits and under the conditions set out by the Council, acting by a qualified majority on a proposal from the Commission and after consulting the European Parliament and the EMI, the EMI shall be consulted by the authorities of the Member States on any draft legislative provision within its field of competence.

7. The Council may, acting unanimously on a proposal from the Commission and after consulting the European Parliament and the EMI, confer upon the EMI other tasks for the preparation of the third stage.

8. Where this Treaty provides for a consultative role for the ECB, references to the ECB shall be read as referring to the EMI before the establishment of the ECB.

   Where this Treaty provides for a consultative role for the EMI, references to the EMI shall be read, before 1 January 1994, as referring to the Committee of Governors.

9. During the second stage, the term 'ECB' used in Articles 173, 175, 176, 177, 180 and 215 shall be read as referring to the EMI.

Article 109g

The currency composition of the ECU basket shall not be changed.

From the start of the third stage, the value of the ECU shall be irrevocably fixed in accordance with Article 109l (4).

Article 109h

1. Where a Member State is in difficulties or is seriously threatened with difficulties as regards its balance of payments either as a result of an overall disequilibrium in its balance of payments, or as a result of the type of currency at its disposal, and where such difficulties are liable in particular to jeopardize the functioning of the common market or the progressive implementation of the common commercial policy, the Commission shall immediately investigate the position of the State in question and the action which, making use of all the means at its disposal, that State has taken or may take in accordance with the provisions of this Treaty. The Commission shall state what measures it recommends the State concerned to take.

If the action taken by a Member State and the measures suggested by the Commission do not prove sufficient to overcome the difficulties which have arisen or which threaten, the Commission shall, after consulting the Committee referred to in Article 109c, recommend to the Council the granting of mutual assistance and appropriate methods therefor.

The Commission shall keep the Council regularly informed of the situation and of how it is developing.

2. The Council, acting by a qualified majority, shall grant such mutual assistance; it shall adopt directives or decisions laying down the conditions and details of such assistance, which may take such forms as:
   (a) a concerted approach to or within any other international organizations to which Member States may have recourse;
   (b) measures needed to avoid deflection of trade where the State which is in difficulties maintains or reintroduces quantitative restrictions against third countries;
   (c) the granting of limited credits by other Member States, subject to their agreement.

3. If the mutual assistance recommended by the Commission is not granted by the Council or if the mutual assistance granted and the measures taken are insufficient, the Commission shall authorize the State which is in difficulties to take protective measures, the conditions and details of which the Commission shall determine.

   Such authorization may be revoked and such conditions and details may be changed by the Council acting by a qualified majority.

4. Subject to Article 109k (6), this Article shall cease to apply from the beginning of the third stage.

Article 109i

1. Where a sudden crisis in the balance of payments occurs and a decision within the meaning of Article 109h (2) is not immediately taken, the Member State concerned may, as a precaution, take the necessary protective measures. Such measures must cause the least possible disturbance in the functioning of the common market and must not be wider in scope than is strictly necessary to remedy the sudden difficulties which have arisen.

2. The Commission and the other Member States shall be informed of such protective measures not later than when they enter into force. The Commission may recommend to the Council the granting of mutual assistance under Article 109h.

3. After the Commission has delivered an opinion and the Committee referred to in Article 109c has been consulted, the Council may, acting by a qualified majority, decide that the State concerned shall amend, suspend or abolish the protective measures referred to above.

4. Subject to Article 109k (6), this Article shall cease to apply from the beginning of the third stage.

Article 109j

1. The Commission and the EMI shall report to the Council on the progress made in the fulfilment by the Member States of their obligations regarding the achievement of economic and monetary union. These reports shall include an examination of the

compatibility between each Member State's national legislation, including the statutes of its national central bank, and Articles 107 and 108 of this Treaty and the Statute of the ESCB. The reports shall also examine the achievement of a high degree of sustainable convergence by reference to the fulfilment by each Member State of the following criteria:

- the achievement of a high degree of price stability; this will be apparent from a rate of inflation which is close to that of, at most, the three best performing Member States in terms of price stability;
- the sustainability of the government financial position; this will be apparent from having achieved a government budgetary position without a deficit that is excessive as determined in accordance with Article 104c (6);
- the observance of the normal fluctuation margins provided for by the exchange rate mechanism of the European Monetary System, for at least two years, without devaluing against the currency of any other Member State;
- the durability of convergence achieved by the Member State and of its participation in the exchange rate mechanism of the European Monetary System being reflected in the long-term interest-rate levels.

The four criteria mentioned in this paragraph and the relevant periods over which they are to be respected are developed further in a Protocol annexed to this Treaty. The reports of the Commission and the EMI shall also take account of the development of the ECU, the results of the integration of markets, the situation and development of the balances of payments on current account and an examination of the development of unit labour costs and other price indices.

2. On the basis of these reports, the Council, acting by a qualified majority on a recommendation from the Commission, shall assess:
    - for each Member State, whether it fulfils the necessary conditions for the adoption of a single currency;
    - whether a majority of the Member States fulfil the necessary conditions for the adoption of a single currency,
    and recommend its findings to the Council, meeting in the composition of the Heads of State or Government. The European Parliament shall be consulted and forward its opinion to the Council, meeting in the composition of the Heads of State or Government.

3. Taking due account of the reports referred to in paragraph 1 and the opinion of the European Parliament referred to in paragraph 2, the Council, meeting in the composition of Heads of State or Government, shall, acting by a qualified majority, not later than 31 December 1996:
    - decide, on the basis of the recommendations of the Council referred to in paragraph 2, whether a majority of the Member States fulfil the necessary conditions for the adoption of a single currency;
    - decide whether it is appropriate for the Community to enter the third stage,
    and if so
    - set the date for the beginning of the third stage.

4. If by the end of 1997 the date for the beginning of the third stage has not been set, the third stage shall start on 1 January 1999. Before 1 July 1998, the Council, meeting in the composition of Heads of State or Government, after a repetition of the procedure provided for in paragraphs 1 and 2, with the exception of the second indent of paragraph 2, taking into account the reports referred to in paragraph 1 and the opinion of the European Parliament, shall, acting by a qualified majority and on the basis of the recommendations of the Council referred to in paragraph 2, confirm

which Member States fulfil the necessary conditions for the adoption of a single currency.

1. If the decision has been taken to set the date in accordance with Article 109j (3), the Council shall, on the basis of its recommendations referred to in Article 109j (2), acting by a qualified majority on a recommendation from the Commission, decide whether any, and if so which, Member States shall have a derogation as defined in paragraph 3 of this Article. Such Member States shall in this Treaty be referred to as 'Member States with a derogation'.

    If the Council has confirmed which Member States fulfil the necessary conditions for the adoption of a single currency, in accordance with Article 109j (4), those Member States which do not fulfil the conditions shall have a derogation as defined in paragraph 3 of this Article. Such Member States shall in this Treaty be referred to as 'Member States with a derogation'.

2. At least once every two years, or at the request of a Member State with a derogation, the Commission and the ECB shall report to the Council in accordance with the procedure laid down in Article 109j (1). After consulting the European Parliament and after discussion in the Council, meeting in the composition of the Heads of State or Government, the Council shall, acting by a qualified majority on a proposal from the Commission, decide which Member States with a derogation fulfil the necessary conditions on the basis of the criteria set out in Article 109j (1), and abrogate the derogations of the Member States concerned.

3. A derogation referred to in paragraph 1 shall entail that the following Articles do not apply to the Member State concerned: Articles 104c (9) and (11), 105 (1), (2), (3) and (5), 105a, 108a, 109, and 109a (2) (b). The exclusion of such a Member State and its national central bank from rights and obligations within the ESCB is laid down in Chapter IX of the Statute of the ESCB.

4. In Articles 105 (1), (2) and (3), 105a, 108a, 109 and 109a (2) (b), 'Member States' shall be read as 'Member States without a derogation'.

5. The voting rights of Member States with a derogation shall be suspended for the Council decisions referred to in the Articles of this Treaty mentioned in paragraph 3. In that case, by way of derogation from Articles 148 and 189a (1), a qualified majority shall be defined as two thirds of the votes of the representatives of the Member States without a derogation weighted in accordance with Article 148 (2), and unanimity of those Member States shall be required for an act requiring unanimity.

6. Articles 109h and 109i shall continue to apply to a Member State with a derogation.

Article 109l

1. Immediately after the decision on the date for the beginning of the third stage has been taken in accordance with Article 109j (3), or, as the case may be, immediately after 1 July 1998:
    –   the Council shall adopt the provisions referred to in Article 106 (6);
    –   the governments of the Member States without a derogation shall appoint, in accordance with the procedure set out in Article 50 of the Statute of the ESCB, the President, the Vice-President and the other members of the Executive Board of the ECB. If there are Member States with a derogation, the number of members of

the Executive Board may be smaller than provided for in Article 11.1 of the Statute of the ESCB, but in no circumstances shall it be less than four.

As soon as the Executive Board is appointed, the ESCB and the ECB shall be established and shall prepare for their full operation as described in this Treaty and the Statute of the ESCB. The full exercise of their powers shall start from the first day of the third stage.

2. As soon as the ECB is established, it shall, if necessary, take over tasks of the EMI. The EMI shall go into liquidation upon the establishment of the ECB; the modalities of liquidation are laid down in the Statute of the EMI.

3. If and as long as there are Member States with a derogation, and without prejudice to Article 106 (3) of this Treaty, the General Council of the ECB referred to in Article 45 of the Statute of the ESCB shall be constituted as a third decision-making body of the ECB.

4. At the starting date of the third stage, the Council shall, acting with the unanimity of the Member States without a derogation, on a proposal from the Commission and after consulting the ECB, adopt the conversion rates at which their currencies shall be irrevocably fixed and at which irrevocably fixed rate the ECU shall be substituted for these currencies, and the ECU will become a currency in its own right. This measure shall by itself not modify the external value of the ECU. The Council shall, acting according to the same procedure, also take the other measures necessary for the rapid introduction of the ECU as the single currency of those Member States.

5. If it is decided, according to the procedure set out in Article 109k (2), to abrogate a derogation, the Council shall, acting with the unanimity of the Member States without a derogation and the Member State concerned, on a proposal from the Commission and after consulting the ECB, adopt the rate at which the ECU shall be substituted for the currency of the Member State concerned, and take the other measures necessary for the introduction of the ECU as the single currency in the Member State concerned.

Article 109m

1. Until the beginning of the third stage, each Member State shall treat its exchange-rate policy as a matter of common interest. In so doing, Member States shall take account of the experience acquired in cooperation within the framework of the European Monetary System (EMS) and in developing the ECU, and shall respect existing powers in this field.

2. From the beginning of the third stage and for as long as a Member State has a derogation, paragraph 1 shall apply by analogy to the exchange-rate policy of that Member State.

[...]

PART FIVE
INSTITUTIONS OF THE COMMUNITY

TITLE I
PROVISIONS GOVERNING THE INSTITUTIONS

CHAPTER 1
The institutions

[...]

Section 4
The Court of Justice

[...]

Article 173

The Court of Justice shall review the legality of acts adopted jointly by the European Parliament and the Council, of acts of the Council, of the Commission and of the ECB, other than recommendations and opinions, and of acts of the European Parliament intended to produce legal effects *vis-à-vis* third parties.

It shall for this purpose have jurisdiction in actions brought by a Member State, the Council or the Commission on grounds of lack of competence, infringement of an essential procedural requirement, infringement of this Treaty or of any rule of law relating to its application, or misuse of powers.

The Court shall have jurisdiction under the same conditions in actions brought by the European Parliament and by the ECB for the purpose of protecting their prerogatives.

Any natural or legal person may, under the same conditions, institute proceedings against a decision addressed to that person or against a decision which, although in the form of a regulation or a decision addressed to another person, is of direct and individual concern to the former.

The proceedings provided for in this Article shall be instituted within two months of the publication of the measure, or of its notification to the plaintiff, or, in the absence thereof, of the day on which it came to the knowledge of the latter, as the case may be.

[...]

Article 175

Should the European Parliament, the Council or the Commission, in infringement of this Treaty, fail to act, the Member States and the other institutions of the Community may bring an action before the Court of Justice to have the infringement established.

The action shall be admissible only if the institution concerned has first been called upon to act. If, within two months of being so called upon, the institution concerned has not defined its position, the action may be brought within a further period of two months.

Any natural or legal person may, under the conditions laid down in the preceding

470

paragraphs, complain to the Court of Justice that an institution of the Community has failed to address to that person any act other than a recommendation or an opinion.

The Court of Justice shall have jurisdiction, under the same conditions, in actions or proceedings brought by the ECB in the areas falling within the latter's field of competence and in actions or proceedings brought against the latter.

Article 176

The institution or institutions whose acts has been declared void or whose failure to act has been declared contrary to this Treaty shall be required to take the necessary measures to comply with the judgment of the Court of Justice.

This obligation shall not affect any obligation which may result from the application of the second paragraph of Article 215.

This Article shall also apply to the ECB.

Article 177

The Court of Justice shall have jurisdiction to give preliminary rulings concerning:
(a) the interpretation of this Treaty;
(b) the validity and interpretation of acts of the institutions of the Community and of the ECB;
(c) the interpretation of the statutes of bodies established by an act of the Council, where those statutes so provide.

Where such a question is raised before any court or tribunal of a Member State, that court or tribunal may, if it considers that a decision on the question is necessary to enable it to give judgment, request the Court of Justice to give a ruling thereon.

Where any such question is raised in a case pending before a court or tribunal of a Member State against whose decisions there is no judicial remedy under national law, that court or tribunal shall bring the matter before the Court of Justice.

[...]

Article 180

The Court of Justice shall, within the limits hereinafter laid down, have jurisdiction in disputes concerning

[...]

(d) the fulfilment by national central banks of obligations under this Treaty and the Statute of the ESCB. In this connection the powers of the Council of the ECB in respect of national central banks shall be the same as those conferred upon the Commission in respect of Member States by Article 169. If the Court of Justice finds that a national central bank has failed to fulfil an obligation under this Treaty, that bank shall be required to take the necessary measures to comply with the judgment of the Court of Justice.

[...]

Article 184

Notwithstanding the expiry of the period laid down in the fifth paragraph of Article 173, any party may, in proceedings in which a regulation adopted jointly by the European Parliament and the Council, or a regulation of the Council, of the Commission, or of the ECB is at issue, plead the grounds specified in the second paragraph of Article 173 in order to invoke before the Court of Justice the inapplicability of that regulation.

[...]

PART SIX
GENERAL AND FINAL PROVISIONS

[...]

Article 215

The contractual liability of the Community shall be governed by the law applicable to the contract in question.

In the case of non-contractual liability, the Community shall, in accordance with the general principles common to the laws of the Member States, make good any damage caused by its institutions or by its servants in the performance of their duties.

The preceding paragraph shall apply under the same conditions to damage caused by the ECB or by its servants in the performance of their duties.

The personal liability of its servants towards the Community shall be governed by the provisions laid down in their Staff Regulations or in the Conditions of Employment applicable to them.

[...]

Appendix 3

PROTOCOLS AND DECLARATIONS
WITH RELEVANCE FOR EMU

Appendix Outline

Protocol on the Statute of the European System of Central Banks and of the European Central Bank

Protocol on the Statute of the European Monetary Institute

Protocol on the excessive deficit procedure

Protocol on the convergence criteria referred to in Article 109j of the Treaty establishing the European Community

Protocol amending the Protocol on the privileges and immunities of the European Communities

Protocol on Denmark

Protocol on Portugal

Protocol on the transition to the third stage of economic and monetary union

Protocol on certain provisions relating to the United Kingdom of Great Britain and Northern Ireland

Prototcol on certain provisions relating to Denmark

Protocol on France

Declaration on Part Three, Titles III and VI, of the Treaty establishing the European Community

Declaration on Part Three, Title VI, of the Treaty establishing the European Community

Declaration on monetary cooperation with non-Community countries

Declaration on monetary relations with the Republic of San Marino, the Vatican City and the Principality of Monaco

Declaration on Article 109 of the Treaty establishing the European Community

Declaration on Articles 109, 130r and 130y of the Treaty establishing the European Community

Declaration on disputes between the ECB and the EMI and their servants

PROTOCOL ON THE STATUTE OF THE EUROPEAN SYSTEM OF CENTRAL BANKS AND OF THE EUROPEAN CENTRAL BANK

THE HIGH CONTRACTING PARTIES,

DESIRING to lay down the Statute of the European System of Central Banks and of the European Central Bank provided for in Article 4a of the Treaty establishing the European Community,

HAVE AGREED upon the following provisions, which shall be annexed to the Treaty establishing the European Community:

CHAPTER I
CONSTITUTION OF THE ESCB

Article 1
The European System of Central Banks

1.1. The European System of Central Banks (ESCB) and the European Central Bank (ECB) shall be established in accordance with Article 4a of this Treaty; they shall perform their tasks and carry on their activities in accordance with the provisions of this Treaty and of this Statute.

1.2. In accordance with Article 106 (1) of this Treaty, the ESCB shall be composed of the ECB and of the central banks of the Member States ('national central banks'). The Institut monétaire luxembourgeois will be the central bank of Luxembourg.

CHAPTER II
OBJECTIVES AND TASKS OF THE ESCB

Article 2
Objectives

In accordance with Article 105 (1) of this Treaty, the primary objective of the ESCB shall be to maintain price stability. Without prejudice to the objective of price stability, it shall support the general economic policies in the Community with a view to contributing to the achievement of the objectives of the Community as laid down in Article 2 of this Treaty. The ESCB shall act in accordance with the principle of an open market economy with free competition, favouring an efficient allocation of resources, and in compliance with the principles set out in Article 3a of this Treaty.

Article 3
Tasks

3.1. In accordance with Article 105 (2) of this Treaty, the basic tasks to be carried out through the ESCB shall be:
   - to define and implement the monetary policy of the Community;
   - to conduct foreign-exchange operations consistent with the provisions of Article 109 of this Treaty;
   - to hold and manage the official foreign reserves of the Member States;
   - to promote the smooth operation of payment systems.

475

3.2. In accordance with Article 105 (3) of this Treaty, the third indent of Article 3.1 shall be without prejudice to the holding and management by the governments of Member States of foreign-exchange working balances.

3.3. In accordance with Article 105 (5) of this Treaty, the ESCB shall contribute to the smooth conduct of policies pursued by the competent authorities relating to the prudential supervision of credit institutions and the stability of the financial system.

Article 4
Advisory functions

In accordance with Article 105 (4) of this Treaty:

(a) the ECB shall be consulted:
- on any proposed Community act in its fields of competence;
- by national authorities regarding any draft legislative provision in its fields of competence, but within the limits and under the conditions set out by the Council in accordance with the procedure laid down in Article 42;

(b) the ECB may submit opinions to the appropriate Community institutions or bodies or to national authorities on matters in its fields of competence.

Article 5
Collection of statistical information

5.1. In order to undertake the tasks of the ESCB, the ECB, assisted by the national central banks, shall collect the necessary statistical information either from the competent national authorities or directly from economic agents. For these purposes it shall cooperate with the Community institutions or bodies and with the competent authorities of the Member States or third countries and with international organizations.

5.2. The national central banks shall carry out, to the extent possible, the tasks described in Article 5.1.

5.3. The ECB shall contribute to the harmonization, where necessary, of the rules and practices governing the collection, compilation and distribution of statistics in the areas within its fields of competence.

5.4. The Council, in accordance with the procedure laid down in Article 42, shall define the natural and legal persons subject to reporting requirements, the confidentiality regime and the appropriate provisions for enforcement.

Article 6
International cooperation

6.1. In the field of international cooperation involving the tasks entrusted to the ESCB, the ECB shall decide how the ESCB shall be represented.

6.2. The ECB and, subject to its approval, the national central banks may participate in international monetary institutions.

6.3. Articles 6.1 and 6.2 shall be without prejudice to Article 109 (4) of this Treaty.

CHAPTER III
ORGANIZATION OF THE ESCB

Article 7
Independence

In accordance with Article 107 of this Treaty, when exercising the powers and carrying out the tasks and duties conferred upon them by this Treaty and this Statute, neither the ECB, nor a national central bank, nor any member of their decision-making bodies shall seek or take instructions from Community institutions or bodies, from any government of a Member State or from any other body. The Community institutions and bodies and the governments of the Member States undertake to respect this principle and not to seek to influence the members of the decision-making bodies of the ECB or of the national central banks in the performance of their tasks.

Article 8
General principle

The ESCB shall be governed by the decision-making bodies of the ECB.

Article 9
The European Central Bank

9.1. The ECB which, in accordance with Article 106 (2) of this Treaty, shall have legal personality, shall enjoy in each of the Member States the most extensive legal capacity accorded to legal persons under its law; it may, in particular, acquire or dispose of movable and immovable property and may be a party to legal proceedings.

9.2. The ECB shall ensure that the tasks conferred upon the ESCB under Article 105 (2), (3) and (5) of this Treaty are implemented either by its own activities pursuant to this Statute or through the national central banks pursuant to Articles 12.1 and 14.

9.3. In accordance with Article 106 (3) of this Treaty, the decision-making bodies of the ECB shall be the Governing Council and the Executive Board.

Article 10
The Governing Council

10.1. In accordance with Article 109a (1) of this Treaty, the Governing Council shall comprise the members of the Executive Board of the ECB and the Governors of the national central banks.

10.2. Subject to Article 10.3, only members of the Governing Council present in person shall have the right to vote. By way of derogation from this rule, the Rules of Procedure referred to in Article 12.3 may lay down that members of the Governing Council may cast their vote by means of teleconferencing. These rules shall also provide that a member of the Governing Council who is prevented from voting for a prolonged period may appoint an alternate as a member of the Governing Council.

Subject to Articles 10.3 and 11.3, each member of the Governing Council shall have one vote. Save as otherwise provided for in this Statute, the Governing Council shall act by a simple majority. In the event of a tie, the President shall have the casting vote.

In order for the Governing Council to vote, there shall be a quorum of two-thirds of the members. If the quorum is not met, the President may convene an extraordinary meeting at which decisions may be taken without regard to the quorum.

10.3. For any decisions to be taken under Articles 28, 29, 30, 32, 33 and 51, the votes in the Governing Council shall be weighted according to the national central banks' shares in the subscribed capital of the ECB. The weights of the votes of the members of the Executive Board shall be zero. A decision requiring a qualified majority shall be adopted if the votes cast in favour represent at least two-thirds of the subscribed capital of the ECB and represent at least half of the shareholders. If a Governor is unable to be present, he may nominate an alternate to cast his weighted vote.

10.4. The proceedings of the meetings shall be confidential. The Governing Council may decide to make the outcome of its deliberations public.

10.5. The Governing Council shall meet at least 10 times a year.

Article 11
The Executive Board

11.1. In accordance with Article 109a (2) (a) of this Treaty, the Executive Board shall comprise the President, the Vice-President and four other members.

The members shall perform their duties on a full-time basis. No member shall engage in any occupation, whether gainful or not, unless exemption is exceptionally granted by the Governing Council.

11.2. In accordance with Article 109a (2) (b) of this Treaty, the President, the Vice-President and the other Members of the Executive Board shall be appointed from among persons of recognized standing and professional experience in monetary or banking matters by common accord of the governments of the Member States at the level of the Heads of State or Government, on a recommendation from the Council after it has consulted the European Parliament and the Governing Council.

Their term of office shall be eight years and shall not be renewable.

Only nationals of Member States may be members of the Executive Board.

11.3. The terms and conditions of employment of the members of the Executive Board, in particular their salaries, pensions and other social security benefits shall be the subject of contracts with the ECB and shall be fixed by the Governing Council on a proposal from a Committee comprising three members appointed by the Governing Council and three members appointed by the Council. The members of the Executive Board shall not have the right to vote on matters referred to in this paragraph.

11.4. If a member of the Executive Board no longer fulfils the conditions required for the performance of his duties or if he has been guilty of serious misconduct, the Court of Justice may, on application by the Governing Council or the Executive Board, compulsorily retire him.

11.5. Each member of the Executive Board present in person shall have the right to vote and shall have, for that purpose, one vote. Save as otherwise provided, the Executive Board shall act by a simple majority of the votes cast. In the event of a tie, the President shall have the casting vote. The voting arrangements shall be specified in the Rules of Procedure referred to in Article 12.3.

11.6. The Executive Board shall be responsible for the current business of the ECB.

11.7. Any vacancy on the Executive Board shall be filled by the appointment of a new member in accordance with Article 11.2.

Article 12

Responsibilities of the decision-making bodies

12.1. The Governing Council shall adopt the guidelines and make the decisions necessary to ensure the performance of the tasks entrusted to the ESCB under this Treaty and this Statute. The Governing Council shall formulate the monetary policy of the Community including, as appropriate, decisions relating to intermediate monetary objectives, key interest rates and the supply of reserves in the ESCB, and shall establish the necessary guidelines for their implementation.

The Executive Board shall implement monetary policy in accordance with the guidelines and decisions laid down by the Governing Council. In doing so the Executive Board shall give the necessary instructions to national central banks. In addition the Executive Board may have certain powers delegated to it where the Governing Council so decides.

To the extent deemed possible and appropriate and without prejudice to the provisions of this Article, the ECB shall have recourse to the national central banks to carry out operations which form part of the tasks of the ESCB.

12.2. The Executive Board shall have responsibility for the preparation of meetings of the Governing Council.

12.3. The Governing Council shall adopt Rules of Procedure which determine the internal organization of the ECB and its decision-making bodies.

12.4. The Governing Council shall exercise the advisory functions referred to in Article 4.

12.5. The Governing Council shall take the decisions referred to in Article 6.

Article 13

The President

13.1. The President or, in his absence, the Vice-President shall chair the Governing Council and the Executive Board of the ECB.

13.2. Without prejudice to Article 39, the President or his nominee shall represent the ECB externally.

Article 14

National central banks

14.1. In accordance with Article 108 of this Treaty, each Member State shall ensure, at the latest at the date of the establishment of the ESCB, that its national legislation, including the statutes of its national central bank, is compatible with this Treaty and this Statute.

14.2. The statutes of the national central banks shall, in particular, provide that the term of office of a Governor of a national central bank shall be no less than five years.

A Governor may be relieved from office only if he no longer fulfils the conditions required for the performance of his duties or if he has been guilty of serious misconduct. A decision to this effect may be referred to the Court of Justice by the Governor concerned or the Governing Council on grounds of infringement of this

Treaty or of any rule of law relating to its application. Such proceedings shall be instituted within two months of the publication of the decision or of its notification to the plaintiff or, in the absence thereof, of the day on which it came to the knowledge of the latter, as the case may be.

14.3. The national central banks are an integral part of the ESCB and shall act in accordance with the guidelines and instructions of the ECB. The Governing Council shall take the necessary steps to ensure compliance with the guidelines and instructions of the ECB, and shall require that any necessary information be given to it.

14.4. National central banks may perform functions other than those specified in this Statute unless the Governing Council finds, by a majority of two thirds of the votes cast, that these interfere with objectives and tasks of the ESCB. Such functions shall be performed on the responsibility and liability of national central banks and shall not be regarded as being part of the functions of the ESCB.

Article 15
Reporting commitments

15.1. The ECB shall draw up and publish reports on the activities of the ESCB at least quarterly.

15.2. A consolidated financial statement of the ESCB shall be published each week.

15.3. In accordance with Article 109b (3) of this Treaty, the ECB shall address an annual report on the activities of the ESCB and on the monetary policy of both the previous and the current year to the European Parliament, the Council and the Commission, and also the European Council.

15.4. The reports and statements referred to in this Article shall be made available to interested parties free of charge.

Article 16
Banknotes

In accordance with Article 105a (1) of this Treaty, the Governing Council shall have the exclusive right to authorize the issue of banknotes within the Community. The ECB and the national central banks may issue such notes. The banknotes issued by the ECB and the national central banks shall be the only such notes to have the status of legal tender within the Community.

The ECB shall respect as far as possible existing practices regarding the issue and design of banknotes.

CHAPTER IV
MONETARY FUNCTIONS AND OPERATIONS OF THE ESCB

Article 17
Accounts with the ECB and the national central banks

In order to conduct their operations, the ECB and the national central banks may open accounts for credit institutions, public entities and other market participants and accept assets, including book-entry securities, as collateral.

Article 18
Open market and credit operations

18.1. In order to achieve the objectives of the ESCB and to carry out its tasks, the ECB and the national central banks may:
  – operate in the financial markets by buying and selling outright (spot and forward) or under repurchase agreement and by lending or borrowing claims and marketable instruments, whether in Community or in non-Community currencies, as well as precious metals;
  – conduct credit operations with credit institutions and other market participants, with lending being based on adequate collateral.

18.2. The ECB shall establish general principles for open market and credit operations carried out by itself or the national central banks, including for the announcement of conditions under which they stand ready to enter into such transactions.

Article 19
Minimum reserves

19.1. Subject to Article 2, the ECB may require credit institutions established in Member States to hold minimum reserves on accounts with the ECB and national central banks in pursuance of monetary policy objectives. Regulations concerning the calculation and determination of the required minimum reserves may be established by the Governing Council. In cases of non-compliance the ECB shall be entitled to levy penalty interest and to impose other sanctions with comparable effect.

19.2. For the application of this Article, the Council shall, in accordance with the procedure laid down in Article 42, define the basis for minimum reserves and the maximum permissible ratios between those reserves and their basis, as well as the appropriate sanctions in cases on non-compliance.

Article 20
Other instruments of monetary control

The Governing Council may, by a majority of two thirds of the votes cast, decide upon the use of such other operational methods of monetary control as it sees fit, respecting Article 2.

The Council shall, in accordance with the procedure laid down in Article 42, define the scope of such methods if they impose obligations on third parties.

Article 21
Operations with public entities

21.1. In accordance with Article 104 of this Treaty, overdrafts or any other type of credit facility with the ECB or with the national central banks in favour of Community institutions or bodies, central governments, regional, local or other public authorities, other bodies governed by public law, or public undertakings of Member States shall be prohibited, as shall the purchase directly from them by the ECB or national central banks of debt instruments.

21.2. The ECB and national central banks may act as fiscal agents for the entities referred to in Article 21.1.

21.3. The provisions of this Article shall not apply to publicly-owned credit institutions which, in the context of the supply of reserves by central banks, shall be given the same treatment by national central banks and the ECB as private credit institutions.

Article 22
Clearing and payment systems

The ECB and national central banks may provide facilities, and the ECB may make regulations, to ensure efficient and sound clearing and payment systems within the Community and with other countries.

Article 23
External operations

The ECB and national central banks may:
– establish relations with central banks and financial institutions in other countries and, where appropriate, with international organizations;
– acquire and sell spot and forward all types of foreign exchange assets and precious metals; the term 'foreign exchange asset' shall include securities and all other assets in the currency of any country or units of account and in whatever form held;
– hold and manage the assets referred to in this Article;
– conduct all types of banking transactions in relations with third countries and international organizations, including borrowing and lending operations.

Article 24
Other operations

In addition to operations arising from their tasks, the ECB and national central banks may enter into operations for their administrative purposes or for their staff.

CHAPTER V
PRUDENTIAL SUPERVISION

Article 25
Prudential supervision

25.1. The ECB may offer advice to and be consulted by the Council, the Commission and the competent authorities of the Member States on the scope and implementation of Community legislation relating to the prudential supervision of credit institutions and to the stability of the financial system.

25.2. In accordance with any decision of the Council under Article 105 (6) of this Treaty, the ECB may perform specific tasks concerning policies relating to the prudential supervision of credit institutions and other financial institutions with the exception of insurance undertakings.

CHAPTER VI
FINANCIAL PROVISIONS OF THE ESCB

Article 26
Financial accounts

26.1. The financial year of the ECB and national central banks shall begin on the first day of January and end on the last day of December.

26.2. The annual accounts of the ECB shall be drawn up by the Executive Board, in accordance with the principles established by the Governing Council. The accounts shall be approved by the Governing Council and shall thereafter be published.

26.3. For analytical and operational purposes, the Executive Board shall draw up a consolidated balance sheet of the ESCB, comprising those assets and liabilities of the national central banks that fall within the ESCB.

26.4. For the application of this Article, the Governing Council shall establish the necessary rules for standardizing the accounting and reporting of operations undertaken by the national central banks.

Article 27
Auditing

27.1. The accounts of the ECB and national central banks shall be audited by independent external auditors recommended by the Governing Council and approved by the Council. The auditors shall have full power to examine all books and accounts of the ECB and national central banks and obtain full information about their transactions.

27.2. The provisions of Article 188c of this Treaty shall only apply to an examination of the operational efficiency of the management of the ECB.

Article 28
Capital of the ECB

28.1. The capital of the ECB, which shall become operational upon its establishment, shall be ECU 5 000 million. The capital may be increased by such amounts as may be decided by the Governing Council acting by the qualified majority provided for in Article 10.3, within the limits and under the conditions set by the Council under the procedure laid down in Article 42.

28.2. The national central banks shall be the sole subscribers to and holders of the capital of the ECB. The subscription of capital shall be according to the key established in accordance with Article 29.

28.3. The Governing Council, acting by the qualified majority provided for in Article 10.3, shall determine the extent to which and the form in which the capital shall be paid up.

28.4. Subject to Article 28.5, the shares of the national central banks in the subscribed capital of the ECB may not be transferred, pledged or attached.

28.5. If the key referred to in Article 29 is adjusted, the national central banks shall transfer among themselves capital shares to the extent necessary to ensure that the distribution of capital shares corresponds to the adjusted key. The Governing Council shall determine the terms and conditions of such transfers.

Article 29
Key for capital subscription

29.1. When in accordance with the procedure referred to in Article 109l (1) of this Treaty the ESCB and the ECB have been established, the key for subscription of the ECB's capital shall be established. Each national central bank shall be assigned a weighting in this key which shall be equal to the sum of:
  - 50% of the share of its respective Member State in the population of the Community in the penultimate year preceding the establishment of the ESCB;
  - 50% of the share of its respective Member State in the gross domestic product at market prices of the Community as recorded in the last five years preceding the penultimate year before the establishment of the ESCB;

  The percentages shall be rounded up to the nearest multiple of 0.05 percentage points.

29.2. The statistical data to be used for the application of this Article shall be provided by the Commission in accordance with the rules adopted by the Council under the procedure provided for in Article 42.

29.3. The weightings assigned to the national central banks shall be adjusted every five years after the establishment of the ESCB by analogy with the provisions laid down in Article 29.1. The adjusted key shall apply with effect from the first day of the following year.

29.4. The Governing Council shall take all other measures necessary for the application of this Article.

Article 30
Transfer of foreign reserve assets to the ECB

30.1. Without prejudice to Article 28, the ECB shall be provided by the national central banks with foreign reserve assets, other than Member States' currencies, ECUs, IMF reserve positions and SDRs, up to an amount equivalent to ECU 50 000 million. The Governing Council shall decide upon the proportion to be called up by the ECB following its establishment and the amounts called up at later dates. The ECB shall have the full right to hold and manage the foreign reserves that are transferred to it and to use them for the purposes set out in this Statute.

30.2. The contributions of each national central bank shall be fixed in proportion to its share in the subscribed capital of the ECB.

30.3. Each national central bank shall be credited by the ECB with a claim equivalent to its contribution. The Governing Council shall determine the denomination and remuneration of such claims.

30.4. Further calls of foreign reserve assets beyond the limit set in Article 30.1 may be effected by the ECB, in accordance with Article 30.2, within the limits and under the conditions set by the Council in accordance with the procedure laid down in Article 42.

30.5. The ECB may hold and manage IMF reserve positions and SDRs and provide for the pooling of such assets.

30.6. The Governing Council shall take all other measures necessary for the application of this Article.

Article 31
Foreign reserve assets held by national central banks

31.1. The national central banks shall be allowed to perform transactions in fulfilment of their obligations towards international organizations in accordance with Article 23.

31.2. All other operations in foreign reserve assets remaining with the national central banks after the transfers referred to in Article 30, and Member States' transactions with their foreign exchange working balances shall, above a certain limit to be established within the framework of Article 31.3, be subject to approval by the ECB in order to ensure consistency with the exchange rate and monetary policies of the Community.

31.3. The Governing Council shall issue guidelines with a view to facilitating such operations.

Article 32
Allocation of monetary income of national central banks

32.1. The income accruing to the national central banks in the performance of the ESCB's monetary policy function (hereinafter referred to as 'monetary income') shall be allocated at the end of each financial year in accordance with the provisions of this Article.

32.2. Subject to Article 32.3, the amount of each national central bank's monetary income shall be equal to its annual income derived from its assets held against notes in circulation and deposit liabilities to credit institutions. These assets shall be earmarked by national central banks in accordance with guidelines to be established by the Governing Council.

32.3. If, after the start of the third stage, the balance sheet structures of the national central banks do not, in the judgment of the Governing Council, permit the application of Article 32.2, the Governing Council, acting by a qualified majority, may decide that, by way of derogation from Article 32.2, monetary income shall be measured according to an alternative method for a period of not more than five years.

32.4. The amount of each national central bank's monetary income shall be reduced by an amount equivalent to any interest paid by that central bank on its deposit liabilities to credit institutions in accordance with Article 19.

The Governing Council may decide that national central banks shall be indemnified against costs incurred in connection with the issue of banknotes or in exceptional circumstances for specific losses arising from monetary policy operations under-taken for the ESCB. Indemnification shall be in a form deemed appropiate in the judgment of the Governing Council; these amounts may be offset against the national central banks' monetary income.

32.5. The sum of the national central banks' monetary income shall be allocated to the national central banks in proportion to their paid-up shares in the capital of the ECB, subject to any decision taken by the Governing Council pursuant to Article 33.2.

32.6. The clearing and settlement of the balances arising from the allocation of monetary income shall be carried out by the ECB in accordance with guidelines established by the Governing Council.

32.7. The Governing Council shall take all other measures necessary for the application of this Article.

Article 33
Allocation of net profits and losses of the ECB

33.1. The net profit of the ECB shall be transferred in the following order:
  (a) an amount to be determined by the Governing Council, which may not exceed 20% of the net profit, shall be transferred to the general reserve fund subject to a limit equal to 100% of the capital;
  (b) the remaining net profit shall be distributed to the shareholders of the ECB in proportion to their paid-up shares.

33.2. In the event of a loss incurred by the ECB, the shortfall may be offset against the general reserve fund of the ECB and, if necessary, following a decision by the Governing Council, against the monetary income of the relevant financial year in proportion and up to the amounts allocated to the national central banks in accordance with Article 32.5.

CHAPTER VII
GENERAL PROVISIONS

Article 34
Legal acts

34.1. In accordance with Article 108a of this Treaty, the ECB shall:
  - make regulations to the extent necessary to implement the tasks defined in Article 3.1, first indent, Articles 19.1, 22, or 25.2 and in cases which shall be laid down in the acts of the Council referred to in Article 42;
  - take decisions necessary for carrying out the tasks entrusted to the ESCB under this Treaty and this Statute;
  - make recommendations and deliver opinions.

34.2. A regulation shall have general application. It shall be binding in its entirety and directly applicable in all Member States.

Recommendations and opinions shall have no binding force.

A decision shall be binding in its entirety upon those to whom it is addressed.

Articles 190 to 192 of this Treaty shall apply to regulations and decisions adopted by the ECB.

The ECB may decide to publish its decisions, recommendations and opinions.

34.3. Within the limits and under the conditions adopted by the Council under the procedure laid down in Article 42, the ECB shall be entitled to impose fines or periodic penalty payments on undertakings for failure to comply with obligations under its regulations and decisions.

Article 35
Judicial control and related matters

35.1. The acts or omissions of the ECB shall be open to review or interpretation by the Court of Justice in the cases and under the conditions laid down in this Treaty. The ECB may institute proceedings in the cases and under the conditions laid down in this Treaty.

35.2. Disputes between the ECB, on the one hand, and its creditors, debtors or any other person, on the other, shall be decided by the competent national courts, save where jurisdiction has been conferred upon the Court of Justice.

35.3. The ECB shall be subject to the liability regime provided for in Article 215 of this Treaty. The national central banks shall be liable according to their respective national laws.

35.4. The Court of Justice shall have jurisdiction to give judgment pursuant to any arbitration clause contained in a contract concluded by or on behalf of the ECB, whether that contract be governed by public or private law.

35.5. A decision of the ECB to bring an action before the Court of Justice shall be taken by the Governing Council.

35.6. The Court of Justice shall have jurisdiction in disputes concerning the fulfilment by a national central bank of obligations under this Statute. If the ECB considers that a national central bank has failed to fulfil an obligation under this Statute, it shall deliver a reasoned opinion on the matter after giving the national central bank concerned the opportunity to submit its observations. If the national central bank concerned does not comply with the opinion within the period laid down by the ECB, the latter may bring the matter before the Court of Justice.

Article 36
Staff

36.1. The Governing Council, on a proposal from the Executive Board, shall lay down the conditions of employment of the staff of the ECB.

36.2. The Court of Justice shall have jurisdiction in any dispute between the ECB and its servants within the limits and under the conditions laid down in the conditions of employment.

Article 37
Seat

Before the end of 1992, the decision as to where the seat of the ECB will be established shall be taken by common accord of the governments of the Member States at the level of Heads of State or Government.

Article 38
Professional secrecy

38.1. Members of the governing bodies and the staff of the ECB and the national central banks shall be required, even after their duties have ceased, not to disclose information of the kind covered by the obligation of professional secrecy.

38.2. Persons having access to data covered by Community legislation imposing an obligation of secrecy shall be subject to such legislation.

Article 39
Signatories

The ECB shall be legally committed to third parties by the President or by two members of the Executive Board or by the signatures of two members of the staff of the ECB who have been duly authorized by the President to sign on behalf of the ECB.

Article 40
Privileges and immunities

The ECB shall enjoy in the territories of the Member States such privileges and immunities as are necessary for the performance of its tasks, under the conditions laid down in the Protocol on the Privileges and Immunities of the European Communities annexed to the Treaty establishing a Single Council and a Single Commission of the European Communities.

CHAPTER VIII
AMENDMENT OF THE STATUTE AND
COMPLEMENTARY LEGISLATION

Article 41
Simplified amendment procedure

41.1. In accordance with Article 106 (5) of this Treaty, Articles 5.1, 5.2, 5.3, 17, 18, 19.1, 22, 23, 24, 26, 32.2, 32.3, 32.4, 32.6, 33.1 (a) and 36 of this Statute may be amended by the Council, acting either by a qualified majority on a recommendation from the ECB and after consulting the Commission, or unanimously on a proposal from the Commission and after consulting the ECB. In either case the assent of the European Parliament shall be required.

41.2. A recommendation made by the ECB under this Article shall require a unanimous decision by the Governing Council.

Article 42
Complementary legislation

In accordance with Article 106 (6) of this Treaty, immediately after the decision on the date for the beginning of the third stage, the Council, acting by a qualified majority either on a proposal from the Commission and after consulting the European Parliament and the ECB or on a recommendation from the ECB and after consulting the European Parliament and the Commission, shall adopt the provisions referred to in Articles 4, 5.4, 19.2, 20, 28.1, 29.2, 30.4 and 34.3 of this Statute.

CHAPTER IX
TRANSITIONAL AND OTHER PROVISIONS FOR THE ESCB

Article 43
General provisions

43.1. A derogation as referred to in Article 109k (1) of this Treaty shall entail that the following Articles of this Statute shall not confer any rights or impose any obligations on the Member State concerned: 3, 6, 9.2, 12.1, 14.3, 16, 18, 19, 20, 22, 23, 26.2, 27, 30, 31, 32, 33, 34, 50 and 52.

43.2. The central banks of Member States with a derogation as specified in Article 109k (1) of this Treaty shall retain their powers in the field of monetary policy according to national law.

43.3. In accordance with Article 109k (4) of this Treaty, 'Member States' shall be read as 'Member States without a derogation' in the following Articles of this Statute: 3, 11.2, 19, 34.2 and 50.

43.4. 'National central banks' shall be read as 'central banks of Member States without a derogation' in the following Articles of this Statute: 9.2, 10.1, 10.3, 12.1, 16, 17, 18, 22, 23, 27, 30, 31, 32, 33.2 and 52.

43.5. 'Shareholders' shall be read as 'central banks of Member States without a derogation' in Articles 10.3 and 33.1.

43.6. 'Subscribed capital of the ECB' shall be read as 'capital of the ECB subscribed by the central banks of Member States without a derogation' in Articles 10.3 and 30.2.

Article 44
Transitional tasks of the ECB

The ECB shall take over those tasks of the EMI which, because of the derogations of one or more Member States, still have to be performed in the third stage.

The ECB shall give advice in the preparations for the abrogation of the derogations specified in Article 109k of this Treaty.

Article 45
The General Council of the ECB

45.1. Without prejudice to Article 106 (3) of this Treaty, the General Council shall be constituted as a third decision-making body of the ECB.

45.2. The General Council shall comprise the President and Vice-President of the ECB and the Governors of the national central banks. The other members of the Executive Board may participate, without having the right to vote, in meetings of the General Council.

45.3. The responsibilities of the General Council are listed in full in Article 47 of this Statute.

Article 46
Rules of procedure of the General Council

46.1. The President or, in his absence, the Vice-President of the ECB shall chair the General Council of the ECB.

46.2. The President of the Council and a member of the Commission may participate, without having the right to vote, in meetings of the General Council.

46.3. The President shall prepare the meetings of the General Council.

46.4. By way of derogation from Article 12.3, the General Council shall adopt its Rules of Procedure.

46.5. The Secretariat of the General Council shall be provided by the ECB.

Article 47
Responsibilities of the General Council

47.1. The General Council shall:
- perform the tasks referred to in Article 44;
- contribute to the advisory functions referred to in Articles 4 and 25.1.

47.2. The General Council shall contribute to:
- the collection of statistical information as referred to in Article 5;
- the reporting activities of the ECB as referred to in Article 15;
- the establishment of the necessary rules for the application of Article 26 as referred to in Article 26.4;
- the taking of all other measures necessary for the application of Article 29 as referred to in Article 29.4;
- the laying down of the conditions of employment of the staff of the ECB as referred to in Article 36.

47.3. The General Council shall contribute to the necessary preparations for irrevocably fixing the exchange rates of the currencies of Member States with a derogation against the currencies, or the single currency, of the Member States without a derogation, as referred to in Article 109l (5) of this Treaty.

47.4. The General Council shall be informed by the President of the ECB of decisions of the Governing Council.

Article 48
Transitional provisions for the capital of the ECB

In accordance with Article 29.1 each national central bank shall be assigned a weighting in the key for subscription of the ECB's capital. By way of derogation from Article 28.3, central banks of Member States with a derogation shall not pay up their subscribed capital unless the General Council, acting by a majority representing at least two-thirds of the subscribed capital of the ECB and at least half of the shareholders, decides that a minimal percentage has to be paid up as a contribution to the operational costs of the ECB.

Article 49
Deferred payment of capital, reserves and provisions of the ECB

49.1. The central bank of a Member State whose derogation has been abrogated shall pay up its subscribed share of the capital of the ECB to the same extent as the central banks of other Member States without a derogation, and shall transfer to the ECB foreign reserve assets in accordance with Article 30.1. The sum to be transferred shall be determined by multiplying the ECU value at current exchange rates of the foreign reserve assets which have already been transferred to the ECB in accordance with Article 30.1, by the ratio between the number of shares subscribed by the national central bank concerned and the number of shares already paid up by the other national central banks.

49.2. In addition to the payment to be made in accordance with Article 49.1, the central bank concerned shall contribute to the reserves of the ECB, to those provisions equivalent to reserves, and to the amount still to be appropriated to the reserves and provisions corresponding to the balance of the profit and loss account as at 31 December of the year prior to the abrogation of the derogation. The sum to be contributed shall be determined by multiplying the amount of the reserves, as defined above and as stated in the approved balance sheet of the ECB, by the ratio between the number of shares subscribed by the central bank concerned and the number of shares already paid up by the other central banks.

Article 50
Initial appointment of the members of the Executive Board

When the Executive Board of the ECB is being established, the President, the Vice-President and the other members of the Executive Board shall be appointed by common accord of the governments of the Member States at the level of Heads of State or Government, on a recommendation from the Council and after consulting the European Parliament and the Council of the EMI. The President of the Executive Board shall be appointed for eight years. By way of derogation from Article 11.2, the Vice-President shall be appointed for four years and the other members of the Executive Board for terms of office of between five and eight years. No term of office shall be renewable. The number of members of the Executive Board may be smaller than provided for in Article 11.1, but in no circumstance shall it be less than four.

Article 51
Derogation from Article 32

51.1. If, after the start of the third stage, the Governing Council decides that the application of Article 32 results in significant changes in national central banks' relative income positions, the amount of income to be allocated pursuant to Article 32 shall be reduced by a uniform percentage which shall not exceed 60% in the first financial year after the start of the third stage and which shall decrease by at least 12 percentage points in each subsequent financial year.

51.2. Article 51.1 shall be applicable for not more than five financial years after the start of the third stage.

Article 52
Exchange of banknotes in Community currencies

Following the irrevocable fixing of exchange rates, the Governing Council shall take the necessary measures to ensure that banknotes denominated in currencies with irrevocably fixed exchange rates are exchanged by the national central banks at their respective par values.

Article 53
Applicability of the transitional provisions

If and as long as there are Member States with a derogation Articles 43 to 48 shall be applicable.

PROTOCOL ON THE STATUTE OF THE EUROPEAN MONETARY INSTITUTE

THE HIGH CONTRACTING PARTIES,

DESIRING to lay down the Statute of the European Monetary Institute,

HAVE AGREED upon the following provisions, which shall be annexed to the Treaty establishing the European Community:

Article 1
Constitution and name

1.1. The European Monetary Institute (EMI) shall be established in accordance with Article 109f of this treaty; it shall perform its functions and carry out its activities in accordance with the provisions of this Treaty and of this Statute.

1.2. The members of the EMI shall be the central banks of the Member States ('national central banks'). For the purposes of this Statue, the Institut monétaire luxembourgeois shall be regarded as the central bank of Luxembourg.

1.3. Pursuant to Article 109f of this Treaty, both the Committee of Governors and the European Monetary Cooperation Fund (EMCF) shall be dissolved. All assets and liabilities of the EMCF shall pass automatically to the EMI.

Article 2
Objectives

The EMI shall contribute to the realization of the conditions necessary for the transition to the third stage of economic and monetary union, in particular by:
- strengthening the coordination of monetary policies with a view to ensuring price stability;
- making the preparations required for the establishment of the European System of Central Banks (ESCB), and for the conduct of a single monetary policy and the creation of a single currency in the third stage;
- overseeing the development of the ECU.

Article 3
General principles

3.1. The EMI shall carry out the tasks and functions conferred upon it by this Treaty and this Statue without prejudice to the responsibility of the competent authorities for the conduct of the monetary policy within the respective Member States.

3.2. The EMI shall act in accordance with the objectives and principles stated in Article 2 of the Statute of the ESCB.

Article 4
Primary tasks

4.1. In accordance with Article 109f (2) of this Treaty, the EMI shall:

- strengthen cooperation between the national central banks;
- strengthen the coordination of the monetary policies of the Member States with the aim of ensuring price stability;
- monitor the functioning of the European Monetary System (EMS);
- hold consultations concerning issues falling within the competence of the national central banks and affecting the stability of financial institutions and markets;
- take over the tasks of the EMCF; in particular it shall perform the functions referred to in Articles 6.1, 6.2 and 6.3;
- facilitate the use of the ECU and oversee its development, including the smooth functioning of the ECU clearing system.

The EMI shall also:
- hold regular consultations concerning the course of monetary policies and the use of monetary policy instruments;
- normally be consulted by the national monetary authorities before they take decisions on the course of monetary policy in the context of the common framework for *ex ante* coordination.

4.2. At the latest by 31 December 1996, the EMI shall specify the regulatory, organizational and logistical framework necessary for the ESCB to perform its tasks in the third stage, in accordance with the principle of an open market economy with free competition. This framework shall be submitted by the Council of the EMI for decision to the ECB at the date of its establishment.

In accordance with Article 109f (3) of this Treaty, the EMI shall in particular:
- prepare the instruments and the procedures necessary for carrying out a single monetary policy in the third stage;
- promote the harmonization, where necessary, of the rule and practices governing the collection, compilation and distribution of statistics in the areas within its field of competence;
- prepare the rules for operations to be undertaken by the national central banks in the framework of the ESCB;
- promote the efficiency of cross-border payments;
- supervise the technical preparation of ECU banknotes.

Article 5
Advisory functions

5.1. In accordance with Article 109f (4) of this Treaty, the Council of the EMI may formulate opinions or recommendations on the overall orientation of monetary policy and exchange-rate policy as well as on related measures introduced in each Member State. The EMI may submit opinions or recommendations to governments and to the Council on policies which might affect the internal or external monetary situation in the Community and, in particular, the functioning of the EMS.

5.2. The Council of the EMI may also make recommendations to the monetary authorities of the Member States concerning the conduct of their monetary policy.

5.3. In accordance with Article 109f (6) of this Treaty, the EMI shall be consulted by the Council regarding any proposed Community act within its field of competence.

Within the limits and under the conditions set out by the Council acting by a qualified majority on a proposal from the Commission and after consulting the European Parliament and the EMI, the EMI shall be consulted by the authorities of the Member States on any draft legislative provision within its field of competence, in particular with regard to Article 4.2.

5.4.   In accordance with Article 109f (5) of this Treaty, the EMI may decide to publish its opinions and its recommendations.

Article 6
Operational and technical functions

6.1.   The EMI shall:
- provide for the multilateralization of positions resulting from interventions by the national central banks in Community currencies and the multilateralization of intra-Community settlements;
- administer the very short-term financing mechanism provided for by the Agreement of 13 March 1979 between the central banks of the Member States of the European Economic Community laying down the operating procedures for the European Monetary System (hereinafter referred to as 'EMS Agreement') and the short-term monetary support mechanism provided for in the Agreement between the central banks of the Member States of the European Economic Community of 9 February 1970, as amended;
- perform the functions referred to in Article 11 of Council Regulation (EEC) No 1969/88 of 24 June 1988 establishing a single facility providing medium-term financial assistance for Member States' balances of payments.

6.2.   The EMI may receive monetary reserves from the national central banks and issue ECUs against such assets for the purpose of implementing the EMS Agreement. These ECUs may be used by the EMI and the national central banks as a means of settlement and for transactions between them and the EMI. The EMI shall take the necessary administrative measures for the implementation of this paragraph.

6.3.   The EMI may grant to the monetary authorities of third countries and to international monetary institutions the status of 'other holders' of ECUs and fix the terms and conditions under which such ECUs may be acquired, held or used by other holders.

6.4.   The EMI shall be entitled to hold and manage foreign exchange reserves as an agent for and at the request of national central banks. Profits and losses regarding these reserves shall be for the account of the national central bank depositing the reserves. The EMI shall perform this function on the basis of bilateral contracts in accordance with rules laid down in a decision of the EMI. These rules shall ensure that transactions with these reserves shall not interfere with the monetary policy and exchange-rate policy of the competent monetary authority of any Member State and shall be consistent with the objectives of the EMI and the proper functioning of the exchange-rate mechanism of the EMS.

Article 7
Other tasks

7.1.   Once a year the EMI shall address a report to the Council on the state of the preparations for the third stage. These reports shall include an assessment of the progress towards convergence in the Community, and cover in particular the adaptation of monetary policy instruments and the preparation of the procedures necessary for carrying out a single monetary policy in the third stage, as well as the

494

statutory requirements to be fulfilled for national central banks to become an integral part of the ESCB.

7.2. In accordance with the Council decisions referred to in Article 109f (7) of this Treaty, the EMI may perform other tasks for the preparation of the third stage.

Article 8
Independence

The members of the Council of the EMI who are the representatives of their institutions shall, with respect to their activities, act according to their own responsibilities. In exercising the powers and performing the tasks and duties conferred upon them by this Treaty and this Statute, the Council of the EMI may not seek or take any instructions from Community institutions or bodies or governments of Member States. The Community institutions and bodies as well as the governments of the Member States undertake to respect this principle and not to seek to influence the Council of the EMI in the performance of its tasks.

Article 9
Administration

9.1. In accordance with Article 109f (1) of this Treaty, the EMI shall be directed and managed by the Council of the EMI.

9.2. The Council of the EMI shall consist of a President and the Governors of the national central banks, one of whom shall be Vice-President. If a Governor is prevented from attending a meeting, he may nominate another representative of his institution.

9.3. The President shall be appointed by common accord of the governments of the Member States at the level of Heads of State or Government, on a recommendation from, as the case may be, the Committee of Governors or the Council of the EMI, and after consulting the European Parliament and the Council. The President shall be selected from among persons of recognized standing and professional experience in monetary or banking matters. Only nationals of Member States may be President of the EMI. The Council of the EMI shall appoint the Vice-President. The President and Vice-President shall be appointed for a period of three years.

9.4. The President shall perform his duties on a full-time basis. He shall not engage in any occupation, whether gainful or not, unless exemption is exceptionally granted by the Council of the EMI.

9.5. The President shall:
   - prepare and chair the meetings of the Council of the EMI;
   - without prejudice to Article 22, present the views of the EMI externally;
   - be responsible for the day-to-day management of the EMI.

   In the absence of the President, his duties shall be performed by the Vice-President.

9.6. The terms and conditions of employment of the President, in particular his salary, pension and other social security benefits, shall be the subject of a contract with the EMI and shall be fixed by the Council of the EMI on a proposal from a Committee comprising three members appointed by the Committee of Governors or the Council of the EMI, as the case may be, and three members appointed by the Council. The President shall not have the right to vote on matters referred to in this paragraph.

9.7. If the President no longer fulfils the conditions required for the performance of his duties or if he has been guilty of serious misconduct, the Court of Justice may, on application by the Council of the EMI, compulsorily retire him.

9.8. The Rules of Procedure of the EMI shall be adopted by the Council of the EMI.

Article 10
Meetings of the Council of the EMI and voting procedures

10.1. The Council of the EMI shall meet at least 10 times a year. The proceedings of Council meetings shall be confidential. The Council of the EMI may, acting unanimously, decide to make the outcome of its deliberations public.

10.2. Each member of the Council of the EMI or his nominee shall have one vote.

10.3. Save as otherwise provided for in this Statute, the Council of the EMI shall act by a simple majority of its members.

10.4. Decisions to be taken in the context of Articles 4.2, 5.4, 6.2 and 6.3 shall require unanimity of the members of the Council of the EMI.

The adoption of opinions and recommendations under Articles 5.1 and 5.2, the adoption of decisions under Articles 6.4, 16 and 23.6 and the adoption of guidelines under Article 15.3 shall require a qualified majority of two thirds of the members of the Council of the EMI.

Article 11
Interinstitutional cooperation and reporting requirements

11.1. The President of the Council and a member of the Commission may participate, without having the right to vote, in meetings of the Council of the EMI.

11.2. The President of the EMI shall be invited to participate in Council meetings when the Council is discussing matters relating to the objectives and tasks of the EMI.

11.3. At a date to be established in the Rules of Procedure, the EMI shall prepare an annual report on its activities and on monetary and financial conditions in the Community. The annual report, together with the annual accounts of the EMI, shall be addressed to the European Parliament, the Council and the Commission and also to the European Council.

The President of the EMI may, at the request of the European Parliament or on his own initiative, be heard by the competent Committees of the European Parliament.

11.4. Reports published by the EMI shall be made available to interested parties free of charge.

Article 12
Currency denomination

The operations of the EMI shall be expressed in ECUs.

Article 13
Seat

Before the end of 1992, the decision as to where the seat of the EMI will be established shall be taken by common accord of the governments of the Member States at the level of Heads of State or Government.

Article 14
Legal capacity

The EMI, which in accordance with Article 109f (1) of this Treaty shall have legal personality, shall enjoy in each of the Member States the most extensive legal capacity accorded to legal persons under their law; it may, in particular, acquire or dispose of movable or immovable property and may be a party to legal proceedings.

Article 15
Legal acts

15.1. In the performance of its tasks, and under the conditions laid down in this Statute, the EMI shall:
   - deliver opinions;
   - make recommendations;
   - adopt guidelines, and take decisions, which shall be addressed to the national central banks.

15.2. Opinions and recommendations of the EMI shall have no binding force.

15.3. The Council of the EMI may adopt guidelines laying down the methods for the implementation of the conditions necessary for the ESCB to perform its functions in the third stage. EMI guidelines shall have no binding force; they shall be submitted for decision to the ECB.

15.4. Without prejudice to Article 3.1, a decision of the EMI shall be binding in its entirety upon those to whom it is addressed. Articles 190 and 191 of this Treaty shall apply to these decisions.

Article 16
Financial resources

16.1. The EMI shall be endowed with its own resources. The size of the resources of the EMI shall be determined by the Council of the EMI with a view to ensuring the income deemed necessary to cover the administrative expenditure incurred in the performance of the tasks and functions of the EMI.

16.2. The resources of the EMI determined in accordance with Article 16.1 shall be provided out of contributions by the national central banks in accordance with the key referred to in Article 29.1 of the Statute of the ESCB and be paid up at the establishment of the EMI. For this purpose, the statistical data to be used for the determination of the key shall be provided by the Commission, in accordance with the rules adopted by the Council, acting by a qualified majority on a proposal from the Commission and after consulting the European Parliament, the Committee of Governors and the Committee referred to in Article 109c of this Treaty.

16.3. The Council of the EMI shall determine the form in which contributions shall be paid up.

Article 17
Annual accounts and auditing

17.1. The financial year of the EMI shall begin on the first day of January and end on the last day of December.

17.2. The Council of the EMI shall adopt an annual budget before the beginning of each financial year.

17.3. The annual accounts shall be drawn up in accordance with the principles established by the Council of the EMI. The annual accounts shall be approved by the Council of the EMI and shall thereafter be published.

17.4. The annual accounts shall be audited by independent external auditors approved by the Council of the EMI. The auditors shall have full power to examine all books and accounts of the EMI and to obtain full information about its transactions.

The provisions of Article 188c of this Treaty shall only apply to an examination of the operational efficiency of the management of the EMI.

17.5. Any surplus of the EMI shall be transferred in the following order:
   (a) an amount to be determined by the Council of the EMI shall be transferred to the general reserve fund of the EMI;
   (b) any remaining surplus shall be distributed to the national central banks in accordance with the key referred to in Article 16.2.

17.6. In the event of a loss incurred by the EMI, the shortfall shall be offset against the general reserve fund of the EMI. Any remaining shortfall shall be made good by contributions from the national central banks, in accordance with the key as referred to in Article 16.2.

Article 18
Staff

18.1. The Council of the EMI shall lay down the conditions of employment of the staff of the EMI.

18.2. The Court of Justice shall have jurisdiction in any dispute between the EMI and its servants within the limits and under the conditions laid down in the conditions of employment.

Article 19
Judicial control and related matters

19.1. The acts or omissions of the EMI shall be open to review or interpretation by the Court of Justice in the cases and under the conditions laid down in this Treaty. The EMI may institute proceedings in the cases and under the conditions laid down in this Treaty.

19.2. Disputes between the EMI, on the one hand, and its creditors, debtors or any other person, on the other, shall fall within the jurisdiction of the competent national courts, save where jurisdiction has been conferred upon the Court of Justice.

19.3. The EMI shall be subject to the liability regime provided for in Article 215 of this Treaty.

19.4. The Court of Justice shall have jurisdiction to give judgment pursuant to any arbitration clause contained in a contract concluded by or on behalf of the EMI, whether that contract be governed by public or private law.

19.5. A decision of the EMI to bring an action before the Court of Justice shall be taken by the Council of the EMI.

Article 20
Professional secrecy

20.1. Members of the Council of the EMI and the staff of the EMI shall be required, even after their duties have ceased, not to disclose information of the kind covered by the obligation of professional secrecy.

20.2. Persons having access to data covered by Community legislation imposing an obligation of secrecy shall be subject to such legislation.

Article 21
Privileges and immunities

The EMI shall enjoy in the territories of the Member States such privileges and immunities as are necessary for the performance of its tasks, under the conditions laid down in the Protocol on the Privileges and Immunities of the European Communities annexed to the Treaty establishing a Single Council and a Single Commission of the European Communities.

Article 22
Signatories

The EMI shall be legally committed to third parties by the President or the Vice-President or by the signatures of two members of the staff of the EMI who have been duly authorized by the President to sign on behalf of the EMI.

Article 23
Liquidation of the EMI

23.1. In accordance with Article 109l of this Treaty, the EMI shall go into liquidation on the establishment of the ECB. All assets and liabilities of the EMI shall then pass automatically to the ECB. The latter shall liquidate the EMI according to the provisions of this Article. The liquidation shall be completed by the beginning of the third stage.

23.2. The mechanism for the creation of ECUs against gold and US dollars as provided for by Article 17 of the EMS Agreement shall be unwound by the first day of the third stage in accordance with Article 20 of the said Agreement.

23.3. All claims and liabilities arising from the very short-term financing mechanism and the short-term monetary support mechanism, under the Agreements referred to in Article 6.1, shall be settled by the first day of the third stage.

23.4. All remaining assets of the EMI shall be disposed of and all remaining liabilities of the EMI shall be settled.

23.5. The proceeds of the liquidation described in Article 23.4 shall be distributed to the national central banks in accordance with the key referred to in Article 16.2.

23.6. The Council of the EMI may take the measures necessary for the application of Articles 23.4 and 23.5.

23.7. Upon the establishment of the ECB, the President of the EMI shall relinquish his office.

PROTOCOL ON THE EXCESSIVE DEFICIT PROCEDURE

THE HIGH CONTRACTING PARTIES,

DESIRING to lay down the details of the excessive deficit procedure referred to in Article 104c of the Treaty establishing the European Community,

HAVE AGREED upon the following provisions, which shall be annexed to the Treaty establishing the European Community:

Article 1

The reference values referred to in Article 104c (2) of this Treaty are:
- 3% for the ratio of the planned or actual government deficit to gross domestic product at market prices;
- 60% for the ratio of government debt to gross domestic product at market prices.

Article 2

In Article 104c of this Treaty and in this Protocol:
- government means general government, that is central government, regional or local government and social security funds, to the exclusion of commercial operations, as defined in the European System of Integrated Economic Accounts;
- deficit means net borrowing as defined in the European System of Integrated Economic Accounts;
- investment means gross fixed capital formation as defined in the European System of Integrated Economic Accounts;
- debt means total gross debt at nominal value outstanding at the end of the year and consolidated between and within the sectors of general government as defined in the first indent.

Article 3

In order to ensure the effectiveness of the excessive deficit procedure, the governments of the Member States shall be responsible under this procedure for the deficits of general government as defined in the first indent of Article 2. The Member States shall ensure that national procedures in the budgetary area enable them to meet their obligations in this area deriving from this Treaty. The Member States shall report their

500

planned and actual deficits and the levels of their debt promptly and regularly to the Commission.

Article 4

The statistical data to be used for the application of this Protocol shall be provided by the Commission.

PROTOCOL ON THE CONVERGENCE CRITERIA REFERRED TO IN ARTICLE 109j OF THE TREATY ESTABLISHING THE EUROPEAN COMMUNITY

THE HIGH CONTRACTING PARTIES,

DESIRING to lay down the details of the convergence criteria which shall guide the Community in taking decisions on the passage to the third stage of economic and monetary union, referred to in Article 109j (1) of this Treaty,

HAVE AGREED upon the following provisions, which shall be annexed to the Treaty establishing the European Community:

Article 1

The criterion on price stability referred to in the first indent of Article 109j (1) of this Treaty shall mean that a Member State has a price performance that is sustainable and an average rate of inflation, observed over a period of one year before the examination, that does not exceed by more than $1\frac{1}{2}$ percentage points that of, at most, the three best performing Member States in terms of price stability. Inflation shall be measured by means of the consumer price index on a comparable basis, taking into account differences in national definitions.

Article 2

The criterion on the government budgetary position referred to in the second indent of Article 109j (1) of this Treaty shall mean that at the time of the examination the Member State is not the subject of a Council decision under Article 104c (6) of this Treaty that an excessive deficit exists.

Article 3

The criterion on participation in the exchange-rate mechanism of the European Monetary System referred to in the third indent of Article 109j (1) of this Treaty shall mean that a Member State has respected the normal fluctuation margins provided for by the exchange-rate mechanism of the European Monetary System without severe tensions for at least the last two years before the examination. In particular, the Member State shall not have devalued its currency's bilateral central rate against any other Member State's currency on its own initiative for the same period.

501

Article 4

The criterion on the convergence of interest rates referred to in the fourth indent of Article 109j (1) of this Treaty shall mean that, observed over a period of one year before the examination, a Member State has had an average nominal long-term interest rate that does not exceed by more than two percentage points that of, at most, the three best performing Member States in terms of price stability. Interest rates shall be measured on the basis of long-term government bonds or comparable securities, taking into account differences in national definitions.

Article 5

The statistical data to be used for the application of this Protocol shall be provided by the Commission.

Article 6

The Council shall, acting unanimously on a proposal from the Commission and after consulting the European Parliament, the EMI or the ECB as the case may be, and the Committee referred to in Article 109c, adopt appropriate provisions to lay down the details of the convergence criteria referred to in Article 109j of this Treaty, which shall then replace this Protocol.

PROTOCOL AMENDING THE PROTOCOL ON THE PRIVILEGES AND IMMUNITIES OF THE EUROPEAN COMMUNITIES

THE HIGH CONTRACTING PARTIES,

CONSIDERING that, in accordance with Article 40 of the Statute of the European System of Central Banks and of the European Central Bank and Article 21 of the Statute of the European Monetary Institute, the European Central Bank and the European Monetary Institute shall enjoy in the territories of the Member States such privileges and immunities as are necessary for the performance of their tasks,

HAVE AGREED upon the following provisions, which shall be annexed to the Treaty establishing the European Community:

Sole Article

The Protocol on the Privileges and Immunities of the European Communities, annexed to the Treaty establishing a Single Council and a Single Commission of the European Communities, shall be supplemented by the following provisions:

502

'Article 23

This Protocol shall also apply to the European Central Bank, to the members of its organs and to its staff, without prejudice to the provisions of the Protocol on the Statute of the European System of Central Banks and the European Central Bank.

The European Central Bank shall, in addition, be exempt from any form of taxation or imposition of a like nature on the occasion of any increase in its capital and from the various formalities which may be connected therewith in the State where the Bank has its seat. The activities of the Bank and of its organs carried on in accordance with the Statute of the European System of Central Banks and of the European Central Banks shall not be subject to any turnover tax.

The above provisions shall also apply to the European Monetary Institute. Its dissolution or liquidation shall not give rise to any imposition.'

PROTOCOL ON DENMARK

THE HIGH CONTRACTING PARTIES,

DESIRING to settle certain particular problems relating to Denmark,

HAVE AGREED upon the following provisions, which shall be annexed to the Treaty establishing the European Community:

The provisions of Article 14 of the Protocol on the Statute of the European System of Central Banks and of the European Central Bank shall not affect the right of the National Bank of Denmark to carry out its existing tasks concerning those parts of the Kingdom of Denmark which are not part of the Community.

PROTOCOL ON PORTUGAL

THE HIGH CONTRACTING PARTIES,

DESIRING to settle certain particular problems relating to Portugal,

HAVE AGREED upon the following provisions, which shall be annexed to the Treaty establishing the European Community:

1. Portugal is hereby authorized to maintain the facility afforded to the Autonomous Regions of the Azores and Madeira to benefit from an interest-free credit facility with the Banco de Portugal under the terms established by existing Portuguese law.

2. Portugal commits itself to pursue its best endeavours in order to put an end to the abovementioned facility as soon as possible.

503

PROTOCOL ON THE TRANSITION TO THE THIRD STAGE OF ECONOMIC AND MONETARY UNION

THE HIGH CONTRACTING PARTIES,

Declare the irreversible character of the Community's movement to the third stage of economic and monetary union by signing the new Treaty provisions on economic and monetary union.

Therefore all Member States shall, whether they fulfil the necessary conditions for the adoption of a single currency or not, respect the will for the Community to enter swiftly into the third stage, and therefore no Member State shall prevent the entering into the third stage.

If by the end of 1997 the date of the beginning of the third stage has not been set, the Member States concerned, the Community institutions and other bodies involved shall expedite all preparatory work during 1998, in order to enable the Community to enter the third stage irrevocably on 1 January 1999 and to enable the ECB and the ESCB to start their full functioning from this date.

This Protocol shall be annexed to the Treaty establishing the European Community.

PROTOCOL ON CERTAIN PROVISIONS RELATING TO THE UNITED KINGDOM OF GREAT BRITAIN AND NORTHERN IRELAND

THE HIGH CONTRACTING PARTIES,

RECOGNIZING that the United Kingdom shall not be obliged or committed to move to the third stage of economic and monetary union without a separate decision to do so by its government and Parliament,

NOTING the practice of the government of the United Kingdom to fund its borrowing requirement by the sale of debt to the private sector,

HAVE AGREED the following provisions, which shall be annexed to the Treaty establishing the European Community:

1. The United Kingdom shall notify the Council whether it intends to move to the third stage before the Council makes its assessment under Article 109j (2) of this Treaty.

    Unless the United Kingdom notifies the Council that it intends to move to the third stage, it shall be under no obligation to do so.

504

If no date is set for the beginning of the third stage under Article 109j (3) of this Treaty, the United Kingdom may notify its intention to move to the third stage before 1 January 1998.

2. Paragraphs 3 to 9 shall have effect if the United Kingdom notifies the Council that it does not intend to move to the third stage.

3. The United Kingdom shall not be included among the majority of Member States which fulfil the necessary conditions referred to in the second indent of Article 109j (2) and the first indent of Article 109j (3) of this Treaty.

4. The United Kingdom shall retain its powers in the field of monetary policy according to national law.

5. Articles 3a (2), 104c (1), (9) and (11), 105 (1) to (5), 105a, 107, 108, 108a, 109, 109a (1) and (2) (b) and 109l (4) and (5) of this Treaty shall not apply to the United Kingdom. In these provisions references to the Community or the Member States shall not include the United Kingdom and references to national central banks shall not include the Bank of England.

6. Articles 109e (4) and 109h and i of this Treaty shall continue to apply to the United Kingdom. Articles 109c (4) and 109m shall apply to the United Kingdom as if it had a derogation.

7. The voting rights of the United Kingdom shall be suspended in respect of acts of the Council referred to in the Articles listed in paragraph 5. For this purpose the weighted votes of the United Kingdom shall be excluded from any calculation of a qualified majority under Article 109k (5) of this Treaty.

    The United Kingdom shall also have no right to participate in the appointment of the President, the Vice-President and the other members of the Executive Board of the ECB under Articles 109a (2) (b) and 109l (1) of this Treaty.

8. Articles 3, 4, 6, 7, 9.2, 10.1, 10.3, 11.2, 12.1, 14, 16, 18 to 20, 22, 23, 26, 27, 30 to 34, 50 and 52 of the Protocol on the Statute of the European System of Central Banks and of the European Central Bank (the 'Statute') shall not apply to the United Kingdom.

    In those Articles, references to the Community or the Member States shall not include the United Kingdom and references to national central banks or shareholders shall not include the Bank of England.

    References in Articles 10.3 and 30.2 of the Statute to 'subscribed capital of the ECB' shall not include capital subscribed by the Bank of England.

9. Article 109l (3) of this Treaty and Articles 44 to 48 of the Statute shall have effect, whether or not there is any Member State with a derogation, subject to the following amendments:
    (a) References in Article 44 to the tasks of the ECB and the EMI shall include those tasks that still need to be performed in the third stage owing to any decision of the United Kingdom not to move to that stage.
    (b) In addition to the tasks referred to in Article 47 the ECB shall also give advice in relation to and contribute to the preparation of any decision of the Council with regard to the United Kingdom taken in accordance with paragraphs 10 (a) and 10 (c).
    (c) The Bank of England shall pay up its subscription to the capital of the ECB as a contribution to its operational costs on the same basis as national central banks of Member States with a derogation.

10. If the United Kingdom does not move to the third stage, it may change its notification at any time after the beginning of that stage. In that event:
    (a) The United Kingdom shall have the right to move to the third stage provided only that it satisfies the necessary conditions. The Council, acting at the request of the United Kingdom and under the conditions and in accordance with the procedure laid down in Article 109k (2) of this Treaty, shall decide whether it fulfils the necessary conditions.
    (b) The Bank of England shall pay up its subscribed capital, transfer to the ECB foreign reserve assets and contribute to its reserves on the same basis as the national central bank of a Member State whose derogation has been abrogated.
    (c) The Council, acting under the conditions and in accordance with the procedure laid down in Article 109l (5) of this Treaty, shall take all other necessary decisions to enable the United Kingdom to move to the third stage.

    If the United Kingdom moves to the third stage pursuant to the provisions of this Protocol, paragraphs 3 to 9 shall cease to have effect.

11. Notwithstanding Articles 104 and 109e (3) of this Treaty and Article 21.1 of the Statute, the government of the United Kingdom may maintain its 'ways and means' facility with the Bank of England if and so long as the United Kingdom does not move to the third stage.

PROTOCOL ON CERTAIN PROVISIONS RELATING TO DENMARK

THE HIGH CONTRACTING PARTIES,

DESIRING to settle, in accordance with the general objectives of the Treaty establishing the European Community, certain particular problems existing at the present time,

TAKING INTO ACCOUNT that the Danish Constitution contains provisions which may imply a referendum in Denmark prior to Danish participation in the third stage of economic and monetary union,

HAVE AGREED on the following provisions, which shall be annexed to the Treaty establishing the European Community:

1. The Danish Government shall notify the Council of its position concerning participation in the third stage before the Council makes its assessment under Article 109j (2) of this Treaty.

2. In the event of a notification that Denmark will not participate in the third stage, Denmark shall have an exemption. The effect of the exemption shall be that all Articles and provisions of this Treaty and the Statute of the ESCB referring to a derogation shall be applicable to Denmark.

3. In such case, Denmark shall not be included among the majority of Member States which fulfil the necessary conditions referred to in the second indent of Article 109j (2) and the first indent of Article 109j (3) of this Treaty.

4. As for the abrogation of the exemption, the procedure referred to in Article 109k (2) shall only be initiated at the request of Denmark.

5. In the event of abrogation of the exemption status, the provisions of this Protocol shall cease to apply.

PROTOCOL ON FRANCE

THE HIGH CONTRACTING PARTIES,

DESIRING to take into account a particular point relating to France,

HAVE AGREED upon the following provisions, which shall be annexed to the Treaty establishing the European Community:

France will keep the privilege of monetary emission in its overseas territories under the terms established by its national laws, and will be solely entitled to determine the parity of the CFP franc.

DECLARATION ON PART THREE, TITLES III AND VI, OF THE TREATY ESTABLISHING THE EUROPEAN COMMUNITY

The Conference affirms that, for the purposes of applying the provisions set out in Part Three, Title III, Chapter 4 on capital and payments, and Title VI on economic and monetary policy, of this Treaty, the usual practice, according to which the Council meets in the composition of Economic and Finance Ministers, shall be continued, without prejudice to Article 109j (2) to (4) and Article 109k (2).

DECLARATION ON PART THREE, TITLE VI, OF THE TREATY ESTABLISHING THE EUROPEAN COMMUNITY

The Conference affirms that the President of the European Council shall invite the Economic and Finance Ministers to participate in European Council meetings when the European Council is discussing matters relating to economic and monetary union.

DECLARATION ON MONETARY COOPERATION WITH NON-COMMUNITY COUNTRIES

The Conference affirms that the Community shall aim to contribute to stable international monetary relations. To this end the Community shall be prepared to cooperate with other European countries and those non-European countries with which the Community has close economic ties.

DECLARATION ON MONETARY RELATIONS WITH THE REPUBLIC OF SAN MARINO, THE VATICAN CITY AND THE PRINCIPALITY OF MONACO

The Conference agrees that the existing monetary relations between Italy and San Marino and the Vatican City and between France and Monaco remain unaffected by the Treaty establishing the European Community until the introduction of the ECU as the single currency of the Community.

The Community undertakes to facilitate such renegotiations of existing arrangements as might become necessary as a result of the introduction of the ECU as a single currency.

DECLARATION ON ARTICLE 109 OF THE TREATY ESTABLISHING THE EUROPEAN COMMUNITY

The Conference emphasizes that use of the term 'formal agreements' in Article 109 (1) is not intended to create a new category of international agreement within the meaning of Community law.

DECLARATION ON ARTICLES 109, 130r AND 130y OF THE TREATY ESTABLISHING THE EUROPEAN COMMUNITY

The Conference considers that the provisions of Article 109 (5), Article 130r (4), second subparagraph, and Article 130y do not affect the principles resulting from the judgment handed down by the Court of Justice in the AETR case.

DECLARATION ON DISPUTES BETWEEN THE ECB AND THE EMI AND THEIR SERVANTS

The Conference considers it proper that the Court of First Instance should hear this class of action in accordance with Article 168a of the Treaty establishing the European Community. The Conference therefore invites the institutions to adapt the relevant rules accordingly.

Appendix 4

SECONDARY LEGISLATION
RELATING TO EMU
(OJ No L332, 31.12.1993)

Appendix Outline

Council Regulation (EC) No 3603/93 of 13 December 1993
specifying definitions for the application of the prohibitions referred to in Articles 104 and
104b (1) of the Treaty

Council Regulation (EC) No 3604/93 of 13 December 1993
specifying definitions for the application of the prohibition of priviliged
access referred to in Article 104a of the Treaty

Council Regulation (EC) No 3605/93 of 22 November 1993
on the application of the Protocol on the excessive deficit procedure annexed to the
Treaty establishing the European Community

Council Decision (93/716/EC) of 22 November 1993
on the statistical data to be used for the determination of the key for the financial
resources of the European Monetary Institute

Council Decision (93/717/EC) of 22 November 1993
on the consutation of the European Monetary Institute by the authorities of the Member
States on draft legislative provisions

COUNCIL REGULATION (EC) NO 3603/93 OF 13 DECEMBER 1993

specifying definitions for the application of the prohibitions referred to in Articles 104 and 104b (1) of the Treaty

THE COUNCIL OF THE EUROPEAN UNION,

Having regard to the Treaty establishing the European Community, and in particular Article 104b (2) thereof,

Having regard to the proposal from the Commission([1]),

In cooperation with the European Parliament([2]),

Whereas Articles 104 and 104b (1) of the Treaty are directly applicable; whereas the terms featuring in Articles 104 and 104b (1) may be specified, if necessary;

Whereas the terms 'overdraft facilities' and 'other types of credit facility' used in Article 104 of the Treaty should be defined, particularly with reference to the treatment of claims existing at 1 January 1994;

Whereas it is desirable that the national central banks participating in the third stage of Economic and Monetary Union should enter such Union having on their balance sheets claims negotiable under market conditions, in particular to give the required flexibility to the monetary policy of the European System of Central Banks and to permit a standard contribution from the various national central banks participating in monetary union to the monetary income to be distributed among them;

Whereas the central banks which, after 1 January 1994, still hold claims against the public sector which are non-negotiable or are subject to conditions which are not market conditions should be authorized subsequently to convert such claims into negotiable fixed-maturity securities under market conditions;

Whereas paragraph 11 of the Protocol on certain provisions relating to the United Kingdom of Great Britain and Northern Ireland stipulates that the Government of the United Kingdom may maintain its 'ways and means' facility with the Bank of England if and so long as the United Kingdom does not move to the third stage; whereas it is appropriate to make provision for the conversion of the amount of this facility into marketable debt at a fixed maturity and on market terms if the United Kingdom moves to stage three of EMU;

Whereas the Protocol on Portugal lays down that 'Portugal is hereby authorized to maintain the facility afforded to the Autonomous Regions of the Azores and Madeira to

1. OJ No C 324, 1.12.1993, p.5; and OJ No C 340, 17.12.1993, p.3.
2. OJ No C 329, 6.12.1993 and Decision of 2 December 1993 (not yet published in the Official Journal).

benefit from an interest-free credit facility with the Banco de Portugal under the terms established by existing Portuguese law'; and that 'Portugal commits itself to pursue its best endeavours in order to put an end to the abovementioned facility as soon as possible';

Whereas Member States must take appropriate measures to ensure that the prohibitions referred to in Article 104 of the Treaty are applied effectively and fully; whereas, in particular, purchases made on the secondary market must not be used to circumvent the objective of that Article;

Whereas, within the limits laid down in this Regulation, the direct acquisition by the central bank of one Member State of marketable debt instruments issued by the public sector of another Member State does not help to shield the public sector from the discipline of market mechanisms where such purchases are conducted for the sole purpose of managing foreign exchange reserves;

Whereas, notwithstanding the role assigned to the Commission pursuant to Article 169 of the Treaty, it is for the European Monetary Institute and, thereafter, for the European Central Bank, pursuant to Articles 109f (9) and 180 of the Treaty, to ensure that national central banks honour the obligations laid down by the Treaty;

Whereas intra-day credits by the central banks may assist the smooth operation of payment systems; whereas, therefore, intra-day credits in the public sector are compatible with the objectives of Article 104 of the Treaty, provided that no extension to the following day is possible;

Whereas the function of fiscal agent exercised by the central banks should not be impeded; whereas, even if clearing by the central banks of cheques issued by third parties for the public sector's account may occasionally involve a credit, Article 104 of the Treaty should not be regarded as prohibiting such operations, provided that they do not result overall in a credit for the public sector;

Whereas the holding by the central banks of coins issued by the public sector and credited to the public sector constitutes an interest-free form of credit for the public sector; whereas, however, if only limited amounts are involved, this practice does not interfere with the principle of Article 104 of the Treaty; whereas, therefore, in view of the difficulties which would arise from total prohibition of this form of credit, it may be permitted within the limits laid down in this Regulation;

Whereas, following unification, the Federal Republic of Germany has particular difficulty in complying with the limit set on such assets; whereas it is appropriate in those circumstances to authorize a higher percentage for a limited period;

Whereas the financing by the central banks of obligations falling upon the public sector *vis-à-vis* the International Monetary Fund or resulting from the implementation of the medium-term financial assistance facility set up within the Community results in foreign claims which have all the characteristics of reserve assets; whereas it is, therefore, appropriate to authorize them;

Whereas public undertakings are covered by the prohibition in Articles 104 and 104b (1);

514

whereas they are defined in Commission Directive 80/723/EEC of 25 June 1980 on the transparency of financial relations between Member States and public undertakings([1]),

HAS ADOPTED THIS REGULATION:

Article 1

1.   For the purposes of Article 104 of the Treaty:
(a) 'overdraft facilities' means any provision of funds to the public sector resulting or likely to result in a debit balance;

(b) 'other type of credit facility' means:
(i)   any claim against the public sector existing at 1 January 1994, except for fixed-maturity claims acquired before that date;
(ii)   any financing of the public sector's obligations *vis-à-vis* third parties;
(iii) without prejudice to Article 104 (2) of the Treaty, any transaction with the public sector resulting or likely to result in a claim against that sector.

2.   The following shall not be regarded as 'debt instruments' within the meaning of Article 104 of the Treaty securities acquired from the public sector to ensure the conversion into negotiable fixed-maturity securities under market conditions of:
–   fixed-maturity claims acquired before 1 January 1994 which are not negotiable or not under market conditions, provided that the maturity of the securities is not subsequent to that of the aforementioned claims;
–   the amount of the 'ways and means' facility maintained by the United Kingdom Government with the Bank of England until the date, if any, on which the United Kingdom moves to stage three of EMU.

Article 2

1.   During stage two of EMU, purchases by the national central bank of one Member State of marketable debt instruments issued by the public sector of another Member State shall not be considered direct purchases within the meaning of Article 104 of the Treaty, provided that such purchases are conducted for the sole purpose of managing foreign exchange reserves.

2.   During stage three of EMU, the following purchases conducted for the sole purpose of managing foreign exchange reserves shall not be considered direct purchases within the meaning of Article 104 of the Treaty:
–   purchases by the national central bank of a Member State not participating in stage three of EMU, from the public sector of another Member State, of marketable debt instruments of the latter,
–   purchases by the European Central Bank or the national central bank of a Member State participating in stage three of EMU, from the public sector of a Member State not participating in stage three, of marketable debt instruments of the latter.

1.   OJ No L 195, 29.7.1980, p.35. Directive as last amended by Directive 93/84/EEC (OJ No L 254, 12.10.1993, p.16).

Article 3

For the purposes of this Regulation, 'public sector' means Community institutions or bodies, central governments, regional, local or other public authorities, other bodies governed by public law or public undertakings of Member States.

'National central banks' means the central banks of the Member States and the Luxembourg Monetary Institute.

Article 4

Intra-day credits by the European Central Bank or the national banks to the public sector shall not be considered as a credit facility within the meaning of Article 104 of the Treaty, provided that they remain limited to the day and that no extension is possible.

Article 5

Where the European Central Bank or the national central banks receive from the public sector, for collection, cheques issued by third parties and credit the public sector's account before the drawee bank has been debited, this operation shall not be considered as a credit facility within the meaning of Article 104 of the Treaty if a fixed period of time corresponding to the normal period of the collection of cheques by the central bank of the Member State concerned has elapsed since receipt of the cheque, provided that any float which may arise is exceptional, is of a small amount and averages out in the short term.

Article 6

The holding by the European Central Bank or the national central banks of coins issued by the public sector and credited to the public sector shall not be regarded as a credit facility within the meaning of Article 104 of the Treaty where the amount of these assets remains at less than 10% of the coins in circulation.

Until 31 December 1996, this figure shall be 15% for Germany.

Article 7

The financing by the European Central Bank or the national central banks of obligations falling upon the public sector *vis-à-vis* the International Monetary Fund or resulting from the implementation of the medium-term financial assistance facility set up by Regulation (EEC) No 1969/88([1]) shall not be regarded as a credit facility within the meaning of Article 104 of the Treaty.

---

1. Council Regulations (EEC) No 1969/88 of 24 June 1988 establishing a single facility providing medium-term financial assistance for Member States' balances of payments (OJ No L 178, 8.7.1988, p.1).

Article 8

1. For the purposes of Articles 104 and 104b (1) of the Treaty, 'public undertaking' shall be defined as any undertaking over which the State or other regional or local authorities may directly or indirectly exercise a dominant influence by virtue of their ownership of it, their financial participation therein or the rules which govern it.
    A dominant influence on the part of the public authorities shall be presumed when these authorities, directly or indirectly in relation to an undertaking:

    (a) hold the major part of the undertaking's subscribed capital;

    (b) control the majority of the votes attaching to shares issued by the undertaking; or

    (c) can appoint more than half of the members of the undertaking's administrative, managerial or supervisory body.

2. For the purposes of Articles 104 and 104b (1) of the Treaty, the European Central Bank and the national central banks do not form part of the public sector.

Article 9

This Regulation shall enter into force on 1 January 1994.

This Regulation shall be binding in its entirety and directly applicable in all Member States.

Done at Brussels, 13 December 1993.

For the Council
The President
Ph. MAYSTADT

517

COUNCIL REGULATION (EC) NO 3604/93 OF 13 DECEMBER 1993

specifying definitions for the application of the prohibition of privileged access referred to in Article 104a of the Treaty

THE COUNCIL OF THE EUROPEAN UNION,

Having regard to the Treaty establishing the European Community, and in particular Article 104a (2) thereof,

Having regard to the proposal from the Commission([1]),

In cooperation with the European Parliament([2]),

Whereas the prohibition of privileged access to financial institutions, as laid down in Article 104a of the Treaty, forms an essential element of the submission of the public sector in its financing operations to the discipline of the market mechanism and so makes a contribution to the strengthening of budgetary discipline; whereas, moreover, it places the Member States on an equal footing as regards public sector access to financial institutions;

Whereas the Council must specify definitions for the application of such prohibition;

Whereas the Member States and the Community must act with due regard for the principle of an open market economy in which there is free competition;

Whereas, in particular, this Regulation cannot affect the methods for organizing markets complying with that principle;

Whereas this Regulation does not seek to interfere with any operation of public financial institutions complying with the same principle;

Whereas Article 104a of the Treaty prohibits measures establishing privileged access; whereas the types of acts concerned by this prohibition should be specified; whereas the commitments freely made by financial institutions in the framework of contractual relations unquestionably cannot be affected;

Whereas the same Article provides that prudential considerations may justify departure from the principle of this prohibition; whereas laws, regulations or administrative actions may not, however, under the cover of prudential consideration, be used to establish disguised privileged access;

1. OJ No C 324, 1.12.1993, p. 7; and OJ No C 340, 17. 12. 1993, p.6.
2. OJ No C 329, 6.12.1993 and Decision of 2 December 1993 (not yet published in the Official Journal).

Whereas public undertakings are covered by the same prohibition; whereas they are defined in Commission Directive 80/723/EEC of 25 June 1980 on the transparency of financial relations between the Member States and public undertakings([1]);

Whereas, for reasons of monetary policy, financial institutions and, in particular, credit institutions may be obliged to hold claims against the European Central Bank and/or national central banks;

Whereas the European Central Bank and national central banks may not, as public authorities, take measures establishing privileged access; whereas the rules on mobilization or pledging of debt instruments enacted by the European Central Bank or by national central banks must not be used as a means of circumventing the prohibition of privileged access;

Whereas, in order to avoid any circumvention of the prohibition, the definitions in Community law of the various types of financial institution should be supplemented by a reference to those institutions engaging in financial activities which have not yet been harmonized at Community level, such as, for instance, branches of third-country establishments, holding and factoring companies, uncoordinated undertakings for collective investment in transferable securities (UCITS), institutions for retirement provision, etc.,

HAS ADOPTED THIS REGULATION:

Article 1

1. For the purposes of Article 104a of the Treaty, 'any measure establishing privileged access' shall be defined as any law, regulation or any other binding legal instrument adopted in the exercise of public authority which:
   - obliges financial institutions to acquire or to hold liabilities of Community institutions or bodies, central governments, regional, local or other public authorities, other bodies governed by public law or public undertakings of Member States (hereinafter referred to as 'public sector'), or
   - confers tax advantages which may benefit only financial institutions or financial advantages which do not comply with the principles of a market economy, in order to encourage the acquiring or the holding by those institutions of such liabilities.

2. Privileged access shall not be regarded as being established by those measures which give rise to:
   - obligations for funding social housing under special terms such as, inter alia, an obligation to centralize funds with public financial institutions, when the funding terms prevailing for the public sector are identical to those for funding of the same nature granted to private borrowers for the same purposes,
   - the obligation to centralize funds with a public credit institution, in so far as such a constraint is an integral part, as at 1 January 1994, of the organization of a particular network of credit institutions or of specific savings arrangements

---

1. OJ No L 195, 29.7.1980, p.35. Directive as last amended by Directive 93/84/EEC (OJ No L 254, 12.10.1993, p.16).

designed for households and intended to provide the whole of the network or the specific arrangements with financial security. The use of such centralized funds must be determined by the management bodies of the public credit institution concerned and comply with the principle of a market economy where there is free competition,

- obligations to finance the repair of disaster damage, provided that the conditions for financing repairs are not more favourable when damage is sustained by the public sector than when it is sustained by the private sector.

Article 2

For the purposes of Article 104a of the Treaty, 'prudential considerations' shall be those which underlie national laws, regulations or administrative actions based on, or consistent with, EC law and designed to promote the soundness of financial institutions so as to strengthen the stability of the financial system as a whole and the protection of the customers of those institutions.

Article 3

1. For the purposes of Article 104a of the Treaty, 'public undertaking' shall be defined as any undertaking over which the State or other regional or local authorities may exercise directly or indirectly a dominant influence by virtue of their ownership of it, their financial participation therein or the rules which govern it.

   A dominant influence on the part of the State or other regional or local authorities shall be presumed when these authorities, directly or indirectly in relation to an undertaking:
   (a) hold the major part of the undertaking's subscribed capital;

   (b) control the majority of the votes attaching to shares issued by the undertaking; or

   (c) can appoint more than half of the members of the undertaking's administrative, managerial or supervisory body.

2. Without prejudice to their obligation as public authorities not to take measures establishing privileged access within the meaning of Article 104a of the Treaty, the European Central Bank and the national central banks shall not, for the purposes of this Article, be considered as forming part of the public sector.

3. 'National central banks' means the central banks of the Member States and the Luxembourg Monetary Institute.

Article 4

1. For the purposes of Article 104a of the Treaty, 'financial institutions' means:
   - credit institutions as defined in the first indent of Article 1 of Directive 77/780/ EEC([1]),

   ---

   1. Council Directive 77/80/EEC of 12 December 1977 on the coordination of the laws, regulations and administrative provisions relating to the taking-up and pursuit of the business of credit institutions (OJ No L 322, 17. 12. 1977, p. 30). Directive as last amended by Directive 89/646/EEC (OJ No L 386, 30. 12. 1989, p. 1).

- insurance undertakings as defined in Article 1, point (a) of Directive 92/49/EEC(^{1}),
- assurance undertakings as defined in Article 1, point (a) of Directive 92/96/EEC(^{2}),
- UCITS as defined in Article 1 (2) of Directive 85/611/EEC(^{3}),
- investment firms as defined in Article 1 (2) of Directive 93/22/EEC(^{4}),
- other undertakings the activities of which are similar to those of the undertakings referred to in the previous indents or the principal activity of which is to acquire holdings of financial assets or to transform financial claims.

2. The following institutions do not form part of the financial institutions defined in paragraph 1:

- the European Central Bank and national central banks,
- post office financial services when they form part of the general government sector defined in accordance with the European System of Integrated Economic Accounts or when their main activity is to act as the financial agent of government, and
- the institutions which are part of the general government sector defined in accordance with the European System of Integrated Economic Accounts or the liabilities of which correspond completely to a public debt.

Article 5

This Regulation shall enter into force on 1 January 1994.

This Regulation shall be binding in its entirety and directly applicable in all Member States.

Done at Brussels, 13 December 1993.

For the Council
The President
Ph. MAYSTADT

1. Council Directive 92/49/EEC of 18 June 1992 on the coordination of laws, regulations and administrative provisions relating to direct insurance other than life insurance (third Directive on insurance other than life insurance) (OJ No L 228, 11.8.1992, p.1).
2. Council Directive 92/96/EEC of 10 November 1992 on the coordination of laws, regulations and administrative provisions relating to direct life assurance (third Directive on life insurance) (OJ No L 360, 9.12.1992, p.1).
3. Council Directive 85/611/EEC of 20 December 1985 on the coordination of laws, regulations and administrative provisions relating to undertakings for collective investment in transferable securities (UCITS) (OJ No L 375, 31.12.1985, p.3). Directive as amended by Directive 88/220/EEC (OJ No L 100, 19.4.1988, p.31).
4. Council Directive 93/22/EEC of 10 May 1993 on investment services in the securities field (OJ No L 141, 11.6.1993, p.27).

European Economic and Monetary Union: The Institutional Framework

COUNCIL REGULATION (EC) NO 3605/93 OF 22 NOVEMBER 1993

on the application of the Protocol on the excessive deficit procedure annexed to the Treaty establishing the European Community

THE COUNCIL OF THE EUROPEAN UNION,

Having regard to the Treaty establishing the European Community, and in particular the third subparagraph of Article 104c (14) thereof,

Having regard to the proposal from the Commission[1],

Having regard to the opinion of the European Parliament[2],

Whereas the definitions of 'government', 'deficit' and 'investment' are laid down in the Protocol on the excessive deficit procedure by reference to the European System of Integrated Economic Accounts (ESA)[3]; whereas precise definitions referring to the classification codes of ESA are required; whereas these definitions may be subject to revision in the context of the necessary harmonization of national statistics or for other reasons; whereas any revision of ESA will be decided by the Council in accordance with the rules on competence and procedure laid down in the Treaty;

Whereas the definition of 'debt' laid down in the Protocol on the excessive deficit procedure needs to be amplified by a reference to the classification codes of ESA;

Whereas Council Directive 89/130/EEC, Euratom of 13 February 1989 on the harmonization of the compilation of gross national product at market prices[4] provides an adequate, detailed definition of gross domestic product at market prices;

Whereas, pursuant to the terms of the Protocol on the excessive deficit procedure, the Commission is required to provide the statistical data to be used in that procedure;

Whereas detailed rules are required to organize the prompt and regular reporting by the Member States to the Commission of their planned and actual deficits and of the levels of their debt;

Whereas, pursuant to Article 104c (2) and (3) of the Treaty, the Commission is to monitor the development of the budgetary situation and of the stock of government debt in the Member States and to examine compliance with budgetary discipline on the basis of criteria relating to government deficit and government debt; whereas, if a Member State does not fulfil the requirements under one or both criteria, the Commission must take into

1. OJ No C 324, 1.12.1993, p.8; and OJ No C 340, 17.12.1993, p.8.
2. OJ No C 329, 6.12.1993.
3. Statistical Office of the European Communities, *European System of Integrated Economic Accounts (ESA)*, second edition.
4. OJ No L 49, 21.2.1989, p.26.

522

account all relevant factors; whereas the Commission has to examine whether there is a risk of an excessive deficit in a Member State,

HAS ADOPTED THIS REGULATION:

SECTION 1
Definitions

Article 1

1.   For the purposes of the Protocol on the excessive deficit procedure and of this Regulation, the terms given in the following paragraphs are defined according to the European System of Integrated Economic Accounts (ESA). The codes in brackets refer to ESA, second edition.

2.   'Government' means the sector of general government (S60), that is central government (S61), local government (S62) and social security funds (S63), to the exclusion of commercial operations, as defined in ESA.

   The exclusion of commercial operations means that the sector of general government (S60) comprises only institutional units producing non-market services as their main activity.

3.   'Government deficit (surplus)' means the net borrowing (net lending) (N5) of the sector of general government (S60), as defined in ESA. The interest comprised in the government deficit is the sum of interest (R41), as defined in ESA.

4.   'Government investment' means the gross fixed capital formation (P41) of the sector of general government (S60), as defined in ESA.

5.   'Government debt' means the total gross debt at nominal value outstanding at the end of the year of the sector of general government (S60), with the exception of those liabilities the corresponding financial assets of which are held by the sector of general government (S60).

   Government debt is constituted by the liabilities of general government in the following categories currency and deposits (F20 and F30), bills and short-term bonds (F40), long-term bonds (F50), other short-term loans (F79) and other medium and long-term loans (F89) as defined in ESA.

   The nominal value of a liability outstanding at the end of the year is the face value.

   The nominal value of an index-linked liability corresponds to its face value adjusted by the index-related capital uplift accrued to the end of the year.

   Liabilities denominated in foreign currencies shall be converted into the national currency at the representative market exchange rate prevailing on the last working day of each year.

Article 2

Gross domestic product means gross domestic product at market prices (GDP mp), as defined in Article 2 of Directive 89/130/EEC, Euratom.

Article 3

1. Planned government deficit figures mean the figures established for the current year by the Member States consistent with the most recent decisions of their budgetary authorities.

2. Actual government deficit and government debt level figures mean estimated, provisional, half-finalized or final results for a past year.

SECTION 2
Rules and coverage of reporting
Article 4

1. As from the beginning of 1994, Member States shall report to the Commission their planned and actual government deficits and levels of government debt twice a year, the first time before 1 March of the current year (year n) and the second time before 1 September of year n.

2. Before 1 March of year n, Member States:
    -   shall report to the Commission their planned government deficit for year n, an up-to-date estimate of their actual government deficit for year n-1 and their actual government deficits for years n-2, n-3 and n-4,
    -   shall simultaneously provide the Commission for years n, n-1 and n-2 with their corresponding public accounts budget deficits according to the definition which is given most prominence nationally and with the figures which explain the transition between this public accounts budgets deficit and their government deficit. The figures explaining this transition which are provided to the Commission shall include, in particular, the figures for net borrowing of the subsectors S61, S62 and S63,
    -   shall report to the Commission their estimate of the level of actual government debt at the end of year n-1 and their levels of actual government debt for years n-2, n-3 and n-4,
    -   shall simultaneously provide the Commission for years n-1 and n-2 with the figures which explain the contributions of their government deficit and the other relevant factors contributing to the variation in the level of their government debt.

3. Before 1 September of year n, Member States shall report to the Commission:
    -   their updated planned government deficit for year n and their actual government deficits for years n-1, n-2, n-3 and n-4 and shall comply with the requirements of the second indent of paragraph 2,
    -   their actual level of government debt for years n-1, n-2, n-3 and n-4, and shall comply with the requirements of the fourth indent of paragraph 2.

4. The figures for the planned government deficit reported to the Commission in accordance with paragraphs 2 and 3 shall be expressed in national currency and in budget years.

    The figures for actual government deficit and actual government debt level reported to the Commission in accordance with paragraphs 2 and 3 shall be expressed in national currency and in calendar years, with the exception of the up-to-date estimates for year n-1, which may be expressed in budget years.

Where the budget year differs from the calendar year, Member States shall also report to the Commission their figures for actual government deficit and actual government debt level in budget years for the two budget years preceding the current budget year.

Article 5

Member States shall, in accordance with the procedure laid down in Article 4 (1), (2) and (3), provide the Commission with the figures for their government investment expenditure and interest expenditure.

Article 6

Member States shall provide the Commission with a forecast of their gross domestic product for year n and the actual amount of their gross domestic product for years n-1, n-2, n-3 and n-4, under the same timing conditions as those indicated in Article 4 (1).

Article 7

In the event of a revision of ESA to be decided on by the Council in accordance with the rules on competence and procedure laid down in the Treaty, the Commission shall introduce the new references to ESA into Articles 1 and 4.

Article 8

This Regulation shall enter into force on 1 January 1994.

This Regulation shall be binding in its entirety and directly applicable in all Member States.

Done at Brussels, 22 November 1993.

For the Council
The President
Ph. MAYSTADT

COUNCIL DECISION OF 22 NOVEMBER 1993

on the statistical data to be used for the determination of the key for the financial resources of the European Monetary Institute

(93/716/EC)

THE COUNCIL OF THE EUROPEAN UNION,

Having regard to the Treaty establishing the European Community, and in particular Article 16.1 and 16.2 of the Protocol on the Statute of the European Monetary Institute annexed thereto,

Having regard to the proposal from the Commission([1]),

Having regard to the opinion of the European Parliament([2]),

Having regard to the opinion of the Committee of Governors,

Having regard to the opinion of the Monetary Committee,

Whereas the European Monetary Institute, hereinafter referred to as 'the EMI', will be established on 1 January 1994;

Whereas the EMI will be endowed with its own resources;

Whereas the size of the resources of the EMI will be determined by the Council of the EMI;

Whereas the resources of the EMI will be provided out of contributions by national central banks in accordance with the key referred to in Article 16.2 of the Protocol on the Statute of the EMI;

Whereas the key for the financial resources of the EMI will be determined before the start of the second stage;

Whereas the statistical data to be used for the determination of the key will be provided by the Commission in accordance with the rules adopted by the Council;

Whereas the rules adopted by the Council in this Decision do not constitute a precedent for other legal acts which the Council could adopt in other areas;

---

1. OJ No C 324, 1.12.1993, p.11; and OJ No C 340, 17.12.1993, p.11.
2. OJ No C 329, 6.12.1993.

Whereas the nature of and sources for the data to be used and the method of calculation of the key must be defined;

Whereas Council Directive 89/130/EEC, Euratom of 13 February 1989 on the harmonization of the compilation of gross national product at market prices([1]) introduces a procedure for the adoption by Member States of data on the gross domestic product at market prices; whereas the Member States must take all the necessary steps to ensure that that data is transmitted to the Commission,

HAS DECIDED AS FOLLOWS:

Article 1

The statistical data to be used for the determination of the key for the contributions by the national central banks to the financial resources of the EMI shall be provided by the Commission in accordance with the rules laid down in the following Articles.

Article 2

Population and gross domestic product at market prices, hereinafter referred to as 'GDP mp', shall be defined according to the European System of Integrated Economic Accounts (ESA) in force. GDP mp shall mean GDP mp as defined in Article 2 of Directive 89/130/EEC, Euratom.

Article 3

The data on population shall be taken for the year 1992. The mean of the total population over the course of the year shall be used in accordance with the ESA recommendation.

Article 4

The data on GDP mp shall be taken for each of the years 1987 to 1991. The data on GDP mp for each Member State shall be expressed in the national currency at current prices.

Article 5

The data on population shall be collected by the Commission (Eurostat) from Member States.

Article 6

The data on GDP mp for the years 1988 to 1991 shall result from the application of Directive 89/130/EEC, Euratom. The data for 1987 shall be collected by the Commission (Eurostat) from Member States, which shall make them consistent with the 1988 to 1991 data on GDP mp.

1. OJ No L 49, 21.2.1989, p.26.

Article 7

1.   The share of a Member State in the population of the Community shall be its share in the sum of the population of the Member States, expressed as a percentage.

2.   The GDP mp data for each year and each Member State expressed in national currencies shall be converted into figures expressed in ecus. The exchange rate used for this purpose shall be the average of the exchange rates for all working days in a year. The daily exchange rate shall be the rate calculated by the Commission and published in the 'C' series of the *Official Journal of the European Communities*.

3.   The share of a Member State in GDP mp of the Community shall be its share in the sum of GDP mp of the Member State[s] over five years, expressed as a percentage.

Article 8

The weighting of a national central bank in the key shall be the arithmetic mean of the shares of the Member State concerned in the population and in the GDP mp of the Community.

Article 9

The various steps of calculation shall use sufficient digits to ensure their accuracy. The weighting of national central banks in the key shall be expressed to four decimal places.

Article 10

The data referred to in this Decision shall be communicated by the Commission to the Committee of Governors of the Central Banks of the Member States before 1 January 1994.

Done at Brussels, 22 November 1993.

For the Council
The President
Ph. MAYSTADT

COUNCIL DECISION OF 22 NOVEMBER 1993

on the consultation of the European Monetary Institute by the authorities of the Member States on draft legislative provisions

(93/717/EC)

THE COUNCIL OF THE EUROPEAN UNION,

Having regard to the Treaty establishing the European Community, and in particular Article 109 (6) thereof, and Article 5.3 of the Protocol on the Statute of the European Monetary Institute annexed to this Treaty,

Having regard to the proposal from the Commission([1]),

Having regard to the opinion of the European Parliament([2]),

Having regard to the opinion of the Committee of Governors,

Whereas the European Monetary Institute, hereafter referred to as 'the EMI', is to be established on 1 January 1994;

Whereas the Treaty stipulates that the authorities of the Member States shall consult the EMI on any draft legislative provision within its field of competence; whereas it is for the Council to set the limits and the conditions of such consultation;

Whereas this obligation on the authorities of the Member States to consult the EMI shall not prejudice the responsibility of national authorities for the matters which are the subject of such provisions;

Whereas this Decision does not concern decisions taken by national authorities in the context of the implementation of monetary policy;

Whereas consultation of the EMI must not unduly lengthen procedures for adopting legislative provisions in the Member States; whereas the time limits within which the EMI must deliver its opinion must, nevertheless, enable it to examine the texts referred to it with the required care; whereas, in duly justified cases of extreme urgency, for example on account of market sensitivity, Member States may set a time limit of less than one month; whereas, in these cases particularly, dialogue between the national authorities and the EMI should enable the interests of both to be taken into account,

---

1. OJ No C 324, 1.12.1993, p.12; and OJ No C 340, 17.12.1993, p.12.
2. OJ No C 329, 6.12.1993.

HAS ADOPTED THIS DECISION:

Article 1

1. The authorities of the Member States shall consult the EMI on any draft legislative provision within its field of competence pursuant to Article 109f of the Treaty and in particular on:
    -   currency legislation, the status of the ecu and means of payment,
    -   the status and powers of national central banks and the instruments of monetary policy,
    -   the collection, compilation and dissemination of monetary, financial, banking and balance of payments statistics,
    -   clearing and payment systems, in particular for cross-border transactions,
    -   rules applicable to financial institutions in so far as they influence the stability of financial institutions and markets.

2. The EMI shall, immediately on receipt of any draft legislative provision, notify the consulting authority whether, in its opinion, such provision is within its field of competence.

Article 2

1. 'Draft legislative provisions' shall mean any such provisions which are legally binding and of general applicability in the territory of a Member State, which lay down rules for an indefinite number of cases and which are addressed to an indefinite number of natural or legal persons.

2. Draft legislative provisions within the meaning of paragraph 1 shall not include draft provisions the exclusive purpose of which is the transposition of Community directives into the law of Member States.

Article 3

Each Member State shall take the measures necessary to ensure effective compliance with this Decision. To that end, it shall ensure that the EMI is consulted at an appropriate stage enabling the authority initiating the draft legislative provision to have the EMI's opinion before taking its decision on the substance and that the opinion received from the EMI is brought to the knowledge of the adopting authority if the latter is an authority other than that which has prepared the legislative provisions concerned.

Article 4

The authorities of the Member States preparing a legislative provision may, if they consider it necessary, set the EMI a time limit for the submission of its opinion which may not be less than one month from the date on which the President of the EMI receives notification to this effect, save in case of extreme urgency. Upon expiry of the time limit, the absence of an opinion shall not prevent further action. Should the opinion of the EMI be received after the time limit, the Member States shall, nevertheless, ensure that it is brought to the knowledge of the authorities referred to in Article 3.

Article 5

This Decision is addressed to the Member States.
Done at Brussels, 22 November 1993.

For the Council
The President
Ph. MAYSTADT

INDEX

Bold page numbers indicate chapter titles and references in the form '276n13' refer to p 276, footnote 13.

International Banking and Finance Law

KLUWER LAW INTERNATIONAL – THE HAGUE / LONDON/ BOSTON